ECONOMICS FOR COMPETITION LAWYERS

ECONOMICS FOR COMPETITION LAWYERS

GUNNAR NIELS

HELEN JENKINS

JAMES KAVANAGH

Oxera

OXFORD

UNIVERSITY PRESS

OXFORD

UNIVERSITY PRESS

Great Clarendon Street, Oxford OX2 6DP

Oxford University Press is a department of the University of Oxford.
It furthers the University's objective of excellence in research, scholarship,
and education by publishing worldwide in

Oxford New York

Auckland Cape Town Dar es Salaam Hong Kong Karachi
Kuala Lumpur Madrid Melbourne Mexico City Nairobi
New Delhi Shanghai Taipei Toronto

With offices in

Argentina Austria Brazil Chile Czech Republic France Greece
Guatemala Hungary Italy Japan Poland Portugal Singapore
South Korea Switzerland Thailand Turkey Ukraine Vietnam

Oxford is a registered trade mark of Oxford University Press
in the UK and in certain other countries

Published in the United States
by Oxford University Press Inc., New York

British Library Cataloguing in Publication Data

Data available

Library of Congress Cataloging in Publication Data
Library of Congress Control Number: 2011922684

Typeset by Glyph International, Bangalore, India
Printed in Great Britain
on acid-free paper by
Ashford Colour Press Ltd, Gosport, Hampshire

ISBN 978-0-19-958851-0

3 5 7 9 10 8 6 4 2

FOREWORD

'There are no useful propositions in economics', wrote the late JK Galbraith, 'that cannot be stated accurately in clear, unembellished and generally agreeable English.' Even allowing for some exaggeration in that observation, it may nonetheless invite scepticism from lawyers—and judges—faced with complex economic evidence in competition cases. However, for those dealing with such cases, an understanding of the economic questions and arguments is increasingly important. In the decade since the European Commission ushered in a 'more economic' approach in its 2000 Guidelines on Vertical Restraints, an economic appreciation of the issues is now influencing all areas of competition law. Indeed, the issues themselves are sometimes framed primarily in economic terms.

This presents a significant challenge for those dealing with competition cases who lack an advanced education, and often any formal training at all, in economics. In meeting that challenge, this new work will be of great assistance. The economic theories, concepts, and techniques relevant to different areas of competition law are explained in approachable language, and mathematical formulae that can cause the lawyer's eyes to glaze over are avoided. Here one can find an explanation of critical loss as applied to market definition; of the different metrics that may be used to measure economic profitability; of the various measures of cost that can be used for the consideration of exclusionary pricing; of the efficiencies that can justify vertical restraints; and of the different theories used to determine FRAND terms of supply. This is not to suggest that the text is always easy for the non-economist: the authors do not adopt a simplistic approach, and their sophisticated analysis and exposition inevitably make certain sections a demanding read. But the result is a rewarding explanation of the economic toolkit that is available to practitioners and decision-makers, and deployed by the economic experts now frequently involved in competition cases.

The structure of the book is based on the competition law of the EU, and a notable inclusion is a discussion of the economic issues in state aid that have hitherto received less attention than they deserve. Moreover, a particular benefit of this work is the copious illustration from decided cases not only from the EU courts and Commission and the UK but also decisions and guidelines of national competition authorities and court judgments from Continental European states, the United States, and beyond. Of some of those judgments the authors are critical, and some of their criticisms are controversial, but that makes this book more stimulating. The authors do not shrink from expressing their view as to how, from an economist's perspective, certain aspects of EU competition law should develop. The book concludes with a discussion of the role of the economist as expert—a valuable reminder for economists themselves of their duty to assist the court and avoid the temptation or inducement to partisan bias.

This work does not concentrate exclusively on the traditional focus for competition economists in industrial organization economics, but usefully extends to the techniques of financial analysis and includes a brief excursus into behavioural economics as a basis for considering consumer behaviour in the context of remedies. Perhaps the approach of behavioural economics might usefully also be applied to the conduct of enterprises, since companies and firms—or at least the individuals who direct them—do not necessarily behave like the rational profit-maximizers of economic models.

Competition law emphatically remains law not economics, as these authors with all their experience of competition litigation recognize. There may be sound policy reasons, whether of practicability or of principle, why the law may depart from a rigid application of economic theory, even when the theory commands general consensus. Courts and competition authorities will sometimes find that contemporary internal documents from the participants provide a more satisfactory basis for determination of the nature and operation of the market than more abstract economic analysis. In some cases, sufficient factual data on which to found a robust economic assessment will be lacking. But competition law continues to evolve. Whether for appropriate application of the developing legal principles or for critical assessment of the expert evidence, a clear understanding of the economic theories, concepts, and arguments remains essential. To that important task, this broad-ranging work makes a very significant and welcome contribution.

Mr Justice Roth
London
January 2011

ACKNOWLEDGEMENTS

This book reflects the collective wisdom and ideas developed in Oxera over the past ten years. We are grateful to all our current and former colleagues for the knowledge and insights they have provided. We wish to express our gratitude to Luis Correia da Silva, Kerry Hughes, and Adriaan ten Kate for giving us immense support and inspiration for the book. We have also received tremendous help from Annabel Atkinson, Kelyn Bacon, Cate Dominian, Elizabete Ernstsone, Leon Fields, and Peter Roth. We thank Luke Adams, Clódagh McAteer, and their colleagues at OUP for asking us to write this book and helping us to produce it. We could not have completed this work without the cooperation, love, understanding, and patience of our families, so a special mention is due for Katie, Annabel, Steve, Ellie, Lucas, Imelda, Rodolfo, and Leandro. Last but not least, we would like to say thank you to all the competition lawyers across the world with whom we have had the pleasure to work over the years. It is you who we constantly had in mind when writing the book. We hope that you will enjoy it.

CONTENTS

TABLES OF CASES

Oftel

Ofwat

UNITED STATES

TABLES OF LEGISLATION

LIST OF FIGURES

LIST OF TABLES

1

INTRODUCTION: STARTING FROM FIRST PRINCIPLES

1.1 COMPETITION ECONOMICS AND YOU

Does one of these descriptions apply to you?

Reader 1—You studied law because you didn't like maths at school. After brief stints in commercial and European law you got involved in competition law, only to discover that the field is littered with economists who throw numbers and statistics at you—and competition authorities even seem to listen to them. Reluctantly, but bravely, you decide that to further your career in competition law you must overcome your aversion to equations and charts and learn some economics. This book will help you with that.

Reader 2—You are a seasoned competition lawyer. Over the last 10–15 years you have noted a gradual but steady shift in the field; it is increasingly relying on economic theories and tools. You discover that having a good grasp of the economics gives you an important edge over your rivals. You decide that you want to gain more insight into the principles behind some of the economic tools that you have already been using to construct your winning legal cases. This book will help you with that.

Reader 3—You are an advocate, a barrister, or a judge. You encounter an economic expert who supports one side's case with rather complex quantitative modelling results. Can you rely on this economist? Are those results robust? Or are they a smokescreen? You realize that economic models may always be something of a black box to you, but you decide that you want to be better equipped to peer inside that box, to shake and rattle it by asking critical questions, and see if it still holds together. This book will help you with that.

Whether you are a practising competition lawyer, a competition official, a member of the judiciary, or a legal scholar, economics matters to you because it matters to competition law. Legal provisions have economic concepts embedded in them. Competition authorities refer to economic principles and analysis in their decisions. Parties on either side of a competition dispute use economic arguments and evidence to support their case. You see this happening whether you practise in Europe, in the Americas, in Australia, or in one of the newer competition regimes in Africa or Asia. The degree of influence of economics has differed historically across jurisdictions—US antitrust has relied on economic thinking for over a century, while in Europe this is a much more recent phenomenon[1]—but nowadays economists are active in almost every competition regime around the world.

1.2 WHAT DOES ECONOMICS CONTRIBUTE TO COMPETITION LAW?

1.2.1 DIFFERENT ROLES

So what is it that economics has to offer? Why is it so influential in competition law? What do competition economists do? In answer to these questions, various roles of economics can be distinguished. Some of these roles are about shaping the legal principles of competition policy. Others are about developing tools and applying empirical techniques to competition cases in practice.

First, it is not an outlandish claim that economic thinking actually provides the main rationale for competition law. The very essence of competition law is based on the economic notion that competition is 'good' and monopoly is 'bad'. This notion itself has existed since long before there were any economists, but economic theory has shown that rivalry among suppliers in a market is something worth promoting and protecting. The founding father of the profession, Adam Smith, was the first to recognize, in 1776,

---

[1] See, for example, Kovacic and Shapiro (2000), Shenefield (2004), and Niels and ten Kate (2004).

that society is economically better off if business people can freely pursue their own self-interest (profit), as, in doing so, they will seek to serve the need of customers—the market mechanism known as the 'invisible hand'.[2] Under pressure from rivals, businesses are forced to make the best products and keep prices and production costs low. A monopolist, in contrast, can artificially restrict output so as to extract higher prices from consumers and may have less incentive to be cost-efficient. Following this line of economic thinking, the objective of competition law is to keep markets competitive and to prevent monopoly situations from arising.

In the same vein, economic logic explains why price-fixing cartels are regarded as the 'supreme evil' in competition law in most jurisdictions, and are treated as a criminal offence in some of them.[3] Unfair on consumers it may be, but is price fixing really the equivalent of stealing or fraud? Philosophically and legally (though note that we are not lawyers), this argument seems hard to sustain—aren't firms in a cartel selling their own products? Rather, the explanation seems to be economic. It was again Adam Smith who recognized that 'people of the same trade' have an inherent tendency to get together and have conversations resulting 'in a conspiracy against the public, or in some contrivance to raise prices'.[4] The harsh treatment that cartels generally receive in competition law is meant to deter would-be price-fixers.

Second, beyond the basic insights into competition and monopoly, economic theory has contributed to a greater understanding of the effects of certain common business practices that regularly become the subject of competition inquiries. When are these practices anti-competitive and when not? The answer is not always obvious. When you are on a flight, chances are that few other passengers in your class have paid exactly the same fare as you. Is such price discrimination between passengers anti-competitive? Or is there some economic efficiency rationale (for example, fewer flights would be available overall if airlines were prevented from filling seats through yield management)? And what if an airport price discriminates between airlines in this manner? When you buy a car it usually comes with a built-in stereo. Is such bundling of cars and stereos anti-competitive, hindering the independent sale of car stereos? (If you are wondering why this is a relevant question, consider that until the late 1950s seatbelts were sold separately from cars, and that while the market for personal satellite navigation systems has been fast growing in recent years, in future the addressable market for independent producers of sat navs may decline as built-in navigation systems become commonplace.) And what if Microsoft bundles Windows Media Player with the Windows operating system? Economics can help you in answering these questions.

It took competition law quite some time to realize that inherent trade-offs between restrictive effects and efficiency benefits must be made. We are talking the 1960s and 1970s (some two hundred years after Adam Smith). In the 1960s, US antitrust law—then

---

[2] Smith (1776), Book IV, Ch II.

[3] This label was given by the US Supreme Court, in *Verizon Communication Inc v Law Offices of Curtis V. Trinko LLP*, No 02–682, 13 January 2004.

[4] Smith (1776), Book I, Ch X.

the most prominent competition regime in the world—was marked by substantial confusion about how best to achieve the goal of keeping markets competitive. Various decisions from that period were, with hindsight, more about protecting individual competitors than protecting competition. In *Brown Shoe* (1962), a merger between two shoe manufacturer-retailers in the USA, the Supreme Court held that competition would be best served by preserving 'fragmented industries and markets', even if this meant sacrificing efficiencies, with consequent 'occasional higher costs and prices'.[5] In *FTC v Procter & Gamble* (1967), a merger concerning the household liquid bleach market, the Supreme Court established the 'entrenchment doctrine', whereby mergers could be prohibited if they strengthened the position of the merging parties vis-à-vis rivals through efficiencies, broader product ranges or greater financial resources.[6] Becoming too efficient was deemed bad. This period was also marked by per se prohibitions of various types of business practice that did not easily fit within the textbook model of perfect competition, such as tying and non-price vertical restraints.

This was when the ideas of the 'Chicago School', led by proponents such as Harold Demsetz, Richard Posner, and Robert Bork, came to the fore (Demsetz, 1974; Posner, 1976; Bork, 1978). They showed that many practices and agreements that restrict the freedom or choice of some parties can be efficient and pro-competitive, and should therefore not be prohibited per se but assessed under a rule of reason. In addition, efficiencies should be welcomed because they benefit consumers, even if they harm individual competitors. These ideas revolutionized US antitrust law in the 1970s and 1980s, resulting in a less interventionist, and more economics-based, approach to business practices and mergers. Since the mid-1980s, competition law in the USA and elsewhere has increasingly been influenced by more modern economic theories of industrial organization (IO), sometimes grouped together under the heading 'post-Chicago'. These theories have provided further insights into the economic effects of the types of business practice that competition law often grapples with, including bundling, tying, predation and leveraging of market power.[7]

Competition law in Europe has now caught up with these ideas (it took some 30 years longer than in the USA). Since the late 1990s, the European Commission, at times spurred on and at times held back by the European courts, has sought to reform all the major pillars of the competition rules: restrictive agreements under Article 101 of the Treaty on the Functioning of the European Union (TFEU), mergers and acquisitions under the EU Merger Regulation, abuse of dominance under Article 102, and state subsidies and aid under Articles 106 and 107. (Throughout the book we will be using the article numbering in the TFEU, even where the original decisions or judgments were made under the numberings of previous treaties.) As discussed in this book, in each case these reforms allowed for greater consideration of economic effects and efficiencies. This 'effects-based' approach to competition policy contrasts with the more legalistic, or 'form-based', approach that

---

[5] *Brown Shoe Co v United States* 370 US 294 (1962).
[6] *FTC v Procter & Gamble* 386 US 568 (1967).
[7] For a discussion, see Sullivan (1995), Hovenkamp (2001), and Kovacic (2007).

had prevailed in European competition law since its inception in 1957.[8] Other jurisdictions are following suit—indeed, some, such as Mexico and South Africa, to some extent adopted more economic approaches before the European Commission did.[9]

1.2.2 WHICH STRANDS OF ECONOMICS?

The third role of economics is that it has made significant contributions to competition law by developing a number of practical tests and criteria that make the application of the law more workable and sound, and by developing a range of statistical and econometric techniques that allow for obtaining robust evidence to back up theories and arguments in actual competition cases. Here we should explain that in the economics discipline there isn't actually a strand called 'competition economics'. At university, economics students do not typically learn about concepts such as market definition and dominance. Instead, 'competition economics' draws from different strands of economics.

By far the dominant strands are those of microeconomics and IO, which are concerned with how markets work, how demand and supply interact, and how rivals react strategically to each other's actions. When you come across a competition economist nowadays, chances are they have an IO background. However, competition economics is not exclusively about IO. Two other important theoretical strands are financial economics and behavioural economics. As we will see in several places throughout this book, finance tools are complementary to IO tools. Yet, in practice, the two sit far from comfortably together—do not be surprised if financial economists and IO economists seem to speak different languages and have completely different approaches to analysing concepts such as market power and cartel damages. This book shows where the two strands may be combined. Behavioural economics, in turn, is a relatively new field in economics that blends ideas from psychology and economics. It has been gaining traction of late—not surprising in a period of financial turmoil in which the rationality of markets is questioned—but has yet to make its mark on mainstream competition economics (we return to this topic in Chapters 9 and 11).

Yet, while the economics that is relevant to competition law draws from different (and sometimes not well-integrated) strands of theory, you may be reassured by the fact that it is mainstream and accepted within those strands. As Areeda and Hovenkamp (2007, p 112) put it:

> Antitrust economics employs what academic economists sometimes denigrate as 'applied economics'. The relation of applied economics to economics as an intellectual discipline is a little like the relationship of the tonsillectomy to the science of surgery or the oil change to the science of automotive engineering. Applied economics as a general matter is hardly at the frontier of economic science, but its very banality supplies the consensus needed to make it a successful antitrust tool.

---

[8] See, for example, Vickers (2005a), and Niels and Jenkins (2005).
[9] See ten Kate and Niels (2006), and Oxera (2005b).

Hence, in competition law you won't normally have to listen to academic economists touting their latest theories—indeed, one of the criteria for admissibility of expert evidence in US courts is that it is based on accepted theories, not untested ones (see Chapter 11). Nor should you expect to see too much disagreement among economists about which theory is best. Rather, when economists disagree it is mostly about how a particular theory has been applied to the particular facts of the case, and how case-specific data has been analysed.

This leads us to another field of economics that has been highly influential in competition law, namely econometrics, which can be described as the application of statistical techniques to economic problems. In the last 10–15 years, the toolkit of quantitative techniques available to economists has expanded significantly and so has the body of underlying theory providing models that can be empirically tested using econometrics. At the same time, real-world data availability has improved—companies keep electronic records in data warehouses, and 'scanner data' is collected for many products sold over the counter—as has computing power. It is fairly standard for economists to seek to apply econometric analysis, testing for statistical patterns and relationships in the available data. Indeed, in some US court cases there has been an expectation that economic experts use econometrics when analysing data (see Chapter 11). Where used appropriately, this can lend an element of greater rigour to competition decisions.

Perhaps the first example of a court case that was highly influenced by the relative merits of the econometric analyses by both sides is the 1997 *Staples/Office Depot* merger case in the USA.[10] This merger concerned two retail chains of large office supply stores. The Federal Trade Commission (FTC) had found evidence in internal documents that the two chains saw each other as direct competitors and that they generally set lower prices in cities where both chains had a presence than in cities where only one of them had a store. The econometric analysis by the FTC confirmed this, showing a statistically significant price difference of more than 5% between cities with just one of these stores and cities with both (taking account of any other factors that may have contributed to the price difference). The FTC concluded from this that the merger would lead to a price increase. Notwithstanding its successful impact in this particular US court case, econometrics has its limitations. It is probably the area in economics that most closely resembles a black box in the eyes of the competition lawyer. In this book we set out those cases where econometrics can be helpful, and also seek to equip you with the means to ask the right critical questions of the econometric analysis that you are presented with in competition cases.

1.3 THE BOOK'S APPROACH TO EXPLAINING COMPETITION ECONOMICS

Competition law is a complex field. As one specialized court put it, 'competition law is not an area of law in which there is much scope for absolute concepts or sharp edges'.[11]

---

[10] *FTC v Staples Inc* 970 F Supp 1066 (DDC 1997). See also Baker (1999).

[11] Competition Appeal Tribunal, Judgment in Cases 1035/1/1/04 and 1041/2/1/04, *Racecourse Association and British Horseracing Board v OFT* [2005] CAT 29 at [167].

This is not the fault of economics. Determining whether a certain business practice or merger has on balance more negative or more positive effects on competition and consumers is difficult because the realities of commercial interactions and markets are inherently complex. Yet economists can do a lot more to help lawyers navigate through the complexities of applying competition law to real-world markets. This begins with explaining economic principles and concepts clearly.

Later in this chapter we try to explain a number of important basic economic concepts in the way of the 'economic naturalist', an approach borrowed (loosely) from Robert Frank, one of a number of contemporary authors of 'popular' economics books (Frank, 2007). The idea is to make the reader think a bit like an economist and develop some economic intuition. We explain the concept of demand and supply curves without drawing any charts—not because some lawyers we know have an aversion to charts, but because we think that this will allow you to think through the drivers of demand and supply in a truly back-to-basics fashion. In the remaining chapters of the book we follow a more conventional approach to explaining economics (and do draw some charts), but throughout we try to keep the expositions relatively straightforward and to avoid the excessive use of economics jargon.

Another feature of the style of this book is that we place emphasis on setting out the underlying economic principles of competition law, rather than on setting out competition authorities' guidelines, decisions or case law. We do not take an integrated or 'holistic' law-and-economics approach in this regard (as some other textbooks do). We do strongly believe that good competition law requires a blend of law and economics (and we like to think of ourselves as competition economists with a reasonable grasp of competition law in various jurisdictions). But we believe that you are best served by this book through reading and learning about economics (you already know about the law). This will allow you to exercise your own judgement and achieve that blend between the two fields. For example, on the topic of vertical restraints (Chapter 6), we focus on the basic economics behind such restraints. This helps you think through from first principles why businesses may impose, and accept, vertical restraints; what positive effects they may have on efficiency and consumers; and what negative effects they may have on competition. You can then judge for yourself how the relevant legal framework would apply in a specific case. The book does not start by setting out what, for example, the European Commission guidelines or European court judgments say on vertical restraints, and then explaining the economics (if any) behind them. We do it the other way round. We start with the principles and then illustrate them with real-world case examples (and also show instances where existing guidelines or case law may not reflect 'good economics'). It follows that the economic principles explained in the book are not specific to any competition jurisdiction—most of them apply globally.

Economics is often about applying common sense, but sometimes it produces counterintuitive results. The back-to-first-principles approach presented here also allows us to reveal some common misperceptions among competition practitioners (both lawyers and economists). For example, why is it relevant for market definition when, after a price increase for a product (eg, online DVD rentals), consumers do not switch to a substitute product (such as bricks and mortar DVD rental), but simply consume less of that product? We address this in Chapter 2. And would a network provider offer its services below cost, without this necessarily amounting to predatory pricing (a relevant issue in abuse of dominance cases in the telecoms and high-tech industries is discussed in Chapter 4)?

1.4 EXPLAINING SOME BASIC PRINCIPLES THE ECONOMIC NATURALIST'S WAY

1.4.1 DEMAND CURVES, WITH NO CHART

Think of a two-dimensional field—it could be any sheet of paper, or this page of the book before you. Call this the 'price and quantity' field. Every point on it represents a particular price and a particular quantity of a particular product (this could be any product: apples, foreign holidays, petrol, electricity, jumbo jets). The higher up we are in the field, the higher the price of the product; at the bottom of your sheet of paper the price is zero. Likewise, as we move from left to right, the quantity of the product increases; to the extreme left of your sheet of paper the quantity is zero. (If we had drawn a proper chart—which we will do in Chapter 2—we would have said that the vertical axis represents price and the horizontal axis represents quantity.)

Somewhere in this field, buyers and suppliers of the product are hoping to meet. Let's start with the buyers—the demand side. What happens to the quantity demanded as we move from bottom to top in the field? It seems logical that as the price of apples goes up, they will be less in demand (fewer consumers will buy apples, and those who still do may buy fewer of them). Some products, like foreign holidays, will lose a lot of demand immediately upon moving upwards in the field (so we shoot rapidly from right to left in quantity as we go up in price). These products are said to be price-sensitive. For other products—such as petrol—we can go quite far up the field (raising price) without changing demand much—ie, we hardly move left in quantity (oil companies and tax authorities have found ways to exploit this price insensitivity). But even for those products there will come a point where demand drops—it may be hard to imagine, but car use does eventually fall when petrol becomes prohibitively expensive, even if only for a small number of 'marginal' consumers who can either switch to other modes of transport or who can simply not afford the higher prices (the concept of marginal consumers is an important one in economics, and we come back to it in Chapter 2).

So it is not unreasonable for economists to conclude that the demand curve in the price and quantity field is downward-sloping from top-left to bottom-right—to the left are those consumers with a higher willingness to pay; to the right are those with a lower willingness to pay.[12] We could draw a straight line, but economists prefer to use a more

---

[12] There are products that sell more when the price is higher, because (perhaps somewhat irrationally) consumers' perception of them changes with price ('price *is* quality'). Examples of such products are diamonds, designer handbags and expensive French wines. Economists call these Veblen goods, after Thorstein Veblen who wrote about this in 1899 (Veblen, 1899). A later classic treatise on these effects was given in Leibenstein (1950).

general shape like a curve (in fact, demand could take any irregular shape, as long as over a sufficiently large distance it slopes downwards as we move to the right). This demand curve is not merely some economist construct—real-world business people will know they can sell a bit more if they lower prices, and lose sales if they raise prices, and will try to find the right price and quantity where their profits are highest.

If you find this straightforward so far, that is a good sign because a lot of the time that economists spend working on competition cases actually involves trying to locate this demand curve. They need this, for example, to delineate the relevant market, to measure market power, or to simulate the price effect of a merger. Economists can normally observe only one price–quantity point in the field, which is the current price and quantity. If they are lucky, they can observe a few more points—for example, if the price has changed from last year, and a different quantity was sold at that price (even then, quantity changes may be due to factors other than price changes). But it is never possible to see the full relationship between price and quantity. Economists have to assess empirically the properties of demand in the vicinity of the price–quantity points they can observe. They will in particular want to know how sensitive demand is to price. The issues of market definition and market power critically turn on this, as shown further in Chapters 2 and 3.

There are additional relevant insights we can obtain through this naturalist thought experiment. We have seen how demand is downward-sloping from top-left to bottom-right. But what determines where exactly we start in our field? In other words, ignoring its slope for the moment, what determines whether the demand curve is located somewhere very high up (or far to the right) in the field or somewhere very low (or far to the left)? The answer to this question is of greater relevance to competition law than many practitioners, including economists, realize. Remember that our price–quantity field represents one product only, and it shows how demand for that product interacts with its price. Take foreign holidays to the Greek Islands. One factor that determines the position of the demand curve to start with is income (usually thought of as household disposable income). As income rises—we all become richer—so does demand for Greek Island holidays, even at the same price—the demand curve as a whole shifts to the right.[13]

More interestingly for competition law purposes, however, the position of the demand curve is also determined by competition from other products—say, holidays to the Maldives. Those products have their own price–quantity field and their own demand curve. But there is a lively interaction between the demand curves of the different products—something that is often overlooked by focusing on just one product. So imagine a whole series of price–quantity fields, one for each sunny destination that

---

[13] Again, there are exceptions. Some products actually sell less when income rises. Economists call these 'inferior goods' or Giffen goods, after Robert Giffen, as first recognized in Alfred Marshall's classic economics textbook of 1890 (Marshall, 1890). Examples of inferior goods are potatoes, other basic foodstuffs, and 'cheap' alcoholic beverages such as Mexican pulque and Japanese shochu, although empirical evidence for such Giffen effects is limited.

holidaymakers might conceivably go to. If holidays to the Maldives (or Madeira or Mallorca) become more popular for some reason (they become cheaper, or the quality of tourist facilities improves), this has the effect of shifting the demand curve for Greek holidays further down and to the left. Higher demand for holidays to the Maldives means lower demand for holidays to the Greek Islands. This interaction between demand curves of different products is the essence of how products can be substituted for each other, and lies at the heart of market definition. We come back to this in Chapter 2.

1.4.2 SUPPLY CURVES, STILL WITH NO CHART

Now let's turn to supply. Is the logic the same as for demand? Does the supply curve slope upwards from bottom-left to top-right, with higher price meaning more supply? Alas, not necessarily. Some economic-naturalist thinking can explain this (still with no chart; you will have to wait until Chapter 2). Take the supply of apples. Assume that entry is easy and cheap—many people can grow their own apple tree and bring their produce to the apple market. This is a basic ingredient of the economic model of perfect competition, to which we turn later. Where in our price–quantity field is this supply located?

The answer depends on the level of cost per unit of quantity. This is intuitive: just as buyers make their buy/don't buy decisions by comparing price to their willingness to pay for the product, suppliers make their supply/don't supply decisions by comparing price to their cost of supplying the product. Suppose it costs €1 to produce and market a kilo of apples. All producers are perfectly happy to sell at that price as they cover all their costs. (You are right to think at this point that this is perhaps rather odd: don't businesses want to make a profit over and above the recovery of costs? Well, economists can live with this theoretical result by assuming that the cost here also includes a 'normal' profit as reward for the producer's investment and risk; we address 'normal' profit in Chapter 3.) So, we have then an unlimited supply of apples at €1 per kilo. The supply 'curve' is a horizontal line at that level. It cannot be any lower or any higher. If the price falls below €1, no apples would be supplied to the market as producers cannot recover their costs. Any price above €1 would immediately attract more suppliers who are willing and able to sell at €1. Suppliers who can be lured into the market only at a price above €1—or who are less efficient and cannot recover their costs at €1—simply wouldn't stand a chance in the market. They would rapidly be forced to exit.

Where do demand and supply meet then? What is the market equilibrium? The downward-sloping demand curve will cross the horizontal supply curve at €1, and market quantity in this 'market equilibrium' is whatever quantity consumers demand at that price of €1. At this point, we have a 'marginal consumer' who is willing to pay exactly €1 per kilo, and gets apples at that price. Consumers to the left of that point get their apples at €1 per kilo too, but are willing to pay more than that. They derive a 'consumer surplus' from their purchase, a concept which we explore further below. In equilibrium (the point where demand and supply meet), the equivalent concept of 'marginal producer' does not really apply here since all producers have the same cost of €1 and the supply curve is horizontal.

From this basic premise that supply curves will often tend to be horizontal, we can explore the circumstances in which they are not. Supply curves can also be upward-sloping (from bottom-left to top-right in our price–quantity field). This occurs when some producers have lower costs than others, but cannot serve the whole market due to capacity constraints (unlike in our apple example, in which all suppliers could produce at €1 per kilo without any constraint on capacity or on the number of suppliers with a tree in their garden). Electricity generation is an example. Say there is one nuclear plant that generates electricity at a price of €5 per MWh (megawatt hour), and has the capacity to produce 1,000 MW of electricity in every hour. However, total market demand is 5,000 MWh during peak hours, so the nuclear plant cannot serve the whole market. There is room for producers with higher costs—say, gas turbine plants producing at €30 per MWh. So our supply curve for electricity is horizontal at the level of €5 from where quantity is 0 MWh to where it is 1,000 MWh. It then makes a step-change up to the level of €30 and is horizontal again as we move further right in quantity. There may be a number of such steps as other generation technologies come into play, such as coal-fired power plants at €35 per MWh and oil-fired plants at €60 per MWh. In these situations, the market price in equilibrium will normally be determined by the level of cost of the higher-cost producers—the 'marginal producers'—who will make only a 'normal' profit (the market price just covers their costs). In peak hours the marginal producers may be oil-fired plants and the market price €60.[14] At the market price, the lower-cost suppliers will make a healthy margin above cost. This raises the interesting question for competition law of whether the low-cost producers have market power in these circumstances (addressed in Chapter 3). There is another complication, however, to which we turn below. The nuclear plant in our example has by far the lowest cost of generating electricity (€5 per MWh versus €30 per MWh for the next cheapest technology), but this ignores the fact that the cost of building the nuclear plant in the first place was rather higher than for the other types of plant.

1.4.3 SOME NOTES ON COST CURVES

The supply curves that we have pictured before us reflect the marginal cost of production—what it costs to produce the next unit of output: an apple or a megawatt of electricity. We discuss different cost concepts (such as marginal costs, incremental costs, and avoidable costs) in the context of pricing abuses in Chapter 4. Here we consider the concept of average total cost—which is the cost per unit of output including fixed costs, ie, those costs that do not vary with output, such as the cost of building a plant—because this has an impact on how many suppliers can operate in the market.

---

[14] Off-peak demand is lower (the demand curve is further to the left) and the gas turbine plants now become the marginal producers, resulting in a price of €30. The higher-cost coal- and oil-fired plants do not sell anything during off-peak hours, but they remain in the market as they can sell during peak hours. In most other markets they would have been forced to exit.

High fixed costs means that there are economies of scale—average total production costs per unit decrease as output increases.

Take the nuclear plant. It costs a lot to build, but then it costs relatively little to generate electricity (€5 per MWh in our example). Say the fixed cost of building the nuclear plant is €3 billion. If it is only ever used to generate 1 MW, that unit of output has an average cost of €3 billion (so the average-cost curve begins very high up to the far left of our price–quantity field). The more electricity the plant generates, the lower the average cost. We saw earlier that the plant has a maximum capacity of 1,000 MWh. The average-cost curve for the firm therefore slopes downwards from the far left of the field to where quantity is 1,000 MWh. To generate more, another nuclear plant would have to be built (or other generation technologies would have to be used, as in the above example). The firm's average-cost curve goes up again as we move further right. The 1,000 MWh point is therefore called the minimum efficient scale of production for the nuclear plant.

This basic logic of minimum efficient scale has significant implications for competition law (again something that practitioners are not always aware of, and economists do not always make explicit). It effectively determines how many suppliers can efficiently operate in the market. Most real-world markets have economies of scale, and this is actually the main reason why they often have only a limited number of suppliers (think of car manufacturers, makers of washing powder, or supermarket chains). Even in apple production there are economies of scale (planting and growing a tree is a fixed cost, so we slightly cheated with our €1 per kilo example), but they are not so pronounced, and hence there is room for many suppliers. However, in the case of electricity generation, if the total market demand size is 5,000 MWh during peak hours, there is room in the market for five nuclear plants. If the market size is 2,000 MWh (for example, in a country that is smaller), only two nuclear plants can operate at the minimum efficient scale. A similar situation occurs in the production of jumbo jets, where globally only two manufacturers remain (Boeing and Airbus), most probably because demand is not there to sustain a third. If the market size is below 2,000 MWh, only one nuclear plant can produce efficiently (a second plant or more costly technologies can still operate to meet the residual demand above 1,000 MWh). If the market size is 1,000 MWh or smaller, a situation of 'natural monopoly' arises—there is room for only one firm in the market.

You can see how this interaction between market size (a demand-side feature) and economies of scale (a supply-side feature) often determines the 'natural' state of concentration in markets. Sometimes having a greater number of suppliers in the market is simply not possible, because it is not efficient—if there are too many suppliers, one or more of them are bound to operate below the minimum efficient scale, and they are the ones compelled to exit the market first if competitive forces are allowed to work freely. Consumers and competition authorities have to live with this economic reality. The same logic also explains a main economic rationale for removing trade barriers in the context of the World Trade Organization or the European internal market—free trade enhances total market size (as producers can sell beyond their national market), and hence allows more companies to achieve minimum efficient scale, promoting competition and efficiency at the same time.

1.4.4 COMPETITION 'GOOD', MONOPOLY 'BAD'

In exploring demand and supply above, we have already touched upon the main features of competitive markets: free entry and exit, and no significant economies of scale in production. No individual supplier can influence the market price. This equilibrium price is determined by the interplay between demand and supply (where the marginal consumer meets the marginal producer). All suppliers are 'price-takers'. Economists have shown that such 'perfect competition' produces desirable outcomes for the economy as a whole. First, production in each competitive market takes place at the lowest level of cost—in the apple example, no supplier with costs higher than €1 per kilo can survive in the market. This is called productive efficiency. It is survival of the fittest. Second, all consumers who are willing to pay a price that covers this cost of production are indeed being served (only those with a willingness to pay less than €1 per kilo of apples do not buy any in the equilibrium situation). This means that the 'right' amount of resources in the economy is allocated to apple production; this is referred to as allocative efficiency. Allocative efficiency can also be interpreted as the maximum number of efficient transactions taking place in the market.

For competition law purposes, it is useful to bear in mind the economic principle that any transaction between a willing buyer and a willing seller is something inherently desirable. Think of that old bicycle that has been stored in your garden shed for years. You are perfectly willing to sell it to someone for €25. Equally there must be someone out there whose willingness to pay for your bike is equal to or greater than €25. If the two of you transact, you both benefit compared with a situation in which the bike remains unused in the shed. Thus, when transactions take place, buyers benefit because the price is at or below their willingness to pay, and suppliers benefit because the price is at or above their cost of supply. As a rule of thumb, competition law should therefore generally look favourably upon business practices that create new markets (new buyer–supplier transactions) altogether, or that on balance enhance market size even if they also have some restrictive effect on the side. We explore this further in Chapters 4, 5, and 6.

Contrast that with monopoly. Suppose, hypothetically, that there is a single producer of apples (note, incidentally, that this is exactly what you are asked to suppose when applying the 'hypothetical monopolist' test for market definition, discussed in Chapter 2). What happens to price and quantity? The monopolist can clearly do better than set the price at €1 and make only a 'normal' profit. It can restrict output, thus creating some artificial scarcity, and raise the price—remember that lower quantity and higher prices go hand in hand when the demand curve is downward-sloping. The monopolist is a price-setter, not a price-taker, and does not need to fear consumers switching to rival producers of apples (there are none). The monopolist reduces output and raises price up to the point where its profits are maximized (technically this occurs where the monopolist's marginal revenue equals its marginal cost; we return to this in Chapter 2, since we said we would keep the present chapter simple). Note here that the sky is not the limit for this monopoly price rise. It is unlikely that the price of apples will go up all the way to, say, €5 per kilo, even under monopoly. Any price increase has two offsetting effects: a higher price means a higher profit margin for each product sold (€5 – €1 = €4 in this case), but it also means fewer sales of apples (if the price rises to €5, we would probably move quite far to the left in our price–quantity field, leaving only those buyers who have a very high willingness to pay for apples).[15] At some price above €1 but below €5—say, at €1.50 per kilo—the monopolist maximizes profit because the loss of customers from raising price any further becomes so large that it outweighs the gain in profit margin (this, in a nutshell, is the concept of 'critical loss' used in market definition, which we address in greater detail in Chapter 2).

So, what are the effects of monopoly on economic welfare? Why is monopoly 'bad'? The first effect that may be considered 'bad' is that the monopolist earns more profit than previously (€1.50 – €1 = €0.50 of profit on every kilo sold). This comes directly at the expense of those customers who still buy apples at the monopoly price. Economists say that there is a redistribution from consumer surplus to producer surplus. Producer surplus is simply the difference between price and costs (it's the same as profit). The concept of consumer surplus is less easy to grasp. Remember that our demand curve represents willingness to pay. At the competitive price, all customers with a willingness to pay of at least €1 buy those apples in equilibrium. These are all customers to the left in our price–quantity field, including those to the far left who are willing to pay as much as, say, €5 or even €10 per kilo. But they have to pay only €1 (thanks to those 'good' competitive forces in the market). They therefore get a surplus of willingness to pay over price (the consumer equivalent of producers' profit)— the consumer who was willing to pay €5 gets a surplus of €4 at the price of €1, and the consumer who was willing to pay €10 gets a surplus of €9. In monopoly, price is increased to €1.50, so consumer surplus for all those who still buy apples is reduced by €0.50 per kilo.

Now, a competition lawyer should be aware that economists do not have any particular reason to condemn such redistribution of surplus. No one among the remaining buyers is actually forced to purchase anything they are not willing to pay for. Most buyers still get a surplus, even those willing to pay €1.51. It is just a smaller surplus than previously (the new marginal consumers who are willing to pay exactly €1.50 no longer get any surplus—they used to get €0.50 surplus at the old price of €1—but they can at least still buy the product at a price they are willing to pay). However, who is to say that €0.50 of surplus in the hands of consumers is better than €0.50 of surplus in the hands of producers (or, more accurately, shareholders, which could include pension funds and private investors)?

Economists have more to say on the second 'bad' effect of monopoly, which is that output is artificially restricted. At the price of €1.50, several consumers who are

---

[15] The consumers who no longer buy apples at this price will divert their money to other products, such as pears and kiwi fruit, thus pushing the demand curve for those products to the right in their respective price–quantity fields. This is demand substitution at work. Even a (hypothetical) monopolist is therefore still constrained to some extent by competition from other products.

perfectly willing to pay the cost of producing the apples are not being served by the monopolist (ie, those consumers who are willing to pay between €1 and €1.49). In a competitive situation they were served, but after the monopoly price rise they are no longer served. They are the previous marginal consumers who are now lost. This represents an allocative inefficiency. Too few of the economy's resources are allocated to the production of apples. No one gains from this, not even the monopolist (as it makes no profit on these sales that are no longer made). The term frequently used by economists to describe this effect is 'deadweight welfare loss' (don't ask why).

The third 'bad' effect is that monopolists may have a 'quiet life'.[16] You may think that free from pressure from any rivals, why would a monopolist do its best to produce efficiently, to bring down production costs, or to bring innovative new products to the market? An economist's answer is that at a cost of, say, €0.80 per kilo, the monopolist may make greater profits than at €1.00 per kilo, so it may still seek to reduce costs purely out of self-interest. Yet an apple monopolist may also pay its managers or (less likely) its pickers and packers a bit more than a competitive supplier could afford. It may face less pressure to invest in that new automated apple-picking technology that would reduce costs. Nor may it have great incentives to make any bioengineering efforts to render its apples that little bit sweeter and juicier. This 'quiet life' effect—where the incentive to reduce costs is outweighed—is possibly the most damaging from the perspective of economic welfare. Monopolistic markets generally lack that rivalrous dynamism that leads to innovation and the introduction of new products.

Unfortunately, this 'competition good, monopoly bad' story is not as black and white as you might think. Ending up with a monopoly may be a bad thing for economic welfare, but having a process in which suppliers *want to become* a monopolist is actually highly desirable. The lure of monopoly profit is what drives suppliers to be innovative. Companies in many real-world markets, be they car manufacturers, soft-drink producers or clothes shops, want to make their product a little bit different from competitors so as to be able to charge a premium. This is why in most markets products are 'differentiated', with each supplier having a degree of monopoly power over its own product (or brand). There is some debate in economics (and in other social sciences) about the merits of product differentiation, especially when it is achieved solely through advertising,[17] but if you doubt whether product differentiation overall is a good thing, imagine a world in which we all had to wear the same clothes or drive the same car. In some markets the gains from successful innovation can be even larger—Ford achieved a decisive cost advantage over rivals with its Model T in 1908, the first car to be mass-produced on assembly lines; companies such as Hoover, Tetra Pak, 3M, Microsoft, and Apple created whole new markets for themselves (at least for a period) by launching innovative products (respectively, the vacuum cleaner in 1908, the tetrahedron milk

---

[16] The phrase 'The best of all monopoly profits is a quiet life' was coined by the economist John Hicks (Hicks, 1935).

[17] See the discussion in Comanor and Wilson (1979), and Becker and Murphy (1993).

packaging in 1953, Post-it notes in 1977, MS-DOS in 1982, and the iPod digital music player in 2001).

This poses some fundamental problems for competition law (it is no coincidence that some of the innovative companies listed above have come under scrutiny by competition authorities over the years). First, competition law should tread carefully when tackling monopolies directly, since such action might affect the desirable incentives that other suppliers have to outperform their rivals in search of monopoly profits. As Judge Learned Hand famously put it in 1945, 'The successful competitor, having been urged to compete, should not be turned upon when he wins.'[18] Instead, competition law should focus primarily on keeping markets sufficiently open and contestable, such that monopoly positions can be challenged over time by new entrants. Second, competition lawyers cannot really rely on evidence of intent in the same way as criminal lawyers can. In competitive markets, intentions to 'pound' a rival 'into the sand' or 'squish him like a bug' may actually be perfectly consistent with a healthy drive to compete.[19] Third, innovative activity is regarded as so desirable that there is a wholly separate area of law—intellectual property law—that creates (temporary) monopolies by awarding patents for inventions and innovations. Copyright law has similar effects. Like competition law, intellectual property law is built on a basic economic premise: that rewarding innovative effort by granting a temporary (often around 20 years) monopoly position to the innovator creates greater incentives to innovate in the first place. The tension with competition law is immediately obvious, and we return to this in Chapters 4 and 5.

1.4.5 A RECAP OF THE CONCEPTS USED SO FAR

If you have followed the line of reasoning in our 'economic naturalist' thought experiment above, you have grappled with the following basic economic concepts: price, quantity, buyers, suppliers, price sensitivity, marginal consumers, willingness to pay, demand curve, substitutes, supply curve, market equilibrium, marginal producers, perfect competition, normal profit, entry, exit, capacity constraint, market power, marginal costs, average total costs, fixed costs, economies of scale, minimum efficient scale, natural monopoly, price-taker, productive efficiency, allocative efficiency, monopoly, hypothetical monopolist, price-setter, profit maximization, critical loss, consumer surplus, producer surplus, deadweight welfare loss, innovation, and product differentiation. You already know more about economics than you realize. Much of the material covered in the remainder of this book builds on these basic concepts.

---

[18] *US v Aluminum Co of America (ALCOA)* 148 F 2d 416 (2d Cir. 1945).

[19] Such intentions are cited in two US predation cases: *US Philips Corp v Windmere Corp* 861 F 2d 695 (Fed. Cir. 1988), cert denied, 490 US 1068 (1999) and *Kelco Disposal v Browning-Ferris Indus of Vermont* 845 F 2d 404 (2d Cir.) aff'd 492 US 257 (1989).

1.5 SOME HEALTH WARNINGS ON COMPETITION, COMPETITION POLICY, AND COMPETITION ECONOMISTS

1.5.1 HEALTH WARNINGS ON COMPETITION

As we have seen, competition can achieve many benefits for society—lower prices, allocative efficiency, productive efficiency, innovation, product variety. Not because producers are altruistic benefactors, but because their self-interested pursuit of profit, combined with pressure from rivals who are after the same, leads them to produce the kind of products that consumers want to buy, and to do so at the most efficient levels of cost. Adam Smith's invisible hand works, by and large. And the good thing is that markets do not need perfect competition to achieve all that (which is just as well, since hardly any real-world market is perfectly competitive, not even that for apples). Sometimes a small number of suppliers, even two, may be sufficient to generate fierce rivalry (though in concentrated markets competition can also be highly ineffective; more on this in Chapter 3). In some markets even a monopolist may be prevented from raising prices by the threat of immediate 'hit-and-run' entry—this concept of 'contestable markets' is largely a theoretical construct, but has been found to apply in competition cases involving helicopter services and local bus services, for example.[20]

However, there are some policy goals that competition *cannot* achieve, and it is important to be aware of these. Competitive markets may fail to serve certain customers where the costs of serving them exceed their willingness to pay. Think of a remote, small mountain village—no bus operator would consider it worthwhile running a service to it, and no postal operator would deliver letters there (the demand and supply curves in our price–quantity field never meet). That is why governments may choose to impose a universal service obligation or grant a subsidy to ensure that such 'essential' services are provided, sometimes in return for a degree of exclusivity (ie, monopoly) for the service provider in question (the state aid issues that such service obligations and subsidies may raise are the subject of Chapter 8). Markets also fail in situations of natural monopoly, as described above. To achieve efficient production, a single supplier is warranted, but then specific constraints such as price caps may be imposed on that monopoly supplier at the same time, often by a sector regulator. The regulation of natural monopolies is not discussed specifically in this book. However, some of the most interesting and challenging competition cases arise in these industries since many natural monopolies—rail infrastructure, gas transportation networks, local telephony networks—interact with competitive layers in the supply chain. We return to this in

---

[20] Competition Commission (2000), 'CHC Helicopter Corporation and Helicopter Services Group ASA: A report on the merger situation', January; and *Chester City Council v Arriva* [2007] EWHC 1373 (Ch), High Court judgment (both are cases in the UK).

Chapter 4. Competition law can also learn some useful lessons from regulation when it comes to designing remedies, a theme dealt with in Chapter 9.

Economic theory has identified several other common types of market failure where competition may not do the job. There may be externalities, where decisions by one market participant do not take into account the impact on other market participants. An example of a (negative) supply-side externality is a factory upstream that dumps its waste into the river, thus affecting a fish farm further downstream. An example of a (positive) demand-side externality is a telephone network or social networking site whose attractiveness to any user depends on how many other users have joined (so no user would join individually if no one else joined; a chicken-and-egg externality)—in the extreme, such network effects can give rise to a situation akin to natural monopoly, with the corresponding competition problems—witness the spate of competition actions against Microsoft Windows in the USA and Europe (as discussed in Chapter 4).[21] Furthermore, markets may not function properly if there is asymmetric information between buyers and suppliers (insurance and used cars are frequently cited examples)— there may be so little trust between them that no transactions take place at all. In a famous article published in 1970, the economist George Akerlof showed how owners of good second-hand cars have difficulty selling them because buyers cannot distinguish good cars from 'lemons' (Akerlof, 1970).

Finally, competition can do little to achieve distributive justice. Competition results in what economists have labelled Pareto efficiency, which means that in equilibrium there are no more transactions whereby one party can be made better off without making another party worse off—all efficient transactions that make both parties better off have taken place (in terms of the earlier example, all used bicycles that people wanted to sell and buy have been sold and bought).[22] But this says nothing about how welfare is distrib-uted. One party may have everything and the other nothing, and this can still be Pareto-efficient. We saw above that, on the demand side, not all consumers may be served by competitive markets. On the producer side things are even harsher. Open markets may offer opportunities to many aspiring entrepreneurs, but the playing field is rarely level (eg, large companies benefit from economies of scale) and not everyone succeeds in the marketplace. Competition inevitably produces winner and losers. The fate suffered by the losers can be unpleasant. This leads us to our health warnings on competition policy.

1.5.2 HEALTH WARNINGS ON COMPETITION POLICY

The first health warning on competition policy is that it should not be equated with competition itself (as it sometimes is). Competition policy is normally aimed at pro-moting and protecting competition. But it can also (unintentionally) stifle competition.

---

[21] *United States v Microsoft*, CA, No 98-1232; and Case T-201/04 *Microsoft Corp v Commission of the Euro-pean Communities*, Judgment of 17 September 2007. These judgments on either side of the Atlantic were made at the end of protracted legal disputes.

[22] This is after the economist Vilfredo Pareto (Pareto, 1906).

Robert Bork of the Chicago School (referred to above) called this the 'antitrust paradox'. Think of competition as a boxing match. The audience wants to see a fierce fight in which the best boxer prevails; it doesn't care particularly about the fate of the loser, as long as a new challenger takes his place rapidly. But in comes the referee. He tells the fighters to treat each other in a gentlemanly fashion. No punches below the belt (prices below cost). No verbal threats revealing an intention to massacre the opponent. The boxer who is slightly bigger and more experienced is told he has a 'special responsibility' not to weaken his opponent any further. And the winner is not allowed any excessive prize money. The result is clear. The audience doesn't get the blood it wanted to see. Weaker fighters stay in the ring much longer than they otherwise would. Stronger fighters feel hampered once they gain the upper hand, so may try a little less hard. And new challengers are deterred because there is not much prize money to be won. The referee's rules may ultimately induce the two boxers to stop making much combative effort and instead agree tacitly to just pretend to be having a fierce fight, and rake in fees paid by viewers. Competition policy can have the same dampening effect on competition in the market. The EU regime has come close to such an antitrust paradox with its imposition of a 'special responsibility' on any dominant firm 'not to allow its conduct to impair genuine undistorted competition on the market',[23] and the way this principle has been applied in many abuse cases. We return to this in Chapter 4. The shoe and liquid bleach mergers in the USA that we referred to above are also good examples; indeed, cases like these in the 1950s and 1960s were the inspiration for Bork's book title.

As noted earlier, competition authorities and courts have to distinguish between business practices that are on balance pro-competitive (they do more good than harm to competition and efficiency) and those that are on balance anti-competitive. The only practices where the line can be drawn reasonably clearly are hardcore price fixing and market sharing between competitors—these practices almost invariably do more harm than good (as discussed in Chapter 5). For all other business conduct, agreements and mergers, competition policy must strike a balance between minimizing the likelihood of prohibiting practices that are in reality pro-competitive (false positives), and minimizing the likelihood of condoning practices that are in reality anti-competitive (false negatives). Economics can help by providing insight into the likely effects of practices and by applying counterfactual and cost–benefit analysis, but economists cannot accurately measure the effects of over-enforcement or under-enforcement. Where the line is drawn is ultimately a matter of policy judgement. In practice this will depend on the degree to which policy-makers have confidence that markets can sort themselves out (a confidence that seems to be weaker in Europe than in the USA), or the degree to which policy-makers have confidence that government intervention can improve markets that cannot sort themselves out (a confidence that seems to be weaker in the USA than in Europe).[24]

---

[23] Case 322/81 *Nederlandsche Banden-Industrie Michelin NV v EC Commission (Michelin I)* [1983] ECR 3461.

[24] It is fair to say (though hard to prove) that competition regimes that follow more economics-based approaches tend to be less interventionist overall than the more legalistic regimes.

There is consensus (even in Europe now) that competition policy should protect the process of competition, not individual competitors. Competition can be very harsh on those companies that can't keep up with the more efficient ones, and competition law is not (or should not be) designed to help them (competition authorities should not over-enforce like the boxing referee above). From an economic perspective, competition policy is not about 'fairness'. Indeed, fairness can be a dangerous beacon when deciding on a course in a competition investigation. Markets are rarely 'fair' in the popular meaning of the word, in terms of the playing field being level and the market outcome equitable. (Is it fair that the likes of Walmart have displaced 'mom and pop' stores all over the world?) Nor is there, from an economic perspective, any particular need for markets to be fair in order to function effectively. Competition authorities that over-emphasize the importance of 'fair play' in markets (or that have the word 'fair' in their name, such as the Fair Trade Commissions in Jamaica, Japan, and South Korea, and the Office of Fair Trading in the UK) may create unrealistic expectations among small businesses and consumers that they will ensure a level playing field and a 'fair' market outcome.

The most frequently stated objectives of competition policy are efficiency, economic welfare and consumer welfare. There has been some debate in certain jurisdictions about whether consumer welfare should have primacy over total welfare, and whether 'consumers' should be taken as end-consumers or also buyers in intermediate markets. Fortunately, efficiency and consumer welfare often go hand in hand and competition can enhance both simultaneously (as we saw earlier in the discussion about the benefits of competition). There are some exceptions. One is price discrimination, which often enhances efficiency by allowing output to be increased, but which does not necessarily improve consumer welfare if it also allows the supplier to extract higher prices from each consumer (see Chapter 4). Another is a merger that results in significant cost efficiencies but also a small increase in price; total welfare may rise, but consumer welfare falls (see Chapter 7).

Historically, competition policy has also been associated with several other goals, such as dispersion of economic power—one of the original goals behind US antitrust law[25]—and economic integration—a major goal of the competition rules in the EU Treaty. However, we have already seen that competition is not necessarily good at achieving objectives other than efficiency. For example, by preventing mergers in concentrated markets and tackling abuses by dominant firms, competition law does contribute somewhat to the dispersion of economic power, but sometimes the forces of competition themselves result in, or require, the emergence of powerful but efficient firms. Likewise, the application of 'standard' competition policy principles to Articles 101 and 102 TFEU will often contribute to the internal-market objective as well (eg, exclusionary conduct by a dominant airline or telecoms operator may have

---

[25] US antitrust started with the enactment of the Sherman Antitrust Act in 1890. While there has been much debate about the objectives of antitrust law ever since, early on it was established that at least one of the main goals was to protect competition and prevent monopolies in the interest of consumers. See *Standard Oil Co of New Jersey v United States* 221 US 1 (1911), a case also discussed in Chapter 9.

negatively affected competitors from both that Member State and other Member States). But sometimes EU competition policy seems to apply criteria that are more specific to the aim of the internal market than to competition as such—for example, in its negative stance towards exclusive car dealerships based on national boundaries (economic theory suggests that such exclusive territories for distributors may have efficiency justifications as well—see Chapter 6).

1.5.3 HEALTH WARNINGS ON COMPETITION ECONOMISTS

Throughout the book we aim to give you a feel for what economics can contribute to competition law, and also for what its limitations are. An important theme is the role that economists play in competition cases. Just as competition and competition policy are not synonymous, there is also a distinction between *economics* and *economists*. Knowledge of economics is essential for any competition lawyer. But economists are not always essential. Competition lawyers are normally able to deal with bread-and-butter competition problems themselves. It is only in the more complex cases that they call in the help of economists (although we have seen that competition cases quite often fall into the complex category). This book aims to equip competition lawyers with the means to handle the bread-and-butter cases, and to understand and use the economist's analyses in the more complex cases.

The other side of the coin is that economists must carry out their analysis reliably and with integrity, and present their results with clarity. We believe that our profession may be lacking somewhat on those fronts. Economists do not always recognize the limitations of their analysis (or do not communicate them clearly). They are sometimes, rightly or wrongly, perceived as hired guns—a perception that is reinforced every time two economic experts are seen to be slinging mud at each other's analysis. We would rather that economists are perceived as experts with integrity who can provide insight into the complicated economics of a competition case. Various mechanisms can be, and have been, implemented to promote best practice in the use and conduct of economists, in order to make their contributions more helpful and credible. We address this topic in Chapter 11.

1.6 THE REMAINDER OF THIS BOOK

This book covers all the major areas of competition law. It is organized such that you can either read it cover-to-cover, or use it as reference when you want to find out about the economics behind specific topics or issues. We follow the structure of most legal textbooks in this field, starting with market definition (Chapter 2) and market power (Chapter 3), two 'building blocks' that are of relevance to most types of competition case. Chapter 4 deals with abuse of dominance, Chapter 5 with cartels and other types of horizontal agreement, Chapter 6 with vertical restraints, and Chapter 7 with mergers. We then have three chapters on topics that you may see less often in standard texts.

Chapter 8 sets out the economics of state aid law, which can be considered part of competition law in the wider sense. Having discussed the economics behind the major provisions of competition law, the next two chapters deal with what happens after an infringement has been found. Chapter 9 discusses the design of remedies for competition problems and infringements, an area that has attracted relatively little scholarly attention thus far compared with the identification of those problems—as one commentator noted, 'Everybody likes to catch them, but nobody wants to clean them.'[26] Chapter 10 deals with the quantification of damages arising from infringements, a topic of increasing interest as private damages claims against infringing parties are on the rise in many jurisdictions. Finally, in Chapter 11 we offer some thoughts on the use of economic evidence in competition cases in terms of best practice and future direction.

---

[26] Comment made by Tad Lipsky at the 2007 Federal Trade Commission hearings on s 2 of the Sherman Act (transcript of 28 March, p 47, at <http://www.ftc.gov/os/sectiontwohearings/docs/transcripts/070328.pdf>). The quote is attributed to William Baxter, the Department of Justice Assistant Attorney General behind the break-up of AT&T in 1982—see Chapter 9.

2
MARKET DEFINITION

2.1 WHY MARKET DEFINITION?

Two Italian producers of women's designer shoes want to merge. Their legal representatives notify the deal to the competition authority, saying it should be cleared because there is plenty of competition remaining post-merger. How should the authority go about assessing whether the merger is anti-competitive? Nowadays the basic approach to such mergers is well established in competition law. First, you define the relevant market. Is the market limited to Italian women's designer shoes or does it include other women's designer shoes, or indeed all women's shoes? Is the market national, or does it cover other countries where these shoes are sold? Second, you analyse the position of the merging parties in the relevant market. Do they have a substantially larger combined market share? Does the merger leave only a limited number of competitors in the market? If the answer to these last two questions is yes, the authority is more likely to find that the merger significantly reduces competition. (We address the topic of mergers more generally in Chapter 7.)

You can see how market definition matters here. If the market is limited to Italian women's designer shoes, and the merging parties have market shares of, say, 30% and 25% respectively, the merger is more likely to be blocked than if the market included all women's shoes, in which the parties have only 3% and 2.5%. A similar two-stage approach is taken in other types of competition case as well—for restrictive agreements and abuse of dominance, the relevant market is first defined, and then it is assessed whether the parties concerned have an appreciable or dominant position within that relevant market.[1]

2.1.1 AVOIDING THE SUBMARKET TRAP

The above basic approach may seem obvious to you. It is how almost all competition authorities around the world assess mergers and anti-competitive practices. But it wasn't always so obvious in the history of competition law. (Nor may it remain so obvious in future, as we explain at the end of this chapter and in Chapter 7.) Courts, authorities, and scholars struggled for a long time to develop the notion of market definition.[2] A high point of confusion about market definition was reached in 1962 with the US Supreme Court ruling in *Brown Shoe*, a merger between two shoe manufacturer–retailers (a case we also cited in Chapter 1 as causing confusion about the objectives

---

[1] We make two observations on terminology here. First, the expression 'relevant market' arose in US antitrust case law in the mid-twentieth century, where the term 'relevant' usually linked the market to a specific case or to a product of a defendant firm—for example, the market relevant for cellophane wrapping. Today, the concept has acquired a specific meaning that goes beyond the simple combination of two common words. Second, a number of commentators have advocated the use of the term 'market delineation', which arguably reflects more accurately what the exercise is about than 'market definition'. However, the latter term has gained the upper hand in common usage and we join the bandwagon in this book.

[2] See Werden (1992).

of competition law).[3] In this ruling the court endorsed the principle of submarkets within relevant markets. It first stated that 'The outer boundaries of a product market are determined by the reasonable interchangeability of use or the cross-elasticity of demand between the product itself and substitutes for it.' So far so good (we explain the concept of cross-elasticity in section 2.3 below). But the court went on: 'However, within this broad market, well-defined submarkets may exist which, in themselves, constitute product markets for antitrust purposes.'[4] The lower court had defined separate relevant markets ('relevant lines of commerce') for men's shoes, women's shoes, and children's shoes, but according to the Supreme Court this did not rule out the possibility that narrower relevant markets could exist at the same time, such as by price, quality or age/sex. In *Brown Shoe* itself such further submarkets were in fact rejected in the end, mainly on the basis that this would not change the analysis as the parties had similar market shares across those submarkets (eg, they had 9.6% of boys' shoes and 7.9% of girls' shoes; we discuss this aspect of market definition in section 2.7 on supply-side substitution and market aggregation). However, several subsequent cases in the lower courts followed the *Brown Shoe* principle and ended up defining submarkets within markets. For example, in *US v Mrs Smith Pie Co* (1976), the market was defined as that for all desserts (based on consumer research), but a separate submarket was then found for frozen dessert pies, and it was in this submarket that the competition concerns were investigated.[5]

It is plain to see that defining a relevant market and then allowing for submarkets within that market is not a very helpful step in the competition analysis. Commentators in the USA were quick to point this out. Some called the submarket principle 'an intellectual monstrosity' with 'little economic justification' (Hall and Phillips, 1964); others observed that 'either there is or there is not a market in which competition may be affected ... If the line of commerce is men's shoes, it should not also be men's golf shoes: if one boundary is right, the other must be wrong' (Hale and Hale, 1966). The submarket concept was eventually abandoned in the USA (although competition authorities in other parts of the world still fall into the submarket trap occasionally). The 1982 US Merger Guidelines paved the way for the hypothetical monopolist test, which is the test on which most competition authorities base their approach to market definition these days, and which we discuss extensively in this chapter.[6] Submarkets cannot exist under this test.

Under the hypothetical monopolist approach, market definition is an intermediate step in assessing the competitive constraints on companies. It analytically tries to separate two types of competitive constraint: competition from *other* products (or geographic areas), and competition from other suppliers of the *same* product (or in the same geographic area). The market definition stage of an inquiry focuses mainly on

---

[3] *Brown Shoe Co v United States* 370 US 294 (1962).
[4] Ibid., at 325.
[5] *US v Mrs Smith Pie Co* 440 F Supp 220 (ED Pa 1976).
[6] Department of Justice (1982), 'Merger Guidelines', 14 June.

the first type, ie, competition from other products. Competition *within* the same product is assessed at a later stage in the inquiry, once the market has been defined. The way to achieve this analytical separation is to pretend that competition within products does not exist at the market definition stage, so as to focus only on competition *between* products. This pretending that competition within products does not exist is achieved by hypothetically monopolizing it (as explained in section 2.4).[7] If the relevant market is defined correctly in this way, the analysis can then focus on competition within that market, without worrying too much about outside products at that stage, or falling into the submarket trap. This is why, in our view, market definition can be a very helpful, and analytically sound, intermediate step in competition analysis.

2.1.2 AVOIDING THE PRODUCT CHARACTERISTICS TRAP

Market definition based on economic principles is about substitution and price pressure between products. It is not about the physical characteristics of products. Of course, physical features will often dictate whether products are substitutable—straw and twigs are not good substitutes for bricks—and they need to be taken into account in any market definition exercise, if only as a sense-check. But a market definition that relies solely on product characteristics can become economically unsound. Products with very different characteristics may still be substitutes in the eyes of the buyers—sugar and high-fructose corn syrup; plastic and glass bottles. One can have endless, and usually inconclusive, debates about market boundaries based on product features. Is chewing gum a relevant market because people like to chew something?[8] Are holiday parks with an indoor pool and sports facilities on site a separate market from holiday parks that have such facilities nearby but not in the park? (See section 2.5.) Moreover, market definition based on product characteristics overlooks the fact that price pressure between products does not require all customers to consider them substitutes. Babies and elderly people with dentures may not switch from bananas to other fruits, but that in itself does not make them a relevant market, as many other people may well see other fruits as substitutes. This may be sufficient for these other fruits to place a competitive constraint on bananas (see section 2.8). In this chapter we will see several examples of a reliance on product features possibly leading to erroneous conclusions about market definition.

---

[7] As we also explain later, the prevailing degree of competition within the product does have an impact on what happens after hypothetically monopolizing the market and hence on your conclusion on competition between products, so the analytical separation is not theoretically pure.

[8] This was the question in the Mexican predatory pricing case *Chicles Canel's SA de CV v Chicle Adams SA de CV*, Mexican Federal Competition Commission, 15 February 1997. See ten Kate and Niels (2006).

2.1.3 BEWARE THE PRODUCT DIFFERENTIATION TRAP

Yet some caution is called for here. The economic theory of market definition works best when products are reasonably homogeneous—for example, apples versus bananas, or cellophane versus other wrapping materials—such that you can test whether one homogeneous group of products competes with another. Market definition works less well when product differentiation is an important feature of the market. Unfortunately from this point of view, many real-world products are differentiated—women's designer shoes, cars, breakfast cereals, mobile telephones, even apples come in different sizes and tastes. Differentiation typically means that there is a spectrum of products that are close but imperfect substitutes. For example, there is a whole range of cars from superminis and small family cars to executive and luxury cars. Likewise, corner shops, shopping centres, and airports are differentiated geographically. Delineating a relevant market on such a spectrum can be difficult, artificial and potentially misleading.

- Difficult: there may be no clear cut-off points along the spectrum. You can buy a new car at virtually every price multiple of €1,000 from around €7,000–€8,000—you get a Kia Picanto or Suzuki Alto for that—to well into the €150,000s, where you start buying variants of the Mercedes SL class, the BMW 7 series, or the Lexus LS series (and that's ignoring the Ferraris, Maseratis, and Rolls Royces that have prices an order of magnitude higher still).

- Artificial: a very wide market for all cars would include not-so-close substitutes such as a Skoda Fabia and an Alfa Romeo Spider in the same market; but very narrow markets—eg, the market for Porsche 911 Carreras—may not be informative for the competition analysis either.

- Potentially misleading: the reliance on market definition as an intermediate step in competition analysis creates the impression that the question is all about products being 'in, or out'—all products outside the relevant market are not close substitutes; all products within the relevant market are equally close substitutes. This is not the case in differentiated product markets. Product substitutability is a matter of degree, and market definition means you have to draw the line somewhere, in the knowledge that the product that is just inside the line may not be so different from the product that is just outside. (In fairness to the US Supreme Court, recognition of the complications that arise in differentiated product markets was probably one of the reasons behind the submarket principle in *Brown Shoe*.)

This need for caution does not imply that market definition is inappropriate in differentiated product markets. It is still often very useful in carrying out a market definition exercise. Several of the aspects of market definition that we discuss in this chapter—supply-side substitution and market aggregation (section 2.7), and chains of substitution (section 2.9)—can be specifically tailored to deal with the challenges of product differentiation. Nevertheless, the usefulness of market definition as an intermediate step is increasingly being questioned, and alternative approaches that focus directly on competitive constraints have been proposed, particularly in merger cases. We come back to this later in the chapter, and in Chapter 7 on mergers.

2.1.4 THE REMAINDER OF THIS CHAPTER

Section 2.2 gives an overview of the possible dimensions of a relevant market, in addition to the standard product and geographic dimensions. Section 2.3 discusses the basic economic principles of demand that are of relevance to market definition, in particular demand systems, substitution, and elasticities. Section 2.4 deals with the hypothetical monopolist test for market definition, as defined in its purest form in the 1992 US Horizontal Merger Guidelines. Section 2.5 explains critical loss analysis, the tool most frequently used to put the hypothetical monopolist test into practice. The subsequent sections address further specific aspects of market definition, namely the cellophane fallacy (2.6), supply-side substitution and market aggregation (2.7), price discrimination markets (2.8), and chains of substitution and further aspects of geographic market definition (2.9). Section 2.10 discusses market definition for complementary products (including aftermarkets and networks) and for bundles, while section 2.11 explains how market definition may depend on the relevant layer of the vertical supply chain. Section 2.12 addresses the question of product migration over time (for example, from narrowband Internet access to broadband) and how this relates to product substitution. Section 2.13 discusses how relevant markets may be defined by reference to features other than price, such as quality and innovation. Section 2.14 sets out some methods and techniques that are often used for measuring substitution and elasticities in practice. Finally, in section 2.15 we return to the question: 'Why market definition?'

2.2 DIMENSIONS OF THE RELEVANT MARKET

2.2.1 THE PRODUCT AND GEOGRAPHIC DIMENSIONS

When you read about relevant markets, you commonly see that they have both a product dimension and a geographic dimension. The relevant product market consists of the group of products that are considered close substitutes—for example, the market for broadband Internet services (whether over cable or fixed-telephony networks). The relevant geographic market is the area in which that group of products is sold or purchased—for example, the market for broadband Internet services in the UK, or in the Greater London area. However, a relevant market may have several dimensions in addition to product and geography. Often these dimensions are implicitly or explicitly considered as part of the product dimension, but sometimes they are overlooked. We list these dimensions here, before turning to the basics of market definition in section 2.3.

2.2.2 TIME OF PURCHASE OR CONSUMPTION

A train journey from Oxford to London at 7.30am is not much different from a train journey from Oxford to London at 10.30am (although the carriages tend to be somewhat more crowded at the earlier time), and yet the two may be in separate relevant markets. Travellers taking the 7.30am are likely to be more time-sensitive than price-sensitive, allowing operators to charge about twice as much at 7.30am as at 10.30am. So not only are you more likely to find a free seat on the 10.30, you are also significantly better off. Such peak versus off-peak market distinctions can be made in many transport, communications, and leisure markets, where peak may refer to the time of day or to the season. Time of purchase or consumption also matters for certain 'perishable' goods such as fresh fruits, newspapers, and sports broadcasting events. In the extreme this may also give rise to different relevant markets—for example, live broadcasting of sports events is generally seen as separate from deferred broadcasting of the same events (unless your team won the cup, in which case you may want to see the whole match over and over again).

2.2.3 PERIOD OF INVESTIGATION

This second additional market dimension is also related to time, but in a different way. It refers to the period of investigation, ie, whether the investigation is forward-looking, backward-looking, or both, and for how long. Merger assessments are forward-looking. They are generally concerned with how the merger will affect competition in the next one or two years. The analysis therefore focuses on competitive constraints in the next one or two years, and market definition should assist in identifying those constraints. Market analyses (and hence market definition exercises) carried out by national regulators under the EU telecoms regulatory framework focus on the next three years, as they must identify suitable regulatory measures for a period of three years.[9] In contrast, investigations into abuse of dominance often relate to the current situation or to the recent past, when the abuse took place. The question is then whether the company in question was dominant in that period. A forward-looking market definition in such cases may overlook the fact that a market has already been monopolized (and market power already exercised), and may erroneously conclude that there are close substitutes at the prevailing price (which is already a monopoly price). This is known as the cellophane fallacy, as explained further in section 2.6.

2.2.4 DIFFERENT CUSTOMER GROUPS

There may be different markets for the same product corresponding to different customers (or groups of customers). This may occur when some customers have a greater choice of alternatives than other customers, and suppliers can exploit this difference by targeting the latter, 'captive', customers with higher prices. This gives rise to price discrimination markets, a topic we discuss in section 2.8.

2.2.5 DIFFERENT DISTRIBUTION CHANNELS

The same bottle of beer can be in a different relevant market depending on whether it is sold in a supermarket or in a bar. The same holds for a pay-TV sports package that may be sold

---

[9] Council Directive (EC) 2009/140 of the European Parliament and of the Council of 25 November 2009 amending Council Directives (EC) 2002/21 on a common regulatory framework for electronic communications networks and services, 2002/19 on access to, and interconnection of, electronic communications networks and associated facilities, and 2002/20 on the authorization of electronic communications networks and services, Art 16(6) of the amended Framework Directive.

to residential customers and to bars. This is not to say that different distribution channels always form separate markets. The main criteria are again the difference in demand patterns and the ability of suppliers to exploit this difference—when you are in a bar you are unlikely to switch to buying a drink in the supermarket, even if it is five times cheaper to do so.

2.2.6 THE VERTICAL LAYER IN THE SUPPLY CHAIN

The same product—a car, a washing machine, a bunch of fresh flowers—may pass through a whole set of intermediaries on its way from producer to end-consumer. The relevant market can be different depending on which layer of the chain is considered (and this in turn will normally depend on where in the chain the competition problem in question arises). This poses difficult questions for market definition, and we discuss these further in section 2.11. One set of questions concerns the relationship between demand by end-consumers and demand by intermediaries—is demand by the intermediary derived from consumer demand? If consumers can switch to substitutes, can the product still be a must-stock item for the intermediary? Another set of questions relates to the importance of intermediaries vis-à-vis end-consumers—should competition law be mainly concerned with end-consumers as opposed to intermediaries? Does it matter if a whole layer of the chain is excluded from the market through the conduct in question if end-consumers are no worse off?

Not all market dimensions identified in this sub-section will be relevant to all competition cases, and sometimes the additional dimensions will be implicitly considered as part of the definition of the product market. Nonetheless, we suggest that it is useful to check explicitly which of these dimensions may lead to further separate markets in any specific case at hand.

2.3 THE DEMAND SIDE: SUBSTITUTION AND ELASTICITIES

A distinction was made above between two types of competitive constraint on companies—one from other products (which is assessed as part of market definition), and one from suppliers of the same product (which is mainly assessed at a later stage in the competition analysis once the relevant market has been defined). Another useful distinction is between demand-side substitution, supply-side substitution and new entry. Demand-side substitution refers to switching behaviour by customers. This is the most immediate competitive constraint that companies face. Supply-side substitution refers to suppliers in neighbouring markets using their existing production facilities to start producing the product in question (or service the geographic area in question). We explain supply-side substitution in section 2.7. It is usually a less immediate constraint on companies than demand-side substitution. Customers are generally quicker to vote with their feet if they are unhappy than wait for other suppliers to come to them. New entry by rivals takes even more time and investment than supply-side substitution, and is therefore the least immediate constraint and not usually considered at the market definition stage. In this section we focus on the demand side.

2.3.1 THE DEMAND CURVE, WITH CHART

In Chapter 1 we saw how customers' responsiveness to price can be captured by the demand curve, how this demand curve is affected by the prices of other, substitute, products, and how this forms the basis for market definition. We elaborate on that here. Figure 2.1 shows the demand curve that we didn't draw in Chapter 1. It represents a very simple demand schedule for, say, women's designer shoes (ignore for the moment any differences between the Italian, French, or Spanish varieties of this product). As with your imaginary price–quantity space in Chapter 1, price is on the vertical axis and quantity on the horizontal axis. According to the demand schedule, no customer buys the shoes if the price is 10, and for every price decrease of 1 monetary unit there is demand by one additional customer (this is a simplification: in demand schedules such as this one the quantity normally refers to number of units of the product and not to the number of customers, but let's just say every customer buys one pair of designer shoes). So if the price is 9 there is one customer willing to pay for the shoes, if the price is 8 there are two customers, etc. If we wrote the formula for this demand schedule (something we generally try to avoid in this book), it would be $q = 10 - p$, where q stands for quantity and p for price. We could also write it as $p = 10 - q$, which is equivalent. The latter is called the inverse-demand relation, since it expresses price as a function of quantity, while the demand relation expresses quantity as a function of price. You may have noticed that Figure 2.1 is drawn as the inverse-demand relation (as price is on the y-axis and quantity on the x-axis) rather than the demand relation. For this possibly counterintuitive way economists draw demand curves, blame Alfred Marshall, who laid the foundations for microeconomic analysis in the late nineteenth century (Marshall, 1890).

The simple demand curve in Figure 2.1 allows us to explore some of the main principles that underlie market definition. As noted in Chapter 1, the exact position of the demand curve in the price–quantity space is influenced by two external factors: income,

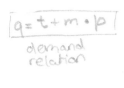

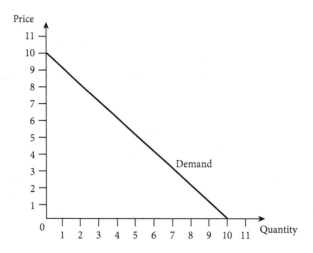

Fig. 2.1 The demand curve

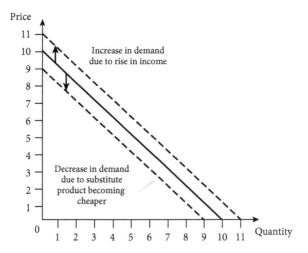

Fig. 2.2 The demand curve shifts

and demand for substitute products. Let's say there is an increase in income in the economy as a whole such that at every price there is now one additional customer who is
willing (and able) to pay for women's designer shoes. The demand curve as a whole
shifts 1 unit to the right (or 1 unit upwards, which is the same; we could write the new
demand formula as $p = 11 - q$). This is shown in Figure 2.2. Now assume that a substitute product—say, mass-produced copies of designer shoes—is reduced in price, such
that customers are lured away from designer shoes; at each price, there is now one customer less for designer shoes. This can also be seen in Figure 2.2.

What this really says is that demand for women's designer shoes is not just a function
of the price of women's designer shoes, but also of income and of the price of substitute
products. It is not unreasonable to assume that such a general relationship can hold for
any product in the real world—how much you buy of a product is influenced by its
price, by the price of alternative products, and by your income. Now picture a whole
demand system in which demand for each good in the economy is expressed as a function of the price for that good, of total income, and of the prices of all other goods in the
economy, ie, not just substitutes (economists have developed several types of demand
system, but the most common is the Marshallian demand system, after the same Alfred
Marshall). For market definition it is obviously the closer substitutes that matter most,
but it is useful to bear in mind that within this demand system (but also in the real
world) all products are to some extent substitutes of each other—any euro you don't
spend on designer shoes you can spend on foreign holidays or French wine instead.
This demand system forms the starting point for the hypothetical monopolist test, as we
explain further in this chapter. Being aware of this demand system helps you understand the basics of market definition, and also some of the common mistakes that are
sometimes made when defining relevant markets.

To help you picture this concept of the demand system, imagine a tablecloth. Each point on the cloth represents a product. Now lift the tablecloth at one specific point, and assume this is like raising the price of that product. The neighbouring products on the cloth are lifted up as well—these are the closest substitutes. The next closest substitutes go up to a lesser extent, and more remote products show no noticeable change. For example, when you lift the tablecloth at the point where apples are, then you may drag up pears and other fruits to some extent as well. Designer shoes are in the demand system too, but probably so far away from the apples that there is no noticeable effect on them from you lifting the cloth. The same would hold if you lifted the cloth at the point where the shoes are—apples are unlikely to be noticeably affected. Market definition is in essence about identifying those products that are close substitutes in the demand system—ie, those products that move together when you lift the tablecloth.[10]

2.3.2 DEMAND RESPONSIVENESS AND ELASTICITY

We noted above that demand-side substitution—ie, by customers—is the most immediate constraint on producers. What matters for market definition is how customers react to changes in price. Other non-price features, such as quality, are generally taken as given for the purpose of market definition (although they may sometimes be considered separately, as discussed in section 2.13). The demand curve in Figure 2.1 shows prices and quantities for a given product quality (changes in quality may have the effect of shifting the curve up or down, just like income and substitute products did in Figure 2.2).

The demand curve captures how customers react to price changes. There are two ways of looking at this: demand responsiveness and demand elasticity. Demand responsiveness can be inferred from the slope of the curve. In Figure 2.1 this slope has an angle of −1 (a 1-unit fall in price leads to a 1-unit rise in demand). If we draw a flatter curve, we would say that demand is more responsive to price (a small price change leads to a bigger change in quantity). The extreme would be a horizontal curve, where even a tiny increase or decrease in price leads to a loss or gain of all demand (this is the demand an individual supplier faces in perfect competition; recall from Chapter 1 that in this case the supplier is a price-taker and faces no choice but to supply at the market price). A steeper curve would represent less responsive demand. The extreme would be a vertical demand curve, where the same quantity is demanded regardless of what price is charged.

A more commonly used measure is the price elasticity of demand. This represents the percentage change in quantity following a 1% increase in price. An elasticity of −2 means that a 1% increase in price leads to a 2% fall in demand. Price elasticity can also be described as the percentage change in quantity divided by the percentage change

$$\frac{quantity \; \varepsilon}{price \; \varepsilon} = price \; elasticity$$

---

[10] Indeed, some authors have proposed a market definition test that focuses purely on which products rise above a certain threshold with the central product on the tablecloth. This would be an alternative to the hypothetical monopolist test, which, in terms of this analogy, focuses on which products prevent the monopolist from lifting the tablecloth. See ten Kate and Niels (2009).

in price. So if a 10% price increase results in a 20% fall in demand, the elasticity is, again, −2.[11] If a 10% price increase results in only a 3% fall in demand, the elasticity is −0.3. More accurately, this measure should be called the own-price elasticity of demand, as it relates the demand for a product to changes in its own price. Another measure that is relevant for market definition is the cross-price elasticity, which represents how demand for one product reacts to changes in the price of another product. If a 10% increase in the price of flights between London and Paris results in a 15% increase in demand for Eurostar train journeys, the cross-price elasticity of rail with respect to air travel between the two cities is 1.5 (15% divided by 10%). Note that the own-price elasticity is usually negative, since price and demand move in opposite directions (in Chapter 1 we said that 'Veblen goods' are the exception to this norm—they are more in demand as they become more expensive). The cross-price elasticity is positive when two products are substitutes—a price increase in one is associated with a demand increase for the other as a result of customers switching (like in the air–rail example above). The cross-price elasticity is negative for what economists call complementary goods—an increase in the price of gin not only reduces demand for gin itself but also demand for tonic water, as people will consume fewer gin-and-tonics. We explain in section 2.4 where in the market definition process own-price elasticities are of relevance and where cross-price elasticities play a role. We return to the role of complements in market definition in section 2.10.

Own-price elasticities play an important part in microeconomic theory and competition analysis. As we explain below in the context of the hypothetical monopolist test, elasticities are directly linked to the price that monopolists set when maximizing their profits. The more elastic the demand to start with, the lower the price that the monopolist can set (intuitively, this is because elastic demand means that customers are responsive to price). If the own-price elasticity lies between 0 and −1, demand is said to be inelastic. Customers do not respond much to price changes—a 10% price increase means customer demand falls by less than 10%. Where demand is inelastic, there is clearly scope for increasing price—indeed, a profit-maximizing monopolist would always do so. In contrast, demand is said to be elastic if the own-price elasticity is greater than 1 in absolute terms—say, −2 or −3 (because the own-price elasticity is a negative number, more elastic means a 'more negative', so smaller, number, which makes it difficult to explain this intuitively as we keep having to add the qualifier 'in absolute terms'). Elastic demand—eg, where a 10% price increase results in a 20% or 30% loss of sales— makes it less attractive for profit-maximizing companies to raise the price.

---

[11] Below and in section 2.4 we explain that if you raise the price by 10%, the elasticity itself may have changed, so this last interpretation of elasticity, while intuitive and therefore often used, is not strictly correct. From a theoretically pure perspective, an elasticity refers only to one specific point on the demand curve, and infinitesimal price changes from that point.

2.3.3 A HEALTH WARNING ON ELASTICITIES

Own-price elasticities must be used and interpreted with care. Competition practitioners (be they lawyers or economists) do not always bear this in mind. The reason is that the elasticity value depends crucially on the price level at which it is measured. Demand for a product can be inelastic when the price is low, and elastic when the price is high.

To see this, consider Figure 2.3, which shows the same demand curve we saw earlier. The (inverse) demand function for this curve was p = 10 – q. We defined the own-price elasticity as the percentage change in demand divided by the percentage change in price. We endeavour to keep algebra to a minimum in this book, but it is useful to explain the steps in calculating elasticities here—see also Table 2.1. The elasticity can be expressed as Δq/q divided by Δp/p (where Δ is the symbol for a very small change, so the first expression shows the change in q divided by q, which gives the percentage change[12]). This can be rewritten as Δq/Δp times p/q. Of these last two expressions, the important one to explain our point here is p/q, ie, price divided by quantity.[13] The fact that the elasticity mathematically depends on the ratio between price and quantity implies that it matters where on the demand curve the elasticity is measured. It also implies that the elasticity increases as price increases, ie, as we move further up the

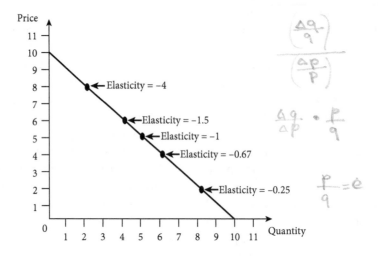

Fig. 2.3 Elasticities vary along the demand curve

[12] Well, it gives the per-unit change. Multiply this by 100% and you get the percentage change. Economists often do not make this distinction explicit as it is easier to speak of the percentage change, but leave out the 'multiply by 100%'.

[13] The other expression, Δq/Δp, represents the functional relationship between price and quantity and is the inverse of the slope of the curve in Figure 2.3 (the slope is Δp/Δq). Technically, Δq/Δp is the first derivative of quantity with respect to price and equals –1 here (this is because the demand function is q = 10 – p; if the demand function had been q = 10 – 2p then Δq/Δp would have equalled –2).

Table 2.1 An elasticity calculation step by step

Description of the step	Result
Demand curve function	$q = 10 - p$
Inverse demand curve function (shown in Figure 2.3)	$p = 10 - q$
Percentage change in demand (we omit multiplying by 100%)	$\Delta q / q$
Percentage change in price	$\Delta p / p$
Own-price elasticity	$(\Delta q / q) / (\Delta p / p) = (\Delta q / \Delta p) \times (p / q)$
Slope (first derivative) of the demand curve	$\Delta q / \Delta p = -1$
Own-price elasticity at $p = 2$ and $q = 8$	$-1 \times (2/8) = -0.25$
Own-price elasticity at $p = 4$ and $q = 6$	$-1 \times (4/6) = -0.67$

demand curve. Take a point at the lower end of the curve, where price is 2 and quantity is 8. Our formula tells us that the elasticity at this point is –1 (see the last footnote) times 2/8, so –0.25. This implies highly inelastic demand. A bit higher up the curve, at a price of 4 and quantity of 6, demand is still inelastic, but less so—the elasticity is –1 times 4/6, so –0.67. At a price of 5 and quantity of 5 the elasticity equals –1. At any point above that, demand is elastic. So at a price of 6 and quantity of 4 the elasticity is –1.5, and at a price of 8 and quantity of 2 the elasticity is –4. All this is on the very same demand curve that has the same slope throughout.

You should therefore treat with some scepticism general statements such as 'the demand for petrol is inelastic' or 'the demand for foreign holidays is elastic'. The demand for petrol may be relatively unresponsive to price changes—and this may be reflected in a relatively steep slope of the demand curve—but whether demand for petrol is inelastic or elastic depends on the point of measurement, ie, whether petrol prices are already high or low.[14] The important implication of this is that the outcome of the hypothetical monopolist test also depends on the point of measurement—a theme to which we return below.

2.4 BRINGING IN THE SUPPLY SIDE: THE HYPOTHETICAL MONOPOLIST TEST

2.4.1 WHERE DOES THE HYPOTHETICAL MONOPOLIST COME FROM?

You saw before that in the demand system, like on the tablecloth, all products are to some extent substitutes and impose price pressure on each other. Market definition is about drawing the line somewhere such that the relevant market includes only the

---

[14] One exception to this is where the demand curve is 'iso-elastic', ie, it has the same elasticity along the whole of the curve. This is a demand curve specification that has some interesting theoretical properties but limited practical value.

closest substitutes which impose the most significant price discipline on each other. There are various methodologies to determine where and how the line is drawn—and some are more economically sound than others—but you should be aware that the line itself will always have an element of arbitrariness.

One way of drawing the line is to simply lift the tablecloth—raise the price of the product in question by, say, 5%—and include in the relevant market for that product those other products that move up in price as well up to a certain (arbitrary) point, say 4% (assuming that the output of those other products stays constant). This approach would look purely at demand interactions between products within the demand system—it does not say anything about any supply-side factors that might cause such a price change in the first place. The debates leading up to the hypothetical monopolist test in the USA, however, focused on the supply side. They centred around the question: which products constrain suppliers in the market from imposing a price increase? An early idea was that of the hypothetical price-fixing cartel—which firms (and products) would need to be included in the cartel such that a price increase would not be undermined by outside competitors? This idea of the hypothetical cartel then made way for the hypothetical monopolist—after all, monopolizing a market outright is generally more effective than cartelizing it. In this approach to market definition, it is the hypothetical monopolist who brings about the price rise in the demand system, and it is the impact on the profitability of the monopolist that determines the likelihood and sustainability of the price rise, and hence the boundary of the relevant market. If it is not profitable (or profit-maximizing—see below) for a hypothetical monopolist to raise price by a small amount—usually 5% or 10%—that must be because too much demand is lost to other products, and the nearest of those substitute products must be included in the market. In other words, so the logic of this methodology goes, a market is something worth monopolizing. In terms of the tablecloth analogy, the relevant market is formed by those products that prevent the hypothetical monopolist from lifting the cloth by 5%–10%.

First introduced in the 1982 US Merger Guidelines, the wording of the hypothetical monopolist test was refined in the 1992 Horizontal Merger Guidelines, published jointly by the Department of Justice and the Federal Trade Commission:

> A market is defined as a product or group of products and a geographic area in which it is produced or sold such that a hypothetical profit-maximizing firm, not subject to price regulation, that was the only present and future producer or seller of those products in that area likely would impose at least a 'small but significant and non-transitory increase in price', assuming the terms of sale of all other products are held constant. A relevant market is a group of products and a geographic area that is no bigger than necessary to satisfy this test.[15]

---

[15] Department of Justice and Federal Trade Commission (1992), 'Horizontal Merger Guidelines', s 1.0, reprinted in 4 Trade Reg Rep 104.

Each of these words in the definition has a specific meaning, and we will dissect it bit by bit. In the first sentence you will recognize the product and geographic dimension of the market (and you know from section 2.2 that you should be checking for additional dimensions as well). Also in the first sentence you see the hypothetical monopolist, ie, the 'only present and future' supplier of those products in that area. Importantly, the monopolist is a profit-maximizing firm (just like any firm in a microeconomics textbook), and there is no regulation that would prevent it from raising prices. The hypothetical monopolist test draws the line for market definition by reference to a 'small but significant and non-transitory increase in price'—now commonly known as 'SSNIP'—that the monopolist 'likely would' impose (assuming no price change for other products). We return to this below. Finally, the text implies that there is a distinction between 'a market' and 'a relevant market' as determined by the 'no bigger than necessary' criterion, a subtlety in the hypothetical monopolist test to which we also return later. There may be various 'candidate' markets, but only one relevant market (and no sub-markets). Below we consider what a hypothetical monopolist 'likely would' do.

Before that, it is worth making some last comments on the notion of the hypothetical cartel. Although market definition now focuses on the hypothetical monopolist, thinking in terms of cartel price increases can still be useful in certain cases. In a US damages action in 1989 against a concrete producer cartel, the question arose as to whether concrete in West Los Angeles was a relevant market. The plaintiff argued that the success of the cartel itself proved the existence of a relevant market. The court agreed:

> As a purely logical matter, French [the plaintiff] is unquestionably correct. A price-fixing conspiracy confined to manufacturers of concrete would not have been able to succeed if concrete were not a distinct product market: when the cartel attempted to raise prices, customers would simply switch to sand, brick, gravel or some other construction material. Similarly, a price-fixing conspiracy confined to firms in West Los Angeles would not have succeeded if West Los Angeles were not a distinct geographic market: when the cartel attempted to raise prices, customers would simply take their business to East Los Angeles or San Diego or Phoenix. If a group of firms is able to fix prices, it is because their customers have nowhere else to turn. Every price-fixing conspiracy thus identifies directly, in a real world context, a group of firms which is insulated from outside competitive pressures. That is precisely what conventional market definition evidence attempts to identify artificially, by the collection and interpretation of economic data regarding the relationship between various demand curves, by common sense assumptions about the interchangeability of similar products, and the like.[16]

So the success of the cartel was seen as proof that the market was no wider than that for concrete in West Los Angeles.

The notion of the hypothetical cartel has recently made a reappearance in economic thinking on market definition. The 2010 Horizontal Merger Guidelines indicate that the US agencies may employ the concept of a hypothetical profit-maximizing cartel

---

[16] *EW French & Sons v General Portland* 885 F 2d 1392, 1402 (9th Cir. 1989) at [65].

instead of a hypothetical monopolist if the pricing incentives faced by the actual suppliers in the market differ substantially from those of the monopolist because they sell products outside the candidate market as well.[17] The example given is where the candidate market is one for durable equipment and the suppliers selling that equipment derive substantial revenues from selling spare parts and service for that equipment. We discuss such situations in section 2.10.

2.4.2 WHAT WOULD THE HYPOTHETICAL MONOPOLIST DO?

You start with the product where the competition concern arises in the first place—let's say women's designer shoes as in the merger at the start of this chapter (we return later to the importance of choosing the right starting point for the test—you might instead choose to start with Italian designer shoes if these are sufficiently differentiated from the other varieties). To define the boundaries of the market you then hypothetically monopolize the supply of women's designer shoes. All of a sudden, instead of multiple suppliers (including your two merging parties) there is only one. Luckily, economic theory tells us exactly what the monopolist is going to do in this candidate market.

As explained in Chapter 1, the monopolist will set its price and quantity at the profit-maximizing level. Here we explain in a bit more detail (and with a chart) how the profit-maximizing point is found. In Figure 2.4, which is the standard monopoly representation that you will find in any microeconomics textbook, the monopolist faces the entire (inverse) demand curve for women's designer shoes (since by assumption there are no other suppliers). The demand function is the same as before, represented by the equation $p = 10 - q$. Assume for now (like economists typically do when analysing this standard monopoly situation) that the monopolist does not need to worry about any shifts in the demand curve (as explained in section 2.3, the demand curve may shift up or down with changes in income or in the prices of other products, but the analysis here abstracts from such changes—in the hypothetical monopolist test this abstraction is covered by the assumption that 'the terms of sale of all other products are held constant').

Profits for the monopolist equal revenue minus costs. Some basic maths (which we don't explain here) means that maximum profit is achieved when marginal profit is zero (profits can no longer be increased further), and this occurs at the point where marginal revenue equals marginal cost. We now set out the steps in calculating this optimal point—see also Table 2.2. Revenue equals price times quantity—so $p \times q$, which equals $(10 - q) \times q$. This means that marginal revenue is $10 - 2q$ (the first derivative of revenue with respect to quantity). The marginal revenue curve is shown in Figure 2.4—it starts at the same point as the demand curve (price equals 10 at zero quantity), but then slopes downward twice as steeply. Now suppose that marginal cost equals 2 per unit of output (so total cost is $2q$). This is also shown in the figure. Total profit is maximized at $q = 4$, since that is where marginal revenue equals marginal cost ($10 - 2 \times 4$ equals 2). At this point,

---

[17] Department of Justice and Federal Trade Commission (2010), 'Horizontal Merger Guidelines', 19 August, p 9.

Table 2.2 Calculating the profit-maximizing point step by step

Description of the step	Result
Inverse demand function	$p = 10 - q$, $\quad p \cdot q$
Monopoly revenue = price × quantity $p \cdot q$	$(10 - q) \times q$
Marginal cost per unit	2
Monopoly profit = revenue − total cost	$(10 - q) \times q - (2 \times q)$
Monopoly marginal revenue (first derivative of revenue with respect to quantity)	$10 - 2q$
Monopoly profits are maximized where marginal revenue equals marginal cost	$10 - 2q = 2$, so $q = 4$ and $p = 6$
Monopoly profit at q = 4 and p = 6 (optimum point)	$(6 \times 4) - (2 \times 4) = 16$
Monopoly profit at q = 5 and p = 5	$(5 \times 5) - (2 \times 5) = 15$
Monopoly profit at q = 3 and p = 7	$(7 \times 3) - (2 \times 3) = 15$

price equals 6 (10 − 4), and the profit margin on each unit equals 4 (price minus marginal cost), so total profit on the 4 units sold equals 16. Total profit is shown in the figure as area A. Another way of describing the profit-maximizing point is that it is where the surface of area A is the greatest. If you set price a bit lower, at 5, total profit falls to 15 (as quantity increases to 5 and the profit margin per unit is 3). If you raise price to 7 and the profit margin to 5, quantity falls to 3 and total profit is also 15. Hence, as a monopolist you cannot do better than set the price at 6 and quantity at 4, making a profit of 16.

Recall from section 2.3 that at this profit-maximizing point of q = 4 and p = 6 the own-price elasticity is −1.5. So the monopolist ends up on the elastic part of the demand curve.

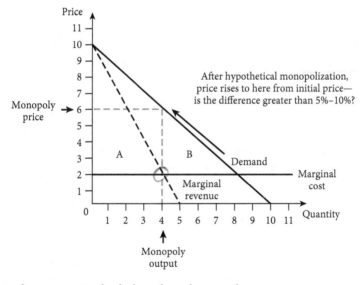

Fig. 2.4 Profit-maximization by the hypothetical monopolist

Contrast this with the perfect competition outcome, where price equals marginal cost, so p = 2, and quantity is 8, and the own-price elasticity equals –0.25. So you are on the inelastic part of the demand curve when there is perfect competition on the supply side. You can see how a monopolist would rapidly move away from there, raising prices and not losing too much custom in the process.[18] Area A in Figure 2.4 reflects a transfer of consumer surplus to producer profit when moving from perfect competition to monopoly. Area B reflects the consumer surplus that is lost because those units are no longer sold even though consumers were willing to pay more than the cost of producing them—area B is the deadweight welfare loss to society resulting from monopoly (the lost consumer surplus accrues to no one; it's wasted) compared with perfect competition.

Back to what this means for market definition. You have seen now at what price and quantity point you end up after hypothetically monopolizing the market. It is the point which the profit-maximizing monopolist 'would' choose. All you need to do next is compare that point with where you started before monopolizing the market, and measure how much the price has changed—is this change 'small but significant'? If the starting point was perfect competition, monopolization of the market in our example would lead to an increase from p = 2 to p = 6, so by 200%—clearly a large and significant increase in price. However, the starting point does not need to be perfect competition; the market pre-monopolization may have been characterized by some form of oligopolistic competition, such that price was already higher than marginal cost. If the market price pre-monopolization was, say, 5, the hypothetical monopolist would impose a price increase of 1 monetary unit to 6, so 20%, which is more than the 5%–10% range for SSNIP. If the market price was 5.75, the change to 6 would represent a 4% increase, so less than 5%–10%. If the market price was 6, monopolization would not result in any price increase. You can see that it therefore matters where exactly you start before applying the hypothetical monopolist test. If the product in question is already priced at the monopoly level, a hypothetical monopolist would not impose any further price increases as that would not maximize its profit. That does not imply that the market is not worth monopolizing, because it clearly is in this case. This result, and the erroneous conclusion you can draw from it, is known as the cellophane fallacy, which we discuss further in section 2.6.

2.4.3 WHY THE 'SS' IN SSNIP?

The term 'SSNIP' has become widely known in competition law. Indeed, the terms 'SSNIP test' and 'hypothetical monopolist test' are used interchangeably. Apart from raising an eyebrow at this somewhat strange abbreviation to describe a price increase, you may have wondered why it has to be a 'small but significant' increase in the first place. Is this for some scientific reason, or is it purely arbitrary? Would the test still work with a large price increase? Another question that springs to mind is why 'small but

---

[18] This is not always the case. Depending on the level of marginal cost, there are markets where even with perfect competition you would be on the elastic part of the demand curve, such that a hypothetical monopolist might not raise prices much further. Products like that are less likely to be worth monopolizing, as we discuss in section 2.12.

significant' is usually interpreted as 5% or 10%? Are there any reasons to prefer 5% over 10%, or vice versa? You will recall from the earlier sections that substitution between products is a matter of degree. It is not all or nothing, one–zero. If you lift the tablecloth high enough, many remote products will move up as well. If you raise the price of women's designer shoes far enough, there comes a point when even the cheaper mass-produced shoes become an attractive alternative. Any cut-off point for such a price increase is inherently arbitrary. You could perform a market definition test that asks if a hypothetical monopolist would raise price by 20%, 50%, or 100%. Conceptually, these are all valid tests. Why do most competition authorities use 5%–10% as the threshold? There are various reasons for this—policy-related, technical, and practical.

First, the policy-related reasons. Competition law is generally concerned with mergers and anti-competitive practices that reduce competition in the market and hence lead to higher prices. How high is too high? Some competition authorities consider that even a 5% increase is already of significant detriment to consumers. For example, the UK Competition Commission stated in its previous (2003) Merger Guidelines:

> The Commission will normally use 5 per cent for the SSNIP test, rather than the more common 5–10 per cent, because in many instances an increase in the price of a product of around 5 per cent (with all other prices unchanged) might reasonably be judged to have a significant effect on customers' expenditure on the product and so provides an appropriate level at which to consider the test. In addition, a 5 per cent increase in price might be expected to have an appreciable effect on a firm's profit margin, the main issue then being whether demand would be reduced to such an extent as to offset the effects of the higher margin.[19]

Of course the hypothetical monopolist is not real and does not impose price increases for real. But the SSNIP threshold is related to the more general concern about price rises. An authority, like the Competition Commission, that applies a 5% threshold can be said to be stricter than an authority that applies a 10% or 20% threshold. A higher threshold for the SSNIP means a greater chance of broader markets being defined and hence a lower likelihood of a finding of market power. Say you found that the hypothetical monopolist for flights between London and Paris would raise prices by 8% to maximize profits. A 5% threshold would mean the SSNIP test is passed and flights between London and Paris are a separate market (and hence you are more likely to consider the merger being investigated to be problematic). In contrast, under a 10% or 20% threshold the test is not passed, and you would include more substitute products in the relevant market. Again, there is no scientifically correct cut-off point, but most competition authorities would generally be concerned about price increases of 5%–10% (and some are concerned at only 5%), so there are policy reasons to define 'small but significant' as 5%–10%.

---

[19] Competition Commission (2003), 'Merger References: Competition Commission Guidelines', [2.8]. The 2010 Guidelines still prefer 5% but are more open to different thresholds: 'When applying the hypothetical monopolist test, the Authorities will normally use a SSNIP of 5 per cent, though they may sometimes use a higher or lower number.' Competition Commission and Office of Fair Trading (2010), 'Merger Assessment Guidelines', September, [5.2.12].

Second, there are some technical reasons for using 5%–10% for the SSNIP rather than a higher threshold. How far the monopolist's profit-maximizing price lies above the initial price depends on the initial own-price elasticity. The more inelastic demand is (before hypothetically monopolizing the market), the more the monopolist will raise prices (and hence the more likely it is that the 5%–10% SSNIP threshold will be met). As explained in section 2.3, elasticities vary depending on the price point at which they are measured. Economists can usually estimate elasticities only at current price levels, not at the (hypothetical) monopoly price level. The estimated elasticities can therefore be used only to test very small price increases above the current price level—hence 5% or at most 10% for the SSNIP threshold. Beyond that it is difficult to know how quickly demand becomes more elastic (so how quickly the profit-maximizing price is reached)—a 20% SSNIP threshold would lead to uncertain results because the elasticity value might differ too much between the starting price point (where we can measure the elasticity) and the point to which price is increased to maximize profits (for which we don't have an estimate). Following this logic, the hypothetical monopolist test would be most accurately applied if the threshold used were 1% or even less. However, from a statistical perspective such a very small increase may not be noticeable or distinguishable from 'noise' in the price data. In statistics, a 5% cut-off point is often used to determine statistical significance, for no 'hard' reason other than 5% being sufficiently different from zero (it is 'significant') while at the same time still being a 'small' number. So, for pragmatic reasons, 5% (or 10%) is neither too small nor too large; it seems about right as a threshold for the SSNIP test.

Third, there are practical reasons for using a SSNIP of 5% or 10%. The hypothetical monopolist test is frequently applied using critical loss analysis (see section 2.5). This in turn often uses evidence from consumer surveys in which respondents are asked how they would react to a SSNIP. Surveys are difficult (but not impossible) to design in such a way that you get objective and meaningful answers (see section 2.14). Some people find it difficult to think in percentages. The clearest way of asking the SSNIP question may therefore be to refer to a 10% price increase, and relate this to a price the respondents actually, or typically, pay. For example, if a commuter train ticket costs €7.50, you can ask what consumers would do if it were raised by 10% to €8.25 (for a period of one or two years; see the discussion on the 'N' in SSNIP below). A hypothetical 5% increase to €7.88 (rounded) or 7.5% increase to €8.06 might be more difficult for survey respondents to relate to. At the same time, there are practical reasons why using 5% for a SSNIP is not necessarily better or worse. The degree of precision with which elasticities and customer switching rates after small price increases can be measured in practice is inherently limited. Any distinction between 5% and 10% may be easily outweighed by the uncertainties in the empirical estimates and would therefore be spurious.

2.4.4 WHY THE 'N' IN SSNIP?

The other aspect of the SSNIP is the 'non-transitory' nature of the price increase. The 'N' in SSNIP is as arbitrary as the 'SS', and the cut-off point is usually chosen for policy and practical reasons. The main rationale for considering a 'non-transitory' as opposed to a transitory price increase is that competition authorities are not normally concerned with transitory market power. Positions of market power tend to be eroded over time (more on this in Chapter 3). If it suddenly starts to rain in a busy market place, vendors who sell umbrellas find themselves controlling a scarce good that is in strong demand, such that they can probably extract a hefty monopoly rent. The same is true for car hire and taxi companies when the European airspace is closed due to volcanic ash, and stranded passengers across Europe desperately try to get home.[20] Such a position of market power will not last, and does not usually merit a separate market definition by time of consumption (the first additional market dimension discussed in section 2.2). Only market power that persists over time is of concern. The small but significant increase in price must therefore be 'non-transitory'. One exception to this is the electricity generation market, where authorities have been concerned about very short, 30-minute, periods of market power and have defined relevant markets accordingly (these 30-minute periods recur more frequently and predictably than the periods of rain or volcanic ash clouds, so in reality in electricity generation the authorities are concerned about a series of regular short periods of market power over a longer time period).[21]

How long is non-transitory? Competition authorities usually refer to a period of one to two years. In some markets, customers may sign contracts with providers for a minimum period, say, six or twelve months. By interpreting non-transitory as one or two years, you would still take into account the fact that customers may switch once the contract expires, even if they can't switch before then. Longer-term contracts, say, for three or five years, are not taken into account—customers on these contracts will be in the hypothetical monopolist's pocket for the duration of the non-transitory period. The length of the period has implications for how strict a competition authority is. A three- or five-year period would imply a less strict approach than one or two years, as market dynamics are given more time to undermine the monopolist's price increase. The hypothetical monopolist for a commuter rail service may find it profitable to raise fares for one year, but not much longer, because at some point beyond one year too many customers would begin to use alternative modes of transport (eg, they might decide to buy a car). If the 'N' is taken as one year, this would still mean a separate relevant market for the commuter rail service, but if the 'N' is greater than one year the market is wider. In terms of the practical reasons for choosing a particular 'N', as with the 'SS', the analysis is likely to be more precise if you take one or two years than if you take longer periods. This is because market dynamics are difficult to predict further into the future—beyond one or two years any analysis is likely to become speculative. Likewise, the profit-maximizing price over a one-year or two-year period would depend on which costs are marginal (variable with output) over the period. Recall that the longer the time

---

[20] One of us paid €3,000 for a taxi ride from Rome to Paris during the April 2010 volcanic ash incident. Economists do not learn about economics only from textbooks.

[21] Competition Commission (2001), 'AES and British Energy'; and Office of Fair Trading and Ofgem (2005), 'Application in the energy sector; competition law guideline'.

period, the more costs become variable, so it becomes more difficult to predict where the monopolist would set the profit-maximizing price.

The Horizontal Merger Guidelines in the USA do not specify the length of 'N'—they refer to 'lasting for the foreseeable future'. The UK Competition Commission's previous (2003) Merger Guidelines stated that the SSNIP 'is assumed to last for the foreseeable future', but then added that the authority 'will typically consider the extent of response which is likely to occur within a year of the price rise (although the exact time period will depend on the nature of the market considered)'.[22] The Canadian Competition Bureau's Merger Guidelines define non-transitory as one year (although with a footnote caveat that market characteristics may sometimes require a different period).[23] Curiously, the European Commission Notice on market definition refers to a 'permanent' increase in price.[24] In line with the description above, this would imply that the Commission takes greater account of long-term market dynamics and tends to define wider markets as a result. However, another possible explanation for the European Commission text would be that the term 'permanent' is simply an alternative (and somewhat inaccurate) way of capturing the concept of 'non-transitory'.

2.4.5 AN ITERATIVE PROCESS: FROM THE FOCAL PRODUCT TO THE 'SMALLEST' MARKET

We have described what the hypothetical monopolist test is: would the hypothetical monopolist impose a SSNIP? Here we discuss the importance of selecting the right start and end point for the test, ie, the right product and geographic area.

Let's begin with the end point. The US Merger Guidelines make a subtle distinction between the definition of a market—which is where a hypothetical monopolist would impose a SSNIP—and the relevant market—which is 'a group of products and a geographic area that is no bigger than necessary to satisfy this test'. In other words, the relevant market is the 'smallest' market in which the monopolist would impose a SSNIP.[25] A hypothetical mobile phone monopolist operating in the whole of Europe would be able to impose a SSNIP, so the whole of Europe would be a market. But a hypothetical mobile phone monopolist in Germany would probably also be able to impose a SSNIP. Which of these two candidate markets is the relevant market? Let's say it's the whole of Europe. We then find that there are so many mobile operators in Europe that none of them has significant market power, and conclude that there is no competition concern. This would be an erroneous conclusion. Within Europe there is at least one 'pocket' of

---

[22] Competition Commission (2003), 'Merger References: Competition Commission Guidelines', [2.7]. The 2010 Guidelines do not indicate how 'non-transitory' should be interpreted. Competition Commission and Office of Fair Trading (2010), 'Merger Assessment Guidelines', September.

[23] Competition Bureau (2004), 'Merger Enforcement Guidelines', September, [3.4].

[24] European Commission (1997), 'Notice on the Definition of Relevant Market for the Purposes of Community Competition Law', 97/C372/03, [17].

[25] The 2010 Horizontal Merger Guidelines no longer refer to this smallest market principle. We think that this may cause confusion, as this is one of the fundamental principles of the hypothetical monopolist test.

market power—in this example, Germany—where a hypothetical monopolist (and possibly real companies as well) can raise prices. Therefore, Germany should be the relevant market. By taking the smallest market you avoid overlooking pockets of market power. It also means that you don't need to worry about submarkets within the relevant market.

So the end point for market definition is to find the smallest market in which the hypothetical monopolist would impose a SSNIP. But what is the starting point? Recall that market definition is not an end in itself, but only an intermediate step in the analysis of competitive constraints. For market definition to be informative, the starting point must always be the product in relation to which the competition case arises. If the case concerns mobile telephony services in Germany—say, two German operators wish to merge—the first candidate product and geographic area to hypothetically monopolize would be mobile telephony in Germany. If the concern arises from a proposed merger between two producers of frozen dessert pies in north-east USA, then that is the hypothetical monopolist's initial domain. The starting point for a relevant market is sometimes called the focal or labelling product (and geographic area).

The focal product can be narrowly defined. After all, you are trying to find the smallest market in which a SSNIP can be imposed in order to identify pockets of market power. Thus, in the merger case at the beginning of this chapter you can start with Italian women's designer shoes (both our merging parties own Italian brands), and hypothetically monopolize that market so as to test whether they face competitive constraints from French or Spanish designer shoes—if the monopolist would impose a SSNIP, the relevant market is indeed confined to Italian designer shoes. However, in section 2.1 we also warned that in markets with differentiated products the whole market definition exercise may become uninformative, especially if the focal products become too narrow (Porsche 911 Carreras, or Prada shoes). We recommend that in these situations you take a view on whether the products concerned are so differentiated that market definition loses value as an intermediate step (because you potentially end up finding that each differentiated product is worth monopolizing and hence in theory constitutes a separate relevant market). If differentiation is that significant, it may be more appropriate to focus the analysis directly on the competitive constraints and closeness of competition between the differentiated products, skipping market definition altogether (we return to this later in the chapter and in Chapter 7 on mergers). However, we think that there is often no need for skipping market definition, because in many differentiated product markets you can still find meaningful groups of products that are reasonably similar and that you can hypothetically monopolize to test the constraints from other groups—for example, top-of-the-range sports cars, Italian women's designer shoes, or even all women's designer shoes. There is an element of judgement that you may have to exercise here.

It is also important to bear in mind that in any competition case there can be more than one focal product (or area). Indeed, you should in principle define a relevant market for any product (or area) where you might suspect a possible competition concern. If a German and a UK mobile telephony operator wish to merge, you have to define a relevant market separately for mobile telephony in Germany as the focal product and mobile telephony in the UK as the focal product. These are two different market definition exercises.

(Note that in this case you may well find that neither relevant market has the other in it, and hence that there are no competitive overlaps between the merging parties. This is one of the rare situations in which a narrow market definition, ie, separate national markets rather than a cross-border one, actually favours the merging parties; normally broader markets favour merging parties, and hence merging parties favour broader markets.)

Likewise, if a producer of frozen dessert pies merges with a producer of ice cream, you have to apply the hypothetical monopolist test to each of these products separately. The two exercises may well lead to the same market definition that has both products in it, for example, a market for all desserts. However, you might also find that substitution is strong in one direction but not the other. Say that frozen dessert pies are not worth monopolizing because consumers switch en masse to ice cream and other desserts if the price is raised, while at the same time, in the market with ice cream as the focal product, a hypothetical monopolist does find it profitable to impose a SSNIP because fewer consumers switch away to other desserts. So ice cream is in the market for frozen dessert pies, but frozen dessert pies are not in the market for ice cream. Alternatively, you might find that ice cream is not worth monopolizing but that fruit-flavoured yogurt is the nearest substitute, so the relevant market for ice cream contains ice cream and fruit-flavoured yogurt (more on the ranking of substitutes below). Again, frozen dessert pies are not in the market for ice cream. If you had started the market definition exercise from only one of these products, you would have observed only a partial view of substitution between the products. If you had defined the market starting only from ice cream, you might have erroneously concluded that the merger is of no concern because frozen dessert pies are in a separate market, as you would have overlooked the fact that, the other way round, ice cream does impose a competitive constraint on frozen dessert pies.

2.4.6 ASYMMETRIC MARKETS

Markets can be asymmetric in this regard—one product may be in the market for another product, even if that other product is not in its market (there is debate among economists about how often such asymmetry occurs, but it is a theoretical possibility and has been found in some competition cases, as discussed below). That is why it is important to make clear which is the focal or labelling product of a relevant market. It is also why a generally worded question such as 'Are frozen dessert pies and ice cream in the same relevant market?' is meaningless—the answer depends on what the focal product is. The right way of asking the question is: 'Is ice cream in the relevant market for frozen dessert pies?', and 'Are frozen dessert pies in the relevant market for ice cream?' In our hypothetical example, the answer to the first question was yes and the answer to the second question no. A case where asymmetric markets were found is the *Bayer–Aventis Crop Science* merger (2000), involving agricultural crop-protection products.[26] The European Commission found evidence of substitution from foliar and

---

[26] European Commission Decision of 12 July 2000 in Case COMP/M 2547.

soil applications of fungicides and insecticides to seed treatment, but not the other way round (from seed treatment to the other applications). The Commission also found another instance of 'one-way substitution'—between two specific types of cereal crop-protection products. Asymmetric markets have also been found in various supermarket inquiries in the UK—larger stores were considered to constrain smaller stores, but not the other way round.[27]

A case where the authority focused too much on the question of whether two products are in the same market, as opposed to whether one is in the market for the other (focal) one, is the 2001 review of competition in the mobile market conducted by Oftel, the UK telecoms regulator (now Ofcom).[28] The focal product was mobile telephony, and one of the market definition questions addressed was whether fixed telephony was a substitute for mobile. The authority presented some consumer evidence suggesting that the constraint from fixed on mobile was limited (eg, the vast majority of mobile calls were short 'convenient' calls of the type that, by definition, could not be made from a fixed line—for example, a call to your partner from the supermarket to clarify the shopping list). But Oftel then also, incorrectly, discussed why mobiles posed limited constraints on fixed telephony—most users still saw fixed telephony as their main method of making calls as the quality of fixed telephony was higher, and fixed users said they would not switch to mobiles even after a large price increase in fixed telephony. It concluded on this basis that fixed and mobile telephony are in separate markets. However, these last pieces of evidence are not informative about whether mobile telephony is constrained by fixed; they would be more relevant in a competition review where fixed telephony was the focal product. A case where an expert made a similar mistake is the 2007 abuse of dominance case before the English High Court concerning local bus services. As pointed out in the judgment:

> [Counsel for the defendants] also made what I regard as a fair point of criticism of [the claimants' expert's] analysis. In any analysis of whether local buses form an exclusive product market, the usual approach is to hypothesise a small but significant non-transitory increase in price for bus services of 5 to 10% and determine what alternative modes of transport (if any) become a substitute. That is the right approach, whereas [the claimants' expert] appeared to regard it as equally relevant to consider whether buses were a substitute for cars. Buses may be competitively constrained by cars, but cars may not be competitively constrained by buses.[29]

The distinction between the focal product and other products is also of utmost importance in later rounds of the test, where the hypothetical monopolist controls multiple products and the question often arises as to whether the SSNIP then applies to all products or only to the focal product. The distinction is not explicitly made in the original formulation of the hypothetical monopolist test in the US Merger Guidelines,

---

[27] For example, Competition Commission (2005), 'Somerfield plc/Wm Morrison Supermarkets plc', September.
[28] Oftel (2001), 'Effective competition review: mobile', 26 September, Annex 1.
[29] *Chester City Council and Chester City Transport Limited v Arriva PLC* [2007] EWHC 1373 (Ch), [157]. We acted for the defendants in this case.

as quoted above. Ten Kate and Niels (2009) therefore proposed a slightly amended wording of the test, as follows (the amendments to the original are in italics):

> A market *for a product at a specific location* is defined as *that* product or a group of products *containing that product* and a geographic area in which it is produced or sold *covering that location*, such that a hypothetical profit-maximizing firm, not subject to price regulation, that was the only present and future producer or seller of those products in that area likely would impose at least a 'small but significant and non-transitory increase in price' *for that product at that location*, assuming the terms of sale of all products not in that group or not in that area are held constant. The relevant market *for a product at a location* is the group of products and geographic area that is no bigger than necessary to satisfy this test.

2.4.7 GETTING TO THE SMALLEST MARKET

You have now seen what the starting and end points are for the hypothetical monopolist test. The way to get from one—the focal product and area—to the other—the smallest market in which a SSNIP would be imposed—is through a process of iteration. You would normally begin with the product market. The geographic market comes later (see section 2.9 on how it is important that the product and geographic market must remain linked in a meaningful way).

You hypothetically monopolize the focal product—say Italian women's designer shoes. The hypothetical monopolist will set the price at the profit-maximizing level (which is likely to be higher than the existing price level because the different producers of Italian women's designer shoes now no longer compete with each other). You then apply the SSNIP question to this candidate market: is this new profit-maximizing price more than 5%–10% higher than the existing price? If the answer is yes, you have found your relevant product market. If the answer is no—for example, the price increase would only be 3%—you must expand the market. Recall that if a SSNIP would not be imposed, that must be because consumers switch to other products in the demand system—it does not matter whether this is switching to close substitutes, such as French designer shoes, or spending income on more remote substitutes, such as theatre tickets or expensive bottles of wine. In keeping with the aim of finding the smallest market, you take the closest substitute for the focal product—say, French women's designer shoes—and bring it within the realm of the hypothetical monopolist. You then apply the SSNIP question again, this time to the new group of products controlled by the hypothetical monopolist. If the answer is now yes, you have found your relevant product market. If the answer is still no, you proceed to the third iteration of the test by including the second closest substitute in the realm of the hypothetical monopolist. And so on.

In reading this explanation of the iterative process, three questions may have occurred to you that we have not yet answered. First, how do I actually assess whether a SSNIP would be imposed? Second, if the test fails in the first iteration, how do I determine what the closest substitute is? Third, from the second iteration onwards, do I apply the SSNIP question to all products controlled by the monopolist or only to the focal product? We answer the second and third questions next in this section. The first question is addressed in section 2.5 where we deal with critical loss analysis. Before that, however, it is worth pointing out that while in theory the hypothetical monopolist test can have several iterations, in practice you'll find that quite often one iteration is sufficient. If you conclude that a hypothetical monopolist of Italian designer shoes would not find it profit-maximizing to impose a small price increase, in all likelihood any real producer of such shoes—including the merged entity—would also not be able to raise price. Hence you have the answer to your competition question, and there is no need to delineate exactly where the boundaries of the relevant market are beyond Italian designer shoes.

2.4.8 RANKING SUBSTITUTES: CROSS-PRICE ELASTICITIES AND DIVERSION RATIOS

As you have by now read several times, many products within the demand system are to some extent substitutes for each other. But clearly some are closer substitutes than others. For the purpose of the hypothetical monopolist test, you need to rank substitute products by how close they are to the focal product. The closest substitute is normally the product that absorbs most of the sales that are lost by the hypothetical monopolist after imposing a price increase. That product poses the strongest competitive constraint on the focal product and is the one that the monopolist, if given the choice, would like to get its hands on most. Once that closest substitute product is grouped with the focal product, the hypothetical monopolist no longer cares about losing sales from the latter to the former because it controls both products. The most significant obstacle to raising the price of the focal product has thus been removed (internalized, as economists would say), and its price will increase more than in the first iteration. You are therefore more likely to find that the SSNIP threshold has been passed. Including the closest substitute first (in the second iteration of the test) is important to meeting the smallest-market criterion. If you included a more remote substitute, you might find that this group of products is still not worth monopolizing and hence continue expanding the market, potentially too widely.

How do you rank substitutes? The standard measure for the degree of substitutability between products is the cross-price elasticity, as we saw in section 2.3. It is defined as the percentage change in the quantity of one product divided by the percentage change in price of the other product. For substitute products, the cross-price elasticity is positive, while for complementary products it is negative. For any two products there are two different cross-price elasticities—the cross-price elasticity of demand for rail services with respect to the price of air travel, and the cross-price elasticity of demand for air travel with respect to the price of rail services. Just as markets can be asymmetric (as you saw above), cross-price elasticities can differ between two products (indeed, an asymmetry between markets is the result of such a difference in cross-price elasticities). So the cross-price elasticity of demand for rail services with respect to the price of air travel may be 1.5, while the other way round it may be 0.5. Which of the two elasticities are you most interested in? For the purpose of the hypothetical monopolist test, the relevant elasticity depends on the focal product. If the focal product is air travel between

London and Paris because there is a proposed merger between two airlines operating on this route, in the hypothetical monopolist test we are analysing the effects of price changes in air travel between London and Paris (as imposed by the hypothetical monopolist). The relevant cross-price elasticity is therefore the one of demand for rail services between London and Paris with respect to the price of air travel—not the one of demand for air services with respect to the price of rail.

Now consider how cross-price elasticities work in the ranking of substitutes. Assume that the own-price elasticity for flights between London and Paris equals –3, and that the hypothetical monopoly airline would therefore not impose a SSNIP (see section 2.5 on critical loss analysis). Say there are currently 500,000 passengers per year on this route. A 10% price increase for one year would result in a 30% fall in passengers. Where do these 150,000 lost air passengers go? We know that the cross-price elasticity of demand for rail services between London and Paris with respect to the price of air travel is 1.5, so the 10% price increase by the monopoly airline would lead to a 15% increase in the demand for rail. The other possible substitute product is car journeys, including a ferry or Eurotunnel journey across the Channel. Say the cross-price elasticity of car journeys between London and Paris with respect to the price of flights is 0.5. Based on cross-price elasticities alone, rail would be the closest substitute. This is one way of ranking substitutes.

Another way would be to assess which substitute product absorbs the greatest proportion of the lost passengers. If 400,000 rail journeys are normally made each year, this increases to 460,000 after the 10% price increase in air travel (60,000 is 15% of 400,000). So 60,000 of the 150,000 lost air passengers switch to rail. If the total number of car journeys between London and Paris each year is 1.4 million, the 10% price increase for air travel means 70,000 (5% of 1.4 million) additional car journeys. By this measure, car journeys are a closer substitute for air travel than rail, because the greatest proportion of the lost air passengers switch to cars. This proportion is commonly known as the diversion ratio—the diversion ratio from air travel to car journeys is 47% (70,000 divided by 150,000); that from air travel to rail is 40% (60,000 divided by 150,000). Diversion ratios are frequently used in merger analysis, especially where differentiated products are concerned (see Chapter 7)—they are a useful measure of the closeness of substitute products, just as they are useful here for ranking substitutes for the purpose of the SSNIP test.

The ranking of substitutes should be straightforward in most cases. In the above example it was slightly complicated because the ranking by cross-price elasticity differed from that by diversion ratio. In practice this is not likely to occur often (diversion ratios are a function of the cross-price elasticity and the size of the market, so only where sizes of markets differ substantially—as here, where there are many more car journeys than rail or air journeys—do you get such differences in order). In any event, in cases such as these where there are two important close substitutes, the precise ranking may not make too much of a difference to the conclusion. Regardless of whether rail or car journeys are the closest substitute, the analysis has already found that air travel between London and Paris itself is not a market worth monopolizing. Hence, if the competition concern arose solely in air travel (say, a merger between two airlines serving the route), you can quickly be reassured that the concern is limited because air travel faces competition from other modes of travel. If the competition concern arose across air and rail—for example, an airline forms a joint venture with a rail operator on the route—you would treat both air and rail in turn as the focal product and assess whether each is in the other's market. When looking at air as the focal product—which is one of the analyses you would undertake—which substitute do you include in the market for air once you have established that air travel by itself is not worth monopolizing? In this case you should probably try both ranking methods to avoid overlooking any competition concerns. Based on diversion ratios, car journeys (including the Channel crossings) are the closer substitute, and you might find that an air–car monopolist would impose a SSNIP. In this case you might conclude that air and rail are not in the same market and hence that the joint venture raises no competition concerns (this also depends on whether air is excluded from the market when you take rail as the focal product, which is the other analysis you would undertake). However, ranked by cross-price elasticities, rail is the closest substitute, and you might find that an air–rail monopolist would also impose a SSNIP (even if this price increase is somewhat smaller than the one imposed by the air–car monopolist). Air–rail is technically the smaller market of the two (a total of 800,000 passengers versus 1.5 million passengers), and hence would be the relevant market, and you would find that the joint venture raises potential competition concerns.

There are two further points to make in relation to the ranking of substitutes and the use of cross-price elasticities. First, in the context of market definition, any sales loss matters to the hypothetical monopolist since it makes the price increase less profitable. In other words, it does not matter to the monopolist whether sales are lost to close substitutes or remote substitutes. In the above example, 130,000 of the 150,000 lost air passengers switched to rail and car journeys; the remaining 20,000 may no longer make the journey at all (and spend their money on other things). Market definition is therefore not only about analysing switching to substitute products. When you design a consumer survey to assess market definition, it is important that you explore whether consumers simply buy less of the product, in addition to whether they switch to substitute products.

Second, it follows from the above that own-price elasticities are of greater interest in market definition than cross-price elasticities. The analysis of critical loss—explored in section 2.5—revolves around own-price elasticities, not cross-price elasticities. This has not always been understood in competition law. Before the hypothetical monopolist test was developed, markets were frequently defined according to whether the cross-price elasticity between two products was high or low—see, for example, the quote from the *Brown Shoe* ruling in section 2.1. The cross-price elasticity in itself provides insufficient information about market definition. Its role is in the ranking of substitutes for the purpose of the hypothetical monopolist test, and this is a rather secondary role. Nonetheless, a measurement of the cross-price elasticity may provide a useful sense-check on the own-price elasticity. This is because there is a theoretical relationship between the two (which we do not elaborate upon here)—within the Marshallian demand system, there is a general rule that the higher the sum of all of a product's cross-price elasticities, the higher (more negative) that product's own-price elasticity will be.

If you see an estimate of own-price elasticity that suggests very elastic demand for a product (a 10% price increase causes a large sales loss), you should also expect to see that product having some high cross-price elasticities with other products, since that sales loss will be mainly absorbed by other products in the demand system.

2.4.9 THE SECOND ITERATION ONWARDS: WHICH OF THE MONOPOLIST'S PRODUCTS DOES THE SSNIP QUESTION APPLY TO?

This is a frequently asked question, and has not been answered very well in competition authorities' guidance or other texts. And yet it is straightforward: even if the monopolist controls multiple products, the SSNIP question should apply only to the focal (label-ling) product as that is the product where the competition concern arises in the first place. Let's return to our Italian women's designer shoes. This is the focal product because two producers of these shoes want to merge. In the first iteration of the test you found that the hypothetical monopolist would impose a 3% price increase—insufficient to constitute a SSNIP. You find that French designer shoes are the closest substitute for the Italian variety. In the second iteration of the test the monopolist controls both Italian and French women's designer shoes. As a result, it now no longer cares about losing sales to French shoes when raising the price of Italian ones—the main constraint on raising Italian shoe prices has disappeared (in economic terms, it has been internalized by the monopolist). At the same time, the monopolist can now raise prices for both of these products if required to maximize profits (remember that in the first iteration the assumption was that the terms of sale of all other products, including French shoes, are held constant). Say the hypothetical monopolist would now impose a price increase on Italian shoes of 13%—a SSNIP. But French shoes increase in price by 4% (the profit-maximizing price, obtained in the same way as in Figure 2.4). So in this example there is no SSNIP on French shoes, despite the monopolization of their supply, the reason being that they face strong competition from other women's designer shoes that the monopolist does not control.

Must you therefore proceed to a third iteration of the test, where the group of prod-ucts controlled by the monopolist includes all women's designer shoes? Suppose you did, and you found that the price of Italian shoes now increases by 15% and that of French shoes by 6% (the monopolist no longer cares about switching from Italian and French to other designer shoes, so can flex prices up a bit further), while the other shoes—monopolized for the first time in this third iteration—increase in price by only 2%. Following the same logic that made you proceed to the third iteration—ie, you require that *all* the hypothetical monopolist's prices must increase—you would eventually reach the conclusion that the market should include all women's shoes, in which the merging parties have a combined market share of only 5.5%. Alas, the logic and the conclusion are wrong. Already in the second iteration, you found a pocket of market power in Italian women's designer shoes. As soon as French shoes, their closest substitute, are added, the monopolist would impose a SSNIP (or even more) on the

Italian shoes. The relevant market for Italian women's designer shoes includes the Italian and French varieties, but no more. It is a market worth monopolizing, especially for the producers of Italian shoes (such as the two merging parties). The fact that you discover in the second iteration that French shoes in themselves are not a market worth monop-olizing (even when taken together with Italian shoes) is irrelevant. You are focused on the scope for price increases in Italian designer shoes, because that is where the compe-tition concerns from the merger arise. So in the second and any subsequent iterations of the hypothetical monopolist test, the SSNIP question is still applicable only to the focal (labelling) product.

If, instead, the merger is between a producer of French shoes and a producer of Italian shoes, you take both as the focal product and carry out two separate market definition exercises. The SSNIP question still applies to the focal product only. For the Italian shoes as focal product you reach the same conclusion as above—the relevant market is that for Italian and French shoes. When French women's designer shoes are the focal product, other designer shoes impose a significant constraint (the monopolist imposes only a 4% price increase, even if Italian shoes are included). The relevant market for French women's designer shoes becomes worth monopolizing only when all designer shoes are includ-ed—a 6% price increase is then imposed on the focal product, as we saw earlier.

2.4.10 PURITY, WITH SOME PRAGMATISM

Thus far we have considered the hypothetical monopolist test in its purest form, which is based on the definition of the test in the 1992 Horizontal Merger Guidelines. There are two major factors in reality that put this theoretical purity under pressure, and call for some pragmatic flexibility if the hypothetical monopolist test is to remain a useful concept for market definition. One factor is the need to put the test into practice. It is difficult enough to estimate elasticities and consumer responses to price changes (more on this in section 2.14). But once you have an estimate, identifying the profit-maximizing price that the monopolist would set gives rise to additional complications. It is easier—as we explain in the next section—to ask simply whether it would be profit-able for the hypothetical monopolist to impose a SSNIP, rather than whether it would be profit-maximizing. This is the essence of critical loss analysis, a commonly used method to make the hypothetical monopolist test workable.

The other factor is that, as we mentioned before, in most markets there is a degree of product differentiation. The test works best when products are homogeneous. One prag-matic adjustment we have already discussed is that, for the purposes of the hypothetical monopolist test, you can to some extent ignore differentiation and group together prod-ucts that may still be considered reasonably homogeneous (top-of-the-range sports cars, or women's designer shoes—no two products in these groups are exactly the same, but overall they constitute reasonably identifiable categories). There are markets, however, where the degree of differentiation is so high that the hypothetical monopolist test in its purest form becomes too uninformative. If that is the case, you should either skip market definition altogether and focus directly on competitive constraints (see section 2.15 and

Chapter 7 on mergers), or you could try some of the critical loss techniques for differentiated products that economists have developed relatively recently (see below).

2.5 CRITICAL LOSS ANALYSIS: 'COULD' OR 'WOULD'?

2.5.1 TWO DIFFERENT HYPOTHETICAL MONOPOLISTS

In section 2.4 we quoted the definition of the hypothetical monopolist test from the 1992 US Horizontal Merger Guidelines. Below are the definitions from the UK competition agencies' Merger Guidelines and the European Commission Notice on market definition. Can you spot the difference?

> In applying the hypothetical monopolist test, the Authorities will assess whether the hypothetical monopolist could profitably raise the price of at least one of the products in the candidate market by at least a small but significant amount over a non-transitory period of time (ie by a 'SSNIP'—a small but significant and non-transitory increase in price).[30]

> The question to be answered is whether the parties' customers would switch to readily available substitutes or to suppliers located elsewhere in response to a hypothetical small (in the range 5%–10%) but permanent relative price increase in the products and areas being considered. If substitution were enough to make the price increase unprofitable because of the resulting loss of sales, additional substitutes and areas are included in the relevant market. This would be done until the set of products and geographical areas is such that small, permanent increases in relative prices would be profitable.[31]

Rather than ask what a monopolist 'would' do to maximize profits—as in the US version—these other versions ask what a monopolist 'could' do profitably. The US version is the theoretically purer one—monopolists maximize profits. The other version is about breaking even—at what point does the monopolist make the same profits as before?

Having two different versions of the hypothetical monopolist test has caused much confusion among competition practitioners (lawyers and economists) in the last 10–20 years. Some may not even have been aware that there was a difference—the EU and UK guidance documents do not mention that their test is different from that in the USA, and even the US agencies switched versions between the 1982 and 1992 guidelines without stating this explicitly.[32] But does it really matter?

Theory tells us that it is not always the case that if a certain price increase is profitable, the hypothetical monopolist would actually impose it. A profit-maximizing monopolist would impose a smaller increase if that led to even higher profits. In fact it can be

---

[30] Competition Commission and Office of Fair Trading (2010), 'Merger Assessment Guidelines', September, [5.2.11].

[31] European Commission (1997), 'Notice on the Definition of Relevant Market for the Purposes of Community Competition Law', 97/C372/03, [17].

[32] The 1992 Guidelines in fact use both versions in different places. The difference between the two versions of the test is made explicit on p 12 of the 2010 Horizontal Merger Guidelines.

shown that the break-even price increase is twice as high as the profit-maximizing price increase (assuming linear demand and constant marginal cost, as we have in our examples). If you go back to Figure 2.4, the monopolist would go to the profit-maximizing price, but could raise price even higher and still make a profit. As a consequence, markets defined using the break-even approach tend to be narrower than those defined using the profit-maximization approach.

In practice, however, the break-even approach, when using critical loss analysis (discussed below), has some advantages, even if it is less theoretically pure. Identifying the price that maximizes the monopolist's profits is less straightforward than identifying the price at which the hypothetical monopolist makes the same profit as currently (ie, the profits made by the suppliers in the market before you hypothetically monopolized it). We note here that economists have also developed a practical means of applying the SSNIP question to the profit-maximizing hypothetical monopolist—this is through the critical elasticity.[33] Recall Figure 2.4. The lower (further to the right) you are on the demand curve, the more inelastic demand is, and the further the monopolist would increase price. There is a 'critical' elasticity level where the resulting price increase is exactly 5% (or 10%). You can apply the hypothetical monopolist test by estimating the actual elasticity and comparing this to the critical elasticity. However, the critical level depends crucially on the shape of the demand curve, ie, whether this is linear or of some other shape. A great advantage of standard critical loss analysis is that it does not depend at all on the shape of the demand curve, and you therefore do not need to make any assumptions about demand. Your results are more likely to be robust.

2.5.2 THE CONCEPT OF CRITICAL LOSS

If you raise the price of a product, two things happen. You sell less of the product, as customers walk away or reduce their purchases. But on the products that you do sell, you make a higher profit margin than before. These two effects therefore work in opposite directions. The first decreases your profits; the second increases them. Any business in the real world faces this trade-off when considering a price increase. And so does a hypothetical monopolist. How do you, and the hypothetical monopolist, know which of the two effects predominates? At what point do the two effects exactly cancel each other out, and leave you with the same amount of profits as before? This is what standard critical loss analysis is about—the critical sales loss is the percentage of sales at which the hypothetical monopolist makes the same profit before and after imposing a SSNIP. If the actual sales loss following the SSNIP exceeds the critical loss threshold, the SSNIP is unprofitable (conclusion: the market is wider). If the actual loss is below the critical loss, the SSNIP is profitable (conclusion: this is a relevant market).

You can already see from the description of the two effects which factors influence this critical loss threshold. The first effect is customers walking away or reducing purchases

---

[33] See Werden (1998).

following the 5% or 10% price increase. So it matters whether you select 5% or 10% as the SSNIP. As explained in section 2.4, either is valid in principle. With a 5% SSNIP you expect there to be a lower actual sales loss than with 10%, but the critical loss threshold will also be lower (see the discussion around Table 2.3 below). The reason why lost sales matter is that the monopolist made a profit margin on them before, and those profits are now lost. So the initial profit margin (as before, defined as price minus marginal cost, divided by price) also matters in determining the critical loss threshold. The second effect of the price increase is the higher margin on remaining sales. The higher margin equals the initial margin plus 5% or 10% (as that is by how much the price has increased; this assumes that marginal costs do not change over this range of output, a simplifying but often not unreasonable assumption). So, in sum, the critical loss threshold depends on only two factors: the percentage SSNIP on which you do the analysis, and the initial profit margin.

This is as far as we can take our verbal explanation of critical loss analysis. Some basic algebra is required to explain the formula for working out the critical loss. A chart also helps. Consider the following. There is a starting situation in which q units of the product are sold at price p. This gives rise to a price–cost margin, m, equal to price minus marginal costs, divided by price—ie, $m = (p-c)/p$. Then there is a SSNIP of x, which is equal to the change in p divided by p ($x = \Delta p/p$)—note therefore that x can be any percentage, even though it is usually 5% or 10%. Suppose that this SSNIP results in a decline in the quantity sold of Δq (Δq is a positive number if there is a sales loss). The two effects of the SSNIP on profits can then be expressed as follows. The fall in quantity, Δq, gives rise to a loss of profits since on each of the units previously sold the profit was m times p—ie, the loss of profit is Δq times m times p. The profit margin on the remaining sales is enhanced by x (the SSNIP)—this extra profit is $(q-\Delta q)$ times x times p. The critical loss question is: what is the maximum decline the quantity may suffer before the price increase becomes unprofitable? The answer: it is the Δq for which the profit gains from the price increase are equal to the loss of profits from the decline in quantity. In other words, it is where the hypothetical monopolist breaks even. A bit of algebra leads us from the break-even equation $(q-\Delta q)$ times p times $x = \Delta q$ times m times p, to the standard expression for the critical loss percentage: $\Delta q/q = x/(x+m)$.[34] Thus, in line with the verbal explanation earlier, the critical loss depends only on the SSNIP percentage used, x, and on the initial price–cost margin, m.

This situation is illustrated in Figure 2.5. F is the starting point, with a price p and a quantity q. Total profits for the monopolist are equal to the area ACFD (points A and C are on the marginal cost curve and a profit margin of p minus A is earned on every unit of q). Then price is raised from p to $(p+\Delta p)$ and output reduces to $(q-\Delta q)$. As above, it is assumed that marginal costs, c, do not change between these two quantities. The profits lost by the quantity reduction correspond to the shaded area BCFE. But there is also a profit gained by the price increase, as represented by the shaded area DEHG. Critical loss analysis is about comparing these two effects. If BCFE is larger in surface than DEHG, the price increase is unprofitable. If DEHG is larger, the increase is profitable. You can see that this depends crucially on the level of Δq. Given the values of q, p and Δp, the larger Δq is, the greater area BCFE

[34] The critical loss formula was first identified in Harris and Simons (1989).

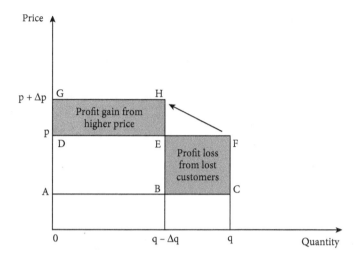

Fig. 2.5 The profit effects of a price increase

becomes, and the more area DEHG gets squeezed. The Δq for which areas DEHG and BCFE have exactly the same surface is the critical sales loss—this is where the monopolist breaks even, ie, would make the same profit before and after the price increase.

You may have noted that Figure 2.5 does not have a demand curve. It just has two price–quantity points, F and H. This is because determining the critical sales loss—and the formula $x/(x+m)$—does not depend on the shape or nature of the actual demand curve at all (other than that it is downward-sloping). It simply follows from an arithmetic comparison between profits before and after a price increase. This is one of the practical advantages of critical loss analysis. The profit-maximization version of the hypothetical monopolist test, while theoretically purer, relies crucially on assumptions that you would have to make regarding the shape of the demand curve in order the find the profit-maximizing price. All you need to know for critical loss analysis is the initial price–cost margin (see Chapter 10 for some practical tips on how to derive price–cost margins from financial information).

Table 2.3 shows the critical loss percentages for 5% and 10% price increases and for different values for the initial price–cost margin. Various points are worth noting in the table. When the initial margin is zero (price equals marginal cost, so no profits are made), the 5% or 10% price increase would be profitable for the monopolist regardless of the sales loss, as any remaining sales now generate a positive profit—hence the critical sales loss is 100%, at which point profit is zero again. The general point is that if you make a higher margin, every lost sale hurts you more. Furthermore, you can see that the critical sales percentage for a 10% SSNIP is higher than for a 5% SSNIP, although not quite proportionately so—the choice between 5% and 10% matters somewhat here (with 5% you tend to find slightly narrower markets than with 10%), but as noted before,

Table 2.3 Critical loss values based on the formula x/(x+m)

Initial price–cost margin (m) (%)	Critical loss for 5% SSNIP—0.05/(0.05+m) (%)	Critical loss for 10% SSNIP—0.1/(0.1+m) (%)
0	100	100
10	33.3	50.0
20	20.0	33.3
30	14.3	25.0
40	11.1	20.0
50	9.1	16.7
60	7.7	14.3
70	6.7	12.5
80	5.9	11.1
90	5.3	10.0
100	4.8	9.1

we would suggest that your ultimate conclusions on market definition should not hinge upon the exact choice of the SS in SSNIP.

Another point is that many of the critical loss percentages in the table imply that a lot of customers do not have to switch—for a 5% SSNIP, the critical loss is less than 20% for any margins above 20%, which means that you may have a result where more than 80% of customers would continue to buy the product. Critical loss analysis is about what customers do at the margin, not what the average or typical customer does. It is still not a market worth monopolizing if switching by the other 20% makes the price increase unprofitable. In this case, those (marginal) customers with choice protect the other (typical) customers who do not have or do not exercise a choice. We also touch upon this general principle, and the difference between captive and non-captive customers, in section 2.8 on price discrimination markets. Moreover, while from one perspective the percentages in the table may seem low, from another they may seem high. They almost all exceed the SSNIP percentage itself (except where the margin is very high). Going back to the elasticities in Figure 2.3, what this implies is that critical loss analysis is not really about testing whether the elasticity is higher or lower than −1. In other words, −1 is usually not a critical level of elasticity—instead, as shown in the table, for an initial margin of, say, 40%, the break-even critical elasticity is −2.2 for a 5% SSNIP (11.1% sales loss divided by 5%) and −2 for 10% (20% divided by 10%).

2.5.3 HOLIDAY PARKS AND HOSPITALS: APPLICATIONS OF CRITICAL LOSS ANALYSIS

The 2001 merger between Gran Dorado (owned by Pierre & Vacances) and Center Parcs, reviewed by the Dutch competition authority (Nederlandse Mededingings-autoriteit, NMa), illustrates how you can get stuck focusing on product characteristics, and how this can be overcome through critical loss analysis.[35] Gran Dorado and Center Parcs both operated self-catering accommodation in holiday parks with a range of facilities (indoor swimming pools, restaurants, playgrounds, etc) in the Netherlands, Belgium, and Germany. These parks are typically used by families for short breaks. The NMa approved the merger, but only after the parties had agreed to sell off a substantial number of parks.

Center Parcs and Gran Dorado were the two largest, and probably best-known, providers of holiday parks in the Netherlands and surrounding regions popular with Dutch short-breakers. Other, smaller players with similar offerings included Landal GreenParks, Zilverberk Parken, and Euroase Parcs. The NMa assessed whether there is a separate market for self-catering accommodation in holiday parks with a range of facilities, or whether other types of accommodation for short breaks are considered good substitutes by consumers. The NMa mainly emphasized the differences in product characteristics. It concluded that other types of holiday accommodation, such as family hotels, hotels for city breaks, hotels close to theme parks, and luxurious camping sites, should not be included in the relevant market because of the significant differences. For example, according to the NMa, parks with bungalows (as the holiday homes in the parks are known in the Netherlands) are mainly visited by larger groups, especially families with children, and also offer a range of facilities for entertainment; in contrast, a hotel primarily offers a place to sleep. It also noted that camping sites would be a substitute for holiday parks only in specific periods of the year and that there could be differences in comfort. Some of the holiday parks, particularly the larger ones, distinguish themselves from the smaller, more basic parks by offering a certain minimum set of facilities on site, such as a 'tropical' swimming pool and various restaurants. Furthermore, the NMa concluded that there are significant differences between the quality and price of the various types of holiday park. Based on these considerations, it provisionally narrowed the market down to those holiday parks that could be considered as four-season holiday villages, which included those operated by Center Parcs and Gran Dorado.

The differences in product characteristics that the NMa emphasized are no doubt of importance to holidaymakers. However, there are several product features that might make the holiday parks more interchangeable to others. For example, customer research carried out by the parties for their own commercial purposes (ie, not specifically for the merger inquiry) showed that for many visitors to the Center Parcs and Gran Dorado parks, walking and cycling through the surroundings outside the parks was one of the main activities during their short break (besides using the pool and other facilities inside the park). Indeed, these holiday parks are typically located in an attractive national park or coastal area, rather than, say, in the middle of an industrial estate. Seen from this perspective, other types of accommodation in such areas—including hotels, holiday homes, and holiday parks with fewer facilities—compete in the same market.

---

[35] NMa (2001), *Gran Dorado–Center Parcs,* Zaak 2209. See also Niels and van Dijk (2006). We advised the merging parties in this case.

Moreover, many alternative providers of short-break accommodation also offer access to facilities such as swimming pools and restaurants nearby, even if these facilities are not on the same site and are operated by third parties. Nor is the self-catering aspect unique to holiday parks. Many hotels now also offer self-catering accommodation (through so-called 'apart-hotels'), and two of Gran Dorado's bigger parks also offered hotel accommodation. An even broader perspective would be to include all accommo-dation for short breaks in the same market. Indeed, the parties regarded Eurodisney as a major competitor. Even if its product offering is quite different—hotel accommoda-tion near a theme park—Eurodisney competes directly to attract families with children for their short breaks, which is inconsistent with the NMa's definition of the market. Indeed, the short-break brochures in which Grand Dorado and Center Parcs advertised also typically included Eurodisney and other options for short breaks. Finally, as to price differences, these were often more marked between holiday parks of a different quality than between a park and, say, hotel, of similar quality—ie, a short break in a top-of-the-range holiday park and a top-of-the-range hotel with similar facilities nearby could have a similar price.

Hence, focusing solely on product characteristics potentially leads to a discussion without end. (Does an indoor pool become a 'tropical' pool when it has a slide and some palm trees?) Yet an even greater shortcoming of this approach is that it fails to address the crucial question for market definition—namely whether a sufficient proportion of consumers consider these products to be substitutes. As noted earlier, products do not need to be perfect substitutes to be in competition with each other, since a small overlap of consumers who are willing to switch can be sufficient. With this in mind, the merging parties undertook a consumer survey to identify empirically the level of sales that a hypothetical monopolist would lose as a result of a SSNIP. This type of survey is often the easiest (and fastest) way to obtain some relevant data on switching behaviour, even though it has shortcomings (see section 2.14), and the results should always be inter-preted with care.

The survey was held among close to 250 short-breakers in the Netherlands, ie, those who had been on any short break in the past three years. In order to focus the minds of the respondents (and hence increase the chance of relevant answers), they were first asked about their current behaviour and preferences in relation to short breaks. Then, before turning to the SSNIP question, respondents were asked which type of short break they were considering for the next two years. Those who (certainly or probably) consid-ered visiting a holiday park with facilities and indoor pool (ie, of the Center Parcs or Gran Dorado type) were asked whether they would still do so after a 10% price increase lasting for two years or whether they would switch to an alternative type of short break, or not go on a short break at all (as noted earlier, the latter also represents a relevant sales loss to the monopolist). To help respondents interpret the question, they were not only informed of the 10% increase but were also given a numerical example of what this, on average, would do to the price they would pay.

The results of the survey indicated that the relevant market is broader than only hol-iday parks with a range of facilities and an indoor swimming pool. This is because 28%

of those who considered a short break in such a park said they would switch to another type of short break, or take no short break at all, after a 10% price increase. This sales loss was clearly higher than the estimated critical loss. Recall that the critical loss depends on the price–cost margin. A rough approximation indicated that the holiday parks had a margin in the range of 60%–80% (this is because a large part of their costs are fixed, ie, they do not vary with sales). Applying the formula, this generates a critical loss of 11%–14% (10% divided by 10% plus 60% equals 14%, and 10% divided by 10% plus 80% equals 11%). You can see that in cases like these there is no need to identify the price–cost margin with great precision—the broad margin range of 60%–80% gener- ates a narrower critical loss range of 11%–14%, and the actual loss in this case is suffi- ciently in excess of the critical level for you to be confident that you are making the right comparison (the only uncertainty would be about the reliability of the survey response, not about the application of the critical loss analysis itself).

The survey also revealed that there was no clear closest substitute. Respondents who said that they would switch were asked what options they would switch to. They men- tioned more than two alternatives on average (this in itself indicates that they see mul- tiple substitutes). Stand-alone holiday homes and apartments had the highest diversion percentage, with 37% and 34%, respectively. Other types of holiday parks—without indoor pool or a pool nearby—were mentioned by 21%–26% of respondents. The dif- ferent types of hotel—for city breaks, family hotels, theme park hotels, and others—all received scores between 18% and 25%. Given that the critical loss analysis indicated that the market should be defined more broadly than just holiday parks with facilities and indoor pools—the focal product—it was not really necessary to proceed to the second iteration of the hypothetical monopolist test including the closest substitute. In the end, the precise market definition was left open, as the NMa approved the merger on the condition that the parties divest a number of their parks.

Critical loss analysis was also used in a merger between two hospitals in the Netherlands in 2005.[36] The NMa commissioned a study on the demand elasticity of patients in order to determine the relevant geographic market in which these hospitals operated. The study estimated a 'time elasticity' of demand—ie, the sensitivity of patients with respect to travel time—but then translated this into a price elasticity of demand so as to compare the results with the critical loss formula (more on this in section 2.13). For one product market—clinical treatments—the study found an actual sales loss of just under 10% after a price increase of 10%, with a confidence interval of +/– 2.8% around this estimate (reflecting statistical uncertainty). Based on a margin estimate of around 70%—reflecting the fact that hospitals have relatively high fixed costs and low marginal costs—the study calculated the break-even critical loss to be around 12.5% (in line with Table 2.3). It concluded from this that the SSNIP was profitable and hence that the geographic market was not wider than the area immediately surrounding the

[36] NMa (2005), *Ziekenhuis Hilversum-Ziekenhuis Gooi-Noord*, Zaak 3897, 8 June. We advised the merging parties on this case too.

two hospitals. However, had the profit-maximization approach been used, a margin of around 70% would imply a critical elasticity around –1.1 (critical loss of 11%). This would be well within the confidence interval around the actual loss, and hence cast some doubt on the conclusion that the SSNIP was profitable. In the end, based on various other factors including this one, the NMa concluded that the hospitals did compete in a wider geographic market and approved the merger. The main lesson from this example is that care should be taken when the actual loss estimates are very close to the critical loss percentage. In these situations it may be useful to cross-check the break-even result against the profit-maximization result.

2.5.4 CRITICAL LOSS IN MARKETS WITH DIFFERENTIATED PRODUCTS

If there is a merger between producers of the same product (as in our example of the Italian women's designer shoes), that product is the focal product for your hypothetical monopolist test. If the merger is between an Italian and a French producer, and there is some concern that these two products compete with each other, you take them both as the focal product and carry out separate tests for each. If both produce men's designer shoes as well, you would carry out four separate hypothetical monopolist tests. You can see that in markets with differentiated products—such as cars and breakfast cereals—you may end up having to perform a very large number of tests, one for each variety of the product. Earlier we explained two paths you could take to avoid this. First, you could to some extent ignore differentiation and group together products that may still be considered reasonably homogeneous (top-of-the-range sports cars, holiday parks with self-catering accommodation). In line with the smallest-market principle, you could do this conservatively and take relatively narrow groups to start with. The hypothetical monopolist test would then be applied to each of the groups as if they consisted of homogeneous goods. Second, you could skip the market definition stage altogether and focus directly on the competitive constraints and closeness of competition between the differentiated products (as discussed in Chapter 7).

Economists have recently developed some tools that provide a third alternative.[37] You can still define the relevant market through the hypothetical monopolist by applying critical loss analysis to a group of differentiated products. In essence this is the same as applying the SSNIP question in the second and subsequent iterations of the hypothetical monopolist test, but here you can potentially take any product in the group as the focal product. You effectively take a shortcut by starting with a monopolist who already controls all the products where competition concerns may arise. You can then apply the break-even SSNIP question to any one of the products in the group, or to all the products. The focus in this new critical loss test for differentiated products is on the diversion ratio between these products—the critical loss formula depends not just on

[37] See Farrell and Shapiro (2008), Daljord, Sørgard, and Thomassen (2008), and ten Kate and Niels (2010).

the SSNIP, x, and the initial margin, m, but also on the percentage of total sales loss after the SSNIP that is diverted to other products within the group as opposed to outside the group. This percentage can be called the intra-group diversion ratio (some economists call it the aggregate diversion ratio, but we believe that this term has more than one meaning). The higher the intra-group diversion ratio, the less the monopolist cares about losing sales of one of its products (as more of these lost sales are captured by the other products), and hence the more profitable the SSNIP.

We can show this in a formula. Recall that the critical loss formula for the standard case (homogeneous products) was x divided by x+m. With differentiated products the critical loss can be expressed as x divided by x+m(1–d), where d is the intra-group diversion ratio. The factor (1–d) has crept into the formula as the percentage of sales that is lost to outside products. To see how it makes a difference, take the critical loss for a 10% SSNIP and 40% margin from Table 2.3—equal to 20% in the standard formula. In the new formula, if d equals zero (ie, 100% of sales is lost to outside products), the formula becomes the same as before, and the critical loss is still 20%. But with a positive intra-group diversion ratio this changes. Say d equals 0.2 (20%). The new formula then gives a critical loss of 24%—this is higher than the 20% you had before, since it takes more sales loss before the monopolist starts to care. If d equals 0.5 the critical loss becomes 33%, and if d is 0.8 the critical loss is 56%. Thus, the more the products under the control of the hypothetical monopolist are each other's closest substitutes, the more the monopolist can profitably increase price. There is still some debate among economists and practitioners about whether in markets with differentiated products it is more informative to use these tools and still define relevant markets, or to skip the market definition stage altogether and use the tools for unilateral effects analysis, which are very similar, as discussed in Chapter 7.

2.6 THE CELLOPHANE FALLACY

2.6.1 BACK TO THE 1950S

The 'cellophane fallacy' is a widely known concept in competition law. Less well-known are the finer details of the original case, which is more than 50 years old. In 1956, the US Supreme Court ruled on a monopolization case brought by the government against Du Pont.[38] Du Pont had a 75% share of US sales of cellophane (the producer of the other 25% had a licence from Du Pont and paid it royalties), but cellophane constituted only 20% of all flexible packaging materials. The decision therefore turned on the definition of the relevant product market. The Supreme Court, unlike the government, considered that there was sufficient evidence of interchangeability between cellophane and other materials (such as paper, film, and foils). There were similarities in functionality, and large user industries such as meat production switched regularly between different

---

[38] *US v EI du Pont de Nemours & Co* 351 US 377 (1956).

types of packaging material. While cellophane was two to three times as expensive as its nearest competitors (glassine and grease-proof papers), the court found that further price increases were prevented by those other materials. Can you see the fallacy in this reasoning?

Cellophane production was already a (near-)monopoly at the time. Du Pont possessed the technology and competition from the other cellophane producer was restricted through an overt agreement and apparent tacit coordination between the two. If the prevailing price was already the monopoly price, a hypothetical cellophane monopolist (Du Pont nearly was one for real) would not raise prices any further, since at the monopoly price other competing products start to bite. But that does not mean that cellophane is not a market worth monopolizing—it could still be a relevant market of its own. Many commentators have pointed this out since. Indeed, three dissenting Supreme Court judges said it in the judgment itself:

> We cannot believe that buyers, practical businessmen, would have bought cellophane if close substitutes were available at from one-seventh to one-half cellophane's price. That they did so is testimony to cellophane's distinctiveness.[39]

The cellophane fallacy can be explained through Figures 2.3 and 2.4. We explained how own-price elasticities depend on where on the demand curve you are to start with. The hypothetical monopolist test assesses the price at which the monopolist maximizes profits, and asks whether this price is at least 5%–10% higher than the initial (pre-monopolization) price. You can see that if the price is already at (or very near to) the monopoly price, the monopolist would not impose a further SSNIP. The logic of the test would then dictate that the market is broader than the product in question, but this could lead to an erroneous conclusion that this product is not worth monopolizing.

2.6.2 IS IT A PROBLEM, AND IF SO, WHAT CAN BE DONE ABOUT IT?

The cellophane fallacy is not normally a concern in merger cases. Competition authorities review whether mergers reduce competition compared with the present situation. It is therefore valid to take the prevailing price level as the starting point for the hypothetical monopolist test where the market is reasonably competitive before a merger. The exception is where markets, pre-merger, are already characterized by a form of (tacit) price coordination between competitors, such that hypothetical monopolization would not lead to significant further price increases, hence giving rise to the cellophane fallacy again. The fallacy is most likely to arise in cases where there is already a dominant company, or more generally where it is suspected that the party or parties under investigation have already exercised some degree of market power. In any such case, competition authorities or claimants can, and often do, invoke the cellophane fallacy to refute attempts by the defendants to demonstrate a wider market based on a SSNIP question applied to prevailing prices. Are they right?

---

[39] Ibid., at [417].

In theory, the cellophane fallacy arises only when prevailing prices are at, or very close to, the monopoly level. If prices are more than 5%–10% below the monopoly level, you would find a hypothetical monopolist imposing a SSNIP—your analysis would not suffer from the cellophane fallacy. The question is: how do you know where prevailing prices lie relative to the monopoly price level? We suggest that the answer to this question cannot be inferred just from the existing market structure (except where you have an unregulated real profit-maximizing monopolist). You cannot say there is a cellophane fallacy just because the market structure does not look perfectly competitive. Prices in oligopolistic markets may lie anywhere between the competitive and monopoly levels. Even companies with very high market shares may still be constrained by competitors (even if small) from raising price all the way up to the monopoly level. In these cases, asking the SSNIP question based on prevailing prices can still provide useful insight into substitution and competitive constraints. You just have to bear in mind that some degree of market power (short of monopoly power) may already have been exercised at those prices. At the very least you can apply a one-way test. If, at the prevailing price level, a monopolist can profitably impose a SSNIP, you can be confident that the market is no wider. If, in contrast, you find that the monopolist cannot profitably increase price, you have to accept that there may be a cellophane fallacy and that the market may be defined too broadly. Ultimately, if there is a high probability that your analysis will suffer from a cellophane fallacy, you may have to conclude that market definition is not a useful intermediate step and instead focus directly on indicators of competitive constraint (as further discussed in Chapter 3).

A frequently cited solution to the cellophane fallacy is to start the hypothetical monopolist test from the competitive price level rather than the prevailing price level. Because the test has its foundations in microeconomic theory, it is tempting to take marginal cost as the competitive price level (since in perfect competition, prices equal marginal cost). However, as we discuss in greater detail in Chapter 3, there are many real-world markets in which prices are set above marginal costs, but which can still be considered competitive—prices above marginal costs may be required to cover fixed costs, or may reflect only a temporary position of pricing power that is eroded over time. Therefore, to get a better approximation of the competitive price level you would need to carry out an analysis of profitability over a longer time period. The problem is, however, that such an analysis makes the market definition stage rather redundant (Niels, 2004). After all, profitability sheds light directly on whether companies can persistently earn high returns without attracting entry or inducing consumer switching. This is precisely how competition law defines market power and dominance—profitability analysis is a direct indicator of dominance, which means that market definition as an intermediate step is no longer required. Indeed, the US Supreme Court itself cited profitability in the 1956 cellophane case as a reason to reject the monopolization claim and, implicitly, reject the presence of a cellophane fallacy (arguably the court referred to less sophisticated techniques of measuring profits than have been developed since—see Chapter 3):

> Nor can we say that du Pont's profits, while liberal (according to the Government 15.9% net after taxes on the 1937–1947 average), demonstrate the existence of a monopoly without proof of lack of comparable profits during those years in other prosperous industries.

Cellophane was a leader over 17% in the flexible packaging materials market. There is no showing that du Pont's rate of return was greater or less than that of other producers of flexible packaging materials.[40]

2.6.3 THE 'REVERSE' CELLOPHANE FALLACY

Just as the cellophane fallacy leads to overly broad markets, economists have identified a phenomenon called the 'reverse' cellophane fallacy, which results in overly narrow markets. This occurs where the prevailing price level is too low to start with. Recall from Figure 2.4 and Table 2.3 that if price is very low (say, at or close to marginal cost), almost any price increase is profitable, and hence the hypothetical monopolist test is easily passed. When may prevailing prices be too low? We would suggest that situations like this are more exception than norm, but theoretical examples are where a predatory price war has been raging in the market in question, or where a product has been subject to a regulatory price cap that is below the point where a reasonable profit is made.

2.7 SUPPLY-SIDE SUBSTITUTION AND MARKET AGGREGATION

2.7.1 WHAT IF THE HYPOTHETICAL MONOPOLIST WERE NOT THE ONLY FUTURE SUPPLIER?

In section 2.3 we explained the distinction between demand-side substitution, supply-side substitution, and new entry. Thus far in this chapter we have dealt with demand-side substitution, ie, switching behaviour by customers. The only supply-side aspect of market definition that has come up at this stage is our hypothetical monopolist, ie, the supplier who imposes the price changes to which customers react. Supply-side substitution is about other suppliers' reactions to the monopolist's price changes. It is usually a less immediate constraint on companies than demand-side substitution (we said before that customers are generally quicker to vote with their feet if they are unhappy than wait for other suppliers to come to them). Nonetheless, it may also render price increases by the monopolist unprofitable.

In the formal definition of the hypothetical monopolist test in the 1992 US Horizontal Merger Guidelines—cited in section 2.4—supply-side substitution is expressly ruled out because the monopolist is the 'only present and future producer or seller of those products in that area'. This version of the test considers only demand-side substitution. However, other jurisdictions tend to also consider supply-side substitution as part of the market definition stage under certain conditions, discussed below. Ultimately, it should not matter too much during which stage of the analysis you consider supply-side substitution since all competitive constraints must be considered (recall that market definition is only

---

[40] Ibid., at [404].

an intermediate stage). In the US approach, those suppliers that are not in the market currently, but that could easily supply-side substitute into it, are taken into account at the point of calculating market shares in that market. This should give the same result as calculating shares in a wider market based on supply-side substitution.

Nevertheless, there are some traps you might inadvertently walk into when relying on supply-side substitution at the market definition stage. We discuss these below. First, we set out how the line is usually drawn between supply-side substitution and new entry (the latter does not form part of the market definition stage; more on this in Chapter 3).

2.7.2 PAPER AND BUSES: ILLUSTRATING THE CRITERIA FOR SUPPLY-SIDE SUBSTITUTION

Paper production is a frequently cited example of supply-side substitution. Paper is usually supplied in a range of qualities, from standard writing paper (uncoated) to high-quality paper (often coated) to be used, for instance, in art books. From a demand point of view, different qualities of paper are not substitutes—a pricey art book cannot be printed on low-quality paper. However, paper plants may be able to manufacture different qualities of paper, switching their existing production facilities at little cost within a short timeframe, if the commercial opportunity arises—for example, if the price of a paper variety they are currently not producing increases by 5%–10%. In such circumstances, the various qualities of paper may be included in the relevant market based on supply-side considerations. The European Commission uses the paper example in its 1997 Notice on the Definition of Relevant Market, and first dealt with the issue in a 1992 merger decision:

Demand-side substitutability

17. There is limited substitutability between uncoated and coated papers because of their different characteristics (such as discolouring and printing quality). In addition uncoated paper is much cheaper than coated paper. The above table shows that the price of the cheapest coated paper is even higher than the price of the most expensive uncoated paper and that coated paper is on average 15% more expensive than uncoated paper.

Supply-side substitutability

18. From the supply side, there is a rather high substitutability. Indeed, since the difference between coated and uncoated paper results from extra processing, the coating processing can be included whenever required. Since the different grades of paper result mainly from the blend used, the coating materials used and some other extra processing, it is relatively easy for a producer to switch from production of one paper type to another. This is particularly true with regard to the older non-integrated machines, which can be used for various kinds of paper production. The high speed, high capacity and highly integrated new mills are also able to switch from production of one paper type to another, although to a lesser extent than older non-integrated machines.[41]

---

[41] Case No IV/M.166, *TORRAS/SARRIO* (1992), OJ C58/00; [1992] 4 CMLR 341.

Bus services are another common example of supply-side substitution, in the context of geographic market definition (paper is an example of product market definition). From a demand-side perspective, point-to-point bus routes would form separate markets. A hypothetical monopolist on the route from your home to your office would be able to increase fares (abstracting from competition from other modes of travel, such as cars, trains, taxis, or walking), because you would not travel somewhere else after a price rise. However, from a supply perspective, bus operators can shift or expand into new routes with relative ease, provided that they have an existing bus depot nearby (where buses can park overnight and receive maintenance). This means that geographic markets for bus services are often defined more widely, covering the whole area that can economically be served from an existing depot.

From these two examples you can see what kind of criteria matter for supply-side substitution. Supply-side substitution requires there to be no significant additional 'sunk' investments or costs of switching. It must be sufficiently swift and it must be of a sufficient scale to constrain the hypothetical monopolist. The first of these criteria refers to a commonly used concept in economics—that of sunk investments. Such investments are different from other investments in that they cannot be recovered upon exit from the market. A typical example is an investment in a new brand by a market entrant, which will lose its value once the company exits the market again (and the brand cannot be sold). In contrast, investments that are not sunk still have value at the point of exit. This matters for entry decisions—if you know you can get rid of your assets for a decent price in the event of your new business venture failing, you are more likely to go ahead than in the situation where you have to scrap the assets. The second criterion relates to timeliness of the supply switch. As with the 'N' in SSNIP there are no hard and fast rules for what is timely, but often the reference is to a one-year period, or simply to existing production facilities being used (existing paper plants or bus depots). Use of existing facilities implies swift entry, and also narrows the first criterion somewhat from no sunk investment to no major investment in new facilities (sunk or not). The 1992 US Horizontal Merger Guidelines call supply-side substitution 'uncommitted entry', which is contrasted with 'committed entry' (the 2010 Guidelines, at p 16, simply refer to 'rapid entrants'). In economic theory, industries without sunk costs and where entry is rapid are sometimes called 'contestable markets'—the possibility of 'hit and run' entry would prevent even a monopolist from raising prices in such markets (and hence, according to the hypothetical monopolist test, they may not be relevant markets in themselves in the first place).

To continue with the bus example, the provision of local bus services has some features of a contestable market. If the operator has a bus depot nearby, adding services to an existing route or opening new routes can be done swiftly (in the UK a new route can be opened 56 days after registration). Any investment in additional buses is not sunk, since there is often a reasonably liquid market for second-hand buses should the operator decide to exit the route (buses can also be leased or rented). With regard to the third criterion mentioned above—scale—in the provision of bus services even entry on a small scale can have a strong competitive impact on a particular bus route—for example, if the entrant runs its service only on the busiest part of a route or during the busiest times of the day. This conclusion was reached in the 2004 OFT decision in the *Arriva/ Wales and Borders Rail* case, where a regional rail franchise was acquired by an operator which also provided local bus services in the area:

> Buses may be bought outright, or leased. Bus depots (and out-stations [secure areas for overnight parking]) may be leased … An existing operator with a local depot is unlikely to face significant barriers to expansion and it is likely that larger operators would take up any profitable routes abandoned (wholly or partially) by Arriva. Where a route is unprofitable (wholly or at certain times) local councils may invite tenders from operators to run the route on a subsidised basis, in which case there is competition for, rather than on, these routes.[42]

2.7.3 THE RISK OF OVERSTATING COMPETITIVE PRESSURE FROM SUPPLY-SIDE SUBSTITUTION

There is something inherently odd about supply-side substitution. Demand-side substitution is about whether consumers see products as substitutes. If they do to a sufficient degree, you put the two products together in the relevant market. Supply-side substitution is not so much about the products as the suppliers of those products. The high-quality paper monopolist is constrained by the producers of low-quality paper because they can also produce high-quality paper, not by the low-quality paper itself. This oddity is one of the reasons why the US Guidelines prefer to focus on demand-side substitution, and then treat suppliers that can supply-side substitute (ie, enter in an 'uncommitted' way) as participants in the market and include them in the market share calculation. As noted earlier, this should ultimately result in the same conclusion as in the approach where you include supply-side substitution in the market definition itself. But there is a risk that you will overstate the competitive pressure from supply-side substitution as a result of this 'oddity'. We highlight the main pitfalls here.

Consider the following example. You have six producers of high-quality paper. The two largest ones (A and B) have 25% of production each, the other four 12.5%, as shown in Table 2.4. Considering demand-side substitution only, you find that a hypothetical monopolist for high-quality paper would impose a SSNIP—customers would not switch to low-quality paper. If the two largest producers were to merge, they would have a combined market share of 50%, sufficient to raise some competition concerns. But you haven't considered supply-side substitution yet. Suppose low-quality paper is produced by completely different companies, but you find that their existing plants and equipment can very easily be switched to produce high-quality paper. So on a supply-side basis the relevant market for the merger should include low-quality paper as well. As you can see from the table, the total market is now two-and-a-half times as large, and the merging parties have a combined market share of only 20%—not enough to warrant

---

[42] Office of Fair Trading (2004), 'Completed Acquisition by Arriva Plc of the Wales and Borders Rail Franchise', 16 March, p 5.

Table 2.4 Stylized example of supply-side substitution

	High-quality paper production (tonnes)	Market share in high-quality paper	Market share in all paper	Market share in high-quality paper plus available low-quality capacity
Producer A	100	25%	10%	21.7%
Producer B	100	25%	10%	21.7%
Producer C	50	12.5%	5%	10.9%
Producer D	50	12.5%	5%	10.9%
Producer E	50	12.5%	5%	10.9%
Producer F	50	12.5%	5%	10.9%
Market size (tonnes)	400	400	1,000	460
Low-quality paper production (tonnes)	600			
Low-quality capacity available for substitution (tonnes)	60 (10% of all low-quality capacity)			

competition concerns. This may well be the correct conclusion. But there is a risk that you have overstated the importance of supply-side substitution as a competitive constraint, and hence understated the scope for the merged entity's market power. You have effectively assumed that all production of low-quality paper can be readily switched to high-quality paper (you have added all 600 tonnes to the relevant market). This may not reflect reality. There may be various reasons why some of the capacity cannot be readily switched—producers of low-quality paper may not want to upset relationships with their existing customers, they may have long-term supply contracts with them, or they may still consider the low-quality market more lucrative despite the price increase in high-quality paper. In essence, this comes down to the scale of the supply-side substitution, the third criterion mentioned above. Suppose producers of low-quality paper would switch only 10% of their capacity to high-quality paper. Then you should count only that available capacity when you calculate market shares. You would find that according to this calculation the merged entity has a 43.5% market share.

2.7.4 THE RISK OF GETTING SUPPLY-SIDE SUBSTITUTION IN THE WRONG DIRECTION

Another potential pitfall with using supply-side substitution is to get the direction of the substitution wrong. This happens when you include all products or geographic areas which suppliers can substitute into, regardless of whether this substitution is towards, or away from, the focal product or area. This leads to overly broad markets, since only supply-side substitution *towards* the focal product or area in question is relevant in capturing the competitive constraints on that product or area.

An example of where such an error was made is the abuse of dominance case before the English High Court involving bus services, as referred to previously. The dispute concerned alleged predation on several local routes in Chester in the north-west of England—this was the focal area. The experts for the claimants and defendants had agreed that the geographic market should be defined based on supply-side substitution, including all existing bus depots that could economically serve routes in Chester (a drive time of 30 minutes was agreed upon as the maximum distance between the depot and the route—see section 2.9 for a discussion on isochrones analysis). However, the claimants' expert subsequently expanded the geographic market by including all areas that could be served from the depots, including areas in the other direction from Chester. This led to an overly broad market (in this case, the defendant had a higher market share in the wider market because it had substantial operations in areas adjacent to Chester). The court agreed with the defendants' expert that this was incorrect:

> [The claimants' expert's] starting point was to identify which depots can economically provide bus services to Chester, whether or not any such depot in fact does so; and that part of the exercise is one with which in principle [the defendants' expert] agrees. He then defined the market as comprising the areas that those depots serve or can serve, and he concluded that for practical purposes that meant it comprises the eight local authority districts in which the depots are situated; and with that approach [the defendants' expert] disagreed. Thus, for example, Arriva's Winsford depot (to the east of Chester . . .) is said to be capable of economically operating into Chester, and the Crew and Nantwich administrative district lying to its south-east (and increasingly remote from Chester) into which services from Winsford are also possible is therefore also said to fall within the geographic market . . .

> The effect of [the claimants' expert's] approach (unlike [the defendants' expert's]) is thus to include in his market depots from which he accepts it would *not* be possible for any operator economically to provide local bus services in Chester . . .

> I accept [the defendants' expert's] opinion . . . that when identifying a geographic market by reference to supply-side considerations it is a mistake to include all geographic areas into which suppliers can substitute regardless of whether this is towards or away from the focal market; and that only supply-side substitution towards the focal market is relevant to capture competitive constraints on that market. The [defendants' expert's] opinion is that [the claimants' expert] has committed the error of overlooking this principle and so has erroneously promoted a broader geographic market than is justified . . . I accept his opinion.[43] [Emphasis in original].

---

[43] *Chester City Council and Chester City Transport Limited v Arriva PLC* [2007] EWHC 1373 (Ch), [163]–[164] and [190]. We acted for the defendants in this case.

2.7.5 MARKET AGGREGATION

Market aggregation is a phenomenon closely related to supply-side substitution. It is one of those pragmatic adjustments to the theoretically pure hypothetical monopolist test that make its application more practical. We started this chapter with a merger between producers of Italian women's designer shoes. We later discussed the question of whether different types of shoes (such as French women's designer shoes) are seen as substitutes and impose price pressure on Italian shoes. But there is another distinction that must be considered. From a purely demand-side perspective, size 38 shoes and size 39 shoes are not substitutable. Thus, on this basis you should define a separate relevant market for each shoe size. Clearly that would be somewhat absurd. Your conclusions on competitive constraints would be exactly the same for each of these size-based markets, since each producer makes and sells all the sizes (except where producers specialize in very large or small shoe sizes)—the competitive conditions are the same. So you might as well aggregate all shoe sizes into one market. The same logic applies to various transport and communications markets, where demand-side considerations would lead to many different point-to-point markets, but where competitive conditions are often similar for all of these markets, and hence for practical reasons you can aggregate them.

2.8 PRICE DISCRIMINATION MARKETS

2.8.1 COMPARING APPLES WITH BANANAS

In the 1978 *United Brands* judgment, the General Court (then Court of First Instance) had to address the question of whether bananas are a separate market or part of a wider market for fresh fruits.[44] The case concerned banana distribution arrangements in the north-west of Europe. There was some statistical evidence that banana demand and prices are under pressure in the summer months when domestic fruits are in ample supply, and during the 'orange season' at the end of the year. The court agreed with the European Commission that these periods of substitution were too limited—bananas are available the whole year round, so candidate substitute fruits would have to be too, it held. Oranges were regarded as too distinct, and apples were seen as interchangeable only to a small degree. The court (and the Commission) reasoned as follows:

> This small degree of substitutability is accounted for by the specific features of the banana and all the factors which influence consumer choice.

> The banana has certain characteristics, appearance, taste, softness, seedlessness, easy handling, a constant level of production which enable it to satisfy the constant needs of an important section of the population consisting of the very young, the old and the sick.[45]

---

[44] Case 27/76, *United Brands Company and United Brands Continentaal BV v Commission*, 14 February 1978.
[45] Ibid., at [30]–[31].

This reasoning may remind you of the holiday park merger discussed in section 2.5, which also sought to define markets primarily based on product characteristics. You can debate at length whether babies, elderly people, and the sick really can't replace bananas with other fruits (our own recent experience would suggest otherwise, but then supermarkets nowadays offer a much greater variety of fruits year round than they did in the 1970s). But more importantly, the court's reasoning misses the point about critical loss. Even if one particular 'section of the population' cannot switch away from bananas, there are other sections that can. If too many of those other customers would switch to apples, oranges and the like after a banana price increase, a hypothetical banana monopolist would not impose such an increase. The very young, the old, and the sick would thus be protected by the less captive customers. Crucially, this is because banana suppliers and retailers are unable to specifically target their captive customers (for a start, babies, the elderly, and the sick may not do their own shopping). If the monopolist raises price, it has to do so across the board to all customers. It cannot price-discriminate, ie, charge a different price to different groups of customers for the same product.

As discussed in section 2.2, price discrimination can give rise to separate markets by (groups of) customers. This may occur when some customers have a greater choice of alternatives than others, and suppliers can exploit this difference by targeting the latter, 'captive', customers with higher prices, without this being undermined by arbitrage (where the non-captive customers can somehow resell the product to the captive ones, or purchase it on their behalf). Banana suppliers are unable to achieve such price discrimination. But other suppliers can. A common example is the travel industry. A flight from London Heathrow to Milan Linate at 7.45am will have a mix of time-sensitive and non-time-sensitive passengers on board. The former have no choice but to be on that particular flight—they have a meeting in Milan at lunch time. The latter passengers could have chosen a different time to fly, or perhaps even a different destination (eg, a city break in Madrid instead of Milan). Airlines are able to exploit this difference since time-sensitive passengers tend to book their tickets less far in advance of flying (airlines tend to raise fares closer to the flight date), and are more likely to demand flexible tickets in case their meeting times change (airlines target this by offering more expensive flexible economy and business tickets). Competition cases involving airlines therefore frequently define separate markets for time-sensitive and non-time-sensitive passengers.[46] Returning to the bananas case, there was perhaps some economic merit in the court's argument that competition from seasonal fruits is not quite sufficient to prevent a banana price rise—it is just that this banana price rise would occur outside those seasons. Rather than applying the criterion that substitute fruits for bananas must be available all year round, the court could have followed the price discrimination logic and argued that bananas still form a separate relevant market during those times of the year in which other fresh fruits are in less ample supply. It would then probably still have found United Brands to be dominant in those periods.

---

[46] The European Commission has made this distinction in several airline merger cases, including *Lufthansa/Swiss* (Case COMP/M.3770) [2005] OJ C204/3.

Where suppliers cannot specifically target the more captive customers, there are no separate price discrimination markets. If you live two minutes' walking distance from a major supermarket, you are probably a captive customer—you wouldn't drive ten minutes to the other major supermarket in town instead. Fortunately for you, the supermarket has no way of distinguishing between you and the next customer in the queue who lives exactly between the two supermarkets and hence has more choice. The supermarket cannot discriminate against you—you and your captive immediate neighbours are 'protected' by other customers who do have a choice. This protection of customers who don't have a choice by those who do is a feature of demand that arises in many markets (this is not to say that supermarkets don't try to price-discriminate; many have developed sophisticated discount schemes through loyalty cards, voucher systems, and the like).

Clearly, price discrimination is a very common business practice (in Chapter 4 we discuss the circumstances in which it may be anti-competitive). It would not make sense to define separate price discrimination markets wherever different prices are charged. You might discover that almost every passenger on your London–Milan flight has paid a different fare, but you would not want to define a separate market for each passenger. Again, some pragmatism is required. The most consistent approach is to consider instances of price discrimination where the captive group of customers is significant (a group of customers worth having a monopoly over, such as time-sensitive passengers), and where the price difference is significant and sustainable for a non-transitory period.

2.8.2 A COMMENT ON THE RELEVANCE OF ABSOLUTE PRICE DIFFERENCES

You have seen that the hypothetical monopolist test is about reactions to relative price changes between products. It is not about absolute price differences. Branded soft drinks may provide a competitive constraint on own-label soft drinks, and hence be included in the market, despite being more expensive. Customers make a price–quality trade-off, so if the price difference between the two products becomes too narrow they may switch from own-label to branded. However, just as differences in product characteristics sometimes provide a useful sense-check on market definition, so do differences in price. For example, if you can buy a business ticket for a flight from London Heathrow to Milan Linate Airport at 7.45am on a Monday for €734, while an economy ticket from London Stansted to Milan Bergamo Airport at 11.55am on a Wednesday costs €82, chances are that these two flight tickets do not provide competitive pressure on each other. You would expect them to be in separate relevant markets. How can you establish this? It may be that there is a break somewhere in the chain of substitution from cheap to expensive flights between London and Milan (see the next section on chains of substitution). Or it may be that you have to define separate markets along various dimensions, such as by geography (the question being which airports you should include around London and which around Milan), by type of customer (time-sensitive versus non-time-sensitive passengers), or by time of flight (peak versus off-peak).

2.9 CHAINS OF SUBSTITUTION, AND SPECIFIC ASPECTS OF GEOGRAPHIC MARKET DEFINITION

2.9.1 CHAINS OF SUBSTITUTION

The relevant market for a focal product or area may be extended to include several indirect substitute products or areas through a chain of substitution. This phenomenon is consistent with the hypothetical monopolist test. Every link in the chain is in essence a next iteration of the test.

To see the logic of the test, consider the example of the holiday park merger in the Netherlands presented in section 2.5. The survey that was used to assist the product market definition also shed some light on the geographic scope of the market. Respondents were asked how far they are willing to travel to their destination for a weekend break (maximum three nights). The question was asked only for weekend breaks because holidaymakers tend to be unwilling to travel as far as they would for breaks of a week or longer—this would therefore identify the narrowest geographic market. On average, the maximum travel time for weekend breaks was four hours and the median answer was three and a half hours (the median is the middle one if you rank all observations in a sample from lowest to highest). This confirmed the view of the merging parties that people are willing to travel for around three to four hours to their weekend breaks. This travel time determines the catchment area of each park—we discuss the use of drive-time-based isochrones below. Respondents were also asked whether they would consider a destination abroad if all prices in the Netherlands for holiday parks with an indoor pool were increased by 10% for two years. It turned out that as many as 65% of customers who considered the holiday in question would indeed go abroad (the Netherlands is a small country—in a three-to-four-hour drive you will have crossed a border regardless of where you start). This high percentage sales loss, together with the maximum travel times mentioned above, indicated that the geographic market cannot be limited to the Netherlands only. Hence, from the perspective of Dutch holidaymakers, the geographic market for short breaks covers at least the Netherlands, Belgium, and some nearby parts of Germany (in particular the Eifel region), and the north of France. This is the first link in the chain of substitution.

Holiday parks in this broader area do not only compete for Dutch custom but also for visitors from neighbouring countries (the Dutch represented only around 45% of customers of Center Parcs at the time, while 30% were German, 15% French, and 10% Belgian). German customers within a three to four hour drive would come from places like Düsseldorf or Hamburg. For them, there are other popular short-break destinations within a three to four hour drive from where they live, including the Ostsee region, Thüringer Wald, or the Schwarzwald, which are in the other direction from the Dutch parks. This means that Center Parcs in the Netherlands and surrounding areas competes directly with holiday accommodation in those other destinations, despite the fact that Dutch holidaymakers are less likely to travel to those destinations. This is the second link in the chain of substitution. This chain could be further extended since, for example, the Schwarzwald competes in turn with nearby destinations in France, Switzerland, and Austria. Following this logic, there could well be a geographic market for short-break destinations spanning large parts of western and central Europe.

Chains of substitution may also arise in product market definition. There may possibly be an all-cars market, from Skoda Fabias to Alfa Romeo Spiders and Porsche 911s, or an all-broadband-Internet-access market that covers all available download speeds from 2Mbit/s. This last example has been confirmed by several European telecoms regulators, including Ofcom, the UK regulator, in a 2010 market review:

> In 2008 we concluded that the [wholesale broadband access market] definition did not have an upper speed limit, i.e. there is a 'chain of substitution' through the available broadband internet access speeds. This means that for an asymmetric broadband internet access product of any given speed, there are lower or higher speed products (the next links in the chain) which are sufficiently close substitutes that products of all speeds are subject to a common pricing constraint.
>
> Current broadband packages available in the market tend to be at specific clusters of speed, such as 2Mbit/s, 8Mbit/s, and 20Mbit/s. One of the key characteristics of broadband packages is the download (and to some extent upload) speeds, with higher speed services commanding higher prices. Therefore for a given speed service, a 5–10% SSNIP would decrease the price differential between the speed of the service in question and the next service up. If there are sufficient consumers who switch up, it would render the SSNIP unprofitable and suggest a single product market between the two speeds.
>
> Our consumer survey shows that given a 10% increase in the price of the package consumers are currently paying, 14% of residential customers and 22% of business customers are willing to switch their broadband service to a different speed package. Given the critical loss factors it would suggest that the original price rise is not likely to be profitable . . .
>
> In addition, end users are almost as likely to switch up to a higher quality service as they would switch down to a lower quality service (around 6%–7%). This further suggests that consumers see the range of price/speed options as potential substitutes should the price of their package increase. As a result there is unlikely to be an identifiable break across the range of speeds available to warrant separate markets for low and high speed services within the current generation broadband access services available in the market.[47]

Ofcom thus found a continuous chain of substitution among prevailing Internet speeds. It then addressed the question of whether the chain might break following the recent introduction of 'super-fast broadband services' that use fibre rather than copper access and offer speeds of 40–50Mbit/s. The regulator considered that in the next few years there would still be one single market, but recognized that over time some breaks in the speed chain may occur because of the continued development and growth of Internet applications that require very high speeds (such as online games and Internet TV). This illustrates the importance of the second time dimension of relevant markets that we introduced in section 2.2: the scope of the market depends on the period of investigation. It also

---

[47] Ofcom (2010), 'Review of the wholesale broadband access markets', March, [3.88]–[3.91].

highlights the complex market definition questions that arise in innovative industries where consumers migrate to new products over time. We return to this in section 2.12. Finally, the example shows a recognition that there may be breaks in the chain of substitution, and that such breaks must be analysed carefully. We discuss this now.

2.9.2 BREAKING THE CHAIN

You should perhaps be somewhat sceptical of chains of substitution that are too long. Remember that in every further iteration of the hypothetical monopolist test, the monopolist gets to control another substitute product (or area), so has a little bit more pricing power than previously. Before long, pricing power would be such that a SSNIP would be imposed for the focal product or (area)—remember that we said in section 2.4 that the SSNIP question still applies only to the focal product or area in these further iterations, so once the price increases there you have a relevant market. For a link in the chain to be strong, the next substitute must place substantial competitive pressure on the product or area that you have just added to the group controlled by the monopolist. If holiday accommodation in the Schwarzwald strongly constrains the holiday parks in the areas surrounding the Netherlands, the monopolist will not be able to increase prices of the latter by much, and this in turn constrains prices in the Netherlands.

One particular situation in which the chain of substitution may be strong is where you have one supplier that competes nationally with several regional suppliers and follows a national pricing strategy. In several European countries, a national telephony incumbent competes with a number of regional cable companies in the provision of telephony and Internet services. The cable operators do not compete directly with each other (often this is for legacy reasons; many of these operations used to be run as monopolies owned by local authorities). But each of them competes with the national operator. Now take the hypothetical situation where one of the bigger regional cable operators reduces the price of a bundled telephony/Internet/TV package (see section 2.10 on market definition for bundles). The national operator decides that it needs to match this decrease because it does not want to lose customers in that region. But that means reducing prices in the whole country, because it always charges the same everywhere (it advertises its packages at the national level, which is one of its competitive advantages over the regional operators). Hence, the other regional cable operators are also forced to lower their prices, so as to keep in line with the national operator. In effect, the first regional operator, through a chain of substitution via the national operator, has placed an indirect competitive constraint on all other regional operators. Clearly, if the national operator decides to abandon its policy of uniform pricing and to flex prices regionally instead (and if regulation allows this), the chain breaks down and different regional markets may be defined.

2.9.3 KEEPING AN EYE ON THE FOCAL PRODUCT

If you have defined the product market based on supply-side substitution, you should still bear in mind the focal product for the rest of your analysis, for example, when assessing the geographic market. Take the following stylized example, based on an abuse of dominance investigation by the water regulator in England and Wales.[48] The investigation concerned the treatment of leachate. A somewhat less glamorous product than Italian women's designer shoes, leachate is the liquid that originates from rain percolating through the different layers of waste on a landfill site. It can be toxic and therefore needs to be treated appropriately before being discharged in the sewer. This occurs mainly at waste-water treatment works. The leachate is normally transported by tanker— 'tankered'—from the landfill site to these treatment works. The complaint concerned access for companies tankering leachate to the waste-water treatment works which were owned by the incumbent regional water and sewerage company. There was discussion about the possibility of supply-side substitution by other treatment works that could treat any liquid waste but that did not currently treat leachate. Such supply-side substitution was deemed feasible overall, although there were some limitations on the available capacity of these other treatment works, and other types of liquid waste were more profitable to treat (recall the paper example in section 2.7). Let's ignore these limitations and assume that the product market is extended to the treatment of all liquid waste, on the basis that any treatment works can treat any type of liquid waste, including leachate. This brings us to the geographic market. Tankering leachate is expensive—it ceases to be economical if the distance between the landfill site and treatment works is greater than 30 miles (see also the sub-section below on transport costs). But most other types of liquid waste are more economical to ship over longer distances—say, up to 60 miles. Given that the product market has been defined as all liquid waste (in this stylized example), should you consider this longer distance when delineating the geographic market?

The answer is no. To see why, consider the (again slightly stylized) situation in which all waste-water treatment works that currently treat leachate and lie within 30 miles of the major landfill sites in the region are owned by the incumbent. Beyond the 30 miles are several other treatment works that could switch (supply-side substitute) to treating leachate, and therefore have been included in your relevant product market. But you can clearly see that leachate cannot be economically tankered to those supply-side substitutes because the distance is too great. If you had taken your product market—treatment of all liquid waste—as the starting point for your geographic market, you would have overlooked the pocket of market power in leachate treatment itself. Your geographic market definition should therefore always refer back to the focal product, ie, the product where the competition concern arose in the first place (in this case treatment of leachate only).

2.9.4 TRANSPORT COSTS AND TRADE PATTERNS AS A BASIS FOR GEOGRAPHIC MARKET DEFINITION

Geographic patterns of supply and demand are often driven by transport costs. It is therefore relevant to consider these costs when delineating geographic markets.

---

[48] Ofwat (2005), 'Investigation into charges for the treatment of tankered landfill leachate by United Utilities Plc following a complaint made by Quantum Waste Management Ltd', Case CA98/01/32, Decision, 20 May. We advised the investigated party.

Concrete is a classic example of an industry where geographic markets are highly local-ized because of transport costs—in-transit mixers generally have to reach the construction site within 90 minutes from loading at the plant to prevent the concrete from becoming hard and unusable. Other products may be more easily shipped—fresh flowers grown in the Netherlands make it in large quantities to homes in the USA and Japan. But even for those products, transport costs matter—air freight charges on Dutch flowers will add to the cost faced by the US purchaser, more so than on flowers grown in nearby Mexico, and this may ultimately affect market definition.

At its simplest, you can incorporate transport costs directly in the hypothetical monopolist test—if transport costs between two regions represent more than 5%–10% of the prevailing prices, a monopolist in one region could increase price by 5%–10% without attracting supply from the other region. The NMa applied this test when reviewing a merger between the only two major sugar producers in the Netherlands (which it ultimately approved).[49] Transport costs for industrial sugar were found to be around €0.08 per tonne/kilometre. With a prevailing price of around €650 per tonne, a 5% price increase might invite imports from a distance of 400 km (5% of €650 equals €32.5; transporting a tonne of sugar over a distance of 400 km costs €32, so becomes attractive with the new price). The NMa also took into account the fact that the new European internal market regime for sugar—promoting greater market integration—might lead to a fall in market prices to around €500 per tonne in the coming years. Assuming the same transport costs, the corresponding distance over which imports would be profitable after a 5% price increase is 300 km, and the NMa took this as the basis to expand the relevant market beyond the Netherlands.

When applying the hypothetical monopolist test with transport costs, the usual cau-tion is required. For example, prevailing prices may already encapsulate the transport cost differential (this is akin to the cellophane fallacy discussed in section 2.6). Likewise, transport costs may change over time, as new technologies or modes of transport are developed (mix-at-site trucks can now deliver smaller amounts of concrete with less time pressure than in-transit mixers, so some concrete customers have greater choice than previously), or the conditions of competition in the transport market change (competition authorities have uncovered an international price-fixing cartel in the supply of air cargo services in recent years, which may have added to the transport cost of products like fresh flowers).[50] The period of investigation is a relevant dimension of the market here, as explained in section 2.2.

Sometimes it may be more relevant to consider transport costs from the perspective of the buyer rather than the supplier. In our holiday park example, the customers travel to the supplier rather than the other way round (this is a purer form of demand-side

[49] NMa (2007), *Cosun–CSM*, Zaak 5703/304, 20 April.

[50] US Department of Justice (2007), 'British Airways Plc And Korean Air Lines Co Ltd Agree To Plead Guilty And Pay Criminal Fines Totaling $600 Million For Fixing Prices On Passenger and Cargo Flights', press release, 1 August; and European Commission (2010), 'Antitrust: Commission fines 11 air cargo carriers €799 million in price fixing cartel', press release, 9 November. Several other competition authorities around the world have investigated this cartel as well (many airlines were involved).

substitution; where it is the supplier that moves, this is more closely related to supply-side substitution). When it is the customers that move, instead of focusing on transport costs as such, you would measure what in transport economics is commonly known as the generalized cost of travel. This is the sum of the monetary costs of a journey (the cost of the ticket if using public transport or the fuel if using the car) and its non-monetary costs. The latter consists mainly of the value of the total time spent on the journey. Calculating this value can take into account many different factors, such as opportunity costs (what else you could have done during that time), or the fact that some of the time spent has a greater 'cost' (waiting at a railway station is more 'costly' than sitting in a comfortable leather seat while on the move).[51]

In addition to using the analysis of transport costs or generalized costs of travel as part of the hypothetical monopolist test, you can use such analysis to delineate specific geographic areas within which you then assess the conditions of competition. In the example of the Dutch sugar merger, the authority drew circles of a 300km radius around each merging party's production facilities. The geographic market was thus extended to include producers in Belgium, France, and Germany—the so-called European 'sugar belt'. In this broader market the two Dutch producers had a share of around 20% (compared with nearly 100% in the Netherlands only). We discuss this further in the next sub-section on isochrones.

An alternative to assessing transport costs is to consider actual trade patterns. If there is a lot of movement of goods between two regions—by either suppliers or buyers—then it is likely that they form part of the same geographic market. A formal approach to this is the Elzinga–Hogarty test, named after two economists who first proposed that a geographic region is likely to be a separate market from other regions if there are few imports—'little in from outside' (LIFO)—and few exports—'little out from inside' (LOFI) (Elzinga and Hogarty, 1973). The test has been widely applied, including in several hospital mergers in the USA, where it was assessed whether hospitals attract patients from far afield.[52] The Dutch sugar merger case also included an analysis of current import and export patterns. The NMa found that imports into the Netherlands from the other countries in the 'sugar belt' were as yet relatively limited, but would be expected to increase under the new EU internal market regime. As with the SSNIP, exactly how you set the threshold for LIFO and LOFI is inherently arbitrary—Elzinga and Hogarty proposed two thresholds at 75% and 90% of supply (according to this logic, if imports and exports as a proportion of total supply are above the threshold, the geographic market is likely to be wider).

Using current trade patterns to define geographic markets can, however, lead to erroneous conclusions. In particular, it misses the basic logic of the hypothetical monopolist test, which is about demand and supply responses to small changes in price. Even if you observe few imports or exports at present, what matters is whether trade would

[51] More background on generalized cost can be found in Button (1993).

[52] One example is *FTC v Tenet Healthcare Corp* 17 F Supp 2d 937 (ED Mo 1998), rev'd 186 F 3d 1045 (8th Cir. 1999).

start to take place *after* the hypothetical monopolist imposes a SSNIP. Another criticism levelled at the Elzinga–Hogarty test—in the specific context of hospital mergers—is that it suffers from the 'silent majority fallacy' (Capps et al., 2001). There may be a significant difference between those patients who travel further afield and those who do not. So even if you observe that many people who live near one hospital travel to other distant hospitals, this does not mean that the first hospital has no market power—it may be that those who do not travel to other hospitals do not have the ability to do so (because of their condition, for example), and the first hospital may be able to exploit its captive customers. In essence this points to the possible existence of price discrimination markets, as discussed in section 2.8. Nonetheless, despite these valid criticisms of the Elzinga–Hogarty test, examining current trade patterns can still provide a useful sense-check for your geographic market definition, just like product characteristics and absolute price differences can provide useful sense-checks for product and geographic market definitions.

2.9.5 ATTACK OF THE ISOCHRONES

Until quite recently, geographic markets were often delineated by drawing circles of various sizes around production facilities or population centres to determine catchment areas—circles with a 30-mile radius around landfill sites for tankering waste or a 300km radius around sugar production facilities for the transport of sugar (as in the examples used earlier). You can see that circles are rather unsophisticated—they may accurately reflect distances as the crow flies, but not how far you can travel in a tanker filled with leachate, a truck filled with sugar, or an empty bus on its way from the depot to the starting point of a route in the early morning (the basis for defining local bus markets, as discussed in section 2.7). Modern technology has allowed for some further sophistication in this type of analysis. Mapping software is now regularly used to delineate more coherent geographic markets that take into account the characteristics of the underlying road network and travel speeds. Instead of circles you get isochrones. An isochrone is a line that joins together all of the points that can be reached within a constant journey time from a given starting location. To draw the isochrones, the drive time first needs to be determined—you can use evidence from surveys, analyse transport costs, or observe existing travel patterns (as discussed in the previous sub-section). There is an inevitable element of judgement in this, but you can always test the sensitivity of your results by drawing slightly broader and narrower isochrones to see whether the competitive landscape within the isochrones changes. Having determined the journey time, the second step is to construct the isochrones. The mapping software will contain a road matrix and a set of speeds for travelling on each road—speeds can be adjusted depending on the type of vehicle, the type of road, and the time of day.

What do you take as the central point of the isochrone? In line with the logic of the hypothetical monopolist test, this should reflect the focal product as closely as possible. In the bus example discussed in section 2.7, the competition concern arose with respect

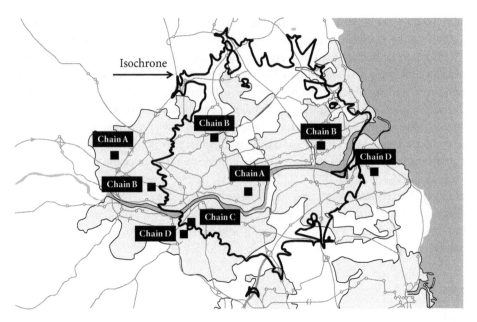

Fig. 2.6 20-minute isochrone for the cinema owned by chain A

to certain routes in the centre of Chester.[53] Based on supply-side considerations, the geographic market was found to include all existing bus depots within 30 minutes' drive time of the routes. In theory, you could draw an isochrone around every point on the route from which the bus can begin service in the early morning. Pragmatically, however, an isochrone around one particular main stop on the route (eg, the central bus station in Chester) will often provide sufficient insight. The next step in the competition analysis is then to analyse market shares and other indicators of competitive strength of the various operators in this geographic market.

In other cases you would draw the isochrones around the relevant outlets in question—each supermarket or holiday park. This gives the catchment area of each outlet, which provides useful information on the competitive constraints they face. For example, in a cinema merger in the UK—*Odeon/UCI* (2005)—the OFT and the parties drew isochrones for a 20-minute drive time around each cinema, a distance considered to reflect the cinema's core catchment area.[54] A 30-minute isochrone was then used as a sensitivity check. (The only part of the country in which isochrone analysis was not used was Central London, where people tend not to drive to the cinema.) Figure 2.6 shows the boundaries of the 20-minute isochrone for a cinema owned by one of the

[53] *Chester City Council and Chester City Transport Limited v Arriva PLC* [2007] EWHC 1373 (Ch).

[54] Office of Fair Trading (2005), 'Acquisition by Terra Firma Investments (GP) 2 Ltd of United Cinemas International (UK) Limited and Cinema International Corporation (UK) Limited', 7 January; undertakings accepted 9 May. We acted for the merging parties in this transaction.

merging parties (chain A) in one of the cities considered. This figure has been drawn using the MapInfo software. The irregular shapes and 'peaks' of the isochrone simply reflect the configuration and speed of the underlying road network. The other merging party (chain B) has two cinemas in the area, while only one competing cinema is present (chain C). The other competing operator in the city, chain D, has no presence in this isochrone. Strictly speaking, such isochrones do not accurately reflect the relevant geographic market, since they are supply-centred rather than demand-centred. Two cinemas do not compete because they are within 20 minutes' drive time of each other, but because they are both within reach (ie, within 20 minutes' drive time) of the same customers. One simple adjustment to the supply-centred isochrones is therefore to perform a 'population re-centring', which comes down to drawing the isochrones around major population centres and then assessing which outlets are within their reach. For pragmatic reasons, you do this only for the major population centres, rather than for every single customer as pure theory would dictate, since a focus on the major centres will usually give a sufficiently clear picture.

2.10 MARKET DEFINITION FOR COMPLEMENTS AND BUNDLES

2.10.1 SUBSTITUTES, COMPLEMENTS, AND BUNDLES

Recall from section 2.3 that substitute products have a positive cross-price elasticity while complements have a negative one. If a 10% increase in the price of flights between London and Paris results in a 15% increase in demand for Eurostar train journeys—a substitute—the cross-price elasticity of rail with respect to air travel between the two cities is 1.5 (15% divided by 10%). If a 10% increase in the price of gin reduces demand for tonic water—a complement in gin-and-tonics—by 10%, the cross-price elasticity of tonic water with respect to gin is –1. Substitutes and complements therefore have exact opposite properties. This has profound implications for the assessment of mergers (as further discussed in Chapter 7). If you merge two substitute products, you can expect them both to increase in price—this is commonly understood and lies at the heart of merger control in competition law. Less well understood is that merging two complementary products has the opposite effect: they decrease in price after the merger. This is why such mergers are often inherently benign to consumers of the product (they may still give rise to competition concerns of a different nature, such as portfolio and foreclosure effects—see Chapter 7).[55]

---

[55] That a monopolist with two complementary goods would reduce prices compared with the situation where each good is controlled separately was first identified by the French economist Antoine Augustin Cournot in 1838—the same Cournot from the famous oligopoly model discussed in Chapter 3 (Cournot, 1838). This 'Cournot effect' is also of relevance in the context of vertical restraints, where it leads to the problem of double marginalization, as explained in Chapter 6.

But first let us explore the implications of complements for market definition. If you expand the hypothetical monopolist's influence by adding a substitute product, prices will go up—the monopolist now no longer cares about losing sales to those substitutes. Following the same logic as above, if you add a complementary product instead, a profit-maximizing monopolist will set a lower price than before. A hypothetical monopolist in the supply of gin would selfishly raise price to extract maximum profits, without caring about the negative effect that this has on tonic water sales. If the monopolist controlled tonic water as well, it would care about lost tonic water sales, and hence would not raise the price of gin by as much when maximizing the profits of both products. This is exactly the opposite effect of adding a substitute product—a complementary product acts as a pricing constraint when it is inside the monopoly group, whereas a substitute product acts as a constraint when it is outside. How do you apply the hypothetical monopolist test here?

The test itself can be readily applied in cases where there are complementary products. The main difficulty lies in choosing the right starting point—in the first iteration of the test, does the monopolist control just one product, or does it control the two (or more) complements? The outcome of the test may differ substantially (a gin monopolist might impose a SSNIP while a gin-and-tonic monopolist might not). The choice will have to be determined by the specific market and the specific competition problem that you are considering. If the real companies in the market supply just one product, your hypothetical monopolist should do so as well—the production and sale of gin by spirits companies are usually separate from those of tonic water, so it is not unreasonable to take gin as the focal product if that is where the competition concern arises, and ignore the complementarities with tonic water at the market definition stage. In contrast, if the real companies normally control two complementary products already, or consumers in the market usually buy the complementary products together (in a bundle), it may be more appropriate to start the test from a hypothetical monopolist that controls both of those products. An obvious, if somewhat absurd, example is that of left shoes and right shoes. They are different products, and they are complements, not substitutes. Shoe producers supply and sell them together, and consumers buy them together. You can therefore safely start your market definition exercise with a hypothetical monopolist who produces both left and right shoes, and ask if it could impose a SSNIP on pairs of shoes.

The same logic holds for bundled products more generally. Bundling occurs when two or more products are sold more cheaply together than individually (this is known as mixed bundling), or when they are sold only together (pure bundling). Bundling is a very common business practice—with a left shoe comes a right shoe, with a car come four wheels and tyres and a stereo, with your mobile phone subscription comes a handset. Bundling has many economic justifications, but it may also raise competition concerns—we address this in Chapter 4. Here we explore how bundling may affect market definition. There is an economic case for defining relevant markets for bundles, as opposed to individual products, where: (i) bundling is pure rather than mixed— the two products are available only as a package, not separately (you can't buy just a right shoe); (ii) the complements are consumed in fixed proportions (one left and one right shoe, one car and four wheels); and (iii) all suppliers in the market sell bundles. However, there are also markets where the picture is more mixed—only some suppliers sell bundles, or bundling is a relatively new phenomenon. An example is the various 'triple-play' and 'quadruple-play' packages that you can get from telecoms providers (fixed telephony, broadband Internet, TV, and mobile telephony). These packages have been on offer for several years and are steadily gaining ground among consumers, but still there are operators in the market with different combinations of services in the bundles (some are traditionally stronger in TV services, others in telephony services), and some customers purchase them while others still obtain individual services from different providers. Here there is no clear-cut case for either defining relevant markets at the level of the individual products or at the level of the bundles. It is probably good practice to do both. This allows you to explore the relative strengths of the different operators in each product separately, and at the same time to assess whether some operators are particularly well positioned in the offering of the bundles (not all providers of the individual services may be able to offer all services in the bundle), and identify any scope for market power in that way.

Below we illustrate how the hypothetical monopolist test might work when there are complementarities between products in two specific types of market—aftermarkets and two-sided platform markets.

2.10.2 MARKET DEFINITION FOR AFTERMARKETS

In most circumstances, you buy a product, you consume it, and that's the end of the story. In some markets, however, buying the product is just the beginning. In order to make full use of it, you subsequently have to buy associated products or services that are complements to the original product. Examples of this include razors and razor blades, printers and cartridges, game consoles and video games, and proprietary software and further upgrades to that software. The same holds for durable equipment (such as photocopiers, machinery, cars, and cash registers), and subsequent maintenance services and spare parts for that equipment. The market in which you buy the associated product or service is commonly referred to as the secondary market or aftermarket. Many competition cases have arisen in aftermarkets. Often they involve complaints that the supplier of the primary product is using its control over that product to exclude independent suppliers from selling the secondary product. A prime example is the *Kodak* litigation in the USA, which lasted from 1987 to 1998—Kodak was found guilty of monopolizing the market for the servicing of its high-volume copier and micrographics equipment.[56] It had a strong position in the supply of this equipment (the primary product), which required extensive, ongoing maintenance (the secondary product).

---

[56] The two main rulings in this case are *Eastman Kodak Co v Image Technical Services, Inc et al.* 504 US 451 (1992), and *Image Technical Services, Inc et al. v Eastman Kodak Co* 125 F 3d 1195 (9th Cir. 1997). A discussion of the economics of the case can be found in MacKie-Mason and Metzler (2009).

Many independent organizations serviced Kodak equipment at the time, in direct competition with Kodak's own national network of service technicians, but then Kodak stopped selling spare parts to these organizations, such that they could no longer provide maintenance services. We discuss abuse of dominance in Chapter 4. The issue addressed here is whether market definition can be a helpful intermediate step in assessing such practices.

Two main questions arise: Does the primary producer have the ability to foreclose the secondary market from competition? And if competition in the secondary market is foreclosed, does the primary producer have the ability to exploit its customers there (in other words, are customers worse off if Kodak keeps the aftermarket to itself)? In essence you want to know what the competitive constraints are on the primary producer. Market definition normally helps in identifying these competitive constraints. In this case, the main market definition question is whether the secondary market is a separate relevant market from the primary market, or whether there is a 'systems market' that includes both the primary and secondary product. However, regardless of how you delineate the market exactly, the source of any market power of the primary producer is its control over the primary product. So even if you conclude that the aftermarket is a separate market, you would still need to explicitly take into account the link between the primary market and the aftermarket.

A systems market would be more appropriate if customers are fully aware at the time of purchase that what they buy is a system, ie, they know that they need to purchase the secondary product or service as well, and take this into account when making the primary purchase decision. One example would be game consoles and video games. When choosing between a Nintendo Wii, a Sony PlayStation 3, and a Microsoft Xbox 360, you (or, more likely, your children) will normally consider which games are available for that console. If the market is a systems one, you could test whether a hypothetical monopolist controlling one system faces competition from other systems—does the Nintendo Wii face a pricing constraint from the PlayStation and Xbox? Does Kodak face strong competition from other producers of high-volume copiers and micrographics equipment? You would also take into account the general logic of complements we discussed earlier—if there were a genuine systems market, and companies priced on a systems basis, Kodak would be constrained from raising the price of the secondary product if that negatively affected sales (and hence profits) of the primary product, and vice versa. This market definition therefore helps you identify cases where any negative effects on customers are limited, ie, cases where system competition is so strong that it constrains any exploitation of market power in the secondary market.

There are other circumstances, however, in which system competition is not sufficiently strong to constrain market power in the secondary market, and where a systems market definition would therefore be less appropriate. This can occur where customers do not fully take the need for the secondary product into account when choosing the primary product, or have insufficient information at the time of the primary purchase. It can also arise when the primary product already has a large installed base of customers who are locked in for the foreseeable future (they would face high switching costs if they were to move to another primary product). You would also be more doubtful about a systems market if there is evidence (as there was in *Kodak*) that the supplier of the primary product does not engage in system pricing. Finally, there may be a separate market for the secondary product if the competitive dynamics of the primary and secondary markets are very different, or where many secondary products are compatible with multiple primary products—for example, spare car parts such as tyres that fit on any make of car, or garages that service any make of car.

2.10.3 MARKET DEFINITION IN TWO-SIDED PLATFORM MARKETS

If you have followed developments in competition law in the last five years, chances are you have heard the term two-sided market. It is one of those economic concepts that suddenly became fashionable among scholars and practitioners. The economic literature on two-sided markets that has snowballed in recent years was originally inspired by a real competition case—the investigations since the late 1990s by competition authorities worldwide into interchange fees in the Visa and MasterCard credit card schemes.[57] We return to interchange fees in Chapter 5. Here we explore the economic properties of credit card schemes—in particular their two-sided nature and the implications for market definition.

Credit card schemes are one among many examples of networks or platforms that face demand from two groups of customer—hence the term two-sided demand—with positive demand externalities existing between these two groups (we explained the concept of externality in Chapter 1). In credit card schemes, these externalities arise between issuers—the participating banks that issue cards to their accountholders—and acquirers—the banks that sign up retailers (more generally referred to as 'merchants') to accept the card scheme. A card becomes more valuable to retailers the more consumers hold and use it, and a card becomes more valuable to have in your wallet the more retailers accept it in their shops. Other examples include video game consoles (externalities between users and game developers), PC operating systems (PC users and applications developers), newspapers (readers and advertisers), and nightclubs and speed-dating events (men and women).

In setting their pricing structure, platforms face the celebrated chicken-and-egg problem—they must 'get both sides on board', but in order to get participants on one side they need to have sufficient participants on the other side. This is not dissimilar to a situation where you have two complementary products—if demand for one goes up, then so does demand for the other. It makes commercial sense to set a pricing structure that optimizes the size of the network. This usually means setting relatively low prices

---

[57] Reserve Bank of Australia (2001), 'Reform of credit card schemes in Australia', December; Visa International—Multilateral Interchange Fee (Case COMP/29.373) Decision of 24 July 2002, [2002] OJ L318/17; and Office of Fair Trading (2005), 'Investigation of the multilateral interchange fees provided for in the UK domestic rules of Mastercard UK Members Forum Limited (formerly known as MasterCard/Europay UK Limited)', Decision, 6 September. We advised one of the credit card schemes in a number of these investigations.

for the more price-sensitive customer side, and relatively high prices for the less price-sensitive side. Likewise, it may imply setting lower prices to the side that is more important in terms of attracting the other side, ie, the side that generates larger network effects. For this reason, 'free' newspapers are free to users and recover costs from advertisers, and some speed-dating events are free to women and thus recover more of their costs from men. There is nothing inherently anti-competitive about these pricing practices. Indeed, to the extent that they have the effect of expanding the platform or network size, they may increase overall welfare compared with the situation where all sides are charged the same price.

A first step in the competition analysis is, as usual, to define the relevant market—does the platform face competitive constraints from other platforms? The hypothetical monopolist test can be used here. We illustrate this with a stylized application to a hypothetical credit card scheme. The first question that arises is what you take as the starting point—a hypothetical monopolist on one side, on the other side, or on both sides? It usually does not make much sense to consider a hypothetical monopolist on one side in isolation. In the context of a credit card scheme, if the question is whether the scheme competes with other payment systems, you want to test competition on both sides. The complementary and network effects between the two sides mean that no real card scheme would set prices on one side without considering the effects on demand from the other side. First, a reduction in the number of card transactions on one side would by definition mean a reduction in transactions on the other side—one retailer transaction necessarily involves one cardholder transaction (the two sides are like complements in this respect). Second, because of the network effects between the two sides, when setting prices, the monopolist would take into account the fact that a reduction in demand on one side also makes the product less attractive for the other side. Applying the hypothetical monopolist test to a credit card scheme is therefore similar to a second-round iteration of the test, where the monopolist controls two products. The main difference with the standard situation is that the two products are like complements, not substitutes.

How do you apply critical loss analysis? You follow the same logic as in standard critical loss analysis, but now take into account two sides of the market. So you test whether the hypothetical monopolist can profitably impose a 5%–10% increase in charges to retailers (known as merchant service charges), a 5%–10% increase in cardholder charges, or a combination of the two that results in an overall increase in the 'system price' of 5%–10%. To determine the critical loss, you need some estimate of the actual sales loss on either side that would result from the price increase, and an estimate of the profit margin.

Let's start with the margin. Suppose that the issuing banks that participate in the scheme (those banks that have relationships with cardholders) incur a cost per transaction of €1.20, and the acquiring banks (those that deal with retailers) a cost of €0.30 (such a cost imbalance between issuing and acquiring banks is not uncommon in payment systems, since the former incur costs such as fraud prevention, bad-debt write-offs, and cardholder loyalty awards). The total 'system cost' is therefore €1.50 per transaction. As to revenues, suppose that issuing banks receive €1.00 per transaction from cardholder charges, while acquiring banks receive €1.50 per transaction from merchant service charges (this revenue imbalance is also not uncommon since retailers tend to have greater willingness to pay than cardholders—indeed, the combination of the cost and revenue imbalances provides the economic rationale for the interchange fees paid from acquirers to issuers, as discussed in Chapter 5). The total 'system price' per transaction is €2.50, so the initial price–cost margin equals €1.00, or 40%.[58]

Now suppose you have evidence on retailers' and cardholders' responses to price increases. A survey among retailers suggests that a 10% increase in merchant service charges would lead to a loss of 15% of total card transactions as the retailers where those transactions take place would cease to accept the card or discourage card payments by imposing a surcharge or minimum purchase value. Econometric evidence on cardholder elasticity of demand suggests that a 10% increase in cardholder charges would lead to a 30% drop in transactions—cardholders are apparently quite prone to switching to other payment methods. The last step in this hypothetical example is for you to compare the actual loss with the critical loss. You have to do this according to the system price and system cost. The merchant service charge (€1.50) represents 60% of the system price (€2.50). A 10% increase in that charge is therefore equivalent to a 6% increase in the system price. This 6% increase leads to a 15% loss in transactions. Applying the critical loss formula of section 2.6 gives you 6% divided by 6% + 40%, which equals 13%, so the actual loss exceeds the critical loss. The cardholder charges (€1.00) represent 40% of the system price. A 10% increase in those charges is therefore equivalent to a 4% increase in the system price. The critical loss for this is 4% divided by 4% + 40%, or 9%, so is again exceeded (transactions fall by 30%). Hence a 10% price increase is unprofitable both on the retailer side and on the cardholder side. This would imply that the market is broader than just credit cards.

2.11 MARKETS ALONG THE VERTICAL SUPPLY CHAIN

As noted in section 2.2, an additional market dimension is the vertical layer in the supply chain. The same product—a car, a washing machine, ice cream, a bunch of fresh flowers—may pass through a whole set of intermediaries on its way from producer to end-consumer. The relevant market may be different depending on which layer of the chain is considered. This in turn will normally depend on where in the chain the competition problem in question arises. If the concern relates to an exclusive distribution arrangement between a washing machine manufacturer and a large retail chain, the product market should be defined with reference to that upstream level of the supply chain. Washing machines are the focal product, and the first question to ask is whether the manufacturer has market power in the supply of washing machines (if it has, the

---

[58] You may work out that if both acquirers and issuers are to earn a 40% margin, the scheme requires an interchange fee paid by acquirers to issuers equal to €1.00 per transaction so as to make up for the cost–revenue imbalance in the scheme (the acquiring banks then receive €0.50 net per transaction while incurring a cost of €0.30, and the issuing banks receive €2.00 net with a cost of €1.20).

arrangements are more likely to have anti-competitive effects—see Chapters 4 and 6). However, it will still be relevant to consider the final layer of the supply chain (the downstream market) as well, which is the layer where you purchase a washing machine from a retail outlet. This is for several reasons, as discussed below.

2.11.1 MARKETS IN DIFFERENT LAYERS AND THEIR INTERACTION

First, even if the upstream market between manufacturer and retail chain is the focal product where the exclusive arrangement arises, this arrangement is likely to have an effect on the final consumer market as well—you as a consumer may face less choice of where to buy your washing machine. The downstream market can therefore be an additional relevant market. In this market you want to analyse the competitive position of the retailer, and the effects of the arrangement on prices and other terms offered to consumers. Second, even if the focus is on the upstream market, the demand in this market—in this case the demand for washing machines—is often largely driven by the demand of final consumers. Whether different types of washing machine— high-capacity versus low-capacity; those with and without a tumble dryer—are close substitutes depends on the preferences of final consumers. The demand of retailers for washing machines is often a 'derived' demand from that of consumers. Retailers will buy and stock the products that consumers want.

Indeed, the main evidence you have on substitution will often relate to consumer behaviour rather than retailer behaviour. If that is the case, you have to exercise some care when applying the hypothetical monopolist test to the upstream market. Suppose you find that if the retail price of washing machines is raised from €500 to €525—a 5% increase—consumer demand falls by 10%. The own-price elasticity of demand for washing machines is –2. Is this price increase profitable? That depends on whether you look at it from the perspective of the retailer or the manufacturer. Recall Table 2.3, which shows the critical loss threshold depending on the initial price–cost margin and the percentage price increase. Suppose that the retailer obtains washing machines from the manufacturer at a wholesale price of €250. The retailer margin is therefore 50% (half of the retail price of €500). From Table 2.3 you can see that the critical loss threshold for a 5% price increase and 50% margin equals 9.1%. The 10% fall in demand (just) exceeds this critical level, which would lead you to conclude that the price increase is unprofitable. However, what you have just determined is that a hypothetical monopoly retailer of washing machines could not impose a SSNIP. The focal question here, in contrast, is whether a hypothetical monopoly manufacturer could profitably increase price. How can you use the consumer evidence from the downstream market to infer any conclusions on this last question in relation to the upstream market? You can use the principle that retailer demand is derived from consumer demand and apply critical loss analysis. The manufacturer might achieve the increase in the retail price from €500 to €525 by increasing the wholesale price from €250 to €275 (assuming that the retailer fully passes on this price increase of €25 to its customers). The wholesale price increase is 10%. The sales loss is still 10%—retailer demand is simply derived demand, ie, retailers only purchase washing machines that they ultimately sell to consumers (with some delay usually). Now suppose that the cost of production of the washing machine is €125, which means that the manufacturer has an initial margin of 50% as well. As you can see from Table 2.3, for a 10% price increase the critical loss threshold is 16.7%, so for the hypothetical monopoly manufacturer this price increase is profitable and the market is no wider than washing machines.

Note that in this example we assumed that the retailer passes on 100% of the whole-sale price increase. However, even if the pass-on rate is lower, your conclusion that the manufacturing layer is worth monopolizing remains unchanged, since a lower pass-on rate means that even fewer sales are lost, so the wholesale price increase is even more profitable. We discuss the economic principles of pass-on in more detail in Chapter 10 on the quantification of damages.

2.11.2 DO END-CONSUMERS ALWAYS MATTER MOST?

Retailer or wholesaler demand is not always fully derived from consumer demand. It may be the case that even where final consumers are willing and able to switch between different products, retailers cannot because some products are 'must-stock' items. For your flight from London to Paris, you can choose among several airlines. But when you book the ticket through a travel agent (something that probably occurs less and less with the rise of Internet bookings), you expect that agent to offer tickets for all the major airlines. So travel agents have less choice than final consumers—often it is the case that each major airline is a 'must-have' for each travel agent. What do you do in situations where consumers have choice (so you don't have to worry about them) but retailers or other intermediaries in the chain do not?

Competition policy is often, implicitly or explicitly, more concerned with effects on final consumers than effects on intermediaries. This is why the analysis of mergers and business practices upstream in a supply chain will frequently consider effects further downstream as well as the effects upstream (as in the washing machine example above). Sometimes you can go a step further and place the main weight of the analysis on the downstream market—you may not care what effect a practice or agreement has on certain intermediaries in the chain, as long as final consumers are not negatively affected. This may occur where the main effect of the practice or agreement is to redistribute profits from one layer in the chain to another—for example, from manufacturer to retailer, or vice versa. Such arrangements are very common and can lead to fierce commercial disputes in which competition law arguments are often invoked, but the final consumer may not always be affected. We discuss this further under vertical restraints in Chapter 6. Some policy judgement may be required in such cases. Is a particular intermediary layer in the value chain really worth preserving? Consider the example of the leachate abuse of dominance case in section 2.9.[59] The complaint was made by an intermediary acting as a broker

---

[59] Ofwat (2005), 'Investigation into charges for the treatment of tankered landfill leachate by United Utilities Plc following a complaint made by Quantum Waste Management Ltd', Case CA98/01/32, Decision, 20 May.

between landfill sites and the providers of leachate tanker and treatment services. The incumbent water and sewerage company, which owned the treatment works and also had its own tanker operations, began to contract with some of the landfill sites directly, thereby 'squeezing' the intermediary broker out of the market. If you take a narrow view on market definition at the layer of intermediary brokerage services, you might find that the broker—given the nature of its activities—had no choice but to deal with the landfill sites and treatment works in that area. If you take a broader view, you might conclude that what matters is whether the landfill sites, as the customers in this market, have sufficient choice (the authority found that they did have some choice, including building their own treatment facilities). The position of the broker as intermediary matters less if you take that view—customers are unharmed, so why care if the broker goes out of business? (In market definition terms, you are implicitly saying that the leachate broker could dedicate itself to other activities instead.)

2.11.3 TURNING THE SUPPLY CHAIN UPSIDE DOWN FOR MARKET DEFINITION

Another issue related to defining markets in the context of a vertical supply chain arose in the European Commission's investigation into loyalty rebates offered by British Airways (BA) to travel agents.[60] When you deal with a case like this, the concern is usually about the effects that such rebates have on competition between airlines, and therefore ultimately on airline users, ie, the passengers. A sensible first stage in your analysis of these competitive effects would therefore be to define the relevant market with airline services as the focal product. You can then assess whether the airline has a dominant position in the provision of flights—if it has, such practices are more likely to produce anti-competitive effects than if it does not (we discuss this in Chapter 4). The European Commission took a different approach. It defined the relevant market the other way round, as that for the provision of air travel agency services, which are purchased from travel agents by airlines. It found that BA had a dominant position as a buyer in that market, with a (declining) market share as a buyer of over 40% of all relevant flights. Perhaps in this case the outcome might have been the same if the Commission had defined the market for the supply of airline services (where the 40% market share would also have been used as an indicator of dominance). But defining the market in the way the Commission did carries the risk of focusing the attention of the competition analysis on the wrong market, ie, it leads you to focus on the effects of the rebates in the travel agent market, while the real concern is with distortions to the supply of airline services to final customers. To capture this concern, defining a market for the supply of airline services is more informative.[61]

---

[60] *Virgin/British Airways*, (Case COMP/D-2/34.780) [2000] OJ L30/1.

[61] A separate competition concern identified by the Commission in this case was the potential distortive effect of BA's discrimination between travel agents. For this concern, defining the market as that for travel agency services may have been informative, as that is where the discrimination had an effect.

2.12 PRODUCT SUBSTITUTION VERSUS PRODUCT MIGRATION

There are markets where consumers migrate from one product to another over time. Many modern examples come from the digital world: consumers migrate from dial-up (narrowband) Internet access to broadband Internet, from analogue TV to digital TV, from VHS to DVD (and now Blu-ray), from traditional cameras to digital cameras, and, to some extent, from letters and faxes to email. However, product migration occurs in other industries as well—for example, from wooden tennis rackets to those made of graphite and other high-tech materials, or from long-distance coach services to low-cost airlines for domestic and regional travel. Sometimes the shift from one product to the next may happen overnight, but often the old and new products live alongside each other for some time. In competition investigations, the question then regularly arises as to whether the two products form part of the same relevant market—are the old and new products regarded as close substitutes? As you have seen in this chapter, the hypothetical monopolist test is defined in terms of relative price changes (can the monopolist increase the price of one product by a small amount without losing too many customers to substitute products?). Product migration is not driven by small price changes. However, this is not to say that it should be ignored when defining relevant markets. Product migration can still have implications for whether a product is worth monopolizing.

Product migration is normally in one direction—from the old product to the new. The question of whether one is in the other's relevant market can arise in two directions, depending on which is the focal product. One direction is to ask whether the old product places a competitive constraint on the new product. At some point in time this becomes a less interesting question. Once you have switched to broadband Internet or digital TV, you are unlikely to ever switch back to the old product (narrowband or analogue TV, respectively). Nonetheless, in the early stages of the new product, the old one may still be very attractive to consumers, such that suppliers of the new product have to compete not only with each other but also with the suppliers of the old product. This may have been the case in the early years of broadband Internet access, when broadband providers had to keep prices low to attract narrowband users.

The more complicated question to ask is whether the new product imposes a pricing constraint on the old product. Two examples in which authorities had to address this question are the analysis of narrowband markets by Oftel, the predecessor to Ofcom, in 2003, and the analysis of the leased-lines market by OPTA, the Dutch telecoms regulator, in 2005. In the first of these cases the following statement was made:

> Oftel's view is that there is not a single market including both narrowband and broadband. While Oftel recognises that customers have moved from narrowband to broadband and that this is likely to continue to some extent in the future, it is not clear that this is substitution in response to a relative price change as such, as opposed to customers upgrading to a higher quality product that was not previously available.[62]

---

[62] Oftel (2003), 'Fixed Narrowband Retail Services Markets: Final Explanatory Statement and Notification', 28 November, [2.6].

Hence, Oftel did not consider product migration to be a relevant form of substitution for the purpose of market definition, since it did not occur in response to relative changes in the prices of both products. It was therefore still concerned with narrow-band services as a separate market from broadband. OPTA used the same reasoning with respect to the leased-lines market. A leased line is a permanently connected communications link between two premises, dedicated to a customer's exclusive use. At the time, business users had begun to gradually switch from leased lines to other data services, such as those based on Internet protocol technology. While these newer data services had more variable capacity and required more outsourcing of network management functions, customers considered them a lower-cost alternative to leased lines. Having noted a high degree of migration from leased lines to the newer data services between 2002 and 2004, OPTA nonetheless concluded that the movement between the products was not relevant for market definition:

> Switching and migration from service A to B does not automatically constitute demand substitution. Demand substitution requires that switching from A to B is caused by changes in the price difference between A and B. In this case, there is price pressure. Migration, however, can result from other factors, such as the emergence of a completely new service (B) or changes in user preferences. Consumers migrate as a result, where this migration no longer depends on further small (5% to 10%) changes in the price difference between A and B.[63]

Do these cases reflect an overly restrictive interpretation of the hypothetical monopolist test? What ultimately matters is whether the old product is a product worth monopolizing. Here, product migration does have relevance. Recall the charts earlier in this chapter. In Figure 2.2 you saw how the demand curve of a product can shift downwards if a close substitute product gains in popularity (or becomes cheaper). Product migration has precisely this effect. The rise of graphite tennis rackets meant that, over time, the demand for wooden rackets declined. The same happened to the demand for dial-up Internet access and VHS players. Going back to Figures 2.2 to 2.4 earlier in the chapter, you can see the consequences of the demand curve shifting downwards. The intersect between demand and marginal costs (which are assumed to remain the same) moves ever further towards the left-hand side of the demand curve. Remember from Figure 2.3 that this left-hand side is the elastic part of the curve. Now consider the more dramatic case in Figure 2.7, where demand has fallen substantially due to migration away from the product—this new demand curve can be expressed as $p = 3 - q$ (previously this was $p = 10 - q$, so for every price point there are 7 fewer buyers). In perfect competition, price would equal marginal cost, so $p = 2$, and quantity would be 1. Hence, even under perfect competition you would already have elastic demand (you may have worked out that at this point the elasticity equals −2). As it is, if perfect competition is the starting point in this example, a hypothetical monopolist would still impose a SSNIP (the monopoly price is 2.5 and monopoly output 0.5, so the price

---

[63] OPTA (2005), 'Ontwerpbesluit huurlijnen' (draft decision leased lines), 1 July, [280] (translated from Dutch).

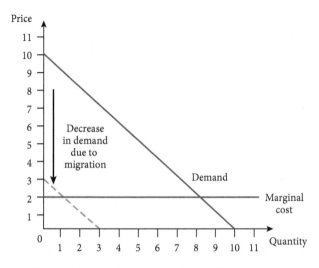

Fig. 2.7 Decrease in demand due to migration to other products

increase compared with a situation of perfect competition is still 25%). But you can see that if the starting price is higher than under perfect competition, or the demand curve falls even further, there comes a point where even a monopolist would not impose a SSNIP. That is the point when the old product is no longer worth monopolizing.

In practice, once it is recognized that product migration does matter for market definition as a matter of principle, the main question becomes whether migration places a sufficiently strong constraint. This depends in part on the speed of migration—does migration become significant within the period covered by the investigation? It may well be that in the examples of Oftel and OPTA such an analysis would have led to the same conclusions as those drawn by the two regulators—indeed, in both cases there were other indications that separate markets could be defined. One reason why the old product could still be worth monopolizing may be that those customers who have not yet migrated to the new one are in fact the less price-sensitive customers—in this case, while the monopolist has lost many customers due to migration, it can still profitably exploit the remaining ones. Such an effect is not captured in Figure 2.7. You might capture it by assuming that migration does not shift the whole demand curve down, as in Figure 2.7, but rather makes it rotate downwards from the point where price is zero and quantity is ten, such that the curves becomes steeper from that point. The profit-maximizing price then remains the same, and only quantity falls. These are all further refinements that you can incorporate into the analysis of your specific case. The important point in this sub-section is that product migration cannot be dismissed as irrelevant for market definition or for the analysis of competitive constraints—product migration is a relevant form of competitive pressure between products.

2.13 MARKET DEFINITION FOR FEATURES OTHER THAN PRICE

2.13.1 IT'S NOT JUST THE PRICE THAT MATTERS

The traditional hypothetical monopolist test focuses on the ability to raise price, and this is what we have discussed so far in this chapter. Raising prices is the most direct, and often most visible, way of exploiting a position of market power, and is usually the main concern of competition authorities. However, products do not compete only on price—they compete on non-price aspects such as quality, design and brand. A hypothetical monopolist can also exploit customers by downgrading those aspects of the product offering and thereby saving costs—for example, it could cut corners on quality or not improve the design of the product. This could equally be of concern to competition authorities, as consumers are negatively affected. In principle, therefore, the logic of the hypothetical monopolist test can be applied to non-price aspects as well. You could ask: would the hypothetical monopolist put into effect a 5%–10% reduction in quality? The difficulty tends to lie in establishing a clear metric for those non-price aspects (how do you measure quality?), and in identifying how a small change in a particular product feature affects the monopolist's profits (does lower quality mean lower costs? Does lower quality reduce demand?). But these difficulties have not prevented economists and competition authorities from using the hypothetical monopolist framework to define relevant markets according to product features other than price.

The UK Competition Commission's (CC) inquiry into the *Sportech/Vernons* merger in 2007 provides an example.[64] Between them, the merging parties operated the major weekly football pools in the UK, which consist of the stakes received from people playing in the pools. Football pools had been very popular, but had shrunk by a factor of 10 since 1994 when the National Lottery was introduced (you could say that this is a form of product migration as discussed in the previous section). The stakes in the pool are influenced by the entry prices set by the pool operators. Only a portion of the pool money goes into the prize fund—the payout ratio is in the range of 20%–25%. Most of the prize fund is paid out to the winning player as a jackpot. Thus, there are three important features of the product—the entry price, the payout ratio, and the size of the jackpot. The hypothetical monopolist test in its purest form would apply to the entry price only. However, the CC considered evidence on the effect of a small but significant deterioration in the merging parties' product offering more generally—ie, a small increase in the entry price, a small reduction in the jackpot, and a small reduction in the payout ratio. Note that for each of these features there is a clear metric (they are all expressed as monetary value) and a directly observable link with the profitability of the operators (the greater the payout, the smaller the profit left for the operator), which

---

[64] Competition Commission (2007), 'A report on the anticipated acquisition by Sportech plc of the Vernons football pools business from Ladbrokes plc', 11 October.

makes the test more straightforward to apply than for some other non-price features. The evidence indicated that not many customers actually switched between the two major pools in response to changes in the product offering. This suggested that the two did not really compete with each other, and this was the main reason why the CC concluded that the merger did not substantially lessen competition. As to competition with other gambling products, there was evidence that many customers would simply play the pools less if the product offerings worsened, but not switch to the National Lottery or other gambling products. The CC drew a somewhat confusing conclusion from this:

> Survey evidence shows that customers who stop playing the pools either save the money or spend it in a wide range of other ways. However, we considered that expanding the market definition to include all alternative uses of disposable income would not be appropriate. We therefore conclude, at this stage, that the market is no wider than the football pools . . .

> In our view, given the wide range of alternative spending or saving products to which football pools customers might switch in response to a price rise, a market definition which took account of all these alternatives would not be workable, even if we thought they were a constraint on pools prices.[65]

In line with the market definition principles set out in this chapter, you would instead conclude that the market *is* wider than football pools—customers who stop playing the pools are a relevant sales loss to the hypothetical monopolist. You cannot determine where exactly the market boundaries lie because there is no clear closest substitute for the football pools, but nor is there any need to do so, because the fact that a hypothetical monopolist in football pools cannot profitably worsen the product offering implies that the merging parties cannot either.

2.13.2 TIME ELASTICITIES IN GEOGRAPHIC MARKET DEFINITION

In section 2.9 we discussed transport costs as a factor in geographic market definition, and how in the case of individual consumers you can analyse the generalized cost of travel, which incorporates monetary and non-monetary costs (mainly the value of the time spent). Transport costs can determine the extent of the geographic market. Economists have taken this a step further and introduced the concept of time elasticity as a substitute for price elasticity in defining relevant markets, specifically in the context of hospital mergers (Capps et al., 2001). In many countries the government regulates the prices charged by hospitals and other healthcare providers, so the main concern when implementing the hypothetical monopolist test is not a price rise but a reduction in the quality of service. However, measuring the quality of healthcare delivery is notoriously difficult and patients generally have little information to judge the quality, which can complicate the market definition analysis. As an alternative to measuring changes in price and quality, the time elasticity approach measures how

---

[65] Ibid.

many consumers would switch to competing healthcare providers in response to a hypothetical 5%–10% increase in travel time to a healthcare provider in a given geographic area. How many patients go to an alternative provider? The increase in travel time does not reflect what the hypothetical monopolist is really going to do—it is not actually going to relocate the hospital—but rather is an approximation for other reductions in quality of service. The willingness to change to alternative providers after hypothetical increases in the travel time gives an indication of the responsiveness in demand to changes in other aspects of the service. The analysis then makes certain assumptions about how the time elasticity relates proportionately to the price elasticity, which in turn allows the identification of a critical loss level above which the increase in travel time (and reduction in quality) becomes unprofitable because too many patients switch elsewhere.

You may get the impression that this is a rather roundabout way of applying the hypothetical monopolist test to non-price aspects of a product. Yet time elasticities have been used in several healthcare merger cases in the USA and Europe, as responsiveness to travel time to hospitals can be measured more easily than reactions to other non-price features of the service. In other markets, customer responses to changes in quality may be assessed more directly than in healthcare, and in some cases you might attempt to use a quality elasticity—the percentage change in demand divided by the percentage change in quality. Would our hypothetical monopolist for Italian women's designer shoes exploit its market power by cutting on quality and design? The principles would be the same as for the time elasticity, and based on the same logic as critical loss analysis. The main challenge is, again, identifying how a small change in quality affects the hypothetical monopolist's profits—if quality worsens, how much extra profit does the monopolist make through saved costs, and how much profit is lost due to customers switching? These questions are generally easier to answer for price changes than for quality changes.

2.13.3 MARKET DEFINITION IN INNOVATION MARKETS

In industries such as high-tech, IT, and pharmaceuticals, companies compete not only, or even mainly, on price, but also on who brings the most innovative products to market. Market power can be reflected in the control over innovative capabilities as much as in the control over prices. How can you capture this scope for market power during the market definition stage of your competition analysis? The US agencies—the DOJ and FTC—have come up with a rather 'innovative' approach: innovation capability is treated as a separate market in itself:

> An innovation market consists of the research and development directed to particular new or improved goods or processes, and the close substitutes for that research and development. The close substitutes are research and development efforts, technologies, and goods that significantly constrain the exercise of market power with respect to the relevant research and development, for example by limiting the ability and incentive of a hypothetical monopolist to retard the pace of research and development. The Agencies will

delineate an innovation market only when the capabilities to engage in the relevant research and development can be associated with specialized assets or characteristics of specific firms.[66]

This principle was applied in the DOJ's review of the proposed merger of General Motor's Allison Division and ZF Friedrichshafen, a German company, in 1993.[67] GM Allison and ZF were the world's two largest producers of medium and heavy automatic transmissions (used in buses, heavy trucks, and similar types of vehicle). ZF was dominant in Europe, whereas GM was dominant in the USA. For the purposes of assessing the merger, the DOJ defined both product markets and innovation markets. The production and sale of transmissions for buses and heavy trucks constituted the relevant product markets, and geographically they were confined to the USA (this was because it was a review by the DOJ; applying the same logic to Europe would probably have resulted in a separate European geographic market as well). In contrast, the innovation market was defined as the worldwide market for technical innovation in the design, development, and production of transmissions. This made a significant impact on the outcome of the case. While GM and ZF did not compete in many of the defined product markets in the USA—and hence the merger caused little concern in those markets— together they controlled most of the relevant worldwide innovation market. The DOJ was concerned that the merger would significantly lessen the competition in innovation. The proposed merger was ultimately abandoned.

Similar innovation markets are frequently considered in the context of technology transfer and licensing agreements. The European Commission tends to define technology markets in such cases:

> Technology markets consist of the licensed technology and its substitutes, i.e. other technologies which are regarded by the licensees as interchangeable with or substitutable for the licensed technology, by reason of the technologies' characteristics, their royalties and their intended use. The methodology for defining technology markets follows the same principles as the definition of product markets. Starting from the technology which is marketed by the licensor, one needs to identify those other technologies to which licensees could switch in response to a small but permanent increase in relative prices, i.e. the royalties. An alternative approach is to look at the market for products incorporating the licensed technology.[68]

Again, conceptually, the approach is very similar to the hypothetical monopolist test.

---

[66] Department of Justice and Federal Trade Commission (1995), 'Antitrust Guidelines for the Licensing of Intellectual Property', p11.

[67] *United States v General Motors Corp* Civ No 93-530, filed 16 November 1993.

[68] European Commission (2004), 'Guidelines on the application of Article 81 of the EC Treaty to technology transfer agreements', Commission Notice, 2004/C101/02, 27 April, [22]. At the time of writing, new guidelines were being consulted on by the European Commission.

2.14 MARKET DEFINITION IN PRACTICE: MAIN EMPIRICAL METHODS

In this chapter you have been reading about the economic principles of market definition. You may still wonder how the conceptual framework of the hypothetical monopolist can be tested quantitatively in practice. Even where quantification is not feasible, the framework itself already helps you in asking the right questions about market definition. However, in many cases, some attempt at measuring whether a small price increase is profitable for the hypothetical monopolist can be made. Critical loss analysis is the basis for this, as explained in section 2.5. Determining the *critical* loss level is relatively straightforward—there is a simple formula for critical loss, and the main bit of empirical analysis you must carry out for this step is to identify the initial price–cost margin, which is one of the ingredients of the formula (see Chapter 10 on how you can obtain margin information from financial accounts). A greater challenge lies in empirically estimating the *actual* sales loss after a price increase, which you then compare with the critical loss to determine whether the price increase is profitable (the term 'actual' is of course not quite accurate because it is still hypothetical, but highlights the contrast with the 'critical' loss that is used as a threshold). This is where economists usually come in with their toolbox of empirical methods to measure customers' responsiveness to price. The aim of this book is not to explain in detail how these tools work; however, this section gives you a flavour of three of the main empirical tools used in market definition: regression analysis, surveys—both often used for measuring price elasticities—and price-correlation analysis. We also indicate how you, as a competition lawyer, can ask some critical questions when you are presented with the results of such empirical analyses. Chapter 10 provides a further discussion of regression analysis and other empirical methods in the context of quantifying damages.

2.14.1 USING REGRESSION ANALYSIS TO ESTIMATE ELASTICITIES

If you want to know how customers respond to price changes, one option is to observe actual prices and quantities for the product. How much of the product customers have actually purchased at different price levels tells you something about their 'revealed preferences' (as opposed to 'stated preferences', which is what you get from surveys, as discussed below). If you have a sufficient number of observations, you may be able to identify the demand curve and price elasticities. Imagine that you observe prices and quantities of the product—say, women's designer shoes—at regular intervals (monthly) over an extended period of time (two years). All observations are plotted in the price–quantity space in Figure 2.8. This is a highly stylized example—in reality you would not get such wide variation in the observed prices (economists like variation in the data, as that generally allows for more robust measurement). While eyeballing the figure already gives you some idea of the relationship between price and quantity (again, you would rarely see this in practice), you need to identify a demand curve that is accurate and

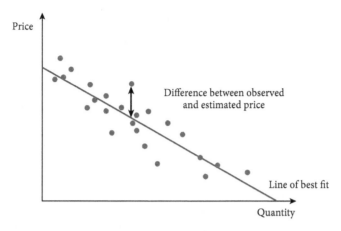

Fig. 2.8 The demand curve as the 'line of best fit'

statistically meaningful. This is where regression analysis comes in. Regression is a generic term for statistical methods that can be used to explain the variation in data using other factors. Economists (some of them specifically trained as econometricians—econometrics is the application of regression to economic data) use a regression to estimate the equation for the demand curve based on the observed prices and quantities.

Recall that the theoretical demand function in Figure 2.1 was expressed as $p = 10 - q$. Using regression analysis, you can estimate a demand function of this form that best matches the dots in Figure 2.8. You start by writing the equation for this line as $p = a - b \times q +$ error term, where a and b are the coefficients to be estimated—a is where the demand curve intersects with the y-axis, usually referred to as the 'constant term' (a = 10 in Figure 2.1), while b is the coefficient that represents the slope of the curve (b = 1 in Figure 2.1). The error term represents the distance from the estimated line of best fit to each of the dots (in Figure 2.8 this difference is illustrated for one particular observation). In other words, it reflects how far off the line you are at each given quantity (some observations are closer to the line than others). 'Line of best fit' means that you want to minimize the differences overall. Statistically, the trick to this involves several steps. First, you draw a line that you think fits reasonably well. Second, at each quantity you take the difference between the line and the actual observation (this can be positive or negative, depending on whether the observation is above or below the line you drew). Third, you take the square of each difference. Squaring has two rationales: you are treating points below and above the line the same (squaring a negative number gives a positive number), and you are giving more weight to the larger differences (as squares get bigger for higher numbers). Fourth, you take the sum of all the squares. Fifth, you follow the above four steps again for other possible lines, until you have found your line of best fit, which is where the sum of the squared differences is the smallest. This is why this approach is called 'ordinary least squares' (OLS) estimation. It is the most commonly used technique in econometrics and you will often see it when empirical studies are presented in competition cases (OLS and other techniques are explained in basic econometrics textbooks[69]). More sophisticated techniques are sometimes used where this suits the nature of the data, but the basic logic remains that the objective of the analysis is to find the line of best fit. When OLS was first developed in the 1930s, econometricians used to calculate the minimum sum of the squares by hand. Fortunately, these days you can use statistical packages such as Stata to do it for you.

In practice, when you are presented with the results of a regression analysis, you will often see that the demand curve is specified in logarithms ('logs') rather than 'levels'— instead of a function 'p = a − b × q + error term', economists often estimate the function 'log p = a − b × log q + error term'. This means that all the price and quantity data has been transformed into logarithms. The logarithm of a number to a given base is the power to which that base must be raised in order to produce that number (10 is often used as the base; 10^3 = 1,000, so the logarithm of 1,000 to base 10 equals 3). The regression then simply tests the relationship between these transformed series instead of the original series. One reason for using this statistical trick is that the log specification is better at capturing the price–quantity interaction when the demand curve is not linear. Another reason is that the coefficient b directly represents the own-price elasticity, rather than just the slope of the curve—ie, it directly gives you the answer you are after (this is due to a mathematical relationship to do with the first derivative of a logarithmic function).

There is a potential problem with the interpretation of the observations plotted in Figure 2.8. Each observation reflects the quantity that was actually purchased at the particular price. These actual outcomes are not just reflective of the demand curve, they are the result of the interaction between demand and supply. Economists refer to this as the endogeneity of prices. When you look at the position of any two dots in the price–quantity field, you cannot tell whether the difference between the two is attributable to a shift *along* the demand curve, or to a shift *of* the demand curve *itself* to the left or to the right. Only shifts along the demand curve are relevant for the estimation of the slope of the demand curve. To isolate the shifts along the curve, economists look for instances where a difference between two observations has resulted from a shift of the *supply* curve rather than of the demand curve. These shifts in supply aid help to highlight all the changes in demand that take place along the same demand curve. A typical cause of a shift in the supply curve is production cost changes. Hence, cost data is often included in the estimation to identify supply changes. In commonly used economics jargon, the cost data is used as an 'instrument' in the regression analysis so as to properly estimate the slope of the demand curve. Using instruments addresses the endogeneity problem. Sometimes other variables can be suitable as instruments—for example, the weather

---

[69] Examples of basic textbooks include Wooldridge (2005) and Gujarati (2009). For technical expositions of how econometrics techniques can be applied to market definition we refer you to Davis and Garcés (2009), Bishop and Walker (2010), and Motta (2004).

conditions at particular times can be used as instruments to explain supply shocks in agricultural products (such as the 2010 ban on Russian wheat exports as a result of the drought). More complex statistical techniques and modelling can also be used to overcome the price endogeneity problem, such as panel data econometrics methods (we explain the basics of these techniques in Chapter 10).

To illustrate how regression analysis is used to estimate elasticities for market definition, consider the merger between Pan Fish and Marine Harvest, two farmers of Atlantic salmon, which was examined by the UK CC (and a number of other national competition authorities) in 2006.[70] An important question in the case was whether salmon farmed in Scotland constituted a product market that was distinct from salmon farmed in Norway. The CC used regression analysis to estimate own- and cross-price elasticities for Scottish salmon. The equation specified by the CC was of the form: 'log of quantity of Scottish salmon = a – b × log of price of Scottish salmon + c × log of price of Norwegian salmon + d × log of income + error term'. Note that this is the demand function where quantity is a function of price, rather than the inverse demand function that is shown in Figures 2.1 and 2.8, where price is a function of quantity. Plugging in the data it had on quantities, prices, and income, the CC could estimate the coefficients a (the constant term), b (the own-price elasticity of demand for Scottish salmon), c (the cross-price elasticity of Scottish salmon with respect to the price of Norwegian salmon), and d (the income elasticity). The CC recognized that prices might be endogenous, so it used exchange rate data as an instrument for Scottish and Norwegian salmon prices. The estimation results indicated that the own-price elasticity for the Scottish salmon was –3.5, and the cross-price elasticity with respect to the price of Norwegian salmon was 3. These estimates suggest that the demand for Scottish salmon is quite sensitive to price, and also that it responds positively and strongly to Norwegian salmon price changes. While the CC did not perform a formal critical loss analysis based on the own-price elasticity estimate, it considered that the own- and cross-price elasticities were high, and concluded that this evidence was consistent with Scottish and Norwegian salmon being in the same product market.

2.14.2 WHAT QUESTIONS CAN YOU ASK WHEN PRESENTED WITH REGRESSION ANALYSIS FOR MARKET DEFINITION?

Estimating elasticities through regression analysis is conceptually straightforward, and generally allows for more robust results than simply plotting a line. Nevertheless, there are often pitfalls and complexities with such analysis (endogeneity of prices, discussed above, is one). High standards need to be met before a regression analysis can be considered robust—economists have developed a reasonably clear idea of what constitutes 'good economic practice'. The econometrics toolbox may always be something of a black

---

[70] Competition Commission (2006), 'Pan Fish ASA and Marine Harvest NV merger inquiry—Final report', 18 December.

box to you, and debates on which particular econometric method is most appropriate in the case at hand can be rather esoteric, but there are things you can do to shake and rattle the box by asking critical questions, and see if it still holds together. The critical questions fall into three main categories (see also Chapter 10 on how to assess empirical methods for quantifying damages, and Chapter 11 on best practice in using economic evidence in competition cases).

First, you can ask questions about the data: what is the data coverage in terms of time period and products or market participants? How frequent is the data (monthly, yearly)? How large is the dataset? Are there enough observations to estimate elasticities robustly using econometric methods? Is the data of good quality (are there many missing observations or measurement errors)? Data coverage must be sufficient to cover the relevant products and time period, and the more observations (and more variance between them) there are, the greater the likelihood of finding statistically significant results. You can see that in the extreme, if you have only two observations, chances are that the line drawn from one to the other will not accurately reflect the demand curve. Even 24 observations, as in Figure 2.8, is on the low side. Second, you can ask questions about the econometric approach: is the econometric method appropriate for the market concerned and in light of the available data (does OLS work, or is a more sophisticated technique needed)? What assumptions underlie the econometric approach? Is the equation specified correctly, and is it in line with economic theory and market reality? Does it solve the price endogeneity problem? If instruments are used for price, are they appropriate? How do the results vary if alternative approaches or specifications are used? The third category consists of questions about the elasticity estimates: are the estimated elasticity values plausible (is the own-price elasticity negative as theory would predict)? How similar or different are they if compared with other available elasticity estimates? Are the estimated coefficients statistically significant? Testing for statistical significance helps in understanding the uncertainty surrounding an estimate and informs about how much weight should be placed on the analysis. You should expect any econometric results to be accompanied by a range of statistical diagnostic tests, which indicate whether the results are statistically significant (one such test is the t-test) and whether they suffer from potential statistical problems such as endogeneity.

2.14.3 USING SURVEY EVIDENCE TO ESTIMATE ELASTICITIES

Customer surveys are an alternative approach to estimating demand elasticities, and are being used increasingly in competition cases. Their appeal is that they can be relatively cheap and 'quick and dirty' (although more sophisticated variants of customer surveys can be more elaborate and expensive), and that they can be used to ask the SSNIP question directly—how would customers react if prices were raised by a small amount? The responses give an indication of the demand loss resulting from a SSNIP, which in turn you can compare with the critical loss. Through surveys you can obtain information on customers' stated preferences, ie, what they say they would do after a price increase, as opposed to revealed preferences, reflecting what they actually did. To ensure that the survey results are reliable, there are a number of rules of good practice you can follow when designing it. These rules have not been widely debated or formalized—a good deal of literature exists on how to undertake customer research, but surveys designed for competition cases tend to have their own specific characteristics. A useful first attempt to document good practice rules has been made by the UK competition agencies in a recent consultation on guidance for the design and presentation of consumer survey evidence in merger inquiries.[71]

A typical survey designed for the hypothetical monopolist test is directed at existing customers of the product in question—those are the customers who the monopolist cares about, and who may defeat an attempt to raise prices. If you have ever been asked to respond to a survey of this nature (by telephone, on the street, or over the Internet), whether for market definition or (more likely) general market research purposes, you may agree that it helps if the survey is not too long and follows a certain logical structure. First, the survey should ask some 'warm-up' questions—about the respondents themselves, about current behaviour and habits, and about why the customer chose the given product and whether alternative products were considered. These questions reveal certain characteristics of customers and help respondents in beginning to think about the product choice situation. Then you can ask the SSNIP questions—how would the respondent react to a SSNIP? This is followed by a number of questions about switching to alternative products. This basic survey structure is illustrated in Figure 2.9.

Several of the case examples discussed in this chapter have relied on survey evidence, including the Dutch holiday parks and hospital mergers (section 2.5). Another case where survey evidence was used to establish the sales loss for the hypothetical monopolist test is the acquisition by LOVEFiLM of Amazon's online DVD rental business, which effectively created a monopoly in this product in the UK—hence the question arose as to whether the relevant product market was limited to online DVD rentals.[72] Internet-based surveys were commissioned on behalf of the acquiring party, canvassing

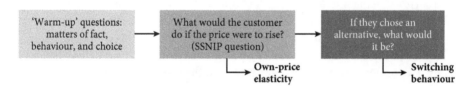

Fig. 2.9 Basic structure of a SSNIP survey

Source: Based on Walters and Reynolds (2008).

---

[71] Competition Commission and the Office of Fair Trading (2010), 'Good practice in the design and presentation of consumer survey evidence in merger inquiries—Consultation', May.

[72] Office of Fair Trading (2008), 'Anticipated acquisition of the online DVD rental subscription business of Amazon Inc. by LOVEFiLM International Limited', ME/3534/08, 8 May. We advised the acquiring party on this transaction.

the views of approximately 2,000 customers of online DVD rental services. First, questions about facts, behaviour, and choice were asked: which providers do you currently rent DVDs over the Internet from? Which of these would you consider to be your main provider? How much per month do you pay for your online DVD rentals from your main provider? The survey then asked the SSNIP question: 'Say that your online DVD provider decided to increase its prices, so that instead of paying £x per month, you had to pay £x + 10% (10% more) per month to receive exactly the same service, what would be your most likely response?' The 'x' was shown here as the price the respondent actually pays for online DVD rentals, as answered in an earlier question. The question on the screen also showed what £x + 10% actually is in money terms. Finally, questions about switching were asked: were you to cancel your online rental contract, how would you meet your demand to see films? The survey results showed that 30%–40% of respondents would switch after a 10% price increase. Since the critical loss threshold of 20–30% was below this actual loss, the relevant market was deemed to be wider than online DVD rental services. There was no clear nearest substitute—alternatives such as renting DVDs from 'bricks and mortar' rental shops, downloading films, and watching fewer films, were all given frequent mentions by switchers. But delineating the precise boundaries of the market was not necessary anyway, since the survey had already indicated that a hypothetical monopolist of online DVD rentals could not raise prices, and therefore neither could the real monopolist that was created by the acquisition. In the end, while there was some discussion about the interpretation of the survey results, the OFT cleared the merger because it found that internal business and strategy documents confirmed that the parties saw other products as their closest competitors, which was consistent with the market being broader than online DVD rentals.

If more time (and budget) is available, you may seek to carry out a conjoint or discrete-choice survey, which is a more sophisticated and generally more robust type of survey. Instead of asking respondents what they would do after a hypothetical price increase, a conjoint survey asks them to choose among products with different characteristics (price being one of these), which more closely resembles the actual choice-making situation that customers often find themselves in. The survey presents customers (or potential customers) with a menu of products that differ slightly from each other in their 'attributes', including price, functionality, and different aspects of quality. Two options are presented each time, and the respondent has to express a preference. By varying the product attributes in each option, a picture emerges of how customers trade off price and other attributes against each other. Econometric analysis can then be applied to the responses in order to estimate a price elasticity (or indeed to estimate an elasticity of demand with respect to any of the product attributes—conjoint analysis is often used for general marketing purposes as well).

Conjoint analysis was used for market definition in Ofcom's review of the pay-TV market.[73] In particular, it sought to understand whether channels containing premium

---

[73] Ofcom (2008), 'Pay TV second consultation—Access to premium content', 30 September, Annex 10.

Package A	Package B
- price: £15 per month	- price: £13.50 per month
- brand: Sky Sports	- brand: Sky Sports
- live FAPL games: YES	- live FAPL games: NO
- other football competitions: NO	- other football competitions: YES
- international cricket: YES	- international cricket: YES
- cricket featuring England: NO	- cricket featuring England: YES
- other sports: motor racing, darts	- other sports: rugby, golf, tennis, motor racing, darts, many others

Which of these options would you prefer?

Fig. 2.10 Stylized example of the choices presented in a conjoint survey

Source: Based on conjoint survey carried out in Ofcom (2008), 'Pay TV second consultation—Access to premium content', 30 September, Annex 10.

content, such as Football Association Premier League (FAPL) matches, constitute a separate market. The discrete-choice survey sought to test the importance of a variety of sports to households' decisions to subscribe to premium sports channels, and to inform on the level of substitution between sports. Respondents were presented with a series of pay-TV sports packages and in each case were asked which of two options they would prefer. Figure 2.10 shows a stylized example of one of these choice situations—two pay-TV sports packages which have as main differences the price and whether they included FAPL matches. After analysing the survey responses, Ofcom concluded that channels containing premium content do indeed constitute separate markets, since channels without such premium content are not seen as sufficiently close substitutes.

2.14.4 WHAT QUESTIONS CAN YOU ASK WHEN PRESENTED WITH SURVEY EVIDENCE FOR MARKET DEFINITION?

Not surprisingly, the use of surveys comes with the necessary health warnings, especially if they are of the 'quick and dirty' variety. There are a number of critical questions you can ask when presented with survey evidence. Where reasonably satisfactory answers can be given to these questions, surveys can make a useful contribution to the analysis, and some weight can be attached to the results.

A first set of questions relates to whether customers would actually do what they say in the survey response. A survey is a means of obtaining stated-preference data, and this may not necessarily reflect the actions that would be taken by customers in a real situation. Customers may overstate their switching when responding to a SSNIP question, leading to an overestimation of the sales loss and thus too wide a relevant market. A careful survey design (as discussed above) should mitigate this potential problem.

Careful phrasing of the questions is equally important—any confusion or ambiguity should be avoided, and questions should be neutral rather than leading. The representativeness of the survey is another critical aspect. Only when the sample is sufficiently large and representative of the relevant population as a whole can you obtain statistically meaningful results. For example, data from a survey may be biased if the survey is conducted in a location that tends to have different types of people passing through it at different times. Thus, carrying out a survey at a railway station on a weekday morning is likely to yield a different sample of travellers (mainly commuters) than if the same survey were carried out at the same railway station during the day at the weekend (mainly leisure travellers). This may bias the answers to the questions since the sample is not truly random and hence not representative. A lot of these potential issues can be resolved if the various parties involved in the case, in particular the merging parties and the competition authority, agree beforehand on the aim, design and wording of the survey (this may not always be feasible). This limits any disputes over the survey to the interpretation of the actual results, and not its design. A final set of questions you can ask relates to whether the survey results are consistent with the other evidence that is available in the inquiry. If yes, you can have confidence in the survey results—in both the holiday park and online DVD rental merger cases, the survey respondents' attitudes to price changes and switching corresponded with internal documents on what the companies themselves saw as their closest demand substitutes.

2.14.5 PRICE-CORRELATION ANALYSIS

Before the concept of the relevant market was developed for the purpose of competition law, economists used to regard a market as something where the 'law of one price' holds. The logic is that products that constitute a market should be priced very similarly. Any price differences within such a market would be removed through a combination of entry (by suppliers who can undercut higher prices), exit (by suppliers who can't compete at lower prices) and arbitrage (intermediaries buying low and selling high). Relevant markets in competition law are more practical and acknowledge that products can place competitive pressure on each other even if prices are not the same. Yet the idea of the law of one price still has its use for market definition, and lies behind price-correlation analysis. If products are close substitutes, and even if they have different prices, you would still expect those prices to move together over time—if some event causes the price of one of the products to change with respect to the other, this will trigger demand and supply substitution (customers switching, intermediaries engaging in arbitrage), and eventually prices will come back into line. The statistical term for such moving in parallel is correlation, as measured by the correlation index, which can take any value between +1 (when there is perfect positive correlation) and −1 (perfect negative correlation, ie, if one goes up the other goes down), with a correlation of zero meaning no correlation at all. The closer the correlation between the price series of two markets is to +1, the more likely it is that the two are in the same relevant market.

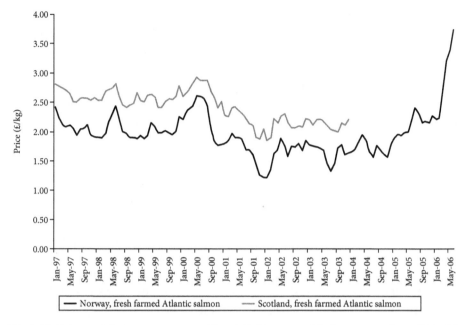

Fig. 2.11 Price correlation to support market definition: monthly farm gate prices of Scottish and Norwegian salmon

Source: Competition Commission (2006), 'Pan Fish ASA and Marine Harvest NV Merger Inquiry—Final Report', 18 December, Fig. 7.

The *Pan Fish/Marine Harvest* merger, which we saw earlier in this section, provides a good illustration of how price-correlation analysis can assist with market definition.[74] To answer the question of whether salmon farmed in Scotland constitutes a distinct product market from salmon farmed in Norway, the CC not only carried out regression analysis (see above) but also considered the correlation between the prices of Scottish salmon and Norwegian salmon over time. This is shown in Figure 2.11. You can see that prices of Scottish and Norwegian salmon tend to move in parallel, ie, they are highly correlated (the correlation coefficient is 0.91). Scottish salmon is consistently priced at a premium, but this does not alter the observation that the prices move in parallel, which suggests that Scottish and Norwegian salmon belong to the same relevant market.

Just like other empirical methods, price-correlation analysis comes with a number of health warnings. The CC was well aware of this: 'while informative, neither the correlation test, nor the extent of co-movement in prices (stationarity) test, can be viewed as definitive evidence of the existence of a relevant market.'[75] The main potential problem

[74] Competition Commission (2006), 'Pan Fish ASA and Marine Harvest NV merger inquiry—Final report', 18 December.
[75] Ibid., at [5.36].

with the price-correlation test is that prices of two products can be correlated over time for reasons other than these products being in the same relevant market—you can have spurious correlation. A frequent cause of spurious correlation is prices being influenced by changes in costs that are common to both products. In the salmon example, it could be that salmon feed prices cause prices of Scottish and Norwegian salmon to move in parallel. However, in this particular case, there were no obvious reasons why prices might have moved in parallel, and the price-correlation results pointed in the same direction as the regression analysis and other evidence. This gives confidence that the conclusion on market definition is the correct one.

2.15 CONCLUSION: WHY MARKET DEFINITION?

Market definition is about whether a product (or geographic area) is in or out. Are French women's designer shoes in the market for Italian women's designer shoes or out? If they are in, you consider them as part of your analysis of competitive constraints in the market. If they are out, you don't. In this regard, market definition is a useful inter-mediate step in the competition analysis, and the hypothetical monopolist test provides a useful threshold for whether something is in or out—based on the question of which products constrain each other from raising price. Without such a threshold, there would be much confusion and lack of clarity on market definition, just like before the 1980s when the hypothetical monopolist test was introduced—submarkets within markets and market definitions based on product characteristics would probably creep up again. Furthermore, having market definition as a standard intermediate step in the analysis contributes to a degree of legal certainty. It assists companies in carrying out self-assessments of risks (or opportunities) under competition law—by defining the relevant market (or different scenarios for relevant markets), a company can calculate its own market share and that of rivals, and thus assess the likelihood of a finding of market power or lack of competition. Market shares measured within a relevant market are still a good (initial) guide to the existence of market power (see Chapter 3).

In this chapter we have explained the basic logic and some of the advanced features of the hypothetical monopolist test for market definition. We have also explained how exercising some judgement is inevitable when setting the threshold of whether some-thing is in or out, and a measure of pragmatism is required when trying to apply the threshold in practice. Sometimes the required degree of judgement and pragmatism will be so high that market definition becomes less useful as an intermediate step. As explained in this chapter, a particular situation in which this may arise is when markets are characterized by a high degree of product differentiation. Asking whether some-thing is in or out can be difficult, artificial, and potentially misleading when products are highly differentiated. The question becomes more about which products are each other's closest substitutes, than about which products are in or out. In these situations you can focus on the analysis of competitive constraints directly, and skip the market definition stage altogether. Rather than asking whether the relevant market contains

Italian, French, or all women's designer shoes, you ask whether Prada and Gucci, prior to a merger, provide a strong competitive constraint on each other. We return to this in Chapter 7 on mergers. Nonetheless, many of the economic concepts and tools underlying market definition that are discussed in this chapter—from demand elasticities and supply-side substitution to isochrones and complements—are also at the heart of the economic questions arising at subsequent stages of competition analysis.

3

MARKET POWER

3.1 THE CORE CONCERN IN COMPETITION LAW

When is a company allowed to give away an additional product for free to its customers? When are two cinema chains permitted to merge? When can a telecoms operator choose to whom it offers access to its intercity broadband network? Under most competition and regulatory laws the answer will depend on whether the company in question has substantial market power. Indeed, at the core of competition law is the control of market power. Most disputes about 'hawkish' versus 'dovish' competition law enforcement revolve around different views of the balance between 'beneficial' market power and market power that is seen as detrimental to consumers.

Market power is the ability of a company to keep price above the competitive level for a sustained period of time without being undermined by consumers switching or competitors entering the market. As we discussed in Chapter 2, a relevant market can be thought of as something worth monopolizing. Here we consider how to determine whether it has indeed been monopolized. Recalling the simple demand framework from Chapters 1 and 2, Figure 3.1 reproduces the basic monopoly picture. A monopolist, or any company with market power, seeks to artificially restrict output. A lower level of output means that customers are paying more for the (now) scarcer product. The actual price is above cost, leading to high profits for the company with market power (represented by area A). The figure shows the extreme case where a company is a monopoly. In this chapter we consider the various degrees of market power and how to identify them.

We saw in Chapters 1 and 2 that pricing above the competitive level leads to a deadweight welfare loss—lost opportunities for consumers and producers to gain from doing business with one another (area B in Figure 3.1). While this might suggest that all non-cost-reflective pricing (and hence all forms of market power) should be deemed harmful and rooted out, the picture is not black and white. A careful balance is required. Companies will generally seek to acquire market power; indeed this is a strong spur to cost efficiency, innovation, and investment. In recognition of this, under competition

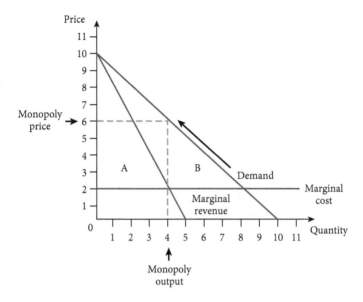

Fig. 3.1 The simple mechanics of market power

law it is not illegal to establish a dominant position through organic growth, investment, or serving customers well. It is only the abuse of such a dominant position that is prohibited. Merger control is designed to prevent positions of market power being established through acquisition, unless there is a strong efficiency rationale that will compensate for the loss of rivalry between two merging parties. Companies must therefore 'earn' their market power and not simply 'buy' it. Chapter 4 discusses abuses of dominance and Chapter 7 looks at the economic principles of merger control.

As with market definition, most competition cases will involve an assessment of market power. It is important therefore to understand the concept, how it can be measured, and when its presence may be problematic. Section 3.2 defines the principle of market power and its different degrees. Section 3.3 examines how to assess market power with reference to market shares and concentration. Section 3.4 looks into the concepts of entry and exit barriers. Market shares and entry barriers form the basis of most assessments of market power. We then go on to look in section 3.5 at the concept of collective dominance, and in section 3.6 at the role of profitability as an indicator of market power. Section 3.7 discusses the issue of buyer power—that is, market power on the buyer side rather than the seller side of the market—and the concept of bidding markets. Finally, section 3.8 considers an area where assessing market power and its consequences is far from straightforward: dynamic, innovative markets.

3.2 WHAT IS MARKET POWER?

3.2.1 IT'S A MATTER OF DEGREE

There are two ways in which market power is generally understood. As described above, the first relates to a company's ability to raise prices above the competitive level. The second relates to its ability to exclude or significantly harm its competitors. These are intimately linked and mirror the two types of abuse of dominance in competition law: exploitative and exclusionary abuses. In an environment where we assume that companies are profit-maximizing, any exercise of market power is ultimately designed to be exploitative, ie, to yield higher profits. However, to achieve this aim, a company may choose to take strategic actions—such as lowering prices or imposing restrictions on access to key inputs—that do not necessarily lead to higher prices in the short run but do harm its rivals. Once its rivals have been excluded or sufficiently damaged, the company is free to exploit that power by increasing its prices and hence its profits.

As described in Chapter 1, in a perfectly competitive market no company has the ability to price above costs, as customers will switch immediately to one of the other myriad suppliers that are pricing at the lower level. Since all suppliers have access to the best available technology to produce the good at the lowest cost, there is no constraint on entry for rivals that see a commercial opportunity. Hence, in this model, no company can behave independently of others because of the inherent market disciplines. In the real world, virtually no market actually works in this way and the difficulty lies in determining how persistent any deviation from these conditions is, and whether market forces, left to their own devices, will address any concerns about market power.

Competition is about gaining market share from your competitors, and therefore harming them in this way. Higher than normal profits provide strong incentives for businesses to take risks. It has been said that profits are the ignition system for our economic engine and therefore competition authorities need to consider carefully when and how they should intervene. Beating a rival to a sale or developing an invention that makes a rival's technology obsolete will result in harm to those rivals. Such activities may also lead to periods where a successful company has higher profits than in a purely competitive market. Ruling such actions illegal may remove the incentives to engage in this beneficial form of dynamic competition.

A practice that is highly desirable when undertaken by a company in an effectively competitive market may be considered heinous when conducted by a company judged to have significant market power. An example is very low pricing. In an effectively competitive market, very low pricing (below direct cost) by a company will be of great benefit to consumers since they reap the advantages of the low prices. The company may wish to continue pricing low for some time to establish its position in a marketplace. However, if that company has strong market power, such a practice (known as predation) might turn out to be detrimental to consumers in the medium to long run—while, initially, consumers benefit from the low prices, the stronger company's main competitors cannot compete and are ultimately forced to exit. At that point, and assuming that competitors cannot easily re-enter the market, the powerful company is free to raise its prices without fear of competitor reprisal. In the end, therefore, consumers suffer from the exploitative higher prices. Competition law needs to be able to distinguish beneficial competition and short-term market power that incentivizes investment, efficiency and innovation, from that which is harmful to consumers in the longer term.

How then can a company raise its prices (the first indicator of market power)? We explained above that the company restricts output, thereby raising prices. This means that the company's customers either cannot (or do not wish to) switch to other suppliers, or there are not enough competitors available. Furthermore, it means that there are reasons why potential competitors cannot easily respond to these opportunities—ie, there are barriers to entry or expansion in the market. This pricing power must also persist for some considerable time to be deemed more than transient market power.

How can a company significantly exclude or harm its competitors (the second indicator of market power)? Again it must have the ability to set (or significantly influence) prices or the conditions of competition in the market, but in this scenario it does this to the detriment of rivals, rather than to its own direct benefit through raising prices. The underlying prerequisites are more or less identical to those of a company wanting to raise price. We shall see in section 3.4 on entry and exit barriers that these considerations underpin most precedents on establishing market power.

It should come as no surprise then that market power is not a 'bright line test', but is best seen as a spectrum. There is no single point where one can say that a company goes from having no market power to having it. Understanding this spectrum helps to assess the extent of concern and the likely need for intervention in any particular situation. In the case of mergers (Chapter 7), even relatively small overlaps between merging parties can sometimes lead to potential consumer harm in the form of price rises or degradation of services. For abuse of dominance, the degree of market power matters for the analysis of the effects of practices on competition (Chapter 4). In the case of certain vertical restraints (Chapter 6), you might wish to intervene only if there is significant market power.

3.2.2 DIFFERENTIATED PRODUCT MARKET POWER

At the 'benign' end of the spectrum, limited market power can arise simply because products are differentiated in some way. Examples are the location and opening hours of corner shops or the location of refreshment sellers on a beach—this last example comes from Hotelling (1929), who identified the importance of product differentiation at a time when economists were still mainly using models of perfect competition and monopoly in homogeneous goods markets. The price that a corner shop charges for a litre of milk is higher than in a major supermarket. In a model of perfect competition this should not be sustainable. In reality, however, the characteristics of the litre of milk include the time cost of purchasing (the time to get to the shop and buy the milk—we discussed this in Chapter 2) and the urgency with which it is required (running out of such essential household items leads to what are known as 'distress' purchases). The customer is willing to pay a premium for the opportunity to buy the milk quickly and immediately. Such market power is arguably of no real concern to competition authorities since the small corner shop is probably part of a broader market, including the large superstores on the outskirts of town, and most customers have the option to purchase their milk elsewhere or as part of their weekly shop and thereby avoid the higher charges. (The story may be different in a small rural village where the shop is truly the only option.)

Similarly, a degree of market power can arise from brand-based differentiation—for example, in groceries, footwear or personal hygiene products. While there may be some quality (and therefore cost) differentials between two bottles of shampoo, these are unlikely to explain fully the price differences. The higher margins indicate market power for the branded product, but where consumers have the option to choose freely across a wide range of such products, these higher margins are usually not of concern under competition law. Where there is effective competition between the brands, this market structure is described as monopolistic competition—each supplier has a monopoly over its own brand, but there are many such suppliers. In theory, the outcome in such markets can be described as follows. Where each brand incurs costs associated with the brand quality—advertising or some form of quality-enhancing investment—we would expect prices to be higher than the marginal cost of production, reflecting the fact that each brand has some market power because customers have strong brand preferences. However, any additional margins earned as a result of the differentiation are competed away in investing in the brand to preserve its differentiating character. In this market environment, prices are in line with average costs and no company makes profits above the 'normal' economic level for its industry (we explain these profit and cost concepts in section 3.6 and Chapter 4). Many real-world markets fit this description (we discuss the importance of product differentiation in Chapter 2), including clothing, restaurants, and service industries. Although any individual good or service purchased will be priced above marginal cost, these types of market are generally not considered to exhibit a problematic degree of market power. We shall see in Chapter 7 that mergers between brands in these markets might, however, give rise to concerns about additional pricing power.

3.2.3 APPRECIABLE EFFECT

The first threshold for market power that features in competition concerns is where there is sufficient influence from a practice or a company for there to be an appreciable effect on competition. This effect is measured through its impact on price, output, choice, innovation, or investment, as all of these parameters of competition can affect the benefits that consumers gain from market activity. The concept of appreciable effect has often been related to the consideration of non-hardcore horizontal and vertical agreements (that is, agreements other than those relating to price fixing, market sharing or bid rigging). In these cases, the positive efficiency benefits of such agreements must be compared with their restrictive effects on competition, and under Article 101(1) the assessment usually concerns whether these restrictive effects are appreciable. No clear thresholds exist for appreciability. European Commission guidance refers to certain market share thresholds below which an agreement may be regarded as not problematic—these range from 10% to 30% depending on the type of agreement (in particular whether it is horizontal or vertical), and are generally below the standard for dominance under Article 102—we discuss this in Chapters 5 and 6.

3.2.4 DOMINANCE

Dominance is the core market power threshold in EU competition law. When a single company is large and powerful enough to have a substantial effect on the market, it is considered to have a significant degree of market power—ie, a dominant position. This is captured in the *United Brands* and *Hoffman-La Roche* judgments, where the European Court of Justice (ECJ) links the ability to behave independently (ie, to set higher prices or worse terms of trade) to the ability to hinder or exclude competitors:

> UBC is an undertaking in a dominant position enjoying a degree of general independence in its behaviour on the relevant market which enables it to hinder to a large extent any effective competition from competitors . . .[1]

> The dominant position thus referred to relates to a position of economic strength enjoyed by an undertaking which enables it to prevent effective competition being maintained on the relevant market by affording it the power to behave to an appreciable extent independently of its competitors, its customers and ultimately of the consumers . . .[2]

These legal definitions do not accord strictly with the underlying economics of market power. In particular, they do not capture the subtleties of market interactions. No company can really behave independently of its competitors and customers; the very nature of a downward-sloping demand curve means that even a monopolist will lose customers as it raises prices. The caveat 'to an appreciable extent' suggests that the independence is not absolute but a matter of degree. In a competitive market, all firms are 'price-takers', ie, each firm has little or no ability to set the price at which its products are sold. Behaving independently of customers and competitors means that a dominant company is not too concerned about whether its customers will find alternative suppliers (or go without), or that its competitors are able to assail its strong market position. The breadth of this definition allows a range of behaviours to be captured as indicators of independence, such as foreclosing competitors, raising prices without concomitant increases in costs, reducing frequency or quality of service, or reducing innovation.

---

[1] Case 27/76 *United Brands v Commission* [1978] ECR 207, [65].
[2] Case 85/76 *Hoffmann-La Roche & Co AG v Commission* [1979] ECR 461, [38].

3.2.5 SUPER-DOMINANCE AND MONOPOLY

The strongest form of unilateral market power is where a company does have a monopoly (or near-monopoly). A level between dominance and monopoly that has been identified in EU law is 'super-dominance', which can be interpreted as 'a position of overwhelming dominance verging on monopoly'.[3] The best-known types of monopoly are natural ones and those that are statutory. A natural monopoly (as explained in Chapter 1) is an industry where the underlying costs of production mean that it is most efficient to have a single producer. In these cases, the economies of scale are so strong that there is room in the market for only one supplier. Standard examples are the physical networks of utility services—water, sewerage, electricity, gas transmission and distribution networks have high fixed costs, but once built can serve each additional customer at low cost. Economies of scale can also arise from the demand-side characteristics of a market, known as network effects, discussed in section 3.4. Statutory monopolies are those where the state has determined that there will be no competition.

Historically, for utility services that were considered to be complementary to much of the rest of the economy (transport, energy, water, and sewerage), public ownership was a solution to the need for subsidy or cross-subsidy to provide these essential services. For other services, such monopolies have been a popular form of state revenue-raising, either through state ownership of the monopoly or through the licence fees extracted from private operators in return for the right to exploit that monopoly. The licences for the first ITV franchises for UK commercial broadcasts were dubbed the original 'licence to print money' because of the scarcity of analogue broadcast spectrum, which meant that there was initially only one (monopoly) channel on which advertising would be carried in each region (this was in the 1950s). Postal services were another statutory monopoly in countries across the world, built on the desire to ensure a universal service (ie, regular delivery of mail to all addresses at an affordable price—see also Chapter 8 on state aid). Early recognition of the difficulty of enforcing a single price for a delivery service from any point to any other point in a country in the presence of competition has meant the persistence of national postal monopolies until very recently. In these cases, states have either retained public ownership to ensure that there is limited incentive to exploit the monopoly power, or in recent years have privatized them (in search of funding and cost efficiency) and subjected them to regulation. Indeed, entire separate legal frameworks exist in most jurisdictions to deal with such industries, although they are usually scrutinized under competition law as well. We do not discuss regulation in detail, although many of the principles of competition economics are relevant in considering the issues of the appropriate boundaries and approach to the regulation of these businesses. Furthermore, as we shall see in Chapter 4, many examples of abuse of dominance arise in these regulated industries. Intellectual Property (IP) rights and the patent system are a further source of

---

[3] Super-dominance was first defined in this way in the Opinion of Advocate General Fennelly of 19 October 1998, in Case C-395/96 P *Compagnie Maritime Belge and Dafra-Lines v EC Commission* [2000] ECR I-1365.

super-dominance or monopoly. In general, while the ownership of these rights does not infringe competition law, in this chapter and in Chapter 4 we will see several examples of IP owners being challenged for anti-competitive practices that appear to be trying to extend the strength or duration of those rights in a manner that does not deliver new products or further innovation.

3.3 ASSESSING MARKET POWER THROUGH MARKET SHARES AND CONCENTRATION

3.3.1 MARKET SHARES AND MARKET POWER

Having considered the different degrees of market power, the next step is determining where on the spectrum a company lies. In each case, a good understanding of the specific market is necessary, starting with the delineation of its boundaries (see Chapter 2). The next step is to look at the market shares of the participants in the relevant market. Market share and concentration measures are central to understanding the nature of existing competition in the market. They can also be a means to determine negative clearance or 'safe harbours'—ie, where a company is so small in a properly defined market that it is highly unlikely to have substantial market power and therefore no enforcement action is taken. But how small should the share be for there to be little concern? Conversely, if a company has a large share, is that synonymous with market power? In the EU there is a strong presumption linking market share to market power:

> The existence of a dominant position may derive from several factors which, taken separately, are not necessarily determinative but among these factors a highly important one is the existence of very large market shares ...

> very large market shares are in themselves, and save in exceptional circumstances, evidence of the existence of a dominant position.[4]

In *AKZO* (1991), the General Court ruled that a company with a stable market share of more than 50% in a relevant market would be deemed dominant unless there were exceptional circumstances.[5] The 40%–50% dominance threshold also appeared in the 2004 Coca-Cola undertakings with respect to exclusivity, rebates, and tying, which apply to those countries where Coca-Cola's soft drinks represent more than 40% of national sales (and more than double the share of the nearest competitor).[6]

The economics tells us that market shares should, in any case, not be seen as the sole answer. While they are a useful summary indicator of the impact a company has in a market, they cannot capture other crucial market characteristics that reveal the force of potential competition. These include the barriers to entry and exit, as discussed

---

[4] Case 85/76 *Hoffmann-La Roche & Co AG v Commission* [1979] ECR 461, [39] and [41].
[5] Case C-62/86 *AKZO Chemie BV v EC Commission* [1991] ECR I-3359.
[6] *Coca-Cola* (Case COMP/A39.116/B2) [2005] Commission Decision of 22 June 2005.

in section 3.4. Taking existing and potential competition together gives a fuller understanding of the competitive constraints faced by a company.

3.3.2 MEASURING MARKET SHARES: NOT AS EASY AS IT MIGHT SEEM

The higher a company's market share, the greater the likelihood that it can set its prices and output with limited constraint from competitors or customers. Market shares are straightforward to calculate in theory. You simply take the output of the relevant firm and divide it by the total market output. But in practice this analysis can be more difficult than it seems. First, market shares in terms of what—turnover (sales), volume (quantity), number of suppliers, number of customers, or capacity? Each of these metrics has its merits and limitations, and the most appropriate one will depend on the specific case at hand. According to the 2010 US Horizontal Merger Guidelines:

> In most contexts, the Agencies measure each firm's market share based on its actual or projected revenues in the relevant market. Revenues in the relevant market tend to be the best measure of attractiveness to customers, since they reflect the real-world ability of firms to surmount all of the obstacles necessary to offer products on terms and conditions that are attractive to customers. In cases where one unit of a low-priced product can substitute for one unit of a higher-priced product, unit sales may measure competitive significance better than revenues. For example, a new, much less expensive product may have great competitive significance if it substantially erodes the revenues earned by older, higher-priced products, even if it earns relatively few revenues. In cases where customers sign long-term contracts, face switching costs, or tend to re-evaluate their suppliers only occasionally, revenues earned from recently acquired customers may better reflect the competitive significance of suppliers than do total revenues.
>
> In markets for homogeneous products, a firm's competitive significance may derive principally from its ability and incentive to rapidly expand production in the relevant market in response to a price increase or output reduction by others in that market. As a result, a firm's competitive significance may depend upon its level of readily available capacity to serve the relevant market if that capacity is efficient enough to make such expansion profitable. In such markets, capacities or reserves may better reflect the future competitive significance of suppliers than revenues, and the Agencies may calculate market shares using those measures. Market participants that are not current producers may then be assigned positive market shares, but only if a measure of their competitive significance properly comparable to that of current producers is available. When market shares are measured based on firms' readily available capacities, the Agencies do not include capacity that is committed or so profitably employed outside the relevant market, or so high-cost, that it would not likely be used to respond to a SSNIP in the relevant market.[7]

---

[7] Department of Justice and Federal Trade Commission (2010), 'Horizontal Merger Guidelines', 19 August, p 17.

The most common measure of market share is turnover or sales value. Sales value is the usual measure when products are differentiated, so that there is a spectrum of pricing in the market. Using sales value allows the different products to be aggregated, with more weight placed on the suppliers of more expensive products. Consider the Nestlé and Perrier merger in 1992. The two companies were both involved in bottling water from a natural spring or source. The European Commission found that market shares in value terms better reflected the market power in the French bottled water market than shares in volumes:

> because the French water market is composed of two categories of products which are very different in terms of price, ie the nationally distributed mineral waters and the local waters, which are mainly spring waters. There exists a wide and constantly increasing price gap between these two categories of waters ... Given this considerable price difference between these two categories of waters and the importance of financial resources in the water market for investment in publicity and marketing, the Commission considers that it is more appropriate to take account of the market shares expressed in value than in volume.[8]

On the other hand, using value market shares may underestimate the competitive significance of lower-price suppliers (as noted in the quote from the US Horizontal Merger Guidelines above). Volume (in terms of units supplied) is a common alternative measure of market shares, especially when the products in question are sufficiently homogeneous.[9] When examining a joint venture between Kemira GrowHow and Terra Industries, two producers of fertilizers and other chemicals, the UK Competition Commission (CC) assessed market shares calculated on the basis of tonnes supplied, for each type of fertilizer or chemical.[10] The number of customers can also be an important volume-based metric for market share calculations, particularly where a firm's strength in the market is driven by serving different customers or groups of customers. In the airline industry, market shares for a given route are typically calculated in terms of the number of passengers flown, as seen in the *Aer Lingus/Ryanair* merger.[11]

Value- and volume-based measures of market share give information about the constraints from other companies based on the choices made by customers. As we know from Chapter 2, supply-side factors can also broaden the market, where suppliers active in closely related markets could easily move to supplying the focal product. A market share measure that captures the capacity of potential suppliers is relevant in such cases

---

[8] *Nestlé/Perrier* (Case No IV/M.190) [1992] OJ L356/1.

[9] In a different context—that of setting fines—competition law usually refers to market shares in terms of the value of sales (we discuss fines in Chapter 9). For example, when investigating a bitumen cartel in Spain, the European Commission considered market shares in terms of volumes of bitumen products, since the parties had a market-sharing arrangement on the basis of volumes, but then used sales value market shares to determine the cartel fines. *Bitumen Spain* (Case COMP/387103), Commission Decision of 3 October 2007 C(2007) 4441 final.

[10] Competition Commission (2007), 'A report on the anticipated joint venture between Kemira GrowHow Oyj and Terra Industries Inc', 11 July.

[11] *Ryanair/Aer Lingus* (Case COMP/M.4439), Commission Decision of 27 July 2007 C(2007) 3104.

since capacity is a better indicator of supply-side substitution, and hence of competitive significance. This principle is reflected in the US Horizontal Merger Guidelines as quoted above, as well as the New Zealand Commerce Commission guidelines:

> where a capacity-based measure of market share produces a significantly lower share of the market for the combined entity than one based on sales volumes, the implied unemployed capacity available to competitors, or to possible market entrants, might be taken into account as a potential constraint on the combined entity from actual or near competitors.[12]

Consider a hypothetical example from the bus sector. There are two operators within a given local market: operator A with a depot with 60 buses and operator B with 40 buses. If operator B runs mainly inter-urban services (with high passenger mileage) and operator A runs mainly local services (with low passenger mileage), a market share based on passenger miles would give the impression that B was the stronger competitor. A capacity-based measure would reveal that operator A has a greater ability to substitute to new routes and is therefore a stronger supply-side competitor than operator B. In Chapter 2 we discussed the *Chester City Council and Chester City Transport v Arriva* predatory pricing case involving local bus services, where it was accepted that the geographic market should be defined in terms of supply-side substitution. The case then turned on the relevant market share metric, with the candidates being bus hours (ie, the hours a bus spends on the road—proposed as a proxy measure for turnover) and capacity (by number of buses and depot capacity). The High Court concluded as follows:

> As regards [the claimants' expert's] 'bus hours' metric, I also regard this as wrong in principle. [The claimants' expert] accepts it has not, so far as he knows, been used before. He produced no material showing a reliable link between bus hours and turnover and I regard the metric as at least an unreliable proxy for turnover. But even if it is to be regarded as a proper such proxy, I also accept [the defendants' expert's] opinion that such a metric is not an appropriate one for measuring market power in a case where the market is being determined on a supply-side basis, even though it may be where it is being determined on a demand-side basis. Turnover measures what operators are *actually* doing, not what they are capable of doing, whereas in a supply-side case the inquiry is what they are *capable* of doing. [The defendants' expert's] opinion, which I regard [the claimants' managing director] as sharing, is that in such a case *capacity* is the best metric for measuring market power. I accept that opinion and agree that a vehicle count is one way of measuring it. I understood [the defendants' expert] also to agree that an alternative way is to measure the bus capacity of particular depots. I find that [the claimants' expert] used the wrong metric in order to ascertain market shares in a wrongly identified market.[13] [Emphasis in original.]

Another example of the use of capacity as the basis for market share calculations is the *Cott/Macaw* (2006) merger in the UK, where the relevant market for PET-bottled own-label carbonated soft drinks (CSDs) was defined on the basis of supply-side

---

[12] New Zealand Commerce Commission (2003), 'Mergers and Acquisitions Guidelines', s 5.2.
[13] *Chester City Council and Chester City Transport Limited v Arriva PLC* [2007] EWHC 1373 (Ch), [191]. We acted for the defendants in this case.

substitution, and the CC concluded that 'For that reason, capacity-based market shares potentially better represent the potential for competition by taking into account each supplier's total capacity to provide own-label PET-bottled CSDs.'[14] However, it acknowledged that market shares based on capacity might overstate some companies' share of capacity available for producing PET-bottled CSDs since the margins might be higher from continuing to produce an alternative product (see also Chapter 2 on how supply-side substitution may be overstated in these circumstances). Hence the Commission also considered market shares in terms of sales value. Indeed, it is not uncommon to compare a number of market share indicators to gain an understanding of the different dimensions of potential market power that a company may have.

A further consideration is how frequently the market shares are measured and over what time period. Competition authorities often use annual market shares, mainly for pragmatic reasons. This may give a good picture of relative market positions over the relevant time period, but may not be appropriate where there are infrequent and large orders, resulting in volatile annual market shares that are uninformative. In this situation, market shares over a longer time period (eg, three or five years) may need to be calculated. One such sector characterized by large and infrequent orders is the aircraft industry. In the merger between Boeing and McDonnell Douglas in 1997, the European Commission examined ten years of market share data, where market share was measured in terms of the order backlog for aircraft still in production, new orders, and net orders.[15] Ten- and five-year time horizons for calculating market shares were also used in the *General Electric/Honeywell* merger, which related to the manufacturing of large jet aircraft engines.[16]

In any case, a snapshot of market shares in one year is normally insufficient. To understand market power and the ability to behave independently of rivals, knowing how market shares change over time is crucial. By looking at a number of years of market share data we can see whether companies jockey for position or if a large company has remained large for some time. The European Court's decision on AKZO's dominance illustrates this point:

> AKZO's market share is not only large in itself but is equivalent to all the remaining producers put together ...

> AKZO's market share (as well as that of the second and third placed producers Interox and Luperox) has remained steady over the period under consideration and AKZO has always successfully repulsed any attacks on its position by smaller producers.[17]

Stability of market shares is a particularly important indicator in high-tech industries characterized by rapid innovation—a theme we return to in section 3.8. In such

---

[14] Competition Commission (2006), 'Cott Beverages Ltd and Macaw (Holdings) Ltd merger inquiry: Final report', 28 March, [5.3]. We advised the merging parties in this inquiry.

[15] *Boeing/McDonnell Douglas* (Case No IV/M.87730) [1997] OJ L336/16; [1997] 5 CMLR 270.

[16] *General Electric/Honeywell* (Case COMP/M.2220) [2004] OJ L48/1.

[17] Case C-62/86 *AKZO Chemie BV v EC Commission of the European Communities* [1991] ECR I-3359.

industries, the dynamics of market shares can often be decisive in a finding of market power. For example, the combined market share for cardiac ultrasound machines in the *Philips/ATL* merger would have been above 40% in a number of national markets. Yet the European Commission concluded that there was no concern because the parties' post-merger market share could be expected to be challenged by innovative competitors, as it had been in the past:

> the cardiac ultrasound market is R&D intensive and largely driven by technological innovations which take place at relatively rapid pace, on average every 4–5 years ... The rapid innovation rate of ultrasound allows competitors, who manage to place a new product on the market, to gain market shares relatively quickly, while established products might lose out. HSG (then HP, Hewlett-Packard) prior to 1998 was by far the market leader in Europe in cardiac ultrasound. Later on, GE and Acuson managed to improve their position significantly ... These developments have resulted in a significant price decrease for top-end equipment but also in a change of market shares of the main competitors (HP lost ground on GE and Siemens/Acuson).[18]

3.3.3 MEASURING CONCENTRATION

In assessing market power, the market share of the company under investigation is not the only statistic of interest. You also want to know the relative size and strength of its competitors, and how many there are. All these aspects can be captured in various measures of concentration—the most common being the number of competitors, Cn measures, and the Herfindahl–Hirschman Index (HHI). The first of these—the number of competitors—is the simplest measure of concentration: the fewer the competitors in a market, the higher the concentration. While easy to dismiss as uninformative (it doesn't tell you anything about the relative strength of these competitors), this measure can be helpful in cases that involve localized markets and where consumer choice matters. In its groceries market investigation, the CC focused on the number of supermarket 'fascias' (ie, brands of competing shops) in each local market:

> The number of competing fascias in a local market provides another indication of the extent of the competitive constraint faced by particular stores within that market. The greater the number of fascias, the greater the number of alternatives to which customers can switch following any weakening of the retail offer at a store. Where a grocery store faces zero, one or two competitor fascias (ie monopoly, duopoly or triopoly stores), and the retailer operating that store has a high market share, that retailer is likely to face little to no competitive constraint in that market.[19]

This fascia count as a concentration measure is based on the assumption that consumers choose to go to a supermarket because of its overall offering, and then do all their

---

[18] *Philips /Agilent Healthcare Solutions* (Case COMP/M.2256), Commission Decision of 2 March 2001.
[19] Competition Commission (2008), 'The supply of groceries in the UK—Market investigation', 30 April, [6.10].

shopping there. They rarely split any one shopping visit across multiple supermarkets. Therefore it is the loss of an option that is important in reducing the competitive constraint on neighbouring supermarkets.

Cn measures of concentration give the combined share of the 'n' largest firms in a market (they were widely used by industrial organization (IO) economists in the 1950s and 1960s but less so now). For example, C4 gives the combined market share of the largest four firms in a market. When assessing the *Cott/Macaw* merger, the CC considered C2 measures in the market for PET-bottled own-label CSDs: the pre-merger C2 ratio was 65%, rising to 89% post-merger, indicating a highly concentrated market (although the CC cleared the merger because it found that buyer power and supply-side substitution would prevent any potential exercise of market power—see also section 3.7).[20]

The most commonly used concentration measure is the HHI, which is calculated by adding the squares of market shares of all the companies in a market. The effect of this squaring is that the index gives more weight to the larger companies. The mechanics of calculating the HHI are shown in Table 3.1. The higher the HHI, the more concentrated the market is. An HHI of close to zero indicates a market with many firms, each having a tiny market share. The maximum HHI is 10,000, which indicates a monopoly (the square of 100 is 10,000). The table shows two industries, each with nine firms, but with quite different distributions of their market shares. The C4 measure is actually the same in both industries—80%. But which of them is the more concentrated? Industry one is dominated by two main suppliers with 35% each, followed by a fringe of much

Table 3.1 Concentration measures: an illustration

	Industry one		Industry two	
	Market share (%)	HHI	Market share (%)	HHI
Firm 1	35	1,225	20	400
Firm 2	35	1,225	20	400
Firm 3	5	25	20	400
Firm 4	5	25	20	400
Firm 5	5	25	4	16
Firm 6	5	25	4	16
Firm 7	4	16	4	16
Firm 8	3	9	4	16
Firm 9	3	9	4	16
Total	100	2,584	100	1,680
C4	80		80	

[20] Competition Commission (2006), 'Cott Beverages Ltd and Macaw (Holdings) Ltd merger inquiry: Final report', 28 March, [7.2].

smaller firms. Competition in industry two seems more evenly balanced between four firms with 20% each. You can see that the high market shares of 35%, when squared, have a big impact on the HHI. As a result, the HHI for industry one is 904 points higher than for industry two.

The HHI is a good summary measure of the size distribution of firms. It reflects both the distribution of the market shares of the larger firms and the composition of the part of the market served by smaller firms. In theory you need information on the shares of all the firms in the market to calculate the HHI, but firms with small market shares have little effect on the overall HHI (eg, if you don't have precise information on the sales of fringe firms 7 to 9, you can combine them in a residual category or assume some average market share for each—either way the result does not change much). Another useful way of interpreting the HHI is that when you divide 10,000 by the HHI you get the equivalent number of equally sized firms in the market. An HHI of 2,500 gives you 10,000 / 2,500 = 4, so the structure of industry one (HHI = 2,584) is roughly equivalent to having four equally sized companies in the market (if all four have 25%, the square of that is 625, and the sum of the squares is 2,500). Industry two (HHI = 1,680) is roughly equivalent to a structure with six equally sized firms (10,000 / 1,680 = 5.95). Finally, we note that the HHI has a theoretical property that economists find particularly interesting. In the standard Cournot model of oligopoly (discussed in section 3.5), there is a direct positive relationship between the HHI and the price–cost margins in the industry—the higher the concentration, the greater the margins earned by the oligopolists, which is an intuitive result.

3.3.4 WHEN IS A MARKET TOO CONCENTRATED?

We have now defined the various measures that are used as a filter for determining when there is likely to be a concern about market power or market concentration. How high is too high? This is in essence a matter of judgement. There are no bright lines. In any event, given that market shares and concentration do not tell you the whole story on market power, thresholds may be useful only as an initial filter or safe harbour. The EU Merger Regulation states that a market share of the merging parties of no more than 25% indicates that the concentration is too low to impede effective competition.[21] In terms of the HHI, the EU approach is that a post-merger HHI of below 1,000 (eg, ten firms each having 10% of the market) would not normally be of concern. A post-merger HHI of between 1,000 and 2,000 and a delta (an increase in the HHI as a result of a merger) below 250 would also generally be allowed. However, a post-merger HHI above 2,000 would require further scrutiny if the delta is in excess of 150 (an HHI of 2,000 reflects a market with five equally-sized firms). In the USA, concentration in merger cases is also measured using the HHI: a post-merger HHI of below 1,500 would

---

[21] Council Regulation (EC) 139/2004 of 20 January 2004 (the EC Merger Regulation), [32].

result in an approval of the merger, whereas a merger resulting in HHI above 1,500 that involves a delta of more than 100 points is said to 'often warrant scrutiny', and a merger resulting in HHI above 2,500 with a delta of more than 200 points is presumed to be likely to enhance market power.[22]

3.3.5 THE LERNER INDEX

If we return once again to Figure 3.1, we can see a potential direct test of market power. Because the key economic element of market power is the ability to price above cost, a seemingly obvious measure is the extent to which prices do indeed deviate from marginal costs. For this, economists have the Lerner index, which is defined as price minus marginal cost, divided by price. This is more commonly referred to as the price–cost margin—indeed this is the margin that is of relevance to the formula for critical loss analysis explained in Chapter 2 and the one for merger simulation analysis discussed in Chapter 7. There is a well-known relationship in economic theory, known as the Lerner condition, which captures the link between the demand conditions facing a company and the extent to which it prices above marginal costs (Lerner, 1934). The less elastic the demand a company (such as the monopolist in Figure 3.1) faces, the higher it will price above its marginal costs. Specifically, the condition states that at the profit-maximizing price, the price–cost margin (Lerner index) is equal to –1 divided by the elasticity. So if the elasticity is –2 (meaning that if the firm raises its price by 10%, it will lose 20% of its demand), we would expect to observe margins of 50% (–1 divided by –2).

As with the logic of the hypothetical monopolist, a company with market power will make a trade-off between raising price to earn higher margins on all products it sells and the fact that the increase in price will reduce sales. The margin it chooses is therefore related to the likelihood of customers switching (and the likelihood of its competitors responding). Where a company has some market power to earn margins and is profit-maximizing, it will not operate on the inelastic portion of its demand curve (we also saw this in Chapter 2).

In microeconomic and IO theory, the Lerner index is a prime indicator of market power; after all, market power is defined in theory as the ability to price above marginal cost. However, this measure may not be directly applicable to competition cases. It focuses on marginal cost as the benchmark, but there are many reasons why companies price above marginal costs even in markets that are effectively competitive. As we saw in Chapter 1, in most industries there are fixed costs that need to be recovered and therefore require a positive price–cost margin (alternatively you can consider long-run marginal or incremental costs which do include fixed costs—see Chapter 4). In section 3.2 we saw the example of monopolistically competitive markets, where margins are positive because companies have some differentiated pricing power,

---

[22] Department of Justice and Federal Trade Commission (2010), 'Horizontal Merger Guidelines', 19 August, p 19.

but where overall those margins are competed down to the level where they cover average total costs. Instead of comparing prices with marginal costs, you need a longer-term perspective. In section 3.6 we discuss how profitability over a longer time period can be used as an indicator of market power. Like the Lerner index, it has the benefit of directly capturing the essence of the definition of market power: the ability to keep price above the competitive level for a sustained period of time without being undermined by consumers switching or competitors entering the market.

The Lerner condition is sometimes used to sense-check other economic evidence on elasticities and consumer responsiveness to price. For example, if you observe that a company has a price–cost margin of around 67% (see Chapter 10 on how you can derive margin information from financial accounts), the Lerner condition would imply that this company faces an elasticity of –1.5 (because –1 / –1.5 = 0.67). If the economists produce evidence that the elasticity is much higher or much lower than this, you can ask some critical questions about how this can be reconciled with the basic Lerner condition. There are some good reasons why the condition may not hold (and the economists would need to make these explicit). One is that the Lerner condition reflects a long-run profit-maximizing equilibrium. Prices at any point in time may deviate from the optimum, because of factors such as the uncertainty surrounding demand conditions and pricing frictions. Companies may also have chosen not to price that particular product at the profit-maximizing level—for example, if they want to increase its sales penetration or promote a complementary product. At times, economists have also used the Lerner condition as a substitute for elasticity evidence (so as more than just a sense-check)—they look at the price–cost margin, and from this derive a direct conclusion on price-responsiveness (the higher the margin, the less elastic the demand). We believe that this is taking the theoretical relationship a step too far.[23]

3.4 ENTRY AND EXIT BARRIERS

3.4.1 POTENTIAL COMPETITION

While market shares and concentration help understand the current competitive constraints that exist in a market, it is also important to assess the potential for new or existing companies to respond to high prices and profits and undermine the market position of the incumbents—potential competition can be as significant as actual competition. Entry and exit barriers are an important determinant of the extent and persistence of market power. We do not differentiate particularly here between entry and exit barriers. An exit barrier (a cost to leave a market), such as laws on minimum redundancy payments, can affect a company's entry decision as much as an up-front investment requirement. In entering a market, a company assesses its risks which include the

---

[23] This use of the Lerner condition in merger cases (specifically in the context of critical loss analysis) has been the subject of a heated debate. See Katz and Shapiro (2003).

costs of failure. Likewise, a company that has made significant up-front investments to gain a market position will not abandon these investments lightly. We also do not draw a real distinction between barriers to entry faced by new competitors and barriers to expansion faced by existing competitors. Both require a similar analysis. When assessing entry barriers you ask the question: What is the source of the market failure that allows a company to acquire and sustain market power without this being undermined by new competitors? The failure could relate to the way customers purchase the product—informational problems, transactional frictions, or the fact that each consumer's demand relates to the demand of other consumers. It could also relate to some aspect of how the product is produced—economies of scale or scope, or investment that cannot be recovered. Barriers to entry are relevant in nearly all competition cases (the exception being per se breaches of competition law, in particular hardcore cartels—see Chapter 5).

What constitutes a barrier to entry into a market, and how can we judge whether entry barriers are high or low? These are questions that depend on the market conditions and are amenable to economic testing. There is no theory or precedent that sets out the exact height of entry barriers that lead to market power. In the economics literature, two definitions of entry barriers have been most prominent. The first, by Bain (1956), states that barriers to entry are:

> the advantages of established sellers in an industry over potential entrants, these advantages being reflected in the extent to which established sellers can persistently raise their prices above a competitive level without attracting new firms to enter the industry.

Bain identified three features of the market that could hinder entry: economies of scale, product differentiation, and absolute cost advantages. Economies of scale mean that the market is characterized by costs that fall as volumes rise, and thus an entrant faces the prospect of entering either at a smaller than optimal scale at a consequent cost disadvantage relative to the incumbent, or at an optimal scale and depressing market prices. Incumbents' absolute cost advantages could allow them to sell profitably at prices below the cost of potential entrants. A different, more narrow, definition of barriers to entry was proposed by Stigler (1968):

> a cost of producing (at some or every rate of output) . . . which must be borne by a firm which seeks to enter an industry but is not borne by firms already in the industry.

This definition does not include economies of scale as a barrier to entry because an incumbent faces (or faced) the same requirement to achieve and maintain economies of scale.

In practice, competition authorities tend to consider a wide range of factors that could constitute a barrier to entry, and do not necessarily make the distinction between the above two definitions. The focus is usually on any barriers that prevent a 'likely, significant and timely' entry. The term 'likely' reflects the fact that entry analysis is inevitably speculative to some extent because it concerns future market developments (any evidence of past instances of entry, or the absence thereof, would add some weight to such forward-looking analysis). For entry to be 'significant', it must be of sufficient scope and magnitude to deter or prevent the exercise of market power by incumbents. Whether entry can be considered 'timely' depends largely on the characteristics and dynamics of the market in question. It also depends to some extent on the competition authority's stance on the relevant timeframe for analysing competition problems—in the same way as the interpretation of the term 'non-transitory' does when applying the hypothetical monopolist test (as discussed in Chapter 2). In its Guidance on Article 102, the European Commission states only that: 'For expansion or entry to be considered timely, it must be sufficiently swift to deter or defeat the exercise of substantial market power.'[24] In its Merger Guidelines the Commission is more specific as to what is a 'timely' entry: it should be achieved within two years.[25]

3.4.2 ABSOLUTE, STRATEGIC, AND EXCLUSIONARY BARRIERS TO ENTRY

IP law, patents, supply licences, planning laws, and other types of legislation can constitute an important barrier to entry into a market. In the case of IP law and certain statutory functions, monopolies are granted by design. In other areas of law it may be an unintended or unfortunate byproduct of some other policy objective. Competition authorities can sometimes intervene in these instances, in their advocacy role or in some countries under specific statutory powers. For example, the CC found that the local planning system and rules—created to control and shape development in order to meet certain economic and social objectives of local governments—constrain entry into local grocery retailing markets by larger supermarkets.[26] (In Chapter 9 we discuss the assessment of the costs and benefits of the remedies imposed by the CC in that case.) Patents constitute an absolute entry barrier, and as such have played an important role as an indicator of market power in several cases. In the *AstraZeneca* (2005) abuse of dominance case, patents were considered to be a significant barrier to entry into a market for Losec, an anti-ulcer medicine.[27] The abuse related to AstraZeneca seeking to extend the patent protection for Losec's active ingredient, omeprazole, by presenting misleading evidence before patent offices in various EU countries. In the *Tetra Pak/ Alfa-Laval* (1991) merger, the Commission found there to be significant entry barriers

---

[24] European Commission (2009), 'Guidance on the Commission's Enforcement Priorities in Applying Article 82 EC Treaty to Abusive Exclusionary Conduct by Dominant Undertakings', 2009/C 45/02, February, [19].

[25] European Commission (2004), 'Guidelines on the assessment of horizontal mergers under the Council Regulation on the control of concentrations between undertakings', 2004/C 31/03, [74].

[26] Competition Commission (2008), 'The supply of groceries in the UK market investigation', 30 April, [7.44].

[27] *AstraZeneca* (Case COMP/A 37.507/F3), Commission Decision 2006/857/EC, [2006] OJ L332/24.

into the market for aseptic carton packaging machines, one of the reasons being that Tetra Pak owned many patents for the production of these machines.[28]

Strategic entry barriers form a broad category and can be described as advantages that are specifically enjoyed by the incumbents. These include economies of scale or scope, reputation, an established distribution and sales network, the existence of sunk costs, informational barriers, and customer switching costs. These factors are largely a result of the nature of the market or the consequence of a position of incumbency. In addition, incumbents' own actions can create barriers to entry. Such practices, which include predatory pricing, margin squeeze, bundling and tying, could in themselves be found to be illegal (rather than just aspects that are considered during the analysis of entry barriers)—see further Chapter 4.

3.4.3 INFORMATIONAL ENTRY BARRIERS

Information on the different products in a given market may be hard to acquire or the product may be fully understood by a customer only once it is purchased (such products are known as an experience goods). These characteristics may make customers more likely to continue to purchase from the current supplier, or from one that comes recommended or has a well-known brand. Such informational barriers therefore make it difficult for new or smaller firms to grow. Transactional frictions may lead to customer inertia and other customer choice biases. These frictions can be as simple as learning the shortcuts on a different mobile phone or as complex as digging up the front garden to lay a new cable to one's home.

Such inertia can lead consumers to be extremely loyal in their purchasing behaviour. Evidence shows that consumers are much more likely to get divorced than to change their bank (see Santander, 2010). Conversely, in some sectors, businesses offer consumers substantial incentives to switch in order to overcome these informational and transactional challenges, which can even lead to concerns of too much switching if these incentives are funded from charges that are protected by entry barriers. Recent inquiries into financial services products in the UK have identified certain informational market failures as a main reason why competition is not effective in these markets. For instance, in the market for payment protection insurance (PPI)—a product that insures borrowers against events that may prevent them from repaying a loan—the CC found that informational factors were a major entry barrier for stand-alone PPI providers:

> The second barrier we found was poor consumer awareness of PPI. We found that a significant number of consumers did not consider PPI before approaching their lender for credit; moreover, a significant number of customers did not know that they could take out PPI from someone other than their credit provider. This low consumer awareness and poor

---

[28] *Tetra Pak/Alfa-Laval* (Case No IV/M068 19 July 1991), Commission Decision 91/535/EEC, [1991] OJ L290/35.

understanding of options restricts the ability of providers of stand-alone PPI successfully to enter or expand into PPI markets.[29]

For store cards, it was found that customers did not understand price and cost information very well and that this was preventing them from switching. Remedies were imposed that enforced common ways of presenting information and clear signals that a product is priced high.[30] Chapter 9 on the design of remedies discusses the new insights from behavioural economics into these informational barriers and consumer biases and their effect on competition.

3.4.4 ECONOMIES OF SCALE AND SCOPE

Economies of scale have been explained in Chapter 1. To recap, markets with this feature exhibit unit costs that fall the more output that is produced. This means that there is some fixed or semi-fixed component of cost. An example is the need to rent a building that is bigger than currently required because the company expects to grow; as the business employs more staff, the average costs of the building per employee will fall since the costs of the building are fixed. This type of scale economy is exhausted as capacity is reached. Where this occurs at relatively low levels of output, it does not constitute a major barrier. This is because if two buildings are required to house the optimal number of staff to serve a given market, this can be done by one firm renting two buildings or two firms renting one building each. Both will observe economies of scale as they build to scale, but these will not significantly hamper entry.

Economies of scope reflect the possibility that it is cheaper to produce a range of products from a common cost base. Banking products are a good example. Once a financial institution has set up its credit-scoring facility to assess the creditworthiness of potential customers, it can easily supply a wide range of loan products using this facility, such as overdrafts, credit cards, and personal loans. Additionally, if it supplies the current account to a customer it has access to crucial information about that customer (income, regular outgoings, location) to feed into its credit-scoring model. An entrant wishing to offer only one product line (for example, just credit cards), would face higher per-product costs for credit-scoring, because it would be more difficult to get the relevant information on a potential customer's credit history and because it cannot spread the fixed costs over different products. (Interestingly there are often agreements between banks to share common datasets on customers, which tend to reduce the scale and scope advantages for incumbents and hence promote competition; but you can see the tension with the prohibition under Article 101 on information sharing between competitors—a theme we explore in Chapter 5.)

Economies of scale (or scope) can act as a barrier to entry in two ways. First, if the entrant can operate only below the minimum efficient scale, it would have a significant

---

[29] Competition Commission (2009), 'Market investigation into payment protection insurance', 29 January, [57].

[30] Competition Commission (2006), 'Store cards market investigation', Final Report, 7 March.

cost disadvantage relative to the incumbent, limiting the degree to which it can compete effectively. Second, even if a potential entrant can enter at the minimum efficient scale, it may be deterred by the knowledge that its entry could lead to excess capacity and consequent price decreases in the market, making the entry unprofitable. Returning to the different definitions of entry barriers by Bain and Stigler, large fixed costs that drive economies of scale and scope would not be considered an entry barrier by Stigler. In particular, if there is a second-hand market for the assets (eg, buildings can be sub-let; machines or databases can be sold), these fixed costs may simply be regarded as a cost of doing business rather than a barrier to entry. Entrants will need to finance entry and this may be seen to be risky, particularly where the next best alternative for use of the assets may have a much lower value, but it is in essence a cost or risk that is faced by the incumbents as well.

3.4.5 SUNK COSTS

Sunk costs constitute perhaps the most important strategic barrier to entry. Chapter 2 defined sunk costs in the context of supply-side substitution. These are costs that have been incurred and cannot be recovered on exit—ie, they have no alternative value. A classic example is advertising and brand investment (although these days brands can sometimes be sold in their entirety just like any other fixed asset, so this type of investment may not always be completely sunk). In the abuse of dominance case brought against Coca-Cola, the Commission found advertising to be an important barrier.

> the strong position of [Coca-Cola] and its respective bottlers (due to high market shares, unique brand recognition and the must stock nature of [Coca-Cola]'s strongest brands and the exceptional breadth of the CSD [carbonated softdrinks] portfolio) is protected from competition by barriers to entry in the form of sunk advertising costs preventing any significant market entry.[31]

Some sunk costs may be absolute barriers, in that it is essential to undertake that investment to enter. This might include building a reservoir to serve a factory's water demand or the costs of meeting regulatory requirements to be allowed a licence to operate in a given market. More commonly, sunk costs are of a strategic nature, in that an incumbent can choose how much of these costs to 'sink' and thereby affect the costs of new competitors entering the market.

A prominent example of sunk costs acting as an entry barrier is in the pharmaceuticals industry. Generic drug producers sometimes have to spend substantial amounts on advertising and marketing in order to establish themselves in a marketplace as effective competitors to the incumbents, which often have a strong reputation built in the years of monopoly supply while still under patent, supported by established marketing and distribution channels. Likewise, in the *Tetra Pak/Alfa-Laval* merger mentioned above,

---

[31] *Coca-Cola* (Case COMP/A.39.116/B2), Commission Decision of 22 June 2005, [25].

the European Commission considered that Tetra Pak's proven track record and reputation formed another substantial entry barrier into the market for aseptic carton packaging machines, in addition to Tetra Pak's patents. An established track record and the
good reputation of the incumbents can make entry into a market difficult for potential
entrants. We note that this kind of entry barrier in itself should not be condemned; to
the contrary, it should be seen as benefiting consumers. But it can still function as an
entry barrier and is therefore relevant to the assessment of market power.

Equipment or plants that are highly industry- or even customer-specific can also
represent a significant entry barrier in the form of sunk costs. When considering a
merger between manufacturers of silicon carbide, the European Commission noted
that the costs of constructing a medium-size silicon carbide processing plant for macro
grains were not only significant, but also involved specific equipment that could be used
only for the processing of abrasive grains.[32]

3.4.6 CONTESTABLE MARKETS

Sunk costs are an important determinant of whether markets are contestable. As
discussed in section 3.3, high market shares do not necessarily equate to market power.
A contestable market is one where even an apparent monopolist has no market power,
because sunk costs do not exist and barriers are so low that the threat of entry is
sufficient to constrain the incumbent. Chapter 2 also considered contestability, in the
context of supply-side substitution and the threat of rapid entry.

The intuition behind the theory of contestable markets is simple yet striking: in
certain cases, the simple *threat* of competition in markets that appear to be concentrated or monopolistic is sufficient to drive prices to the competitive level. Since Baumol
first presented the theory of contestability in 1982, it has attracted considerable attention and criticism, in terms of both its theoretical rigour and its applicability (Baumol,
1982). Contestability requires that there are no entry barriers and in particular no sunk
costs. Otherwise the potential loss from writing off the sunk costs would have to be
weighed against the profits derived from entry and would act as a significant deterrent.
The absence of barriers to entry and exit allows for 'hit and run' entry—any profit
opportunity that arises because an incumbent raises its price above costs, no matter
how short-lived, can be fully and costlessly exploited by a new entrant. It is also
necessary that there is some period of time in between a new entrant arriving in the
market and a response by the incumbent to reduce its price back to the competitive
level. It is during this time that the entrant makes the profit that gives it the incentive to
enter. Once the incumbent lowers its prices, profits are reduced to the normal level and
the entrant then costlessly leaves the market with its accumulated profits.

The initial proponents of the theory suggested that its clearest application was in
airline markets where aircraft could be transferred from one route to another at

[32] *Saint-Gobain/Wacker-Chemie/NOM* [1997] OJ L274/1, [184].

negligible extra costs. Indeed, the theory was used to justify several high-profile horizontal mergers in the US airline sector in the early 1980s. However, some of the evidence gathered since then shows that fares in fact rose sharply post-merger on routes where market shares were high, and suggests that the sunk costs required in setting up ground support for a new route were overlooked (Shepherd, 1988).

Perhaps a clearer example is the provision of local bus services, as also explained in Chapter 2. If an operator has a bus depot nearby, adding services to an existing route or opening new routes can be done swiftly (in the UK a new route can be opened 56 days after registration). Any investment in additional buses is not sunk since there is often a reasonably liquid market for second-hand buses should the operator decide to exit the route (buses can also be leased or rented). Even entry on a small scale can have a strong competitive impact on a particular bus route—for example, if the entrant runs its service only on the busiest part of a route or during the busiest times of the day. This conclusion was reached in the 2004 OFT decision in the *Arriva/Wales and Borders Rail* case, where a regional rail franchise was acquired by an operator which also provided local bus services in the area.[33]

Another example of where contestability was relied upon to clear a merger is the acquisition by CHC Helicopter Corporation (CHC) of Helicopter Services Group ASA (HSG) in 2000.[34] Even though this acquisition created a duopoly in the market for the supply of helicopter services to oil and gas installations on the UK continental shelf, the CC found that this did not have a detrimental effect on the public interest, the primary reason being that the helicopter services market remained contestable. Barriers to entry were found to be low since entrants did not suffer any cost disadvantage compared with the incumbents; regulatory barriers were low and there were no issues around the availability of airport capacity. Helicopter firms operating in other geographic markets were thus considered to be potential hit and run entrants. Finally, the CC found that the long-term price contracts that incumbents were tied into meant that they could not adjust their prices rapidly in response to any hit and run entry. This would ensure that incumbents set a competitive price ex ante, and not merely in response to the actual development of competition. Interestingly, this case was reviewed in 2005 as part of an ex post evaluation of merger decisions.[35] This review suggests that the original clearance may have been over-optimistic in its assessment of the low barriers to entry. Post-merger prices did rise and customers found the quality of service to be lower. One sponsored new entrant did emerge, but one of the buyers incurred significant costs to facilitate this. With this entrant active in the market, prices fell and quality of service

[33] Office of Fair Trading (2004), 'Completed Acquisition by Arriva Plc of the Wales and Borders Rail Franchise', 16 March.
[34] Competition Commission (2000), 'CHC Helicopter Corporation and Helicopter Services Group ASA: A report on the merger situation', January.
[35] Office of Fair Trading (2005), 'Ex post evaluation of mergers', March.

rose again. If the market were truly contestable, this actual entry would not have been required as the mere threat of entry would have kept prices low.

We return to the concept of contestable markets in Chapter 7, presenting examples of mergers that have been allowed despite apparently high levels of concentration post-merger. While the conditions for a finding of a fully contestable market may be rare, it illustrates that caution should be exercised in assuming that high market shares will be sufficient to presume market power. Where barriers to entry are low, making hit and run entry relatively easy, the threat of entry can be a strong constraint on incumbents.

3.4.7 NETWORK EFFECTS

Network effects are a form of economies of scale driven by the demand characteristics of a product rather than the supply side. A network effect is where the benefit that one consumer receives from a network product is affected by how many other consumers have also joined. Economists call this a positive demand-side externality—positive because users influence each other's demand positively; externality because each user does not take into account that positive effect on others when making an individual decision on whether to join the network. We came across this concept in Chapter 2 on market definition, which is rendered more complicated by the presence of such effects.

Network effects can sometimes be easily exhausted—for example, at a restaurant. Your demand for a restaurant (especially one you've never visited before) can be positively influenced by the number of people already eating there. First, it is an information signal and, second, your enjoyment is enhanced by the atmosphere of a restaurant which has a reasonable number of patrons. However, such network effects do not lead to significant market power. The positive benefits you receive from the presence of others quickly turn to negative effects if the restaurant is too crowded, and even if that were not the case, there is a natural limit, given the capacity of a restaurant, which is well below the total market size. There is plenty of room in the market for other restaurants.

Now let's take the example of social networking sites. The benefit of being a member of such a site depends on how many others are members. In general, the more members there are, the more benefits there are, as it is more likely that you will be able to link up with current friends and past acquaintances. In early 2008, no one site was significantly more popular than another. MySpace had the most visitors, around 100 million per month, while Facebook was only a little behind. Enthusiastic early adopters may even have been members of more than one site. Over time, however, Facebook has pulled ahead, becoming the largest of the sites and establishing a critical mass that makes it more attractive to every new potential member. By early 2010—so within a space of only two years—Facebook had more than five times as many monthly visitors as its nearest rivals.[36] This critical mass becomes a serious barrier to entry and expansion for

---

[36] To see this effect, go to: <http://www.businessinsider.com/chart-of-the-day-unique-visitors-social-networking-sites-2010-4>, where you can see Silicon Alley Insider Chart of the Day, 'Unique Visitors On Global Social Networking Sites'.

all other sites. A new entrant cannot simply steal a few customers from Facebook and build up slowly over time. The network effect means that an entrant must be able to establish a critical mass quickly to become a viable competitor. Indeed, most of Facebook's direct rivals have declined in size. Twitter and LinkedIn did manage to grow because both have differentiated themselves from Facebook to provide a different type of social networking service rather than compete head-to-head with Facebook.

Markets where standardization brings benefits can also exhibit significant network effects that lead to strong and enduring barriers to entry. Microsoft is the classic example—its success in the market for PC operating systems has led to it being the global standard, and competition authorities have worried about this:

> Microsoft's dominance presents extraordinary features in that Windows (in its successive forms) is not only a dominant product on the relevant market for client PC operating systems, but it is the *de facto* standard operating system product for client PCs.[37]

Do network effects mean the end of all competition? Not necessarily. They may be exhausted well below the total market size—as in the restaurant example above. Microsoft has been found to be virtually super-dominant as a result of the network effect in PC operating systems. Yet even Windows never achieved a 100% share of all PCs in the world, as other operating systems, such as Apple Mac OS, continue to exist alongside it, again mainly because they have to some extent differentiated themselves.[38] In other markets, several platforms can coexist (and compete) despite the presence of network effects. An example of this is the video game console market, with Nintendo Wii, Sony PlayStation 3, and Microsoft Xbox 360 all currently maintaining a position in the market (in section 3.8 we discuss how this current situation differs dramatically from that ten years ago when the UK Monopolies and Mergers Commission believed that Nintendo and Sega had durable positions of market power because of network effects).

Networks can also interconnect and standards can be made interoperable. In this way, different producers can compete with each other within the confines of that common network, platform, or standard. Manufacturers of Blu-ray disc players can compete with each other as Blu-ray has now become the accepted new industry standard for high-definition video, so all discs will operate on this standard. Sometimes interoperability or interconnection can be achieved through commercial negotiation (see also Chapter 5), and sometimes it requires government intervention. The main point here is that interoperability, however achieved, means that competing companies can benefit from the same network effects. Significant parts of the IT sector are now based on 'open source', which means that access to the source code and other proprietary information is open to others, who can modify and develop the software or hardware further. Prominent examples include the Linux operating systems and the

---

[37] *Microsoft* (Case COMP/C-3/37.792), Commission Decision of 24 March 2004, [472].
[38] Ibid., [432].

Mozilla Firefox Internet browser. Thus, the presence of network effects does not inevitably result in insurmountable entry barriers.

Two-sided network effects are a specific form of network effects that can raise barriers to entry (we explained this concept in Chapter 2). They arise where platforms bring together two different types of customer in some form of common pursuit. Examples are dating agencies and nightclubs bringing together men and women; payment systems bringing together retailers and customers; or a newspaper bringing together advertisers and readers. Entry barriers of this type were found in the market for printed classified directory advertising. Yell was the largest producer of such services in the UK. It issued a regionally varied publication delivered to all homes with classified advertising and had been subject to price regulation. In 2006 the CC concluded that this price regulation needed to continue. Although the Internet was becoming an increasingly important constraint on Yell's business, it was still considered to be in a separate market. Within the market for classified directory advertising in the UK, Yell was found to have a market share of 75% and to benefit from strong barriers to entry and expansion in the market arising from the two-sided network effects that exist:

> entry barriers are high and include the network effect referred to above and the need to establish a strong brand identity . . .

> the incumbency position of the largest player is reinforced by the network effects present in this market. Other providers wishing to expand have to build usage in order to attract advertisers. This requires investment, particularly in usage advertising, and acts as a barrier to expansion.[39]

A few years later, the Dutch competition authority (NMa) approved a merger between the only two providers of paper-based classified directories in the Netherlands partly because the provision of such advertising services over the Internet was considered a close substitute.[40] In section 3.8 we return to the topic of assessing market power in innovative markets.

3.5 COLLECTIVE DOMINANCE, TACIT COLLUSION, AND EFFECTIVE COMPETITION

The discussion so far has concentrated on unilateral, single-firm market power. But market power can also arise in markets with only a few large suppliers that do not compete very vigorously. This results in a situation of collective dominance or lack of effective competition, which can be of concern in abuse of collective dominance cases

---

[39] Competition Commission (2006), 'Classified Directory Advertising Services market investigation', 21 December, [54(a)]. We advised the investigated party during this inquiry.

[40] NMa (2008), 'European Directories—Truvo Nederland', Decision in Case 6246, 28 August.

(see Chapter 4), in market investigations in the UK under the Enterprise Act 2002 (which deal with markets where competition is not effective; various examples of this are discussed throughout the book), and in particular in merger cases. In oligopolistic markets, the relationship between total market demand and economies of scale means that there is room for only a limited number of firms in the market (as explained in Chapter 1). No one firm can act independently of the others, but each can influence market outcomes in some way. In this section we outline the economics of oligopoly markets. We then go on to consider the situations in which these firms are likely to coordinate their actions so as to achieve the same outcome as a monopolist would. For collective dominance or tacit collusion to exist, the market must be an oligopoly, but we shall see that this is not a sufficient condition.

3.5.1 OLIGOPOLISTIC MARKETS

The core economic models of duopoly—a market with two firms—were developed in the nineteenth century by two French economists. These models are easily extendable to a larger numbers of firms (oligopoly). Cournot's (1838) model assumes that there are capacity constraints in production so the two firms commit in advance to the production quantity and then place their product in the market, which clears at a price where supply meets demand. The firms make identical products. Real-world examples that come close to this model include package tour operators booking a year ahead the number of charter flights and hotel rooms they think they will sell in the following holiday period (see the *Airtours* case below); and law firms that must determine their levels of employment of competition lawyers in advance of selling their services in the market, since the training of staff to the requisite standard takes months or years.

In deciding on the level of output, each firm recognizes that its profit will depend on the choice made by the other firm. Through assuming the other firm will behave in a similarly rational, profit-maximizing manner, each can choose an optimal output level, given its knowledge of market demand and its assumption that the other firm will not change its output. Each then effectively behaves like a monopolist on its residual demand, ie, the amount of the demand left after the other firm's production decision. Because of the capacity constraints, the two firms cannot adjust their choices once the behaviour of their rival is revealed. Without going into detail on the mathematics of the model, the result is an intuitive one: output, price, and profits in Cournot oligopoly will lie somewhere between those of the competitive market and a monopoly market. The essence of the Cournot model is that the two firms are still competing with one another but they recognize their interdependence. This means that they can achieve prices above the competitive level and can exploit some market power. However, this market power falls short of what could be achieved if there were a monopoly, as neither firm has the incentive to restrict its output to (half) the monopoly level because each knows that the other will then produce more and capture a greater market share. This results in a market output greater than the monopoly level. Achieving a joint-profit maximizing output would require coordination (tacit or explicit) between the two—see below. Interestingly, if the Cournot approach is extended to more than two firms in a market then with each additional firm the Cournot solution moves further away from the monopoly outcome, increasing total output until it approaches the competitive level. In terms of the Lerner index (see section 3.3), the price–cost margin in the Cournot model increases directly with the HHI (the more concentrated the market, the higher the margin).

Bertrand (1883) altered the assumption that there are capacity constraints and in so doing dramatically changed the predictions of the market outcomes under duopoly. He posited that instead of choosing output in advance, the duopolists chose their price. Without capacity constraints they are able to adjust their price once they see the choice made by their rival. Bertrand's model shows that, under these conditions, price and output will be the same as in the competitive equilibrium. To see why, imagine that one firm chooses a price that is 5% lower than its rival's. With no capacity constraints, the cheaper firm captures all the demand for the product, as we also assume that customers are perfectly informed. The more expensive firm then seeks to adjust its price below that of its rival in order to steal back the demand. This interaction continues until the price is at the level of costs and neither firm can profitably undercut the other. The conclusion is that even in a market with only two firms you can get effective competition. Understanding the characteristics of the market will be central to knowing which outcome is more likely. The more sticky the output and price are, the more the Cournot predictions are likely to hold. In general, the Cournot approach has been found to be the better predictor of actual market outcomes. Yet IO economists now more commonly use Bertrand as their base model, but with differentiated goods. In the differentiated Bertrand model, prices are raised further above marginal cost the more differentiated the products are.

Since the seminal works of Cournot and Bertrand there have been many extensions of these models. Variants we have already seen are where there are more than two firms or where products are differentiated (heterogeneous) rather than homogeneous. The assumption on what firms expect their rivals to do can also be varied (referred to as 'conjectural variation'). The standard assumption described above is that firms see their rivals' choices as fixed, in quantities (Cournot) or prices (Bertrand). This can be changed to expectations that, in Cournot, quantity changes will be fully met by rivals at one extreme—which will result in a monopoly outcome—or at the other extreme that changes will be fully offset by rivals—ie, if one firm increases its quantity, it expects others to reduce their quantities proportionately; this leads to an outcome resembling perfect competition.

The Cournot and Bertrand models are static oligopoly models. Like the standard monopoly, monopolistic competition and perfect competition models that we saw previously, they refer to only one time period. Firms select their output or price, the market clears, and that's it. These models have provided significant insight into the outcomes that you can expect in markets that are neither monopolistic nor perfectly competitive. Of greater interest for our purposes here are dynamic oligopoly models, based on game theory. These take the Cournot and (more commonly) differentiated Bertrand models as the starting point, but then play these games over and over again. This opens the possibility of signalling, reputation, and retaliation effects between the firms, and hence allows us to analyse tacit collusion. We turn to this topic now.

3.5.2 TACIT COLLUSION: THE PRISONER'S DILEMMA AND HOW OLIGOPOLISTS CAN OVERCOME IT

Dynamic oligopoly theory deals extensively with tacit collusion. For the purposes of competition law, tacit collusion can also be referred to as collective or joint dominance, coordinated effects, concerted practices, or conscious parallelism—the economics are essentially the same. In markets with certain characteristics, firms may naturally recognize their shared incentive to limit production and raise prices without any formal communication. Given the absence of any formal coordination or communication, it is economics that is at the core of these cases. To identify the existence of this type of market power it is important to assess the market structure and, within this, the behaviour of these firms. We do not discuss the issues that arise from formal coordination, such as in a price-fixing or market-sharing cartel—these practices are covered in Chapter 5. The economic principles of explicit coordination are in fact the same as those covered here; the difference is that, in those cases, firms use formal mechanisms (contracts or cartel agreements) to enforce the common policy—here we look at where such outcomes are tacit and self-policing.

So, if the two oligopolists in the market recognize their interdependence, will they always find a cosy solution that benefits both, where they don't compete too hard but settle on a price and output that maximizes their joint profits? Unfortunately for the oligopolists—and fortunately for consumers—the answer is no. The mere recognition of their interdependence is insufficient. Effective coordination requires more than that. This is because oligopolists face a fundamental problem that they cannot overcome without some form of collusion: the attractiveness of cheating on each other. To understand this point, it is useful to think of a simple, often-examined, example from game theory known as the prisoner's dilemma. Game theory is a branch of mathematics that looks at strategic interactions between players and predicts behaviour in response to the structure of the game and its incentives. It is commonly used in economics in trying to understand firms' behaviour and lies at the heart of modern IO theory. Given the set-up of a game, players may have dominant strategies, that is, strategies that give a player its highest pay-off regardless of the strategic choice made by the other player. If both players have a dominant strategy, the outcome is thus predictable; this is known as a Nash equilibrium, after the pioneering work in this area by the mathematician John Nash (1950).

Figure 3.2 shows this game in the form of a pay-off matrix. The set of strategies available for the two duopolists, firm 1 and firm 2, is to price either 'high' or 'low'. Both move simultaneously. There are four possible outcomes to this game. If firm 1 decides to price high and firm 2 prices low, firm 1 receives a pay-off of zero while firm 2 gets the whole

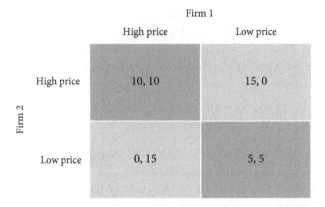

Fig. 3.2 Pay-off matrix for the oligopoly (prisoner's) dilemma game

market for itself and receives €15. We are in the bottom-left cell of the matrix. If it is firm 1 that undercuts firm 2's attempt to price high, we are in the top-right cell and the pay-offs are reversed (both firms have exactly the same size and costs in this example). If both price low, they get €5 each (bottom-right cell). If both price high, they get €10 (top-left). You can see that this (10, 10) cell is the joint preferred outcome for both firms. Let's say it is the joint-profit-maximizing outcome, while the bottom-right cell represents the competitive outcome (which can be Cournot or Bertrand; this does not really matter here). Will they reach the joint desired outcome of (10, 10)?

Consider firm 2's preferred choice given each of firm 1's possible strategies. If firm 1 prices high, firm 2 will prefer to price low, steal the market and earn high returns (it gets €15, rather than just €10 if it also prices high). If firm 1 prices low, firm 2 will again prefer to price low, rather than have the market stolen from it and earn nothing if it prices high (the €5 thus obtained is better than zero). This means that firm 2's dominant strategy is to always price low, regardless of what firm 1 does. The game is symmetric, so firm 1 has the same dominant strategy of pricing low. They therefore end up in the bottom-right of the matrix, each obtaining a profit of €5. Clearly not what they had hoped to achieve.

Looking at the market, both companies would like to reach the point where they both price high, and therefore both obtain the high profits of €10 each. However, this is not a stable equilibrium because each could gain even more by cheating and pricing low while the other prices high. This incentive to compete and undercut one's rival is present even in a duopoly, and it shows that collusion is not necessarily the natural outcome in an oligopolistic market. The more firms there are in the market, the more likely it is that one of them will find the temptation to cheat irresistible. This fundamental oligopolist dilemma is good news for consumers and competition authorities. The original prisoner's dilemma has two prisoners who committed a crime jointly, but are interrogated separately, and who get the choice between 'confessing' and 'not confessing'. The game has the same pay-off structure, with confessing being like pricing low and not confessing like pricing high. Ideally they would both like not to confess and walk free, but the temptation for both to confess and get a reward while the other gets locked up proves too tempting, so both end up confessing. You may notice some similarity with the leniency policy for cartel infringements that has been introduced, successfully, by many competition regimes around the world—the first company to blow the whistle on the cartel gets immunity from fines, and many cartelists have succumbed to the temptation. We discuss this in Chapter 5.

Alas, oligopolists (and the economists modelling their behaviour) have a number of ways of getting round the dilemma. In the real world, they do not play the Cournot or Bertrand game only once. Rather, they meet each other time and time again in the same market, or indeed in other markets. Dynamic oligopoly takes account of the fact that the nature of rivalry between oligopolists is not limited to a single game in a single time period. The dynamic interaction over time allows the firms to learn about their rival's behaviour, and between them the firms could reach an implicit understanding about behaviour that is in their common interest. These interactions provide the scope for coordination, signalling, and reputation building. Importantly, no explicit collusion is required; firms can anticipate the likely reactions of their rivals. For example, if firm 1 always prices low when firm 2 prices low, but responds to an increase in firm 2's price by likewise increasing its price, firm 2 may note this behaviour and continue to price high. In this case the two firms have reached the joint profit nirvana of (10, 10). But firm 2 will still have an incentive to cheat and diverge from this 'high'–'high' outcome to earn higher profits of €15 for a while. If firm 1's response is then rapidly to price low as well, both firms gain only €5 in the next period and end up not trusting each other anymore.

Hence, members of the oligopoly need to devise an effective retaliation mechanism in order for 'high' pricing to be the economically sustainable outcome. A 'low' price reaction to another firm's divergence is a form of retaliation or punishment, even though both firms suffer the consequences. In general, for sustained collusion the cost from the punishment needs to exceed the gain from divergence, so will be influenced by the difference in return between the two strategies (here €15 – €10 = €5) and the speed with which a firm can retaliate (over how many periods the €15 return is earned, ie, how long before cheating is detected and acted against). Because of all the interdependencies in terms of the rewards for cheating, speed of punishment, and the discount rate of the firms (ie, the degree to which they value future profits less than current profits), these dynamic oligopoly models give a wide range of predictions of the likelihood of tacit collusion. However, they do provide useful insight into the kind of conditions you need in the market for tacit collusion to be sustainable. These conditions have made their way into EU case law on collective dominance, in particular the *Airtours* judgment, to which we turn now.

3.5.3 THE *AIRTOURS* CONDITIONS

In *Gencor* (1999) the General Court (then Court of First Instance) defined collective dominance as the 'relationship of interdependence' between the parties of an oligopoly that 'encourages them to align their conduct in such a way as to maximise joint profits'.[41] The General Court's assessment of the European Commission's decision to block Airtours' proposed acquisition of First Choice further confirms this approach to joint dominance.[42] In this case, the Commission had pretty much relied on oligopolistic interdependence in the market in a static sense, with tour operators behaving like Cournot oligopolists setting quantities (as we noted above). The General Court stated that this was insufficient, and that collective (or joint) dominance arises when the adoption of a long-lasting common policy by the members of an oligopoly is 'possible, economically rational, and hence preferable'.[43] It translated this into guidance in the form of the following three conditions that need to be met to support a concern of collective dominance. First, the members of the 'dominant oligopoly' must have the ability to monitor the other members (transparency). This makes economic sense: the market must be sufficiently transparent such that members can coordinate without communication and can easily detect deviations so there is limited opportunity for cheating. Second, suitable retaliation mechanisms must exist should one of the oligopolists cheat. Third, the reaction of current and future competitors, as well as consumers, should not destabilize the outcome of the common policy. This basically means that all suppliers in the market must participate and entry barriers must be high.

In assessing whether these conditions are met, an understanding of the nature of the oligopoly and the market is necessary. As we have seen in our earlier discussion of oligopoly theory, a wide range of outcomes is possible within these market structures. The following questions and indicators are of relevance in assessing which of these outcomes is most likely. First, can the members collude tacitly, ie, without communication? And will they notice when a rival defects on the implicit agreement? Indicators of this are: transparent pricing (this makes it easier to coordinate prices and to detect cheating by the other oligopoly members); and whether products are homogeneous (if they are, the oligopolists will understand each other's cost structures and competition and coordination need to focus only on price). Second, do the members have a punishment mechanism with which to retaliate? Indicators of this are: excess capacity (this is the easiest way to retaliate, by being able to quickly increase production and therefore lower the market price in response to cheating); multi-market contact (retaliation can occur in another market where the firms also compete); and the speed of price adjustment (if prices or output choices are committed significantly in advance and cannot be easily altered, the ability to retaliate will be restricted). Third, is the oligopoly sufficiently stable to reward tacitly colluding members over a reasonable period of time? Indicators that would be supportive of this are: where only very few firms compete in the market (EU case law has called this 'tight' oligopoly', a term that does not really exist in the economic theory of oligopoly); high entry barriers and inelastic demand; and

---

[41] Case T-102/96 *Gencor v Commission* [1999] 4 CMLR 971, [276].

[42] Case T-342/99 *Airtours plc v EC Commission* [2004] ECR II-1785.

[43] Ibid., at [61].

stable demand and low levels of technological change (these again ensure that the coordinated outcome can persist).

One of the challenges with analysing oligopoly markets is known as the 'topsy-turvy principle'. Indicators such as excess capacity can signal that the market will be very competitive, as firms will have a strong incentive to price low to capture market share and earn revenue to cover the fixed costs of operation. However, as set out above, excess capacity may be the means by which a tacitly collusive equilibrium is supported. It is precisely the fact that fierce competition can result in very low prices (because of the excess capacity) that gives extra inducement to tacitly collude and keep the prices high.

3.5.4 CASES OF COLLECTIVE DOMINANCE: MINING, TOUR OPERATORS, AND RECORDED MUSIC

Against this framework we can consider some cases to understand the assessment of tacit collusion. The merger of two major platinum and rhodium mining companies, Gencor and Lonrho, was blocked on the basis of collective dominance.[44] Although this decision was taken before *Airtours*, it meets the criteria set out therein. The market was found to meet the transparency requirements as there was only moderate growth in demand, a mature production technology, and firms with very similar cost structures. It was also a 'tight' oligopoly with significant barriers to entry—the merged entity and one other firm would have accounted for a combined market share of around 80%. The international commodity nature of the products meant that there was significant price transparency and the firms had financial links and multi-market contacts, so detection of deviation would be relatively swift and certain. Retaliation would be possible because of significant excess capacity and the homogeneous nature of the metal products.

We have set out the economic principles that underlie *Airtours*, but what was the result of the factual application of these principles to this case? Airtours and First Choice were two major package tour operators based in the UK. The Commission's disputed decision stated that a merger is to be blocked on the grounds of collective dominance when the degree of interdependence between the oligopolists is such that it is rational for them to restrict output.[45] The Commission did not consider the presence of a retaliation mechanism to be a condition for collective dominance. This conclusion was at the core of the Court's rejection of the prohibition decision: competing oligopolists will always have an incentive to restrict output, but the degree of restriction will be greater if there is coordination among the oligopolists. The Court reassessed the facts and concluded that the merger would not lead to a jointly dominant market structure. The Court did not consider the market to be transparent, since flight and accommodation commitments were negotiated on a confidential basis at least one year in advance. Rival tour operators would not necessarily know the full range of locations that others

---

[44] Case T-102/96 *Gencor Limited v Commission* [1999] ECR II-753.
[45] *Airtours/First Choice* (Case IV/M.1524) [2000] OJ L93/1, [54].

had developed until the brochures for the next holiday season were released. Thus it would be hard to coordinate tacitly on output choices. Most importantly, retaliation was considered to be difficult. Since capacity choices were made more than a year ahead, there was limited excess capacity for firms to use for punishment of a rival that deviated from the collusive outcome. Adding extra capacity late in the annual process (once the brochures of rivals had been produced) was expensive, difficult, and generally of lower quality. Hence the core criteria to maintain the collusive equilibrium were not met.

In another case that reached the European courts, Sony had sought to acquire the BMG music business, leading to a concentration in the market for recorded music. The merged entity would have a market share of 20%–25% and the industry would move from five to four major international players. The Commission cleared the merger, rejecting the alleged risk of collective dominance post-merger.[46] The General Court overturned this decision after an appeal by Impala, an association of independent music producers, forcing the Commission to re-examine the case.[47] The Court's main concern was that this was indeed a market in which joint dominance was likely to be a concern. The Commission found that the products were not homogeneous, as different majors focused on different genres. While there was reasonable transparency of pricing, there was frequent discounting of list prices that undermined this transparency and would likely disrupt attempts to coordinate. There was a possible mechanism for retaliation—via exclusion of a major's recording artists from compilation albums—but there was little evidence that this had ever been used. The Court disagreed with the Commission's assessment. It found that the market was in fact sufficiently transparent for effective monitoring by members of the 'dominant oligopoly' to take place. Even in the absence of direct evidence of transparency in the market, the Court considered that the fact that prices were closely aligned and in excess of competitive levels was sufficient, given that there was no alternative reasonable explanation for these features. The General Court's assessment of past pricing behaviour led it to conclude that tacit coordination was likely to be already present in the market. Yet in the end the Commission reinstated its clearance. This case illustrates that, even when using the same framework and analysing the same facts, judgements can differ markedly in terms of whether tacit collusion is likely to exist in the future.[48]

3.6 PROFITABILITY AS A MEASURE OF MARKET POWER

3.6.1 PROFITABILITY CAPTURES THE ESSENCE OF MARKET POWER

The most direct means of measuring market power is to understand the relationship between the costs of the company and the prices it charges, since the essence of market

---

[46] *Sony/BMG* (Case COMP/M.3333) [2005] OJ L62/30.

[47] Case T-464/04 *Independent Music Publishers and Labels Association (Impala association internationale) v EC Commission* [2006] ECR II-2289.

[48] For a discussion of the economics of this case, see Pilsbury (2007).

power is the ability to charge high prices and earn high profits for a sustained period of time without being undermined by consumers switching or competitors entering the market. In the theoretical world of perfect competition, prices would equal marginal cost. In the real world, fixed costs are present even in competitive markets and so the profit mark-up over marginal cost may need to be high to cover these fixed costs. Prices and costs may also fluctuate over time. So if not through a simple price–cost comparison, how can you measure market power directly? The answer is through profitability analysis. In competitive markets, companies are expected to make profits in the long run that are broadly in line with the minimum returns required by investors (ie, the cost of capital). Profits above the cost of capital would invite entry by new competitors, and profits below would induce exit. It is the presence of high profits that normally signals to other firms to enter the market. Hence, observing returns that are persistently and significantly above of the competitive level captures the essence of market power. It tells you that there is a profitable opportunity that is not being exploited by new entrants, from which you can deduce that entry barriers are significant and that some degree of unilateral market power or lack of effective competition (tacit collusion) is keeping profits high.

Over shorter time periods, however, profits could diverge from the cost of capital for a variety of reasons, not all of which are necessarily related to market power or anti-competitive practices—for example, economic cycles, windfall gains that are not related to a company's main operations, or temporarily high profits in dynamic, innovative markets. Therefore, in addition to the cost of capital, information on returns made by appropriate comparator companies or industries may be considered as benchmarks for the profitability assessment. The idea is to examine profits made in companies or industries that are known to be competitive but that otherwise face similar economic circumstances to the company of interest. These comparators will indicate how returns are expected to vary but for the alleged market power (Oxera, 2003a).

Profitability can provide important insights into the degree of competitiveness in a market as a whole, as well as into the market power of individual companies. This is particularly relevant for oligopolistic markets where no single company is dominant, but where the competition authority may be concerned about the (limited) degree of competitive pressure that the few companies in the market impose on each other, as we saw in section 3.5. Economic theory predicts that some oligopolistic markets can be very competitive, leading to prices close to costs, while others can exhibit prices close to monopoly levels. In both situations, assessing profitability can shed light on the degree of competition in a way that other techniques cannot. Persistent and high profits are consistent with the presence of entry barriers. An incumbent may have access to specific knowledge or other resources that enable it persistently to produce more efficiently than its rivals, which do not have access to the same resources. Or entrants may face other entry barriers, as discussed in section 3.4, such as economies of scale, sunk costs, or lack of access to essential inputs.

Profitability analysis has been a well-established, if evolving, component of competition cases in the UK for many years. In particular, the CC's market investigation guidelines suggest that where profitability is persistently and substantially above the competitive benchmark for a company that constitutes a significant proportion of the market, there is prima facie evidence of the presence of significant entry barriers.[49] The use of profitability analysis by other competition authorities has been more limited compared with the UK. We saw in Chapter 2 that the US Supreme Court referred to DuPont's profitability as an indicator of its monopoly power in the famous cellophane case of 1956, but the use of profitability analysis is less fashionable in the USA these days.[50] The European Commission conducted a profitability analysis as part of its review of the extent of competition in the payment cards and retail banking industries in the EU.[51] The Dutch competition authority has conducted profitability analysis in a number of cases, but this was to show an abuse of dominance, not as an indicator of market power (see Chapter 4, where we will also explain that there is an important difference between these two uses of profitability analysis).

The techniques of profitability analysis are used not just in competition investigations. They are also employed by credit rating agencies, investors, and for investment appraisal by companies. However, there is a distinction between accounting profitability, which simply uses accounting data to calculate profitability ratios at a point in time, and economic profitability, which typically measures profitability over the economic lifetime of the assets in question. It is the latter form of profitability that can provide the most meaningful and reliable information about the state of competition in a market. Profitability assessment and its tools are of relevance to a wide range of competition policy issues. We present it here as part of the economics toolkit for assessing market power—whether a company can raise prices consistently and profitably above competitive levels. However, there are many aspects of competition investigations where profitability may be relevant: the assessment of margin squeeze or excessive pricing as abuse of dominance (see Chapter 4), failing-firm analysis in a merger context (Chapter 7), state aid and subsidies (Chapter 8), the ability of a company that has infringed competition law to pay the fine (Chapter 9), and the quantification of damages (Chapter 10).

In a competition inquiry, profitability analysis should be used in conjunction with other indicators of market power such as market shares and entry barriers. This is the general framework within which profitability analysis is (intended to be) used in UK competition investigations. Knowing that profits look higher than competitive benchmarks for a company for a given period can give support to the results from the other bits of market assessment that will have been undertaken. Where high profits are found, they may be explained by a lack of competition, or they may reflect superior efficiency or temporary high profits in a dynamic market. Conversely, where profits do

---

[49] Competition Commission (2003), 'Market Investigation References: Competition Commission Guidelines', CC3, June.

[50] *US v EI du Pont de Nemours & Co* 351 US 377 (1956).

[51] European Commission (2006), 'Interim Report I: Payment Cards', 12 April and 'Interim Report II: Current Accounts and Related Services', 17 July.

not seem to exceed the benchmarks, this may mask a lack of competition that is resulting in a lack of efficiency, depressing measured returns.

What are the practical stages in analysing profitability for the purpose of assessing
market power? There are three steps. First, what is the relevant measure of profitability?
Second, how easily can we measure it, using standard accounting data? Third, how can
we tell if our estimated profits are too high or too low? We answer these three questions
in this section, first looking at the definition of measures of profitability and then
considering asset valuation and accounting issues that arise in calculating the preferred
metrics. We next look at the appropriate benchmarks for competitive returns. Finally,
we consider issues around the interpretation of the results. In particular, if high profits
are found, are they due to market power or superior efficiency? What indicators would
suggest that returns are the appropriate reward for innovation or investment?

3.6.2 MEASURES OF PROFITABILITY

A number of metrics can be used for the profit performance of a company. Commonly
used measures include return on capital employed (ROCE), return on sales (ROS), and
gross margins. In the context of economic profitability analysis, the conceptually correct approach is to apply the internal rate of return (IRR) and net present value (NPV)
measures.[52] These measures reflect the way in which companies make investment
decisions in real-world markets. The intuition is that the IRR and NPV match the pattern of cash flows associated with economic activities—an initial cash outflow followed
by a series of net cash inflows in subsequent periods. IRR and NPV are the standard
theoretical methods of investment appraisal, and also the ones most commonly used in
the business world. In a survey of 392 chief financial officers of companies in the USA
and Canada, Graham and Harvey (2001) found that around 75% always or almost always
use the IRR or NPV as their evaluation technique. The NPV of a stream of earnings into
the future tells you how much those earnings are worth to someone today. The value will
differ depending on how risky those earnings are and how patient the person is. These
aspects are captured in the discount rate used to calculate the NPV (we explain the
logic of discounting in Chapter 10 as well). Let's take a simple example where you
are promised a stream of earnings for five years of €100 per year, with each payment
to arrive at the start of each year. Being impatient, your discount rate is 10%. Your
valuation of each more distant year reduces (alternatively, we could say that your
next-best alternative for the money would be to put it in the bank and earn 10% interest
per year on it). So while today's €100 is worth that to you, next year's is worth only
€90.91 currently and the fifth payment you receive is worth only €68.30. The NPV of
that promised income is €416.99. This means you would be prepared to give only
€416.99 today to receive the rights to the €500 income over five years. This can be
thought of as an investment project. With a discount rate of 10%, the NPV would be

---

[52] See, for example, Oxera (2003a) and Morris (2003).

zero if you invested €416.99 and then received five payments of €100 as a reward for the investment.

If now you consider that the future income may be risky, your discount rate will increase. If it increases to 20%, your NPV of the promised income is only €358.87, with the fifth €100 payment having a value of €48.23. With this higher discount rate, the maximum you would be prepared to invest (ie, the point at which your NPV is zero) is €358.87 to receive the future income. The IRR is linked to this NPV concept. For a given investment and costs and revenue streams, it tells you the discount rate that would mean the NPV is zero. For example, a grocery supplier may decide to invest in some research into a new ready-meal product. There will be a period of initial cash outflows while the product is being developed and marketed, followed by a series of net cash inflows in subsequent periods while it is being sold. There is uncertainty over the future revenues, so the grocery supplier asks itself what the return on this project is by calculating the discount rate that would make the company indifferent to making the investment. This is the IRR.

The IRR and the NPV therefore take into account the inflows and outflows of an activity over time, and reflect the economic principle of the time preference of money (Kay, 1976 and Edwards et al., 1987). As the CC noted in its market investigation into store cards:

> Financial theory underlying investment decision making, valuation and related matters focuses on the amounts and timing of the cash flows of the activity and leads to the conclusion that the most satisfactory basis for assessing rate of return is a calculation of the IRR on a DCF [discounted cash flow] basis.[53]

A company would choose to undertake an investment if the IRR is greater than the company's cost of capital or its hurdle rate for new projects. The cost of capital reflects the return required by investors to invest in the company's activities rather than elsewhere. If the IRR is greater, this means that the return is more than enough to compensate the company for the risk it will face in undertaking the investment.

This investment appraisal principle can be applied to the concept of competitive markets. In theory, free entry and exit should eventually lead to a market outcome in which the returns made in the market are equal to the cost of having to remunerate providers of capital to the company or industry. Consider the example of the investor above. If the NPV of the cash flows, obtained using the cost of capital as the discount rate, were positive, or the IRR of the activity were greater than the cost of capital, it would be profitable to invest and enter the market. Other investors would make the same decision. With each additional entrant, the market returns fall (because of increased price competition) until the point at which the IRR equals the cost of capital (or the NPV equals zero). By contrast, if the IRR were persistently and substantially

---

[53] Competition Commission (2006), 'Store cards market investigation', Final Report, Appendix 8.4, [14].

above the competitive benchmark, this would indicate the existence of entry barriers and hence market power.

For the purposes of competition analysis, there is usually a need to measure the IRR over a specific period during the lifespan of an economic activity, rather than over the entire period of a project or business activity. This is not only because you usually will not have data for the entire lifetime of the company (for example, if the grocery supplier we saw previously was formed in the 1950s, and shows no signs of exiting the market any time soon), but also because you are normally interested in current market power (so you want to assess profitability for only a limited but significant number of past and future years—see below). In practice, therefore, a 'truncated IRR' can be calculated using accounting information on net cash flows during the period under consideration.[54] Since only a segment of the lifespan of an investment is considered, the initial asset value is treated as a cash outflow and the residual value at the end of the period is treated as an inflow (as if the activity were sold off at the end). The intuition is that we are taking a snapshot of the company's assets at two moments in time, and then calculating the returns within the time period, including changes to the company's asset base.

The key information required to measure the truncated IRR or NPV is, first, cashflow data for the activity in question over a reasonable length of time; and second, estimates of the value of assets employed in that activity at the start and end of the truncated period. Cash flow data is normally available from a company's audited accounts. It might be more tricky to obtain if the competition concern relates to a particular line of business that is not separately reported in accounts, in which case cost- and revenue-allocation exercises are required. A company's management accounts may provide the relevant information for this. The truncated IRR and NPV are not straightforward to measure. Valuing assets may be complicated, if, for example, the business employs a lot of intangible assets. These problems are often, but not always, capable of resolution.

3.6.3 ACCOUNTING VERSUS ECONOMIC MEASURES OF PROFITABILITY

ROCE is the profit earned by a company divided by the level of capital employed in the business over the same period. Usually the period for the calculation is a year; where the period of interest is longer, a series of annual ROCE estimates is produced. The profit used is normally an accounting return based on profit before interest and tax but after depreciation and amortization (technically termed EBIT—earnings before interest and tax). This profit figure is divided by the capital employed, which is usually taken as fixed assets less net liabilities. See also the diagram and discussion of ROCE in Chapter 8. An alternative measure is return on equity (ROE).

---

[54] This method was developed in Edwards et al. (1987).

The ROCE or ROE calculation produces a percentage that represents the return achieved as a proportion of the capital employed. In order to determine whether these returns are reasonable, it is necessary to have a benchmark, and for ROCE this is usually taken as the cost of capital of the company in question (for ROE it is the cost of equity). However, the ROCE is not very informative on the underlying economic profitability of an activity. In fact, the annual ROCE measures are very likely to differ from the IRR. The main reason is that the numerator and the denominator in the calculation of ROCE are sensitive to variations in accounting practices (over time and across companies). In contrast, the truncated IRR calculation uses actual cash flows in each year rather than earnings. Cash flows are a relatively 'hard' statistic, so the profile of returns are not sensitive to accounting schedules. The EBIT figure in the ROCE numerator is particularly affected by the choice of depreciation schedules and accruals. Accruals are costs (or revenues) incurred (or earned) in one period but paid for (or received) in cash in another period. They can cause a significant wedge between the actual cash inflows and outflows in a period and the revenues and costs, and hence profits, assigned to that period. The denominator in the annual ROCE estimate is highly sensitive to depreciation schedules. This can affect the usefulness of year-to-year (or company-to-company) comparisons of ROCE over a particular period of time. For example, in its inquiry into train leasing, the CC noted that:

> because [the train lessors] operate asset-intensive businesses, accounting returns are very sensitive to the accounting depreciation applied to those assets, which may not reflect their economic value. We also noted that as an asset ages, its NBV [net book value] declines and where the rental remains constant this will lead to an increase in ROCE, which may not accurately reflect the economic profitability of the asset.[55]

In the classified directory advertising services market investigation, the CC also expressed its preference for the truncated IRR and recognized the limitations of the ROCE-based measures.[56]

The literature has established a theoretical relationship between the IRR and ROCE.[57] In short, the IRR can be expressed as a weighted average of the ROCEs. However, the weights that would have to apply to the ROCE are highly specific, and if all the information is available to calculate the average ROCE in this way, that same information might as well be used to estimate the IRR directly. Therefore, from an economic perspective, the ROCE is not the best measure of profitability, despite the fact that several past competition cases have relied on it.

In certain circumstances it may be appropriate to use other measures of profitability, including accounting ratios such as return on sales (ROS) and gross margins. These are essentially snapshots of a company's performance at particular points in time.

---

[55] Competition Commission (2009), 'Rolling Stock Leasing Market Investigation', Final Report, 7 April, Appendix 6.4, [2]. We advised one of the three investigated parties in this inquiry.

[56] Competition Commission (2006), 'Classified Directory Advertising Services market investigation', 21 December.

[57] See Kay (1976) and Peasnell (1982).

ROS measures earnings as a proportion of sales. Gross margins are sales net of the cost of goods sold (gross profit) as a proportion of sales. Different companies may include different items in the category of 'cost of goods sold' in their accounts, so comparisons of gross margins across companies must be made carefully. Gross margins may be more robust than ROS where overheads are difficult to allocate. These accounting ratios are often easier and more convenient to obtain than the IRR or ROCE, particularly in cases where it is difficult to estimate the assets employed. However, the ROS and gross margin measures in themselves do not give much useful information for the purpose of assessing entry barriers, since they do not take into account the capital and risk that is involved in the activity.

For example, in its inquiry into retail banking, the European Commission requested annual revenue and cost data over the period 2000–04 for the payment card activities of 203 issuing and acquiring banks across the then 25 Member States.[58] (Issuing banks issue cards to cardholders; acquiring banks deal with the merchants that accept the cards for payment.) Where necessary, these institutions were required to allocate revenue and costs between their various activities. Profitability was measured with the use of a cost mark-up (revenue minus costs, divided by costs) for each of the companies that submitted data, and the Commission used this profit ratio to measure the distribution of profitability of financial institutions, as well as the differentials between countries and how the profit ratio evolved over time. The analysis led the Commission to conclude that profitability in the issuing of payment cards (credit and debit) was high and sustained over time. However, the range for the estimated cost mark-ups was typically very large—for example, between around –50% and 132% in the issuing of credit cards. Since capital costs are excluded from the cost mark-up, it is difficult to compare results across different banking activities—capital costs would be likely to be higher in issuing than on the acquiring side, as a result of banks' need to provision against default by cardholders.[59]

3.6.4 ASSET VALUATION

As we have set out, profits reflect the returns that investors gain from investing in a business. This investment is reflected in the value of the assets that are created and so these assets are a key element of calculating returns. The value of assets (such as buildings, machinery, brands) acts as a 'denominator' in the analysis of returns, against which cash flows are compared. Thus, for a given level of cash flows, the higher the value of the underlying assets, the lower the returns. The most readily available estimates of asset values are from audited accounts, which normally provide figures based on depreciated historical costs. Unfortunately, these do not necessarily form the right basis for valuing

---

[58] European Commission (2007), 'Communication from the Commission: Sector Inquiry under Art 17 of Regulation 1/2003 on retail banking', COM (2007) 33 final, 31 January.

[59] European Commission (2007), 'Commission staff working document accompanying the Communication from the Commission', SEC (2007) 16, 31 January, p 126.

assets when trying to assess the state of competition in a market. Indeed, the 'rules' by which assets should be valued when it comes to examining profitability in a competition setting differ from accounting conventions.

In the context of economic profitability analysis, the value-to-the-owner principle, as defined by Edwards et al. (1987), provides the correct basis for choosing between the various approaches to asset valuation. This principle requires assets to be valued at *the minimum loss that a firm would suffer were it deprived of the use of that asset*. The basis for this rule is that economic profitability concerns the cost of entry into a market and, therefore, it is appropriate to value assets according to the lowest cost of entry. If profitability still appears persistently and substantially above a competitive benchmark (eg, the cost of capital), when profitability is measured on this basis, this is indicative of limitations in the competitive process, as otherwise there would have been new entry to compete away the excess returns. The value-to-the-owner principle therefore forms the basis for the opening and closing asset values that you need for the truncated IRR calculation. You can also use this economic asset valuation to adjust the ROCE calculations (where asset values are in the denominator)—this will generally improve the usefulness of the ROCE estimations compared with using accounting values, and may bring the ROCE estimates more in line with the IRR.

The usual result of applying the value-to-the-owner principle is the modern equivalent asset (MEA) value, defined as the lowest cost of purchasing assets today that can deliver the same set of goods and services as the existing assets (this is also sometimes referred to as the depreciated replacement cost value). This may sound complicated, but MEA valuation answers a straightforward question: if the same 'output' were to be produced by a modern asset using the best available technology, what is the cost of providing that asset? Effectively, this approach allows technical efficiency to be built into the valuation, taking into account that an entrant may make use of the latest technology.

The historic cost of an asset, as reported in the accounts, may bear little resemblance to the MEA value of that asset. Furthermore, book values of assets may omit intangible assets, which can sometimes be a substantial part of a company's capital base. Intangible assets (such as brand value and human capital) are by convention typically not included on the balance sheet of companies, although recent developments in accounting standards are changing this somewhat. Failing to identify and account for intangible assets when measuring economic (as opposed to accounting) profitability could result in incorrect profitability results, and therefore wrong conclusions as to how effective competition in the market is.

According to the value-to-the-owner principle, a company's intangible assets should be valued as capitalized costs. In order for costs to be capitalized (ie, treated as capital expenditure that created an asset rather than ongoing operating costs), they need to involve an upfront commitment of capital, which over a relatively long term would be at risk of not being recovered. There are three criteria for recognizing intangible assets used by the CC: it must comprise a cost incurred now, primarily to obtain earnings in the future; this cost must be additional to those necessarily incurred at the time in running the business; and it must be identifiable as creating such an asset separate from any that arises from the general running of the business.[60]

In the case of home credit providers, the CC identified four possible categories of intangible assets: an experienced and trained workforce; the customer base; knowledge of customers' creditworthiness; and IT systems. It rejected the inclusion of corporate reputation (or brand) or start up losses as an intangible asset. The CC used the concept of 'deprival value' to measure intangible assets, which is in line with the principle of the value to the owner and values assets according to the cost to a business of being deprived of its use. It valued intangible assets in each of these areas by identifying what parts of the operating costs in these areas should be capitalized, and then capitalizing these over the estimated economic lifetime of the asset. The CC used a number of simplifying assumptions, which to some extent opened it up to criticism—for example, the useful economic lifetimes for each of these intangible assets ranged from one-and-a-half-years to five years, but the CC made a simplifying assumption that all home credit intangible assets had a useful economic lifetime of three years.

3.6.5 ACCOUNTING AND ALLOCATION ISSUES ARISING IN PROFITABILITY ASSESSMENTS

Profitability assessments rely on accounting data, and this can pose practical problems. Companies prepare accounts for purposes such as internal management and external reporting, which means that they cannot always be readily used for competition investigations. In addition, established accounting principles leave sufficient flexibility for accounting policies to differ across companies, across countries, and over time. For these reasons, a key challenge for competition authorities is to interpret and, if necessary, adjust, the available accounting data in such a way as to provide meaningful insight into the economic profitability.

The need to consider the relevant costs gives rise to the question of which costs should be included and to what extent. If companies produced only one good or service, this would be a relatively straightforward process; all the costs incurred would be directly and exclusively attributable to the good in question. Such costs are known as 'direct' costs. In general, direct costs include, for example, labour and materials used to produce that good or service. In the case of a single output, direct costs also include all overheads and any other general company expenses.

However, in reality, companies often supply more than one product and potentially operate in both upstream and downstream markets. Naturally, some costs will be shared across outputs and are not obviously related to the specific output. These are known as 'indirect' costs, and include, for example, costs of assets that are used to produce

---

[60] Competition Commission (2002), 'The Supply of Banking Services by Clearing Banks to Small and Medium-sized Enterprises' (Cm 5319), 14 March; Competition Commission (2006), 'Classified Directory Advertising Services market investigation', 21 December; Competition Commission (2006), 'Home credit market investigation', 30 November.

multiple products and overhead costs. There are two distinct types of indirect cost: joint and common. Joint costs are incurred when the production of one product simultaneously involves the production of one or more other products that cannot be separated from the first product. Common costs arise when two or more products are produced together, even though they can be produced separately. An example of a joint cost is the slaughter of a sheep which produces both a fleece and mutton. Production of the fleece automatically produces the mutton as well. An example of a common cost is a person in a human resources department of a business with a number of different divisions. The human resources person can deal with only one staff issue at a time, but it may be sufficient to have this one person who splits the time across all the divisions of the business. Thus, a common cost can be allocated to different parts of a business in line with how it is used. A joint cost, however, cannot meaningfully be allocated between its different outputs.

Some method of allocation is required for the indirect costs. Economic theory can guide the process, but it does not point to an unequivocally correct way of allocating costs across the various outputs. Different approaches may yield different results—there is a worked example of this in Chapter 8. As such the sensitivity of results to the allocation assumptions made should be tested. Broadly, cost allocation can be based on three types of cost drivers (either separately or in combination). The first type is input-based drivers where indirect costs are apportioned based on known inputs. An example of using this approach is the allocation according to a single cost driver such as labour input or floor space used. Another example is to use equi-proportionate mark-up (EPMU) across all products based on the direct costs of each product. If €50 of indirect costs had to be allocated across two products, each with €40 and €60 of direct costs respectively, €20 (40%) would be allocated to the first product and €30 (60%) to the other. This approach has the advantage of recovering indirect costs in equal proportion to the underlying direct costs of each output. The second option is output-based drivers where allocation is based on production or sales volumes. For example, if the same €50 of indirect costs had to be allocated across the same two products, which are produced in equal proportions, €25 (50%) would be allocated to each. The third option is value-based drivers, which use demand factors such as prices, revenues or consumers' willingness to pay. For competition purposes, value-based cost drivers should be used with caution, as a circularity problem may arise. If revenue is used as an allocator for costs, excessively high profits tend to be overlooked, since higher prices lead to higher levels of cost allocated to that line of business and, consequently, lower estimates of profitability. See Chapter 8 for a discussion of cost allocation in a state aid context.

3.6.6 WHAT IS THE COMPETITIVE BENCHMARK?

As noted earlier, in competitive markets, characterized by free entry and exit, companies are expected to make profits in the long run that equal the minimum returns required by investors (the opportunity cost of capital). The final step in the analysis is therefore to compare the estimated IRR (or a series of annual ROCE estimates) with the cost of capital and/or the returns of appropriate comparator companies.

The cost of capital is, as the name suggests, an estimate of the price the company must pay to raise the capital that it has employed. Profits above the cost of capital would encourage entry by new competitors, and profits below it would induce exit. Hence, returns that are persistently and significantly above the cost of capital are an indication of barriers to entry. The cost of capital could take the form of an interest rate on debt, or a dividend rate on equities, or more commonly, a combination of the returns on the two of forms of capital. The cost of capital is typically expressed as the weighted average cost of capital (WACC), which, as the name implies, is a weighted average of the cost of debt and the cost of equity. It is usually calculated based on the capital asset pricing model (CAPM). For unquoted companies or lines of business, estimates of the cost of capital for comparator listed companies may be suitable. The cost of debt is relatively simple to calculate, given the existence of interest schedules and extensive contracts in the financial marketplace. The return to equity is more complex. At the heart of CAPM is an average measure of the returns actually achieved by holders of equity over a relatively long period of time, compared with the alternative investment in a risk-free bond—usually taken as government bonds in the jurisdiction concerned. This calculation produces a return for the stock market as a whole, and is a proxy for the return to investment that is normal in a competitive market. To make a comparison with an individual company or industry, a correction factor is needed to compensate investors for any difference in the risk profile between the stock market as a whole and the company or sector in question. This relative risk coefficient is known as the beta. Chapter 8 gives a worked example of calculating a WACC. The output of the WACC calculation is a cost of capital (measured in percentage terms) that can be compared with IRR (or ROCE), also measured as a percentage.

In analysing profitability, it is appropriate to compare returns with the cost of capital at the time when the investment decision was made (ie, with the ex ante cost of capital). The use of the ex ante cost of capital reflects the opportunity costs faced by investors when they were committing capital to the investment. Therefore, when assessing the profitability of individual investments, it is appropriate to compare the IRR with the cost of capital at the beginning of the IRR period—ie, when the investment is assumed to have been made. When assessing profitability of a company as a whole, the cost of capital will not stay fixed but will change over time—in this regard a company can be thought of as a bundle of investment decisions taken at different points in time.

Over relatively short time periods, profits may well diverge from the cost of capital for a variety of reasons, not all of which are necessarily related to market power or anti-competitive practices. Therefore, in addition to the cost of capital, the returns made by appropriate comparator companies or industries which operate in a competitive environment can also be considered as benchmarks for the profitability assessment. If the profits of the company under investigation are in line with those of competitive comparators they may not indicate a competitive problem, even if they are above the cost of capital.

The cost of capital is frequently used by the CC as a benchmark for assessing profitability, for example, in its investigation into the classified directory advertising services market:

> Effective competition should put pressure on the profit levels of these companies so that they move towards their cost of capital in the medium to long run. In comparing profits to the weighted average cost of capital (WACC) we applied two profitability measures; return on capital employed (ROCE) and internal rate of return (IRR).[61]

In the CC's inquiry into the supply of banking services to SMEs, the cost of equity was considered the appropriate measure of profitability due to the nature of the industry (the total capital on banks' balance sheets includes deposits from accountholders, which are not relevant capital for the purposes of profitability analysis). A profitability gap of 9%, 10%, and 12% in 1998, 1999, and 2000 respectively between the returns on equity and cost of equity of the four largest clearing groups was considered to indicate a lack of competition in the market.[62] A further example is the home credit market investigation in which the CC concluded that the 5%–13% profitability gap between the ROCE of S&U and Provident and the cost of capital of other typical large home lenders partly reflected prices that were higher than they would be in a competitive market.[63] In the OFT's 1996 assessment of BSkyB's profitability, the IRR was compared with the cost of capital, and the 'excess return' of 10.3% was considered high and, according to OFT, would not be sustained in a competitive market.[64]

As set out above, profitability measures can also be benchmarked against suitable comparators that reflect the profits that would have been achieved in a competitive environment. Comparators should be selected so that they are subject to a reasonable degree of competitive pressure and operate in industries with similar cost structures and risks. For example, in its investigation into classified directory advertising services, the CC's benchmarking analysis involved a comparison of Yell's returns with a sample of more than 4,000 publicly listed companies, and with smaller sub-sets of companies derived on the basis of their similarity in terms of selected quantitative risk metrics (eg, cost structure, revenue volatility, beta) as well as by excluding outlier companies (eg, companies with a ROS higher than 100% or with negative asset values).[65]

---

[61] Competition Commission (2006), 'Classified Directory Advertising Services market investigation', 21 December.

[62] Competition Commission (2002), 'The Supply of Banking Services by Clearing Banks to Small and Medium-sized Enterprises' (Cm 5319), 14 March.

[63] Competition Commission (2006), 'Home credit market investigation', 30 November.

[64] Office of Fair Trading (1996), 'The Director General's review of BSkyB's Position in the Wholesale Pay TV Market', December.

[65] Competition Commission (2006), 'Classified Directory Advertising Services market investigation', 21 December, Appendix 7.1.

3.6.7 USE AND INTERPRETATION OF THE RESULTS OF THE PROFITABILITY ASSESSMENT

The application of the IRR methodology is straightforward if good data on cash flows and MEAs is available, and if the objective is to establish the existence of market power or lack of effective competition. Good data is likely to be available for established industries with historical data over a long period of time. In these circumstances it is possible to obtain meaningful insight into whether profits are above the competitive level, and hence whether there is a competition problem that needs to be addressed.

However, the results of a profitability assessment may still raise a number of interpretation issues. In some instances, where high profits are found, it may not be clear whether these are due to a lack of competition or to superior efficiency or temporary high profits in a dynamic market. Likewise, profits that do *not* exceed the competitive benchmarks may not necessarily imply a lack of market power, since they may be due 'X-inefficiencies' (inefficiencies from a monopoly position). Again, in these situations, cross-checks could be made. For example, the profitability assessment could be extended to a longer time period. Temporary positions of market power and high profits are commonplace in well-functioning markets, and, indeed, provide appropriate price signals and incentives to companies. However, in a truly competitive market, profits would be expected to be eroded over time by new entrants. Therefore, where high profits are persistent over a very long period, this is consistent with the market not functioning properly.

If profits are high due to superior efficiency or temporary positions of market power, there may not be an immediate competition problem. The cost advantage of superior efficiency (eg, managerial skill or economies of scale) can be the reason why a company has achieved legitimate market power, as can other advantages (eg, a strong brand); however, this does not exclude the possibility that once achieved, this market power may be exercised and abused (through exclusionary practices; not through extracting high profits). In this regard there is an important distinction that competition authorities or practitioners often fail to make: that between condemning high profits in their own right, and using high profits as indicator of market power. Here we are discussing the latter. From an economic perspective, high profitability is a useful indicator of market power or lack of effective competition, but that does not mean that those high profits should be prohibited directly (a theme we return to in Chapter 4 when we discuss excessive pricing as an abuse of dominance). In line with this, a well-established principle in competition law is that market power as such is not prohibited; only the abuse of it is. This is a particularly sound principle if market power is indeed acquired through superior efficiency. Yet that does not preclude that this efficiency does constitute a source of market power than can be abused—not by exploiting it (efficient companies deserve high profits as a reward for their efforts), but by using the market power derived from the efficiency advantage in some other way, thereby unduly extending the position of dominance.

Successful innovation could lead to high returns (ie, returns significantly above the cost of capital) because individual winning innovations may generate significant returns as compensation for the risk of failure taken at the time of the investment. Consider a stylized example of a risky investment with the following characteristics:

- in the successful (upside) scenario, the company earns a high return (30%);
- in the unsuccessful (downside) scenario, it earns a low return (0%);
- the expected return (ie, the average of different scenarios) is 15%;
- the expected return is assumed to be in line with the ex ante cost of capital (15%).

If the upside scenario occurred, the ex post profitability analysis of this stylized example would show a significant profitability gap—ie, 15% (30% ex post return minus 15% ex ante WACC). Given that the expected returns were in line with the cost of capital, high actual returns in this example provide compensation for bearing risks at the time of the investment.

Fortunately we can distinguish to some extent between highly innovative, risk-taking companies and less innovative ones. The first feature of innovation is that companies in such markets tend to undertake investments which require a significant upfront commitment of capital for a relatively long time period against the prospect of uncertain future demand. In the event that such investments prove successful and the realized demand is high, ex post returns could significantly exceed the cost of capital. However, if the investment fails, the capital committed upfront could be lost with no return. Where investments are scalable to changes in demand or demand uncertainty is low, a significant difference between actual returns and the cost of capital would not be expected, even if demand turns out to be high. With these characteristics, downside risks are relatively low, as the company would be able to scale back its investments in response to a demand shock.

The second feature of innovation is that if there is competition at the onset of the investment, the successful innovator would be expected to change over time and different companies would be expected to bring their products profitably to the market. Accordingly, returns persistently in excess of the cost of capital would suggest a deviation from a well-functioning market since it would indicate that there may be limited competition at the onset of each investment. For example, the CC chairman, Peter Freeman, confirmed that persistency of high returns is an appropriate indicator of market power in innovative markets (Freeman, 2004).

> We accept that . . . high profits may be attributable to superior entrepreneurial activity, successful innovation, and more efficient techniques of production and organisation . . . That is not to say that . . . high returns necessarily indicate a high level of efficiency or that adequate conditions for competition can always be expected . . . Each case requires an assessment of the economic circumstances . . .

> In high-tech markets (especially where there are network effects), the situation is potentially much more difficult, not least because the very high ex ante risks of failure arguably mean that the ex post returns to 'winning' firms and technologies should similarly be high. This may in some instances limit the usefulness of using profitability measures in such markets, at least in a short term or static sense. This does not mean that competition

authorities should abandon any attempt to look at profitability performance, especially where high profits might be expected to persist over the longer term, but it does mean that facile assumptions should be avoided.

An example where the CC (in its former incarnation as the Monopolies and Mergers Commission (MMC)) explicitly discussed the case for innovation in the form of high-risk investments is the investigation into indirect electrostatic photocopiers in the UK. The MMC recognized in its profitability analysis that Rank Xerox was highly innovative:

> At the time when Rank Xerox began to market plain paper copiers in this country, the Xerox group had already undertaken a great deal of costly research and development which had been by no means assured of success; and even when a commercially marketable machine had been developed there was no certainty that it would be commercially and technically successful. In its early days the production and marketing of plain paper copiers must therefore be regarded as having been a high risk industry. On this account alone relative high profits could be justified for a period to allow adequate reward for the risks accepted. However, Rank Xerox has now become firmly established and, although new techniques and new machines are still being developed, the period of particularly high risk and the need to compensate for such risk have in our view passed. In making this point we do not imply that the industry is now free from risk. An example of continuing risk is the fact that a recently introduced machine has not achieved the targets set for it. There must also be some risk involved in the launching of the company's latest machine, the 9200. But such risks are in our view not risks of the severity involved in the original development and marketing of plain paper copiers.[66]

3.6.8 IS PROFITABILITY ANALYSIS 'TOO DIFFICULT'?

The reluctance to consider profitability is often put down to conceptual and measurement issues. While these certainly mean that caution should be exercised when undertaking profitability assessments and drawing conclusions from them, it is not particularly different from good practice for most of the other economic indicators and techniques commonly used in competition law. We believe that the difficulties of profitability analysis are overstated. The theoretical framework for such an analysis has been developed (centred around the truncated IRR and asset valuation on a replacement cost basis) and, perhaps exceptionally in economics, a whole lot of good financial data is out there, in published company accounts, management accounts, and financial markets. Thousands of business and investment decisions are made every day based on this data by the very companies that we scrutinize under competition law. It would be a waste if this data were completely ignored in the competition analysis. Measurement and interpretation problems are also prevalent in other economic techniques, such as the estimation of demand elasticities for market definition or the use of game theory to assess market conduct. Sometimes these techniques can be used and sometimes they cannot.

---

[66] Monopolies and Mergers Commission (1976), 'Indirect electrostatic reprographic equipment—A report on the supply of indirect electrostatic reprographic equipment', December.

Therefore, profitability analysis should be seen as one among a number of complementary economic indicators and techniques that can be considered together in a competition case. When used in a case, it can follow the same principles of best practice in the use and presentation of economic evidence in competition proceedings—a theme discussed in Chapter 11. In addition to using profitability as an indicator of market power, the techniques of profitability and financial analysis are already being used in other contexts in competition law, including pricing abuses (see Chapter 4), state aid (Chapter 8), the setting of access remedies and fines (Chapter 9), and the quantification of damages (Chapter 10). In this regard, the debate about whether profitability analysis is too difficult is to some extent no longer relevant—it is already part of the economics toolkit for competition law.

3.7 BUYER POWER AND BIDDING MARKETS

3.7.1 WHAT HAPPENS WHEN BUYERS HAVE THE POWER?

In what we have discussed so far we have used the term market power to mean seller market power. We now consider the opposite case of buyer market power. As with a strong seller, a strong buyer can restrict its demand in order to pay a lower price for inputs. We will also look at countervailing buyer power, where buyer strength can offset supplier strength through bargaining, especially in the context of bidding markets. Many markets have only a few buyers (or even one), who can exercise buyer power over suppliers. The question of supermarket buyer power has been scrutinized in many jurisdictions, both under competition law and in more general policy debates. There are other examples of high buyer concentration, including large broadcasters negotiating TV rights with programme makers, the government procuring defence or pharmaceutical products, and, a famous example in the USA, elite universities jointly determining the financial aid that individual students receive for agreeing to attend a certain university (Blair and Harrison, 1993, pp 8–10).

Buyer power has been characterized in one of two ways. The first is 'monopsony power' as the mirror image of monopoly power—a powerful buyer can force prices down below the competitive level by withholding demand. Pure monopsony is the demand-side analogue of monopoly, and therefore has the same detrimental effects that are usually associated with monopoly. A monopolist restricts supply in order to increase price. A monopsonist will restrict its demand for a given product in order to lower the price it pays. If it achieves this, there will be a deadweight loss arising from the fact that production is lower than it would be in the competitive situation. The other characterization is 'bargaining power'—rather than the powerful buyer lowering the market price overall, the more powerful buyers can negotiate and keep to themselves greater individual discounts than less powerful buyers.[67] The measures of buyer

---

[67] For a useful overview, see Doyle and Inderst (2007).

power that you can use are similar to the measures of market power we have already seen. As with market power, market definition is important (you may need to define the market from the perspective of a hypothetical monopsonist, something we touched upon in Chapter 2). You can then use buyer market shares and concentration measures. Another relevant factor may be the size of the buyer relative to suppliers.

There are some differences between buyer and seller power. Recall from Chapter 1 that demand curves tend to slope downwards but supply curves are often horizontal. Downward-sloping demand means that a monopolist that restricts output can be guaranteed to raise price. In contrast, if supply curves are flat (which occurs when the same production technology is available to many competitors and economies of scale are limited), the monopsonist may gain little from restricting demand as it will not result in a significant decrease in price. This may mean that there is relatively little benefit to a strong buyer from 'monopsonizing' the market. Another difference relates to the effects on producer and consumer welfare. Unlike seller market power, buyer power, even if it exists, may not necessarily reduce consumer welfare. If buyer power leads to lower input prices and the buyers face effective competition in downstream markets, the lower price will be passed on to consumers. There may be some detriment associated with the deadweight loss in the input market, but consumer welfare downstream is enhanced through the lower prices (we discuss the issue of pass-on in Chapter 10 on quantifying damages). Even if only some buyers get access to lower input prices, to the extent these are passed on to consumers, this will also be of benefit to consumers.

One potential theory of harm arising from bargaining power is known as the 'waterbed effect'. The concern is that suppliers are forced to charge smaller retailers higher prices to compensate for supplying larger retailers at lower prices. This may force smaller retailers to exit because they cannot compete with the larger ones that have bargaining power. In practice there has been little empirical support for this concern. A further theory of harm that may arise in the upstream market is that the use of buyer power to extract large discounts could damage the long-term incentives of suppliers to invest and innovate, and could potentially lead to the exit of suppliers. If this effect occurred, the product range on offer to consumers might decrease. That said, theoretical and empirical evidence indicates that incentives for suppliers to innovate might increase when they face strong buyers, as this is one way of gaining bargaining power in negotiations. The question of retailer buyer power was analysed by the CC in the 2008 grocery market investigation.[68] There had been some concern about a reduction in the number of smaller retailers. The Commission found that, despite the undoubted strength of the big retail chains, the financial viability of grocery suppliers was not under threat, there was no evidence of decline in investment and innovation, and there were no major barriers to entry and expansion for smaller suppliers.

---

[68] Competition Commission (2008), 'The supply of groceries in the UK—Market investigation', 30 April.

The interaction between large buyers and large sellers is frequently examined in the context of market power assessments, especially in mergers. Where buyers are potentially able to resist the pressure from the market power of strong sellers, this is known as 'countervailing buyer power'.[69] In order for a buyer to place strong competitive pressure on a large supplier, it must have a credible threat to find an alternative supplier. This will be enhanced if the buyer is able to enter the upstream market itself or sponsor upstream entry by a third party, or if small rival suppliers can easily expand. This can prevent the exercise of seller power. It is even better for consumer welfare if the buyers compete vigorously and hence pass the cost savings they extract from suppliers on to consumers.

3.7.2 COUNTERVAILING BUYER POWER IN BIDDING MARKETS

A particular form of countervailing buyer power that has become a common defence in competition cases—especially mergers—is that the market is a 'bidding market'. In such a market, any prevailing large market shares do not necessarily imply market power, and the presence of two or three potential competitors (bidders) can be enough to keep prices in check because competition is *for* the market rather than *in* the market. A bidding market (for jet engines) was central to the much-debated *General Electric (GE)/Honeywell* case (see also Chapter 7).[70] This example highlights the difficulty of assessing market power in a bidding market: if a company wins an auction for a large contract, it may become a near-monopolist for the duration of that contract. However, if the market is contestable, the winning company does not necessarily have market power and may not win the next contract. As evidence of GE's alleged market power, the European Commission had argued that 'on 10 out of the last 12 platforms for which airframe manufacturers offered exclusive positions, GE managed to place its products'.[71] It also argued that current market shares are a good proxy for present and future market power because winning contracts allows companies to invest in R&D, and because incumbency can play a role in buyers' future purchasing decisions. In contrast, the US Department of Justice, which also reviewed the merger, argued that static market shares are a weak indicator of competitive conditions in the market, and that GE's high market share was mainly due to one particularly large contract that had recently been won (Majoras, 2001).

What are the criteria for judging the nature of a bidding market? Strong countervailing buyer power requires that the buyer has some form of credible threat to remove its business from the seller. Thus, for a bidding process to achieve effective competition even though there are few suppliers and only one winner, it needs to reflect this constraint. We saw in section 3.2 that contestability requires low barriers to entry and exit (no sunk costs) and that prices adjust more slowly than quantity. Here we are looking at competition *for* the market (winner-takes-all bidding), so the barriers-to-entry

---

[69] This theory was developed in Galbraith (1952).

[70] Case T-210/01 *General Electric Company v EC Commission* [2005] ECR II-5575.

[71] *General Electric/Honeywell* (Case COMP/M.2220) [2004] OJ L/48/1, at [45].

requirement still holds but there is no head-to-head competition on price and quantity. Four main criteria determine whether a bidding process is likely to deliver a contestable market (Klemperer, 2005, p 6):

(1) competition is winner-takes-all—the bidder wins all or none of the contract;

(2) competition is lumpy—each contract is large relative to a bidder's total sales;

(3) competition begins afresh for each auction—there is no 'lock-in' of customers and the incumbent supplier has no major advantages; and

(4) entry is easy.

Each of these represents a dimension of a market that will lie somewhere on a spectrum: from markets with no bidding aspects at one extreme, to those that are 'pure' bidding markets at the other. A schematic representation of bidding versus ordinary markets can be achieved if the above four criteria are simplified into two dimensions—see Figure 3.3. The first dimension encompasses criteria one and two, and can be summarized as the 'size of contract' (the horizontal line in the figure). This involves various aspects of the bidding process, such as its frequency (if auctions are frequent, the relative importance of each contract decreases); the size of the contract relative to that of the overall market and of market participants; and the number of contracts awarded within each auction. The second dimension encompasses criteria three and four, and can be described as the 'ease of entry' (the vertical line in the figure). This dimension covers not only the entry barriers to a market (eg, sunk costs), but also the incumbency effects of the existing supplier that won the last contract (eg, reputation or know-how). One of the differences between competition in the market and competition for the market (bidding processes) is that in the latter the buyer can seek to encourage entry and lower entry barriers through the design of the process itself. There is some tension over the

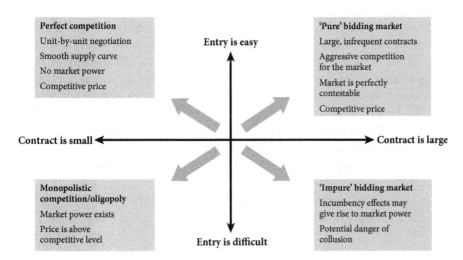

Fig. 3.3 The economic characteristics of bidding markets

optimal size of the contract where a buyer is unsure of the ease of entry: for bigger contracts (which have a large value and long duration) you will get keener bidding if entry
is easy, but if entry is difficult it is probably preferable to have smaller contracts in order
to prevent incumbency advantages embedding the position of one supplier.

If a bidding market is 'impure', the number of bidders will affect the competitiveness
of the market—the more bidders the better. However, adding further bidders may not
contribute significantly to competition if these bidders are weak. If the market has the
character of a 'pure' bidding market, even one credible alternative bidder might be
enough to ensure vigorous bidding competition. For this to be the case there must be no
significant incumbency advantages—this is captured by criterion three. Evidence for
this would be where more than one company has won contracts in the past or where
there is not much specific knowledge acquired in fulfilling previous contracts that new
bidders cannot obtain. Part of the reason why there may actually be few markets that
meet the bidding market defence is that if the first and second criteria hold (ie, contracts
are large and of a winner-take-all kind), the third criterion is less likely to hold: incumbency advantages may be more significant for large contracts that leave only one supplier in the market. Once the supplier gains a clear advantage in a market, other
companies may stop trying to bid against it. Economies of scale in large contracts may
also make it more difficult for new bidders to displace an incumbent.

In the *GE/Honeywell* case, the European Commission argued that GE had incumbency
advantages such that winning a contract would make it more likely that it would win subsequent contracts. This argument clearly depends on the sector in question: if winning
a contract gives a company market know-how, or if the company needs to undertake
substantial investment, lock-in is more likely. This was the case in the second contest to
operate the National Lottery franchise in the UK, in 2000. By that time Camelot, the
incumbent operator that had won the first contest in 1994 against seven other bidders,
had developed substantial learning-by-doing and reputation advantages. Only one other
bidder took part, and lost.[72]

Some of the characteristics that will make a bidding process contestable and give the
buyer strong countervailing power may also make a market more prone to collusion.
Along the 'size of contract' dimension in Figure 3.3, there is a sliding scale of contracts:
at one extreme are very large, infrequent tenders for the whole market and at the other
are very small, frequent tenders for single units. In the middle of this sliding scale—
especially if entry is not easy—there is a greater risk of collusion than in ordinary
markets. The bidding process makes the market more transparent and gives companies
the opportunity to communicate; the more frequent the auctions, the more credible
punishment strategies become, which again favours collusion. In Chapter 5 we discuss
cases of collusion in the form of bid rigging.

Two UK cases are instructive in seeing how the line can be drawn for the bidding
market defence. Both concerned mergers between suppliers that faced countervailing

---

[72] See Klemperer (2005).

buyer power by large supermarkets. In *Cott/Macaw* (2006), the CC cleared the merger even though the merging parties would have a market share of nearly 70% in the production of own-brand CSDs.[73] The homogeneous nature of the products, the retailers' ability to shift to alternative suppliers of their own-brand CSDs (they owned all the rights associated with the product flavour), and the fact that retailers controlled the nature of tendering for supply, all led the Commission to conclude that the merger was not problematic. A subsequent appraisal of this merger decision in 2009 confirmed that the Commission's assessment was correct and that indeed it may have underestimated the incentives for entry (Deloitte, 2009, p 65).

In contrast, the completed merger of Stonegate Farmers and Deans Food Group (trading as Noble) was unwound after the CC found in 2007 that there was likely to be a substantial lessening of competition. The two parties were direct competitors in the supply to UK retailers of fresh and liquid egg products and their post-merger market share was 60%–70% in shell eggs and over 50% in liquid eggs. Because of the nature of egg production, the barriers to entry were significant as a supplier would need to build up its stock of egg-producing hens. Retailers, despite their important position as buyers, could not easily switch to alternative egg suppliers. As a consequence the Commission found that:

> Among the main concerns expressed by some retailers were that there would be difficulty in switching due to limited availability of eggs and to no other suppliers having sufficient capacity to provide an alternative to Noble; and hence that there would be a loss of competition and adverse effects on prices and innovation ...

> Given the difficulty in switching supplier, the limited prospects for entry and expansion we have noted above and the reluctance to import, the effects of the merger would therefore appear likely materially to reduce retailers' bargaining power which may be expected in this particular instance adversely to affect final consumers.[74]

Claiming that a market is a bidding market is not sufficient to justify that buyers will have strong countervailing power. Competition issues must be analysed in very much the same way as in an ordinary market. 'Pure' bidding markets may not be particularly common; however, many markets have some bidding characteristics, and these will be relevant for assessments of market power and effective competition.

3.8 MARKET POWER, INVESTMENT, AND INNOVATION

3.8.1 A DIFFICULT TRADE-OFF

We now return to one of the most difficult trade-offs for competition law: how to assess market power in markets where investment is risky but potentially lucrative

---

[73] Competition Commission (2006), 'Cott Beverages Ltd and Macaw (Holdings) Ltd merger inquiry: Final report', 28 March.

[74] Competition Commission (2007), 'Stonegate/Deans merger inquiry: Provisional findings report', January, [4] and [14].

when successful. Markets characterized by innovation are the prime example of this. Innovation—finding new things to do or new ways to do existing things—is a strong driver of long-run economic welfare. The Lisbon agenda in Europe was focused on improving productivity, and since the 1990s many governments in Europe and elsewhere have sought to implement microeconomic reforms (deregulation, privatization, liberalization of trade) to drive economic growth through productivity and innovation. Competition law is seen as an important tool to support and facilitate innovation, and there is a continuing debate about which type of market structure is most conducive to innovation. At one end is the Schumpeterian support for monopolies to deliver 'creative destruction': each new innovation destroys the monopoly rents generated by previous innovators (Schumpeter, 1942) and at the other end is Arrow's theory that highly competitive markets are most likely to yield innovation: a monopolist might innovate less than competitive firms because a monopolist has more to lose from radical change (Arrow, 1962). The more recent empirical literature has found an 'inverted U' shape relationship between the degree of competition and the degree of innovation—ie, oligopolies may be more innovative than monopoly or perfect competition. Too much competition will dissipate the post-innovation profits and hence reduce the rewards from trying to escape intense competition by innovation, whereas too little competition will leave the pre-innovation profits too high (the quiet life of the monopolist as we saw in Chapter 1). Which effect dominates will turn out to depend on technological characteristics of a sector or industry (Aghion et al., 2005). Meanwhile, there is a long history of competition enforcement in dynamic industries where successful innovation has led to companies having very strong market positions, which are then heavily scrutinized. In this section, we consider the trade-offs inherent in acting on concerns about market power.

We saw in section 3.6 that where there is a significant risk of failure, high returns are necessary to reward those willing to take such risks. The award of IP rights for innovation recognizes this: because it is costly and risky to research and develop a new product, an innovator is given monopoly rights over the commercialization of the idea for a period of time. In fact, having a patent or an IP right is no guarantee of an actual monopoly of the type we have been analysing in this chapter. Designing a new type of kitchen tap may be patent-protected, but because it competes with a wide range of other taps that are sufficiently close substitutes, the patent may confer no pricing power. Similarly an innovation may not be amenable to IP protection but may yield its developer a position of significant market power. The communication protocols in dispute in the *Microsoft* case were not protected by IP, yet Microsoft has been able to prevent others from interoperating with its systems and this has been found to give it significant market power.[75] While there is not always a one-to-one mapping between IP and true monopoly, a clear tension exists between competition and IP law, as successful innovation, protected by IP, may erect absolute entry barriers that reduce competition in existing or

---

[75] *Microsoft* (Case COMP/C-3/37.792), Commission Decision of 24 March 2004, [432].

new markets. We return to this in Chapter 4 on abuse of dominance and Chapter 9 on the design of remedies. The complex trade-off between competition and innovation is also touched upon in other places, including in Chapter 5 (in the context of technology and licence agreements) and Chapter 8 (state aid in innovation market failures).

3.8.2 DYNAMIC RIVALRY

We have emphasized in a number of places that price is not the only parameter of competition. This is particularly the case in dynamic markets where companies tend to compete mainly through innovation. By offering the most innovative products, companies aspire to gain a competitive edge over their rivals, or indeed to create whole new markets for themselves. The benefits of such advantageous market positions can then be reaped, up to the point when rivals catch up or create new products that render the existing ones obsolete. With such dynamic rivalry, the standard tools for market definition and dominance need to be applied with caution. Chapter 2 highlighted that market definition based around the products that are currently in the market may not be fully informative if there is a possibility that those products will be substantially modified, or even replaced, over the next one to two years (the time period over which a market is usually defined). In assessing market power, a company with a very high market share, or even 100%, today may not be in the same position in a year's time—strong market positions can be eroded quickly. Likewise, companies may currently be competing fiercely with each other to develop products and services that have not yet fully made it to market, again making it difficult to define markets based on current product features. Within a few years it may be that one company has exited the market while the other has captured a large proportion of demand.

It is difficult for anyone, including competition authorities and judges, to evaluate future developments in dynamic markets. Competition authorities should therefore exercise caution when assessing dominance based on current market positions or product features. The 1995 report by the UK Monopolies and Mergers Commission on the video game consoles market serves as a healthy reminder of this principle.[76]

Investigating this market between January 1994 and March 1995, the MMC found that it was dominated by Nintendo and Sega, which held a combined market share of nearly 100% for consoles (hardware) and around 40% for games (software). The MMC concluded that 'Nintendo and Sega remain well placed to retain their dominant position in the market and derive profit from it.'[77] However, the report was outdated almost from the time of its publication. In the same year, Sony launched its highly successful PlayStation game console in Europe, which would go on to sell over 100 million units worldwide—more than any console to date other than its successor, PlayStation 2 (the

---

[76] Monopolies and Mergers Commission (1995), 'Video games: A report into the supply of video games in the UK', March.

[77] Ibid., at [1.4].

contemporaneous rival console, Nintendo 64, sold 33 million units).[78] PlayStation rep-resented a whole new 'generation' of consoles at the time (for example, it had CDs con-taining the necessary software, rather than cartridges). Several further generations of game consoles have since been developed. Microsoft also successfully entered the game console market in 2001, with Xbox, while Sega, one of the two 'dominant' companies in 1995, exited the market in that same year. This is the archetypal example of how tempo-rary market power can be mistaken for a more permanent kind, where innovation involves 'creative destruction', with a successful new product making an existing one obsolete.

High-tech firms have long histories of disputes with competition authorities because of their positions of market power. IBM is a famous example (see, for example, Pugh, 1995). Post-World War II, IBM's product line consisted of tabulators, card punch machines, accounting machines, scales, typewriters, and time-recording systems, and it had a strong market position in many of these. In 1946, it began developing a new technology—computing—investing around 9% of its revenue in R&D in this area. In 1956, it signed a consent decree with the Department of Justice regarding a range of restrictive practices, particularly in relation to the sales of tabulators and card punches. At that point, this market was in decline and it is unlikely that the consent decree was a significant restriction on IBM as its past product line was competitively constrained by the new computing products coming to market. IBM was then scrutinized again from 1969 to 1984, in both the USA and Europe, over concerns about interoperability of its CPUs (central processing units) and its bundling practices in the mainframe market. The case was dropped in the USA in 1982 and settled in Europe in 1984, with IBM agreeing to offer access to its interface protocols and not to bundle other products with its CPU (reminiscent of the remedies in the recent *Microsoft* case—see Chapters 4 and 9).[79] By that time, however, IBM's market position had already diminished, and the company suffered a serious decline through the 1980s and 1990s, finding itself out-flanked by the innovations in PCs and servers that were the source of market power for the likes of Microsoft and Intel. IBM, through some renewed innovative efforts, man-aged to regroup and moved into software. Perhaps to come full circle, in 2010 the European Commission again opened proceedings against the company.[80] It was alleged to have abused a dominant position in the mainframe market through tying and dis-criminatory pricing practices.

Were the concerns about IBM's market power founded? Doesn't the *IBM* case demonstrate that all positions of market power will one day be eroded? Will the same hold for Microsoft, which the European Commission has found to be super-dominant on the basis of a strong and enduring near-monopoly position in the market for

---

[78] Sources: <http://www.scei.co.jp/corporate/data/bizdataps_e.html> and <http://www.nintendo.co.jp/ir/en/library/index.html>.

[79] Bull EC 7/8-1984, point 1.1.1 *et seq.*

[80] European Commission (2010), 'Commission initiates formal investigations against IBM in two cases of suspected abuse of dominant market position', press release, IP/10/1006, 26 July.

PC operating systems? Is its Windows operating system vulnerable to the same risks of being made obsolete by a new technology? The network effects are stronger with Microsoft than, for example, games consoles, as its market power is embedded more deeply. Households replaced their consoles more easily than the MMC anticipated—indeed, today many households have multiple gaming platforms. In the server market, once a business has set up its systems using a Microsoft operating system, moving away involves significant switching costs. The communication benefits of being able to interface easily with other machines are also very strong. However, even Microsoft faces competitive threats, and in the last few years the issue of whether the advent of web-based technology would make PC operating systems obsolete has been much debated. Furthermore, in devices that increasingly compete with PCs, such as set-top boxes and mobile phones, Microsoft has faced strong competition from other operating systems, thus further eating into the dominance of Windows.

Practices designed to hamper the successful innovations of others may be a legitimate focus of competition law, but is it more beneficial to everyone to allow companies the benefits of the market power that accompanies successful innovation? Economics would highlight that the long-term benefits of dynamic efficiency can easily outweigh any short-term losses of allocative efficiency from high pricing. Judging when to intervene to preserve and support dynamic rivalry (for example, by obliging companies to offer up protocols allowing others to interoperate with them) and when to allow market forces to run their course is inherently difficult. In Chapters 4 and 9 we provide some economic principles that may assist in making such judgements.

4

ABUSE OF DOMINANCE

4.1 SUCCESSFUL COMPETITOR OR DANGEROUS MONOPOLIST?

4.1.1 A LONG-STANDING CONCERN

Monopoly has always been recognized as a problem in law and commerce. Back in 1602, Darcy, a member of Queen Elizabeth's court, received an exclusive licence to sell all playing cards in England. This arrangement was apparently secured in part by the Queen's concern that card playing was becoming a problem among her subjects, and her hope that having one person controlling the trade would regulate the activity. When an alternative supplier, Allin, sought to make and sell his own playing cards, Darcy sued in court to prevent this competition and protect his monopoly.[1] The court ruled against Darcy and determined that the Queen's granting of a monopoly was invalid. It argued that while she intended to permit this monopoly for the public good, she must have been deceived because such a monopoly can be used only for the private gain of the monopolist. The court worried about the conduct of the monopolist, referring to what we these days would call foreclosure and exploitative abuses: the court said that such a monopoly prevents persons who may be skilled in a trade from practising their trade, and that the monopolist would raise prices and have no incentive to maintain the quality of the goods. As we saw in Chapter 1, the very essence of competition law is based on the economic notion that competition is 'good' and monopoly is 'bad'. The judges of the early seventeenth century also clearly recognized the detriments of monopoly: higher prices, lower quality, and less incentive to innovate. The *Darcy* ruling put a temporary stop to the granting of state-sanctioned monopolies, until King James I (who reigned from 1603 to 1625) began to grant them again.

Four hundred years later, courts and competition authorities still worry a great deal about the effects of monopolies in network and infrastructure industries, technology markets, state-owned activities, and other areas. Competition is by nature a process of 'creative destruction' whereby smaller, less efficient or plain unlucky companies will fail and exit the market when confronted with larger, more efficient, or lucky rivals. Philosophies differ on whether successful dominant companies should be disliked or admired, and what, if anything, competition law should do about them. Recall the analogy of the boxing match in Chapter 1. By intervening too much, the referee can actually dampen the intensity of the fight and leave spectators (consumers) worse off. What is the optimal degree of intervention? A guiding principle in US antitrust law is that 'the successful competitor, having been urged to compete, should not be turned upon when he wins.'[2] But what if the dominant company is successful not only on its own merit but also because, like Darcy, it has benefited from a state-granted monopoly (these days, for example, via previous state ownership or a patent)? Competition authorities

---

[1] *Darcy v Allin* 77 Eng Rep 1260 (QB, 1602).
[2] *US v Aluminum Co of America* 148 F 2d 416, 430 (2nd Cir. 1945).

do not usually attack positions of monopoly or market power directly (structural remedies are rare outside merger control—see Chapter 9), but they do step in when dominant companies engage in anti-competitive behaviour aimed at protecting or extending such positions.

In Europe, Article 102 policy and case law on abuse of dominance have traditionally been influenced by the 'ordo-liberal school'. This school of thought emphasizes individual freedom as the primary objective of competition law, and considers that the presence of dominant companies weakens the competitive process and reduces the economic freedom of other market participants. The notion that the mere existence of dominant companies is a threat to competition has been deeply embedded in EU law. A dominant company has traditionally been regarded as the proverbial bull in a china shop—it must be restrained to prevent it from inflicting further damage to its already fragile surroundings. As formally established in *Michelin I*, a dominant company has a 'special responsibility not to allow its conduct to impair genuine undistorted competition on the common market.'[3] This view on how competition works is somewhat outdated. Economic theory and practical experience over the past 30–40 years have shown that competitive dynamics can function well even if a market has some very large suppliers. Indeed, large companies or temporary positions of market power can improve competitive dynamics and incentives to innovate (see Chapter 3). The theory has also established that certain behaviour can have positive efficiency effects, even if practised by dominant companies. In other words, using the bull in a china shop analogy to describe dominant companies does not fit well with modern thinking on how markets work. EU competition law has recognized this and has introduced some significant changes to the treatment of abuse of dominance through a combination of policy reforms and court rulings in the last decade, as discussed in this chapter.

4.1.2 FORM VERSUS EFFECT

EU case law on abuse of dominance has historically established a two-step approach, where dominance is first determined and then the practice is assessed mainly on the basis of its *form* rather than its *economic effects*. Once a company is found to be dominant, its 'special responsibility' not to impair competition means it cannot engage in certain forms of behaviour, such as pricing below variable cost, tying its products, or offering loyalty rebates. This virtual per se prohibition, combined with the low (and mainly market-share-based) threshold for dominance that has often been applied (see Chapter 3), has led to a rather interventionist abuse of dominance regime in Europe. Little consideration has been given to the actual and potential effects of these practices on competition and consumer welfare.

This has begun to change—to some extent in case law, but in particular through the European Commission's policy efforts to reform the approach to Article 102, culminating

---

[3] Case 322/81 *Nederlandsche Banden-Industrie Michelin NV v Commission* [1983] ECR 3461 (*Michelin I*).

in the publication in 2008 of formal guidance on Article 102 (then 82).[4] This guidance endorses a test for abuse of dominance that examines the economic effects of practices. It also builds on the principle—long accepted in US antitrust—that competition law should protect the competitive process in the market, not individual competitors. Aggressive commercial behaviour by dominant companies should not be ruled illegal merely because it affects competitors. Rather, the analysis should focus on the effects of the behaviour on competition and consumers. If the functioning of competition is not threatened (ie, if a monopoly position is unlikely to be achieved or sustained) or if the practice generates efficiencies that benefit consumers, intervention may not be required even if individual competitors are harmed. The effects-based approach should eventually lead to a more economically sound, and less interventionist, approach to abuse of dominance. Nonetheless, there is the potential for increased legal uncertainty (some businesses and lawyers would prefer to keep the traditional form-based approach). A 'special responsibility' falls on the economics profession to produce clear and workable criteria for assessing economic effects under Article 102 and its equivalents in national competition laws. The aim of this chapter is to take you through the economic principles and methods relevant to effects-based approaches in abuse of dominance cases.

4.1.3 STRUCTURE OF THIS CHAPTER

Section 4.2 presents the main economic principles for assessing unilateral exclusionary conduct, including the threshold for intervention and the tests to identify competitive effects (exclusionary effects from vertical agreements as opposed to unilateral conduct are discussed in Chapter 6 as well, but from an economic perspective there are many commonalities). Section 4.3 is also of general application, explaining the cost benchmarks that can be used to assess exclusionary conduct, especially in relation to the various types of below-cost pricing. Section 4.4 deals with predatory pricing, a classic type of abuse. This section is also relevant for other types of abuse that are variations on predation. Section 4.5 addresses price discrimination, a practice that is very common and often welfare-enhancing, but may sometimes have exclusionary effects. Section 4.6 discusses loyalty-enhancing discounts and rebates, and exclusive dealing. The next sections explore margin squeeze (4.7), bundling and tying (4.8), and refusal to supply and essential facilities (4.9).

While interventions under the abuse of dominance rules tend to focus on exclusionary behaviour (ie, conduct that harms competition in a market), the underlying legislation in Europe also condemns exploitative conduct that is directly at the expense of customers. Article 102 covers practices which consist of 'directly or indirectly imposing unfair purchase or selling prices or other unfair trading conditions', and equivalent provisions exist in competition legislation elsewhere (though not in section 2

---

[4] European Commission (2008), 'Guidance on the Commission's Enforcement Priorities in Applying Article 82 EC Treaty to Abusive Exclusionary Conduct by Dominant Undertakings', December.

of the US Sherman Act). Little clarity exists on the criteria that can be applied to such exploitative abuses (and the European Commission's Guidance on Article 102 does not cover it). In section 4.10 we take you through the relevant economic principles and cases of excessive pricing as a specific form of exploitative abuse.

4.2 GENERAL PRINCIPLES FOR ASSESSING EXCLUSIONARY CONDUCT

This section covers several topics of general application for abuse of dominance: the nature of an effects-based approach; the relevance of the degree of dominance; the test for assessing exclusionary conduct; the possibility of abusing collective dominance; and the use of a dominant position in one market to harm competition in a related market.

4.2.1 WHY THE EFFECTS-BASED APPROACH IS DIFFERENT

The basic characteristics of an effects-based approach to abuse of dominance are fourfold. First, the degree of dominance matters. Practices such as below-cost pricing and refusal to supply are more likely to have an anti-competitive effect if the perpetrator has a very high degree of dominance (or even 'super-dominance') than if it just passes the threshold for dominance. Second, the degree of foreclosure matters. It is not just the nature or form of the conduct, but also its incidence—the extent to which the dominant company is applying it in the market. For instance, in the case of selective price cuts (eg, targeted discounting or 'fighting brands'), the direct link between dominance and the likelihood of success of predation breaks down—the dominant company is not using the full weight of its market power to exclude rivals, so the existence of dominance in itself would not be sufficient to conclude a high likelihood of success of the predatory strategy. Third, only conduct that would exclude 'as-efficient' competitors is abusive. This principle seeks to draw the line between exclusionary conduct that simply reflects 'competition on the merits' and exclusionary conduct that is harmful to consumers. Fourth, exclusionary behaviour can still be justified on the grounds of necessity, meeting competition, or efficiency. The efficiency defence recognizes the economic principle that some restrictive practices may be justified to achieve efficiencies (a theme we see in Chapters 5 and 6 as well).

The *Virgin v British Airways* case illustrates how an effects-based approach to abuse of dominance can result in a different outcome from a form-based approach. In 1993, Virgin lodged a complaint before the European Commission, and in 1994 before a US court, claiming that British Airways (BA) had used incentive schemes to foreclose the market and impede its growth.[5] Using an effects-based test, the US court concluded that BA's discount schemes had not harmed competition and it therefore rejected

---

[5] *Virgin Atlantic LTD v British Airways PLC* 257 F 3d 256 (2d Cir. 2001); and *Virgin/British Airways* (Case COMP/D-2/34.780) [2000] OJ L30/1.

the complaint. The opposite conclusion was reached by the Commission, which focused the analysis on the structure of the schemes—ie, their *form* rather than their effects on competition.

Under the schemes, travel agents could qualify for 'performance rewards' and other bonuses, and for funds from BA for marketing and staff training courses (we discuss loyalty rebates in section 4.6). The schemes were generally linked to the yearly growth in the sales of BA tickets by the travel agent, and were structured to pay rewards retro-actively on all ticket sales once the performance target was met, not just on the incremental sales above the target. In 1997, BA held 40% of Heathrow Airport's slots and operated around 60% of all international routes from the airport. Virgin was a smaller operator, with 2% of slots at the same airport and 5.5% of airline sales in the UK. The US court considered that Virgin had failed to demonstrate that BA's behaviour harmed overall competition. It also stated that BA's discounts had not prevented Virgin from becoming a successful airline; it had even become the leading operator on the London–New York route in 1995. Furthermore, the schemes could have only a marginal impact on the competition between travel agents since 'truly loyal' agents (defined as those who booked more than 80% of their UK–US ticket sales with BA) represented less than 5% of the total sales. The court also held that rewarding customer loyalty promotes competition on the merits. In contrast, the Commission focused on the form of the incentive structures offered by BA. Of particular concern was the retroactive nature of the discounts, which might induce travel agents who are close to the sales target to promote BA rather than rival airlines. In condemning these schemes, the Commission stated that:

> Such commission schemes carried out by a firm enjoying a dominant position as a purchaser of services from travel agents are illegal, regardless of any possibility for the travel agents or competing airlines to minimize or avoid their effects.[6]

This reflects the principle previously established in EU law that a dominant company is allowed to offer discounts that relate to efficiencies only (eg, cost savings for large orders), but not to encourage loyalty. It ignores the potential reductions in the prices of the tickets offered to final consumers or improvements in the quality of the service offered by sales agents. In contrast with the US judgment, the commercial success of rivals was not given much importance in the Commission's decision. Although the Commission recognized that rival airlines had been gaining market share in the UK, it stated that 'it can only be assumed that competitors would have had more success in the absence of these abusive schemes.'[7] Finally, to determine further whether there had been an abuse of dominance, the Commission used a principle of EU law that establishes that a dominant company has an obligation not to discriminate—BA's loyalty schemes discriminated between travel agencies. Price discrimination is discussed in section 4.5.

---

[6] *Virgin/British Airways* (Case COMP/D-2/34.780) [2000] OJ L30/1, at [102].
[7] Ibid., at [107].

4.2.2 RELEVANCE OF THE DEGREE OF MARKET POWER

The first stage in any competition investigation into alleged abuse of dominance is to define the relevant market and then to assess whether the company in question has a dominant position. These topics were covered in Chapters 2 and 3. The assessment of the degree of dominance is always a useful first step in the analysis of the effects of an alleged abuse. The 'one-size-fits-all' dominance threshold is too low to allow for automatic inferences of anti-competitive effects, and anti-competitive effects depend on a sustained position of market power. The definition of dominance (see Chapter 3) states that a dominant undertaking can act to an appreciable extent independently of competitors, both actual and potential. This should imply that the undertaking has current and future market power. In existing EU case law, much of the dominance analysis has been backward-looking. Yet for allegations of predation and certain other types of abuse it is also important to examine the dynamic structural features of the market so as to assess whether future market power does in fact follow from an abuse of current market power. Dominant positions acquired through aggressive actions are less of a concern if over time they are likely to be eroded by new entry. This will depend on entry barriers, which were explained in Chapter 3.

EU case law has focused very much on market share thresholds (combined with some indications of entry barriers), with 40%–50% market share being the rule of thumb. In *AKZO* (1991), the General Court ruled that a company with a stable market share of more than 50% in a relevant market would be deemed dominant unless there were exceptional circumstances.[8] The rule of thumb also appeared in the 2004 Coca-Cola undertakings with respect to exclusivity, rebates and tying, which apply to those countries where Coca-Cola's soft drinks represent more than 40% of national sales (and more than double the share of the nearest competitor).[9] Such thresholds may have a useful policy function as a safe harbour—we won't go after you if you have less than 40%–50% of the relevant market—but they are not very informative for the analysis of effects. As we explained in Chapter 3, from an economic perspective, market power is a matter of degree—Microsoft Windows has market power, but so has a small corner shop (provided that there are few other shops nearby). Dominance is just one threshold, and the degree of dominance matters when it comes to assessing pricing behaviour—a very aggressive price cut is more likely to be detrimental to competition if the company has 95% of the market than if it has 40%. The fact that the degree of dominance matters has to some extent been recognized in EU case law, which has developed the concept of 'super-dominance' (see Chapter 3).

4.2.3 TESTS FOR DETERMINING WHETHER CONDUCT HAS ANTI-COMPETITIVE EFFECTS

It is broadly accepted that the threshold for intervention against abuse of dominance should start from the premise that harm to competitors, without harm to the competitive

---

[8] Case C-62/86 *AKZO Chemie BV v EC Commission* [1991] ECR I-3359.
[9] *Coca-Cola* (Case COMP/A.39.116/B2), Commission Decision of 22 June 2005.

process, does not constitute anti-competitive conduct. But what does this mean? How do we know whether the competitive process is harmed? Various options have been considered as thresholds for intervention.[10]

Perhaps the most natural way of judging whether harm occurs to the competitive process is to watch the outcome from competition. This means that examining the net effects on consumer welfare is one option for a threshold. As Chapter 1 described, when the competitive process works well it delivers higher consumer welfare, so when it is harmed you would expect to see a reduction in consumer welfare. The test would therefore ask whether the conduct reduces competition to the detriment of consumers, without creating efficiencies that are sufficient to offset this detriment. This would be similar to the substantial lessening of competition criterion often used in merger control (see Chapter 7). Such a test has the attractive property that it fits with the general objective of competition policy to maximize consumer welfare. It has the downside that judging net effects on consumer welfare is complex. For courts or competition authorities to evaluate all possible anti-competitive effects and offsetting efficiencies would be a laborious exercise, although not impossible (it is done for mergers). It would also be rather costly for businesses to do this in respect of all aspects of their conduct in all markets where they may exceed or come close to the dominance threshold. It would result in legal uncertainty and possibly lead to excessively cautious behaviour, dampening aggressive but desirable competitive moves. The consumer welfare test should therefore be seen as a guiding principle for other, more practical tests for assessing abusive behaviour. The other tests can be seen as a means of practically implementing the consumer welfare test.

The second option is a profit sacrifice test. This asks whether the conduct in question is commercially irrational 'but for' the expectation that rivals are excluded or disciplined. A variant of this is the 'no economic sense' test. These tests are most suitable in the context of predation and similar practices which involve a temporary sacrifice of profits in the expectation of greater future profits (see section 4.4). The advantage of the profit sacrifice test is that it is conceptually simpler than assessing consumer welfare—the focus is only on the financials of the dominant company, not on the ultimate effects on consumers. It is a fairly straightforward test to apply if the challenged conduct has an unambiguous exclusionary rationale, but not if the conduct has the effect of generating legitimate profits as well as profits from excluding competitors (ie, the conduct makes 'some' rather than 'no' economic sense). It can be difficult to separate these benefits. Think of an exclusive-dealing case where the dominant company wants retailers to stock its product but not those of its rivals, and has to pay those distributors more than it otherwise would, or of a predation case in which the company is dominant in one market and engages in below-cost pricing in a new market where network effects are important. Here the profit sacrifice test may not work well, since the conduct can be commercially rational with or without exclusionary effect—either way, profits will be

[10] Useful discussions on the various tests can be found in Elhauge (2003), Vickers (2005a), Werden (2006), and Department of Justice (2008), 'Competition and Monopoly: Single-firm Conduct Under Section 2 of the Sherman Act', September, Ch 3. The DOJ withdrew this report in 2009, but the chapter on standards for exclusionary conduct remains a useful contribution to the debate.

made (the efficiency rationale for exclusive dealing is discussed in Chapter 6 in the context of vertical restraints). An additional point to make here is that not all types of abuse involve a profit sacrifice. A dominant company can make its competitors' lives difficult through practices that are not necessarily costly to it, such as certain forms of refusal to supply (see section 4.9) and loyalty rebates (see section 4.6)—economists have lumped these practices together under the heading 'raising rivals' costs' (Salop and Scheffman, 1987). The profit sacrifice test would not work in these instances.

The third option is an 'as-efficient competitor' test. This asks whether the conduct would exclude a rival that is as efficient as the dominant company. It is usually put into practice by asking whether the prices charged by the dominant company meet its own costs or, in the case of margin squeeze (see section 4.7), whether the dominant company's downstream business would be profitable if it had to pay the wholesale price charged by its upstream business. The as-efficient competitor principle seeks to draw a line between conduct that simply reflects competition on the merits and exclusionary conduct that is harmful to consumers. Conduct that involves the dominant company cutting its prices down to, but not below, its own costs is beneficial to consumers and will only tend to exclude rivals that are less efficient—ie, rivals with higher costs. The test works best in pricing cases, but less well in bundling and tying, where it is not clear whether a rival that does not produce all the products in the bundle should qualify as equally or less efficient (it normally has a disadvantage, since it cannot benefit from economies of scope between all the bundled products)—see section 4.8.

The principle that only conduct that would exclude as-efficient competitors is abusive has been reflected in EU case law on predatory pricing since *AKZO* (1993), which states that predation can be presumed if a dominant company sets prices below average variable cost (AVC).[11] Other cost floors have since been proposed and used—the Commission's 2008 Guidance document emphasizes average avoidable cost (AAC) and long-run incremental cost (LRIC)[12]—but these all fit in the framework of the as-efficient competitor test (we explain the main cost concepts in section 4.3). If prices are above the chosen cost benchmark, equally efficient companies—those with similar costs—can still compete in the market. The Commission's Guidance is clear in its support for the as-efficient competitor test:

> Vigorous price competition is generally beneficial to consumers. With a view to preventing anti-competitive foreclosure, the Commission will normally only intervene where the conduct concerned has already been or is capable of hampering competition from competitors which are considered to be as efficient as the dominant undertaking.[13]

Practical problems with this test can arise in markets where an incumbent company faces competition from new entrants that do not enjoy the same scale advantages, and

---

[11] Case C-62/86 *AKZO Chemie BV v Commission*, [1991] ECR I-3359; [1993] 5 CMLR 215.

[12] European Commission (2008), 'Guidance on the Commission's Enforcement Priorities in Applying Article 82 EC Treaty to Abusive Exclusionary Conduct by Dominant Undertakings', December.

[13] Ibid., at [23].

are therefore not as efficient, or at least *not yet* as efficient. The Guidance document leaves the door open for a finding that, when network or learning effects exist, a competitor that is currently less efficient than the dominant company may be foreclosed by 'particular price-based conduct'.[14] The implication of this statement is that even prices above average total cost (ATC) could possibly be deemed predatory. This raises difficult policy questions, since it could lead to the protection of inefficient companies. It may also be impractical for compliance—how is a dominant company to know its competitors' costs in order to benchmark whether its prices fall below that level? One area where this 'not-yet-as-efficient' competitor standard has been implemented is in markets that are in the process of being liberalized, where a former state monopoly is the dominant company and new entrants are expected to gain scale advantages, and hence become more efficient, over time. We return to this issue in section 4.7 on margin squeeze, where regulators have used the concept of a 'hypothetical reasonably efficient' competitor in place of the 'as-efficient' competitor in some situations.

If we settle on the as-efficient competitor test as the main criterion in abuse cases, the next question is how to measure the 'as-efficient' costs. In section 4.3 we explain the main cost benchmarks.

4.2.4 ABUSE OF COLLECTIVE DOMINANCE

Given that Article 102 refers to abuses by 'one or more undertakings', dominance is not necessarily only a matter of single-firm conduct. Abuse cases based on collective dominance are rare, and this has a logical reason: collective dominance is more commonly associated with collusion (explicit or tacit) than with exclusionary practices. Explicit collusion and concerted practices among competitors are caught under Article 101 (discussed in Chapter 5). This includes collective boycotts (which in effect are similar to a refusal to supply by an individually dominant company). Tacit collusion is more difficult to address under Article 101, a reason why merger control (discussed in Chapter 7) seeks to prevent the creation of conditions that allow for tacit collusion (these conditions are discussed in Chapter 3).

The legal test for a collective dominant position requires two or more companies that are independent economic entities to be united by some economic links such that they adopt the same conduct in the market. In *Cewal* (1993), the Commission found an abuse of dominance by a shipping conference which tried to eliminate its main independent competitor on a certain route by signing exclusive agreements with the port authorities, establishing loyalty arrangements with clients, and employing so-called 'fighting ships'.[15] The role of these ships was to target the competitor with selective price cuts, avoiding the need to lower the incumbent companies' prices across the board. The shipping conference established a Special Fighting Committee which saw to it that freight tariffs were modified

---

[14] Ibid., at [24].

[15] *Cewal*, [1993] OJ L34/20. This decision was upheld in Cases T-24/93 etc *Compagnie Maritime Belge Transports SA v Commission* [1996] ECR II-1201; [1997] 4 CMLR 273.

with respect to the prevailing conference tariffs, in order to offer lower rates than the competitor for vessels sailing on the same date. The difference between the fighting tariff and the prevailing tariff was absorbed by all conference members.

Yet shipping conferences are rather exceptional, since they could act almost as one entity while benefiting from a block exemption from Article 101 (this privilege was removed in 2006[16]). For collective dominance more generally, you can see that parallel conduct motivated by economic links (and yet without amounting to a concerted practice) is likely to be rare, and found only where there are contractual links between the companies involved which give them shared economic interests. For example, consider clubs organizing a sports league which behave in parallel when selling TV rights, or companies that may behave in parallel as a consequence of cross-shareholdings. For the most part, such arrangements are treated under Article 101 or as joint ventures under merger control. Where collective dominance issues do arise under Article 102, it is important to establish the link between dominance and the effects on competition: are all the collectively dominant companies adopting the same conduct at the same time, such that the full force of their dominant position is utilized? We return to the relevance of this link between dominance and effects in sections 4.4 (on predatory pricing).

4.2.5 DOMINANCE AND ABUSE IN RELATED MARKETS

EU case law determines that a dominant position in one market can be abused in a related market. There is no clear definition of a 'related market' and the term tends to be interpreted quite widely. The principle was first set out by the European Court of Justice in the *Tetra Pak II* case by reference to 'associative links':

> The relevance of the associative links which the Court of First Instance [now General Court] thus took into account cannot be denied. The fact that the various materials involved are used for packaging the same basic liquid products shows that Tetra Pak's customers in one sector are also potential customers in the other. That possibility is borne out by statistics showing that in 1987 approximately 35% of Tetra Pak's customers bought both aseptic and non-aseptic systems. It is also relevant to note that Tetra Pak and its most important competitor, PKL, were present on all four markets. Given its almost complete domination of the aseptic markets, Tetra Pak could also count on a favoured status on the non-aseptic markets. Thanks to its position on the former markets, it could concentrate its efforts on the latter by acting independently of the other economic operators . . .

> Accordingly, the Court of First Instance was right to accept the application of Article 86 [now 102] of the Treaty in this case, given that the quasi-monopoly enjoyed by Tetra Pak on the aseptic markets and its leading position on the distinct, though closely associated, non-aseptic markets placed it in a situation comparable to that of holding a dominant position on the markets in question as a whole.[17]

---

[16] European Commission (2006), 'Competition: Commission welcomes Council agreement to end exemption for liner shipping conferences', press release, 26 September.
[17] Case C-333/94 *Tetra Pak v Commission* [1996] ECR 1-5951 at [29]–[31].

From an economic perspective a related market will be one of two types. The first is where markets are linked vertically. Where a company has control of a key input into a downstream market in which it is competing with other suppliers, this might enable it to foreclose the downstream market. The second is the *Tetra Pak II* situation where markets are linked horizontally—a company has dominance in one product market and uses it to acquire dominance or strengthen an existing dominant position in a related market. The horizontal link between markets will be strongest when two products are complements (vertically related products are by nature complements—see also Chapters 2 and 6). An example of vertically related markets would be the market for the collection and sorting of letters—which is a (potentially) competitive activity in countries that have liberalized the postal services sector—and the market for access to the incumbent's delivery network (which has aspects of a natural monopoly). An example of horizontally related markets would be the market for the delivery of general letters and that for business-to-business mail services. In the *De Post-La Poste* case, the Belgian incumbent, which was dominant in the market for the delivery of 'normal' letters, was found by the European Commission to have abused that position with the aim of eliminating a competitor in the neighbouring market for business-to-business mail services.[18] From an economic perspective, this 'related market' principle makes sense, since 'leveraging' of market power from one market to another (vertically or horizontally) can be a rational strategy. However, it is incorrect to assume that a dominant position in one market automatically gives a company the ability to behave anti-competitively in another market. It is important to establish a clear link between the two markets and identify the mechanism through which the position in one market can be used to advantage in the other. We return to this topic in sections 4.4 (on predatory pricing) and 4.8 (on bundling and tying).

4.3 COST BENCHMARKS FOR EXCLUSIONARY CONDUCT

In line with the as-efficient competitor test, cost benchmarks can help you distinguish between situations in which the dominant company's pricing would force the exit of as-efficient rivals, and situations in which that pricing would exclude only less efficient rivals. The starting point for testing below-cost pricing was proposed by Areeda and Turner (1975, p 712):

> marginal-cost pricing by a monopolist should be tolerated even though losses could be minimized or profits increased at a lower output and higher price, for the reasons, among others, that marginal-cost pricing leads to a proper resource allocation and is consistent with competition on the merits. Neither reason obtains when the monopolist prices below marginal cost.

---

[18] *De Post-La Poste* (Case COMP/37.859) Commission Decision 2002/180/EC, [2002] OJ L61/32.

This principle gained widespread acceptance in the US courts and later in competition regimes elsewhere. Several other cost benchmarks have been used in competition law as well, including a number of variants of marginal cost. As discussed in this section, the European Commission's Guidance on Article 102 expresses a preference for two cost benchmarks: AAC and LRIC (the Commission uses the term long-run average incremental cost, or LRAIC).[19] EU case law refers to AVC and ATC.[20] As regards the USA, 'modern antitrust courts look to the relation of price to "avoidable" or "incremental" costs as a way of segregating price cuts that are "suspect" from those that are not.'[21] This section provides explanations of all these cost concepts, starting with marginal cost.

4.3.1 MARGINAL COST

Marginal cost is the cost of producing the last unit of output. It normally refers to the change in total cost caused by producing a unit of output in the short run, ie, the period in which a company does not change its fixed costs, such as its plant. As we saw in Chapter 1, as long as price exceeds marginal cost, each additional sale will make a contribution to profit. Suppose a dominant company produces 150 units at a variable unit cost of €8, and sells them at a price of €45. In order to combat entry it decides to expand output to depress the market price. As such it produces an additional 50 units at a variable cost of €10 per unit and now sells 200 units at a price of €25 (the additional units cost slightly more to produce because the existing plant has a capacity of 150, so an additional, somewhat less efficient, machine must be hired). Since the company would have sold 150 units absent the alleged exclusionary conduct, the potentially exclusionary increment is 50 units. The dominant company's marginal cost (the cost of producing the last unit) is €10, and the pricing strategy is profitable on this basis. Table 4.1 illustrates.

Marginal cost is not always as straightforward as in our example in Table 4.1. What is the marginal cost of a seat on your flight from London to Milan at 7.45am? There is no unique answer to this question. It depends on two dimensions: the relevant marginal (or incremental) unit of output, and the relevant time period. The more you expand these two dimensions, the more costs are included in your measure of marginal (or incremental) cost. If the plane is about to take off and has an empty seat, the marginal cost to the airline of filling that seat is close to zero (the weight of the extra passenger will add a fraction to the fuel costs). If the relevant increment is the scheduled 7.45am flight as a whole, you include the costs of flying the plane, including fuel, crew and variable airport charges. If the relevant increment is the whole London–Milan route, yet more costs become part of the marginal (incremental) cost, including the costs of

---

[19] European Commission (2008), 'Guidance on the Commission's Enforcement Priorities in Applying Article 82 EC Treaty to Abusive Exclusionary Conduct by Dominant Undertakings', December, [26].

[20] Case C-62/86 *AKZO Chemie BV v Commission* [1991] ECR I-3359; [1993] 5 CMLR 215.

[21] *Barry Wright Corp v ITT Grinnell Corp* 724 F 2d 227, 232 (1st Cir. 1983).

Table 4.1 Marginal cost

Initial production	150 units
Expanded production following entry	200 units
Alleged exclusionary output	50 units
Variable costs (€)	
Variable cost on initial units	8
Variable cost on additional units (including the last unit)	10
Cost benchmark (€)	
Marginal cost	10

setting up additional service facilities at either airport. In any abuse case where cost benchmarks are used, it is therefore crucial to identify the increment and timeframe that would be most informative on whether an as-efficient competitor can effectively compete in the market.

In economics, marginal cost will normally refer to the cost of the last unit of output—ie, in the airline example the relevant unit of output would be the marginal seat, and the relevant marginal cost would therefore be close to zero. But you can see that this is somewhat unsatisfactory for a below-cost pricing case—if marginal cost indicates the cost of only a single unit, comparing price with marginal cost tells us only whether the dominant company is losing money on the very last unit produced. We are usually interested in whether the dominant company's alleged exclusionary strategy makes sense across the whole increment of potentially exclusionary output, not merely on the last unit of that output. Marginal and incremental costs are thus closely related concepts; the difference being that the latter relates to a larger increment than just the last unit of output.

4.3.2 AVERAGE VARIABLE COST

AVC is the sum of all the costs that vary with the quantity of a particular good, divided by the total quantity. Typical costs that vary with changes in output are materials, fuel and labour. The AVC is usually applied in a short-term context, taking production capacity as given and excluding all fixed costs. But it can also have a time dimension—as time passes, a higher proportion of a company's fixed costs tend to become variable, making AVC an increasing function of time. As such, using AVC requires (sometimes difficult) determinations of whether a particular cost is fixed or variable. Continuing with our example, the AVC of the activity as a whole is €8.50 per unit—(150 units at €8 per unit + 50 units at €10 per unit), divided by 200 total units; see Table 4.2.

AVC was suggested by Areeda and Turner (1975) themselves as a more workable proxy for marginal cost. It is a better match for the information typically contained in a company's accounts and therefore easier to calculate. As noted in section 4.2, the European Court of Justice used AVC as a cost benchmark in *AKZO*.[22] One issue to

---

[22] Case C-62/86 *AKZO Chemie BV v Commission* [1991] ECR I-3359; [1993] 5 CMLR 215.

Table 4.2 Average variable cost

Initial production	150 units
Expanded production following entry	200 units
Alleged exclusionary output	50 units
Variable costs (€)	
Variable cost on initial units	8
Variable cost on additional units	10
Cost benchmark (€)	
Average variable cost	8.5
Marginal cost	10

watch is that AVC normally measures the average over the product's entire output, not just of the incremental output that is the focus of the exclusionary conduct claim. This can be adjusted as necessary by looking at the AVC of the incremental amount of output—in Table 4.2 this would be €10 instead of €8.50.

4.3.3 AVERAGE AVOIDABLE COST

AAC covers all the costs, including both variable costs and product-specific fixed costs, that could have been avoided if the company had not produced a discrete amount of additional output. Normally this refers to the amount that could have been avoided by not engaging in the exclusionary strategy. The absence or presence of avoidable losses is a good indicator of whether the dominant company is making or losing money on this increment. A failure to cover AAC indicates that the dominant company is sacrificing profits in the medium term (since it cannot cover the relevant fixed costs) and that an equally efficient competitor cannot serve the targeted customers without incurring a loss. Unlike LRIC (discussed next), AAC omits all fixed costs that were already *sunk* before the time of the predation—ie, costs that can no longer be avoided, such as product-specific brand advertising. (We explained sunk costs in Chapter 2 in the context of supply-side substitution.) Consequently, AAC will generally be lower than LRIC.

Continuing with the above example, the dominant company's AAC is €20 per unit—(€500 for avoidable product-specific fixed costs + 50 units at €10 per unit), divided by 50 units. Here the avoidable fixed cost is the cost of hiring a machine used to produce the 50 additional units. It is a fixed cost in this context because it is incurred regardless of whether 50, 30, or 10 extra units are produced, but it is still an avoidable cost. See Table 4.3.

Helpfully, by including all costs that the company could have avoided by not producing the additional units, using AAC as a benchmark circumvents the difficult issue of whether a particular cost is strictly fixed or variable (you are interested only in the increment). Still, there is scope for debate over what is an avoidable cost—for example,

Table 4.3 Average avoidable cost

Initial production	150 units
Expanded production following entry	200 units
Alleged exclusionary output	50 units
Variable costs (€)	
Variable cost on initial units	8
Variable cost on additional units	10
Fixed costs (€)	
Cost of plant that can be avoided (machines that don't need to run)	500
Cost benchmark (€)	
Average variable cost	8.5
Marginal cost	10
Average avoidable cost	20

in the *Intel* rebates case (discussed in more detail in section 4.6) there was extensive discussion of what were the relevant costs for AAC.[23]

In its Guidance on Article 102, the Commission has proposed that prices below AAC indicate that the dominant company is sacrificing profits in the short term and that an equally efficient competitor cannot serve the targeted customers without incurring a loss.[24] AAC therefore establishes the price floor for the provision of a good or service to a targeted group of customers for a limited period of time. Avoidable cost makes sense in most cases as it gets at the 'sacrifice' of predation: the company would have been better off producing nothing and avoiding these costs than producing the units of output at a price below AAC.

4.3.4 LONG-RUN INCREMENTAL COST

LRIC is the change in total costs resulting from the production of an increment in the quantity of output, which can be the whole output of the product in question or just the incremental output associated with the exclusionary conduct. The Commission's Guidance refers to LRIC as 'the average of all the (variable and fixed) costs that a company incurs to produce a particular product.'[25] But if we want to understand the profitability of the exclusionary conduct it can be more appropriate to calculate the LRIC of just the additional output associated with exclusion. You can see here that the increment matters. Unlike AAC, LRIC includes all product-specific fixed costs even if those costs were sunk before the period of predatory pricing, ie, LRIC includes both recoverable and sunk fixed costs.

---

[23] *Intel* (Case COMP/C-3/37.990), Commission Decision of 13 May 2009 D(2009) 3726 final, [1036]–[1153].
[24] European Commission (2008), 'Guidance on the Commission's Enforcement Priorities in Applying Article 82 EC Treaty to Abusive Exclusionary Conduct by Dominant Undertakings', December, [26].
[25] Ibid., at n 2.

Continuing with our example, think of the dominant company responding to the threat of entry—first it takes out newspaper advertising to promote its product and expands its factory space, and subsequently it lowers prices and expands output. The advertising and factory expansion are associated with the alleged exclusionary output and form part of LRIC. They do not form part of AAC—even if the additional 50 units are never produced, these costs can no longer be avoided once incurred. In our example the LRIC of the incremental output is €40—(€500 for plant + €500 for advertising + €500 for factory space + 50 units at €10 per unit), divided by 50 units. In our example it is also easy to calculate the LRIC of the whole product (ie, all 200 units) rather than the relevant increment, which in this case is €38.50—€2,000 for plant + €2,000 for advertising + €2,000 for factory space + (150 units at €8 per unit + 50 units at €10 per unit), divided by 200 total units. See Table 4.4. You can see that LRIC in this example comes close to ATC. A main difference between the two (not reflected in our example) is that ATC is based on current or past costs, whereas LRIC it is forward-looking and may therefore incorporate any expected shifts in costs (eg, in telecoms the costs of network and equipment keep falling, so that the LRIC for a brand new telephony network may be lower than the ATC of the current network). Another difference (which is reflected in the example) is where the company produces multiple products and the ATC of a product may include an allocated part of a company's overhead costs, while the LRIC of that particular product does not.

Pricing below LRIC can be economically rational apart from any exclusionary effect. As LRIC includes all product-specific sunk costs, a company pricing below that cost can

Table 4.4 Long-run incremental cost

Initial production	150 units
Expanded production following entry	200 units
Alleged exclusionary output	50 units
Variable costs (€)	
Variable cost on initial units	8
Variable cost on additional units	10
Fixed costs (€)	
Cost of plant that can be avoided (machines that don't need to run)	500 for 50 units; 2,000 for all units
Cost of brand advertising (sunk)	500 for 50 units; 2,000 for all units
Common cost of factory attributable to this product	500 for 50 units; 2,000 for all units
Cost benchmark (€)	
Average variable cost	8.5
Marginal cost	10
Average avoidable cost	20
Long-run incremental cost	40 for 50 units; 38.5 for all units

still generate a positive cash flow (ie, it would cover its variable costs and hence make a contribution to the recovery of its already-sunk fixed costs). Such sales, which a LRIC or ATC standard might condemn as exclusionary, would therefore be potentially profitable and hence might reflect commercially rational behaviour. In its Guidance, the European Commission has therefore proposed that prices above AAC but below LRIC indicate that an equally efficient competitor *could be* foreclosed from the market—there is no presumption of foreclosure as is the case with prices below AAC.[26] LRIC serves in most cases as a price floor above which concerns about exclusionary below-cost pricing are unlikely to materialize.

LRIC has been deemed to be of particular relevance to network industries (as is also reflected in price and access regulation in these industries—see Chapter 9). In its 1998 notice on the application of the competition rules to the telecommunications industry, the Commission indicated that LRIC could be an appropriate cost floor for predation cases:

> In the case of the provision of telecommunications services, a price which equates to the variable cost of a service may be substantially lower than the price the operator needs in order to cover the cost of providing the service. To apply the AKZO test to prices which are to be applied over time by an operator, and which will form the basis of that operator's decisions to invest, the costs considered should include the total costs which are incremental to the provision of the service. In analysing the situation, consideration will have to be given to the appropriate time frame over which costs should be analysed. In most cases, there is reason to believe that neither the very short nor very long run are appropriate.

> In these circumstances, the Commission will often need to examine the average incremental costs of providing a service, and may need to examine average incremental costs over a longer period than one year.[27]

In *Deutsche Post* (2001), the Commission found the incumbent postal operator in Germany guilty of predatory pricing (and of cross-subsidy and granting fidelity rebates). It determined that:

> [A]ny service provided by the beneficiary of a monopoly in open competition has to cover at least the additional or incremental cost incurred in branching out into the competitive sector. The Commission considers that any cost coverage below this level is predatory pricing which falls foul of Article 82 of the EC Treaty [now Article 102 TFEU].[28]

4.3.5 AVERAGE TOTAL COST

ATC is the sum of fixed and variable costs, divided by total output. In our example the dominant company manufactures several products. It has allocated a share of the cost

---

[26] European Commission (2008), 'Guidance on the Commission's Enforcement Priorities in Applying Article 82 EC Treaty to Abusive Exclusionary Conduct by Dominant Undertakings', December, [26].

[27] European Commission (1998), 'Notice on the application of competition rules to access agreements in the telecommunications sector—Framework, Relevant Markets and Principles' [1998] OJ C265, [114]–[115].

[28] *Deutsche Post AG* (Case COMP/35.141) Commission Decision 2001/354/EC, [2001] OJ L125/27.

of its overheads to the product which is subject to the exclusionary conduct claim. The overheads would include a share of investment in company-wide branding and head office costs. Thus we have €7,000 total fixed costs for this product, €1,000 of which is the allocated overhead. The €1,000 is not included in the LRIC because it is not incremental to producing the product in question. So the ATC is €43.50—(€7,000 total fixed cost + (150 units at €8 per unit + 50 units at €10 per unit)), divided by 200 total units. See Table 4.5.

Prices above ATC are not exclusionary under the as-efficient competitor test since they allow any efficient competitor to make a profit. There are two possible challenges to this conclusion. One is in the case of structured or targeted discounts, where prices can exceed ATC if measured against all units sold to a customer, but below cost (even below AAC) if measured against the 'contestable' units only. We explain this point in section 4.6. The second challenge is where the dominant company enjoys positive network effects or economies of scope that a competitor cannot currently replicate. In this case, while the competitor's costs are higher than those of the dominant company, a competition authority may take a dynamic view on costs, ie, whether in the absence of the alleged exclusionary conduct or when competition is more established, the rival could overcome its disadvantage and become 'as efficient'—see sections 4.2 and 4.7 on the concept of a 'hypothetical reasonably efficient' competitor that has been used in place of the 'as-efficient' competitor.

What is the conclusion in this example? The dominant company's initial price of €45 covered ATC. The new price of €25 is above the AAC of €20 but below the LRIC of €40 (or €38.50 if the LRIC is measured for the whole product). It is therefore capable of

Table 4.5 Average total cost

Initial production	150 units
Expanded production following entry	200 units
Alleged exclusionary output	50 units
Variable costs (€)	
Variable cost on initial units	8
Variable cost on additional units	10
Fixed costs (€)	
Cost of plant that can be avoided (machines that don't need to run)	2,000
Cost of brand advertising (sunk)	2,000
Common cost of factory attributable to this product	2,000
Allocated overheads (not incremental to this product)	1,000
Cost benchmark (€)	
Average variable cost	8.5
Marginal cost	10
Average avoidable cost	20
Long-run incremental cost	40 for 50 units;
	38.5 for all units
Average total cost	43.5

foreclosing an as-efficient entrant since prices are below the level of costs that this entrant would have to incur to build up the same production capability. However, pricing below LRIC but above AAC can be commercially rational without intent to foreclose. In addition, an efficient competitor that is already in the market can also price at €25, cover its avoidable costs and make a €5 per unit contribution to the recovery of its already sunk fixed costs. Cost benchmarks are useful in this type of pricing abuse case, but must be considered in conjunction with other evidence on market structure and conduct, as we shall see in the remainder of this chapter.

4.3.6 PROFITABILITY TESTS FOR BELOW-COST PRICING

One specific issue in predation and margin squeeze is the allocation of costs over time—the question being what costs are within the alleged period of below-cost pricing. Where genuine investment is required in a particular year, it would be incorrect to assume that losses in that year represent below-cost pricing, since that investment is relevant to revenues not only in that year but in future years. The treatment of costs should reflect these conditions. Rather than price–cost comparisons you can analyse the profitability of the product over a longer timeframe, using the techniques of profitability analysis described in Chapter 3. Investments should be amortized or depreciated according to their economic use—for example, operational costs (marketing or promotional costs) that are front-loaded within a project lifetime, but may justifiably be recovered over a number of years. The correct way to account for these is to amortize them over a period linked to the underlying output they are supporting. Only then may any remaining observed losses be treated as an indication of below-cost pricing.

A potential problem of profitability analysis in exclusion cases is that it does not easily distinguish between future profits arising from normal competition and future profits that result from a successful predatory strategy. We come back to this in section 4.4. We note that considering profitability in these cases is still more appropriate than a simple price–cost comparison; it can provide useful insight into the drivers of the losses that you observe in the early years (do they reflect a genuine investment to stimulate subsequent demand?), and the profits you observe in subsequent years (do they depend on the exit of competitors?).

Another challenge is that the results of the profitability test—or indeed of any price–cost test—may be sensitive to specific assumptions or accounting approaches. In a margin squeeze case relating to the broadcaster BSkyB, the Office of Fair Trading (OFT) included as a relevant cost the investment in supplying set-top boxes to new subscribers, and amortized this cost over an average subscriber lifetime of ten years.[29] However, alternative amortization periods might also have been valid—for example, based on the useful lifetime of a set-top box (which is less than ten years due to the

---

[29] Office of Fair Trading (2002), 'BSkyB Investigation: Alleged Infringement of the Chapter II Prohibition', OFT Decision, CA98/20/2002, 17 December, [463].

impact of changing technology). Such changes would have an appreciable impact on the results of a margin squeeze or predation test. If the set-top box were instead amortized over five years, the relevant costs for the benchmark would have been higher and profitability lower. Further examples of profitability analysis in margin squeeze cases are given in section 4.7.

4.4 PREDATION

4.4.1 WHAT IS PREDATION, FROM AN ECONOMIC PERSPECTIVE?

Predatory pricing is one of the most debated business practices in competition law. Intuitively, there seems nothing wrong with a low price since that is exactly what competition is supposed to bring about. Still, ever since the enactment of the first competition laws, the notion has existed that a company might unduly force its rivals out of the market by setting low prices. An early predation case was that against Standard Oil, which eventually resulted in the break-up of the company in 1911 (as discussed in Chapter 9 on the design of remedies). One accusation levied against Standard Oil was that 'it frequently cuts prices to a point which leaves even the Standard little or no profit, and which more often leaves no profit to the competitor, whose costs are ordinarily somewhat higher.'[30]

From an economic perspective, predatory pricing involves a dominant company deliberately incurring short-term losses to eliminate competitors or to prevent entry into the market, in order to be able to charge monopolistic prices in the long term. This is difficult to distinguish from fierce but healthy price competition. Pricing low, and even below cost, is a common commercial practice—for example, when companies enter a new market, launch a new product, or wish to gain market share. Predatory pricing is to some extent a self-deterring practice—predation pays off only if the predator can subsequently raise prices sufficiently to recover the previous losses, making enough extra profit thereafter to justify the risks. These risks are not small, since even the exit of a rival does not by itself destroy the rival's assets. Those assets might be acquired by entrants who can spring up to take the defunct company's place, unless there are entry barriers which prevent such a resurgence of competition. As such, while complaints about predation may be frequent—companies often cry foul when they see a rival undercutting them—actual instances of predatory pricing are not. Indeed, according to the Canadian 1992 Predatory Pricing Enforcement Guidelines:

> in the period 1980 to 1990 the Director [of Investigation and Research] received some 550 complaints alleging an offense under the predatory pricing provisions. Of those complaints, only 23 resulted in formal inquiries under the [Competition] Act, four were referred to the Attorney General, and only three resulted in the laying of charges.[31]

---

[30] *Standard Oil Company of New Jersey v United States* 221 US 1 (1911).

[31] Director of Investigation and Research (1992), 'Predatory pricing enforcement guidelines'. The latest version of these guidelines was published in 2008.

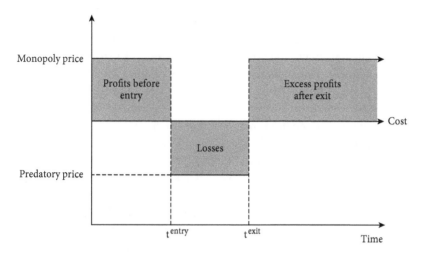

Fig. 4.1 The three stages of predatory pricing

How can you distinguish predatory pricing from instances of aggressive but desirable low pricing? Predatory pricing can be conceptualized as a three-stage process, as shown in Figure 4.1. In the first stage you have a monopolist (or a dominant company that is happy to tolerate some smaller rivals in the market). The second stage is where the dominant company engages in below-cost pricing against a new or existing competitor. In the third and final stage, the rivals have been forced out of the market and the dominant company can reap monopoly profits again. Any standard for assessing predatory pricing needs to take into account these three stages. The dominance criterion in essence considers the first stage: does the alleged predator have a dominant position in the market to start with? This makes economic sense and may seem obvious. However, in some cases the predation allegation relates to a new or related market where the predator is not (yet) dominant, and in these cases the likelihood of successfully completing the three stages may be lower—this is not always taken into account in practice, as we will see below. The cost and profit benchmarks that we discussed in section 4.3 focus on the second stage. Is the alleged predator indeed pricing below cost and hence incurring losses? The 1993 *AKZO* judgment determined that prices below AVC should be presumed to be predatory, prices in the range between AVC and ATC can be predatory if set in the context of a plan aimed at eliminating a competitor, and prices above ATC do not normally indicate predation.[32] Section 4.3 has set out the other benchmarks that have been considered in competition law, including AAC, LRIC and profitability over a longer timeframe. The use of cost benchmarks is in line with the as-efficient competitor test as set out in section 4.2.

[32] Case C-62/86 *AKZO Chemie BV v Commission* [1991] ECR-I 3359; [1993] 5 CMLR 215.

Another set of criteria that we discuss in this section focuses on the third stage, where the losses of the second stage are being recovered. If the concern about abuse of dominance is harm to consumers and not harm to competitors, it makes sense to ask if this third stage is actually likely to be reached, and if so, whether it will last a long time. In other words: is successful predation feasible? If not, there is limited consumer harm (in fact, consumers benefit from low prices in the second period), and the practice usually deters itself (although some harm may have been done to competitors in the second period). This logic is reflected in the recoupment test, which we discuss in more detail below. One advantage of this focus on the third stage is that complex price–cost comparisons for the second stage may be avoided if it is clear that the third stage is unlikely to be reached. A disadvantage is that it can be speculative if it refers only to future market developments—most predation complaints are made during the second stage (although investigations that take a long time may stretch into the third stage, in which case you can observe directly whether there is recoupment, but at the same time it may be too late to prevent any competitive harm).

4.4.2 LEGITIMATE REASONS FOR BELOW-COST PRICING

As illustrated in Figure 4.1, what you observe in cases of predation is a period of below-cost pricing, followed by a period of high prices. The trouble is that this pricing pattern can be consistent with normal commercial behaviour—for example, in the case of the introduction of a new product or where a product exhibits positive network effects (as discussed in Chapters 2 and 3). New products are often introduced at a discount, or even given away for free—according to *The Complete MBA for Dummies*, 'Giving your products away can be a great pricing strategy' (Allen and Economy, 2000). With network effects the case for doing so is even stronger. A new network product needs to reach critical mass, and one way to achieve this is by setting very low prices, giving the product away for free, or even paying early adopters. Prices are raised once critical mass has been achieved. Consumers are better off compared with the situation where the network does not get established at all. This economic logic might apply even if the network product faces no competition; in other words, monopolists may have legitimate reasons to price below cost. You can see that the AVC or other cost and profitability benchmarks may not be very informative in such cases.

If the new product does face competition—say, from a rival network product that seeks to achieve critical mass at the same time—the rational pricing strategy might provoke allegations of predatory pricing. When two new network products compete in this way, not only are price–cost tests of limited assistance, but it is also difficult to establish whether one of them is dominant since both are new to the market. Instead you could consider whether one of the providers has a dominant position in a related market which it can use to gain an undue advantage over its rival (eg, through cross-subsidy or bundling), but you would need to be explicit about the link between dominance and abuse in the two markets. In contrast, in a situation where a company already has a dominant position in the market itself, loss-leading a new product in that market seems less likely to be justifiable. A non-dominant company has more reasons to price below cost—switching costs make it rational to persuade customers to change supplier by offering an attractive discount.

Another rational reason for companies to price certain products below AVC or AAC may arise with multi-product offerings. It can be efficient to set different mark-ups for different products due to product complementarities. In restaurants, for example, the main meal can be good value but the side orders and drinks expensive. Similarly, when you buy a new car, the basic model can be priced competitively but the optional extras such as air conditioning and electric windows can be costly. With respect to aftermarkets, where a customer buys a product that results in follow-on purchases in a related market (see also Chapter 2), it is common practice to subsidize the initial expenditure in order to acquire the customer. Pricing low in the primary transaction is offset by the expected tenure of the customer. In supermarkets, so-called known-value items (KVIs, such as milk or bread) may be priced as loss-leaders to attract customers to the store where high-margin products are also available. In all these situations you observe a pattern like in Figure 4.1, except that the profits are not made in stage 3 on the same product but simultaneously in stage 2 on other products. Pricing one of the products below the relevant cost floor is in itself not harmful in these situations; you would again have to focus on the scope for recoupment of the losses, not in stage 3 but in the other products during stage 2—we return to this below. Incidentally, we note that some countries, such as Austria, Belgium, Germany, France, and Ireland, have (or had) specific legislation that outlaws below-cost pricing by retailers per se—loss-leading on KVIs is not allowed if it involves selling below the purchase price of these items. From an economic perspective this is a rather protectionist measure that may serve to shield smaller retailers from the competition from larger supermarket chains, but that has been shown to result in higher retail prices and produce negative effects on competitive dynamics.[33] Applying the normal competition law standards to these practices seems more suitable from an economic perspective.

4.4.3 STRUCTURAL TESTS: RECOUPMENT AND FEASIBILITY OF PREDATION

For decades, a general agreement on how to distinguish fierce but legitimate price competition from the relatively rare instances of actual predatory pricing was hard to find among academics and practitioners. Much of it comes down to different views on how effectively markets work and on how governments can correct them while minimizing enforcement errors. A false positive—ie, labelling a practice predatory when in fact it is not—leads to welfare losses, as prices are kept too high and inefficient suppliers are sheltered from price competition. On the other hand, a false negative—allowing prices that are in fact predatory—results in some short-run allocative inefficiency, as well as

---

[33] See Oxera (2005a), Collins and Oustapassidis (1997), and Nielsen (1997).

the social costs of monopoly in the longer run. More recently there has been some convergence of predatory pricing standards across competition regimes globally. This convergence starts with the recognition that structural conditions in many markets do not allow for predation—in terms of Figure 4.1, in many markets you may never reach stage 3 (or stage 3 is very short-lived as new entrants come in). Analysing the structural features of the market at first can be an efficient way of dealing with predation complaints.

This logic can be seen in the US Supreme Court's *Brooke Group* judgment of 1993, which established the 'recoupment test' as the primary standard for predatory pricing cases, relegating cost-based tests and inquiries into intent to a second stage:

> Recoupment is the ultimate object of an unlawful predatory pricing scheme; it is the means by which a predator profits from predation. Without it, predatory pricing produces lower aggregate prices in the market, and consumer welfare is enhanced. Although unsuccessful predatory pricing may encourage some inefficient substitution toward the product being sold at less than its cost, unsuccessful predation is in general a boon to consumers . . . That below-cost pricing may impose painful losses on its target is of no moment to the antitrust laws if competition is not injured.[34]

The recoupment test means that intervention is required only if those prices are likely to be offset (ie, recouped) at a later stage through monopoly profits. Strictly speaking, in terms of Figure 4.1, the recoupment test comes down to measuring whether the losses in stage 2 are outweighed by the subsequent profits in stage 3. It is a matter of comparing the size of the rectangle in the middle to that on the right (although the profits in stage 3 are later in time and therefore need to be discounted—see Chapters 3 and 10). In this sense, predation strategies are similar to any other financial investment decision—predation is the initial investment followed by payback once market power is achieved or restored—and this calls for a financial analysis (Elzinga and Mills, 1989).

However, the test can also be applied more pragmatically. Rather than regarding it as a rigid mathematical exercise, the US Department of Justice (DOJ) has referred to the recoupment test as 'a valuable screening device to identify implausible predatory-pricing claims'.[35] In EU competition law, the feasibility of recouping losses is now also recognized as a relevant factor in predatory pricing cases, although it had previously been rejected and is still not given the same decisive importance as it is in the USA (EU competition law has usually assumed that recoupment is feasible once dominance is established).[36] The UK authorities have generally given weight to the structural features of the market. The Competition Commission (CC) (when analysing an allegation of

---

[34] *Brooke Group Ltd v Brown & Williamson Tobacco Corp* 509 US 209 (1993).

[35] Department of Justice (2008), 'Competition and Monopoly: Single-firm Conduct Under Section 2 of the Sherman Act', September, p 69. As noted before, the DOJ withdrew this report in 2009, but this point about the recoupment test remains valid.

[36] In *France Télécom*, the ECJ acknowledged for the first time that recoupment can be a relevant factor in the assessment but it rejected the Opinion of Advocate General Mazák in this case that recoupment should be a necessary condition. Case C-202/07 P *France Télécom v EC Commission* [2009] ECR I-2369.

exclusionary low pricing in the context of a market investigation into the grocery sector, so not an abuse of dominance case) stated that for below-cost selling to be considered predatory, it is necessary to show that:

> barriers to entry or re-entry into convenience store and specialist grocery retailing are high so that new convenience or specialist grocery stores could not open in response to a weakening of the retail offer by large grocery retailers and prevent recoupment of the losses incurred during the predation stage.[37]

Incidentally, the logic of recoupment (aligned with a certain scepticism towards predation complaints) is not new. In 1904, the economist AC Pigou made the following comment in the context of 'dumping', a practice in international trade that has some similarities with predation:

> Destructive dumping into England from abroad does not take place, and for a very simple reason. The only purpose of that policy is to secure the control of the supply, and therewith the power to extract monopoly prices . . . In the British market, if a German Kartel or an American Trust kills British competitors, what advantage has it? It is still prevented from reaping its reward by the presence of sellers from other foreign countries. It will not, therefore, be worth its while to 'dump' unless it has not merely an American or a German, but a world-embracing monopoly.[38]

We now turn to how the structural characteristics of the market can be assessed when using the recoupment test as a screening device. We note here that such screening may not always be sufficient. There are cases where the market structure does lend itself to successful predation—ie, there is a serious risk that you end up in stage 3 of Figure 4.1. In those cases a full analysis of costs and other relevant factors will be required.

4.4.4 DETERMINANTS OF THE FEASIBILITY OF PREDATION

In which circumstances is it likely that the third-stage monopoly profits outweigh the losses from the predatory pricing stage? You can see that from the perspective of the predator, stage 2 must be short and stage 3 must be long—predation must be 'quick and dirty'. If stage 2 drags on, the dominant company keeps building up losses and the prospect of ever recouping these losses diminishes. Driving out competitors through low prices is usually more costly for the predator than for its victims because it has a higher market share. In the *Deutsche Post* case the below-cost period was six years, which seems rather long for there to be predatory pricing of the quick and dirty kind (in this case, the incumbent may have been able to enjoy higher profits in related markets during this period—a different type of recoupment).[39] At the other extreme, in *Aberdeen Journals*, the OFT formally found predation during only one month, which seems on the short side (indeed predation was not successful as the competitor remained in

---

[37] Competition Commission (2008), 'Groceries Market Investigation, Final Report', 30 April, [5.57].
[38] Quoted in Viner (1923), p 120.
[39] *Deutsche Post AG* (Case COMP/35.141) Commission Decision 2001/354/EC, [2001] OJ L125/27, at [36].

the market).[40] We discuss this case in more detail below. Another factor of importance is the proportion of customers that are offered low prices. The ability to exclude rivals from the market and ultimately affect consumer welfare largely depends on the proportion of the market that is foreclosed. If a dominant company with 60% of the market targets only 10% of its customers with a discount, the foreclosure effect is probably much weaker than if it offered the discount to its entire customer base—this is why practices such as targeted discounts and loyalty rebates (discussed below and in section 4.6) are generally not of the quick and dirty predation kind.

Next you would consider the structural features of the market. Successful predatory pricing requires having market power now (during the predation period) and in the future (during the recoupment period). As to current market power, the dominant company must expand output in order to depress the overall market price and put pressure on its rivals. To have a strong impact on market price, it needs a substantial market share from the start. A company with 90% of the market will find this easier than a company with only 40%—again, the degree of dominance matters. Moreover, if market demand is elastic, the dominant company must take on extra sales at a loss in order to satisfy the new demand that is created at the lower price, apart from the extra sales it has to take over from its victims as they exit. A company planning to initiate a predatory pricing campaign must therefore have sufficient capacity to expand output beyond current levels. Normally, the more excess capacity (beyond current output) a predator needs, the more costly predation will be, and hence the more difficult it will be to recoup losses. Finally, just as the dominant company needs a source of funds for predation, so an intended victim can prolong the price-cutting period by using its own reserves, obtaining outside financing, or engaging in long-term relationships with clients. The financial position of non-dominant firms in the market is therefore relevant to assessing the feasibility of predation.

As to future market structure, the costs of predation must be offset by recoupment via future monopoly profits, but such profits depend on an expectation of enhanced market power via the exclusion of rivals. As we noted above, even if current competitors are forced to exit, a monopoly price cannot always be sustained long enough because of entry by new competitors, re-entry by former rivals, or the threat of it. Recoupment of predatory losses is thus possible only if there are high barriers to entry for potential competitors. However, driving rivals out of the market simultaneously requires low barriers to exit for actual competitors. Such asymmetry between entry and exit conditions may not occur frequently since a high entry barrier may give a significant option value to remaining in the market, hence dampening incentives to exit. For example, if you know that your company's assets will go at fire-sale prices should you exit, you may hang on longer in the market than a company which can achieve good resale prices (eg, where assets are not firm-specific, such as property).

---

[40] Decision of the Director General of Fair Trading, *Predation by Aberdeen Journals Ltd*, No CA98/5/2001, [2001] UKCLR 856.

The role of entry barriers as a determinant of future market power is more important in predatory pricing cases than in other types of competition case. Analyses of vertical restraints or refusals to deal, for example, principally focus on current market power. Future market power is important for merger reviews, but also depends on factors such as the merging companies' market shares. In contrast, future market power in predation cases depends first and foremost on entry barriers, and not on market shares as such, since the alleged predator must be assumed to have a market share close to 100% after the predation period. A different situation arises where you do not have monopoly recoupment (the traditional case) but rather oligopoly recoupment. The latter is relevant when predation is meant to maintain discipline in an oligopolistic pricing scheme rather than to establish a monopoly. That is, one or more oligopolists target defectors, or new entrants, with low prices until the latter adhere to the pricing scheme. The target companies do not necessarily have to exit the market; they just have to be disciplined. The *Brooke Group* case quoted above was in fact one of alleged oligopolistic predation in the tobacco market. The Supreme Court considered that oligopoly recoupment is even more difficult than monopoly recoupment, since it requires extensive coordination between competitors during both the predation and the recoupment periods.

4.4.5 REPUTATION EFFECTS: ACHIEVING RECOUPMENT BY SCARING OFF FUTURE ENTRANTS

In a predation case there is a further relevant entry barrier: the predatory strategy may send a signal that the dominant company will price aggressively in response to any future entry. This provides another means to achieve recoupment. The argument is intuitive. Even when it is easy to open the door to a house and step inside (there are no entry barriers), you may think twice about it if you see the pathway to the house littered with corpses. Economics, and in particular game theory, has formalized this logic, and identified the circumstances in which it is most likely to apply.[41] This is therefore the place to introduce you to some basic game theory.

Figure 4.2 shows a game tree. There are two players—the incumbent and a potential entrant—and they move sequentially (in Chapter 3 you saw an oligopoly game where the two rivals moved simultaneously). The entrant first decides whether to enter or stay out. Then, if the entrant comes in, the incumbent decides whether to 'fight' by pricing low and expanding output or to simply 'share' the market. The pay-offs to the two players are shown at the bottom for each possible outcome of the tree. Consider the left tree first. Here the entrant faces a 'normal' incumbent. For this incumbent, fighting the entrant is costly, ie, it requires below-cost pricing. There are three outcomes of this tree. To the left, the entrant stays out and the incumbent reaps monopoly profits of 10 (the entrant's pay-off is 0). In the middle, the incumbent fights the entrant and both make a

---

[41] The leading works are Selten (1978), Kreps and Wilson (1982), and Milgrom and Roberts (1982). For a critique, see ten Kate and Niels (2002).

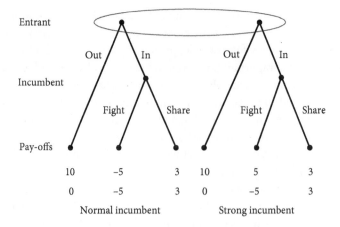

Fig. 4.2 A game tree: reputation effects in predation

loss of 5. In the outcome to the right, the incumbent accommodates entry and both players make a profit of 3. If this game on the left-hand side of the figure were played by itself and only once, the incumbent would never fight, because fighting is always more costly than sharing the market. Knowing this, the entrant will always enter. Predation does not work. However, what if the entrant does not know whether it faces a 'normal' incumbent or a 'strong' incumbent? As shown on the right-hand part of the tree, by strong incumbent we mean one that has an efficiently low cost base and spare capacity. This strong encumbent can successfully fight entry by just undercutting the entrant's costs (but not its own costs) and keep the market to itself—in the figure it gets a positive pay-off of 5 from fighting. (Other models feature an incumbent that is 'crazy', ie, it gets some positive utility from picking a fight, but the effect is the same as for the strong incumbent.) The entrant's lack of information regarding whether the incumbent is strong or weak is denoted by the ellipsoid at the top of the figure—the entrant does not know in which part of the game tree it is playing. Such imperfect information is not an unrealistic assumption; entrants may generally not know what the incumbent's cost base really is like. Importantly, in this situation, 'normal' incumbents can create a repu-tation—or essentially bluff—that they are strong (or crazy), and thereby scare off future entrants.

The incumbent's interest is therefore to try to signal to all entrants that it is strong. Imagine that the incumbent is a multi-product firm. Predating in one market can bring wider benefits if it establishes a reputation as a strong incumbent that will always fight predation across its other key markets. Recoupment is no longer just about future prof-its for the product that is subject to predation, but also about protecting profits earned in other markets in which the incumbent is dominant.

This logic of reputation effects has been given some weight in the assessment of entry barriers in a number of abuse and merger cases (ie, it is not restricted to analysing recoupment in predation cases). The European Commission's merger decision on *Ryanair/Aer Lingus* stated that:

> The Commission's investigation showed that Ryanair has a reputation of engaging in aggressive competition in case of new entry to Ireland, notably by temporarily lowering prices and expanding its capacity in order to drive out the new entrant on routes to or from Ireland. The likelihood of aggressive retaliation is relevant because it has the factual consequence that potential entrants are likely to be deterred from entry and that it is less likely that a dominant firm will be constrained by the threat of new entry.[42]

The logic can also be seen in the Commission's decision in *Microsoft*, albeit that the reputation being established is for exclusionary tying (we return to this case in Chapter 9 on the design of remedies):

> Microsoft's tying of [Windows Media Player] also sends signals which deter innovation in any technologies which Microsoft could conceivably take interest in and tie with Windows in the future. Microsoft's tying instils actors in the relevant software markets with a sense of precariousness thereby weakening both software developers' incentives to innovate in similar areas and venture capitalists' proclivity to invest in independent software application companies. A start-up intending to enter or raise venture capital in such a market will be forced to test the resilience of its business model against the eventuality of Microsoft deciding to bundle its own version of the product with Windows.[43]

A US court that ruled on *Microsoft* made a similar comment:

> Most harmful of all is the message that Microsoft's actions have conveyed to every enterprise with the potential to innovate in the computer industry. Through its conduct toward Netscape, IBM, Compaq, Intel, and others, Microsoft has demonstrated that it will use its prodigious market power and immense profits to harm any firm that insists on pursuing initiatives that could intensify competition against one of Microsoft's core products. Microsoft's past success in hurting such companies and stifling innovation deters investment in technologies and businesses that exhibit the potential to threaten Microsoft. The ultimate result is that some innovations that would truly benefit consumers never occur for the sole reason that they do not coincide with Microsoft's self-interest.[44]

Thus, the incentives to deter entrants are enhanced if the predator is active in several markets—either sequentially in time, or in a number of geographic or product markets. However, bear in mind that the predator may be bluffing if it is using predation in one market to signal strength in other markets. Ultimately, in the game-theoretical

---

[42] *Ryanair/Aer Lingus* (Case COMP/M.4439), Commission Decision of 27 July 2007 C(2007) 3104.

[43] *Microsoft* (Case COMP/C-3/37.792), Commission Decision of 24 March 2004, [983].

[44] *US v Microsoft*, Civil Action No 98-1232 (TPJ), US District Court for the District of Colombia, Court's Findings of Fact, 5 November 1999.

logic, bluffing works only if weakness is never revealed (ie, entry is always fought). Even Microsoft has not always managed to fight off entrants for some of its products and thereby revealed that it is perhaps not the 'strong' or 'crazy' incumbent of the theoretical models. Another question is whether the act of bluffing itself should be considered abusive. Any aggressive act might in theory add to a company's reputation, and in game theory the predatory acts do not necessarily involve below-cost pricing (any undercutting of the entrant may do). From this perspective the cost benchmarks discussed in section 4.3 seem more suitable for identifying practices that exclude as-efficient competitors. The reputational effects may be useful additional indicators when assessing recoupment or entry barriers more generally.

4.4.6 RECOUPMENT IN A RELATED MARKET

We mentioned above that recoupment does not have to be sequential in time; it can also occur in a related market. An example is the *Napp* case in which the OFT found that the dominant company had engaged in predatory and excessive pricing in the supply of sustained-release morphine (the excessive pricing part of this case is discussed in section 4.10). The OFT finding was upheld on appeal by the Competition Appeal Tribunal (CAT).[45] Napp and its economists had argued that below-cost sales of morphine to hospitals were not anti-competitive because the losses would be recouped through the higher-priced sales to consumers in the pharmacy or 'community' sector (in Chapter 11 we discuss the CAT's view on the role of the economists in this case). The question is whether this is a defence against alleged predation, or actually evidence in favour of finding a predation abuse.

Napp's dominant position was established through its successful patenting of the first sustained-release morphine product, called MST, launched in 1980. Unlike a standard new medicine, it was not the underlying chemical entity that was under patent but the sustained-release delivery mechanism. Sustained-release products generally exhibit more differentiation in patient use than other medicines. Hence doctors often continue to prescribe the same brand once it is found to work well with a patient, even after the patent has expired. If the product were not prescribed by brand, the pharmacist dispensing the prescription could substitute a cheaper generic version. In order to overcome the entry barrier of prescribing habits, a new entrant needed to penetrate the hospital market to become the first product prescribed. Given the centralized tendering process in hospitals, entering at lower prices would be an effective means of displacing the incumbent. When a competitor sought to do this in 1996, Napp's response was to meet (but not necessarily 'beat') its price, but this was sufficient to make the entrant's offer unattractive, given that the hospitals would have to incur some switching costs in terms of staff retraining and system modifications.

---

[45] *Napp Pharmaceutical Holdings Limited and Subsidiaries v The Director General of Fair Trading* (Case 1001/1/1/01) [2002] Comp AR 13.

The central defence mounted by Napp was that loss-leading in the hospital market was a sensible business practice (and is indeed common in the pharmaceutical sector), since it led directly to more valuable prescriptions in the community sector once the patient had left hospital. Napp claimed that the pricing structure therefore passed a 'net revenue test'—there was no loss-making price if the lifecycle of the patient was taken into account. Napp further claimed that the same strategy was open to its rivals; indeed it was the main competitor that had initiated the strong discounting to hospitals. Napp also made the point that it faced a single purchaser, the NHS, in both the hospital and community sectors. This single purchaser could trade off the benefits of cheaper prices in one sector against higher prices in the other.

The CAT rejected the relevance of the net revenue test, highlighting the test's similarity to the recoupment test. Exclusionary behaviour in the hospital market (comparable to stage 2 in Figure 4.1) had enabled Napp to charge high prices in the community sector (comparable to stage 3) without fear of significant competition. So both tests show the pattern of Figure 4.1, but then lead to the opposite conclusion: under the recoupment test you conclude that predation is feasible, while the net revenue test purported to show that there was no profit sacrifice in the first place:

> The net revenue test, as applied simplistically by Napp, provides no yardstick for distinguishing between what is legitimate, and what is abusive, behaviour on the part of a dominant undertaking. For instance, a monopolist driving away new entrants by predatory pricing is likely to maximise his net revenue by so doing, for example by avoiding loss of market share and erosion of prices in the profitable market where he holds a monopoly. Yet plainly such behaviour does not cease to be abusive merely because it is profitable for the monopolist to engage in it.[46]

Thus, the particular circumstances of this case show that the structural conditions were present for predatory pricing to be feasible, but not in the standard manner. Dominance in the hospital market, although it was found to exist, was not the crucial aspect of determining the feasibility of the predation. This market had relatively low entry and exit barriers. Instead, the case turned on the dominant position in the market where the losses were to be recouped—the community market—which had very different entry characteristics.

4.4.7 TARGETED DISCOUNTS

Targeted discounting is a form of predation whereby a company specifically targets a group of customers and charges them less than other customers. It is also a form of price discrimination (see section 4.5). The objective of such a practice is to induce the more price-sensitive customers not to switch to a competitor or a potential new entrant. A company offering targeted discounts can sometimes recoup losses

---

[46] Ibid., at [259].

immediately—while it charges below-cost prices to one group of customers, it charges above-cost prices to another. The main competition concern in relation to targeted discounts is that they may lead to the exclusion of actual or potential competitors from the market.

In fact, many of the major EU predation cases were actually about targeted discounts rather than predation in the market as a whole (eg, the *AKZO* and *Cewal* cases discussed earlier). From a legal perspective, the selectivity involved in targeted discounts has traditionally been taken as proof of predatory intent (below we come back to the relevance of intent). From an economic perspective, the ability to exclude rivals depends on the same factors as predation generally. What makes targeted discounting in fact less likely to be anti-competitive is that the degree of foreclosure is lower. If a dominant company with 60% of the market offers discounted prices to only 10% of its buyers or on only some of its products, the foreclosure effect is weaker than if all buyers or products were targeted. We see this illustrated in the *Aberdeen Journals* case, discussed below. In section 4.6 we discuss loyalty discounts and rebates.

4.4.8 THE (LIMITED) RELEVANCE OF INTENT

Intent is a subjective concept. Sometimes intent is inferred if an incumbent reduces the price after entry, forcing the new competitor to exit, and subsequently raises the price back to its original level. However, such behaviour may also occur in competitive circumstances. After all, new entry has the effect of increasing overall market output and confronts the incumbent with the choice to reduce price or cede market share. If the incumbent's price decrease is down to the level of its own cost, only entrants with higher costs will leave the market. So rather than intent, it is the cost benchmarks discussed in section 4.3 that help you identify instances where an as-efficient competitor is excluded. In addition, aggressive boardroom talk and internal memos revealing intentions to 'squish' rivals 'like a bug', 'pound them into the sand' or do other nasty things to them—we showed in Chapter 1 that phrases such as these at times show up as evidence in predation cases—may also be entirely consistent with fierce but healthy competition. A situation where competitors talk about each other using this language is preferable over one where they cosily tolerate each other and veer towards tacit collusion.

Thus, any evidence of an intentional predatory strategy is of limited use from an economic point of view. At best it adds some colour to the picture that the claimant or competition authority is presenting when bringing a predation case. It may also be used to confirm suspicions or to point to further areas of investigation. As noted earlier, the *AKZO* test in EU case law states that prices in the range between AVC and ATC can be predatory if set in the context of a plan aimed at eliminating a competitor, so evidence of intent is considered to be important. In contrast, in *Brooke Group* the US Supreme Court held that no matter how strong and unambiguous the evidence of intent, predation could not be established unless objective market factors showed that recoupment is possible.[47] An earlier lower court decision, *AA Poultry Farms* (1989), had already rejected intent as a basis for liability in predatory pricing cases:

> Firms 'intend' to do all the business they can, to crush their rivals if they can ... Entrepreneurs who work hardest to cut their price will do the most damage to their rivals, and they will see good in it ... If courts use the vigorous, nasty pursuit of sales as evidence of forbidden 'intent', they run the risk of penalizing the motive forces of competition.[48]

4.4.9 THE 'MEETING THE COMPETITION' DEFENCE

Companies under investigation may seek to justify their pricing behaviour on the grounds that they are defending their own commercial interest in the face of actions taken by competitors. There is economic logic to this 'meeting the competition' defence. We saw above that an incumbent facing a new entrant that has come in at a lower price must choose between meeting that price and ceding market share. Yet the defence has its limitations if meeting the competition means having to cut prices *below* the relevant cost benchmark. This can occur in one of two situations: where the entrant has lower costs than the incumbent, or where the entrant itself engages in (temporary) below-cost pricing in order to gain a foothold in the market. In the first situation, the as-efficient competitor principle could be applied in reverse: the entrant is the more efficient competitor and should be allowed to gain market share from the incumbent, so it still makes sense to prevent the latter from pricing below its own costs. The second situation is less clear-cut. Both competitors' prices are clearly not sustainable because they are below cost, and allowing only the entrant and not the incumbent to do this (on the basis that the latter is dominant) would be a form of entry assistance.

In *France Télécom SA v Commission*, the General Court (and later the ECJ as well) upheld the Commission's decision that Wanadoo Interactive (WIN), a subsidiary of France Télécom, abused its dominant position in the French residential broadband market by charging below-cost prices for Internet services. With respect to the 'meeting the competition' defence put forward by France Télécom, the General Court stated that:

> It must be pointed out first of all that the Commission is in no way disputing the right of an operator to align its prices on those previously charged by a competitor. It states in recital 315 of the decision that '[w]hilst it is true that the dominant operator is not strictly speaking prohibited from aligning its prices on those of competitors, this option is not open to it where it would result in its not recovering the costs of the service in question ...

> WIN cannot therefore rely on an absolute right to align its prices on those of its competitors in order to justify its conduct. Even if alignment of prices by a dominant undertaking on those of its competitors is not in itself abusive or objectionable, it might become so where it is aimed not only at protecting its interests but also at strengthening and abusing its dominant position.[49]

---

[47] *Brooke Group Ltd v Brown & Williamson Tobacco Corp* 509 US 209 (1993), at [224]–[225].
[48] *AA Poultry Farms, Inc. v Rose Acre Farms, Inc.* 881 F 2d 1396 (7th Cir. 1989), cert. denied, 494 US 1019 (1990).
[49] Case T-340/03 *France Télécom SA v Commission*, at [176] and [187].

The idea of meeting the competition can been used in a different manner: competition authorities could impose a pricing rule whereby the incumbent company is allowed to meet but not beat the competition—in other words, it can match a rival's price offers but not undercut them. Again this is a form of entry assistance. It may be suitable in liberalizing markets where competition still needs to be established, but it also carries some risk of dampening price competition and protecting inefficient suppliers.

4.4.10 NEWSPAPER WARS: THE ECONOMIC PRINCIPLES ILLUSTRATED

The *Aberdeen Journals* (2001) case provides a useful illustration of several of the economic principles discussed in this section.[50] The evidence collated by the OFT seemed to paint a clear enough picture. Aberdeen Journals Limited, previously a monopolist in the local newspaper market in Aberdeen, sought to get rid of a new entrant, Aberdeen Independent Limited, which had introduced a free-of-charge weekly newspaper. Internal memoranda revealed that Aberdeen Journals' parent company had specifically set aside funds to fight the entrant. Management was told to 'please keep your foot on their neck'. Its own free newspaper, the *Herald & Post*, was 'pitched against the Independent', 'with a view to denying the *Independent* all commercial oxygen', and 'to neutralise them'. Aberdeen Journals even considered acquiring its rival, while trying to convince it 'that we will not allow the *Independent* to break even'. Hence there was plenty of evidence on intent. But what about the analysis of economic effects?

Aberdeen Journals published three local newspapers in the Aberdeen area, two of which were paid-for daily titles, and one (the *Herald & Post*) was a free-of-charge weekly title. It was the only publisher of paid-for newspapers in the area. The *Herald & Post* faced competition from the *Aberdeen & District Independent* (the *Independent*), launched in 1996. Considering both paid-for and free newspapers, Aberdeen Journals had a local market share of over 70% by value and over 60% by volume. The OFT determined as follows:

> Aberdeen Journals, dominant on the market of supply of advertising space in both paid-for and free local newspapers in Aberdeen or the circulation area of the *Herald & Post*, supplied advertising space in the *Herald & Post* at below average variable cost. This raises a presumption of predation that Aberdeen Journals has failed to rebut by providing an objective justification. The Director therefore finds that Aberdeen Journals predated for the period from 1 March until 29 March 2000.[51]

Thus, the OFT considered paid-for and free local newspapers to be in the same relevant market. However, it also stated that its allegation would hold even if separate markets were defined for the two types of newspaper. Aberdeen Journals would still have abused its dominant position in the paid-for market (where it has a monopoly) by behaving

---

[50] Decision of the Director General of Fair Trading, *Predation by Aberdeen Journals Ltd* (No CA98/5/2001) [2001] UKCLR 856. This was the first OFT decision on this matter. There was a subsequent decision after the CAT had sent the case back to the OFT. However, this section focuses on the economic principles and how they apply to the facts of the case rather than on the proceedings as such.

[51] Ibid., at [116].

predatorily in the 'associated' market for advertising space in free newspapers. Does this accord with economic theory? It is clear from the evidence that Aberdeen Journals 'pitched' only its own free newspaper, the *Herald & Post*, against the *Independent*. It aggressively reduced prices of advertising space in the *Herald & Post*, but not in its two paid-for newspapers. The OFT described the *Herald & Post* as a 'fighting title'—a reference to the 'fighting brands' and 'fighting ships' we mentioned earlier. However, from an economic point of view, there is something inherently implausible about 'fighting brand' allegations that involve predation in only a segment of a broader market. To see this, consider two product segments, A and B. Suppose these segments are determined to be in the same relevant market because the degree of demand-side and supply-side substitution between the two is significant. There are two reasons why predation in only one segment—say, segment A—is unlikely to be successful.

First, the principles of market definition set out in Chapter 2 determine that segments A and B are included in the same relevant market if the price in segment A cannot be raised profitably because a significant number of consumers would switch to segment B (or producers in B would redirect production capacity to A). The implication is that predation in segment A cannot take place without inducing a significant number of customers to switch from B to A. Hence, the aggressive price decrease in segment A would significantly affect the predator's own sales in segment B. In addition, if there is a high degree of supply-side substitution as well as demand-side substitution, nothing would prevent a rival in segment A from redirecting its goods to segment B. Applying this reasoning to the case at hand, it is clear that the reduction in price of advertising space in the *Herald & Post* would be expected to affect the prices for Aberdeen Journals' own paid-for titles, if indeed paid-for and free local newspapers were in the same market. The fact that apparently no such substitution took place is an indication that the two products were actually in separate markets.

Secondly, if predation takes place only in segment A, the relationship between the predator's market share and the feasibility of predation breaks down. As we discussed in this section, a predator needs a high market share from the start in order to have a sufficient impact on the overall market price (without a high market share, price must be set very low for a sustained period, making predation more costly). However, with fighting brands, the predator does not use the full weight of its market share in the combined A and B market for the predatory campaign. Aberdeen Journals was not using its full 60%–70% share of the market to fight the *Independent*, since only prices for its free newspaper were lowered. Therefore, the general principle that a high market share means a high likelihood of success of predation cannot be applied to this case.

The fact that the price war took place only in free newspapers and not in paid-for titles rather seems to suggest that the two were in different relevant markets. In the market for free newspapers, Aberdeen Journals stated that it had a share of between 28% and 35%, while the *Independent* had 65%–72%. If this is correct, then it is difficult to see how Aberdeen Journals could successfully predate against the *Independent*, which had a much stronger market position. Indeed, you would have expected that after four years of fighting (it started in 1996), Aberdeen Journals had taken away a lot more market share from the *Independent*. But what about the OFT's statement that its finding of predation is actually not sensitive to the exact market definition, ie, even if there were two separate markets there would still be an abuse? This is consistent with *Tetra Pak II*, as referred to earlier. However, predating from an associated (or neighbouring) market is not that straightforward. The usual relationship between market share and the economic impact (and hence likelihood of success) of predation does not hold in this form of predation. Aberdeen Journals was not using its dominance (monopoly) in the paid-for market as a weapon in the predatory campaign against the *Independent*, since it did not lower the prices of its paid-for titles. It reduced advertising rates for its free title, the *Herald & Post*, which had only 28%–35% of the free newspaper market.

Therefore, in order to make the case that predation takes place from a neighbouring market, a competition authority or claimant needs to show explicitly how linkages between the two markets actually facilitate such predation. Using monopoly profits in one market to subsidize losses in the other market would be an example of such a link, but the OFT did not make this cross-subsidy argument. A linkage identified by the OFT was that 'Aberdeen Journals is part of a major newspaper group that has the funds required for predation in an associated market to be feasible'.[52] This is basically a 'deep-pocket' argument. The fact that it could fund the losses made on the *Herald & Post* for four years was taken by the OFT as evidence of Aberdeen Journals' (or its parent's) deep pockets. However, the relevance of the deep-pocket argument is limited. For an assessment of the economic impact of predatory pricing, it is in principle irrelevant where the predator's losses are funded from. It is also difficult to demonstrate that the predator has deeper pockets than its victims. Indeed, internal memoranda suggested that Aberdeen Journals was somewhat disappointed about the 'stalemate' after four years of fighting: 'Our response to [the owner of the *Independent*] was very vigorous and most publishing entrepreneurs would not have been able to fund these losses over four years.' This seems to suggest that the *Independent* may have had some deep pockets of its own.

From the evidence presented by the OFT, it appears that the *Aberdeen Journals* case does not really fit the picture of quick and dirty predation. The internal memoranda show that Aberdeen Journals had repeatedly been over-optimistic about its chances. In mid-1996 it believed that the *Independent* would cease publication by Christmas that year. In May 1998 it expected to be successful in closing down its rival over the next 18 months to two years. Yet by March 2000, the *Independent* apparently still had a share of more than two-thirds in the free newspaper market. Furthermore, the OFT found there to be predation during only one month—only from 1 March to 29 March 2000 were advertising rates for the *Herald & Post* below AVC (this may in part be explained by the fact that the Competition Act 1998 came into force only on 1 March 2000). After that, Aberdeen Journals apparently increased prices again. In fact, even during March 2000 it had imposed an increase in its advertising rates and subsequently lost a few customers. All this is again inconsistent with a successful, quick and dirty predatory pricing strategy, despite the factual evidence that such a strategy was indeed intended.

---

[52] Ibid., at [51].

4.5 PRICE DISCRIMINATION

4.5.1 WHAT IS PRICE DISCRIMINATION?

Price discrimination can be defined as the sale of different units of the same product at price differentials that do not correspond to any cost difference. This definition includes the sale not only of identical products to different customers at varying prices, but also of identical units to the same buyer at different prices (eg, electricity suppliers and water companies charging lower tariffs for each additional block of demand), and charging the same price for transactions entailing different costs (eg, uniform geographic pricing in postal services). Charging customers different prices that reflect differences in costs is *not* included. We discussed price discrimination in Chapter 2 on market definition, showing that it can sometimes give rise to separate price discrimination markets.

For price discrimination to be feasible the seller must have some control over price. For this reason, the fact that a company is able to price-discriminate is sometimes taken as an indication of a degree of market power (but not necessarily a very high degree, given how common price discrimination is in many markets and industries). Also, the seller must be able to divide its customers into groups or markets with different price elasticities of demand—ie, groups that react differently to a price change. It must therefore have enough information about customers' willingness to pay so that it can segment the market. Finally there must be no scope for arbitrage—the resale by low-price customers to high-price customers—as this would undermine the company's ability to price-discriminate.

Economists distinguish three types of price discrimination. First-degree (or perfect) price discrimination occurs where the seller charges each consumer the maximum amount it is willing to pay. The seller thus captures the entire consumer surplus. This practice is rare because it requires perfect information about each customer, but it might be approximated in some bargaining situations—eg, haggling for a second-hand car. Savvy sales people may extract each customer's willingness to pay during the bargaining process (you may have heard the advice 'never pay the sticker price on a car'—but this is what facilitates price discrimination: the actual price is set as a variable discount to the sticker price). Second-degree price discrimination (sometimes more generally called non-linear pricing) occurs when a company offers a selection of deals and allows each customer to choose the one that most suits them. Carnet tickets (books of ten single tickets on the Paris Metro) offer a lower unit price than buying single tickets individually. Mobile phone users can choose from among a variety of price packages, tailored to light or heavy users, to users who mainly make calls or to those who mainly use the phone for text messaging or Internet browsing. Volume discounts and loyalty rebates are also forms of second-degree price discrimination. The last type is third-degree price discrimination. Usually a company does not have sufficient information to price-discriminate perfectly; instead, it may be able to segment its market and price each segment differently. Student discounts and regional variation in pricing are examples of this. The company charges different prices to consumers with different observable characteristics (such as gender, age, or location). Targeted discounts (discussed in section 4.4) are a form of third-degree price discrimination.

4.5.2 WHAT ARE THE BENEFITS OF PRICE DISCRIMINATION?

Price discrimination is a very common business practice. You see it everywhere. Travellers pay a varying price for the same type of seat on an aeroplane; providers of sports and leisure facilities offer discounts to pensioners and students; a holiday villa in France may cost half as much if you book it for the first week of September instead of the last week of August; university libraries pay lower fees than law firms for academic journals and economics books.

Economic theory also shows that in many circumstances price discrimination enhances economic welfare and efficiency by increasing total market output compared with a situation of uniform pricing. This output expansion is welfare-enhancing in its own right—in Chapter 1 we explained the economic principle that any transaction between a willing buyer and a willing seller is inherently desirable. Price discrimination also offers an effective means for suppliers to recover the fixed costs of production. In a market with many small suppliers producing a homogeneous product, the most efficient outcome is achieved if price equals marginal cost. However, in many industries such pricing would not allow companies to recover their fixed costs. In these circumstances, charging non-uniform prices can expand the market that is served and allow suppliers to recover fixed costs more effectively than by raising prices across the board. At the same time this enhances economic welfare as it allows sales to customers or markets that would not be served under uniform pricing. It is well established in economic theory that the most efficient departure from marginal cost pricing is a 'Ramsey' form of price discrimination, where customers with the greater willingness to pay and the less elastic demand are charged higher prices.[53] The Ramsey logic originally referred to taxation but applies to pricing generally: by charging higher prices to the less elastic customers, the distortion of such high pricing (or taxation) is minimized because the negative effect on output is smallest. If you charged the higher price to the elastic customers instead, the negative effect on output would be larger.

The benefits of price discrimination can be explained by reference to the standard monopoly representation in Chapters 2 and 3—see Figure 4.3, which is similar to Figures 2.4 and 3.1, where the monopolist set the same price for all customers. It earned a profit equal to area A. In addition, compared with a situation of perfect competition there is a deadweight loss—area B—that benefits no one. What happens if the monopolist is able to price-discriminate? Take first-degree discrimination. The savvy monopolist is able to bargain with its customers one by one and extract their maximum willingness to pay. The first customer is charged a price of 9, the second customer a price of 8, the third customer a price of 7, and the fourth customer a price of 6. The fourth customer pays

---

[53] See, for example, Baumol and Bradford (1970).

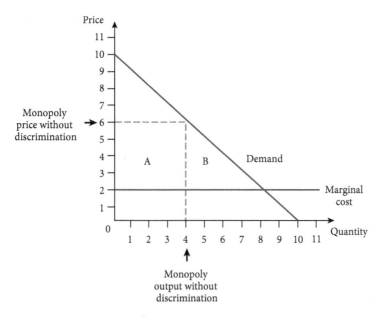

Fig. 4.3 What happens if the monopolist can price-discriminate?

the same price as under single-price monopoly, but the other three customers now pay more. They still benefit from buying the product at a price they are willing to pay, but the monopolist has extracted the consumer surplus that they previously obtained. However, the monopolist does not stop there. It can still profitably sell to the fifth customer at a price of 5 in the safe knowledge that it can keep prices for the first four customers unchanged (thanks to the ability to engage in first-degree price discrimination). Indeed, the monopolist can sell all the way to customer eight where the price still covers its marginal cost. Therefore, under first-degree price discrimination by a monopolist, output and total welfare are exactly the same as under perfect competition—there is no deadweight welfare loss. The only catch is that this total welfare now ends up in the monopolist's pockets, but if you are indifferent to how welfare is distributed between consumers and producers (as economists are in theory), this is still the preferred outcome. If it seems unfair, think of customers five to eight who now get to buy the product whereas previously they could not.

Second- and third-degree price discrimination can have similar output-expanding effects. Just think about how many mobile phone subscriptions would be sold if we all had to buy exactly the same price package, or ask yourself whether airlines would offer as many flights as they currently do if every passenger had to pay the same fare. When publishers try to extract more revenues from a book by first issuing a hardcover edition at a high price (those keenest to get their hands on the book will purchase it at that price), followed by a cheaper paperback edition, the result may be an increase in the total quantity sold compared with a strategy of a single price.[54] Hollywood studios do the same by issuing their films sequentially in different 'windows': cinemas, premium pay-TV channels, DVD rental and sale, and finally free-to-air TV.

Another example of third-degree price discrimination having positive output effects is the supply of on-patent medicines at different prices to different countries. Countries with a lower willingness or ability to pay, or stricter government procurement and pricing rules, can be charged a lower price and hence still be served, while price remains high in the other countries. This output expansion is efficient and it can also be said to be fair—the poorest countries get their medicines cheap (at marginal cost, say), while the high profit margins in the rich countries allow the pharmaceutical companies to recover their fixed R&D costs. Under a single price, some of those poorest countries might not be served at all. These strategies of price discrimination across national markets give intermediary companies the incentive to exploit arbitrage opportunities by engaging in parallel trade (also known as grey imports), thus undermining price discrimination. Attempts by pharmaceutical companies to deter such parallel trade have given rise to a different type of abuse of dominance case, as discussed below.

Finally, we note that from a competition law perspective, price discrimination has an additional benefit in oligopolistic markets: it can scupper attempts at tacit and explicit collusion. It is difficult for cartel members to detect cheating in a market where companies can offer selective, secretive discounts to their customers. Given that collusion is one of the prime concerns of competition law and perhaps the most difficult to tackle (see Chapter 5), such discounting practices are quite desirable. In all, economists see price discrimination as a benign phenomenon in many circumstances.

4.5.3 WHAT ARE THE CONCERNS ABOUT PRICE DISCRIMINATION?

These welfare-enhancing effects of price discrimination explain why competition law does (or should) not condemn price discrimination by dominant companies per se, but rather assesses its effects on welfare and competition. There are four main reasons why competition law may be concerned about price discrimination. First, charging excessively low prices to some but not all customers may have the effect of excluding competitors from the market. Second, charging one customer more than another may distort competition between those customers if they compete with each other in a downstream market. The US Robinson–Patman Act of 1936, which specifically addresses price discrimination, calls this secondary-line injury to competition while the first effect is called primary-line injury. Third, a dominant company may be seen to be exploiting the group of customers to which it charges the higher price. Finally, when policy-makers have set the objective of creating a 'single market', competition law may prevent companies from segmenting markets and engaging in price discrimination. In Europe, this concern has led to a hostile attitude by the authorities towards attempts

---

[54] Knowing this, what do you make of the pricing strategy for this book?

by companies to carve out national markets and prevent parallel imports, as discussed further below.

How can each of these concerns be addressed? For the first and the third, the answer to this question can be given swiftly. Complaints about exclusion of competitors through price discrimination can normally be assessed as predatory pricing or targeted discounting (see section 4.4). Whether the investigated company charges higher prices to other customers or markets is usually not of major importance in the assessment of economic effects of such discounting; the relevant question is whether the low prices charged are excessively low, not whether they are discriminatory as such. Likewise, if the concern is about the exploitation of some customers you can deal with this along the lines of an excessive pricing inquiry (see section 4.10).

From an economic perspective, secondary-line injury is the main concern about price discrimination (and indeed about non-price forms of discrimination, such as discriminatory access conditions). Article 102 itself also seems to emphasize this concern. Paragraph (2)(c) states that an abuse of dominance may consist of 'applying dissimilar conditions to equivalent transactions with other trading parties, thereby placing them at a competitive disadvantage.' This implies that the favoured and the affected customers must be competing with each other in a downstream market for there to be an abuse. In its *United Brands* (1978) and *Hoffmann-La Roche* (1979) judgments, the ECJ explicitly established that secondary-line injury is the relevant criterion for applying Article 102(2)(c).[55] In *United Brands*, the Court found that price discrimination between national markets by the dominant supplier of bananas in Europe placed certain downstream distributors at a competitive disadvantage.

Price discrimination with downstream effects will be of greatest concern if the relevant product is an essential input for downstream producers and if the favoured customer is a subsidiary or affiliated company of the provider of the essential input. This situation commonly arises in network and utility industries such as telecoms, rail, gas and electricity. Often these concerns are addressed through sector-specific regulation. Many regulated companies in these sectors have specific conditions in their licences prohibiting undue discrimination or undue preference, on both price and other terms and conditions. Under competition law, price discrimination is usually assessed more narrowly than under regulation as competition authorities consider the economic effects on customers and competition, while sector regulators often have to consider its social or distributive effects as well. In Chapter 9 we discuss the main insights from the field of regulation for the design of remedies in competition law, including the regulation of access and instances where vertical separation was considered the most effective remedy to deal with pervasive discrimination problems.

So are price discrimination cases under EU law limited to situations where downstream competition is hindered? The answer is no. In a case against the organizers of the

---

[55] Case 27/76 *United Brands v Commission* [1978], and Case 85/76 *Hoffmann-La Roche & Co AG v Commission* [1979] ECR 461.

1998 Football World Cup in France, the Commission imposed a fine for discrimination against residents outside France in the ticket sales.[56] Arguably there is no downstream competition between the favoured football fans in France and the affected fans elsewhere, at least not in the commercial sense. While fundamentally a discrimination case, the Commission treated this as a practice that directly prejudiced the interests of certain consumers, and hence it considered the absence of any effect on the structure of competition to be irrelevant.

4.5.4 PRICE DISCRIMINATION AND PARALLEL TRADE

Anyone who travels abroad a lot will have observed that there are often significant price differentials between countries. This is true for all kinds of products, including beverages, electronic goods, designer-labelled goods, and pharmaceuticals. A natural market response to such price discrimination is to try to undermine it through arbitrage. In the context of international trade this can be done in the form of parallel or grey imports. In turn, a natural response to parallel imports is to take measures to stop them, through commercial or legal means. The question of whether such measures are anti-competitive or welfare-enhancing has been the subject of various competition cases, and is closely linked to the welfare effects of price discrimination, as explained below.

Formally, parallel imports are goods brought into a country without the authorization of the copyright, patent, or trademark owner, after those goods have been placed into circulation in another market by that owner or an authorized distributor. We understand that exhaustion is one of the basic principles of IP law. Once trademarked goods are 'put on the market', the trademark owner is no longer allowed to control the further distribution of these goods. It has 'exhausted' its distribution right by the first sale of the goods. A controversial issue is whether the exhaustion should be national, international or regional. The first type means that rights are exhausted only with respect to the countries in which the goods were put on the market. If the applicable law recognizes only national exhaustion, a parallel importer would infringe the relevant trademark right in the importing country. Thus, the ability of IP owners to prevent parallel trade remains intact under national exhaustion. International exhaustion means that rights are exhausted when goods are first sold in a market anywhere in the world. If a jurisdiction adopts this rule on exhaustion, IP owners cannot stop parallel imports into the jurisdiction. Regional exhaustion is adopted by the EU as an intermediate policy. Rights are exhausted when goods are first sold in any market in the European Economic Area (EEA). Parallel trade is thus allowed for goods put on the market within the EEA but not for goods put on the market elsewhere.

In the *Silhouette* case (1998), the ECJ ruled on the parallel imports of branded sunglasses.[57] An Austrian discount chain, Hartlauer, had bought a consignment of Silhouette

---

[56] *1998 Football World Cup* (Case IV/36.888) [2000] OJ L5/55.

[57] Case C-355/96 *Silhouette International Schmied GmbH & Co KG v Hartlauer Handelsgesellschaft mbH* [1998] ECR I-4799.

sunglasses from a company in Bulgaria (then outside the EU and EEA), which had previously bought them from Silhouette International in Austria. Hartlauer was charged in an Austrian court on the grounds that the trademark rights for the sunglasses had not been exhausted by the act of selling the consignment to the Bulgarian company, and that Silhouette therefore could prohibit Hartlauer from selling them in Austria. The ECJ ruled that community-wide—ie, regional—exhaustion of rights was the proper interpretation of the 1989 EU Trade Marks Directive. Several cases have followed this principle since, including one where a number of UK supermarkets (including Tesco and Costco) had bought perfumes and jeans that Davidoff and Levi Strauss had placed on markets outside the EEA.[58]

The economic arguments against parallel trade are closely linked to those of protecting IP rights generally. Arguments for limiting exhaustion derive from the belief that this provides a higher economic reward to companies that invest in the quality or image of their products, and that this incentive is necessary to maintain the range of products and the quality of goods and associated services that consumers expect. Parallel importers may undermine this by free-riding on the marketing and service efforts of authorized distributors, thereby reducing the incentive to make those efforts in the first place. We return to this free-rider theme in Chapter 6 in the context of vertical restraints.

Another issue that these parallel trade cases highlight—and the one that is of relevance to this section—is the desirability of price differences between markets. Parallel trade arises only because prices in one country are lower than in another. Sometimes this may be due to transient phenomena such as exchange-rate movements, where parallel traders are able to react more quickly than the trademark holders or authorized distributors. A more fundamental cause, however, is that the trademark holder wishes, as a matter of commercial policy, to sell goods at different prices in different markets— it wishes to exploit opportunities to engage in price discrimination, made possible by differences in the ability or willingness of consumers to pay for the product, or differences in wealth or tastes. We saw above that price discrimination is often benign and that it can enhance welfare. The *Silhouette* principle, by imposing certain restrictions on parallel trade, implicitly recognizes that price discrimination by an IP holder is a legitimate business practice. However, where parallel trade *within* the EU (or EEA) is concerned, the EU's stance changes because the internal-market objective comes into play. Parallel imports are all of a sudden seen in a much more favourable light (and price discrimination is seen unfavourably). This has been reflected in a number of abuse of dominance cases against pharmaceutical companies that took actions to prevent parallel trade of their products between Member States.

Parallel importers buy medicines under patent in Member States where wholesale prices are relatively low, and sell them at a higher price in other Member States—a form of international arbitrage. Parallel trade in pharmaceuticals in the EU was worth

---

[58] Cases C-414/99 to C-416/99 *Zino Davidoff SA v A & G Imports Ltd and Levi Strauss & Co and Others v Tesco Stores Ltd and Others* [2001] ECR I-8691.

approximately €4.3 billion in 2006 (European Federation of Pharmaceutical Industries and Associations, 2008). You can see why pharmaceutical companies have an incentive to try to prevent it. In one long-running case, a Greek wholesaler complained about GlaxoSmithKline's (GSK) refusal to supply it with three of its patented products (Imigran, Lamictal, and Serevent). The Greek competition authority initiated an investigation and subsequently referred several questions to the ECJ. Advocate General Jacobs advised that the patent holder would not automatically infringe Article 102 by refusing to supply because the conduct might be justified in light of sector-specific factors. The Advocate General's advice motivated the Greek competition authority's decision in favour of GSK. At a subsequent stage of the legal proceedings, Advocate General Colomer expressed his opinion that GSK's conduct did infringe Article 102 because of GSK's failure to justify its actions economically. The argument that parallel trade has negative effects on R&D investments was in principle accepted, but GSK's conduct was considered to be disproportionate. The final ruling of the ECJ on 16 September 2008 determined that a producer of pharmaceuticals must be in a position to protect its own interest if orders from distributors are 'out of the ordinary'. The court ruled that GSK's actions would constitute an infringement of Article 102 when orders were at 'ordinary' levels, but left it to national courts to ascertain whether the orders in this particular case would be ordinary in relation to the requirements of the market.[59]

So is price discrimination by pharmaceutical companies desirable or should parallel trade be allowed? Price-setting mechanisms in the pharmaceutical sector are different from those in many other industries. New medicines brought to the market are afforded patent protection which confers a temporary monopoly on its holder (historically this was often for 20 years, although this may differ across jurisdictions and products). Patent holders are thus not constrained by competition when setting prices during this period (although they may still be constrained by national price regulations). The rationale behind patent protection is that for there to be sufficient incentives to invest in pharmaceutical research, the costs of R&D and drug testing need to be recovered, and returns from successful drugs must be sufficient to compensate for the costs of unsuccessful drug developments. Wholesale prices for pharmaceutical products have traditionally differed within the EU—for example, they are on average higher in Germany, the Netherlands, and the UK than in Greece and Spain.[60] This is a situation of third-degree price discrimination. An important question is why manufacturers are able to charge higher prices in some EU Member States than in others. Is it due to differences in price elasticity of demand or willingness to pay, as in the standard theory of price discrimination? In the case of pharmaceuticals, wholesale price differentials for patented drugs mainly reflect differences in the way countries regulate their pharmaceutical

---

[59] Case C-53/03 *Synetairismos Farmakopoion Aitolias & Akarnanias (Syfait) and Others v GlaxoSmithKline plc and GlaxoSmithKline AEVE* [2005] ECR I-4609; Joined Cases C-468/06 to C-478/06, Opinion of Advocate General Ruiz–Jarabo Colomer in *Sot. Lélos kai Sia EE and Others v GlaxoSmithKline AEVE Farmakeftikon Proïonton, formerly Glaxowellcome AEVE* [2008] ECR I-7139.

[60] London School of Economics (2004), table 3.2.

markets and how prices are determined in negotiations between governments and the industry. Price-setting mechanisms are thus not driven so much by differences in customers' ability and willingness to pay, but rather by state intervention. The importance of regulatory pricing restrictions driving increased opportunities for parallel trade was also acknowledged in the ECJ judgment:

> it cannot be ignored that such State intervention [price regulation] is one of the factors liable to create opportunities for parallel trade.[61]

Parallel imports thus create a tension between the principle of autonomy of Member States in setting pharmaceutical prices and the creation of a single European market. Price differentials in the EU are due to the Member States each regulating their own pharmaceutical prices, while the principle of free movement of goods within the EU allows traders to arbitrage those differences.

Overall, these abuse cases involving parallel trade in pharmaceutical products are complex because they are judged under several different criteria. There is an IP law angle (should IP holders be entitled to exploit their rights as they see fit?), and there are various political angles (should each Member State be allowed to set its own price levels?; is it right that some countries get the medicine cheap while others end up paying the bill for the R&D costs?; is it appropriate for the rules to be different depending on whether the trade is inside or outside the EU?). The economic test is relatively simple in this context: are total sales of medicines higher or lower under price discrimination or with parallel trade? Another relevant question for the effects analysis in these cases relates to R&D investment—is price discrimination between countries an efficient mechanism for pharmaceutical companies to recover their R&D costs, and would they invest less in R&D if such discrimination were undermined by parallel trade? Economic analysis can shed some light on these questions and assist courts in weighing up the various legal arguments that are often put forward in these disputes.

4.6 LOYALTY REBATES, DISCOUNTS, AND EXCLUSIVE DEALING

4.6.1 SOME DEFINITIONS FIRST

Price discounts and rebates are ubiquitous. Many different types of supplier—small and large—offer them in one way or another. Buyers rarely complain about them because they get a lower price. The rationale for these pricing practices is that they make buyers less likely to switch to competitors. If offered by a dominant undertaking, rebates may have the effect of foreclosing rivals from the market.

---

[61] Joined Cases C-468/06 to C-478/06, *Sot. Lélos kai Sia EE and Others v GlaxoSmithKline AEVE Farmakeftikon Proïonton, formerly Glaxowellcome AEVE* [2008] ECR I-7139, at [67].

Loyalty rebates involve a discount or a rebate payment to a purchaser in return for remaining loyal to the supplier. Whether we refer to this as a 'discount' or 'rebate' is of little importance, as what matters is the final price to the purchaser. This form of discount structure is a common feature in many intermediate product markets. Some retail stores make a substantial proportion of their profits through rebates from product manufacturers, and car dealerships often rely on the rebates offered to them by car manufacturers. Loyalty rebates are granted to customers depending on their past purchasing behaviour. They can take the form of increasing discounts, typically in discrete jumps, when purchases over a defined reference period exceed a given threshold. In *Tyco* (2006), a US monopolization case, a typical offer involved 40% off if the customer bought 90% or more of its requirements from Tyco, but only a 16%–18% discount otherwise.[62] This case related to sales to hospitals of pulse oxymetry sensors (used to monitor the oxygenation of a patient's blood), in which Tyco had a market share in excess of 65%. The US court ruled that the possible loss of Tyco's higher discounts on all of a hospital's sensor purchases effectively forced hospitals to deal exclusively with Tyco. This is sometimes referred to as the 'suction' effect of loyalty rebates.

Unconditional discounts are granted on every purchase regardless of the past purchasing behaviour of the buyer. In this case, rather than a company determining which customers will be charged which prices, the supplier offers a menu of prices at different volume levels and customers 'self-select' their preferred volume/price trade-off. Unconditional discounts are a form of second-degree price discrimination (as described in section 4.5), and you can see that they are less likely to have an exclusionary effect than loyalty rebates.

Exclusive dealing is when a manufacturer agrees with its distributors to be their exclusive supplier. A computer manufacturer might sell PCs to retailers only if they agree not to carry computers produced by any other manufacturer. These arrangements are commonplace and can be efficiency-enhancing where, for example, they prevent other manufacturers from free-riding on investment and sales efforts made. We discuss these efficiency effects in Chapter 6 on vertical restraints. In this chapter we focus mainly on the potential foreclosure effects of such arrangements. Some loyalty rebate and discounting schemes may have such strong effects that they become de facto exclusive dealing.

The general 'theory of harm' with all these practices is that they can foreclose access to customers or distribution channels—see Figure 4.4. An important aspect of the effects-based test approach to abuse of dominance is to ask whether the degree of foreclosure is significant. This will depend on the degree of dominance, on the form and design of the practice in question (a discount or an exclusive dealing arrangement) and on the proportion of distributors or customers that are effectively foreclosed. Discounts and rebates can constitute a form of predatory pricing and therefore the

---

[62] *Masimo Corp v Tyco Health Care Group, LP*, No CV 02-4770 MRP, 2006 WL 1236666 (CD Cal. 22 March, 2006).

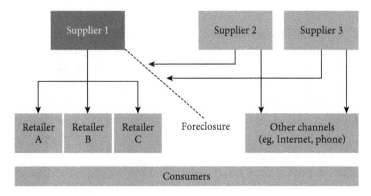

Fig. 4.4 Foreclosure effects

economic principles set out in section 4.4 are of relevance here too. But there are some additional considerations that are specific to discounts and rebates. Foreclosure through discounting may be feasible if the product in question is a leading brand and a 'must stock' item for a retailer (say 70% of its shelf space will always be devoted to the leading brand), and the discount is structured to induce purchasers to satisfy all their needs beyond that 'non-contestable' percentage by purchasing from the dominant company only. In this case, prices that are above cost on average may, due to the structured discount, be effectively below cost on the portion of business (30%) for which rivals can compete. As we explain below, these discounts may effectively foreclose such a large portion of distribution channels and customer demand that competitors cannot achieve efficient scale, thereby enabling the dominant company to maintain its market position.

Even if offered by dominant companies, discounts, rebates and exclusive dealing can benefit consumers in the same way as other types of efficiency-enhancing forms of vertical restraint and non-linear pricing. In terms of vertical effects, a supplier may use discounts to induce a retailer to increase its selling efforts (see Chapter 6). In terms of non-linear pricing, as we explained in section 4.5 it can be efficient for a company to recover joint or fixed costs by charging different customers different amounts for the same product. This is because the undertaking may be able to recover a higher proportion of its costs from the less price-sensitive customers while offering higher discounts to the more price-sensitive customers.

4.6.2 LOYALTY REBATES: EFFECTS

Loyalty rebates take many forms, but most share the characteristic that the percentage discount given to the consumer increases, usually in discrete jumps, when purchase volumes exceed a target level (often based on an increment above the purchases in a previous reference period). The form of loyalty rebate that has received most attention in competition law is retroactive rebates, where discounts apply not only to the customer's purchases above the target but retroactively to all purchases—these have also been referred to as 'back to dollar one' or 'rollback' rebates. We saw the *Virgin v British Airways* example in section 4.2. Non-retroactive rebates apply only to the units purchased above the target (ie, incremental units) once the buyer has exceeded the threshold. An example of a non-retroactive rebate would be 'buy your normal requirement at full price, and get additional units at 50% off'. In that situation, the discount does not roll back to the first unit. A retroactive rebate would be 'buy your normal requirement at full price, or buy extra and get *all* purchases at 30% off'. In that case, the discount applies back to the first unit purchased.

Loyalty schemes may make discounts conditional on exclusive purchasing—whereby buyers receive the discount only if they source all their needs from the supplier. Alternatively, discounts may be conditional on purchasing a certain quantity of units, where the quantity target is a large share of the buyer's needs—eg, a dominant company offering a discount to a buyer conditional on purchasing 80% of its needs from that company. Finally, discounts can be made available on the condition that the buyer purchases a given amount of another product from the supplier. An example is the *PeaceHealth* (2008) case, involving hospital care in Lane County, Oregon.[63] PeaceHealth had a very high market share in tertiary-care services (approaching 90% in certain sub-specialities). In the related markets for primary and secondary acute-care hospital services, PeaceHealth competed with McKenzie, but the latter did not provide tertiary services. McKenzie complained about PeaceHealth's offers of bundled service packages to some customers (insurance companies). These bundled offerings provided discounts on all services if insurance companies made PeaceHealth their sole preferred provider for primary, secondary, and tertiary care. Thus the discount on tertiary care was offered only if a customer also purchased primary and secondary care from PeaceHealth. The US district court considered this to be anti-competitive, but the verdict was overturned on appeal, with the appeal court ruling that the lower court improperly instructed the jury by not requiring it to consider whether PeaceHealth's discounted price was below cost. We discuss bundling and tying in section 4.8.

Loyalty rebates can in theory allow a dominant company to strengthen its position by hindering the expansion of rivals or foreclosing entry. In the short run, the buyers that are offered the discounted prices are less likely to switch, which makes it more difficult for rivals to attract and retain customers. The dominant company may be able to recoup its losses immediately by charging higher prices in other markets. Alternatively, it may be able to recoup its losses in the longer run (when the threat of entry has diminished) by charging high prices to those consumers initially offered the lower prices.

A landmark case in the EU concerning loyalty rebates was the Commission decision in *Michelin* in 2001, as successfully upheld on appeal in 2003.[64] Michelin had a rebate scheme whereby a tyre dealership would become eligible for a range of stepped rebates

---

[63] *Cascade Health Solutions v PeaceHealth* 515 F 3d 883 (9th Cir. 2008).

[64] *Michelin* (Case COMP/E-2/36.041/PO) [2002] OJ L143; Case T-203/01 *Manufacture Française des Pneumatiques Michelin v EC Commission* [2003] ECR II-4071.

depending on the total quantity of Michelin products. The Commission concluded that the rebate had a loyalty-inducing effect, which acted to foreclose the market to competitors:

> thanks to its [high] market shares, Michelin was able to absorb the cost of these rebates, while its competitors were unable to do likewise and therefore had to either accept a lower level of profitability or give up the idea of increasing their sales volume.[65]

More generally the Commission concluded that loyalty rebates by dominant companies are acceptable only if they are cost-related, ie, they 'correspond to the economies of scale achieved by the firm as a result of the additional purchases which consumers are induced to make'.[66]

Is this approach too restrictive? An effects-based analysis would suggest it is. Loyalty rebates may not have significant anti-competitive effects even if they are offered by a dominant company and not cost-related. Assessing the effects on competition of a loyalty rebate scheme involves two main steps (not necessarily in order): you have to determine the strength of the loyalty-enhancing effects of the scheme, and you have to assess the degree of foreclosure. The first step focuses on the form of the scheme and assesses whether there are strong incentives for the retailer to respond to the scheme and sustain or increase its loyalty to the dominant supplier (this step therefore combines a form-based with an effects-based approach). Without strong incentives the competing suppliers can overcome the power of the loyalty rebates by offering their own rebate schemes. The degree of non-linearity in the pricing structure is a key determinant of the strength of the incentives created, as we explain below. The second step assesses whether the foreclosure effect is substantial. This involves analysing the degree of market power of the company under investigation—does it really sell 'must stock' products or control a 'non-contestable' part of the market?—and whether competing suppliers have viable alternative routes to the market. The degree of foreclosure should be substantial and significantly impede rivals' access to the distribution chain. We discuss the two steps in more detail below.

4.6.3 WHAT DETERMINES THE STRENGTH OF THE LOYALTY-ENHANCING EFFECT?

The loyalty-enhancing effects of a rebate scheme will depend on the following factors. First, whether the discount is offered on the condition that the buyer purchases exclusively from the dominant company or sources most of its needs (say, 80%) from the dominant company. The exclusionary effect is stronger in these cases. The second factor is the level and structure of the threshold. If the threshold at which a discount applies is set above the amount that a buyer would normally purchase from the dominant company, the rebate may enhance the customer's loyalty by inducing it to purchase more

---

[65] *Michelin* (Case COMP/E-2/36.041/PO) [2002] OJ L143, at [241].
[66] Ibid., at [216].

than it would otherwise in order to benefit from the scheme. Thresholds that are targeted at each customer (eg, individualized targets for large customers based on the purchases made in the previous period) are more likely to have a loyalty-enhancing ('suction') effect than volume thresholds that are set at the same level for all customers. The level of the threshold matters where the resulting price of some or all units sold to a customer is below an appropriate measure of cost—we return to this topic below. In general, the higher the rebate as a proportion of the total price and the higher the threshold as a proportion of a customer's purchases, the greater the loyalty-enhancing effect. The third factor is the length of the reference period—the period over which volumes are assessed for the purposes of calculating the rebate to which a customer is entitled. The case law is relatively unclear in relation to the duration of such reference periods. In principle, reference periods of one or several years are considered more loyalty-enhancing than a monthly or quarterly reference period, because customer switching decisions may be delayed by the length of the reference period. For example, as a result of the *Virgin v British Airways* case discussed in section 4.2, the Commission required airlines to restrict the period when discounts could be offered to corporate customers and travel agents to no more than six months.[67]

4.6.4 WHAT DETERMINES THE DEGREE AND LIKELIHOOD OF FORECLOSURE?

If in the previous step it is concluded that the rebate scheme has a strong loyalty-enhancing effect, the question is still whether it would foreclose an entrant who is as efficient as the incumbent. Here 'foreclose' means that the rivals cannot access customers and as a result cannot reach efficient scale or compete effectively. When assessing the degree and likelihood of foreclosure, you can use the same structure and conduct criteria that are relevant to the feasibility of predation—eg, does the dominant company have a high market share, and what is the relevant strength of the competitors? Testing for foreclosure in rebate cases raises some additional questions—what is the effective price faced by a customer once the loyalty rebate kicks in? And at what level are the quantities of sales covered by the practice likely to have a significant anti-competitive effect?

In *Concord Boat Corp v Brunswick Corp*, several boat builders in the USA challenged Brunswick's discount programme on boat engines (we also discuss this case in Chapter 10 on quantifying damages).[68] Brunswick had about 75% of the market for recreational boat engines. Boat builders who agreed to buy a certain percentage of their engine requirements from Brunswick for a certain period received a discount on the list price for all engines purchased—the discount was therefore a retroactive loyalty rebate. Because some of the boat builders' customers apparently preferred Brunswick

---

[67] European Commission (1999), 'Commission Sets Out its Policy on Commissions Paid by Airlines to Travel Agents', press release, 14 July.
[68] 207 F 3d 1039 (8th Cir. 2000).

engines, it was claimed that they had to purchase a significant percentage of their engine needs from Brunswick.

How should you apply economic tests to Brunswick's conduct? You can see that there may be a 'non-contestable' portion of the demand amount that would be purchased from Brunswick irrespective of whether it faces competition from equally or more efficient companies. Brunswick has some brand loyalty among boat owners which creates a derived demand for its engines at the level of boat builders. Let's say that this brand loyalty is enough to create a portion of non-contestable demand (ignoring for the moment the evidence that certain customers did in fact switch more than 70% of their purchases). The concern is that the non-contestable portion of demand can be used to create leverage over the contestable portion.

In order to now calculate the effect of the rebate, you need to know the effective price charged over the 'relevant range', which varies depending on the type of rebate. For incremental rebates, the relevant range is the incremental purchases being considered. For retroactive rebates such as Brunswick's, the relevant range is the contestable portion of demand. Let's say that the contestable portion of demand is 25%, in line with the combined market share of Brunswick's rivals. Assume that there is a total demand of 100 units for the Brunswick engines. The price for an engine before the rebate is $100,000 and after the rebate it is $90,000. The effective price charged over the contestable portion of demand is therefore $60,000. To see this, consider that the first 75 units were priced at $100,000 and hence generated revenues of $7.5 million. Now customers purchase 100 units and the loyalty rebates kick in—they pay $90,000 per unit, generating revenues of $9 million. So the additional 25 units, which are assumed to be the contestable part of the market, have generated additional revenues to Brunswick of $1.5 million ($9 million – $7.5 million). The effective price for each of these units was therefore $60,000 ($1.5 million divided by 25). You can also calculate the effective price using the following equation:

$$\text{effective price} = (\text{discounted price} - (\text{undiscounted price} \times \text{non-contestable share}))/\text{contestable share}$$

$$= (\$90,000 - (\$100,000 \times 75\%)) / 25\% = \$60,000$$

The effective price on the contestable units is therefore much lower than the headline price. Table 4.6 shows how the effective price for this rebate scheme will vary according to the proportion of demand that is contestable—the smaller the contestable share, the lower the effective price on that share of demand. If the whole market is contestable then price is just the same as the headline discount price, and you can apply the normal predatory pricing standards to the rebates.

Based on the as-efficient competitor test, the rebate scheme is more likely to have a foreclosure effect if the effective price is below the AAC for the dominant company. Prices above LRIC are usually acceptable, as they would allow an as-efficient competitor to compete profitably. For prices between AAC and LRIC, the European Commission would investigate whether there are 'counterstrategies' available to rivals—for example,

Table 4.6 Calculating the effective price of a loyalty rebate

Contestable share (%)	Non-contestable share (%)	Effective price ($)
100	—	90,000
50	50	80,000
40	60	75,000
30	70	66,667
25	75	60,000
20	80	50,000

their capacity to also use a 'non-contestable' portion of their own buyers' demand as leverage to decrease the price for the relevant range.[69] Where no counterstrategies are available, the Commission will regard the rebate scheme as capable of foreclosure.

This whole logic depends on the premise that there is indeed a 'non-contestable' portion of the demand of each customer for which smaller competitors cannot compete. If there isn't (100% of the market is contestable), the case becomes one of normal predatory pricing, as we noted above. It depends on how much demand could be switched from the dominant company, which is something that must be tested as part of the effects analysis. In its Guidance on Article 102, the Commission defines the contestable share of demand as follows:

> For retroactive rebates, it will generally be relevant to assess in the specific market context how much of a customer's purchase requirements can realistically be switched to a competitor (the 'contestable share' or 'contestable portion'). If it is likely that customers would be willing and able to switch large amounts of demand to a (potential) competitor relatively quickly, the relevant range is likely to be relatively large. If, on the other hand, it is likely that customers would only be willing or able to switch small amounts incrementally, then the relevant range will be relatively small. For existing competitors their capacity to expand sales to customers and the fluctuations in those sales over time may also provide an indication of the relevant range. For potential competitors, an assessment of the scale at which a new entrant would realistically be able to enter may be undertaken, where possible. It may be possible to take the historical growth pattern of new entrants in the same or in similar markets as an indication of a realistic market share of a new entrant.[70]

So the contestable share should be defined according to the amount of demand that customers are willing and able to switch to a competitor. Where the dominant company has a truly 'must stock' brand, this switchable amount may be low, but in other cases, where products are less differentiated and consumers have less brand loyalty, the switchable amount could be high—potentially much higher than would be indicated by

---

[69] European Commission (2008), 'Guidance on the Commission's Enforcement Priorities in Applying Article 82 EC Treaty to Abusive Exclusionary Conduct by Dominant Undertakings', December, [44].
[70] Ibid., at [42].

competitors' combined market share. Indeed the contestable share may be customer-specific since some customers will have strong brand loyalty (or derived demand for brand loyalty) and others may not. In the *Concord Boat* case the court concluded that the plaintiffs had not offered sufficient evidence for a jury to determine that Brunswick's market-share discounts were anti-competitive. This was partly on the basis that at least two customers who previously had purchased more than 80% of their engines from Brunswick had in fact switched to a competitor for more than 70% of their purchases—an indication that the contestable part of the market was large.

Finally, caution is required regarding the interpretation of the link between the contestable share and the foreclosure effect. The calculation of the effective price in Table 4.6 implies that the smaller the relevant range, the greater the effective discount would be per unit of output, and therefore the greater the likelihood that the effective price would fall below any particular cost threshold. In other words, under this test, if there is room for only very small competitors in the market, intervention against rebates is more likely. A broader view is required which takes account of the general competitive dynamics in the market—switching behaviour, barriers to entry and other elements determining the company's ability to foreclose competition. Testing the effective price on the non-contestable part of the market alone is not sufficient to condemn loyalty rebates as exclusionary.

4.6.5 THE *INTEL* REBATES CASE: CHALLENGES IN EFFECTS-BASED TESTS

The strengths and weaknesses of the test discussed above are highlighted in a 2009 decision by the European Commission, which found that the rebates offered by Intel were capable of foreclosing the market to competitors.[71] This was one of the first cases where the Commission explicitly applied the as-efficient competitor test to exclusionary rebate schemes. At the same time, the case highlights the challenges you may face when conducting such analysis to determine the effects of the alleged conduct.

The Commission's decision followed from an investigation against Intel that started in 2004 after repeated complaints by its main competitor, AMD, about Intel's marketing arrangements with five major PC manufacturers (Dell, HP, Acer, NEC, and IBM/Lenovo) in the period 2002–07. The specific products concerned were computer processors of the x86 architecture, which are the industry-standard processors for the Windows and Linux operating systems. Intel and AMD have been the only manufacturers of x86 processors since 2000 as all others previously operating in this market had exited by then. The Commission found that Intel was dominant in the supply of x86 processors, with a market share of over 70%, and that it had abused this dominant position by imposing 'naked' restrictions on purchases of AMD products and by offering

[71] *Intel* (Case COMP/C-3/37.990), Commission Decision of 13 May 2009 D(2009) 3726 final.

rebates conditional on customers purchasing a target level of processors from Intel. The conditions for these rebates were individualized and warranted exclusive or near-exclusive purchases from Intel. For example, NEC was required to purchase 80% of its requirements from Intel in order to receive the rebates, and the threshold for Dell and Lenovo was 100%. The Commission found that Intel had targeted the most important PC manufacturers, leaving AMD with very limited access to alternative routes to the market. The Commission concluded that the rebates formed part of a long-term strategy on Intel's part to foreclose AMD, and that under existing case law the loyalty rebates constituted an abuse.

To support its conclusion and to determine the extent to which the rebates were capable of foreclosing AMD, the Commission undertook an extensive analysis using the framework of the as-efficient competitor test. In this context the test involves determining whether a competitor that is as efficient as Intel (ie, has the same level of production costs), but without as broad a sales base, can profitably operate in the market in the presence of Intel's rebate schemes. To illustrate the effect of conditional rebates on a competitor, consider the stylized example in Figure 4.5. Suppose that Dell's total requirement for processors is 100 units, and that AMD and Intel both produce processors that can fulfil this need. Intel's unit price (the undiscounted price) is €5, but it offers a rebate of 20% to Dell if 100% of its requirements are purchased from Intel—so Dell would pay a price of €4 instead of €5 for 100 units. Dell is in principle willing and able to purchase from AMD up to 40% of its demand (40 units in this example)—this is the contestable share of Dell's demand. What would you do if you were Dell?

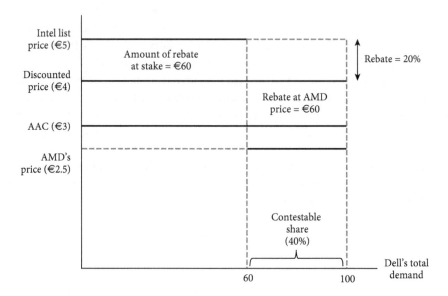

Fig. 4.5 Stylized example of the as-efficient competitor test in *Intel*

If Dell goes ahead and switches to AMD for those 40 units, it would no longer receive the Intel rebate of €1 per unit and would therefore lose a total rebate of €60 on the remaining units it continues to buy from Intel. In order for Dell to be 'compensated' for this loss and hence to actually buy the 40 units from AMD, the effective price offered by AMD has to be €2.50 or lower, as per the effective-price formula:

effective price = (discounted price − (undiscounted price × non-contestable share))/ contestable share

$$= (€4 − (€5 × 60\%)) / 40\% = €2.50$$

At a price of €2.50 instead of €4 for these 40 units, Dell would be exactly compensated for the loss of the Intel rebate, and hence it would be indifferent about purchasing from Intel or AMD—(€4 − €2.50) × 40 also equals €60. Can AMD really compete at this price? In this example, an effective price below the AAC of €3 implies that AMD would not be able to remain viable in the market and compete for Dell's contestable share (as illustrated in Figure 4.5). You can conclude that the rebate forecloses an as-efficient competitor that has access to only 40% of the market. Again you can see how crucial the exact proportion of 'non-contestable' demand is in these calculations.

This example also illustrates how a retroactive rebate implicitly involves leveraging market power from the non-contestable segment to the contestable segment of the market. The same logic was used by the European Commission:

> Intel is an unavoidable trading partner. The rebate therefore enables Intel to use the inelastic or 'non-contestable' share of demand of each customer, that is to say the amount that would anyhow be purchased by the customer from the dominant undertaking, as leverage to decrease the price of the elastic or 'contestable' share of demand market to lower the price in the contestable market, that is to say the amount for which the customer may prefer and be able to find substitutes.[72]

So how did the Commission determine the extent of the foreclosure effect due to such leveraging? It used the framework of the stylized example above but in an extended form. Instead of calculating the effective price and then comparing it to the AAC, it applied a different version of the same test, where the focus was on market shares rather than price. The aim was to work out the extent of potential foreclosure on a customer-by-customer basis. This worked as follows. First, the Commission determined the share of a PC manufacturer's demand that would be required by AMD to price just at AAC and at the same time compensate the customer for the loss in rebates from Intel. This is called 'the commercially viable share'. Obtaining this is just a matter of rearranging the effective price formula above:

commercially viable share = (undiscounted price − discounted price) / (undiscounted price − AAC)

for example: CVS = (5 − 4) / (5 − 3) = 50%

---

[72] Ibid.

Second, the Commission estimated the contestable share—40% in this example. The commercially viable share was then compared with the contestable share to determine the foreclosure effect. If the contestable share of a PC manufacturer's demand were less than the commercially viable share, an as-efficient competitor would not remain viable and the rebate would be capable of foreclosing the market. So in our stylized example we reach the same conclusion as before—the contestable share of 40% is lower than the commercially viable share of 50%, and hence foreclosure is predicted. The Commission followed these steps for each PC manufacturer and generally found the contestable share to be lower than the commercially viable share.

A key assumption in the Commission's analysis was the loss in rebate if a buyer switches its purchase to AMD. For instance, based on Dell's internal documents the Commission assumed that Intel would reduce the rebates by 50% if Dell attempted to purchase from AMD, while Intel argued that this was purely speculative and that the reduction would have been much lower. In the case of HP, on the other hand, the Commission assumed that the entire rebate would be terminated—this was supported by the provisions in an agreement between Intel and HP highlighting the conditionality of the rebates. Intel submitted that this was unrealistic and that a substantial part of HP's rebates were in fact 'non-conditional'.[73]

Another key assumption was the contestable share, including the appropriate time horizon over which to assess the contestable share. With a one-year window the contestable share would be low due to the short-run constraints that would prevent a PC manufacturer from shifting a large share of its purchases. Over a longer time period the constraints to switching (eg, adapting a new technology) would tend to dissipate. The Commission decided that a one-year horizon was appropriate because of the rapid rate of innovation in this market, the consequent short shelf life of the end-products, and the limited long-run visibility of market participants. Intel argued that strategic decisions are made with a two-to-three-year horizon in mind, and hence that the one-year window was not appropriate.

The as-efficient competitor analysis in *Intel* shows both the strengths and weaknesses of this test in loyalty rebates—it has the advantage of generating clear thresholds according to a specified formula, but the disadvantage is that the numbers cannot be relied upon unless you are comfortable with the assumptions behind them. Applying an effects-based test to look at whether rivals are in fact being excluded from the market would usually help figure out whether the numbers are meaningful. Despite its endorsement of the as-efficient competitor test (see section 4.2) and all the work on the numbers (about a third of the 518-page decision is on this test), the Commission reiterates in *Intel* the position in EU case law that the as-efficient competitor test is not indispensable for a finding of infringement, and that the use of conditional rebates by Intel was per se indicative of foreclosure. Indeed, in condemning Intel's rebates the Commission

---

[73] Ibid., at [1299]–[1301].

took the somewhat old-fashioned approach of citing the 1979 decision on *Hoffmann-La Roche*:

> an undertaking which is in a dominant position on a market and ties purchasers—even if it does so at their request—by an obligation or promise on their part to obtain all or most of their requirements exclusively from the said undertaking abuses its dominant position within the meaning of article 82 EC [now 102 TFEU], whether the obligation in question is stipulated without further qualification or whether it is undertaken in consideration of the grant of a rebate. The same applies if the said undertaking, without tying the purchasers by a formal obligation, applies, either under the terms of agreements concluded with these purchasers or unilaterally, a system of fidelity rebates, that is to say discounts conditional on the customer's obtaining all or most of its requirements—whether the quantity of its purchases be large or small—from the undertaking in a dominant position.[74]

The General Court took the same position of citing *Hoffmann-La Roche* in the *Tomra* rebates case—a 2010 judgment handed down a year after the Commission's decision in *Intel*—although it acknowledged that economic analysis should be a part of the overall conclusion:

> the Commission, in the contested decision, correctly considered the individualised quantity commitments not only in a purely formal way from the legal point of view but also taking into account the specific economic context in which the agreements in question operated. That was the basis for the Commission's conclusion, in the contested decision, that the agreements concerned were capable of excluding competitors . . . It follows from all the foregoing that the plea alleging a manifest error on the part of the Commission in holding that non-binding quantity commitments could infringe Article 82 EC [now 102 TFEU] must be rejected.[75]

4.6.6 UNCONDITIONAL VOLUME DISCOUNTS

Volume discounts are an example of second-degree price discrimination: a dominant company offers a menu of prices at different volume levels and customers 'self-select' the volume/price trade-off they desire. Unlike with loyalty rebates, the 'depersonalized' rebate threshold of a volume discount will be too high for some buyers and too low for others—in other words it will be insufficiently specific to keep all purchasers loyal to the dominant company. Smaller customers may never reach the required threshold, while the larger buyers may purchase considerably more than the required threshold. In these circumstances the discount system is unlikely to have a foreclosure effect since a large buyer would not lose the rebate by switching to an alternative supplier for part of its demand, and small buyers would be unaffected by the whole scheme. Traditionally, EU case law has considered unconditional volume discounts to be relatively benign, especially when it is shown that they are cost-reflective.

---

[74] Case 85/76 *Hoffmann-La Roche* [1979] ECR 461, at [89].
[75] Case T-155/06 *Tomra Systems ASA and Others v European Commission* [2010] ECR 297–301.

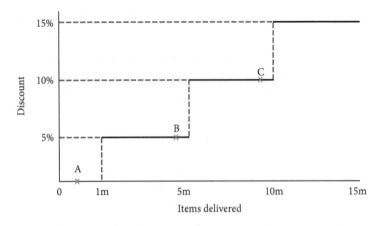

Fig. 4.6 Illustration of stepped volume discounts

In 2000, the UK telecoms regulator Oftel (now Ofcom) condemned the volume discounts offered by Vodafone to mobile service providers and resellers, after establishing that they were based on a stepped structure, increasing in accordance with subscriber levels. Oftel was concerned that the thresholds for discounts were set very high and that a company offering mobile telephony services over Vodafone's network could make a reasonable return only if it secured the maximum discount. Oftel closed the case after Vodafone changed the terms on which the wholesale service was supplied.[76]

From an economic perspective the concern about volume discounts arises only if they are not cost-reflective *and* if they are designed to mimic the structure and effect of a loyalty rebate scheme. This does occur if most customers purchase more or less the same amount of output, and the threshold at which the discount kicks in is set close to this output level. Say that 90% of an incumbent postal operator's bulk-mail customers each send around 5 million items per year, and that the incumbent offers a 10% discount to customers sending precisely this quantity of items every year. In this case, rivals could be excluded from the market for the same reasons outlined above in relation to loyalty rebates. Similar effects might occur if the discounts are stepped and customers can be classified into groups depending on the volume of output purchased. Figure 4.6 provides a stylized example of this type of scheme. There are three steps in the discount structure: at 1, 5, and 10 million mail items per year. Customers which send may fewer mail items than the 1 million threshold—such as Customer A in the figure— are not really affected by the discount scheme. However, customers such as B and C, which are close to the higher discount thresholds (of 5 and 10 million items, respectively), may have an incentive to stay with the incumbent operator and indeed enhance their

---

[76] Case BX/633/141 *Pre-pay Services on the Vodafone Network*. See Oftel (2000), 'Competition Bulletin', Issue 15, March.

volumes so as to hit the target and receive a bigger discount. Whether this has any fore-closure effect depends on similar analysis to that we saw above in relation to loyalty rebates. The difference is that assessing the discount scheme has a pre-condition—you first need to know the distribution of customer demand and hence check whether the discount scheme gets close to mimicking the individualized thresholds that would characterize loyalty rebates.

4.6.7 EXCLUSIVE DEALING

As discussed in more detail in Chapter 6, an exclusive deal between a supplier and a distributor is often benign in terms of its effect on the competitive process. While exclusivity will diminish intra-brand competition (between retailers of the same brand), it can foster inter-brand competition (between brands). In particular, exclusivity may allow the chosen retailer to invest resources in promoting the supplier's product without fear that competing retailers will free-ride on these efforts. Exclusive dealing is of concern to competition law if it places enough distributors in the hands of the dominant supplier to foreclose competing firms from the market—as illustrated in Figure 4.4 above. In these circumstances, exclusive dealing can be a tool for the dominant company to raise entry barriers since it becomes more expensive and difficult for potential rivals to obtain sufficient retail distribution.

An exclusive distribution arrangement between a supplier and distributor is more likely to foreclose competition the greater the degree of market power of the supplier and the greater the distributors' importance relative to other sales channels. Two cases where the foreclosure effects from exclusive dealing were considered to be significant in this regard are *Dentsply* (2005) in the USA and *Unilever* (2006) in the EU, involving exclusive dealing in the markets for false teeth and impulse ice cream, respectively.[77] Dentsply had a stable market share of 75%–80% for a number of years and its dealer network represented 80% of all laboratory dealers, so the US appellate court ruled in 2005 that its exclusivity requirements on those dealers were anti-competitive. Unilever's freezer cabinet exclusivity was condemned by the European Commission and Courts both as a restrictive agreement under Article 101 and as an abuse of dominance under Article 102. Like Dentsply, Unilever had had a market share in the Irish market for ice creams of close to 80% for several years, and around 40% of retail outlets were effectively foreclosed to competitors. These restrictive effects were found to outweigh the possible efficiency benefits of vertical restraints (see Chapter 6).

There are several issues to assess in determining whether exclusive dealing is likely to have anti-competitive effects in an Article 102 context. First, since these are vertical agreements, relevant upstream and downstream markets must be defined and dominance established in the upstream market. Second, the link between the particular

---

[77] *United States v Dentsply International, Inc.* 399 F 3d 181 (3d Cir. 2005); and Case C-552/03 P *Unilever Bestfoods (Ireland) Ltd, formerly Van den Bergh Foods Ltd v Commission* [2006] ECR I-9091.

agreements and their impact on sales and brand must be established. The ability to influence customers is likely to differ across the distribution channels: large retailers, Internet retailers, and small outlets may all have different attributes. Third, you have to identify the extent of the exclusionary practice and the ability of rivals to replicate the benefits of these contracts or to find alternatives. While the agreements themselves are exclusive, it may be feasible for rivals to offer similar exclusive arrangements to distributors. This is a question of assessing whether rivals can replicate the dominant company's agreements.

Consider agreements with retailers that specify monetary payments by the dominant company in exchange for compliance with the terms of the exclusivity. Retailers usually want something in return for the exclusivity; the supplier cannot just impose it. What you often see in practice is that the exclusivity is not made explicit but is achieved implicitly through the structure of the payments. The *Tyco* case referred to above is an example (here the buyers were customers rather than distributors, but the effect is the same).

Imagine an agreement involving confectionary retailing under which outlets are awarded free chocolate bars by a dominant company, OxChoc, if the outlets sell only OxChoc chocolate bars. The value of the payments as a proportion of total sales is 1 free chocolate bar for every 40 sold; this translates into a discount of 2.4% of the full value of chocolate retail sales (1 chocolate bar divided by 41). Say that OxChoc has a 90% market share, and its only rival has 10%. If any one retailer takes the rival's chocolate bars, it will lose the OxChoc discount. Assume that if a retailer starts to stock the rival chocolate bars it will choose (at least initially) to buy only 10% of its needs from the rival. To compensate the retailer for losing the OxChoc discount, the rival must offer a 24% discount (ie, 24% times the 10% share equals an average discount across all chocolate sales of 2.4%). This implies that, in order to compensate for the incentives provided to a retailer by the OxChoc agreement, the rival must offer retailers a discount that is ten times more generous.

Exclusive dealing agreements sometimes contain clauses that grant the dominant company first right of refusal to respond to any offers made by rivals. In this case, even if a rival did attempt to match OxChoc's incentives, perhaps in instances where the incentive rate was relatively low, OxChoc could increase the amount of discount it offered at relatively little cost, and substantially increase the discount the rival would have to offer. Again, exclusivity is achieved de facto. For example, were OxChoc offering a 2% discount, the rival would have to offer at least a 20% discount to make an alternative incentive scheme equally attractive to the retailer. However, if, in response to this approach, OxChoc increased this discount to only half the level offered by the rival (ie, 10%), the rival would have to literally give away its products to match that value. This is a rather extreme example where the retailer is unwilling (perhaps because OxChoc is a 'must-stock' item) to give OxChoc's rival any chance to become its main supplier. If the rival could get a higher share of sales at the retailer the effects would dissipate. But it is clear that a dominant market position increases the risk of exclusive dealing having a foreclosure effect. Before condemning OxChoc's exclusive dealing it is appropriate to consider the countervailing benefits of vertical agreements. We return to this topic in Chapter 6.

4.7 MARGIN SQUEEZE

4.7.1 WHAT IS MARGIN SQUEEZE, AND WHY IS IT A PROBLEM?

Margin squeeze is a form of vertical leveraging whereby a vertically integrated company attempts to exploit a position of dominance in an input market to restrict competition in a competitive downstream market. The company lowers its downstream price or raises the price of the input. These actions, either on their own or together, have a similar effect: they reduce the margin earned by downstream rivals such that they cannot profitably compete or are forced out of the market. This has the effect of enhancing the market power of the integrated company in the downstream market. Various cases in Europe have established margin squeeze as an abuse of dominance, including *Deutsche Telekom* (2003), which concerned the price of unbundled access to local loops, and *Genzyme* (2004), in relation to the downstream market for the drug Cerezyme and its associated home-delivery service.[78]

As illustrated in Figure 4.7, the basic conditions of a margin squeeze are that the company is vertically integrated and dominant in the relevant upstream market such that downstream competitors have a degree of reliance on the company's upstream input.

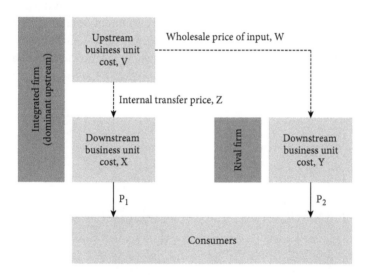

Fig. 4.7 Illustration of a margin squeeze

[78] *Deutsche Telekom AG* (Case COMP/C-1/37.451, 37.578, 37.579), Commission Decision 2003/707/EC, [2003] OJ L263/9; and Competition Appeal Tribunal (2004), *Genzyme Limited v the Office of Fair Trading*, Judgment, CAT 4, 11 March.

One way of abusing its position would be for the integrated company to discriminate in favour of its own downstream business, setting upstream price W above the internal transfer price Z. This form of discrimination can cause secondary-line injury to competition and has been of concern in many vertically integrated network and utility industries (see section 4.5 and Chapter 9). However, even in the absence of price discrimination—ie, W equals Z—there can be harm to competition through margin squeeze. This occurs if the dominant company sets a margin between the wholesale price W of the input and its retail price P_1 in the downstream market that is so low that a downstream competitor relying on the wholesale input is unable to compete, even if it has a unit cost Y equal to unit cost X—ie, even if it is an as-efficient downstream competitor. Note that in this assessment only the P_1 – W margin matters, as that is what defines rivals' potential revenues. The internal transfer price Z within the dominant company is irrelevant for the assessment of margin squeeze.

Figure 4.8 shows the margin squeeze concept a different way. On the left-hand panel there is no margin squeeze—the difference between the wholesale price charged to the entrant and the incumbent's retail price is sufficient to cover the costs of an as-efficient entrant. Since these costs are, by definition, the same as those of the incumbent, the above statement is equivalent to saying that the costs of the incumbent's downstream arm are adequately covered by the retail–wholesale margin—this downstream arm is not making losses at the given prices. Compare this to the right-hand panel, in which the vertically integrated incumbent has 'squeezed' the entrant from two directions, lowering its retail price and increasing its wholesale price. The as-efficient entrant can no longer compete as its potential revenues are defined by the incumbent's retail margin, which is now below the incumbent's retail costs.

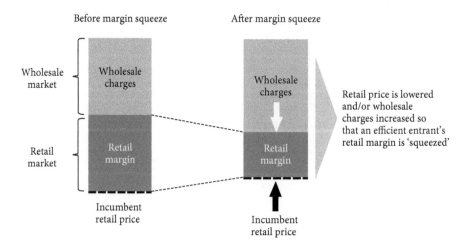

Fig. 4.8 A different illustration of a margin squeeze

While the margin squeeze concept is relatively easy to grasp, the mechanics of margin squeeze tests and their practical application by regulatory and competition authorities raise many economic issues that are far from straightforward. At the heart of these issues lies the need to balance the objective of promoting efficient entry into the market with a desire to provide incumbent companies with sufficient flexibility and incentives to compete and invest. This is a trade-off that is not easily resolved and indeed one which regulators and competition authorities may approach differently, as discussed in this section.

4.7.2 HOW TO ASSESS MARGIN SQUEEZE UNDER COMPETITION LAW

Until recently there has been little guidance on how to assess margin squeeze, let alone whether it constituted a distinct form of abuse under Article 102, separate from predation or excessive pricing. Early EU cases (*National Carbonising*, 1976; *British Sugar/ Napier Brown*, 1988; and *Industrie des Poudres Sphériques*, 2000) provided some useful pointers but left many economic and legal questions unanswered.[79] In the telecoms sector, a 1998 Commission Notice on the application of competition rules to access agreements shed some light on the nature of margin squeeze assessment by identifying two tests that could be applied.[80] First, under the as-efficient competitor test, a margin squeeze could be demonstrated by showing that the dominant company's own retail operations could not trade profitably on the basis of the access price charged to its competitors by the wholesale operating arm of the dominant company. Second, under the 'hypothetical reasonably efficient operator' test, a margin squeeze could be demonstrated by showing that the margin between the price charged to retail competitors for access and the price which the dominant operator charges in the retail market is insufficient to allow a hypothetical reasonably efficient retail service provider to make a normal profit.

In 2008, the General Court judgment in the *Deutsche Telekom* case provided greater clarity and guidance.[81] It confirmed that margin squeeze was a distinct pricing practice that can constitute an abuse under Article 102, and endorsed the conceptual and practical approach followed by the Commission in assessing the existence of a margin squeeze. The Commission's approach, as articulated in the *Deutsche Telekom* and *Telefónica* cases, is based on the following principles.[82] First, the investigated company must be vertically integrated and active in both wholesale and retail markets. Furthermore, it must be dominant in the relevant wholesale market, although it does not need to be

---

[79] *National Carbonising* [1976] OJ L35/6; *Napier Brown v British Sugar* (Case no IV/30.178) [1988] OJ L284, 41–59, Commission Decision of 18 July 1988; Case T-5/97 *Industrie des Poudres Sphériques* [2000] ECR II-3755, Judgment of the Court of First Instance of 30 November 2000.

[80] European Commission (1998), 'Notice on the application of competition rules to access agreements in the telecommunications sector—Framework, Relevant Markets and Principles' [1998] OJ C265, at [117] and [118].

[81] Case T-271/03 *Deutsche Telekom AG v EC Commission* [2008] ECR II-477.

[82] *Wanadoo España v Telefónica* (Case COMP/38.784), Commission Decision of 4 July 2007.

dominant in the retail market that is affected by the alleged margin squeeze. Second, the existence of a margin squeeze will be assessed on the basis of the as-efficient competitor test, using the dominant company's own retail costs and its retail and wholesale charges in order to assess the profitability of its retail operating arm. Regarding costs, retail costs will be estimated according to the LRIC of providing the relevant product under investigation (see section 4.3). Third, the margin squeeze test will be applied across the full range of products offered by the investigated company in the relevant retail market. This is an important point in telecoms where companies tend to sell bundles (eg, broadband, telephone, and television). It means that the retail price will be calculated across the full range of products, and that a margin squeeze would not be found if, for example, only the broadband price fails the test but the full range of products combined meets it (bundling is discussed in section 4.8).

The Commission's approach also recognizes two methods for measuring the profitability of the dominant company's downstream arm—a period-by-period approach and a discounted cash-flow approach (this is in essence the same as the NPV method discussed in Chapter 3). The former measures profitability in each year. It is better suited to mature and stable markets where year-on-year profitability measures may be a reasonable guide for economic profitability. The latter measures profitability across the lifetime of an investment, and is better suited to growing or dynamic markets where initial investments are expected to be recovered by a future stream of profits. In the *Telefónica* case, the Commission applied both approaches and reached the same conclusion under each.

These *Deutsche Telekom* and *Telefónica* principles are somewhat at odds with the approach adopted by various sector regulators in the determination of ex ante margin squeeze rules. For example, in the context of setting prices for wholesale broadband access products, both Ofcom in the UK (2004) and ComReg in Ireland (2005) applied the reasonably efficient competitor test, estimated retail costs on the basis of fully allocated costs, and undertook the analysis at the level of each individual product offered by BT and eircom, respectively.[83] These regulatory approaches usually represent a more onerous test from the perspective of the incumbent operator since they have the effect of increasing the required margin between retail and access prices, thereby providing greater room for entry into the market. At the end of this section we discuss why a difference exists between competition law and regulation with respect to the approach towards margin squeeze.

4.7.3 INCENTIVES FOR MARGIN SQUEEZE: ENHANCED MARKET POWER UPSTREAM OR DOWNSTREAM

As with any case of below-cost pricing, the dominant company's incentives to engage in a margin squeeze abuse are not entirely straightforward, and the issue of incentives is an important element in margin squeeze cases. A margin squeeze case differs from a pure

[83] See Ofcom (2004), 'Direction Setting the Margin between IPStream and ATM Interconnection Prices', 26 August; and ComReg (2005), 'Consultation on Retail Minus Wholesale Price Control for the WBA Market', Consultation Paper 05/67, 19 August.

predatory pricing case since the dominant company is not necessarily losing money overall. It may be profitable throughout the period of the margin squeeze, as it can choose to take its profit upstream while setting a downstream retail price that would be insufficient to cover its downstream costs. The analysis of recoupment is therefore different.

A first motivation of margin squeeze is to gain market power in the downstream market. If a margin squeeze successfully excludes competitors downstream by eliminating their opportunity to compete on price, it will enable the vertically integrated company to acquire or maintain market power in the downstream market. In any margin squeeze, the downstream competitor is also a customer of the upstream business. Excluding this rival reduces profits upstream since a customer is lost and fewer sales are made. Engaging in a margin squeeze is profitable only where the reduction in demand for the dominant company's products upstream is offset by additional revenues elsewhere. Normally this depends on extracting sufficient additional profit downstream to cover the loss of profit on sales of upstream units to rivals. This is subject to the degree of market power the dominant company will be able to exercise in the downstream market—ie, whether it will be able to increase retail prices profitably. In the situation where the downstream market is highly competitive, with low barriers to entry and a low degree of product differentiation, margin squeeze may be an unprofitable strategy. The company is better off taking its monopoly profits upstream and allowing output to be maximized downstream by the most efficient downstream operator. If the downstream market is not perfectly competitive, the incentive to monopolize it is greater.

A second motivation behind margin squeeze is to maintain market power upstream. This strategy involves removing competitive constraints on upstream prices arising from the purchasing behaviour of downstream rivals, enabling the dominant company to acquire or maintain significant market power in the upstream market. Consider a hypothetical example of a broadband market. The upstream product is the network that runs from broadband customers through to their Internet service providers networks. The upstream operator has market power since it is assumed that it currently has no rivals in the market for network infrastructure. The downstream product is consumer broadband, and is supplied by a range of service providers—including the downstream arm of the upstream monopolist—which all purchase network access from the upstream monopolist. This downstream market is reasonably competitive, characterized by homogeneous products and similar levels of efficiency among firms. A potential entrant into the upstream market would have to build a rival network, making a considerable sunk investment to operate in this market. Assuming that the downstream market is currently fragmented, it is difficult for any potential entrant to be guaranteed sufficient demand to recover its sunk costs in building a network since its potential share of the market for the upstream input is uncertain. Winning a small share of the market for supplying network access is not enough to justify the network investment, and as a result there will be no entry in the absence of sufficient guaranteed downstream demand, even if a potential entrant is more efficient than the monopolist. In these circumstances, by excluding downstream rivals, the vertically integrated company can make sure that no rival finds it profitable to enter the upstream market. This helps the company maintain its upstream market power, and is profitable so long as the expected profit forgone through the margin squeeze is outweighed by the expected profit from maintaining upstream market power.

4.7.4 WHOSE COSTS SHOULD BE USED IN THE MARGIN SQUEEZE TEST?

As mentioned above, there are two main tests for margin squeeze. Both ask whether the retail margin of the dominant company's downstream business is unreasonably low. The first test is to use the costs of the dominant company's downstream business—this is in line with the as-efficient competitor test. The second test is to use the costs of a hypothetical reasonably efficient competitor. The as-efficient competitor test is based on the downstream costs of the dominant company. This test is also called the 'imputation test' because you 'impute' the costs of the as-efficient competitor from the costs of the dominant company. A margin squeeze exists where:

Retail price – wholesale price < dominant firm's downstream cost.

This is the standard test for margin squeeze in competition law, and has been used in the *Deutsche Telekom* and *Genzyme* cases referred to above, as well as in the *BSkyB* case discussed in section 4.3. It provides the conditions for efficient entry by rival companies. The second test is based on the costs of a hypothetical reasonably efficient downstream operator, and says that a margin squeeze exists where:

Retail price – wholesale price < a hypothetical reasonably efficient operator's downstream cost.

This has been used primarily in markets that are in the process of liberalization. Although economic literature suggests that monopoly power can bring about managerial inefficiency, a dominant company may nonetheless have a lower downstream unit cost due to economies of scale that cannot be replicated by rival companies. Where this is true—typically in network industries such as telecoms—the use of this test promotes the entry of operators that are 'not yet' efficient. From a consumer welfare perspective, the justification for using this test is that using the entrants' cost may deliver longer-term gains. Using the higher cost base of the entrant initially leads to a short-term inefficiency and potentially higher prices, as it protects the less efficient player. But as the entrants establish themselves and begin to compete in the downstream market, allocative efficiency increases because downstream competition delivers more cost-reflective prices.

In a decision by the UK telecoms regulator Ofcom concerning BT's pricing of its line-rental product, BT Together, the regulator applied multiple cost tests to assess the margin squeeze allegation, including both the imputation test and the hypothetical reasonably efficient operator test.[84] Although it rejected the use of the reasonably efficient

---

[84] Ofcom (2004), 'Investigation Against BT about Potential Anti-competitive Exclusionary Behaviour', Decision of the Office of Communications, Case CW/00760/03/04,12 July.

operator test, Ofcom did modify its imputation test to exclude structural cost advantages derived from BT's inherited customer base. Ofcom's ruling suggests that where a dominant company's unit cost is lower than that of its rivals due to scale or scope economies, where it formerly held a legal monopoly position, it is reasonable to adjust its cost base for features of market structure that are not due to 'competition on the merits'. This sets up a counterfactual market structure under 'normal' competitive conditions. In line with this approach of creating a counterfactual, Ofcom modified its analysis of BT's downstream costs by adding in a 'local calls disadvantage' to take account of the scale economies and lower interconnection costs enjoyed by BT at the local exchange level, thus combining the imputation test and the reasonably efficient operator test.

4.7.5 THE RELEVANT PERIOD OF TIME OVER WHICH TO ASSESS A MARGIN SQUEEZE

A margin squeeze test can require the calculation of future profit margins for the downstream business since a static analysis of profit margins can be misleading where one-off start-up costs are important. For example, where heavy investment is required in a particular year, it would be incorrect to assume that the losses in that year represent a margin squeeze since that investment is relevant to revenues not only in that year but in future years. For an appraisal that includes start-up investments by companies entering the market, genuine investments in future revenues should be amortized or depreciated according to their economic use—for example, operational costs (marketing or promotional costs) that are front-loaded within a project lifetime, but may justifiably be recovered over a number of years. The correct way to account for these is to amortize them over an appropriate period, linked to the underlying output they are supporting. For example, if the downstream business invests in supplying set-top boxes to new subscribers, this investment can be amortized over the average subscriber lifetime. Deciding which of the dominant company's costs are 'genuine' investments in future revenues is not always straightforward. Changing the depreciation profile of investments can have an appreciable impact on the results of the margin squeeze test by changing the forward-looking cost profile of the downstream business.

4.7.6 DEALING WITH COMMON COSTS IN MARGIN SQUEEZE ASSESSMENT

Problems of allocating common costs across multiple downstream products have arisen in several cases, notably *Deutsche Telekom*.[85] (We also discuss cost allocation in Chapters 3 and 8.) At the downstream level, it makes sense to use the dominant company's incremental downstream cost for each product, allowing a company selling

---

[85] *Deutsche Telekom AG* (Case COMP/C-1/37.451, 37.578, 37.579) Commission Decision 2003/707/EC, [2003] OJ L263/9.

multiple downstream products to benefit from economies of scope by spreading its costs across several products. However, if competitors enter only with a single product, they will find it difficult to compete against a vertically integrated company with several retail products. In this scenario, some allowance could be made for common costs as well as incremental costs, in particular if there is a regulatory policy interest in promoting competition. Conducting the margin squeeze test at a less aggregated level might, however, encourage inefficient entry by a single-product company. A 'combinatorial' test can be used to assess the sensitivity of the margin squeeze test results to requiring each product to recover all common costs as well as incremental cost, and compare this with the result from using incremental cost alone.

The issue of such downstream economies of scope arose in *Deutsche Telekom*, where the incumbent argued that calculation of end-user prices should include both access charges and charges from telephone calls, since both are 'derivative' products in relation to wholesale access. The European Commission rejected this argument, based on its definition of network access as a separate relevant market. However, it may be argued that this rejection is appropriate only if rivals could not profitably duplicate Deutsche Telekom's balance between access and call charges—for example, by allowing high-volume users to opt for a higher access fee that is offset by lower call charges, or by selling a bundle of services (eg, voice, broadband, and television).

Similar complex issues relating to the sale of downstream products in bundles have arisen in several cases, including that of BSkyB. Since BSkyB supplies basic pay-TV channels only in bundles with premium channels, the OFT concluded that 'to separate revenues derived by DisCo [BSkyB's downstream arm] from the distribution of basic channels . . . would involve arbitrary allocations.'[86] It therefore included revenues from basic channel subscriptions in the analysis of the margin squeeze on BSkyB's provision of its premium channels. However, rivals to BSkyB complained that the higher margins on BSkyB's basic sales could be cross-subsidizing lower premium margins and that if premium channels were considered in isolation, the squeeze would be deeper. This example illustrates the point that the bundling of two products, such as premium and basic channels, or access and call charges, means that a rigorous separation of costs and revenues for each product is made more difficult, and the conduct of a margin squeeze test made more susceptible to dispute. We discuss bundling in section 4.8.

In the presence of multiple downstream products sharing common costs, the issue of whether margin squeeze damages competition and consumer welfare is no longer straightforward, as there can be a conflict between efficient pricing strategies for a multi-product company and pricing structures that satisfy a margin squeeze test by not excluding competitors. This conflict derives from the usual benefits of price discrimination, as we now explain.

---

[86] Office of Fair Trading (2002), 'BSkyB Investigation: Alleged Infringement of the Chapter II Prohibition', OFT Decision, CA98/20/2002, 17 December, p 106.

4.7.7 IS THERE AN EFFICIENCY DEFENCE TO MARGIN SQUEEZE?

In theory, there are cases where a vertically integrated company's failure to meet a margin squeeze test is not necessarily the result of a strategy to exclude competitors, and might in fact cause no harm to economic welfare. For example, the failure can be a by-product of an efficient pricing structure. If the vertically integrated company sells to two downstream markets, with the same unit costs but different consumer preferences and elasticities, a greater proportion of fixed costs in the upstream market can be recovered from the product with the lower elasticity. This means that the company will charge a higher mark-up on this product than on the more price-sensitive product. With a requirement that rival firms must have access to the upstream input at a price that allows them to compete in the retail market, this pricing structure is made insupportable, even though it was not the result of anti-competitive intent and has led to higher output. In the situation where the vertically integrated company must supply the wholesale input at one price, inefficient entry may occur in the high-margin product, and the company's price for the low-margin product must rise. This in turn reduces demand for the low-margin product and forces the high-margin product to make a greater contribution to common cost.

Although *Deutsche Telekom* appears to show that, legally, abuse of dominance can be found solely from the finding of margin squeeze, other decisions have rejected an abuse of dominance allegation even with a finding of margin squeeze, on the basis that the margin squeeze has not had an appreciable negative effect on competition. Examples are the *BSkyB* case referred to above, and Ofcom's case on mobile on-net calls, which stated that:

> in the circumstances of this case, given the keen competition that exists between mobile operators and mobile service providers in the provision of non-PSTN products [ie, mobile calls] and the countervailing buyer power of the business customers that purchase non-PSTN products, Ofcom considers that the conduct [margin squeeze] in question does not amount to an abuse. Accordingly, there has been no infringement of the Chapter II prohibition or Article 82 of the EC Treaty (now Article 102 TFEU).[87]

The need for an effects-based test in addition to the imputation test also derives from the practical problems with conducting a robust imputation test. As previously discussed, the results of the imputation test can rely on contestable assumptions where start-up investments are recovered over a period of time; where the allocation of common costs between an upstream and a downstream business is problematic; or where downstream rivals do not supply the same range of products as the vertically integrated company.

4.7.8 MARGIN SQUEEZE ASSESSMENTS UNDER COMPETITION LAW AND REGULATION

As we saw at the start of this section, competition law and regulation have applied somewhat different approaches to margin squeeze. At the heart of this divergence lies a

---

[87] Ofcom (2004), 'Suspected Margin Squeeze by Vodafone, O2, Orange and T-Mobile', Decision of the Office of Communications, Case CW/00615/05/03, 21 May, at [215]–[216].

perceived difference in the objectives of ex ante regulation and ex post application of competition law. Unlike competition authorities, sectoral regulators often have a statutory duty to promote competition in the markets they regulate. In setting the ex ante margin for BT's wholesale broadband access product, Ofcom described this difference as follows:

> in terms of a margin squeeze analysis ex post competition law would tend to start from a presumption that the appropriate standard against which the dominant firm should be assessed is one of equally efficient competitors i.e. analysing the margin such that an equally (or more) efficient competitor to BT could enter and compete effectively with BT in the relevant downstream services markets. However . . . the context for the setting of a margin for [wholesale broadband access] is one of ex ante regulation which has as its objective the promotion of competition. Given this objective, Ofcom has concluded that a modification of this conceptual approach is warranted.[88]

Hence, relying largely on the objective of promoting competition, Ofcom decided to uplift BT's costs to capture the impact of a reasonably efficient entrant's lower market share; to employ ATC as the relevant cost standard to account for an entrant's reduced ability to benefit from the same economies of scale as BT; and to implement an ex ante margin squeeze test on each individual product supplied by BT in order to avoid an entrant having to replicate BT's product mix in order to be viable. These adjustments were intended to provide potential entrants with a sufficiently large margin on a product-by-product basis to ensure that they would have the incentives and ability to enter the market and operate viably.

The method adopted by Ofcom in this case could be regarded as a form of entry assistance. From a market liberalization perspective, this may be justified during the early stages of competition in a market, but would be expected to be rolled back as soon as competitors are established in the market. Consistent with this view, in May 2008 Ofcom withdrew the ex ante price control obligations from BT's wholesale broadband access products. However, there is a risk of taking the entry assistance argument too far. By definition, the full suite of adjustments required to implement the hypothetical reasonably efficient competitor test involves modelling a hypothetical operator that is less efficient than the vertically integrated incumbent. The authority should be able to articulate the pro-competitive benefits of promoting 'less efficient' entry so that these benefits can be assessed against the risk of diminishing the investment incentives and pricing freedom of the incumbent operator.

There is a pro-competitive rationale underpinning the principles adopted in the *Deutsche Telekom* and *Telefónica* cases under Article 102. (Incidentally, the Commission also established in these cases that the presence of sector regulation does not exempt the incumbent operator from the application of competition law.) The as-efficient competitor test is consistent with the principle that competition should take place on the merits, and this is therefore compatible with the exclusion of less efficient rivals. Similarly, the use of LRIC rather than ATC as a cost floor for the retail activity is consistent with the principle that, in

---

[88] Ofcom (2004), 'Direction Setting the Margin between IPStream and ATM Interconnection Prices', 26 August, [2.4].

the long run, a rational profit-maximizing company would have no economic reason to provide a service below its LRIC. Prices above LRIC but below ATC provide flexibility to the incumbent operator to recover common and joint costs based on demand differences.

In *Telefónica*, the Commission argued that the application of an aggregated products approach—where the degree of aggregation corresponds to the full range of products offered in the relevant retail market—can be consistent with a new entrant's internal decision-making process, in that its assessment of the profitability of its investment takes into account the complete range of products that it is able to offer in the relevant retail market. In addition, the aggregated approach is consistent with the competition policy principle that the existence of anti-competitive effects should be tested at the level of a relevant market. Indeed, from an economic perspective, it would be difficult to argue that anti-competitive foreclosure leading to consumer harm could be successful in a narrow segment of a relevant market when an aggregate margin squeeze test is showing healthy margins overall. From the supply side, entrants would be able to switch production to other segments of the market; from the demand side, consumers would have a range of products from which to choose other than the products that may be subject to a squeeze.

To find a middle ground between the approaches of competition law (as-efficient competitor) and regulation (hypothetical reasonably efficient competitor), it is possible to implement margin squeeze tests at different levels of aggregation, reflecting different entry strategies that competitors could adopt. Such an approach was taken by Ofcom in 2008 when it investigated an allegation that BT had engaged in a margin squeeze by raising its wholesale prices for number translation services.[89] While rejecting the application of the margin squeeze test on the individual products that the claimant contended were subject to a squeeze, Ofcom applied three different margin squeeze tests at different aggregation levels, corresponding to the most commonly observed business models of BT's retail competitors. The lowest level of aggregation that Ofcom used in this case corresponded to what it considered to be the narrowest plausible relevant retail market: a bundle of local calls, calls to mobiles, and number translation services calls. It did not find evidence of a margin squeeze under any of these tests.

4.8 BUNDLING AND TYING

4.8.1 SOME DEFINITIONS FIRST

Bundling and tying have long been analysed—and hotly debated—in economic theory and in competition law. In economic terms, these practices can be defined as follows:

- Products A and B are *bundled* if the price of the two products sold together is less than the sum of their individual purchase prices. It is useful to distinguish

---

[89] Ofcom (2008), 'Complaint from Energis Communications Ltd about BT's Charges for NTS Call Termination', August.

between *pure bundling*, where the products are offered only as a package, and *mixed bundling*, where the individual components are offered separately as well as in a bundle.

- Product B is *tied* to product A if a supplier refuses to sell product A (the 'tying good') unless the customer also purchases product B (the 'tied good') from that supplier.

Tying can occur when the tying product is designed such that it works properly only with the tied product and not with the alternatives offered by competitors—this is 'technical tying'. Contractual tying occurs when the customer that purchases the tying product commits to also purchase the tied product (and not the alternatives offered by competitors). Tying can be in variable proportions, in which case the amount of product B purchased varies with the intensity of use of product A—an example is razors and razor blades, where the amount of razor blades purchased depends on how often the razor is used. Or tying can be in fixed proportions between the amounts of product B and product A purchased—an example is cars and car tyres, where a new car will come fitted with four tyres. Bundling is always in fixed proportions. Tying in fixed proportions is equivalent to pure bundling since the outcome for the consumer is the same (you cannot buy the car without the four tyres). For this reason we can discuss the economics of bundling and tying for the most part without drawing a distinction between the two terms. Table 4.7 summarizes these definitions.

Table 4.7 Definitions of bundling and tying

Conduct	Definition	Example
Bundling	**A and B are sold together, at a price less than the sum of A and B individually**	
Pure bundling	A and B are available *only* as a package	New car (A) and tyres (B)
Mixed bundling	In addition to the package, A and B are sold *separately*	Word processor (A) and spreadsheet (B) Mobile phone (A) and network agreement (B)
Tying	**B is tied to the purchase of A**	
Variable proportions	The amount of B purchased varies with the *intensity of use* of A	Photocopier (A) and service agreement (B) Razor (A) and razor blades (B)
Fixed proportions (equivalent to pure bundling)	A and B are purchased together	New car (A) and tyres (B)

4.8.2 BUNDLING AND TYING: WHAT IS THE CONCERN?

Companies commonly use price bundling as a strategic marketing tool. Be it a shrink-wrapped package of shampoo and conditioner or a package of broadband, TV, and telephony services, bundling is a common business practice. In theory, there are several legitimate justifications for bundling and tying, including the cost efficiencies due to economies of scope, savings on transaction costs, the assurance of quality, and convenience for consumers. Bundling or tying is of particular concern under competition law only if a company is thought to be using its dominant position in one market to capture market power in another market (leveraging), or to protect its position in the original market (entry deterrence). Sometimes you may also see complaints about bundling as an unfair pricing strategy. Sellers can charge relatively high prices to buyers with a high valuation for one product but a low valuation for the other, while retaining sales to buyers with more moderate valuations by offering a discount on the bundle. This concerns only the exploitation of consumers, not the exclusion of competitors (see section 4.10 on excessive pricing and section 4.5 on price discrimination). So we are left with a simple theory of harm—bundling is of concern when it protects a dominant position in the original market or when it leverages that dominant position into a related market.

Earlier we drew a distinction between horizontal and vertical leveraging. Bundling and tying can be used for both. Unlike predation, bundling and tying do not need to involve profit sacrifice now in expectation of higher profits later—they can just be about perpetuating a monopoly position. There is a good example of this in the 2008 section 2 report by the US Department of Justice, regarding a hotel that is the sole accommodation on a paradise island:

> a tie may result in a firm with monopoly power in one market acquiring a monopoly in a second market or perpetuating its monopoly in the tying product. For instance, the only hotel on an island may tie accommodations and meal packages to its guests. If there are an insufficient number of island residents to support a second restaurant, the hotel may be able to extract greater profit through its tie of accommodations and meals because the tie enables the hotel also to monopolize restaurant services. The hotel thus would extract monopoly profits from not only its guests (the purchasers of the original monopoly product—accommodations) but also island residents (who would buy only the second product—restaurant food).[90]

The paradise island hotel profits because it successfully prevents competition emerging from an independent restaurant, which, but for the tie, would be able to achieve efficient scale by selling meals to hotel guests as well as island residents. In the presence of the tie, hotel guests obtain meals in the hotel at zero marginal cost (having paid for the tied combination of full-board meals and accommodation), which discourages them from trying out an independent restaurant whilst on holiday. You can see that bundling and tying are in this sense just another form of exclusionary pricing, where the effective price of the tied good faced by consumers is below the costs of an as-efficient competitor

---

[90] Department of Justice (2008), 'Competition and Monopoly: Single-firm Conduct Under Section 2 of the Sherman Act', September, p 83. The DOJ withdrew this report in 2009.

that can supply only the tied product (meals) but not the tying product (accommodation). The hotel guests will not be thrown out of the hotel if they seek sustenance elsewhere, but they have a strong price incentive to remain loyal to the hotel's restaurant.

Whenever bundling as a means of leveraging market power is the focus of antitrust concern, it is important to analyse clearly the motivation for bundling and to understand whether it is exclusionary in intent and effect. Economic theory implies that bundling practices should not be condemned per se. When the motivation for bundling is largely for efficiency reasons, the effect on consumer welfare is likely to be positive, even if competitors are harmed. However, when bundling is used strategically in an attempt to leverage market power, harmful effects cannot be ruled out, even if the practice also leads to efficiency gains. Usually an economic analysis of the specific market setting can help identify which effect predominates.

4.8.3 TYPES OF BUNDLING, AND WHETHER THEY RAISE CONCERN

There are basically four market situations in which anti-competitive effects of bundling could arise.

Horizontal bundling within one product market—this occurs when the two bundled products form part of the same relevant market. The products can be substitutes, in which case the bundling should be seen as a volume discount or price discrimination, and the competition analysis can be undertaken accordingly (see sections 4.5 and 4.6). The two bundled products can also be complements, which implies that competition in this market is between bundles (otherwise, the complementary products would not have been considered part of the same market). This may occur in markets where bundling is a common practice across different suppliers, and consumers are sufficiently well informed to take the whole bundle into account when making a purchase decision. We discussed this in Chapter 2 on market definition. In this situation, the competition analysis can be undertaken at the level of competing bundles, rather than focus on bundling as a competitive issue in its own right.

Horizontal bundling over two product markets—this is the more common situation where a supplier bundles products that are in different (not vertically-related) relevant markets. The competitive concern with bundling is that a position of market power in one of these products might be leveraged into the market for the other product (or that the bundling serves to protect existing market power in any of these markets). The bundled products can be either independent products or complements. In the case of complements the likelihood of anti-competitive effects tends to be higher (although the potential efficiency gains from bundling complements may also be larger).

Vertical bundling over two product markets—bundling may take place over two vertically related product markets. For example, in telecoms, a network access product is often combined with a retail service (eg, calls and access in fixed telephony; handset and calls package in mobile telephony). As with horizontal bundling of complements, the competitive concern is that bundling can be used in this way to leverage market power in one market (usually the network market) into the other.

Combined vertical and horizontal bundling of retail products that are offered using the same upstream network—this arises where the bundle includes different (not necessarily related) products offered over the same network—for example, telephony, TV, and Internet services using the same fixed line. The network access product itself might also be bundled into the same package. This form of bundling can have anti-competitive effects in any of the downstream product markets since leveraging could occur by virtue of a position of market power in the upstream market or in one of the downstream markets.

Pure bundling is more likely to be observed when products are complements (customer values for the bundle are greater than the sum of the values for the individual products) rather than substitutes (customer values for the bundle are less than the sum of the valuations for the individual products). For example, a computer and a printer are complements since customers have added value for a printer when they have a computer and vice versa. On the other hand a bottle of Pepsi and a bottle of Coke are substitutes. Since a consumer who has a Coke has relatively little use for a Pepsi, the value of the bundle is less than the sum of the values of the individual products. If substitute products are bundled, there will probably be some buyers who intend to use only one of the two products in the bundle and discard the other. Still the seller will be incurring the costs of producing both products. For this reason pure bundling ends up being a less attractive commercial strategy for substitutes than for complements.

Sometimes a product that is a complement for one group of customers can be a substitute for a different group of customers. Similarly, products that customers regard as complements today might be regarded as substitutes tomorrow. Search engines may be an example of products that sophisticated users might regard as substitutes while less experienced users regard them as complements. The Netscape Internet browser was an example of a product that started off as a complement to the Windows operating system but threatened to become a substitute over time.

4.8.4 SUPPLY-SIDE EFFICIENCIES OF BUNDLING AND TYING

A mixed bundle is bought by consumers because of the discount (or the added value) it gives relative to the purchase of stand-alone products. Bundling can therefore be welfare-enhancing as it leads to lower prices for consumers. Why would a producer be interested in bundling products and offering them at a discount? There are several possible efficiency reasons: because the bundle leads to cost reductions; because the bundle allows price discrimination whereby the producer is able to increase profits; or because of quality considerations. We deal with price discrimination efficiencies further below, as these arise on the demand side.

On the supply side, bundling can lead to a reduction in the production and distribution costs through economies of scope. Bundling is a way to save costs within the product portfolio of the company. For example, it is cheaper to deliver a suite of software packages on a single CD than to send out each one separately. Cost reductions can also arise from economies of scope at the retail level. Think of a bundle of telephone line rental and broadband—advertising this bundle reduces the need to invest in marketing each of these products separately. Similarly the company would need to send one bill only for the use of both services.

A further reason for a supplier to tie products or services is to increase the (perceived) quality or to maintain the reputation and brand of the supplier. A company might find it important to secure the use of separate products together for quality reasons. For instance, by coordinating the interfaces and the commands, a bundled software suite can offer improved functionality and simplicity. Tying a maintenance contract to a complex piece of machinery can ensure that maintenance is carried out by trained personnel only, giving the manufacturer confidence to offer a longer warranty. In being offered two or more products together, consumers have to spend less time searching for the right offer or worrying that the various products will not work together properly, and a supplier doesn't have to worry that a complementary good outside its control (whether associated software or maintenance) will damage customers' perceptions of the quality of its main product.

The issue of quality was addressed in *Jerrold*, a 1961 case in the USA.[91] Back in the 1950s Jerrold made community antenna systems for towns located a long way from TV transmitting stations. To ensure the proper functioning of the system, Jerrold would not sell separate parts but only whole systems, and only on the condition that it installed and serviced the system. It also required exclusive use of Jerrold equipment whenever capacity was added. The Supreme Court affirmed the trial court's finding that Jerrold was justified, on quality-control grounds, in tying the sales of cable TV systems to installation and maintenance services. According to the Court, the tying of goods and service was justified by a 'sound business reason'. The per se law against tying was overruled in this case. The Court upheld a requirement that buyers of TV systems purchase the complete system, as well as the installation and repair service, on the grounds that the tie assured that the systems would function and thereby protected the seller's business reputation.

4.8.5 DEMAND-SIDE EFFICIENCIES OF BUNDLING AND TYING

There is a large body of economic literature on how bundling may be used as a price-discrimination tool to extract more surplus.[92] Most of the literature stresses the importance of bundling as a means of reducing inefficiencies in pricing. Recall from section 4.5 that, to practise price discrimination, the producer must have control over prices, the ability to limit resale, and the ability to distinguish between different consumers. Bundling can be used to fulfil this last condition—by offering different prices for customers who buy different combinations of goods, a seller can separate buyers according to their demand characteristics in a way that might not be possible with independent

---

[91] *United States v Jerrold Electronics Corporation* 365 US 567; 187 F Supp 545 (1961).
[92] See, for example, Adams and Yellen (1976); Schmalensee (1982); Bakos and Brynjolfsson (1999). For an accessible overview see Nalebuff (2003).

pricing of all goods. This discrimination allows the seller to increase profits by extracting greater revenue from those buyers who are most willing and able to pay.

Table 4.8 gives a simple example of where prices for telephony and TV services are based on consumer willingness to pay. There are two types of consumer: those with a higher willingness to pay for making calls and those who value watching TV more. Without bundling, telephone services will be priced at €9 per month and bought only by 'talking' consumers. (Alternatively, they could be sold to both types of consumers at €2 per month, but you can see that this is very unattractive to the service provider.) TV services will be priced at €10 per month and bought only by 'watching' consumers. Say there are only two consumers, one of each type—in this case total revenue will be €19, and only two services are sold (one of each). The company offering telephony and TV can increase its profits and output by bundling telephony and TV together for €12. Now both 'talking' and 'watching' consumers will buy both services (since the combined price matches the sum of their willingness to pay). The company's revenue is then €24, which is more than when offering the products separately, but output has also increased (four services are sold, as both consumers purchase the two services).

In practice, demand-side efficiencies are the result of any output expansion effects (and, hence, increase in economies of scale) that bundling might generate. Such increases in output and revenues may be due to pure market expansion, in which case bundling may attract new customers who were previously not purchasing any product on a stand-alone basis. Complementary goods are more likely to be candidates for a pure market expansion effect. Alternatively, bundling may attract existing customers who were previously purchasing only a subset of the products included in the bundle, as in the case of our 'talking' and 'watching' consumers. Another example is a ticket to the ballet and a ticket to a wrestling match. A customer who has a high value for one of these tickets may be less likely to have a high value for the other, and bundling may induce the ballet goer to give wrestling a try. The products are not complements, but still bundling has an output expanding effect.

Mixed bundling may come at the expense of existing sales. In this context it is useful to distinguish between the impact on rivals' sales (business stealing) and an individual company's own sales (cannibalization). The business stealing effect is where the incumbent's output increases at the expense of its competitors. Clearly the risk of potential harm to competition is greater when business stealing effects dominate the market expansion effects described above. Since bundles are priced below the sum of the relevant stand-alone prices, the existence of bundles will to some degree 'cannibalize' a proportion of existing stand-alone revenues.

Table 4.8 Efficiency benefits of bundling: telephony and TV package

	'Talking' consumers	'Watching' consumers
Willingness to pay for telephony (€)	9	2
Willingness to pay for TV (€)	3	10
Willingness to pay for both telephony and TV (€)	12	12

These effects can be illustrated with the aid of Figure 4.9. An individual consumer's willingness to pay for broadband and fixed telephony is represented by a point in the willingness-to-pay field—a consumer near the top-left corner of the field has a low willingness to pay for telephony and a high one for broadband; a consumer near the bottom-right values telephony a lot and broadband a little. The maximum valuation that any consumer has for either product is assumed to be €25. There are two pricing strategies shown: one (on the left-hand side) where there is no bundling and each product is sold at €20; and the second (on the right-hand side) where there is mixed bundling and consumers can purchase each product separately at a unit price of €20, or both products in a bundle at a discounted price of €32. Consider the left-hand side first. At the separate prices of €20 there are four categories of consumer, as represented by the four rectangles: consumers in the bottom-left rectangle buy nothing because their willingness to pay for either service is below €20; those in the top-left rectangle purchase only broadband; those in the bottom-right only telephony; and those in the top-right buy both products.

The overall market expansion effect arising from bundling is represented by the sum of area A, B, and C. Before the introduction of the bundle, this group of consumers was not purchasing either product on a stand-alone basis because their willingness to pay for each product was below the retail price of €20. However, their combined valuation for both products is above €32 and they are therefore willing to purchase the bundle of broadband and fixed telephony. Examples of consumers in area A are those who value broadband at €19 and telephony at €13, and those who value both services at €16. Similarly, areas B and C represent consumers who were previously purchasing only one product on a stand-alone basis and are now purchasing both products on a bundled basis. From the supplier's perspective, this represents additional revenues of €10 per customer. Area D, on the other hand, shows the cannibalization effect that may

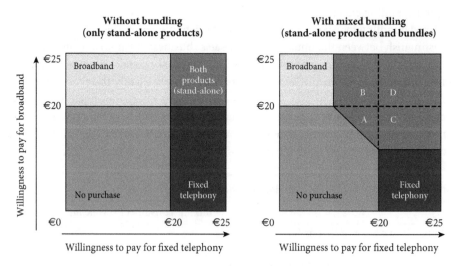

Fig. 4.9 Demand-side effects arising from mixed bundling

arise from bundling. These consumers were spending €40 in total when purchasing products on a stand-alone basis, and are now spending €8 less by purchasing them in a bundle.

4.8.6 BUNDLING AND TYING TO PROTECT AN EXISTING MARKET POSITION

Bundling and tying may protect an existing market position in the tying product if it creates new entry barriers. Pure bundling commits a company to a stronger price and investment reaction. This is because a failure to sell in the tied/bundled market product will also entail losing a sale in the tying/bundling market product. This commitment to a stronger price or investment reaction may hold back potential competitors, and therefore create an entry barrier. When rivals cannot match the supply of the bundle or tie, they will attract only consumers who prefer one product instead of the bundle. If the products are strong complements, this entry barrier might be significant since potential competitors have to offer a whole bundle where consumers strongly prefer the two products together. This could make it necessary for a potential rival to play the game 'bundle against bundle'. Entrants must either seek out the small number of consumers who do not value the tying product, or must compete bundle for bundle, which might not be possible because they cannot replicate the dominant company's position in the tying product. This occurs where there are economies of scale or scope needed to match the bundle.

A similar situation arises if there are network effects, which mean that there is a greater benefit to a good or service as the number of users increases. As a mobile network gets more subscribers, it becomes more valuable since users can call more destinations and be called by more people. Bundling can be used to deny competitors these network effects. Say there are two mobile network operators with a 45% market share each and two new smaller operators with 5% each. The operators currently charge a similar termination fee for calls on each other's network. Consumers do not care which network is used by the person they call. As long as incoming and outgoing traffic are broadly in balance, payments of termination fees balance out between the networks. The two larger operators can change this situation by introducing a bundle in which calls within the same network will not be charged a termination fee. Therefore, consumer prices for calls on the same network will be lower than off-net calls. Networks with a large number of users have an advantage over small networks—you can now call many more people at lower prices. The two smaller operators may not be able to lower their on-net prices to give a high discount because most of their calls will be off-net (ie, to one of the other networks, as they have only 5% of subscribers). The bundle extends the network effect for the two large networks, which can create barriers to enter or expand in the market.

4.8.7 BUNDLING AND TYING TO LEVERAGE MARKET POWER

The hypothesis that bundling can lead to leverage of market power was criticized by the Chicago School in the 1970s (see Chapter 1), on the basis that there is only 'one monopoly rent' in the vertical supply chain and this can be extracted from the monopolized market. If a company enjoys a monopoly in some input market, the full monopoly rent can be extracted by pricing that input at the monopoly level. Attempting to leverage that market power—for example, by bundling another product with the monopolized input—may shift some of the profit to the market for the bundled product, but total profits will not be increased. If the market for the bundled product is competitive, the Chicago School argument means that a monopolist in the bundling market will not be able to increase, and may even reduce, its profits by attempting to bundle a good that is in a competitive market. A monopolist is likely to prefer competition in the complementary product market because a lower price for the complement will lead to increased demand for the monopoly product. This is more likely to occur in the case of tying a monopoly product and a complement that is always used in fixed proportions with the monopoly product. This influential insight changed the previously hostile stance towards bundling and tying in competition law—these practices are not always as harmful to consumers as thought, and may produce efficiency benefits as well. The point is in essence related to the economic concept of double marginalization, which provides an important rationale for vertical restraints. We explain this concept in Chapter 6.

Since then, economic insights into bundling and tying have developed. A reassessment of the Chicago School position gained force with Whinston's examination of the role of bundling as a foreclosure strategy (Whinston, 1990). Whinston showed that the Chicago School's criticism depends on the tied market being characterized by perfect competition and the absence of scale economies in production. The incentives to adopt a foreclosure-based bundling strategy are different when the tied good market is oligopolistic as a result of scale economies. When a monopolist in the tying market faces a competitor in the tied market offering a product subject to strong scale economies and imperfect competition (eg, switching costs), bundling can be used to monopolize the tied market. By bundling, the monopolist reduces the sales of the rival company's tied product and can force that rival to exit the market. This is the paradise island example given earlier, where the independent restaurant cannot achieve minimum efficient scale since hotel guests buy a bundle and have no incentive to venture beyond the hotel's restaurant, thereby preserving the hotel restaurant's monopoly.

Yet even if the motivation to bundle is attempted foreclosure, bundling can benefit consumers. For example, when the strategic motivations to attempt foreclosure include the incentive to undercut rivals, even if competitors are harmed as a result, this does not necessarily lead to a conclusion that consumers will suffer—consumers may benefit from lower prices. The reasoning for this is as follows. A company supplying two complementary products will have incentives to sell these two together at a *lower* combined price than were they to be sold separately. When prices are set separately, a price rise for one creates a negative externality for the complementary product. Selling the products in a bundle eliminates this externality, and avoids double marginalization. This is analogous to a situation where a vertically integrated monopolist produces a more efficient outcome than separate monopolists of the upstream and downstream products. In the latter case, the monopoly price charged by the upstream company leads to an inefficient use of inputs. When the products in a bundle are complements and competition for both products is imperfect, bundling can lead to lower overall prices, higher levels of demand and increased consumer welfare—it is the Chicago School argument again.

When considering issues relating to the leverage of market power through bundling, it is therefore important to analyse the market. A first step in assessing the anti-competitive effects of bundling is to analyse the degree of market power. For anti-competitive effects to arise, the company in question must at least have some degree of market power in one of the products included in the bundle. Otherwise, bundling would be unlikely to have a significant effect on competitors or consumers in the first place, and hence any positive effects of bundling are likely to prevail. When a restaurant offers a free bottle of wine, the impact on competition is unlikely to be material. In addition, even if the bundling company has a dominant position in market A, it may be unlikely to successfully leverage this power if another company has a very strong position in market B, or if the bundle has only a limited impact on the whole of market B. For example, if the bundling company has, as yet, a very small market share in market B, or if there is a sufficient degree on independent demand for product B—ie, buyers that do not need product A.

An investigation by Oftel (now Ofcom) into BT's unmetered off-peak Internet packages is a good example of a case where a regulator analysed the circumstances in which bundling was taking place and, despite initial concerns, decided that it would not create a competition problem.[93] In 2000, BT introduced new tariffs for dial-up Internet access. These included two new packages offering unmetered off-peak Internet access calls, namely BT Surf Together and BT Talk & Surf Together. BT Surf Together provided the lower voice call prices available in the BT Together package as well as unmetered off-peak Internet access calls. BT Talk & Surf Together extended the BT Surf Together package to include unmetered off-peak local voice calls. Oftel's concern was that the tariff structure announced by BT might result in a restriction of competition in the relevant product markets—a form of horizontal leveraging from BT's dominance in the market for residential calls on fixed networks into Internet access markets.

The horizontal leverage argument suggests that if BT offers bundled services such as BT Talk & Surf Together, it would oblige competitors in Internet access also to provide voice services in order to be able to compete in Internet access. BT's packages were in the form of mixed, rather than pure, bundling. In Oftel's view, testing for the existence of horizontal leveraging (from retail voice into retail Internet access) would require analysing whether the marginal price of Surf in the packages was sufficiently high to cover the LRIC of providing Surf. For the horizontal leverage to be detrimental, it would be necessary that market power in the voice market was abused through excessive pricing of voice calls, and that the lower price for Internet access call origination led to a

---

[93] Oftel (2001), 'Investigation by the Director General of Telecommunications into the BT Surf Together and BT Talk & Surf Together Pricing Packages', 4 May.

significant decrease in competition in this market by inducing exit. Oftel rejected the complaint about horizontal leveraging because it was not clear that BT was pricing Surf below cost in the packages.

4.8.8 PRICE-COST TESTS FOR BUNDLING

The test for assessing pricing below cost in the case of bundling is to consider whether the price of the bundle covers the sum of the appropriate costs (whether LRIC or AAC) of each of the component products when offered separately—the cost benchmarks explained in section 4.3 are of relevance here as well. If this is the case, the bundle is unlikely to raise predation concerns. If the price does not cover the separate costs, the next step would be to consider the cost efficiencies generated by bundling the two components, and whether with these efficiencies the price of the bundle does cover costs.

Consider an example where only Ginco makes gin, but both Ginco and Tonics 'R' Us make tonic, and consumers must use both products for their gin-and-tonics. Ginco's AAC is €10 for the gin and €2 for tonic, while AAC for Tonics 'R' Us tonic is €1.50. So Tonics 'R' Us is more efficient than Ginco in the production of tonic. Ginco prices gin and tonic at €15 and €3 respectively if bought separately, but offers a bundled price of €16 if the products are bought as a Ginco package. This is above Ginco's AAC of €12 for both products. However, in order for Tonics 'R' Us to compete for tonic sales, it must persuade consumers to buy its tonic while paying the unbundled price of €15 for Ginco's gin. This means that Tonics 'R' Us can charge no more than €1 for tonic, which is below both Ginco's AAC for tonic and Tonics 'R' Us' own, lower, AAC. The potential harm to the competitive process in this example comes from the structure of Ginco's prices, which results in all or most consumers buying both products from Ginco because the price of the bundle is lower than the prices they would have to pay to acquire the bundled goods separately.

Another way of looking at this is to ask what the effective price of Ginco's tonic is if the entire discount is attributed to this product (this is sometimes called the 'attribution test'). The discount is €2, being the difference between the price of the bundle and the sum of the unbundled prices. Attributing this discount entirely to Ginco tonic (priced at €3 on a stand-alone basis) tells us that Ginco is selling the bundled tonic at €1, which is below the relevant measure of Ginco's cost (its AAC is €2). This is a slightly more complicated way of saying the same thing as above—ie, that the incremental price that Ginco charges for including tonic in the bundle (€1) is less than Ginco's incremental cost, and therefore less than the cost of an as-efficient competitor.

The attribution test is informative for the as-efficient competitor test but does not in itself prove anti-competitive effects. For example, a car dealer that gives away a free tank of fuel with the car certainly fails the attribution test for the car and fuel bundle, but there is neither an anti-competitive intent nor effect since the fuel market is quite competitive and not prone to being foreclosed by one car dealer. The concern with leverage is therefore where as-efficient competitors are foreclosed, not on the sole basis of a price–cost test, but also on the basis of an assessment of the competitive conditions in the market subject to the alleged leverage. In *LePage's*, a manufacturer of private-label transparent tape charged that 3M maintained a monopoly in the market for transparent tape through a bundled-rebate programme for large retail chains.[94] The court did not require LePage's to prove that either it or a hypothetical equally efficient competitor could not meet the discount without pricing below cost. Rather, the jury instructions, which the appeals court upheld, provided that conduct is illegal under section 2 of the Sherman Act when it 'has made it very difficult or impossible for competitors to engage in fair competition'.

4.9 REFUSAL TO SUPPLY AND ESSENTIAL FACILITIES

4.9.1 A DIFFICULT TRADE-OFF

The concept of refusal to supply covers a broad range of practices, such as a refusal to supply products to existing or new customers, refusal to license IP rights, and refusal to grant access to an essential facility or a network. Exclusive dealing (discussed in section 4.6 and Chapter 6) is a form of refusal to supply as well. Typically, competition problems arise when the dominant company competes in a downstream market with the buyer that it refuses to supply. In principle, refusal to supply can be the imposition of unreasonable conditions in return for the supply, rather than an outright denial of access. In this sense, the discounting, margin squeeze, and bundling cases of sections 4.6 to 4.8 can also be seen as a form of refusal to supply where the price of the important input is raised to a level that in effect prohibits rivals from competing in the downstream market. In this section we focus on the more specific issues of refusal to grant access to an essential facility and refusal to license IP rights.

The economic concern with prohibiting refusal to supply is that forcing access to a product diminishes the incentives to invest in that product. If a dominant company denies a rival access to an input, it can often appear that consumers would be better off if the dominant company were forced to deal with its rival. However, there is a trade-off: the dominant company, if forced to deal with the rival, may be less willing to spend the necessary time and resources to innovate in the first place. For this reason, cases of refusal to supply are usually difficult, and from an economic perspective often involve trading off a short-run gain in competition and consumer welfare against long-run harm to incentives for investment and innovation.

In *Trinko* (2004), the US Supreme Court found that an alleged failure by Verizon to share its local telephone network with competitors did not constitute an illegal refusal to deal under the antitrust laws:

> Firms may acquire monopoly power by establishing an infrastructure that renders them uniquely suited to serve their customers. Compelling such firms to share the source of their advantage is in some tension with the underlying purpose of antitrust law, since it may

---

[94] 324 F 3d 141 (3d Cir. 2003) (en banc). We also discuss this case in Chapter 10 on quantifying damages.

lessen the incentive for the monopolist, the rival, or both to invest in those economically beneficial facilities. Enforced sharing also requires antitrust courts to act as central planners, identifying the proper price, quantity, and other terms of dealing—a role for which they are ill suited. Moreover, compelling negotiation between competitors may facilitate the supreme evil of antitrust: collusion. Thus, as a general matter, the Sherman Act 'does not restrict the long recognized right of [a] trader or manufacturer engaged in an entirely private business, freely to exercise his own independent discretion as to parties with whom he will deal.'[95]

The focus in *Trinko* was AT&T's access to the local telephony loop and associated facilities operated by Verizon Communications, the incumbent local exchange carrier in New York State. The case began in 2000 when a lawyer (Curtis Trinko), a customer of AT&T, filed a class action suit against Verizon on behalf of all AT&T customers in the area, on the basis that Verizon was blocking AT&T access in a manner designed to deter customers from buying their telephony services from companies other than Verizon. It was alleged that this constituted a breach not only of the US Telecommunications Act 1996—which sets out sector-specific regulations—but also of section 2 of the Sherman Act. In line with existing US case law, but perhaps in somewhat starker language, the Court set out the principles against which it views monopoly power and behaviour:

> The mere possession of monopoly power, and the concomitant charging of monopoly prices, is not only not unlawful; it is an important element of the free-market system. The opportunity to charge monopoly prices—at least for a short period—is what attracts 'business acumen' in the first place; it induces risk taking that produces innovation and economic growth. To safeguard the incentive to innovate, the possession of monopoly power will not be found unlawful unless it is accompanied by an element of anti-competitive *conduct*.[96] [Emphasis in original.]

In other words, monopoly power in itself is not a reason to intervene, nor is the exploitation of such power through monopoly prices (we discuss this topic in section 4.10). US antitrust law places greater scrutiny on exclusionary conduct (ie, when monopoly power is used to exclude competitors from the market). In *Trinko*, the Supreme Court strongly rejected the imposition of obligations on companies with market power to deal with competitors. Thus, when it comes to the trade-off between requiring access to facilitate competition on the one hand, and maintaining incentives to invest on the other, the Supreme Court favours the latter. The other problem identified by the Supreme Court with a refusal to supply case is that if a court or competition authority orders a dominant company to supply a rival, it must say something about the terms on which that supply will take place. In this way the court or authority risks becoming like a regulator who must monitor commercial conduct on an ongoing basis. In Chapter 9 we discuss some of the challenges of remedying a refusal to supply. We also show that the

---

[95] *Verizon Communications Inc. v Law Offices of Curtis V Trinko, LLP* 540 US 398, 416 (2004), [407]–[408] (quoting *United States v Colgate & Co* 250 US 300, 307 (1919)).
[96] Ibid., Part III.

insights and experiences from the field of regulation can be of assistance in competition law, and that competition authorities in Europe and elsewhere do not necessarily shy away from using competition law to address problems of access to network and infrastructure bottlenecks (these problems exist and cause economic detriment; the US Supreme Court's position leaves them unaddressed).

One case in the past where the Supreme Court ruled against a refusal to deal practice was *Aspen* (1985), where a company owning three mountain areas in the Aspen skiing region terminated a joint-ticketing agreement with a rival that owned one mountain.[97] In *Trinko*, the Court sought to constrain the application of this precedent by describing it as being 'at or near the outer boundary of Section 2 liability' under the Sherman Act. The Court also distinguished *Trinko* from *Aspen* by stating that Verizon's access product would be new, as opposed to an existing product already sold in the market.

The European Commission's position is that refusal to supply will be an enforcement priority under Article 102 if 'the refusal relates to a product or service that is objectively necessary to be able to compete effectively on a downstream market'; 'the refusal is likely to lead to the elimination of effective competition on the downstream market'; and 'the refusal is likely to lead to consumer harm.'[98] Such circumstances may occur when the product or service is an essential input to the downstream market, also called an 'essential facility'. We turn to this concept now.

4.9.2 THE CONCEPT OF AN ESSENTIAL FACILITY

The conditions under which a service or facility will be deemed essential were confirmed by the ECJ in *Bronner*:[99] first, if the refusal of the service is likely to eliminate all competition—eg, because it is physically and economically impossible to replicate the facility or service. Second, if the service or facility is indispensable to an equally efficient company's business (ie, access is essential, rather than simply 'nice to have'). For example, in *Ladbroke*, the General Court viewed televized sound and pictures of the horse races to be an 'additional' feature to the existing service for those placing bets, not an essential one.[100] Finally, if there is no objective justification for the refusal to supply the facility or service. The conditions for a facility to be deemed essential are thus relatively strict, representing a higher standard than dominance.

In the *Bronner* case, an Austrian court referred to the ECJ the question of whether the refusal by a newspaper group to allow the publisher of a competing newspaper access to its home-delivery network, or to do so only if it purchased from the group certain additional services, constituted an abuse of a dominant position. The Court held that the refusal to grant access to a distribution facility would constitute an abuse only if there

---

[97] *Aspen Skiing Co v Aspen Highlands Skiing Corp* 472 US 585, 601 (1985).

[98] European Commission (2008), 'Guidance on the Commission's Enforcement Priorities in Applying Article 82 EC Treaty to Abusive Exclusionary Conduct by Dominant Undertakings', December, [81].

[99] Case C-7/97 *Oscar Bronner v Mediaprint* [1998] ECR I-7791.

[100] Case T-504/93 *Tiercé Ladbroke v Commission* [1997] ECR II-923.

was no real or potential substitute for it. In other words, it is not sufficient that the dominant undertaking's control over the facility gives it a competitive advantage. Rather, the duplication of the facility must be impossible or extremely difficult owing to physical, geographical or legal constraints. An essential facility therefore shares economic characteristics with a natural monopoly, whereby the total income generated in the market in question would not make investment in two facilities profitable. The Court concluded that the newspaper home-delivery service was not an essential facility because the market could potentially support another nationwide distribution system. The Court did not consider it material that it would be uneconomic for a newspaper with limited circulation to establish a nationwide distribution system. Rather, for the system to be deemed an essential facility, it would have to be demonstrated that the market could not sustain a competing system at all (the natural monopoly characteristic). The Court also pointed out that there were alternative, even if less convenient, means of distributing newspapers, such as mail deliveries and conventional newspaper retail outlets.

After *Bronner*, the concept of essential facility played a pivotal role in two cases involving Deutsche Bahn AG (DB), the railway infrastructure manager and main train operator in Germany. In 2003, the German competition authority, Bundeskartellamt, initiated proceedings against DB on account of its refusal to include timetable and fares information in its information systems on two long-distance routes operated by the Connex group (Gera–Berlin–Rostock and Zittau–Berlin–Stralsund). Until then, DB had been the sole provider of long-distance passenger rail services in Germany. Connex was the first competitor to enter this market, on a limited scale. DB's refusal was directed specifically at Connex because the timetables of rail companies competing in the short-distance rail passenger sector were included in DB's information systems. Since Connex had also brought proceedings against DB before the civil law courts, the case was ultimately resolved by a decision of the Berlin Court of Appeals.[101] The Court concluded that DB had a dominant position in the market for the provision of services to railway undertakings, notably in respect of the provision of customer information via timetables. DB was not permitted to discriminate against competitors by refusing to include their services in the timetables. However, the Court also concluded that Connex had no right to ask DB to publish its fares in addition to the timetable information, because it was not essential for fare information to be supplied via the incumbent's information systems in order for the new operator to be successful. Fare information could also be communicated to customers by the new operator itself.

In a second timetable case in 2004, the Regional Court of Berlin confirmed DB's obligation to include in its timetables the train services of competitors.[102] Again the Court stressed that DB had a dominant position in the market for customer information via timetables. In light of the expectations of the general public as regards the

---

[101] Decision of the Kammergericht [KG] (Berlin) of 26 June 2003, 2 U 20/02 Kart.
[102] LG Berlin, Judgment of 27 April 2004, 102 O 64/03 Kart.

exclusivity and completeness of the timetables provided by the former monopolist DB, the service that it offered could not be replaced in any appropriate way by competitors' own services. According to the Court, there was no de facto competition to the information services offered by DB. Furthermore, it found that there was no objective justification for DB excluding from its timetables and other information sources the train services of competitors. The Court did acknowledge that a dominant undertaking could not be obliged to implement measures in favour of competitors that would be uneconomical from a business point of view, and could not be forced to facilitate the activities of a competitor to its own detriment. However, according to the Court, in this context a balance needed to be struck between the parties' competing interests. Among other things, this balancing of interests had to take account of whether the owner bore considerable entrepreneurial risks in creating the infrastructure in question, or whether it was created in the framework of a legally protected monopoly. After considering all these factors, the Court concluded that the inclusion of competitors in the DB timetable was an essential service.

In the USA, the Supreme Court in *Trinko* clarified that its conclusion (to reject the complaint regarding refusal to supply) would have been the same even if the issue had been dealt with under the so-called essential facilities doctrine. The Court stressed that it had never recognized such a doctrine and that, in any case, where access was provided for by sectoral legislation, the doctrine serves no purpose under competition law. The US version of the doctrine had its origins in a 1912 case involving railroads.[103]

4.9.3 THE *IMS HEALTH* CASE: THE TENSION BETWEEN COMPETITION LAW AND IP RIGHTS

The inherent trade-off between requiring access to facilitate competition on the one hand, and maintaining incentives to invest on the other, also arises in the area of IP law. Patents and copyright, which are designed to protect IP, at the same time confer monopoly rights to the owner for a defined period (we also saw this in section 4.5 with respect to parallel trade). This may not always sit well alongside measures to promote competition and open markets. The question then remains as to when a dominant undertaking may be required to offer its IP to its rivals. Case law suggests that a refusal to license IP would be objectionable only if competition in a secondary (related) market were eliminated, and the refusal prevents the emergence of a new product for which there is potential consumer demand. We now look at one of the key cases in this area: *IMS Health* (2004).[104]

The case involved two American companies, IMS Health and NDC Health, which collected data on sales of pharmaceutical and healthcare products in Germany. This information was sold on to pharmaceutical manufacturers, which used the data in the

---

[103] *United States v Terminal Road Ass'n* 224 US 383 (1912).
[104] Case C-418/01 *IMS Health GmbH & Co OHG v NDC Health GmbH & Co KG* [2004] ECR I-5039.

development of their sales and marketing strategies. The ECJ was asked by a German national court to consider whether a refusal by a dominant undertaking to license its IP to a rival can be considered an abuse of a dominant position. At the heart of the issue was a specific geographical structure used to provide data to the pharmaceutical companies. This structure was originally designed by IMS, the first company to collate and market such data in this way. It presented the data to the customer in 'bricks' that correspond to a designated geographical area. IMS held the copyright over the original brick structure, but NDC acquired knowledge of the design through the acquisition of a venture, PII, which had been set up by a former manager of IMS. PII had encountered considerable difficulty in marketing regional data on pharmaceutical products using a different brick structure: customers were not prepared to buy information based on a different structure, perhaps put off by the investment they had made in helping to design the original structure and by any switching costs they might incur. PII therefore reverted to a brick structure that was very close to that designed and owned in copyright by IMS, at which point legal proceedings were brought and a German court prohibited PII (and therefore NDC) from using any kind of brick structure derived from the IMS brick structure. IMS refused to license the brick structure, and NDC complained to the European Commission that IMS's refusal to grant a licence was an abuse of dominance.

The German court referred three questions to the ECJ for preliminary ruling. Is refusal by the dominant undertaking to grant a licence to use the brick structure abusive if potential customers will reject any product not based on that system (ie, is the brick structure an essential facility)? Is it relevant to consider the extent to which IMS Health, the dominant undertaking, involved customers in the design of the brick structure (and in so doing, may have helped create dependency on its system)? Are switching costs faced by customers of the data service relevant to the question of abusive conduct by a dominant undertaking? The ECJ chose to address the second and third questions first, since these seek to clarify the relevant criteria for determining whether access to the brick structure is essential or indispensable for a potential competitor. Using the precedent set by *Bronner*, the ECJ determined that both the degree of participation by the users in the development of the brick structure, and any potential switching costs that customers would face were they to switch to a rival brick system, are relevant factors in determining whether the IMS brick structure is indispensable for the marketing and sale of pharmaceutical data.

With respect to the first question, the Court held that Article 102 does not per se oblige a dominant company to license its IP; a refusal to license is not necessarily an abuse. Referring to *Magill*,[105] the ECJ articulated three cumulative conditions that must be satisfied for a refusal to license to constitute an abuse—namely, where the refusal is:

- preventing the emergence of a new product for which there is potential consumer demand;

---

[105] Joined Cases C-241/91 P and C-242/91 P *Radio Telefis Eireann and Independent Television Publications Ltd v Commission* [1995] ECR I-743 (the *Magill* case).

- unjustified; and

- excluding any competition in a secondary market and therefore reserving the relevant market for the incumbent.

The ECJ left it for the German courts to determine whether these three conditions were met in this case.

4.9.4 THE *IMS HEALTH* CASE: THE ECONOMICS

IMS had established itself as the de facto market standard and saw no benefit from allowing access to its IP, even for a fee. It preferred to earn its monopoly rent through its own direct interaction in the retail market rather than through IP licence fees. The first condition set out by the ECJ—that the refusal is preventing the emergence of a new product for which there is potential consumer demand—appears to force the dominant undertaking to allow development of competition in an adjacent market, but not directly in its own market. Otherwise, if the entrant's product were in the same relevant market, the dominant undertaking would effectively be forced to create competition in its own market. This is exactly where IP law is intended to provide protection.

On the second condition—whether the refusal has no objective justification—the ECJ makes no specific observations. It could be harder to show that a refusal to allow access is unjustifiable in the case of IP compared with other instances where, for example, technology networks are involved. In such a case, an undertaking could argue that access could damage the integrity of its network; hence a refusal could be objectively justified. The main reason not to license IP would be a commercial one.

The third ECJ condition—that the refusal excludes any competition in a secondary market—appears to be intimately linked to the first condition. Moreover, there may be an uncomfortable relationship between the two: if the product must be new, it must be differentiated from the existing products. This raises the question of whether it is in the same relevant market as the existing product or service (a question we addressed in Chapter 2). If it is, is it sufficiently 'new' to comply with the first condition? If the new product or service is sufficiently differentiated to be in a separate relevant market, could that result in not affecting the competitive position at all, therefore reserving the relevant market for the incumbent?

Finding the point that balances these two conditions may be difficult, and accordingly the EU legal position on refusal to license IP remains relatively unclear. Comparing the *Trinko* ruling with *IMS Health* suggests that courts will continue to take different views on these points. In *Trinko* the US Supreme Court stated that:

> The specific nature of what the 1996 [Telecommunications] Act compels makes this case different from *Aspen Skiing* in a more fundamental way. In *Aspen Skiing*, what the defendant refused to provide to its competitor was a product that it already sold at retail . . . In the present case, by contrast, the services allegedly withheld are not otherwise marketed or available to the public. The sharing obligation imposed by the 1996 Act created something brand new . . . they are brought out on compulsion of the 1996 Act and offered not to

consumers but to rivals, and at considerable expense and effort. New systems must be designed and implemented simply to make that access possible—indeed, it is the failure of one of those systems that prompted the present complaint.[106]

Thus, the US Supreme Court saw in *Aspen* that refusal to supply an *existing* downstream competitor suggested a willingness to forsake short-term profits in order to achieve recoupment at a later date, whereas with *Trinko* there was no forsaking of existing profits since the Verizon access had not previously been supplied. As such, a line could potentially be drawn between *Trinko* and *Aspen* to say that a withdrawal of supply would be worse than never supplying. But the ECJ's condition appears to draw the opposite conclusion—that refusal to supply is more likely to be condemned when the refusal is preventing the emergence of a new product, which by definition has never had access. From an economic perspective, it does not necessarily matter whether access is withdrawn or never granted, since if an abuse case turned on this issue it could change a dominant company's incentives to the detriment of consumers. What matters most is the effects of the refusal on competition and efficiency in the round, ie, in both the primary and the associated market, and in both the short and long run.

Striking the wrong balance in cases that concern competition law and IP could potentially distort the market to the disbenefit of consumers. Obliging access to IP could mean that companies may be less incentivized to innovate and more prepared to wait until they can take advantage of (free-ride on) someone else's R&D efforts. However, allowing a company to maintain a monopoly over the provision of that good or service may be damaging to the development of competition and of new products. The solution to these trade-offs, insofar as there is one, is to think through whether a remedy for refusal to supply can be applied that minimizes the undesirable effects of forcing access. We address this further in Chapter 9, which deals with access remedies in general and with FRAND (fair, reasonable, and non-discriminatory) access remedies to IP licences in particular.

4.10 EXCESSIVE PRICING

4.10.1 SHOULD EXCESSIVE PRICES BE PROHIBITED, AND IS COMPETITION LAW THE RIGHT TOOL?

The previous sections have dealt with abuse of dominance practices that have the effect of *excluding* competitors. The harm to consumers from these practices is only indirect: they result in weakened competition, which in turn means higher prices, lower quality, and less product variety and choice. The rules on abuse of dominance in EU competition law also cover practices that directly *exploit* consumers, in particular excessive pricing. If the main objective of competition law is to promote consumer welfare, prohibiting excessive prices surely makes perfect sense. Or does it? The answer to this

---

[106] *Verizon Communications Inc. v Law Offices of Curtis V Trinko, LLP* 540 US 398, 416 (2004), Part III.

question is surprisingly complex and controversial for a host of practical, legal, economic, and ideological reasons. US antitrust law does not prohibit excessive pricing by dominant companies (it is concerned with exclusionary conduct only—see the forceful Supreme Court quote from the *Trinko* case in section 4.9). But even in the EU and individual Member States, competition cases against excessive pricing are rare. In this section we present some economic insights on excessive pricing and explain why, from an economic perspective, these cases pose some problems, but perhaps not the problems that many commentators normally focus on.

To start with, we note that a prohibition of excessive pricing can be economically sound. Even the most free-market-minded economists would accept that monopoly poses a problem. If there is no prospect of that monopoly being removed or undermined through market forces—for example, because it is a natural or statutory monopoly—welfare and efficiency can be improved through capping prices. This is why in many countries, including the USA, elaborate price regulation mechanisms have been set up for monopolies in network and utility industries (such as rail, telecoms, energy, water, and postal services). There is extensive experience with price regulation, and detailed conceptual and practical approaches have been developed (we discuss these in Chapter 9 in the context of designing remedies). Arguments that price regulation is inappropriate or impossible to implement in practice are therefore somewhat overstated. Rather, the two main policy questions are, first, where to draw the line between regulating and not regulating prices, and second, if a price control is deemed appropriate, whether sector-specific regulation is required or competition law can be relied upon to do the job. Setting up a specific regulatory structure for price control is costly, but it is the path most chosen in network industries because it has several advantages: companies have certainty ex ante that their price will be regulated, and a regulator with detailed knowledge of the sector can perform the difficult balancing act between capping prices at competitive levels and allowing the regulated company to make a sufficient return such that it continues to have incentives to invest and provide good quality. How does competition law fare in comparison?

Competition law certainly does not do well in terms of providing legal certainty on how excessive pricing will be treated. There is a prohibition, but it has no clear criteria and is not often enforced. What should a dominant company do? Act contrary to its commercial instincts (and to economic textbooks) by not setting prices at the profit-maximizing level? Or act as usual and hope no competition authority will come after it? EU case law is not very enlightening, and the European Commission's guidance on abuse of dominance expressly ignores the topic.[107] Article 102 itself states that abuse may include 'directly or indirectly imposing unfair purchase or selling prices or other unfair trading conditions'. In *General Motors* (1975), the ECJ determined that an abuse might exist if the price imposed is 'excessive in relation to the economic value of the

---

[107] European Commission (2008), 'Guidance on the Commission's Enforcement Priorities in Applying Article 82 EC Treaty to Abusive Exclusionary Conduct by Dominant Undertakings', December, [7].

service provided' (the case related to the price charged for the inspection of imported vehicles, an activity for which the Belgian authorities had granted a legal monopoly).[108] This was expanded upon in *United Brands* (1978)—a case we saw in previous chapters—where the ECJ related 'economic value' to production costs and determined that the question to be asked is:

> whether the difference between the costs actually incurred and the price actually charged is excessive, and if the answer to this question is in the affirmative to consider whether a price has been charged which is either unfair in itself or when compared to other competing products.[109]

However, the concepts of 'economic value' and 'unfair' have caused a good deal of confusion (incidentally, both *General Motors* and *United Brands* are cases where the ECJ actually overruled a finding of excessive pricing by the European Commission). In *United Brands*, the ECJ stated that alternative ways may be devised to determine what is economic value or an unfair price (adding that 'economic theorists have not failed to think up several'). A number of national competition authorities and courts, in particular in the UK, the Netherlands, and South Africa, have tried to come up with ways to interpret these concepts and apply them in cases of excessive pricing. The European Commission has also carried out a number of investigations. In the next sub-sections we set out the economic considerations that played a role in these cases. Perhaps the main conclusion is that they have provided greater clarity on what excessive pricing is *not* than on what it is.

4.10.2 RELIANCE ON THE MARKET INSTEAD OF INTERVENING: TAMPONS, CONDOMS, AND POST OFFICE BOXES

As explained in Chapter 1, monopoly pricing creates allocative inefficiency in the form of a deadweight welfare loss to society—prices are too high and output is too low compared with the competitive market outcome. Forcing the dominant company to set prices at the competitive level reduces the welfare loss. However, you can see that from a longer-term perspective prohibiting excessive pricing can be counterproductive. While allocative efficiency may be improved, dynamic and productive efficiency could be affected. High prices signal to entrants where new business opportunities lie. The very prospect of high profits is what drives companies to reduce costs and introduce new products and technologies to become market leader. The prospect of those profits being regulated once a dominant position is obtained may distort these incentives. Leave markets alone, and over time dominant positions tend to be eroded by new entry. Again, the high profit made by the incumbent company is precisely what attracts those entrants. Regulatory control of those profits may distort this efficient signalling function of prices, and may thus paradoxically slow down the process of erosion of

---

[108] Case 26/75 *General Motors Continental NV v EC Commission* [1975] ECR 1367.
[109] Case 27/76 *United Brands v Commission* [1978] ECR 207; [1978] 1 CMLR 429.

market power. Hence, the crucial question in each specific case is whether new competitors are indeed likely to enter the market, and in what timeframe. Economics can help here — it can identify the competitive dynamics in the relevant market and whether there are inherent natural monopoly characteristics or other barriers that make entry difficult. However, the question of whether to regulate or not to regulate is to a large extent also a matter of policy judgement and ideology. It depends on how much faith you have in the ability of market forces to erode positions of market power, and how long you are prepared to wait for that process to happen.

There are several past cases where competition authorities considered intervening against excessive prices set by a company with apparently persistent market power, but ultimately decided not to in order to give market forces a chance. In a 1985 inquiry into the tampons market, the Monopolies and Mergers Commission in the UK (MMC, now the CC) found prices to be excessive, but did not recommended price controls because it expected that effective competition would develop by itself and new competitors would enter the market.[110] In the markets for pest control services and for credit card services, the MMC investigated concerns about excessive pricing but then focused its remedies on removing the structural market imperfections that facilitated the excessive pricing in the first place (such as a lack of customer information and the presence of regulatory entry barriers), rather than controlling those prices directly.[111] This way the lack of entry was addressed directly and market forces could then be expected to solve the problem. In 1998 the Dutch competition authority (NMa) investigated the introduction of rental charges for post office boxes by PTT Post, as the postal incumbent was called then (post office boxes were outside the regulated postal services).[112] It concluded that those charges would in fact enhance competition in this market by attracting entry (in addition to its finding that the charges were not excessive). In an inquiry into the market for scientific publishing, the UK OFT found indications of high prices and profits, but decided not to intervene 'for now' because a number of market developments pointed to potentially increased competition and new entry.[113]

In 2002 the OFT opened an abuse of dominance investigation related to excessive pricing by the makers of Durex condoms.[114] Condoms had been the subject of various monopoly inquiries, and resultant price regulation, during the 1970s and 1980s. The last such inquiry by the MMC, in 1994, had resulted in price liberalization, in light of new entry and the fall in Durex's market share from 95% to around 75% during the 1980s.[115] The OFT closed the case in 2005 without finding an abuse, noting that it (like the MMC

[110] Monopolies and Mergers Commission (1985), 'Tampons' (Cmnd 9479).
[111] Monopolies and Mergers Commission (1988), 'Pest Control Services' (Cm 302); and Monopolies and Mergers Commission (1989), 'Credit Card Services' (Cm 718).
[112] *Case 13/Complaints against PTT Post*. See NMa (1999), 'NMa Annual Report 1998'.
[113] Office of Fair Trading (2002), 'The Market for Scientific, Technical and Medical Journals', Statement, September.
[114] Office of Fair Trading (2005), 'Competition Case Closure Summaries', Issue 19, June. We advised the defendant in this investigation.
[115] Monopolies and Mergers Commission (1994), 'Contraceptive Sheaths' (Cm 2529), March.

previously) found 'evidence of emerging competition'—Durex's market share had fallen
further (if slowly) to around 60% in 2002, and several new brands had entered the UK
market, including Trojan, the market leader in the USA. The OFT observed that in such
circumstances, 'any potential remedies such as a price cap could stifle such entry and
hinder rather than help the competitive process.' The OFT also highlighted a methodological problem with determining excessive pricing in this case: to judge whether there
was an abuse, it would need to develop an estimate of the value of the Durex brand. Brand
is one of the 'intangible assets' employed by the company, and therefore forms an important part of the analysis of the economic returns made by the company on its investment.
As discussed in Chapter 3, in competitive markets, investing in intangible assets such as
customer acquisition and workforce skills can be as important as investing in tangible
assets, but valuing intangibles can be difficult. The OFT considered that 'a robust valuation would require substantial additional time and expense'. We discuss below whether and how profitability analysis can shed light on inquiries into excessive pricing.

4.10.3 COMPARISONS WITH OTHER PRICES: BANANAS, FUNERAL
SERVICES, AND MORPHINE

As noted above, one interpretation of *United Brands* is that an assessment of excessive
pricing may be based on a comparison with other prices (the quote above refers to
prices of 'competing products'). There was evidence that United Brands' Chiquita
bananas were 20%–40% more expensive than unbranded bananas (although only 7%
more expensive than the brands of its main rivals). The Commission placed great weight
on the fact that prices in Germany, Denmark, and the Benelux countries were up to
twice as high as in Ireland, and considered Ireland to be a valid benchmark as United
Brands still seemed to make profits there. The Commission considered that United
Brands could and should drop prices by 15%. The ECJ ruled that the Commission failed
to analyse the cost of production of bananas when determining the economic value,
and therefore the Court considered the price comparisons to be insufficient. In a case in
1988 involving funeral services in France, the ECJ did consider that price comparisons
between regions can form a basis for assessing whether prices are excessive.[116] In the
town of Charleville-Mézières in the north of France, the local commune had granted an
exclusive concession to the defendant to provide 'external' funeral services—defined as
'the carriage of the body after it has been placed in the coffin, the provision of hearses,
coffins and external hangings of the house of the deceased, conveyances for mourners,
the equipment and staff needed for burial and exhumation and cremation', but excluding 'internal services' (religious services) and 'unregulated services' ('non-essential'
funeral services such as the supply of flowers and marblework). Such exclusive concessions were allowed under French law, and had been granted by around 5,000 of 36,000
communes in France. The exclusivity itself was not challenged, but the ECJ considered

---

[116] Case 30/87 *Corinne Bodson v SA Pompes funèbres des régions libérées* [1988] ECR 2479; [1989] 4 CMLR 984.

that in principle the behaviour of the concessionaries could distort competition. One complaint in this case related to excessive pricing. The ECJ found that because over 30,000 communes did leave the provision of funeral services to market forces, it must be possible to compare prices between communes with and without concessions and to use this as the basis for determining whether prices by concessionaires are unfair in the context of Article 102.

In a 2001 case concerning the forwarding and delivery of UK mail in Germany, Deutsche Post was found guilty of excessive pricing after the European Commission had compared cross-border tariffs with domestic tariffs.[117] The Commission could not analyse the costs of the service directly because Deutsche Post had only introduced a transparent cost accounting system (separating, among other things, the regulated from the non-regulated services) after the period of the alleged abuse. As an approximation, the Commission therefore relied on a then recent notification by Deutsche Post and other postal operators of the REIMS II agreement (under Article 101), which related to the delivery of cross-border mail. According to the notification, the average costs of forwarding and delivering cross-border mail would be equivalent to 80% of the domestic tariff. For the cross-border services in this case, Deutsche Post actually charged the same as the full domestic tariff, and the Commission ruled that the economic value of the services was at most 80% of the price charged. (For various reasons, the Commission imposed a symbolic fine of only €1,000, and Deutsche Post undertook to change its behaviour.)

In *NAPP*, the OFT determined that a pharmaceutical company had charged excessive prices for its sustained-release morphine product, MST, in the 'community' (pharmacy) market. This was in combination with predatory pricing in the hospital market, as discussed in section 4.4. The finding was upheld by the CAT.[118] The OFT found that NAPP's gross profit margin on MST sales (80%) was more than 10 percentage points higher than the margin earned by its next most profitable rival (after allowing for cost differences), and also much higher than the margins NAPP made on other drugs (which were on average between 30% and 50%). Furthermore, NAPP's MST price was 40% higher than that of the highest-priced rival. The OFT also highlighted the persistency of excessive pricing—MST prices had not fallen since the expiry of NAPP's patent in 1992, and effective competition from new entrants had not developed. However, the *NAPP* case did not subsequently set a trend for more excessive pricing cases by the OFT (we saw above the example of the condoms inquiry that was abandoned). This may be because *NAPP* was not a pure excessive pricing case as such. Rather, the OFT found excessive pricing in the community market in combination with predatory pricing by NAPP in the hospital market. According to the OFT, one of the main reasons why entry in the community market did not take place despite excessive pricing was because

---

[117] *Deutsche Post AG—Interception of cross-border mail* (Case COMP/C-1/36.915), Commission Decision 2001/892/EC, [2001] OJ L331/40.

[118] *Napp Pharmaceutical Holdings Limited and Subsidiaries v Director General of Fair Trading* [2002] CAT 1, 15 January 2002.

NAPP charged excessively low prices in the hospital market, where sustained-release morphine products are usually prescribed initially.

4.10.4 EXCESSIVE PRICING BASED ON EXCESSIVE PROFITS: DEBIT CARDS IN THE NETHERLANDS

The NMa for a number of years was quite active in the pursuit of excessive pricing cases. Earlier we saw the post office boxes case (where it did not intervene in the end), which was followed by cases involving airlines and airports. In 2004 the NMa imposed a fine of €30 million on Interpay, at the time the provider of network services for transactions in the PIN debit card network, for excessively charging retailers for these services.[119] The PIN network had achieved a strong position among the various payment methods in the Netherlands. The interesting aspect of this case is that the NMa determined the existence of excessive pricing by analysing the profitability of Interpay. It commissioned an accounting firm to measure the return on capital employed (ROCE) for PIN services over the period 1998–2001. The NMa found that the annual ROCEs over this period were well in excess of the cost of capital which it had estimated, and therefore concluded that an abuse had taken place over that period. However, the Appeals Advisory Committee subsequently agreed with the criticisms raised by the parties against the NMa's decision.

As to the assessment of excessive pricing, the main shortcoming of the NMa's approach (also highlighted by the Advisory Committee) was that the returns over the period 1998–2001 do not provide an accurate picture of the economic profitability of the PIN network services. The test set out by the NMa for excessive pricing was that the difference between prices and costs should be disproportionate, such that capital providers will have sustained excessive returns on the capital they have invested and the risks they have incurred. However, if this is the correct test, it should take account of any investments and risks incurred by the capital providers (in this case the banks that owned the PIN system) before 1998. The PIN system was set up in 1989 under conditions of uncertainty. Until the mid-1990s, it was not guaranteed that the system would become successful (it had to gain a critical mass of users among both retailers and consumers, and faced some competition from rival card networks). Start-up losses were made for a number of years. From an economic (as opposed to accounting) perspective, these start-up losses should also be treated as investments. It could be shown that an appropriate return on these investments had not yet been achieved by 1998, which was the start of the period assessed by the NMa (possibly because that was the year the Dutch Competition Act came into force—a legal not economic reason). An analysis of profitability over the whole period 1989–2001, incorporating the earlier start-up losses, demonstrated that the PIN network services had achieved an internal rate of return (IRR) in line with the appropriate cost of capital. (As discussed in Chapter 3, for an analysis of

---

[119] See the NMa's primary decision. NMa (2004), 'Besluit van de directeur-generaal van de Nederlandse Mededingingsautoriteit als bedoeld in artikel 62 van de Mededingingswet, nummer 2910/638', 28 April. We advised the defendant in these proceedings.

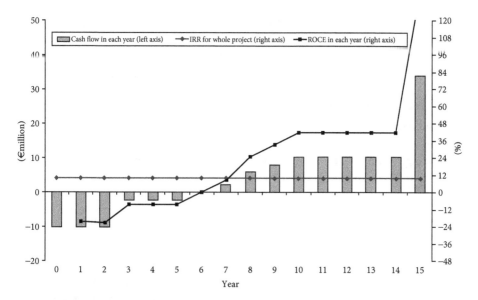

Fig. 4.10 Profitability of a stylized investment project—IRR versus ROCE

Note: The project is assumed to have a cost of capital of 10%. The cash flow in the last year includes the closing asset value.

this type, it is more appropriate to use the IRR rather than the ROCE as the measure of economic profit.) This means that the excessive pricing test set out by the NMa was not met, and hence that no abuse could be established.

To illustrate this point, consider Figure 4.10, which shows a stylized investment project over 15 years with start-up losses (negative cash flows) in the early years and higher returns (positive cash flows) in later years, once the project has become successful. This investment project has a cash-flow profile similar to the PIN system, but the figures are hypothetical. Overall the project makes an IRR of 10%—ie, discounting all the cash flows of the project at 10% gives a net present value (NPV) of exactly zero. This is a 'truncated' IRR over the 15-year period; after year 15, the activity still continues, but the investor 'sells off' the assets in year 15 (the high increase in cash inflow in that year that can be seen in the figure reflects the closing asset value). Assume that the cost of capital is also 10%. This means that the project overall makes a 'normal' return. But consider the annual ROCEs—this profit measure fluctuates from very negative in the early years to very positive in the later years, reflecting the profile of the project's cash flows which are initially low and then increase.[120] Looking only at the ROCEs in the later years, as the NMa did, does not give the correct answer.

---

[120] The capital base for this project is assumed to be in steady state from year 4, ie, new investment equals depreciation. The volatility of the ROCE is therefore not driven by depreciation in this example. If there were a one-off investment followed by straight-line depreciation, the volatility of ROCE would be even greater.

In 2005, following the first appeal stage, the NMa withdrew the fine it had imposed. In the same year, the point about having to analyse the relevant time period was also reflected in another NMa decision, on excessive pricing of basic radio and TV packages by cable companies. Here the NMa had again found high accounting profits over a small number of years. Nonetheless, the NMa then stated that no abuse could be established because the cable companies' returns may have been lower in earlier periods, and may not be sustainable due to the rapidly changing nature of TV markets.[121] These debit card and cable-TV cases represented a significant shift in the NMa's approach to excessive pricing—it has not brought any such cases since (as far as we are aware), hence leaving many open questions about how to assess excessive pricing under Article 102.

4.10.5 OTHER INTERPRETATIONS OF ECONOMIC VALUE: PORTS, HORSERACING DATA, AND STEEL

The cases from the UK and the Netherlands that we presented above (except *NAPP*) sought to determine excessive prices through a comparison with costs or through profitability analysis. Other cases have rejected this approach as too narrow an interpretation of 'economic value'. One such case concerned the Port of Helsingborg, which was accused by ferry operators of setting excessive charges.[122] The European Commission rejected the complaint. It considered that excessive prices could not be established through a simple cost-plus approach. The Commission did assess price–cost margins and profitability of the port. During this exercise, it encountered some practical problems with the allocation of the port's large fixed costs between ferry and other services, and with finding a suitable benchmark for profitability. The Commission said that there were 'insuperable difficulties' with finding benchmarks for profitability.[123] We believe that this overstates the point as the financial tools to estimate such benchmarks are well established—see Chapters 3, 8, and 10. In the end it concluded that prices did appear to exceed costs by a significant margin, but then proceeded to assess whether these prices were also 'unfair'. It drew a comparison with the prices charged for other services at the port and with prices charged to ferry operators at other ports, and found on this basis that prices were not excessive. A final step in the Commission's assessment of economic value was to take into account the fact that the land used by the port for the ferry operations is very valuable in itself, and that ferry operators 'benefit from the fact that the location of the port meets their needs perfectly'.[124] Hence, the Commission attached weight to the value that the product represented to the *purchaser*, rather than only to the cost of the *supplier*. This is a theme that was also central in the following UK case concerning horseracing data.

---

[121] NMa (2005), 'Case number 3528 (UPC) and 3588 (Casema)', September 2005.

[122] *Scandlines Sverige AB v Port of Helsingborg* (Case COMP/A.36.568/D3), Commission Decision of 23 July 2004.

[123] Ibid., at [156] and [225].

[124] Ibid., at [209].

The British Horseracing Board (BHB) was accused of charging excessive prices to Attheraces (ATR), a broadcaster, for pre-race data that could be used in broadcast services overseas (data for broadcasting in the UK and Ireland was subject to a different arrangement). Broadcasters and bookmakers require this data, and the BHB had a monopoly over it. The trial judge determined that the competitive price would be one where BHB recoups the cost of producing its database (about £5 million) together with a reasonable return on that cost, and that the actual price was excessive because it was higher than this competitive price. The Court of Appeal rejected this cost-plus approach to excessive pricing. Following a reasoning similar to that in *Scandlines v Port of Helsingborg*, the court took into consideration the value that the product in question represented to the purchaser:

> we conclude that, in holding that the economic value of the pre-race data was the cost of compilation plus a reasonable return, the judge took too narrow a view of economic value in Article 82 [now 102]. In particular he was wrong to reject BHB's contention on the relevance of the value of the pre-race data to ATR in determining the economic value of the pre-race data and whether the charges specified by BHB were excessive and unfair.[125]

ATR's new broadcast service intended to make a profit and it had shown a willingness to pay substantial amounts for other media rights for the service. The pre-race data had value to ATR because it was related to British horseracing, which represented a core part of the content of the broadcast service. In contrast, the production costs of the data as such are relatively low because it becomes available as a by-product of the organization of horseracing (it is not a product that is produced for its own sake). There was therefore a wide gap between the costs of producing the data and the commercial value of the data to the purchaser, who used it as an input to a commercial end-service. In essence, therefore, the dispute was over who would get the bigger share of the pie—the BHB or ATR—rather than about the total size of the pie (ie, consumers get the end-service regardless of how the pie is divided higher up the supply chain). The Court of Appeal considered that in these circumstances the upstream provider is entitled to charge a price that reflects the value to (and willingness to pay of) the intermediary downstream:

> We appreciate that this theoretical answer leaves the realistic possibility of a monopoly supplier not quite killing the goose that lays the golden eggs, but coming close to throttling her. We do not exclude the possibility that this could be held to be abusive, not least because of its potential impact on the consumer. But Article 82, as we said earlier, is not a general provision for the regulation of prices. It seeks to prevent the abuse of dominant market positions with the object of protecting and promoting competition. The evidence and findings here do not show ATR's competitiveness to have been, or to be at risk of being, materially compromised by the terms of the arrangements with or specified by BHB.[126]

---

[125] *Attheraces v British Horseracing Board* [2007] EWCA Civ 38, at [218].
[126] Ibid., at [217].

From an economic perspective, saying that economic value means the value to the purchaser comes close to saying that no price can ever be excessive. Recall from Chapters 1
and 2 that the price that customers pay reflects their willingness to pay. If prices are very
high, some customers may no longer buy the product, and those who still do get less
consumer surplus out of it, but purchasers would—by definition—never pay more than
what they are willing to pay. Hence, they never pay more than the economic value of the
product to them. In the context of pricing in intermediary markets, such as in *Attheraces*,
this may be sensible because end-consumers are not always harmed by disputes over the
sharing of the pie upstream. But too broad an interpretation of economic value as customer
willingness to pay would make the excessive pricing prohibition rather superfluous. The
Court of Appeal acknowledged this tension and made the following comments (using the
'on the one hand' expression that is so often associated with economists):

> On the one hand, the economic value of a product in market terms is what it will fetch. This
> cannot, however, be what Article 82 and section 18 [of the Competition Act 1998] envisage,
> because the premise is that the seller has a dominant position enabling it to distort the mar-
> ket in which it operates ... On the other hand, it does not follow that whatever price a seller
> in a dominant position exacts or seeks to exact is an abuse of his dominant position.[127]

Yet another interpretation of economic value was put forward by the South African
Competition Tribunal in the *Mittal* case (2007), although this was subsequently overturned by the Competition Appeal Court (2009).[128] Mittal represented around 80% of
steel production in South Africa, a legacy from previous ownership and support by the
state. Its production exceeded total demand in the South African market. It exported its
surplus production at low prices in order to remain competitive in overseas markets
(transport costs are high). At the same time it set its domestic prices at 'import parity',
ie, the level at which imports were priced (which includes the high transport costs). The
difference between the domestic and export prices was 50%–60%. Two customers in
the gold mining sector filed a complaint before the Tribunal. Section 8(a) of the
Competition Act in South Africa prohibits excessive pricing by a dominant company to
the detriment of consumers. The Act defines an excessive price as one that is higher
than the economic value (echoing EU case law). Mittal argued that its prices could not
be excessive because its profitability was not high. The Tribunal was reluctant to determine what the right or wrong price level was. It said that it 'should at once dispel the
notion that the term "economic value" is intended to impute a cost-based theory value,
much less one that is rooted in any particular version of cost'.[129] Instead, it interpreted
economic value as having been determined by the free interaction of demand and
supply in a competitive market, and set out a market structure test for excessive pricing:
the market must be 'uncontested' (with a position of monopoly or super-dominance),

---

[127] Ibid., at [205]–[206].
[128] *Mittal Steel South Africa Limited and ors v Harmony Gold Mining Limited and Durban Roodeport Deep
Limited* (Case No 70/CAC/Apr07) Competition Appeal Court of South Africa, 29 May 2009.
[129] Ibid., at [21] (Competition Tribunal as cited by the Competition Appeal Court).

'incontestable' (subject to insurmountable entry barriers), and unregulated (not subject to price regulation). The Tribunal found these conditions to hold, and considered Mittal to be 'one of those rare firms endowed with sufficient market power to charge excessive prices'.[130] It then focused on Mittal's arrangements with its exporting affiliate, which obtained the steel at the lower export price, but was prevented from selling it in the domestic market. It was this conduct that the Tribunal deemed abusive (calling the economics behind the conduct 'disarmingly elementary', 'the first principle of monopolistic conduct').[131] Because of this approach, the Tribunal considered it unnecessary to assess the 'volumes of expert evidence' on the relationship between prices and costs. The Competition Appeal Court found this structural test to be unsatisfactory and noted that:

> The erroneous approach of the Competition Tribunal also explains why Mittal ends up in the anomalous and wholly impractical position of having been found guilty of and heavily fined for excessive pricing, without any finding of which prices for which of the variety of products were excessive, nor of the period in which the excessive prices were charged, nor of what a non-excessive price would have been, nor of the amount of the excess which it was found to have charged, nor any indication of how—in changing market conditions, eg where production costs may have risen, or supply and/or demand may have changed— an 'excessive price' would in future be determined.[132]

The Appeal Court sent the case back to the Tribunal, but it was then settled between the parties. Hence, the *Mittal* case, having received widespread international attention following the Tribunal decision, in the end has not shed much further light on how competition law can assess excessive pricing.

4.10.6 ARTICLE 102 AS A STICK: TELECOMS, STOCK EXCHANGES, AND ELECTRICITY

In a number of instances, competition authorities have obtained pricing commitments from dominant firms after opening an investigation into excessive pricing. In 1997, the European Commission achieved this result in an inquiry into charges set by Belgacom for access to telephony subscriber data.[133] The inquiry was closed when Belgacom agreed to charge on an average cost basis rather than as a function of the purchaser's turnover (note that this original charging structure might well have been in line with the criteria applied in *Attheraces*, as discussed above). Other examples are the OFT inquiry in 2004 into the fees charged by the London Stock Exchange to companies that list on the exchange, and the commitments by Enel, the Italian electricity incumbent, in 2010, following an inquiry by the Italian competition authority into excessive prices

---

[130] Ibid., at [17].
[131] Ibid., at [18].
[132] Ibid., at [54].
[133] European Commission (1998), 'XXVIIth Report on Competition Policy (1997)', p 26.

in Sicily.[134] Whether Article 102 can be effective as a 'stick' to keep the prices by dominant companies in check is an important policy question in the area of regulation. When it is proposed that a regulatory price control on a particular company be removed, Article 102 is often seen as the fallback option should market forces fail to keep prices in check. The above cases seem to have been successful in using the Article 102 stick, but it does not always work. We saw the Dutch debit card example above. Another example is the inquiry into excessive mobile roaming charges, where the European Commission in the end decided to bypass competition law and impose a specific price control directly.[135]

4.10.7 COMMON MISPERCEPTIONS: WHAT ECONOMICS CAN AND CANNOT SAY ABOUT EXCESSIVE PRICING

As you can tell from this section, the current state of affairs of the excessive pricing prohibition under Article 102 and equivalent provisions in national competition laws is not a happy one. There is no clarity on the criteria to determine whether prices are excessive. There is not even consensus on the fundamental question of whether 'economic value', the test established by the ECJ, means the costs of production incurred by the seller or the value of the product to the buyer. Competition authorities bring these cases only sporadically or not at all. Dominant companies find it difficult to assess whether they should maximize profits as usual or exercise some self-restraint. Most legal and economic commentators would agree that interventions against excessive pricing under competition law should be rare, and some would advocate removing the prohibition of excessive pricing altogether (thus mirroring the situation in the USA). This may well be an appropriate policy choice, but we believe such a choice should be taken for the right reasons. Some of the arguments against the prohibition are based on misperceptions of what economics can and cannot say about excessive pricing.

As we noted earlier, a prohibition of excessive pricing can be economically sound if there is no prospect of market forces removing or eroding a monopoly position. Economics can assist with identifying the circumstances in which this arises (eg, does the activity have natural monopoly characteristics; are there significant entry barriers?). Many countries, including the USA, have extensive experience with regulating prices of particular activities using well-established economic tools. Good outcomes have (often, not always) been achieved through regulatory structures where an agency with detailed knowledge of the sector controls prices while at the same time allowing the regulated company to make a sufficient return so as to preserve its incentives to invest and

---

[134] Office of Fair Trading (2004), 'London Stock Exchange issuer fees', March; and Autorità Garante della Concorrenza e del Mercato (2010), 'A423—ENEL—Dinamiche Formazioni Prezzi Mercato Energia Elettrica in Sicilia', press release, 5 August. The OFT inquiry took place under the competition provisions of the Financial Services and Markets Act 2000 but analysed excessive profits in the same way as in Article 102 cases. We advised the defendant in these proceedings.

[135] Regulation (EC) No 717/2007 of the European Parliament and of the Council of 27 June 2007 on roaming on public mobile telephone networks within the Community and amending Directive 2002/21/EC.

provide good quality. Arguments that price regulation is always inappropriate or impossible to implement are overstated. The main point to be aware of—and this may well be a decisive factor in any cost–benefit analysis of intervention—is that such regulatory structures are costly to set up and maintain (we discuss cost–benefit analysis in Chapter 9).

The second misperception is that excessive pricing cannot be prohibited because it is too difficult to measure profitability. Many commentators—and some of the cases discussed in this section—point to the conceptual and practical difficulties of measuring economic (as opposed to accounting) profits, of allocating costs, and of determining the competitive benchmark. However, as discussed in Chapter 3, a theoretically sound framework for assessing economic profitability in competition law exists, and addresses most of the conceptual and practical problems.[136] The framework is not straightforward to apply, and in some cases it can't be applied (the same holds for every economic technique discussed in this book), but that is no reason to reject it outright since in those cases where it is feasible to apply the framework it can provide useful insight. Interestingly, the ECJ said pretty much the same in *United Brands*:

> While appreciating the considerable and at times very great difficulties in working out production costs which may sometimes include a discretionary apportionment of indirect costs and general expenditure and which may vary significantly according to the size of the undertaking, its object, the complex nature of its set up, its territorial area of operations, whether it manufactures one or several products, the number of its subsidiaries and their relationship with each other, the production costs of the banana do not seem to present any insuperable problems.[137]

In the condoms, debit cards, and stock exchange cases mentioned above, a detailed profitability analysis was undertaken in line with the economic framework we have outlined, and played a central role in the ultimate outcome. (As mentioned, some conceptual issues arose but could be resolved within the framework—in the condoms case the main difficulty was the valuation of the brand which could be done in different ways, while in the debit card case the main dispute centred around the relevant time period for the profitability analysis.) In all, therefore, it is correct to say that *if* the relevant test for excessive pricing is taken as 'cost-plus' or profitability in excess of the competitive level, economics does provide the relevant tools for applying the test, in the same way that costs and profitability can be measured in cases of excessively low pricing, as discussed in sections 4.3 to 4.7.

The real problem with measuring economic profitability—and this is also often misunderstood—is not that it is too difficult to do. It is that the method for measuring economic profitability that we described in Chapter 3 is not meant to measure excessive prices as such, but rather to assess the existence of entry barriers and market power (that is why we explained it in Chapter 3, not here). The method determines profitability

---

[136] Oxera (2003a).
[137] Case 27/76 *United Brands v Commission* [1978] ECR 207; [1978] 1 CMLR 429, at [254].

with reference to replacement costs and the cost of entry—if profits are found to be excessive compared with the costs that an entrant would face, this indicates that entry barriers exist (profitable opportunities are not taken up by entrants). While this can be a powerful tool to assess market power, it does *not* in any way help in forming a judgement on whether prices are too high; that is ultimately a policy or legal judgement. Only if profits are in line with the benchmark (as they were in the debit card case) could one draw the conclusion that there is no competition problem, and hence infer that there is no excessive pricing under Article 102 either. Again, therefore, like the case law itself, economics can provide greater clarity on what excessive pricing is *not* than on what it is. There is no excessive pricing when profits are in line with the competitive level. But when profits are excessive, the economics tells you only that you have a problem of market power, not that you should prohibit those excessive prices as an abuse of dominance.

5

CARTELS AND OTHER HORIZONTAL AGREEMENTS

5.1 ARE ALL CARTELS BAD?

Consider the following cases:

(a) senior and junior managers of three producers of methionine, an amino acid that is used in chicken and pig feed, regularly meet in different European cities to agree price rises and exchange commercially sensitive information;

(b) the chairmen of Sotheby's and Christie's, the art auction houses, meet at their private residences in London and New York and agree to raise the commissions payable by sellers at the auctions;

(c) Ford and Volkswagen, normally rivals, get together and form a joint venture for the production of multi-purpose vehicles;

(d) a number of supermarket chains have individual agreements with tobacco manufacturers that the retail price of a tobacco brand should be linked to that of competing brands;

(e) the member banks of a credit card scheme agree amongst themselves the per-transaction fee to be paid by the bank that acquired the retailer to the bank that issued the card to the customer;

(f) suppliers of industrial electrical generators and equipment allocate the winning bids in procurement tenders for their products according to the phase of the moon.

These are real-world examples of horizontal agreements between competitors. The odd one out in this respect is agreement (d), which is vertical rather than horizontal (we deal with vertical agreements in Chapter 6), but like the others it has been scrutinized by competition authorities for its potential to enable horizontal collusion. All are explicit agreements, distinguishing them from tacit collusion which we discussed in Chapter 3. Which of these agreements would you consider to be in breach of competition law per se? What does economics have to say about this?

5.1.1 A LONG-STANDING CONCERN

Competition law has always looked unfavourably upon horizontal agreements, especially when they come in the form of price fixing, market sharing, or bid rigging among competitors. The US Supreme Court has referred to such hardcore cartels as the 'supreme evil of antitrust'.[1] The then EU Commissioner for Competition stated in 2009 that 'under any analysis, cartels cause terrible damage' (Kroes, 2009). And the concern about cartels is not a new one. Back in 1776, Adam Smith famously wrote:

> People of the same trade seldom meet together, even for merriment and diversion, but the conversation ends in a conspiracy against the public, or in some contrivance to raise prices.[2]

In other words, business people cannot help themselves. Put two competitors together in a room (smoked-filled or otherwise) and the temptation to fix prices or share markets will prove too much. Less well known is the comment that Smith made immediately following the above quote:

> It is impossible indeed to prevent such meetings, by any law which either could be executed, or would be consistent with liberty and justice.

Two-and-a-half centuries after Adam Smith we obviously do have a law that prevents (most) business people from meeting with their competitors and conspiring against the public—competition law. This law can be 'executed' effectively—most jurisdictions prohibit hardcore cartels per se, and competition authorities have enforced this prohibition with vigour, by raiding the cartelists' premises, imposing hundreds of millions of euros in fines, and sending some executives to jail (see also Chapter 9 on the design of remedies). This tough action has no doubt had a strong deterrent effect on

---

[1] *Verizon Communications Inc v Law Offices of Curtis V Trinko, LLP* 540 US 398, 408 (2004).
[2] Smith (1776), Book I, Ch X.

many other would-be cartelists, in a way that still seems quite 'consistent with liberty and justice'.

The per se prohibition of hardcore cartels has economic merit. By restricting output and raising prices, a cartel has the same negative effects as a monopoly: it distributes welfare from consumers to producers and reduces allocative, productive and dynamic efficiency in the market (see Chapters 1 and 2). A cartel formed by a group of competing producers is in many ways worse than a full merger between those producers, because a merger normally brings with it some efficiencies in the form of integration of production processes. Hardcore horizontal agreements usually produce no (or limited—see below) efficiencies that can offset the negative effects on competition. By prohibiting such agreements per se, competition law has created a good deal of legal certainty— many business managers are fully aware that they need to steer clear of talking to competitors about prices—with relatively little risk of over-enforcement, ie, there will not be many instances where the per se prohibition catches agreements that are in reality welfare enhancing (if the line between hardcore cartels and other horizontal agreements is drawn correctly—see below).

5.1.2 'HARDCORE' AND 'NAKED' CARTELS VERSUS OTHER HORIZONTAL AGREEMENTS

However, there is some debate among legal and economic commentators as to where the boundaries should be drawn between hardcore cartels and other horizontal agreements. Of the above examples, you might place agreements (a), (b), and (f) in the first category—they involved price fixing, information sharing, and bid rigging. But what about (c), (d), and (e)? Even the most fervent proponents of a non-interventionist competition policy agree that cartels are bad and merit a per se treatment, but some would prefer to see the class of 'hardcore' cartels to be narrowly circumscribed. Robert Bork (1978, p 263) of the Chicago School (see Chapter 1), argued that only 'naked' cartel agreements should be illegal per se:

> The rule should be restated so that it is illegal per se to fix prices or divide markets (or to eliminate rivalry in any other way) only when the restraint is 'naked'—that is, only when the agreement is not ancillary to cooperative productive activity engaged in by the agreeing parties. Only then is the effect of the agreement clearly to restrict output. Many price-fixing and market-division agreements make cooperative productive activity more efficient, and these should be judged, according to the circumstances, by the standards applicable to internal growth or by horizontal merger rules.

Bork cites the Supreme Court ruling in *Sealy* (1967) as an example of a per se cartel prohibition under section 1 of the Sherman Act 1890 (which prohibits 'every contract, combination in the form of trust, or conspiracy, in restraint of trade'), where in reality the agreement constituted 'cooperative productive activity'.[3] A number of producers of

---

[3] *United States v Sealy, Inc* 388 US 350 (1967).

bedding products and mattresses across the USA decided that there was commercial benefit in advertising nationally, and together set up the Sealy trademark for that purpose. This was then used to license other producers, fix retail prices, and allocate exclusive territories among the licensees. Bork argued that this arrangement constituted 'cooperative productive activity' that was capable of producing efficiencies—it enabled economies of scale in national advertising, helped to standardize products, and prevented free-riding by manufacturers on each other's local sales efforts (a common justification in vertical restraint cases, as discussed in Chapter 6)—and therefore that the Supreme Court should not have ruled it illegal.

Competition law tends to include more types of agreement in the 'hardcore' category than Bork proposed through his definition of 'naked' versus 'ancillary' agreements. The per se prohibition in US antitrust law often refers to 'naked' restraints in line with Bork, but is sometimes applied more broadly (as it was in *Sealy*). Article 101(1) TFEU prohibits 'all agreements between undertakings, decisions by associations of undertakings and concerted practices which may affect trade between Member States and which have as their object or effect the prevention, restriction or distortion of competition'. EU case law under Article 101(1) has identified a class of 'obvious restrictions of competition such as price-fixing, market-sharing or the control of outlets'.[4] These face a virtual per se prohibition (they may still be considered for exemption under Article 101(3), although in practice this is very unlikely since it would need to be demonstrated that efficiencies are created and passed on to customers). One leading legal text identifies the following horizontal agreements that would fall in the 'restrictions by object' box: price fixing, exchanging current and future price information, market sharing, limiting output, limiting sales, and collective exclusive dealing (Whish, 2009, p 120).

While there is ongoing debate in both the USA and Europe about the exact boundaries of 'hardcore' (or 'naked' or 'object') cartel agreements, there is consensus in competition law that those horizontal agreements that are clearly *not* hardcore do not warrant a per se prohibition. R&D, joint production, and other types of cooperation agreement—including example (c) above—may generate significant benefits in terms of technological progress, efficiencies, and greater choice for consumers. Likewise, in some industries competitors need to agree on a common standard or a common set of rules in order for the industry to function effectively—agreement (e) is an example. Rather than prohibit these types of agreement per se, competition law has developed a set of mechanisms to take into account their potential benefits, and this is where economic analysis often comes in. The traditional mechanism in Europe is to assess the efficiency benefits under Article 101(3), and see if they outweigh the restrictive effects identified under Article 101(1). In recent years the potential beneficial effects of some types of horizontal agreement have also been assessed directly under Article 101(1), where the question asked is whether the agreement is restrictive of competition in the first place. This requires a counterfactual analysis (a specialism of economists): if the competitive

---

[4] Cases T-374/94 etc *European Night Services v Commission* [1998] ECR II-3141; [1998] 5 CMLR 718.

situation would be worse in the absence of the agreement (eg, the new product would not be launched at all, or the payment system would not work), you can conclude that the agreement in itself does not restrict or distort competition.

5.1.3 STRUCTURE OF THIS CHAPTER

In this chapter we discuss both cartels and non-hardcore horizontal agreements. Because, as we noted above, economic theory supports the per se prohibition of hardcore cartels, there is not that much more to say on the topic here. The main economic theory of collusion was addressed in Chapter 3 in the context of coordinated effects—the economic conditions in which collusion is most likely to be sustained do not differ much between tacit and explicit collusion, so the theory presented in Chapter 3 is of direct relevance to hardcore cartels as well. Section 5.2 reviews the main economic characteristics of cartels—what makes them tick? The section also addresses 'hub-and-spoke' and other types of information-sharing arrangements which differ from the traditional types of hardcore cartel but have received extensive scrutiny from competition authorities in recent years. You can also read about hardcore cartels in Chapter 9 on the design of remedies, where we discuss the setting of optimal fines and the assessment of the costs and benefits of cartel enforcement actions, and in Chapter 10 on damages, where we explain how you can quantify the harm suffered by the victims of cartel infringements.

In section 5.3 we illustrate the economic questions that arise when assessing the pros and cons of non-hardcore horizontal agreements by discussing three particular types of such agreements: joint purchasing and selling; R&D and technology licensing agreements; and agreements between member banks in a credit card scheme. Finally, in section 5.4 we explore how economics might assist competition authorities with cartel enforcement. Economists have developed quantitative tools that can spot trends and patterns in data and these can also be applied to identify cartel behaviour. In addition, the policy of leniency for cartelists who report the cartel to the authorities—introduced in many competition regimes, often with great success—can be framed in terms of the economics of incentives.

5.2 ECONOMIC CHARACTERISTICS OF HARDCORE CARTELS

5.2.1 NATURE AND TYPES OF AGREEMENT

As you can see from the quote by Adam Smith, cartels existed long before economics began as a discipline. Over the centuries business people have devised a wide variety of methods to form cartels—both before and after the practice was prohibited under the first competition laws (after the prohibition the methods required more savvy and creativity to avoid detection). In Chapter 3 we described the basic economic principles of collusion, including the tension that cartelists face between sticking together (the course most profitable for all) and cheating on each other (very profitable for the cheat in the short run but not for the others). There we discussed it in the context of tacit collusion, but the principles are the same for explicit collusion. To recap, the attractiveness of collusion is influenced by two forces. On the one hand, there are the benefits of collusion in the form of higher profits compared with a competitive outcome—the higher these profits, the stronger the incentives to form and maintain a cartel. On the other hand, there are immediate benefits from deviating from the collusive agreement—the higher the benefits of cheating are to individual cartelists, the more difficult it is to sustain the cartel. Participants in explicit cartel agreements face additional tensions that do not arise in the case of tacit collusion. Compared with the tacit variant, an overt agreement may make it easier to agree on the joint profit-maximizing price and to monitor any cheating. However, because they know explicit agreements fall foul of the law, participants must trade off the benefits of the cartel against the risk of being caught and the punishment that follows (we discuss this in section 5.4 and Chapter 9).

Cartelists have different forms of agreement to choose from. These forms can be broadly classified as price fixing, output restriction, market or customer sharing, and bid rigging. Yet the harmful effects of cartels are broadly the same for each type (as discussed in Chapter 10). You would expect a cartel to select the form that suits the industry best. Where cartels target quantities directly rather than prices, this will often be because it is easier or more effective to monitor quantities (any restriction in output normally results in a corresponding rise in price). Where cartelists operate in different geographic markets or where customers are diverse, some form of market or customer sharing may be most effective, again because it may be easier to implement the cartel in this way. Such customer allocation cartels give each cartel member a degree of monopoly power over its allocated customers, allowing it to restrict output and increase price (again causing similar harm to other forms of cartel). Bid rigging is a specific type of cartel agreement that you see in markets where contracts are awarded through some form of bidding process (note that bid rigging is not confined to bidding markets, discussed in Chapter 3). If all cartel members agree on bid prices or allocate tenders, the effect may be similar to that of a direct price-fixing cartel.

Are there any common patterns in the many cartels that have been uncovered by competition authorities? Economic theory indicates that cartels are most straightforward to sustain in concentrated industries with a small number of suppliers that have similar cost structures, homogeneous products, stable and inelastic demand, and limited technological progress. Collusion is also easier if there is a degree of transparency in market prices and sales, such that any deviations from the agreement can be detected. These structural features of the industry are also what you look for when analysing tacit collusion and coordinated effects (see Chapter 3).

The usual suspects that tend to meet the above description are basic industrial goods and commodities. Many cartels have indeed been found in these industries: synthetic rubber, vitamins, lysine, methionine, bitumen, paraffin wax, sugar, cement, and hydrogen peroxide are but a few recent ones. Take methionine—our example (a) in section 5.1.

Three companies—Aventis (formerly Rhône-Poulenc), Nippon Soda Company, and Degussa—controlled most of the European production of this homogeneous good. The cartel, fined by the Commission in 2002, was in place from 1986 to 1999.[5] The cartel participants met in secret three to four times a year. There were 'summit meetings' among top-level managers and 'technical meetings' at the more junior manager level. The cartelists exchanged information on sales volumes and production capacity and used the information to determine fixed target prices and minimum prices for methionine in each national market. They also agreed specific price increases. The target prices were based on the cartelists' assessment of the willingness to pay in each market (just the thing a textbook monopolist would do). The cartelists on occasion agreed to limit imports from outside Europe to support the price level in Europe.

Yet cartels are not limited to basic industries. A number of recent examples occurred in markets where customers have highly specific requirements and put their orders out for tender—lifts and escalators, gas-insulated switchgear, heavy electrical equipment (the 'electrical conspiracy' discussed below is a much older example of such a cartel). In this category the construction industry seems particularly prone to bid rigging, and cartels have been uncovered in several countries, including the Netherlands, Japan, the USA, and the UK. Bid rigging has also occurred in industries such as defence, agricultural products, financial products, and pharmaceuticals. Other cartels are formed in service sectors as diverse as driving schools, banks, supermarkets, air cargo, and art auction houses—the Sotheby's and Christie's case we mentioned as example (b) in section 5.1.[6] A cartel case concerning local waste collection in New York City illustrates that competition law enforcement sometimes strays into the murkier parts of society as well (the convicted cartelists were 'captains' in the Gambino and Genovese crime families—apparently organized crime not only produces 'drug cartels' but runs some commercial ones too).[7] In sum, it would seem that few industries are immune to hardcore cartel formation.

5.2.2 CONCERTED PRACTICES AND INFORMATION-SHARING ARRANGEMENTS

Explicit cartel agreements are clearly prohibited. In contrast, tacit collusion or coordinated behaviour among competitors is more complicated to address under competition law since, in the absence of proof of communication or intent, it can be difficult to distinguish this from normal business conduct. In between these two forms of collusion lies a range of behaviours and practices that can have the effect of enabling collusion.

---

[5] *Methionine* (Case C.37.519) [2003] OJ L255/1. Upheld by the European courts in Case T-279/02 [2006] ECR II-897 and Case C-266/06 [2008] ECR I-0081.

[6] See US Department of Justice (2001), 'Former Chairmen of Sotheby's and Christie's auction houses indicted in international price-fixing conspiracy', press release, 2 May; and European Commission (2002), 'Commission rules against collusive behaviour of Christie's and Sotheby's', press release, 30 October.

[7] See 'Trash Haulers Plead Guilty In Cartel Case', *New York Times*, 23 July 1997.

Competition law has long struggled to draw the line between what can be prohibited and what cannot. The Article 101 prohibition applies to cases where there has not necessarily been a formal agreement but price fixing or market sharing has been achieved through more informal means, which are often placed under the heading 'concerted practices'. These are defined by the European Court of Justice as:

> a form of coordination between undertakings which, without having reached the stage where an agreement properly so-called has been concluded, knowingly substitutes practical cooperation for the risks of competition.[8]

The wording 'knowingly substitutes practical cooperation for the risks of competition' can be found in many cartel decisions by the European Commission and national competition authorities. Economics can assist in explaining the rationale and effects of such concerted practices, and hence provide some guidance as to the circumstances in which they are likely to be anti-competitive.

One such practice is the sharing of commercial information between competitors. Sometimes there is little doubt that this is done with the aim of forming or supporting a cartel (as in the methionine and auction house examples), but in other situations information exchanges may have more benign motives—for example, the monitoring of industry developments generally. While they may not be anti-competitive by object, such exchanges may have anti-competitive effects. Some economic questions could help in forming your judgement. How frequent is the exchange of information? The less frequent the better, in terms of it being less likely to have anti-competitive effects. What is the degree of disaggregation of the information? The more aggregate it is the better, as less information is revealed about the behaviour of individual suppliers. Does the information exchange relate to historical, current or future pricing data? Historical is better; future is worse. Economists are sometimes involved in such cases to analyse pricing and volume data and see if the exchange of information has had any observable effects in the market (see Chapter 10 for an overview of the methods and models that can be used for this).

Cartels may put in place certain mechanisms to try to stabilize the agreement while avoiding the need for regular communication (and hence reduce the risk of being caught). A particularly inventive mechanism was that of the famous US 'electrical conspiracy' in the 1950s through which General Electric, Westinghouse, and other rivals rigged bids for government and private procurement contracts for heavy electrical equipment. The Department of Justice investigation found that the representatives of the cartelists held meetings and agreed to rotate the prices of their bids to correspond with the phases of the moon. Each manufacturer would thus periodically be the lowest bidder and get its agreed share of the market, while keeping ongoing communication between the cartelists limited.[9]

This degree of inventiveness in sharing information was possibly matched by the bidders in the auctions for radio spectrum organized by the US Federal Communications

---

[8] Cases 48/69 etc *ICI v Commission* [1972] ECR 619; [1972] CMLR 557, [64].
[9] See the coverage of this cartel in 'Business: Rigging the Bids?', *Time Magazine*, 9 February 1960, and 'Corporations: The Great Conspiracy', *Time Magazine*, 17 February 1961.

Commission (FCC) in 1996–97. These were for more than 1,000 spectrum licences covering 493 cities or regions across the USA. Three bidders—21st Century Telesis, Omnipoint, and Mercury PCS—settled a case with the FCC in which they were said to have colluded through coded bids. The scheme worked as follows. Each of the regions had a three-digit code assigned by the FCC. If one of the companies wanted the licence in market 302, for example, and another had bid on it, the first company would submit a bid in another market known to be important to the second company, and end the bid price with the numbers 302 (eg, it would bid something like $2,500,302). The message was clear: if you stop bidding in my market, I'll stop bidding in yours. The scheme allowed the bidders to share information without direct communication. In fact it turned the FCC into an unwitting participant, since at the end of each bidding round the authority would announce both the identity and the amount of the highest bidders, thus divulging the information relevant to the collusive arrangement.[10]

Other indirect collusion mechanisms that you often observe in practice are meeting-the-competition and most-favoured-customer policies. When companies promise you that they 'will match any price' if you find the product cheaper elsewhere, you may wonder what the catch is. Is this just some clever marketing ploy by a company counting on the fact that most customers will not bother to compare prices so actively? Sometimes it is, and you can benefit as a customer if you do make the effort. But meeting-the-competition policies are also a means by which cartelists can signal to each other that any price cut by one of them will be matched (after it has been duly reported by a customer). Most-favoured-customer policies have similar effects. The term is borrowed from the World Trade Organization (WTO) rules for international trade, which establish the principle of the most-favoured nation: any preferential access granted to imports from one WTO member must be granted to other members as well. Most-favoured-customer clauses that promise you any discount that is offered to other customers, even retrospectively, may again appear attractive to buyers. However, they can also be used by a supplier to signal to fellow cartelists that it is not minded to give its customers many discounts in the first place, and hence that they need not worry too much about defection from the cartel agreement. General Electric and Westinghouse introduced most-favoured-customer policies in the aftermath of the electrical conspiracy (perhaps as a substitute for their previous explicit collusion), but several years later were forced by the government to abandon them.[11]

5.2.3 HUB-AND-SPOKE AND SIMILAR ARRANGEMENTS

In recent years, competition authorities have taken action in a number of cases where vertical price and information-sharing agreements were considered to facilitate horizontal price fixing—the so-called 'hub-and-spoke' arrangements. These come in

---

[10] Federal Communications Commission (1997), 'Notice of Apparent Liability for Forfeiture, In Re Applications of Mercury PCS II LLC', FCC-97-388, 28 October. The companies in question breached the FCC auction's anti-collusion rule 47 CFR, s 1.2105(c).

[11] See Scherer and Ross (1990), p 212.

different guises. Sometimes the hub is a manufacturer, and through its vertical agreements with competing retailers (the spokes) it can facilitate collusion between them. In other cases the hub is a retailer and the concern is about collusion between manufacturers. There can also be combinations of these two.

An example of such a case is the retailing of replica football kit in the UK.[12] The Office of Fair Trading (OFT) investigated the agreements between Umbro, a manufacturer of such kit, and a number of retailers. It concluded that the retailers (the 'spokes') would signal to each other via Umbro (the 'hub') that they would not cut prices (eg, it was thus established that a Manchester United replica shirt should sell at £39.99 across all retailers). To give an example of how the agreement worked, when the European football championship in 2000 was approaching, JJB Sports, the largest sportswear retailer in the UK, was keen to avoid a price war for the England replica shirt, in particular with Sports Soccer, a discount retailer. A series of telephone conversations took place between JJB Sports and Umbro, and between Umbro and Sports Soccer, wherein confidential price information was exchanged. There was no direct communication between JJB Sports and Sports Soccer. However, as a result of these discussions, JJB Sports and Sports Soccer avoided discounting the England replica shirts. By the start of Euro 2000 it was apparently very difficult to purchase such shirts for less than £39.99. Umbro was thus said to have acted as a conduit to allow retailers to confirm to each other that they would not sell below the agreed price levels. (Incidentally, after England's premature exit from the Euro 2000 tournament, Sports Soccer swiftly reverted to discounting the shirts.)

In a case involving tobacco sales, the OFT determined that the bilateral agreements between a number of retailers and the two main tobacco manufacturers (Imperial Tobacco and Gallaher) constituted an infringement of the Chapter I prohibition of the Competition Act 1998 (the equivalent of Article 101):

> The Infringing Agreements comprised in each case an agreement and/or concerted practice between each Manufacturer and each Retailer whereby the Manufacturer co-ordinated with the Retailer the setting of the Retailer's retail prices for tobacco products, in order to achieve the parity and differential requirements between competing tobacco brands that were set by the Manufacturer, in pursuit of the Manufacturer's retail pricing strategy. The Infringing Agreement between each Manufacturer and each Retailer restricted the Retailer's ability to determine its retail prices for competing tobacco products.[13]

The OFT found that the parallel vertical agreements with retailers allowed the manufacturers to maintain certain desired pricing relativities between their own and each other's brands, and hence constituted a restriction of competition at the horizontal level, despite the fact that no direct horizontal agreements were in place.

---

[12] Office of Fair Trading (2003), 'Decision of the Office of Fair Trading No. CA98/06/2003: Price-fixing of Replica Football Kit', 1 August, Case CP/0871/01.

[13] Office of Fair Trading (2010), 'Decision of the Office of Fair Trading: Case CE/2596-03 Tobacco', 15 April, [1.4]. We advised one of the retailers in these proceedings.

As can be seen from this last case there are similarities between hub-and-spoke agreements and resale price maintenance, in that a series of vertical agreements may be used to facilitate horizontal collusion. We discuss resale price maintenance in Chapter 6.

5.3 NON-HARDCORE HORIZONTAL AGREEMENTS: COUNTERFACTUAL ANALYSIS

5.3.1 JOINT PURCHASING AND SELLING

Sometimes competitors join forces to collectively negotiate the prices of an input. An example is a cooperative of retailers jointly purchasing products from suppliers. Joint purchasing can bring benefits of economies of scale or other efficiencies, which in turn can lead to lower prices for consumers. Is that sufficient reason to allow such agreements? Joint purchasing may be of concern if the cooperating parties have a high degree of buyer power in the input market and market power in their own product markets. In that case, any lower purchase prices or other efficiencies that are achieved through joint purchasing may not be passed on to consumers. Buyer power in the purchasing market may also give rise to foreclosure of other competing purchasers.

The Dutch bitumen cartel is one example where joint purchasing was judged to have amounted to price fixing and where the claimed efficiency benefits were refuted.[14] The European Commission concluded that eight out of the nine suppliers of bitumen (including BP, Shell, and Total) and the six largest road construction companies, had an arrangement whereby the suppliers and the purchasers jointly agreed on prices and rebates for the bitumen in a series of meetings during the period 1994–2002. The purchasers of the bitumen argued that these price agreements were a case of joint purchasing, falling within the scope of Article 101(3), which states that restrictive agreements may nonetheless be allowed if they produce efficiencies that benefit customers. The Commission rejected this for a number of reasons. One was that the suppliers did not in fact purchase anything collectively, but merely agreed on prices—no real efficiencies in joint purchasing were achieved.

As with joint purchasing, joint selling agreements can be beneficial for consumers in certain circumstances. Arguments concerning the pro-competitive nature of such agreements played an important role in the European Commission's investigation in 2001–02 of producers of gas from the Norwegian continental shelf.[15] Since 1989, the Norwegian gas producers had sold their gas through a single seller, the Gas Negotiation Committee (Gassforhandlingsutvalget, GFU). The Commission concluded that these producers were in breach of Article 101(1) since they fixed the prices and quantities of the gas sold. This signalled an end to the GFU agreement, although a fine was not imposed.

---

[14] *Bitumen–NL* (Case COMP/38.456), European Commission Decision of 13 September 2006.

[15] European Commission (2001),'Commission Objects to GFU Joint Gas Sales in Norway', press release IP/01/830, June; and European Commission (2002), 'Commission Successfully Settles GFU case with Norwegian Gas Producers', press release IP/02/1084, July. We advised the parties in this inquiry.

The GFU had two permanent members, Statoil and Norsk Hydro, Norway's largest gas producers, and was occasionally extended to certain other Norwegian gas producers. It engaged in a joint operating and selling agreement, and negotiated the terms of all supply contracts with buyers on behalf of all natural gas producers in Norway. A number of studies have shown that, in certain circumstances, such joint operating and selling agreements in the gas industry can be efficient.[16] The development of any gas field entails significant, long-term project investment and there are associated risks in the construction costs, added to which are the considerable price and volume risks associated with the marketing of the gas itself. These costs imply that investors in such projects will be looking for a relatively high return. Joint selling arrangements, in conjunction with joint operating arrangements, allow the burden of these risks to be shared between the participants, so that the risk borne by any one group of investors is sufficiently moderate. This leads to a reduction in financing costs and can ensure that investment and development become feasible in the first place—this is relevant for the counterfactual analysis under Article 101(1).

This therefore raises the question of whether the gas producers could have developed the gas field with only a joint operating agreement, ie, without a joint selling agreement—this is one possible counterfactual. The answer is possibly not. A joint operating agreement provides each participant in the agreement with a veto over the development of the field. Consequently, if there is too much uncertainty for any one participant regarding the future sales of the gas from the field, the whole development could be threatened. In this situation, the additional joint selling arrangement reduces the degree of volume uncertainty for the participants in the project by ensuring that every participant has a means of selling the gas produced.

Another factor to consider in the economic analysis of this case—whether under Article 101(1) or 101(3)—is that the Norwegian producers in the GFU sold a large proportion of their gas to the European market, in which they represented less than 15%–20% of all capacity and faced competition from gas producers from other countries. In all, this case illustrates that joint purchasing and selling agreements do not seem to warrant a per se prohibition. The economic effects of such agreements would need to be assessed on a case by case basis through counterfactual analysis under Article 101(1) or through the analysis of efficiencies and customer benefits under Article 101(3).

5.3.2 R&D AND TECHNOLOGY LICENSING AGREEMENTS

R&D is a costly and often time-consuming activity aimed at bringing new products or processes to the market. It suffers from a well-known market failure problem: once public, the fruits of the R&D can often be used by other parties without additional cost, making it difficult for the innovator to appropriate the returns from the R&D activity. IP rights have been created to address part of the problem: innovators are granted

---

[16] See, for example, Dinnage (1998).

patents for a sustained period (typically around 20 years) to allow them to reap the fruits of their efforts and hence incentivize them to make such efforts in the first place. This still does not always solve the problem of the magnitude of risk and costs involved in R&D, and sometimes a form of state support is required—see Chapter 8. In other instances companies seek collaboration with their competitors. This is where the application of Article 101 to R&D agreements comes in.

What is the concern? One potential competition problem relates directly to the R&D market itself. In Chapter 2 you saw that innovation capability may be treated as a separate relevant market in its own right, and hence the R&D agreement may limit competition in that market. An example mentioned in Chapter 2 is the Department of Justice's review of the proposed merger of General Motor's Allison Division and ZF Friedrichshafen, a German company, which together controlled most of the worldwide innovation market for the design, development, and production of transmissions.[17] R&D agreements may have similar effects of reducing competition in innovation markets. Another concern is that R&D cooperation could affect competition in the final product market, even where the agreement is strictly limited to the R&D component and not to subsequent commercialization of the products. An economic analysis by Martin (1995) concluded that R&D joint ventures increase the likelihood of tacit collusion in the product market. This is because where companies expect the joint venture to be more profitable than independent R&D activity, the threat of the venture being broken up by one of the parties helps to sustain tacit collusion in the final product market. He concludes that 'Common assets create common interests, and common interests make it more likely that firms will non-cooperatively refrain from rivalrous behaviour.'

However, competition law has in general looked more benignly upon R&D agreements between competitors, especially if there is sufficient remaining competition in the innovation and final product markets. An example of R&D cooperation between competitors is the *Ford/Volkswagen* case examined by the European Commission in 1992—a joint venture agreement was set up to develop and produce a multi-purpose vehicle (MPV) in Portugal, and the Commission concluded as follows:

> The cooperation between Ford and VW will not lead to an elimination of competition in the MPV segment. Having regard to the leading position of the Renault 'Espace', it will, on the contrary, stimulate competition through the creation of an additional choice in this area and lead to a more balanced structure in the MPV market segment. There will also be increased competition concerning price and quality over the next five to ten years with the further penetration of the segment by Japanese producers as well as other new entrants.[18]

Once successfully developed, new technologies are often exploited by licensing the IP rights to other suppliers, including competitors. Such licence agreements frequently fall under Article 101, and the rules are clarified in the Technology Transfer Block Exemption

---

[17] *United States v General Motors Corp* Civ No 93-530 (D. Del) filed 16 November 1993.

[18] 93/49/EEC: Commission Decision of 23 December 1992 relating to a proceeding pursuant to Art 85 of the EEC Treaty (Case IV/33.814—Ford/Volkswagen), [37].

and its accompanying Guidelines.[19] The general principle remains that IP holders should be free to exploit their rights as they wish, but that they should not distort competition in doing so (we saw this principle in abuse of dominance cases involving IP in Chapter 4). Another principle recognized by the European Commission is that IP licensing is generally pro-competitive. The rules make a distinction between agreements involving competitors and non-competitors. For the latter type, the criteria applied are similar to those for vertical restraints in general, which we discuss in Chapter 6. As to agreements between competitors, a number of 'hardcore restrictions' are identified that cannot be exempted: price fixing, output restriction, customer and market allocation, and non-compete restrictions. With technology agreements there is often a difficult line to be drawn between customer or market allocation clauses, which are deemed anti-competitive, and 'field of use' restrictions. These are commonly included in technology licences and serve the legitimate purpose of preventing the licensee from exploiting the IP for uses other than those specified in the licence. The degree of market power and strength of competitors also play a role in the assessment. Exclusivity in licences is usually accepted, but in agreements between competitors there is greater concern if the exclusivity is reciprocal than if it is non-reciprocal, as reciprocity creates mutual commitments not to supply third parties and may facilitate collusion. In terms of restrictive effects in innovation markets, the Commission Guidelines seek to provide some legal certainty by stating that Article 101 is 'unlikely to be infringed where there are four or more independently controlled technologies in addition to the technologies controlled by the parties'.[20] This approach may be somewhat conservative, and not often will there be four different technologies competing directly in the same innovation or product market.

While there is an extensive set of rules for technology licensing between two parties, there is less clarity on how Article 101 applies to agreements involving multiple parties. Such multi-party arrangements are very common in the high-tech and telecoms industries as many products—mobile handsets, memory chips, digital video equipment—require common technology standards which usually incorporate a large number of different patented technologies. Competitors must license their technologies to each other in order for the market to function effectively. Counterfactual analysis is again called for: are more competitive outcomes achieved with or without the licensing agreements? The two main mechanisms through which multi-party licensing can be achieved are technology (or patent) pools and standard-setting organizations (SSOs). The Commission Guidelines set out some principles that would apply in these cases and that would seem broadly in line with accepted economic principles. The Guidelines recognize that technology pools can be pro-competitive in that they reduce transaction costs and limit the problem of double marginalization by keeping the cumulative IP

---

[19] Regulation 772/2004, [2004] OJ L123/11; and European Commission (2004), 'Guidelines on the application of Article 81 of the EC Treaty to technology transfer agreements', Commission Notice, 2004/C 101/02, 27 April. At the time of writing, new guidelines were being consulted on by the European Commission.

[20] Ibid., at [131].

royalties in check (we explain the problem of double marginalization in Chapter 6).[21] Such positive effects must be weighed against the possible restrictive effects on competition. The Commission states that it would look more favourably upon pools that include patents that are complements rather than substitutes, and that are essential (ie, the products cannot be manufactured without them). It would also take into account the market position of the pool relative to competing technologies, and whether the pool or SSO is open to third parties joining. A potential advantage of SSOs signalled by the Commission is that safeguards and independent bodies may be put in place to limit the exchange of commercially sensitive information between the participants. In Chapter 9 on the design of remedies we discuss another economic aspect of standard setting, namely the setting of fair, reasonable, and non-discriminatory (FRAND) licence royalties.

5.3.3 COOPERATION AMONG BANKS IN PAYMENT CARD SCHEMES

Payment and clearing systems in the banking sector are examples of activities that require cooperation and coordination between competitors in order to function properly. This need for cooperation makes these systems different from a hardcore cartel, but there are still concerns about an elimination of competition among the banks in related markets. This fine balance between cooperation and competition has been extensively analysed in the various investigations into interchange fees set by payment card schemes. We discuss these investigations here to illustrate the economic principles that you may apply to these cases.

Visa and MasterCard are two well-known global credit card schemes. Less clear to the average cardholder is how they function. Thousands of banks around the world participate in the schemes. Known as four-party card schemes, they involve two types of bank and two types of customer—issuing banks that have a direct relationship with the cardholders, and acquiring banks that have a direct relationship with the retailers (or, more broadly, merchants) that accept payments with the card (often, participant banks have both issuing and acquiring activities, but it is still useful to distinguish between the two types). This contrasts with three-party, or proprietary, schemes such as American Express, which have a direct relationship with both types of customer.

Every card transaction always involves, by definition, a cardholder and a merchant (we discussed in Chapter 2 what this implies for market definition for payment systems). Say you use your credit card to make a payment of €100 in a merchant's shop. The acquiring bank credits the merchant's account with €100 minus a merchant service charge (MSC), for example 2% (so the merchant receives €98, having sold a product in its shop for €100). The issuing bank adds the full €100 to your balance, a statement of which is sent to you periodically (you can then choose whether to pay the balance in full or to take up the option of extended credit, which will incur interest). Still in relation to the same transaction, the issuing bank credits the acquiring bank for €100, minus the

---

[21] Ibid., at [210] *et seq.*

so-called interchange fee, for example 1%. So the acquiring bank receives €99, of which €98 is paid on to the merchant, as explained above. This interchange fee is seen as a multilateral agreement between the banks that participate in the scheme, which is why it has become subject to scrutiny from competition authorities around the world.

The multilateral interchange fee (MIF) is not new to competition law. The *NaBanco* ruling (1986) in the USA essentially gave the principle of the MIF a clean bill of health.[22] In Europe, Visa (then Ibanco) had notified its MIF arrangements to the European Commission in 1977, but with little resulting action. Interchange fees again became the focus of attention in the late 1990s, with investigations by the European Commission (following a complaint in 1997 by EuroCommerce, a large retailer association), the OFT (following notification in March 2000 of MasterCard's UK domestic rules), and the Reserve Bank of Australia together with the Australian Competition and Consumer Commission.[23] Since then, investigations into interchange fee arrangements have been carried out in many jurisdictions in the EU and elsewhere, including Spain, the Netherlands, Portugal, Poland, Switzerland, and Israel. Interchange fees were also the centre of attention in the European Commission's sector inquiry into retail banking in 2006–07.[24] Below we discuss the interchange case in the UK in which, in June 2006, the Competition Appeal Tribunal set aside the OFT's earlier prohibition decision.[25] While this case had a favourable outcome for the card schemes, it did not stop the tide of competition authority action against interchange fees—the European Commission prohibited the MasterCard interchange fees in 2007 and the OFT started another investigation.[26] However, the case usefully illustrates the economic principles and counterfactual analysis that are relevant when assessing whether the agreement constitutes a restriction of competition in the first place.

Why the concerns about interchange fees? The most direct allegation against interchange is that it constitutes price fixing by banks at the expense of retailers and ultimately consumers. The banks that participate in the scheme jointly agree on the MIF to be paid by acquirers to issuers. Acquirers will typically pass this fee on through their charges to retailers, which in turn will reflect those charges in their retail prices. One problem with this argument, however, is that the MIF does not really fit the description

---

[22] *National Bancard Corp v VISA USA Inc* 779 F 2d 592 (11th Cir. 1986).

[23] Reserve Bank of Australia (2001), 'Reform of credit card schemes in Australia', December; *Visa International—Multilateral Interchange Fee* (Case COMP/29.373), Decision of 24 July 2002, [2002] OJ L318/17; and Office of Fair Trading (2005), 'Investigation of the multilateral interchange fees provided for in the UK domestic rules of Mastercard UK Members Forum Limited (formerly known as MasterCard/Europay UK Limited)', Decision, 6 September.

[24] European Commission (2006), 'Interim Report I: Payment Cards', 12 April; and European Commission (2007), 'Sector Inquiry under Article 17 of Regulation (EC) No 1/2003 on retail banking (Final Report)', 31 January.

[25] Competition Appeal Tribunal (2006), 'MasterCard UK Members Forum Ltd et al. versus OFT', Judgment on Setting Aside the Decision, 10 July. We advised the card scheme in these proceedings.

[26] Cases *MasterCard* (COMP/34.579), *EuroCommerce* (COMP/36.518), and *Commercial Cards* (COMP/38.580), Commission Decision of 19 December 2007; and Office of Fair Trading (2006), 'OFT to Refocus Credit Card Interchange Work', press release, 20 June.

of a standard price-fixing cartel. Some sort of agreement between issuing and acquiring banks is necessary for the scheme to operate. The MasterCard and Visa schemes have a so-called 'honour-all-cards' rule, which means that merchants who agree to accept, say, MasterCard, must accept all payments with cards carrying the MasterCard logo, regardless of who, or where, the issuing bank is. Merchants can do this in the certainty that their payment will be guaranteed, and the acquirer in turn can do this because of the existing agreement with the issuer (multilaterally via the scheme). Without such an agreement, the scheme would not function. Furthermore, the standard concern with cartels is that they increase price and correspondingly decrease output, thus creating a deadweight loss to society. However, the MIF has the effect of *increasing* output, ie, increasing the uptake and usage of the card. This is because it is a mechanism through which a card scheme can balance prices and costs between the two types of customer (merchant and cardholder), such that usage can be increased (see below). From a competition law perspective, trying to make your product more attractive and enhance its sales is an inherently pro-competitive activity, fundamentally different from a cartel, the nature of which is to artificially restrict output.

In credit card schemes this output expansion is typically achieved by offering cardholders and merchants certain attractive features (an immediate settlement and payment guarantee for merchants, and an interest-free period plus low or no annual fees for cardholders). Cardholders benefit from the fact that the card is attractive to merchants so they can use it widely; merchants benefit from the fact that the card is attractive to cardholders (in Chapter 2 we discussed these two-sided network effects and their implications for market definition). While the standard features of the card product are attractive to both users, the costs of providing the product tend to fall disproportionately on the issuing bank. Thus the MIF is a mechanism by which merchants (via the acquirers) can be made to bear a greater share of the costs of the scheme.

Indeed, one of the main concerns of the OFT, and also the Reserve Bank of Australia, was precisely that the MIF leads to an *excessive* usage of credit cards, ie, excessive output expansion rather than artificial output reduction as with standard cartels. By increasing the proportion of scheme costs that are recovered through the merchants, issuers can make the card 'artificially' attractive to cardholders through loyalty points, cashback, and other benefits. This way, the allegation goes, the economy ends up with too many credit cards, at the expense of cheaper payment systems such as cash and debit cards. (This raises the debate about the economy-wide costs and benefits of the various payment systems, which is far from resolved—for example, using cash is not costless either.) In the view of the competition authorities, the bill for this expensive payment system is ultimately faced by those consumers who do *not* pay by credit card, as merchants pass on the MSC (and hence the MIF) to the overall prices in their stores.

From the above it follows that proponents and opponents of the MIF in fact agree that its effect (and object) is to increase usage of the card scheme by recovering some of the issuer costs through merchants rather than cardholders. This is in line with the economic theory of interchange. Baxter (1983) was the first to provide an economic explanation of interchange fees, and showed that four-party payment systems have historically tended to set inter-bank fees of this type, ie, well before the advent of credit cards.[27] Baxter recognized that card schemes involve joint demand between merchants and cardholders (ie, demand arises in fixed proportions) and joint supply between acquirers and issuers. The execution of a card transaction necessarily results in a service to the two sets of customers. This means that the costs underlying the service are joint costs, which have to be allocated to merchants and cardholders in some way. For the scheme to function at the optimal size, the total willingness of the merchants and cardholders to pay would need to equal the sum of the acquirers' charge (ie, the MSC) and the issuers' charge (to cardholders). Only by coincidence, Baxter noted, would the costs of issuers be exactly equal to the optimal issuer charge at that optimal size. More likely is that a cost–revenue imbalance exists between issuers and acquirers at that point, and a transfer from one to the other is needed to balance this. This transfer is achieved through the interchange fee.

Baxter showed that setting the interchange multilaterally tends to be more efficient than a system of bilateral agreements between issuers and acquirers, in particular because of the large number of banks involved. He gave various reasons why in credit card schemes it is more likely that the optimal MIF flows from acquirers to issuers rather than the other way round, mainly because a greater proportion of the scheme's costs fall on issuers (processing costs, protection against cardholder default, and the costs of the interest-free credit period offered to cardholders), and because cardholders typically have a low willingness to pay (cash and other payment methods are often 'free' at point of use for consumers). This is the case for most credit card schemes today; indeed, three-party schemes such as American Express also tend to recover more of their costs from merchants than from cardholders, but do not require an interchange fee to balance costs and revenues between the two sides because of their proprietary nature (and hence they are not caught under Article 101).

Baxter's theory still lies very much at the heart of the more recent literature on interchange. In a literature overview by Rochet (2003), Baxter's interchange fee is recognized as one that maximizes social welfare under particular assumptions. Other articles expand on Baxter's ideas and explore in greater detail the welfare effects of the MIF under different conditions (eg, depending on the nature of competition between acquirers or issuers). Another feature covered in the literature in addition to joint demand and joint supply is that of the two-sided network effects we mentioned earlier. Indeed, the new literature on the MIF rapidly spawned a whole new area of interest in economics, namely that of two-sided markets (we introduced this area in Chapter 2). Seen from this perspective, credit card schemes are no different from other 'platforms' that exhibit two-sided network effects, ranging from estate agents (house buyers and sellers) and directory services (users and advertisers) to game consoles (players and programmers) and dating agencies (men and women). All these platforms face the challenge to get

---

[27] This is the same William Baxter who in 1982, as the Department of Justice Assistant Attorney General, broke up AT&T into one national and seven regional telephony operators to settle a long-running antitrust investigation—see Chapter 9.

both sides on board, and frequently set lower (or zero) prices to one side and recover costs from the other side—for example, some newspapers are free to readers but charge to advertisers. Credit card schemes—whether three-party or four-party—follow the same pricing logic.

Although there is still a debate in the economics literature about whether a MIF is always set at the socially optimum level, it has generally been accepted that it has the effect of *increasing* the usage of the payment system, as noted earlier. Moreover, the insight from the theory of two-sided markets sheds a somewhat more benign light on the MIF than the cartel allegation—if dating agencies and American Express can set pricing structures to get both sides on board, why can't Visa and MasterCard? The fact that the latter need an agreement among the participating banks to achieve such a pricing structure would seem of secondary importance from this perspective; and yet that is the reason why these agreements fall under Article 101.

In these cases of multilateral agreements, there has been a certain shift of emphasis in EU case law away from Article 101(3) to Article 101(1), where the burden of proof falls on the competition authority or claimant. Specifically, in order to show that an agreement restricts competition in breach of Article 101(1)—ie, before considering the exemption criteria under Article 101(3)—competition with a multilateral agreement (the factual) must be compared with competition without a multilateral agreement (the counterfactual). In determining the counterfactual it is necessary to adopt a realistic view of what is feasible and practical. The requirement for an appropriate counterfactual follows from the General Court's judgments in *Métropole* (2001), which refers to the operations being 'difficult or even impossible to implement' in the absence of the agreement, and *O2 (Germany) GmbH & Co v Commission* (2006), which states that:

> The Court finds that the Commission failed to fulfil its obligation to carry out an objective analysis of the competition situation in the absence of the agreement. In order to be able to make a proper assessment of the extent to which the agreement was necessary for O2 to penetrate the 3G mobile communications market, the Commission should have considered in more detail whether, in absence of the agreement, O2 would have been present on that market.[28]

Interestingly, the *NaBanco* (1986) ruling in the USA applied the logic of counterfactual analysis—it considered that the fixing of fees through the payment system should be treated as part of an integrated arrangement that would not be available if the fees were not fixed. The OFT's counterfactual in its 2005 MIF decision was essentially a situation in which the participating banks would agree bilateral interchange fees instead of MIFs. To support this position, the OFT referred to the EFTPOS debit cards in Australia and credit cards in Sweden as examples of systems that functioned effectively with bilateral agreements instead of a MIF. Against this, the parties argued that the OFT had not sufficiently analysed the counterfactual, and pointed to a number of reasons why the counterfactual of bilaterals would not work, and would be worse for competition than having

---

[28] Case T-112/99 *Métropole Télévision (M6) v Commission* [2001] ECR I-2459; and Case T-328/03, *O2 (Germany) GmbH & Co, OHG v Commission* [2006] ECR II-1231.

a MIF. In particular, bilateral negotiations in the absence of a fallback MIF would be complex, slow, and uncertain, given the large number of banks involved, and would raise barriers for new banks that wished to enter as issuer or acquirer. Furthermore, bilateral interchange fees in the counterfactual could well be higher than the MIF. This is because once a transaction takes place, the acquirer has no option but to settle the transaction with the issuing bank of the particular cardholder, thereby giving issuers certain bargaining power to increase interchange fees, possibly beyond the level that is optimal to the scheme as a whole—the MIF can in fact be seen as a mechanism to keep this 'externality' in check.

On appeal before the CAT, the OFT changed its position on the counterfactual, no longer taking this as a situation with bilateral agreements between member banks, but rather a situation in which banks could deal with one another 'at par' (characterized as a zero interchange fee)—issuers would simply recover their costs from cardholders, and acquirers from merchants. This change in approach eventually meant that the OFT case was set aside for legal reasons. The new counterfactual was therefore not analysed in detail, but if you consider the economic justifications described above for having a positive interchange fee, it is difficult to see how a card scheme would work more effectively or competitively in this counterfactual of the zero interchange fee. In any event, the case serves to illustrate the importance of conducting a counterfactual analysis to determine whether a non-hardcore horizontal agreement actually constitutes a restriction or distortion of competition under Article 101(1), rather than (or in addition to) considering the potential efficiencies and customer benefits of the agreement under Article 101(3). This is a theme we will also see in Chapter 6 on vertical restraints.

5.4 FINDING CARTELS: CAN ECONOMICS HELP?

5.4.1 LENIENCY: INCENTIVE THEORY AT WORK

In 2007, ABB, one of the companies involved in the gas-insulated switchgear cartel, escaped a €215 million penalty by spilling the beans to the European Commission.[29] Its ten co-conspirers were fined a total of €750 million. From 1988 to 2004 these companies had been rigging bids for procurement contracts. You may conclude that ABB got a good deal: it reaped the benefits of the cartel for many years, and then confessed in time to qualify for immunity from fines under the leniency rules while making its competitors pay (note that ABB has nonetheless been sued for damages by purchasers of the cartel—a theme discussed in Chapter 10). To an economist this is incentive theory at work. Companies respond to incentives (see also the discussion on optimal fines in Chapter 9). This is why the leniency programmes in several competition regimes have been so successful as a means of uncovering cartel activity. In the majority of

---

[29] Commission Decision relating to a proceeding under Art 81 of the EC Treaty and Art 53 of the EEA Agreement, *Gas Insulated Switchgear* (Case COMP/38.899) [2008] OJ C5/7.

European Commission cartel decisions in recent years there has been some form of leniency for one or more of the cartelists. The catch is that you have to be the first to report the cartel and provide sufficient evidence to the authorities—subsequent whistleblowers may get some reduction in the fine too if they cooperate with the investigation. When Spain introduced its leniency rules in February 2008 there were queues of business people (or rather the competition lawyers representing them) outside the offices of the national competition authority hoping to be the first to report their particular cartel.[30]

As discussed in section 5.2 and Chapter 9, potential and actual cartelists will trade off the benefits of collusion against the risk and severity of punishment. Leniency programmes have a significant impact on this calculation. The risk of punishment is substantially increased—secret meetings may be possible to organize without the authorities ever finding out, but it takes quite a bit of mutual trust among cartelists for them not to be constantly worried about one of them running off to the authorities in exchange for immunity. Many companies have made the trade-off and decided to report their cartel to the authorities in exchange for leniency.

From a policy perspective, leniency programmes are very attractive. Cartels are notoriously difficult to detect without a whistleblower. Significant investigative powers and resources are required. Leniency means that a substantial part of the detection and evidence gathering is made easier by the information provided by the whistleblower. This is also an argument for allowing leniency applications *after* investigations have started, as occurs in the EU, as this still has the benefit of enabling the authority to achieve a successful outcome more efficiently. We note that under the current rules in Europe, whistleblowers such as ABB may escape the fine but they are not immune to subsequent damages claims by those who have suffered harm from the cartel. From an incentives perspective, therefore, the European Commission's policy of promoting such private actions for damages—discussed in Chapter 10—does run somewhat counter to the leniency policy.

Economists have sought to develop theoretical and empirical analysis to explore how the leniency rules are working and how they may be improved. One suggestion has been that the first party applying for leniency should receive not just immunity from fines but also a financial reward, to be paid out of the fines collected from the other cartelists (Spagnolo, 2004). The intuition behind this is that such rewards make leniency applications even more attractive. This may be particularly relevant for individual whistleblowers given the potentially detrimental effects that their actions can have on their careers or personal circumstances. However, aside from the ethical questions that this raises about rewarding collusive activities, there may also be a risk of encouraging speculative applications that could waste authorities' time. Another theoretical point made is that leniency can actually result in some undesirable effects—because it lowers the expected costs of

---

[30] 'El primer chivato de un cártel aguarda a las puertas de la CNC', news story on <http://www.cincodias. com>, 28 February 2008.

participating in cartels, leniency may, perversely, make it more attractive for companies to form a cartel (Motta and Polo, 2003). On the other hand, the possibility of leniency may encourage companies to keep evidence of cartel involvement that they might otherwise be tempted to destroy. A company with limited documentation of its cartel participation will risk being unable to secure leniency, or obtaining it on less favourable terms.

Empirical analysis of the effects of leniency is made difficult by the covert nature of cartels. A challenge facing the assessment of any policy is the analysis of what would have happened in its absence (more on cost–benefit analysis in Chapter 9). With a leniency policy there is the fundamental problem that the counterfactual is not directly observable since the policy's detection and deterrence effects are on an unknown number of current and prospective cartels. What you can observe is the number of actual investigations, the number of cartels that are discovered, and the punishments that are imposed. If only a few cartels are discovered, this could be due to effective deterrence; however, it is also consistent with poor detection and a large number of undiscovered cartels. One hypothesis might be that, following the introduction of leniency, the number of cartels detected will rise but then fall again after a while as the increased detection rate leads to deterrence of subsequent cartel activity. In assessing the detection effect there is also a self-selection issue to disentangle. Cartel members are more likely to make pre-investigation leniency applications if detection is probable, and therefore may belong to cartels that are close to discovery anyway. An example is where the discovery of an international cartel in one jurisdiction leads to leniency applications in another.

A number of empirical studies have analysed the effects of the 1996 introduction of the leniency programme by the European Commission (Brenner, 2009; Stephan, 2009). There is some evidence that the duration of investigations, which is a proxy for their cost, has been reduced as a result of leniency—this is consistent with the point made earlier that the information provided by whistleblowers saves the competition authorities time and effort. Fines in cartel cases that made use of the leniency programme have been found to be higher, which could be because leniency allows the Commission to construct a more robust case. Another finding is that the duration of cartels involving full immunity was longer than those involving partial immunity, suggesting that leniency helps uncover the more durable cartels. The number of new cartel investigations per year has increased substantially since the introduction of leniency. However, nearly three-quarters of cartel cases that the Commission opened between 1996 and 2005 as a result of leniency applications had already been under investigation in the USA.

5.4.2 EXPERIMENTAL ECONOMICS: LENIENCY AND CARTEL STABILITY

Another set of empirical studies on leniency makes use of experiments, a tool that is increasingly popular among economists, especially where real-world situations are difficult to analyse. Participants in experimental studies make decisions in a controlled setting in return for some reward. The results are monitored electronically and the controlled environment enables multiple trials of the same scenario, allowing a picture to be built up of typical behavioural responses. The participants (usually students) are tested to ensure that they understand the rules of the experiment, and the results may be linked to a financial reward to ensure that they have a stake in the outcome (apparently students can be effectively motivated in this way). An experimental setting allows the creation and stability of cartel behaviour to be monitored under different types of enforcement policy. In experimental cartel studies, participants usually take the roles of the companies setting prices at intervals over time. They are able to discuss price setting among themselves in a structured way so as to allow for the possibility of collusion. The role of the competition authority is reflected in the introduction of a certain probability of detection and fine imposition. This is then supplemented by offering the opportunity of leniency, where a proportion of the fine will be waived. Over many experimental trials this allows a picture to be built up of how prices and cartel formation differ according to the probability of detection and the scale of the fine, with or without leniency.

These experimental studies show that introducing leniency does indeed have the expected effect of reducing cartel stability and prices (Apesteguia et al., 2006; Hinloopen and Soetevent, 2006; Oxera, 2008a). Leniency was found to reduce cartel formation, to increase defection by cartel members, and to increase the price cuts implemented by defectors after leaving the cartel. According to Hamaguchi and Kawagoe (2005), the likelihood of a leniency application is higher the more companies there are in the cartel, but the stability of cartels is not affected by whether the fine reduction is available only to the first company coming forward, or to subsequent ones as well. This suggests that creating this race to be the first may not have much added benefit over and above having the leniency policy in the first place. It provides some support for the Commission's policy of giving the greatest fine reduction to the first applicant but then to also grant some reductions to latecomers who agree to cooperate fully with the inquiry.

5.4.3 ECONOMISTS AS DETECTIVES?

Thanks to the economist Steven Levitt, our profession has gained some reputation among the wider public for having an ability to spot trends and patterns in data that no one else can see. In the 2005 popular economics book *Freakonomics* (Levitt and Dubner, 2005), Levitt described the academic research in which he systematically analysed a large database of test results from the Chicago public school system, revealing that teachers had cheated in around 5% of cases by changing some answers on the students' test forms—teachers had an incentive to cheat because they were rewarded according to their students' performance (Jacob and Levitt, 2003). Another of his studies analysed results from sumo wrestling in Japan and confirmed suspicions of match rigging (Duggan and Levitt, 2002). Such economic studies have not made a significant impact on competition law as yet. However, there is increasing interest in using quantitative tools to help detect cartels.[31]

---

[31] For an overview, see Harrington (2008).

The techniques used for this type of analysis are similar to those for quantifying cartel damages—discussed in Chapter 10—except that here you employ them to detect a cartel in the first place. One important distinction in cartel spotting is that between structural and behavioural features of the market. Focusing on structural features such as those mentioned in section 5.2 (high concentration, homogeneous goods, inelastic demand, etc) may help you identify markets that are more prone to cartelization than others, but it does not get you much closer to identifying actual cartel behaviour, especially since such behaviour may occur in a wide variety of markets, as we saw in section 5.2. Analysing behaviour seems more promising in this regard. There are two main stages to this (see Harrington, 2008). The first is analysing whether something odd is going on, such as company behaviour not being in line with competitive behaviour, or there being structural breaks in prices or bidding patterns for which there is no apparent 'normal' explanation (such as a change in costs). In competitive industries prices tend to respond to cost and demand shocks; a finding to the contrary could be indicative of cartel behaviour. The second stage is then verifying that the oddity can indeed be ascribed to collusion. One way of testing this is to explore whether the behaviour of the (suspected) colluding suppliers is different from that of suppliers that are not in the cartel (eg, suppliers in other geographic markets). Another is to assess whether models of collusion fit the data more closely than models of competition.

One prominent study where the comparator method has been applied is that by Porter and Zona (1993), an analysis of bid rigging in highway construction contracts tendered by the New York State Department of Transportation. The authors had data on 116 auctions between 1979 and 1985. There were five suspected members of the bidding cartel. A model of 'normal' bidding behaviour was estimated using variables such as a company's backlog of projects won in the past but not yet completed, other indicators of available capacity, and location. This model did pretty well in explaining the bidding behaviour by the non-cartel companies. In contrast, the suspected colluders showed a statistically significant deviation from this competitive behaviour. It was also found that the suspects' bid prices had no systematic relationship with their costs, which indicated that they often put in artificially high bids (rather than not bid at all) just to create an appearance of bidding competition. Another study by the same authors analysed bid rigging in the supply of school milk in Ohio (Porter and Zona, 1999). This used data relating to costs, such as the distance between the milk-processing plant and the school, to explain competitive bidding behaviour (eg, bids can normally be expected to increase with the distance to the school, since transport costs are higher). Three suppliers in one particular area were suspected of bid rigging. Other suppliers (mostly in more distant regions) were not. The study indicated that the bidding behaviour differed systematically between the suspected colluders and the others—the colluders' bids bore no systematic relationship with costs, while those of the unsuspected suppliers did. Harrington (2008) notes that it was ironic that the cartelists' decision to make 'phantom' bids rather than not bid at all ultimately provided the relevant data to help demonstrate the collusion. Other studies have sought to detect cartels by identifying bidding behaviour that fits collusive models more closely than competitive models, for example, in wheat auctions in India and timber auctions in the north-west of the USA (Banerji and Meenakshi, 2004; and Baldwin et al., 1997).

A main conclusion that can be drawn from these studies is that cartel detection through economic analysis of data seems most promising in auction markets. The rules of the game are reasonably clear in these markets, such that competitive and collusive behaviour can be readily identified and distinguished. In other types of market this may be more difficult. Good data on the relationship between bids and the underlying costs is also usually required. Another conclusion is that the most informative studies seem to have been those where there was already a suspicion of collusion, such that the behaviour of the suspects could be compared with that of unsuspected suppliers. Economists will have greater difficulty detecting a cartel from scratch.

This leaves the policy question of whether competition authorities should apply economic techniques to systematically screen markets for cartel behaviour. We mentioned above that a review of the structural features of markets would be insufficient and therefore any such screening would have to focus on behavioural patterns. Tax authorities systematically analyse data to identify fraudulent tax returns. Financial regulators do the same for insider trading on stock markets. Should competition authorities follow their example? One difference is that competition authorities do not collect data in the same systematic and comprehensive manner. Another is that tax and financial authorities usually know a fraudulent tax return or an instance of insider trading when they see one, or at least they know when to investigate a case further. When odd patterns in pricing and bidding data are detected, there are still many other possible explanations for these patterns besides cartel behaviour that must be explored before competition authorities can open a formal investigation on this basis. It is too early to say whether economists will ever play a prominent role as cartel detectives. Yet in some cases—such as those involving bid rigging in New York highway construction and Ohio school milk contracts—a sophisticated economic analysis showing that cartel behaviour is the most likely explanation for observed patterns in the data can be a powerful piece of evidence for competition authorities to use when bringing a cartel action.

6

VERTICAL RESTRAINTS

6.1 BUSINESS PRACTICES, THE LAW, AND THE ECONOMICS

Dentsply, the leading manufacturer of false teeth in the USA (sold under the Trubyte brand), refused to supply its products to independent dental-product dealers if they sold competing false teeth. Pronuptia de Paris, the French maker of wedding dresses and accessories, granted its franchisees in Germany exclusivity in their territories, but did not allow them to open other shops or sell competing wedding dresses. Turf TV, a new broadcast service to bookmaker shops in the UK and Ireland, signed up exclusive media rights with roughly half of the British racecourses before its launch (horseracing being the most important TV content on display in bookmaker shops). Volkswagen did not allow its dealers in Italy to sell cars to people living outside Italy. To a business person these may seem like everyday examples of producers trying to organize and control their supply and distribution channels. To competition practitioners these are

vertical restraints that have been famously challenged (some successfully, some unsuc-
cessfully) under competition law.[1]

There has always been certain tension between competition law and business arrangements that span along vertical supply chains. Section 1 of the US Sherman Act of 1890
prohibits 'every contract, combination in the form of trust, or conspiracy, in restraint of
trade', without making a—rather important—distinction between horizontal contracts
between competitors and vertical contracts between companies that operate at different
layers of the supply chain. The same is true for Article 101(1) TFEU, which prohibits 'all
agreements between undertakings, decisions by associations of undertakings and concerted practices' which may affect trade between Member States and which have as their
object or effect the prevention, restriction or distortion of competition'. In the USA, it was
recognized in the early decades after the Sherman Act that horizontal price-fixing agreements are particularly harmful and therefore merit a per se prohibition (as discussed in
Chapter 5). But for a long time vertical agreements also received hostile treatment in US
antitrust law. This changed with the 1977 Supreme Court ruling in *Continental TV Inc v
GTE Sylvania, Inc*.[2] Sylvania, a manufacturer with a 1%–2% share of colour TV sales in
the USA, had adopted a new franchise plan in the early 1960s whereby it reduced the
number of franchisees and did not allow them to sell outside their franchise area. The
court looked benignly upon this practice, and overruled an earlier per se prohibition
of such location and customer restrictions in vertical contracts, citing a number of
economists who had demonstrated that such restrictions can enhance competition and
efficiency.[3] In Europe, such a change in stance, and the recognition that vertical agreements are inherently different from horizontal ones, also took some time. In a 1966 ruling,
the European Court of Justice accepted that exclusivity granted to a distributor may not
infringe Article 101(1) where it is necessary to penetrate new markets.[4] The *Pronuptia de
Paris* ruling by the General Court in 1986 accepted that some, but not all, restrictions
in franchise agreements are necessary for legitimate commercial purposes such as
protection of the brand. Yet a more economic approach towards vertical agreements was
adopted only at the end of the 1990s when the European Commission issued a Block
Exemption Regulation and Guidelines on Vertical Restraints.[5]

---

[1] *United States v Dentsply International, Inc* 399 F 3d 181 (3d Cir. 2005); Case 161/84 *Pronuptia de Paris
GmbH v Pronuptia de Paris Irmgard Schillgallis* [1986] ECR 353; [1986] 1 CMLR 414; *Bookmakers Afternoon
Greyhound Services Limited & Ors v Amalgamated Racing Limited & Ors* [2008] EWHC 1978 (Ch), 8 August;
and Case IV/35.733 *VW* [1998] OJ L124/60.

[2] 433 US 36 (1977).

[3] The per se prohibition that was overruled came from *United States v Arnold, Schwinn & Co* 388 US 365
(1967), which concerned the distribution of bicycles. One economist (who was a lawyer and judge too) extensively quoted by the Supreme Court is Richard Posner, a leading figure of the Chicago School, which was
highly influential in changing antitrust law towards a more economics-based approach in the 1970s, as discussed in Chapter 1 (Posner, 1976).

[4] Case 56/65 *Société Technique Minière (LTM) v Maschinenbau Ulm GmbH (MBU)* [1966] ECR 235.

[5] Regulation 2790/99 on the application of Art 81(3) of the Treaty to categories of vertical agreements and
concerted practices, [1999] OJ L336/21; [2000] 4 CMLR 398; and European Commission (2000), 'Guidelines on
Vertical Restraints', [2000] OJ C291. Both the Block Exemption Regulation and the Guidelines on Vertical
Restraints were amended in 2010.

What triggered these changes in the treatment of vertical restraints under competition law? Economics did. It's not that economists suddenly discovered something that nobody had ever thought of before. They simply highlighted with formal analysis what business people have known for centuries—if you want your products to reach consumers smoothly and efficiently, it can make sense to enter into agreements with your suppliers and distributors, and such agreements necessarily contain certain commitments and restrictions for one or both parties. Vertical agreements do not always have sinister anti-competitive motives. Nor, more importantly, do they always have negative effects on consumers—quite the opposite, economics has shown that vertical agreements very often contribute to greater efficiency and consumer welfare. The *Sylvania* ruling relied heavily on insights from the Chicago School and other contemporaneous economists. It held that even if the reduction in the number of Sylvania retailers affected *intra-brand* competition—between sellers of Sylvania TVs— any market power by retailers was still constrained by *inter-brand* competition—from other TV brands (in particular RCA, which at the time had a market share of 60%–70%; Sylvania had only 1%–2%, and through its aggressive franchise plan managed to grow this to 5%). Moreover, the court acknowledged that vertical restraints can promote inter-brand competition by allowing the manufacturer to achieve efficiencies in the distribution of its product. Sylvania used the restraints to induce the more competent and aggressive retailers to engage in promotional activities and provide service and repair facilities, while at the same time preventing free-riding on these efforts by rival retailers.

Since the 1970s, economists have developed a deeper theoretical and empirical understanding of vertical restraints. The newer theories are often rooted in principal-agent theory, where the supplier is the principal and the distributor is the agent, and vertical contracts are used to align incentives and resolve information asymmetries between the two. This literature has actually identified a greater variety of circumstances where the economic efficiency justifications for vertical restraints may not necessarily hold. Nevertheless, many economists would still agree that vertical restraints generally serve the purpose of making the distribution of goods more efficient, and that they are of concern only when inter-brand competition is weak.

This leaves competition law with the challenging task of assessing whether, and in what circumstances, the efficiencies and competition-enhancing effects of vertical agreements outweigh the anti-competitive effects. In this chapter we set out the basic economic principles of vertical restraints. Section 6.2 deals with the economic rationales for vertical restraints. Section 6.3 discusses their possible anti-competitive effects. We also provide some thoughts on how the economic principles might best be incorporated into the legal assessment. Is there a case for applying the same standards to vertical restraints as to abuse of dominance (discussed in Chapter 4)? Is the economic analysis of pro-competitive effects relevant only when you are considering whether a restrictive agreement can be justified, or also at the stage when you assess (through counterfactual analysis) whether an agreement constitutes a restriction of competition in the first place? Is there support for competition law's harsh treatment of resale price maintenance—where a supplier imposes the price at which the distributor can sell the product—compared with other types of vertical restraint?

6.2 ECONOMIC RATIONALES FOR VERTICAL RESTRAINTS

6.2.1 THE PROBLEM OF DOUBLE MARGINALIZATION

Economists in the nineteenth century not only developed formal models showing the problem of monopoly (as discussed in Chapters 1 and 2), they also discovered what is worse than a monopolist: a succession of monopolists. If, on its way from producer to end-consumer, a product passes through a series of intermediaries, and each intermediary wishes to earn a profit margin on top of the costs incurred, you get the situation known as double (or multiple) marginalization—a problem first identified in 1838 by French economist Antoine Augustin Cournot (the same Cournot of the famous oligopoly model we saw in Chapter 3).[6] Vertical agreements (and vertical integration, as discussed in Chapter 7) can be used as a means to overcome the double marginalization problem.

The pepper trade in the fifteenth century illustrates the problem. Peppercorns travelled a long way from the fields of Southern India to north-west Europe. This trade route had existed since at least the time of the Romans, but in medieval Europe there was a very strong demand for pepper and other spices from the mysterious East. Arab and Indian ships would take peppercorns up the Red Sea and Persian Gulf. They would then be transported over land to important trading hubs in the Levant and Egypt, such as Damascus and Alexandria, controlled (interchangeably) by local rulers or bigger powers, in particular the Mamluk Sultanate and the Ottomans. Access to Europe was controlled by Venice (which faced periodical challenges to its position from rival city states such as Genoa). Every time the peppercorns changed hands, the price went up, as each trader wanted to earn a healthy profit margin. And so did each local ruler imposing a duty on trades. By the time they reached the kitchens of (rich) consumers in the Low Countries, France, and Britain, the price had multiplied many times. What was essentially a basic commodity in South Asia became a luxury good in Europe (used as currency and status symbol as much as for culinary purposes). Too many middlemen all wanted their slice, and all would have liked the others to reduce prices.[7]

---

[6] Cournot (1838). The 'Cournot effect' referred to a situation in which complementary goods are sold separately, which is analytically similar to having the same good sold by successive intermediaries. The first paper to formalize the double marginalization problem in the context of a vertical chain was Spengler (1950).

[7] You can find accounts of the history of the spice trade not only in history or culinary books. Economic history has developed as a separate branch in economics (with a Nobel Prize in 1993 for two leading proponents, Robert Fogel and Douglass North), applying economic theory and quantitative methods in order to explain economic and institutional changes in the past. Economists have extensively studied 15th-century prices of pepper and other spices from contemporaneous sources. The exact price differential for pepper between Asia and Europe is difficult to identify and prices fluctuated wildly over the century (often due to wars and other

An important finding in economics is that such a situation of multiple profit margins on top of each other is bad for everyone involved. End-consumers clearly face a very high price, which only some are willing (and able) to pay. Because of this high price, the last intermediary—the local merchant in Antwerp or York—sells only a small amount of the product, and by implication purchases only a small amount from the previous merchant. And so it goes all the way back to the original producer. The producer and every intermediary in the chain all sell less pepper than they would like. Consumers would already be better off if only one, or a few, of the intermediaries kept any price rise limited to the level of costs incurred (marginal cost), without charging a monopoly premium on top. As to the intermediaries, economics shows that as a group they would be best off if only one of them charged a monopoly price and the rest passed the product on at cost. This single marginalization maximizes the total profits in the chain. It also benefits consumers, since the final price is lower—they pay only one monopoly premium, not multiple ones. Obviously, for the single marginalization approach to work, the intermediaries need some mechanism to coordinate their pricing and share the monopoly rents—this is where vertical agreements (and vertical integration) come in. In the fifteenth century, the scope for such coordination among the rivalrous traders and rulers would have been rather limited (and they wouldn't have heard of Cournot). The best attempt at achieving a single monopoly was when the Portuguese bypassed the whole overland trading route by reaching South Asia over sea (Columbus had sailed the wrong way in 1492, but Vasco da Gama was successful in sailing east round the Cape of Good Hope in 1498 and establishing a new trading route). The Portuguese did not manage to establish a lasting monopoly—the overland route via Venice remained an active one, and later the Spanish, Dutch, and English weighed in with their naval power. This rivalry did eventually succeed in making pepper and other spices more affordable to the average European consumer.

Coordination between the vertical partners in a supply chain can overcome double marginalization. The most direct form of coordination can be achieved through vertical integration (vertical mergers are discussed in Chapter 7). A looser form is through vertical agreements. Suppliers may restrain their distributors from setting prices above a certain level, possibly in return for a side payment (reflecting a share of the greater total profits) or some other concession. Another method is quantity forcing, whereby the supplier requires the distributor to purchase or sell a minimum number of products that corresponds to the single marginalization output. A third type of vertical restraint to avoid double marginalization is for the supplier to set a two-part charge to the distributor—a fixed and a variable charge. This method has some sophisticated economic theory behind it, but the principle is often applied in the real world as well. The supplier sells the product to the distributor (say, a franchisee) at a price per unit that equals marginal cost. This way the franchisee still buys the optimal quantity of the product,

inconvenient disruptions to trade), but a factor of 15 has been mentioned. If you are interested in this field of economics, see Lane (1968) and O'Rourke and Williamson (2006).

avoiding the output-reducing effect of double marginalization. The franchisee is then the one in the chain who gets to set a profit margin on top of its costs, but the supplier extracts the profits thus earned through the fixed franchise fee.

6.2.2 VERTICAL RESTRAINTS AS OUTCOME OF BARGAINING ALONG THE CHAIN

Another, more prosaic, rationale for vertical restraints is that they may simply reflect a quarrel between supplier and distributor. In the real world, fights over how the pie is shared occur all the time. The outcome usually depends on who has greater bargaining power. As explained above, the total pie in the chain would be largest if only one party charged the monopoly price—but which party will achieve this? At one extreme of the bargaining power scale are markets where very large suppliers deal with very small distributors (large airlines and small travel agents may be an example, though perhaps more in the past than at present). The supplier keeps the monopoly profit; the distributors recover only their marginal costs. At the other extreme are markets with very small suppliers who have no choice but to deal through very large distributors (farmers and supermarket chains are a frequently mentioned example). Here the distributor gets to keep the profits and the suppliers recover only their marginal costs. In between are situations where the bargaining power is more balanced, either because both parties have a strong market position (in which case vertical restraints can be used to avoid the otherwise inevitable double marginalization), or because both operate in very competitive markets (in which case there are fewer competition concerns to start with, as both would set price closer to marginal cost).

If a vertical restraint has an impact only on who it is that gets the biggest share of the pie, it does not necessarily have a negative effect on the consumer. What ultimately matters, from an economic perspective at least, is the effect of the restraint on consumers and on competition in the market overall. If there is one layer in the chain that earns a monopoly rent, it does not matter much to end-consumers which layer it is—final prices and quantities are the same regardless. This is not to say that all vertical restraints are of this nature. Sometimes the interests of the supplier and distributor are more aligned, and the two may conspire against the interest of the consumer. It may also be that even if the complaint is motivated by a struggle over the rents, there are still negative effects on consumers. This is discussed in section 6.3. In any event, when you are presented with a complaint by one of the parties about a vertical agreement, it is always worth checking whether it is motivated mainly, or only, by a dispute over the rents in the vertical chain, and it should not be automatically assumed that there is a competition problem. The European Commission has recognized this principle in the context of the food supply chain, where disputes between suppliers and supermarkets over vertical contracts are particularly common:

> Contractual imbalances associated with unequal bargaining power are tackled through policy tools other than competition law instruments, such as, for example, contract law,

common agricultural policy, SME [small and medium-sized enterprises] policy, or unfair commercial practices laws. Most Member States have already enacted specific laws dealing with such issues and have established legal protective mechanisms for all contractual parties in the context of their commercial laws. EC antitrust law is not concerned with particular outcomes of contractual negotiations between parties unless such terms would have negative effects on the competitive process and ultimately reduce consumer welfare. It is not the aim of EC competition rules, as currently devised, to interfere in the bargain struck between contractual parties, in the absence of proven competitive harm.[8]

6.2.3 FREE-RIDER PROBLEMS

A basic justification for vertical restraints centres around the free-rider problem. There are two categories of free-riders: rival suppliers and rival distributors. Economists often express the problem in terms of an externality—one party makes an effort, thereby benefiting another (external) party which does not contribute to the effort itself. In economics jargon, vertical restraints are a means to internalize the externality and align the interests of the parties along the supply chain.

As to the first free-rider category (rival suppliers), a supplier may wish to promote the effective distribution of its products by making investments in the distribution channel—it may provide general training to the sales staff, or invest in the look and feel of the distribution outlets (ice cream producers may provide retail shops with a freezer cabinet; Pronuptia de Paris may assist franchisees with the interior design of the sales outlets). The value of this investment would be diminished if rival suppliers then used the same outlets without contributing to the investment—they would be free-riding. As a result, the first supplier may not wish to make the investment in the first place. Consumers may be worse off if this affects the distribution channel (fewer shops would sell ice cream; the experience of buying a wedding dress would not be the same). Vertical restraints can be used to prevent this free-rider problem. The supplier may require the distributor not to sell rival products. This is commonly referred to as exclusive dealing or single branding. Unilever imposed such restraints on the retail outlets to which it had provided freezer cabinets free of charge—no competing ice cream brands were allowed in the cabinets.[9] A softer variant of exclusive dealing is where the manufacturer requires that its product represent a minimum percentage of the retailer's sales. Pronuptia de Paris imposed this on its franchisees—they had to purchase 80% of their wedding dresses and

---

[8] European Commission (2009), 'Competition in the food supply chain', staff working document accompanying the Communication from the Commission to the European Parliament, the Council, the European Economic and Social Committee and the Committee of the Regions on 'A better functioning food supply chain in Europe', COM(2009) 591, p 18.

[9] Case C-552/03 P *Unilever Bestfoods (Ireland) Ltd, formerly Van den Bergh Foods Ltd v Commission* [2006] ECR I-9091. Under some pressure from the European Commission, during the investigation stage, Unilever also offered retailers the option to hire the freezer cabinet instead of getting it free of charge, but not many retailers took up this option. Case Nos IV/34.073, IV/34.395, and IV/35.436 *Van den Bergh Foods Limited* (98/531/EC), 11 March 1998.

accessories from Pronuptia, together with a certain proportion of cocktail and evening dresses, and could purchase the remainder only from suppliers approved by Pronuptia.

As to the second free-rider category (rival distributors), a supplier may want its distributors to provide pre- and after-sales services to consumers if it believes that this enhances the sales or the reputation of its products. You may value the retailer giving you a demonstration of the technical features of the latest stereo or PC, or allowing you to test-drive a new car. This costs money (sales staff time is money), and the retailer will want to recover this cost. Now suppose that after the demonstration or test drive you can go to the discount dealer next door where no such pre-sale service is provided and buy the same product at a lower price—the discount dealer is effectively free-riding on the full-service retailer's efforts. This can lead to a situation where the latter is unwilling to provide any pre-sales services at all. Again, the effectiveness of the supplier's distribution channel is diminished, and consumers may be worse off if, as a result, no one gives them product demonstrations anymore. Several forms of vertical restraint can be used to prevent this free-rider problem. The supplier may grant each distributor an exclusive territory, such that there are no discount dealers next door (Sylvania and Pronuptia de Paris both used milder variants of exclusive territories in their franchise systems). Alternatively, the supplier may impose a minimum retail price (a vertical restraint commonly referred to as resale price maintenance or vertical price fixing), such that any discounting by dealers is ruled out.

All these vertical restraints addressing the second free-rider problem are intended to reduce intra-brand competition between distributors. But note that there is some tension with the double marginalization rationale we saw earlier: reducing intra-brand competition means giving each distributor a bit more market power, which may bring you back to the problem of having too many profit margins in the chain. You may also have noted that the free-rider justification for vertical restraints sounds a bit outdated in some industries. Nowadays when you buy a new stereo or computer you can access a number of pre-sales services online—product demonstrations, product reviews, user guides (though some manufacturers and consumers may still prefer the old days of product demonstrations by sales staff, and test drives in new cars are more difficult to do online). Likewise, post-sales services (repairs, maintenance) can be charged for directly by retailers. This shows that market dynamics in distribution channels change over time, and that economic arguments for and against vertical restraints must be applied carefully to the specific facts of the case at hand—a per se justification for vertical restraints on the basis that they resolve a free-rider problem seems as inappropriate as a per se prohibition; the free-rider problem must be shown to be of some importance first, and then weighed against the possible anti-competitive effects of the restraint.

One US case where the relevance of the free-rider problem was tested against the specific facts of the case involved the vertical restraints imposed by a retailer, Toys 'R' Us, rather than a manufacturer.[10] The Federal Trade Commission (FTC) had found that

---

[10] *Toys 'R' Us, Inc v Federal Trade Commission* 221 F 3d 928 (2000). For a more detailed discussion of the economic aspects of this case, see Scherer (2009).

Toys 'R' Us, a 'giant in the toy retailing industry', had orchestrated a horizontal agreement among a large number of toy manufacturers through the creation and enforcement of multiple vertical agreements in which each manufacturer promised to restrict supply of its products to low-priced warehouse club stores, on the condition that other manufacturers would do the same. The appeals court upheld the FTC's findings, and dismissed the free-rider argument put forward by Toys 'R' Us in defence of the restraints. Until the late 1980s, Toys 'R' Us accounted for approximately 20% of all toy sales in the USA, but enjoyed a particularly strong position because it was basically the only specialist retailer that offered a full range of toys in its stores (around 11,000 individual toy items). As stated by Judge Diane Wood (a well-known commentator on antitrust law) in the judgment:

> The toys customers seek in all these stores are highly differentiated products. The little girl who wants Malibu Barbie is not likely to be satisfied with My First Barbie, and she certainly does not want Ken or Skipper. The boy who has his heart set on a figure of Anakin Skywalker will be disappointed if he receives Jar-Jar Binks, or a truck, or a baseball bat instead. Toy retailers naturally want to have available for their customers the season's hottest items, because toys are also a very faddish product, as those old enough to recall the mania over Cabbage Patch kids or Tickle Me Elmo dolls will attest.[11]

This market position came under threat in the early 1990s when warehouse clubs—which had a low-price image just like Toys 'R' Us—began to offer a full range of toys, allowing customers to readily compare prices (as the name suggests, warehouse clubs provided only very basic retail services and sold at low prices, though only to members who paid an annual fee of around $30). This threat prompted Toys 'R' Us to impose vertical restraints on manufacturers and to induce a manufacturer boycott of the warehouse clubs. The vertical restraints in these cases were somewhat different from those in 'standard' cases in that they were driven mainly by the retailer, and not by the manufacturer. Toys 'R' Us was seen as a critical outlet for toy manufacturers, even for the large ones such as Hasbro and Mattel. One of the defences put forward by Toys 'R' Us was that its actions were a legitimate response to free-riding by the warehouse clubs. The appeals court found that the free-rider justification did not apply in this case:

> Here, the evidence shows that the free-riding story is inverted. The manufacturers wanted a business strategy under which they distributed their toys to as many different kinds of outlets as would accept them: exclusive toy shops, [Toys 'R' Us], discount department stores, and warehouse clubs. Rightly or wrongly, this was the distribution strategy that each one believed would maximize its individual output and profits. The manufacturers did not think that the alleged 'extra services' [Toys 'R' Us] might have been providing were necessary. This is crucial, because the most important insight behind the free rider concept is the fact that, with respect to the cost of distribution services, the interests of the manufacturer and the consumer are aligned, and are basically adverse to the interests of the retailer (who would presumably like to charge as much as possible for its part in the process).

---

[11] Ibid., at [2].

What [Toys 'R' Us] wanted or did not want is neither here nor there for purposes of the free rider argument. Its economic interest was in maximizing its own profits, not in keeping down its suppliers' cost of doing business. Furthermore, we note that the [FTC] made a plausible argument for the proposition that there was little or no opportunity to 'free' ride on anything here in any event. The consumer is not taking a free ride if the cost of the service can be captured in the price of the item. As our earlier review of the facts demonstrated, the manufacturers were paying for the services [Toys 'R' Us] furnished, such as advertising, full-line product stocking, and extensive inventories. These expenses, we may assume, were folded into the price of the goods the manufacturers charged to [Toys 'R' Us], and thus these services were not susceptible to free riding. On this record, in short, [Toys 'R' Us] cannot prevail on the basis that its practices were designed to combat free riding.[12]

6.2.4 THE HOLD-UP PROBLEM

The hold-up problem is another classic rationale for vertical restraints. Sometimes new business ventures require close coordination and combined efforts between two parties at different layers of the vertical chain. Take the example of a low-cost airline approaching an under-utilized regional airport and convincing it that there is a commercial opportunity to develop and grow the airport. Low-cost airlines have done this successfully across Europe in the last decade. The two parties sign a ten-year agreement that contains certain commitments and restrictions on both sides. While somewhat different from the standard manufacturer–retailer relationship, the airport and the airline are in a vertical relationship (the former provides an input to the latter), and this is therefore a form of vertical agreement. For the venture to succeed, the airport first needs to invest significantly in upgrades to its passenger terminal and handling facilities. Before it incurs the investment, it requires some guarantees that the airline is indeed going to use the airport. The airline therefore commits to base a minimum number of aircraft at the airport for the duration of the agreement (a base is the airport where an aircraft stays overnight and is maintained; this has the advantage that the first outbound flight and last inbound flight of the day can be scheduled there). The airline even agrees to not fly from the main rival airport in the vicinity for the ten years—a form of exclusive dealing. In the absence of these upfront commitments by the airline, the airport would run the risk of being held to ransom by the airline after the completion of the investment (if there are no other interested airlines to use the airport capacity). Economists call this a hold-up problem—like the free-rider problem, it is an externality that can be internalized by means of a vertical restraint.[13] At the same time, to make the venture a success, the airline must invest significantly in setting up the base and also in the promotion of the airport as a

---

[12] Ibid., at [7]–[8].

[13] Some confusion perhaps exists as to whether the term hold-up refers to the actual investment being held up (as in obstructed or delayed), or to the party making the investment subsequently being held up by the other party (as in robbed at gunpoint). Whichever of these interpretations is correct does not really matter, since they both capture the essence of the problem: sub-optimal relationship-specific investment in the absence of vertical restraints.

new destination or departure point. This investment is highly specific to the new venture, and would have to be written off if the airport didn't stick to its part of the deal (the investment in upgrades). To reassure the airline, the airport guarantees, in the agreement, that the airline would get substantial discounts on its landing and handling charges. This avoids a hold up of the airline's investment.

Thus, the hold-up problem has two main (closely related) characteristics: the required investment is highly specific to the vertical relationship, and it is sunk (ie, not recoverable upon exit). As is so often the case (you saw this in Chapter 2 as well with respect to sunk investment and supply-side substitution), both these characteristics are usually a matter of degree. The investment by the airport in its terminal and handling facilities is largely sunk—the full value cannot be recovered should the airport cease to operate. However, it is not necessarily relationship-specific, since the facilities can also be used to serve other airlines (once other airlines have been attracted to the airport). The airline's investment in setting up the base and advertising the new flights from the airport is both sunk and relationship-specific (but probably lower in magnitude). Given these characteristics, the investments by both parties require some mutual assurances, and vertical restraints are a means to provide these. A more extreme example of relationship-specific investments resulting in hold-up problems would be where the airport organizes a competitive tender for a new railway service to be set up between the airport and the nearest city. The owner of the railway would want some guarantees from the airport about minimum usage of the service before building it. It may also seek to restrain the airport from setting up bus services that would compete with the railway. For its part, the airport would want assurance that the railway, once established, does not charge monopoly prices and thereby reduce the number of passengers (a combination of the hold-up and double marginalization problems). Again, an ex ante vertical agreement between the airport and the rail operator can solve these problems.

6.2.5 OTHER DISTRIBUTION EFFICIENCIES ACHIEVED THROUGH VERTICAL RESTRAINTS

There are other efficiencies in distribution that vertical restraints may seek to achieve. Suppliers may want to restrict the number of distributors in each area if there are economies of scale in distribution. Car manufacturers tend to limit the number of dealers to one or two in each major town, not 10 or 15—market demand would be too small to justify too many dealers, each with their own showroom and service facilities. A vertical restraint imposing some form of exclusive territory for each distributor makes commercial sense in these situations. An additional efficiency is that such a restraint can also provide distributors with greater incentives to promote the product. This is especially important when a supplier seeks to enter a new geographic market. The distributor with the exclusivity has the right incentives to do its best to promote the product, and will share in the rewards if it succeeds. This means that the interests of the principal and the agent are aligned, as recognized by the European Court of Justice in the 1966 *Société Technique Minière v Maschinenbau Ulm* judgment referred to earlier.

Restraints that limit intra-brand competition may also induce distributors to maintain optimal (from the supplier's perspective) stock levels. A publisher launching a new title, supported by an advertising campaign, will want bookshops to keep a sufficient number of copies in stock in order to avoid disappointed customers in the event of the book becoming a bestseller. Bookshops, however, may be reluctant to order too many copies—should the title not be successful, they would run the risk of other bookshops beginning to discount, and their inventory ending up in the bargain basement. Resale price maintenance, and to some extent exclusive territories, can prevent such early discounting and hence reduce the inventory risk to distributors (against this, you might say that in many countries the scrapping of minimum book prices has led to a vast expansion of outlets that sell books at accessible prices, including supermarkets and Amazon.com).

Finally, a well-known justification for vertical restraints is that they can assist in protecting the supplier's brand and reputation. We saw earlier that the *Pronuptia de Paris* ruling accepted that certain restrictions in franchise agreements are necessary in order to achieve legitimate commercial purposes such as protection of the brand. Suppliers like Pronuptia want to be associated with a certain image, and it matters to them how the retail outlets that sell their goods convey this image—design, decoration, other products being sold there. Likewise, manufacturers of products such as cars and washing machines may want to control which spare parts are used on their products, or who provides repairs and maintenance for them, if they perceive a risk to their reputation should something go wrong with a third-party supplier. You can see how this kind of restraint may lead to concerns about foreclosure of the spare parts and maintenance markets (aftermarkets)—in section 6.3 we explain how this concern is not very different from foreclosure concerns that are dealt with as abuse of dominance, as discussed in Chapter 4.

6.2.6 IS A RESTRAINT A RESTRICTION?: COUNTERFACTUAL ANALYSIS UNDER ARTICLE 101(1)

You have seen that vertical restraints can have various possible economic rationales and positive effects on competition and efficiency. A legal question that arises is at what stage of the analysis you can take these positive effects into account and weigh them up against the possible negative effects on competition. The EU competition rules (and national statutes modelled after them) have a structure where vertical agreements that prevent, restrict or distort competition are prohibited under Article 101(1) TFEU, but may, under Article 101(3), be exempt from this prohibition if they contribute to greater efficiency and customers receive a fair share of the benefits. While there are additional conditions under Article 101(3)—related to indispensability of the restriction and to remaining competition—in essence this two-part structure to Article 101 allows efficiencies to be taken into account in the second part as potentially offsetting the restrictive effects found under the first part.

The economic rationales of vertical restraints may also be taken into account under Article 101(1) itself. In many circumstances, a vertical restraint on one party's freedom is not a restriction of *competition*. This occurs when the competitive situation in the absence of the restraint is worse than with the restraint. Counterfactual analysis is called for here, which is where economics comes in (we also discussed this in Chapter 5 in the context of horizontal agreements). As summarized by the English High Court in the *Turf TV* judgment concerning exclusive broadcast rights:

> When considering the alleged effect on competition, an economic approach is called for. The approach must be realistic. There must be a proper market analysis of the position with the relevant restriction and the position in the absence of the relevant restriction. Not every restriction on conduct amounts to a restriction on competition, much less to a significant restriction on competition.[14]

In the *Pronuptia de Paris* ruling of 1986, the General Court stated that 'the provisions of franchise agreements for the distribution of goods which are strictly necessary for the functioning of the system of franchises do not constitute restrictions of competition for the purposes of Article 85(1)' (this is now Article 101(1); the ruling was two Treaty article re-numberings ago).[15] The court found this to apply to provisions that prevent the know-how and assistance provided by the franchisor from benefiting its competitors (akin to the free-rider problem discussed earlier), and provisions that establish the control necessary for maintaining the identity and reputation of the franchisor. However, customer or location restrictions in the franchise agreement were considered to restrict competition. The *Turf TV* judgment found that Article 101(1) did not apply because a degree of exclusivity over broadcast rights was necessary for a new entrant planning to take on an incumbent broadcaster which had controlled the market for 20 years:

> I find that the Claimants' argument as to foreclosure by preventing existing purchasers of rights from increasing their market share stands arguments as to competition on their head. Before AMRAC [Turf TV] entered the market, there was a monopoly purchaser of LBO rights. After AMRAC entered the market, there are two purchasers of LBO rights. That appears to be pro-competitive activity and not anti-competitive activity ...

> The evidence clearly showed that a course would receive less revenue from granting non-exclusive rights to two operators as compared with granting exclusive rights to one operator. What was happening in that period was that competition between BAGS/SIS on the one hand and AMRAC on the other took the form of competition to take exclusive licences. That activity was how a competitive market worked, not anti-competitive behaviour ...

> It is commonplace for media sports rights to be sold on an exclusive basis. When there is competition for the purchase of such rights, exclusivity is favoured by the purchaser and by the seller, for proper commercial reasons. Exclusivity gives the purchaser the ability to differentiate his service downstream. Exclusivity gives the seller greater revenue. Where there is competition, the grant of exclusive rights is the natural form for that competition to take.[16]

---

[14] Case 161/84 *Bookmakers Afternoon Greyhound Services Limited & Ors v Amalgamated Racing Limited & Ors* [2008] EWHC 1978 (Ch), 8 August 2008, [452]. We acted as economic experts for the defendants in these proceedings.

[15] *Pronuptia de Paris GmbH v Pronuptia de Paris Irmgard Schillgallis* [1986] ECR 353; [1986] 1 CMLR 414, summary, [2].

[16] Case 161/84 *Bookmakers Afternoon Greyhound Services Limited & Ors v Amalgamated Racing Limited & Ors* [2008] EWHC 1978 (Ch), 8 August 2008, [452], [465], and [468].

From an economic perspective, considering the counterfactual situation in the absence of the vertical restraint makes sense as part of the assessment under Article 101(1). It allows you to ask whether a restraint is a restriction in the first place—if the competitive situation was worse in the absence of the restriction (for example, there was a monopoly for 20 years in the provision of broadcasting services to bookmakers before Turf TV entered), the answer to this question is no. Carrying out such a counterfactual analysis under Article 101(1) gives greater weight to the inherent efficiencies and competition-enhancing effects that vertical restraints can bring about. The balancing approach between Article 101(1) and Article 101(3) also acknowledges the efficiencies. However, it implicitly assumes that vertical agreements are inherently restrictive—Article 101(1) comes before Article 101(3)—and that they should be allowed only if the defendant can show that there are offsetting efficiencies, which can be a high hurdle in practice. The burden of proof under Article 101(1) is on the claimant or competition authority; under Article 101(3) it is on the defendant.

6.3 ANTI-COMPETITIVE EFFECTS OF VERTICAL RESTRAINTS

6.3.1 FORECLOSURE OF SUPPLY OR DISTRIBUTION CHANNELS

Arguably the main competition concern about vertical restraints is that they may be used to foreclose access of competitors to inputs or distribution channels. Dentsply was accused of foreclosing the access of rival false-teeth manufacturers to independent dental-product dealers; Unilever of shutting out rivals from the impulse ice cream market by denying them access to freezer cabinets in retail outlets. Turf TV was accused of foreclosing the rival broadcaster from access to important horseracing content. Hence, you may wonder (as we often have), isn't this foreclosure concern exactly the same as that relating to abuse of dominance? And if so, should the analysis of the economic effects of vertical restraints not be the same as that for abuse of dominance, which we outlined in Chapter 4? From an economic perspective, there may well be good arguments to treat vertical restraints the same as abuse of dominance. An exclusive distribution arrangement between a supplier and distributor is more likely to foreclose competition the greater the degree of market power of the supplier and the greater the distributor's importance relative to other sales channels. Dentsply had a stable market share of 75%–80% for a number of years and its dealer network represented 80% of all laboratory dealers, so the US appellate court ruled in 2005 that its exclusivity requirements were anti-competitive. Unilever's freezer cabinet exclusivity was condemned by the European Commission and courts both as a restrictive agreement under Article 101 and as an abuse of dominance under Article 102—like Dentsply, Unilever had had a market share in Ireland of close to 80% for several years, and around 40% of retail outlets were effectively foreclosed to competitors. These restrictive effects were found to outweigh the possible efficiency benefits (the Commission considered that the freezer exclusivity did not promote inter-brand competition, and that without it there would still be plenty of freezer cabinets left in the market). Turf TV signed up approximately half of the exclusive British horseracing rights, but the court did not prohibit the restraint because Turf TV was a new entrant facing an incumbent which had been a monopolist for 20 years. All these factors are no different from the ones you look at when assessing an alleged abuse of dominance. We therefore refer you to Chapter 4 for additional discussion of the economic principles that are relevant to the foreclosure effects of vertical restraints.

We know of only one competition statute that explicitly treats vertical restraints and abuse of dominance under the same standard. Article 10 of Mexico's Federal Law of Economic Competition (enacted in 1992 and amended in 2006) places all business practices that are not hardcore cartel agreements in the category of 'relative monopolistic practices'—so these include vertical and unilateral practices. Article 11 then states that for these practices to be considered anti-competitive, it must be shown that the responsible party has substantial market power, which is comparable to a dominance standard. EU policy towards vertical restraints also identifies foreclosure as one of the main concerns arising from vertical restraints. The Commission's Guidelines on Vertical Restraints stress that foreclosure is more likely the greater the degree of market power of the supplier and the distributor.[17] The guidelines also state that 'if inter-brand competition is fierce, it is unlikely that a reduction of intra-brand competition will have negative effects for consumers', and even go as far as saying that 'single branding obligations are more likely to result in anti-competitive foreclosure when entered into by dominant companies.'[18] Yet the Commission stops short of equating the analysis of foreclosure under Article 101 to that of abuse of dominance:

> For vertical agreements to be restrictive of competition by effect they must affect actual or potential competition to such an extent that on the relevant market negative effects on prices, output, innovation, or the variety or quality of goods and services can be expected with a reasonable degree of probability. The likely negative effects on competition must be appreciable ... Appreciable anticompetitive effects are likely to occur when at least one of the parties has or obtains some degree of market power and the agreement contributes to the creation, maintenance or strengthening of that market power or allows the parties to exploit such market power. Market power is the ability to maintain prices above competitive levels or to maintain output in terms of product quantities, product quality and variety or innovation below competitive levels for a not insignificant period of time. The degree of market power normally required for a finding of an infringement under Article 101(1) is less than the degree of market power required for a finding of dominance under Article 102.[19]

---

[17] European Commission (2010), 'Guidelines on Vertical Restraints', 2010/C 130/01. In line with this emphasis on the degree of market power to assess foreclosure, the block exemption for vertical agreements does not apply where the supplier or distributor has a market share in excess of 30%. Commission Regulation (EU) 330/2010 of 20 April 2010 on the application of Art 101(3) of the Treaty on the Functioning of the European Union to categories of vertical agreements and concerted practices (a document usually referred to as the Block Exemption Regulation).

[18] European Commission (2010), 'Guidelines on Vertical Restraints', 2010/C 130/01, [102] and [133].

[19] Ibid., at [97].

The reason why the required degree of market power is less than for a finding of dominance is not given. From an economic perspective, if foreclosure is the concern, the same criteria are relevant—under both sets of rules you need to test whether the supplier has a high degree of market power (dominance may be a useful cut-off point for this purpose—see Chapter 4) and a significant part of the distribution channel is foreclosed. One formalistic difference is that Article 101 is about agreements between two parties while Article 102 is about unilateral conduct. However, the means by which a practice arises—by mutual agreement or by one party imposing it, or some combination of the two—does not really matter much when it comes to assessing the effects the practice has on competition. Under the current legal framework, just because there happens to be an agreement between two parties, a lower threshold for intervention is applied than if the conduct were unilateral.

There may be policy reasons for applying a lower threshold under Article 101 than for abuse of dominance. Negative effects on prices, output or product variety may occur in situations where there is no abuse of dominance—it all depends on how you interpret the term 'appreciable'. Let's go back to the example in section 6.2 of the regional airport and the railway built specifically for it. To get round the hold-up problem, as part of the ten-year agreement the airport provided some guarantees on minimum usage—it took on some of the railway's volume risk, confident in its plan with the low-cost airline to develop the airport and attract passengers. But on top of this volume guarantee, it was agreed that the airport would not set up or accept bus services competing with the railway. Now we are seven years into the agreement. The airport development has been a great success. In fact, so many passengers are now using the airport that the railway service has become something of a bottleneck, and while the railway operator at the time gave some assurances that it would keep its fares low, it is clear that passengers, and the airport and airline, would now benefit from a bus service being set up to run alongside the railway. But the agreement prevents the airport from doing so for another three years (bus operators could use bus stops outside the airport's boundaries, but then passengers would have to walk quite far with their luggage). Clearly, the current restriction on bus services (seven years into the agreement) has an appreciable negative effect on consumers. Considering this under Article 102, you would find that the airport faces significant competition from larger airports in the area (so is not dominant), while the railway would be dominant only in a narrowly defined market for public transport to and from the airport (the market may be wider and include private cars). Under the lower 'appreciability' standard of Article 101 you may more easily address this concern. In this case, the relevant question would be whether the restriction was necessary or indispensable at the time of signing the agreement, when both parties were facing a hold-up problem (you cannot just assess the current situation, seven years after signing the agreement).

This is a question that courts and competition authorities are regularly faced with in Article 101 cases, and the complexity lies in having to assess the position the parties were in at the time the agreement was made. It will not be disputed that, back then, restraints were necessary to a certain degree in order to shield the railway operator from the volume risk associated with building the new line. But this does not mean that *all* restraints agreed at the time were strictly needed to overcome the hold-up problem. Some restraints may have been included for other reasons. The clauses in an agreement such as this one will have been influenced by factors such as the relative bargaining position of the two parties. It may well be that the railway operator would have made the investment had the airport provided only the minimum usage guarantee, and that the restriction on competing bus services was included simply because the airport came under time pressure to get a deal signed (ie, the reason it was included was not because the hold-up problem made it necessary). In situations such as these, competition policy may want to intervene at thresholds below those for abuse of dominance—and may succeed in making consumers better off. But applying lower thresholds also means having to engage more often in the complex balancing of the restrictive effects of vertical agreements against their efficiency benefits.

Another situation in which competition authorities may want to intervene without there being an abuse of dominance is where distribution channels are foreclosed by a 'network' of vertical agreements. If there are, say, ten suppliers with a 10% market share each (so no one is dominant), and every distributor in the market deals exclusively with one of the ten suppliers, the distribution channel is as foreclosed to a new supplier wishing to enter as in a situation where a monopoly supplier has such exclusive deals. The European Court of Justice confirmed this principle of cumulative foreclosure (sealing off) in 1991 in a case concerning a vertical agreement between a brewery and the owner of a pub in Frankfurt:

> A beer supply agreement is prohibited by [Article 101(1) TFEU] if two cumulative conditions are met. The first is that, having regard to the economic and legal context of the agreement at issue, it is difficult for competitors who could enter the market or increase their market share to gain access to the national market for the distribution of beer in premises for the sale and consumption of drinks. The fact that, in that market, the agreement in issue is one of a number of similar agreements having a cumulative effect on competition constitutes only one factor amongst others in assessing whether access to that market is indeed difficult. The second condition is that the agreement in question must make a significant contribution to the sealing-off effect brought about by the totality of those agreements in their economic and legal context. The extent of the contribution made by the individual agreement depends on the position of the contracting parties in the relevant market and on the duration of the agreement.[20]

Concerns about distribution channels being foreclosed through the cumulative effect of separate exclusivity deals were also at the heart of the UK government's intervention in the vertical structure of the beer market in 1989. This followed a report by the Monopolies and Mergers Commission (MMC, now the Competition Commission).[21] The MMC found

---

[20] Case C-234/89 *Stergios Delimitis v Henninger Bräu AG* [1991] ECR I-935 [1992]. This case was two EU Treaty re-numberings ago, so the original text referred to Art 85(1) of the EEC Treaty.

[21] Monopolies and Mergers Commission (1989), 'The supply of beer', March. This investigation was carried out under the Fair Trading Act 1973, which was superseded by the Enterprise Act 2002. Both statutes allow(ed) the UK competition authorities to intervene in markets where there is a perceived competition problem but not necessarily an infringement under Art 101 or 102 TFEU.

that 75% of pubs in the UK were owned by brewers, and sold only their beer. Another 12.5% of pubs were tied to a particular brewer through an arrangement that granted exclusivity in exchange for a loan at below market rates of interest. There were six national brewers who represented three-quarters of the beer market (Allied, Bass, Courage, Grand Metropolitan, Scottish & Newcastle, and Whitbread)—none of them had a dominant position. The brewers argued that the exclusivity allowed them to control the product quality from the producer through to the consumer, and that it allowed thousands of small entrepreneurs into the pub business with minimal capital expenditure. But the MMC responded: 'Eloquently though the industry's case has been put, we are not persuaded that all is well.'[22] It considered that the exclusivity restricted consumer choice and that it foreclosed independent manufacturers and wholesalers of beer and other drinks from having access to the pub distribution channel. Over time, the MMC found, the vertical structure served to 'keep the bigger brewers big and the smaller brewers small'. As a remedy it recommended a ceiling of 2,000 on the number of pubs or other beer-selling premises which any brewery may own and the elimination of all loan ties and of ties for low-alcohol beers, wines, spirits, ciders, soft drinks, and mineral waters. The government then issued the 'Beer Orders' in December 1989 in order to enforce the vertical separation in line with the MMC recommendations. Eventually around 14,000 premises were sold off by the national brewers (no regional or local brewer met the ceiling). While carried out under competition rules that are separate from Article 101 TFEU (and its national equivalents), the UK beer case is an example of where a competition authority intervened because a series of vertical agreements had the cumulative effect of foreclosing the beer distribution channel, without there necessarily being a supplier with a significant degree of market power or a dominant position.

6.3.2 VERTICAL RESTRAINTS TO FACILITATE HORIZONTAL COORDINATION

Consumers benefit when there is competition at the product supply level—when producers of false teeth, wedding dresses, toys, cars, and beer all strive to make the highest-quality products at the lowest cost. Take the degree of horizontal competition between suppliers—inter-brand competition—as given for a moment (say, there is only one major producer of false teeth and ten major car manufacturers). Then consider that all these suppliers face the challenge of getting their products to the consumer through distribution channels. We saw in section 6.2 that there are many ways in which suppliers use vertical restraints to ensure that their products are distributed effectively. Distribution thus constitutes another layer of potential competitive pressure, but this can be analysed almost independently from the degree of horizontal competition between suppliers that exists in the first place. Your competition analysis will still show that there is a problem of concentration at the product supply level in the market for false teeth, and less of a

---

[22] Monopolies and Mergers Commission (1989), 'The supply of beer', March, [1.18].

problem in the market for cars, regardless of the vertical restraints. Vertical restraints are therefore not usually of major concern as long as inter-brand competition remains vibrant. Following this logic, your analysis of vertical restraints can focus mainly on their effects on the existing inter-brand competition.

One situation in which vertical restraints may affect inter-brand competition is where distribution channels are foreclosed—we saw this in the previous sub-section. Another situation is where vertical restraints are used to soften horizontal competition between suppliers. You can see this from the perspective of suppliers. Let's say they agree (tacitly or openly) to keep prices high and not get too much in each other's way. This cosy arrangement could still be undermined if their distributors don't play along. The last thing the colluding suppliers want is for their distributors to start discounting the products or playing different suppliers' products off against each other in their shops. Resale price maintenance may be used in these circumstances to prevent distributors from undercutting the price levels agreed among the suppliers. The effect is to diminish inter-brand competition. Such pricing restrictions may also make prices in the market more transparent, which is a condition for successful collusion (see Chapters 3 and 5). Other types of vertical restraint that prevent distributors from competing too aggressively, such as exclusive territories, may equally be used to protect or reinforce horizontal coordination among suppliers. In markets where the supply layer of the chain is more competitive, vertical restraints may be used as a mechanism to facilitate coordination among larger retailers. In Chapter 5 we discussed the 'hub-and-spoke' collusion mechanism as an example of this. The *Toys 'R' Us* case discussed in section 6.2 above represents yet another variant of the use of vertical agreements to achieve horizontal coordination (in this case a retailer achieving a boycott of rival retailers by manufacturers).

6.3.3 RESALE PRICE MAINTENANCE: A 'HARDCORE' RESTRAINT?

You saw in section 6.2 that resale price maintenance can have positive effects of efficiency in distribution, just as other types of vertical restraint can. Preventing distributors from discounting may provide them with better incentives to promote the product, to offer pre-sales services or to keep optimal stock levels. You can also see the difference with horizontal price fixing—horizontal cartels eliminate inter-brand competition; resale price maintenance eliminates only intra-brand competition, and does not directly affect inter-brand competition (it may possibly dampen it, as discussed above).

Yet competition law has invariably treated resale price maintenance with hostility, at least until very recently. The US Supreme Court outlawed the practice in its 1911 *Dr Miles* judgment.[23] Dr Miles Medical Company produced proprietary medicines by means of 'secret methods and formulas', and determined the prices at which wholesalers and retailers could sell them. The justifications put forward by Dr Miles were not unlike those discussed in section 6.2. Independent pharmacists needed a fair profit in

---

[23] *Dr Miles Medical Co v John D Park & Sons Co* 220 US 373 (1911).

return for promoting the products; the big department stores had begun a cut-price system which created 'much confusion, trouble, and damage' and 'injuriously affected the reputation' and 'depleted the sales' of Dr Miles's medicines; and, for these reasons, without resale price maintenance the majority of pharmacists would be unwilling to keep the medicines in stock. The Supreme Court would have none of this and imposed a per se prohibition because it considered that resale price maintenance had as its sole purpose the restriction of competition and fixing of prices. However, 96 years and much criticism from economists later, the Supreme Court overruled *Dr Miles* in the 2007 *Leegin* judgment.[24] Leegin is a designer and manufacturer of women's leather accessories (belts, handbags, shoes), which it sells to independent, small boutiques and speciality stores across the USA under the Brighton brand (launched in 1991). In 1997, Leegin implemented the 'Brighton Retail and Promotion Policy', which involved refusing to sell Brighton products to retailers that discounted below its 'suggested retail prices'. The justification for such a policy was to provide retailers with a margin that allowed them to offer top-quality customer service. Leegin also expressed concern that discounting harmed Brighton's brand image and reputation. In 1998, Leegin introduced the 'Heart Store Program', where it offered a number of incentives to retailers in exchange for selling at its suggested prices. One disgruntled retailer—Kay's Kloset—sued Leegin when its supply contract was suspended because it had sold below the suggested price, and was awarded damages under the *Dr Miles* per se prohibition. However, the Supreme Court subsequently determined that vertical price restraints are to be judged under a rule of reason, stating that:

> Economics literature is replete with procompetitive justifications for a manufacturer's use of resale price maintenance, and the few recent studies on the subject also cast doubt on the conclusion that the practice meets the criteria for a per se rule. The justifications for vertical price restraints are similar to those for other vertical restraints.[25]

In Europe, resale price maintenance is considered a 'hardcore' vertical restriction that cannot qualify for a block exemption.[26] However, the latest Commission Guidelines on Vertical Restraints do acknowledge its potential efficiency benefits, such that individual exemptions may be granted under Article 101(3).[27] The main potential harmful effect of resale price maintenance that is now emphasized in the guidelines (but that must still be balanced against the potential efficiency benefits) is that it may facilitate collusion among suppliers or distributors, in line with the principles set out in the previous sub-section. This is slightly different from the emphasis in *Dr Miles*, which was on the fixing of resale prices in its own right without reference to collusion concerns.

---

[24] *Leegin Creative Leather Products, Inc v Psks, Inc, dba Kay's Kloset . . . Kay's Shoes* 551 US 877; 127 S Ct 2705 (2007).

[25] Ibid., at [2] Syllabus/[2708].

[26] Commission Regulation (EU) 330/2010 of 20 April 2010 on the application of Art 101(3) of the Treaty on the Functioning of the European Union to categories of vertical agreements and concerted practices, Art 4(a).

[27] European Commission (2010), 'Guidelines on Vertical Restraints', 2010/C 130/01, [225].

Two variants of this vertical restraint are maximum resale prices and recommended resale prices. These practices raise fewer competition concerns than standard resale price maintenance where minimum prices are set, and they are generally treated more favourably under competition law. In terms of efficiencies, maximum resale prices in particular seem a useful mechanism to address the problem of double marginalization—distributors are prevented from raising prices too much. As to potential negative effects, you could check if the maximum or recommended resale prices serve a function as focal points to facilitate horizontal collusion among suppliers or distributors in the same way that standard resale price maintenance may.

6.3.4 EXCLUSIVE TERRITORIES IN THE EU: A 'HARDCORE' RESTRAINT?

The prices of new cars have always varied significantly across EU Member States, much to the chagrin of consumers, and of the European Commission. In the 1990s, many savvy VW and Audi drivers in Germany decided to order a new car from dealers in northern Italy, where prices were 20%–30% lower. Volkswagen clamped down hard on its Italian VW and Audi dealers through its vertical agreements in order to prevent such cross-border selling. Their sales were closely monitored, their bonuses cut if they were caught selling to non-residents, and scripts handed out on what they should say to baffled customers as to why they could not possibly buy their car in Italy. The Commission considered this to be a restriction of competition by object under Article 101(1)—a particularly harsh treatment, which only hardcore cartels and resale price maintenance have received—and fined the car maker €102 million (reduced to €90 million on appeal).[28] BMW, General Motors, and DaimlerChrysler were punished for similar practices. The Commission's actions against such export restrictions in vertical agreements have covered a wide range of products, from consumer electronics and sports equipment to alcoholic beverages and pharmaceuticals. Why this strict approach, especially since in section 6.2 we discussed how exclusive territories for distributors may, in theory, provide the right incentives and improve distribution efficiencies? Wasn't Volkswagen entitled to reassure its German car dealers, who were understandably disgruntled by this unplanned intra-brand competition from their Italian counterparts?

The answer here lies not so much in the economics of vertical restraints as with the objective in the EU Treaty of creating a single market. Restrictions on dealers that prevent the movement of goods across borders do not sit well with this broader European policy objective, even if they have some efficiency rationale. This does leave the European Commission with a conundrum: it does not wish to rule out territorial restrictions per se, and therefore has to draw the line somewhere. The way it has sought

---

[28] Case T-62/98 *Volkswagen AG v Commission* [2003] ECR II-2707; [2000] 5 CMLR 853, upheld on appeal to the European Court of Justice in Case C-338/00 *Volkswagen AG v Commission* [2003] ECR I-9189; [2004] 4 CMLR 351.

to do this is by reference to 'active' and 'passive' sales.[29] Active sales are defined as actively approaching individual customers through means such as direct mail and other targeted advertising methods. Passive sales means responding to unsolicited requests from individual customers, or engaging in general advertising. Restrictions on active sales may qualify for the Block Exemption under certain circumstances, but restrictions on passive sales may not. You can see how this line may not always be clear-cut. Presumably, VW may legally prevent its Italian dealers from distributing leaflets in Germany, but not from selling to Germans who happen to walk into their showroom. And what about the growth of sales over the Internet? According to the Commission's Guidelines, using a website to advertise and sell products is a form of passive sales, but territory-based banners on third-party websites are a form of active sales into the territory where these banners are shown. Suppliers and distributors may be forgiven if they find it complicated to assess whether their online sales and advertising strategies infringe competition law.

The cases against export restrictions in car distribution agreements have highlighted another issue where the current legal treatment of vertical restraints is not necessarily consistent with the economics. Article 101 covers agreements between undertakings. It does not cover vertical restraints between companies that share a degree of legal own-ership, ie, where supplier and distributor are vertically integrated, or where the dis-tributor acts as an 'agent' for the supplier. The Commission Guidelines contain a detailed explanation of when a vertical agreement can be considered an agency agreement (in essence, distributors are considered agents when they bear very limited financial and commercial risk in relation to the agreement in question).[30] Again, from an economic perspective, the effects on efficiency and competition are in principle the same, and yet the legal treatment is different. A clear example of where this leads to a somewhat odd result is the *DaimlerChrysler* case—the restrictions imposed on Mercedes-Benz dealers in Germany were in essence the same as those in the *Volkswagen* and other cases, but the General Court annulled the fine imposed on DaimlerChrysler because it was estab-lished that the German dealers acted as agents of the car maker—DaimlerChrysler bore the principal risk; the dealers did not buy the cars for resale, were not required to hold a stock of new vehicles, and did not set the resale price.[31] Some economists (including ourselves) have always been a bit puzzled by these legal distinctions, and have won-dered whether they may in fact lead companies to adopt certain forms of vertical rela-tionship purely because they receive a more favourable treatment under competition law—do the EU rules on vertical restraints push some suppliers towards more vertical integration or agency arrangements than they otherwise would have chosen?

---

[29] European Commission (2010), 'Guidelines on Vertical Restraints', 2010/C 130/01, [51] *et seq.*
[30] Ibid., at [12]–[21].
[31] Case T-325/01 *DaimlerChrysler AG v Commission* [2005] ECR II-3319; [2007] 4 CMLR 559.

6.4 CONCLUSION: QUESTIONS FOR COMPETITION LAW

Industries tend to do a reasonable job at organizing their vertical supply chains effectively and efficiently. Vertical agreements and restraints are an integral part of this—they assist in overcoming the inherent economic problems of double marginalization, free-riding, and hold-up. A number of empirical economic studies have shown that where, in contrast, competition authorities or governments have intervened in the prevailing vertical relationships, the resulting market outcomes have not always made consumers better off (Lafontaine and Slade, 2008). The vertical separation and untying of exclusivity between brewers and pubs in the UK in 1989 has been shown to have produced mixed results: some increase in consumer choice, but also in beer prices. In part this is because the new market structure saw the development of large pub chains that began to act as intermediaries between brewers and pubs, which created problems of bargaining power and exclusivity in its own right (Waterson, 2009; Slade, 1998).

Competition authorities have increasingly recognized the economic benefits of vertical restraints and have sought to balance them against the potential negative effects on competition. From an economic perspective, the main harmful effects of vertical restraints are the potential foreclosure of distribution channels and the facilitation of horizontal coordination between suppliers or distributors. This raises some questions about the treatment of vertical restraints in EU competition law in particular, as addressed in this chapter. If foreclosure is the main competition concern, why not treat vertical restraints in the same way as abuse of dominance? By and large this seems a sensible policy approach, although there are some situations where competition authorities may wish to intervene at lower thresholds. And if what matters is the economic effect of vertical restraints on efficiency and competition, why treat vertical agreements any differently from vertical restraints that are imposed unilaterally by one party, or from restraints on agents or otherwise vertically integrated distributors? Overall, while the approach to vertical restraints has become more economics-based, the way competition authorities strike the balance between positive and negative effects still seems overly complicated at times. A greater number of competition issues might be addressed through counterfactual analysis under Article 101(1) to explore whether there is a restriction of competition in the first place. This may reduce the number of cases where you consider efficiency benefits under Article 101(3) only, or where you have to assess the somewhat complicated criteria for whether the agreement qualifies for a Block Exemption.

7

MERGERS

7.1 WHAT CAN ECONOMICS ADD TO MERGER CONTROL?

Two independent companies—like our Italian producers of women's designer shoes in Chapter 2—decide that their strategic interests will be best met under common ownership. The rationale for such consolidation is that the merged entity is expected to be more profitable than the two companies continuing separately. Such increased profitability may come from many sources—synergies, efficiencies, cost savings, a better range of brands—but of concern to competition authorities is the rationale that consolidation eliminates the rivalry between the two companies. Across many jurisdictions, this is now codified as a concern over whether a merger will lead to a substantial lessening of competition (SLC)—a term used in the USA, Australia, New Zealand, and the UK; variations on this are a substantial lessening or prevention of competition, as used in Canada and South Africa, and a substantial impediment to effective competition (SIEC), as used in the EU. Such an SLC or SIEC could take the form of an increase in price or a reduction in output, choice, quality, or innovation.

Merger analysis is a large component of most competition authorities' workload. It involves making difficult trade-offs. Mergers and acquisitions can enhance competition and efficiency. They can create a form of rivalry between management teams—where one set of managers is not operating a company efficiently, others can step in to improve it. Mergers between small companies can create a stronger competitor to the larger companies in the market; acquisitions can allow companies to gain a foothold in new product or geographic markets and increase competition there. Combining two companies can create synergies in production. Shareholders would be expected to have every incentive to scrutinize the merger plans carefully and accept them only if long-term profitability is increased. A competition authority therefore has to differentiate between pro-competitive deals and ones that are targeted at enhancing market power—although mergers can often result in both effects simultaneously. The added challenge is that the analysis of the effects of a merger is necessarily forward-looking. To understand the impact of consolidation, you must analyse how the market will evolve with and without the merger—this requires a counterfactual analysis.

How does an authority make sure that its threshold is right, ie, that it neither blocks too many mergers that would have efficiency benefits, nor allows too many deals that enhance market power? One approach would be to prohibit all mergers. Companies that want to grow would have to do so organically, through competitive effort. Such a policy might actually stimulate healthy competition and would also save enforcement costs. Yet outright prohibitions of mergers are relatively rare. Competition law recognizes the point made above that many consolidations have as a rationale an underlying efficiency improvement, and that economic welfare and consumers are not at risk as long as the merger does not substantially reduce competition. Testing for an SLC begins with market definition and the assessment of market power, as discussed in Chapters 2 and 3. In this chapter we explain the additional economic principles and analyses that are of relevance to merger assessments. Even if a merger does reduce competition, the authorities are normally keen to preserve its welfare-enhancing aspects. So, instead of prohibiting it, they may require undertakings that can remedy any identified harm. Structural remedies will generally be preferred, such as the divestment of businesses or brands, but behavioural remedies such as access requirements may also be acceptable where they have limited compliance and monitoring costs. We return to this in Chapter 9 on the design of remedies.

If you arrived at this chapter having read the earlier ones—in particular Chapters 2 and 3—you will already have a good understanding of the economic concepts and tools used in merger cases: market definition, market concentration, entry conditions, the likelihood of coordination between competitors, and the countervailing bargaining power of customers. This chapter complements Chapters 2 and 3 (and Chapter 9 on remedies). We start in section 7.2 by exploring the principles behind the (now relatively uniform) tests used by competition authorities in deciding whether a merger is anti-competitive. We then go on in section 7.3 to discuss counterfactual analysis, including cases where one of the merging parties is a failing firm (ie, it would exit in the absence of the merger, hence requiring a counterfactual that is different from just the pre-merger situation). In section 7.4 we discuss the analysis of unilateral effects, which is the central theory of harm that arises in horizontal mergers (ie, mergers between direct competitors). Post-merger, will the merged entity have both an incentive and the ability to increase price or reduce quality, or would sufficient competitive constraints remain? (Coordinated effects, the other theory of harm under the SLC test, are discussed in Chapter 3.) Section 7.5 considers non-horizontal mergers—ie, those that are vertical, diagonal or conglomerate in nature. Concerns about vertical mergers revolve around the possible foreclosure of rivals, so we focus on the ability and incentive of the merged entity to engage in such foreclosure. Finally, in section 7.6, we look at how efficiencies can be dealt with in the merger context, in particular how they can be identified and then balanced against the negative effects on competition.

7.2 WHAT IS THE TEST FOR JUDGING A MERGER TO BE ANTI-COMPETITIVE?

7.2.1 DOMINANCE VERSUS SLC

US antitrust law established one of the earliest frameworks for merger control. Section 7 of the Clayton Act 1914 prohibits mergers where 'the effect of such acquisition may be substantially to lessen competition, or to tend to create a monopoly.' Thus, there are two criteria for judging when a merger is anti-competitive: it leads to a monopoly or near-monopoly position, or it substantially lessens competition. US merger control has traditionally focused on preventing market structures that would be prone to tacit collusion, precisely because such collusion is difficult to address directly under competition law (see Chapter 3 on the criteria for tacit collusion and Chapter 5 on horizontal agreements).

In contrast, EU merger control originally focused on the first criterion, ie, it sought to prevent the creation or strengthening of dominant positions. This led to some confusion as to whether situations of tacit collusion or lack of effective competition were also covered by the rules; the answer was yes, by referring to them as collective or joint dominance (see Chapter 3). The SIEC test adopted under the 2004 Merger Regulation captures coordinated effects more explicitly.

A dominance or monopoly test focuses on the market position of the merged entity. An SLC or SIEC test allows a wider range of potentially welfare-reducing distortions to be considered, covering both coordinated and unilateral effects. It focuses on what competition is lost as a result of the merger, and can also balance the positive and negative effects. Apart from tacit collusion and a lack of effective competition post-merger, the SLC test covers situations where a merger reduces competition significantly but does not create a dominant position for the merged entity. This can occur, for example, in a merger between the second- and third-largest companies in the market where these two compete more vigorously with each other than with the unchallenged market leader. This type of unilateral effect was in essence the theory of harm in the *Heinz/Beech-Nut* merger in 2000, which we discuss in section 7.4. Such mergers were believed to have been outside the scope of the old dominance test (this oversight in EU merger control was termed the 'unilateral effects gap').

Another type of merger that is caught under the SLC test but not the dominance test is where a large company acquires a small but very aggressive competitor. An example is the acquisition of tele.ring by T-Mobile Austria, examined by the European Commission in 2005.[1] This combined the second- and fourth-largest providers in the Austrian mobile telephony market. At 30%–40%, their post-merger market share would be smaller than that of the largest provider, Mobilkom (which had 35%–45%), and tele.ring itself had a market share of 10%–20%. According to the HHI (explained in Chapter 3), the market was concentrated, and the increase in the HHI of 500–600 would be enough to raise concern under the SLC or SIEC test. However, the merged entity would not be dominant, since it would be smaller than Mobilkom. The Commission also concluded that the nature of the mobile telephony market was not conducive to tacit collusion. On this basis, the merger was unlikely to create or strengthen a joint dominant position between T-Mobile and Mobilkom. The Commission did, however, find evidence of an SIEC on the basis of tele.ring's competitive behaviour before the merger, noting that 'tele.ring, as a maverick, has a much greater influence on the competitive process in this market than its market share would suggest.'[2] Using an aggressive entry strategy, tele.ring had cut prices and doubled in size in just a few years prior to the merger. This had prevented the two larger operators from enjoying a cosy oligopoly. By removing this constraint, the merger would reduce the intensity of competition. It is worth emphasizing that the Commission did not allege that T-Mobile and

---

[1] *T-Mobile Austria/Tele.ring* (Case COMP/M.3916), Commission Decision of 26 April 2006.
[2] Ibid., at [129].

Mobilkom would actually collude post-merger, only that a move from a competitive to a duopoly market would result in potentially significant price rises. The merger was cleared with remedies relating to the divestment of spectrum and mast sites, with the Commission concluding that these remedies would strengthen H3G, one of the other smaller operators, and might recreate the pre-merger competitive dynamics.

7.2.2 THE CONSUMER WELFARE STANDARD IN MERGER CONTROL

An associated question is whose welfare should be protected through merger control? As we discussed in Chapter 1, there can be a tension between protecting consumer welfare and using a total welfare standard that encompasses producers and consumers. From an economic perspective, additional welfare is created whenever a market transaction takes place at a price that covers the producers' costs and that the consumers are willing to pay. Merger control aims to deliver benefits to consumers—that is, to keep prices close to costs and quality high. Not all competition regimes give as much weight to producer welfare in their assessments. This tension is most clearly seen in the treatment of merger efficiencies. If weight is attached to producer surplus as well as consumer surplus, merger efficiencies are seen as beneficial in and of themselves. With a consumer welfare standard, only those efficiencies that are passed on to consumers are considered relevant. Figure 7.1 illustrates the comparison between the total welfare and consumer welfare standards. It shows the straightforward (if rather unlikely) example of a merger leading to a monopoly from a starting point of perfect competition.

You can see from Figure 7.1 that marginal costs are lower after the merger, so the merger does generate efficiency gains for the merging companies. But because of the

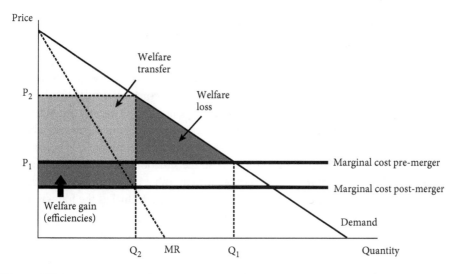

Fig.7.1 Efficiencies versus market power in mergers

market power created by the merger, prices still rise from P_1 to P_2. From a total welfare perspective, only the triangle marked 'welfare loss' would be of concern in this merger, and this would be balanced against the efficiencies rectangle marked 'welfare gain'. You can undertake a simple welfare analysis based on this figure: if the area of the welfare loss triangle is greater than the welfare gain rectangle, the merger harms total welfare; if the efficiencies rectangle is greater, total welfare increases. But if consumer welfare is the standard used by the competition authority, the result is different. The authority would be concerned that the post-merger price increases despite the cost efficiencies, and that there is a welfare transfer from consumers to the merging companies. In this framework the fall in marginal cost would have to be very large for there to be no net price increase after the merger. Otherwise, the efficiency gains would be considered insufficient, even if they compensated for the deadweight welfare loss in the triangle. This effectively means that merger control using a consumer welfare standard can block mergers that would actually enhance total welfare.

7.3 THE COUNTERFACTUAL

7.3.1 WHAT WOULD HAPPEN WITHOUT THE MERGER?

Counterfactual analysis plays an important role in different areas of competition law—in horizontal and vertical agreements (Chapters 5 and 6) to assess whether there is a restriction of competition; in the assessment of state aid (Chapter 8); and in the quantification of damages (Chapter 10). In merger cases, the idea of a counterfactual is to isolate and assess the effect of the specific transaction. You need to compare the market outcome resulting from the merger with the situation that would have prevailed in the absence of the merger. The difference between the two tells you whether there is an SLC in the post-merger state of the world. In most cases, the counterfactual will be the conditions of competition prevailing before the merger. In these cases the SLC assessment can be undertaken by considering the likely impact of the merger on the market as it stands (or in the case of an already completed merger, the situation before completion). Evidence on behaviour under existing market conditions will be relevant for thinking through what the likely future behaviour of companies might be.

However, the past or prevailing market situation is not always a good proxy for what would happen in the future in the absence of the merger, due to potential imminent changes in the structure of competition. Here the analysis becomes more complicated because you have to compare two situations that do not exist: the situation with the merger, and the counterfactual situation without the merger, but with the other imminent changes that have not occurred yet. Having set out the principle of the counterfactual as the framework for assessing mergers, the EU Guidelines on Horizontal Mergers identify situations where the prevailing market conditions may not be the appropriate counterfactual:

> In assessing the competitive effects of a merger, the Commission compares the competitive conditions that would result from the notified merger with the conditions that would have

prevailed without the merger. In most cases the competitive conditions existing at the time of the merger constitute the relevant comparison for evaluating the effects of a merger. However, in some circumstances, the Commission may take into account future changes to the market that can reasonably be predicted. It may, in particular, take account of the likely entry or exit of firms if the merger did not take place when considering what constitutes the relevant comparison.[3]

We consider below two situations where future competitive conditions might differ from the prevailing conditions—first, where new entry might be expected, and second, where the target firm might exit the market (ie, it is a failing firm).

7.3.2 FUTURE MARKET ENTRY IN THE ABSENCE OF THE MERGER

The following cases illustrate how the counterfactual might differ from the prevailing pre-merger situation as a result of market dynamics and entry. In the *Glaxo Wellcome/ SmithKline Beecham* merger in 2000, the European Commission explored whether the counterfactual should include products that were expected to enter the market in the short term regardless of the merger:

> In the pharmaceuticals industry, a full assessment of the competitive situation requires examination of the products which are not yet on the market but which are at an advanced stage of development, (normally after large sums of money have been invested). These products are called pipeline products.[4]

This new entry in the counterfactual is subtly different from the general entry analysis that you carry out in the market power stage (see Chapter 3), since it is entry that does not depend on, or is not triggered by, the merger. You then compare competition in the counterfactual with that after the merger (as noted above, you have to compare two situations, neither of which currently exists). In *Glaxo Wellcome/SmithKline Beecham* the focus was on anti-viral medicines. Although there was a pipeline of products from other companies, the Commission did not consider it to be sufficiently strong to constrain the merged entity. Indeed, there were concerns that the merger would make it more difficult for the pipeline products to achieve their market potential. In other words, the merger would reduce competition not only in the actual market but also in the counterfactual market. In the end the parties agreed to make divestments in this product category.

In 2007, the UK Competition Commission (CC) investigated the completed acquisition by Greif UK—the largest manufacturer of industrial steel containers in the UK—of the steel drum and closures business of Blagden Packaging Group.[5] The merged entity's market share of large steel drums was 85%. The CC found that, pre-merger, of all the competitors in the relevant market, Blagden had posed the most significant competitive

---

[3] European Commission (2004), 'Guidelines on the assessment of horizontal mergers under the Council Regulation on the control of concentrations between undertakings', [2004] OJ C31/03, [9].

[4] *Glaxo Wellcome/SmithKline Beecham* (Case COMP/M.1846), Commission Decision of 8 May 2000.

[5] Competition Commission (2007), 'Greif Inc and Blagden Packaging Group', 17 August.

constraint on Greif—the CC's analysis of the extent of switching showed that Greif and Blagden had lost more custom to each other than to any other company. Furthermore, there was limited competitive constraint from smaller producers or imports. However, this pre-merger market situation did not tell the whole story. The CC considered that the merged entity would be constrained in future by a new steel drum manufacturing line run by Schütz Group, a competitor, at its new industrial packaging facility in the Netherlands. Schütz Group stated that the line would have been installed in the absence of the merger—ie, in the counterfactual—but that it brought forward the installation by 18 months because of the merger. This new rival plant was capable of supplying large orders from UK customers, and the CC's analysis showed that imports from Schütz Group could be competitive for some types of steel drum and for some UK customers (see Chapter 2 on how transport costs can influence the extent of the geographic market). The merger was therefore cleared.

The third example is the 2010 merger between ticketing agent, Ticketmaster Entertainment, and venue owner and promoter, Live Nation, which was scrutinized in both the USA and UK. The CC cleared the deal unconditionally, but had initially raised concerns in relation to horizontal and vertical effects.[6] This was predominantly a vertical merger in the supply chain for live music events. (We consider vertical theories of harm in section 7.5.) One theory of harm specific to the UK was that the merger would also have a horizontal effect through a loss of potential competition in the supply of tickets for live music events. Prior to the merger, Live Nation had entered into an agreement with another ticket agent, CTS Eventim, which had been a strong player in the German market but was new to the UK. The potential horizontal harm was that the merger might prevent CTS's planned entry. This represented an unusual theory of harm since the counterfactual being used was not the pre-merger situation but the future market in which there would be increased competition as a result of CTS's entry. The CC therefore carried out a detailed analysis of this counterfactual, assessing the likelihood of the contract with Live Nation being a necessary and sufficient stepping stone for CTS to enter the UK market. It also explored whether the merger would remove the rationale for that contract (both Live Nation and CTS publicly expressed their intention to honour the agreement irrespective of the merger with Ticketmaster). Live Nation's ultimate commercial aim was to sell tickets directly to consumers using its own website, powered by CTS's ticketing platform. As part of the agreement, CTS would be allocated a proportion of the tickets to events promoted by Live Nation. However, this in itself would not be sufficient to make CTS capable of constraining the two larger companies, Ticketmaster and See Tickets. The CC noted that CTS establishing itself in the UK market as a large-scale ticket retailer would depend on its own efforts and abilities, and that its chances of success would not be affected significantly by the merger. It concluded that the agreement between Live Nation and CTS was neither necessary nor

---

[6] Competition Commission (2010), 'Ticketmaster and Live Nation', 7 May. We advised a third party in this inquiry.

sufficient to ensure the successful large-scale entry of CTS, and that therefore there was no SLC from the merger in this regard.

7.3.3 THE FAILING-FIRM DEFENCE

The failing-firm defence is often put forward by merging parties when the target firm is in distress. In times of economic recession this issue comes to the fore more frequently. To the merging parties (and possibly the authority as well), a failing-firm defence is highly attractive as it can avoid the need for an in-depth consideration of the effects on competition. If, in the counterfactual, the target firm no longer exists then (it can be argued) the merger changes nothing about the competitive landscape. However, the fact that a firm is in difficulty and would be unlikely to survive with its pre-merger strength is not sufficient to conclude that the correct counterfactual is the market without the target firm. Competition authorities need to consider what would have happened to the target firm and its assets in the absence of the merger.

A key issue in applying such a defence is not only that the target company would exit, but that its productive or specialized assets would exit with it. The same principles apply if the target business is a failing division or stand-alone business unit of a company, rather than the entire company. The proposed merger is then justified on the grounds that it is the only way of maintaining the assets of the failing firm in the market. The US Merger Guidelines highlight the importance of the final whereabouts of the failing firm's assets:

> a merger is not likely to enhance market power if imminent failure . . . of one of the merging firms would cause the assets of that firm to exit the relevant market. This is an extreme instance of the more general circumstance in which the competitive significance of one of the merging firms is declining: the projected market share and significance of the exiting firm is zero. If the relevant assets would otherwise exit the market, customers are not worse off after the merger than they would have been had the merger been enjoined.[7]

In the absence of the merger, would the target firm really exit the market? Would its assets be bought by another firm? Or could it recover, albeit with a lag, to become a viable business and competitor in the market? As recognized by the UK Office of Fair Trading (OFT), failing-firm counterfactuals 'are easily the subject of self-speculation—relatively easily alleged but difficult, given the informational asymmetries, to verify independently'.[8] Not surprisingly, therefore, the requirements for qualifying as a failing firm are quite stringent and cases in which the failing-firm defence has been accepted are relatively infrequent. Most jurisdictions explicitly spell out the necessary and sufficient conditions for a successful application of the defence. The degree of stringency when applying this defence varies across jurisdictions. However,

---

[7] Department of Justice and Federal Trade Commission (2010), 'Horizontal Merger Guidelines', August, p 32.

[8] Office of Fair Trading (2008), 'Restatement of OFT's Position Regarding Acquisitions of "Failing Firms"', December, p 3.

the main issues examined are broadly consistent, and can be classified into two conditions: exit of the target business in the absence of the merger is inevitable in the near future; and there is no realistic and substantially less anti-competitive alternative outcome than the proposed acquisition.

The first condition—requiring that exit is inevitable in the near future—usually arises for businesses in financial difficulties, although it can also be due to a change in corporate strategy or managerial inefficiency. Competition authorities recognize that evidence on a company's viability should be evaluated in the context of the prevailing economic and market conditions, and that a downturn affects the financial health of the target and the availability of alternative purchasers. Implicit in this criterion is the condition that the assets of the target business would exit the market as well. The parties also need to show that the financial difficulties are not temporary and cannot be rectified easily by restructuring the business. This will involve examining the company's financial documents (such as the balance sheet) as well as board minutes, management accounts, and strategic plans, to determine what steps the management has taken to recover the company's situation. In economic terms this can be interpreted as there being no investor willing to provide the necessary capital for the business to remain a going concern.

As is apparent, the evidential burden in satisfying this condition can be considerable and these cases are likely to draw on evidence of the financial health of the target firm, using certain financial metrics and ratios that are well established in financial analysis. A general metric is the estimated likelihood of default as reflected in the investment grade of the business. Credit rating agencies use financial tests to assess the risk of creditors not receiving the interest and principal in a timely manner, as these factors typically lead to default. As an example, in one survey the AA-rated debt had a default rate of only 0.03%, whereas 25.7% of CCC-/C-rated firms had actually defaulted (Altman and Narayanan, 1997). More detailed metrics of interest would be those relating to profitability, liquidity and solvency. The relevant profitability metrics would analyse a firm's ability to generate economic value by realizing the returns required by debt and equity investors. These measures can be based on historical performance as well as future expectations. For liquidity, the relevant financial ratios can approximate a firm's ability to meet its short-term obligations, such as interest payments, from current cash flows. An illiquid but potentially solvent firm (ie, one that cannot obtain funding for short-term liabilities, but whose overall liabilities do not outweigh its assets) might not be able to survive as a going concern if investors are unwilling to commit additional funding. Finally, for solvency, the relevant measures would capture a firm's ability to repay its fixed financial obligations, including the principal on its debt. In this context, it should be possible to assess whether the company could earn the required return on additional financial capital that would need to be raised to remedy temporary financial difficulties.

As stated above, the rationale for the failing-firm defence is that the proposed merger allows productive assets to be retained in the market in a way that does not reduce competition compared with the counterfactual of exit. The second condition requires that there is no realistic and substantially less anti-competitive alternative outcome from the firm's decline. If the target business could be sold to one or more other purchasers (albeit potentially for a lower price), this might represent a viable alternative counterfactual. These could be existing competitors or new entrants. In the case of a sale to a new entrant, the counterfactual is likely to be similar to the pre-merger competitive conditions (it's just that the firm in question has a new owner). If the assets would have been dispersed across several existing firms, this could suggest a counterfactual with one fewer competitor, but with each remaining competitor becoming slightly stronger (with more assets). To satisfy this second condition, parties need to show either that these alternatives are not feasible or that the competitive situation will not be better under these scenarios.

A European Commission case where the failing-firm defence was successful is the merger in 2001 of BASF with Eurodiol and Pantochim, two Belgian companies owned by the Italian SISAS Group, where both the subsidiaries and the parent company were in the process of liquidation.[9] Even though this merger enhanced BASF's dominant position in the market, the European Commission considered that it met the conditions of the failing-firm defence. It was satisfied that the target companies were going to exit the market and that, in spite of the best efforts by the Tribunal de Commerce of Charleroi to find suitable buyers under the Belgian pre-bankruptcy regime, only BASF had made an approach to acquire the targets. The criterion regarding the exit of the assets of the target business was also satisfied since the two plants operated as a whole and could have not been sold independently. Hence it was considered that these assets would have exited the market had BASF not made the offer to acquire Eurodiol and Pantochim.

A high-profile case where the failing-firm defence was not accepted, but many might have thought that it would be, is the one in which Lloyds TSB (one of the 'big four' UK high-street banks) acquired HBOS in 2008. HBOS was also a significant player in retail banking (itself the product of a merger between a large building society, Halifax, and the Bank of Scotland). HBOS was in distress as a result of liquidity issues and exposure to toxic assets as part of the general financial crisis affecting many financial institutions at the time. Because of the potential systemic risks, the UK Secretary of State for Business intervened in the public interest, taking control of the ultimate decision of whether to approve the merger. He asked the OFT for a report on the competition effects of the transaction. The OFT found that this acquisition resulted in an SLC that was not easily remediable. Central to this conclusion was the chosen counterfactual. The OFT concluded that, given the unprecedented volatility in the financial markets, using pre-merger competitive conditions was not appropriate, but nor did it consider that the competitive constraints from HBOS would be completely eliminated. It judged the appropriate counterfactual to be that the state would step in to ensure HBOS did not collapse, and then, in the medium term, when that support was no longer required and was withdrawn, HBOS would be sold to another bank with no existing strong position

---

[9] *BASF/Eurodiol/Pantochim* (Case COMP/M.2314) [2002] OJ L132/45.

in the UK, or HBOS would return to viability. Thus the OFT did not consider that this case met the requirements for treating HBOS as a failing firm with no alternative options. The acquisition was cleared by the Secretary of State on the basis of its benefits to the financial stability of HBOS and the UK financial system as a whole, despite the SLC identified by the OFT.[10]

In some cases, the conditions can be applied to stand-alone business units rather than a whole company; one such example is the OFT's decision to clear the acquisition by Tesco of five stores from Kwik Save, another retailer.[11] The OFT used information from all related parties and independent consultants to determine that four of the Kwik Save stores were insolvent and would have closed in the absence of the transaction. The first condition for the failing-firm defence was therefore met (exit was inevitable in the near future). Moreover, even though all major grocery chains were invited to bid for the stores, Tesco was the only bidder, suggesting that there was no alternative buyer. The OFT also considered whether competitive conditions would have been preferable in the situation where the target stores exited and their assets were sold. It concluded that in the case of exit, the number of grocery convenience retailers in the area would not be greater relative to the merger. The transaction would allow the continuation of the stores as grocery retailers, thus preserving choice for local consumers. Hence, the second condition (no less anti-competitive alternative) was also satisfied and the deal was cleared.

In another case, the failing-firm defence was (nearly) accepted but was not considered to be the most relevant counterfactual because it was alleged that the target was failing due to the predatory behaviour of the acquiring party. In November 2009, the CC found that there had been an SLC from Stagecoach's completed acquisition of Preston Bus, a rival bus operator in Preston in the north of England. The CC required Stagecoach to divest a reconfigured Preston Bus business. The decision was appealed to the Competition Appeal Tribunal (CAT), which upheld the CC's finding of an SLC, but questioned the counterfactual.[12] The background to the case was that Stagecoach first approached Preston Bus in 2006 with an offer to purchase the business. The offer was rejected. Following this, Stagecoach developed a plan for expansion in the Preston area and launched a number of local bus services in direct competition with Preston Bus in 2007. Both Stagecoach and Preston Bus incurred losses as a result of this competition. After a year of unprofitable services Preston Bus suffered financial difficulties, and decided to sell. It approached a number of major bus companies for the sale, but Stagecoach made an offer in October 2008 which Preston Bus accepted. Stagecoach submitted that Preston Bus was a failing firm and that, on liquidation, it was highly unlikely that any other company would purchase its assets to provide local bus

---

[10] Department for Business, Enterprise and Regulatory Reform (2008), 'Decision by Lord Mandelson, the Secretary of State for Business, Not to Refer to the Competition Commission the Merger Between Lloyds TSB Group plc and HBOS plc Under Section 45 of the Enterprise Act 2002', 31 October.

[11] Office of Fair Trading (2007), 'Anticipated acquisition by Tesco Stores Limited of five former Kwik Save stores (Handforth, Coventry, Liverpool, Barrow-in-Furness and Nelson)', 11 December.

[12] *Stagecoach Group PLC v Competition Commission* [2010] CAT 14, 21 May 2010.

services in Preston. The CC concluded that the counterfactual should be assessed against the most recent period of 'normal' competition, ie, before Stagecoach entered. Therefore, the counterfactual would be that of Preston Bus profitably running the local services and Stagecoach running inter-urban services outside Preston—in essence, the situation that existed about 18 months before the merger. The CAT rejected the CC's decision to ignore the events of the June 2007–September 2008 period for the purposes of constructing the counterfactual. It did not overturn the CC's finding that the counterfactual would not have been a complete exit by Preston Bus, but concluded that the alternative put forward by the CC (the competition prevailing before Stagecoach's entry) was not correct. As a result the CAT found that the CC's remedy was disproportionate.

7.4 UNILATERAL EFFECTS IN HORIZONTAL MERGERS

7.4.1 UNILATERAL EFFECTS ANALYSIS AS PART OF THE SLC TEST

This section focuses on horizontal mergers. Their main effect is to remove a company from the market, potentially reducing rivalry due to the structural change. We have seen that, in assessing horizontal mergers, SLC-type tests are very broad and allow for consideration of a wide range of effects. The first step is to articulate the theories of harm that might arise from the merger.

At a high level, the main theories of harm that are considered in horizontal mergers are unilateral and coordinated effects. The former refer to the changes in market behaviour that would be profitable for the merged entity, assuming a normal competitive response from the remaining competitors. Such effects (such as price rises) may also benefit the other market participants, but are not dependent on their cooperation. Concerns about unilateral effects arising from mergers are central in many inquiries. The most common assessment in unilateral effects is regarding whether the merging parties will have both the incentive and the ability to raise prices post-merger, but such effects also encompass a reduction in quality, customer choice, or innovation. An example of a broad set of potential unilateral effects being examined is Project Kangaroo, a proposed joint venture of video-on-demand (VOD) activities between three UK broadcasters (BBC, Channel 4, and ITV).[13] The joint venture was blocked by the CC for a number of reasons, including a concern that, in addition to potential price rises (or a reduction in the free content available), there was a serious risk of reductions in the quality of service offered by the three broadcasters and in their innovative activity as a result of the loss of rivalry from the joint venture.

---

[13] Competition Commission (2009), 'BBC Worldwide Limited, Channel Four Television Corporation and ITV plc', February. There were other findings of potential harm from the joint venture relating to vertical effects and the role of the parties as purchasers in particular markets.

Concerns about coordinated effects relate to a merger reducing competition by increasing the probability that, post-merger, companies in the same market tacitly coordinate their behaviour in order to raise prices or restrict output. These coordinated effects may arise where a merger situation reduces certain competitive constraints in a market (such as removing a maverick competitor), thus increasing the probability of competitors colluding, or where it facilitates transparency or retaliation, making a coordinated outcome more stable and therefore more likely. Coordinated effects were also found in the assessment of Project Kangaroo. Because the three joint-venture partners compete as suppliers of secondary television content to others, the CC was concerned that being partners would facilitate tacit coordination, allowing for strategies to be aligned across the joint venture and the individual partners (particularly ITV and Channel 4). This would result in less favourable terms for third parties. The economic framework for assessing coordinated effects is set out in Chapter 3; the difference from unilateral effects is that it is not only the merged entity that alters its behaviour—coordinated effects require the remaining competitors to adjust their behaviour as well.[14]

In this section we examine unilateral effects and consider the types of modelling that can be undertaken to determine how a merger may affect pricing and other strategic behaviour of the merged business. We first consider mergers of producers of homogeneous products, where the core analysis of market definition and market power comes to the fore. We then look at the complexities that arise when the merger is between two companies supplying differentiated products. In these cases you need to analyse how close the competition is between the two companies before drawing conclusions about the likely unilateral effects. Diversion analysis is used here as the key factor in understanding the likely impact on consumers. This feeds into models that simulate the likely effect on pricing behaviour resulting from the loss of rivalry.

7.4.2 UNILATERAL EFFECTS IN HOMOGENEOUS PRODUCT MARKETS: MARKET DEFINITION AND CONCENTRATION

Merging two companies combines their market strength and removes the rivalry that previously existed between them. Merger assessment needs to judge whether this is likely to lead to adverse effects on consumers. Where the products sold by the two companies are similar, adding together their market shares is an appropriate indicator of the potential additional force that the merged entity will have in the market. Assessing such mergers will mean that there is a strong focus on market definition and market share analysis, in line with the principles set out in Chapters 2 and 3. In homogeneous product mergers,

---

[14] The difference is not as clear-cut as it may seem. With unilateral effects, competitors also adjust their behaviour in the post-merger situation but do so with regard to their own optimal price and output, not through coordination. The main distinction is therefore a theoretical one, similar to what we saw in Chapter 3. Unilateral effects are based on static oligopoly theory—prices and outputs change from one competitive outcome to the next as the number of firms in the market is reduced by one. Coordinated effects relate to dynamic oligopoly theory, where firms seek to avoid competitive outcomes by tacitly colluding.

the greater the concentration resulting from the merger, the more likely it is that there will be a competition case to answer.

As we saw in Chapter 2, accurately defining the relevant market needs careful consideration of geographic aspects, demand- and supply-side substitutes, and whether other product attributes are sufficiently different to lead to different markets (eg, the time of purchase or the distribution channel). Chapter 2 also highlights the need to use the timeframe appropriate to the case at hand and to bear in mind that markets may be asymmetric (ie, one product may provide a greater competitive constraint on another than the other way round). The principles outlined in Chapter 2 are directly relevant when assessing mergers of reasonably homogeneous products (market definition becomes more complicated in markets with significant product differentiation).

Usually, the narrower the relevant market, the fewer companies there are, and hence the greater the likelihood of concerns about high concentration, but there are exceptions. In Chapter 2 we saw a case involving local bus services in Chester, where the defendant had a higher market share in the wider market because it had substantial operations in areas adjacent to Chester, whereas the claimant had a stronger position in the city itself. Another example provided in Chapter 2 related to geographic market definition in mobile telephony, where a merger between a German and UK operator would not be seen as problematic if the two countries were considered to be separate geographic markets. Such a situation also arose in the USA when Ovation Pharmaceuticals (now Lundbeck) purchased the drug NeoProfen from Abbott Laboratories. As the deal fell below the US reporting threshold, it was not scrutinized by the Federal Trade Commission (FTC) in advance, but was investigated after completion. Neoprofen is used to treat a potentially life-threatening heart defect affecting around 30,000 premature babies per year. A year before buying NeoProfen, Ovation had completed a deal with Merck & Co for the rights to Indocin, a similar drug. According to the FTC, Indocin was the only other drug available to treat the same heart condition as NeoProfen and, post-acquisition, Ovation raised the price of Indocin from $36 per vial to $500 while setting the price of NeoProfen at $483.[15] The FTC challenged the acquisition. However, the District Court found that the two drugs were not in the same relevant market as they were not bio-equivalent and their Food and Drug Administration approvals and side effects were different.[16] Prescribers testified that the price changes would not induce them to switch between the two drugs in treating the particular heart problem. Therefore the Court did not find an SLC. This is an example of where a finding of narrower markets in fact led to fewer SLC concerns, as it removed the alleged overlap between the merging parties.

Having defined the market, you can use the metrics and thresholds for market shares and concentration presented in Chapter 3. The first check is whether it is possible to conclude that the merging companies have such a small market share within any

---

[15] FTC File No 081-0156, 16 December 2008.
[16] *FTC v Lundbeck, Inc.* Civil No 08-6379 (D Minn, 31 August 2010).

reasonable market definition that there will be little chance of any unilateral effects. Market share assessment can be used here as a form of negative clearance, or as a filter to identify those cases that require further analysis. The EU Merger Regulation states that a market share of the merging parties of no more than 25% indicates that the concentration is too low to constitute an SIEC.[17] The EU approach is also that a post-merger HHI of below 1,000 (eg, ten firms each having 10% of the market) would not normally be considered problematic, and a post-merger HHI of between 1,000 and 2,000 and a delta (an increase in the HHI as a result of the merger) of below 250 would generally result in clearance. However, a post-merger HHI of above 2,000 would require further scrutiny if the delta is in excess of 150. In the USA, a post-merger HHI of below 1,500 would result in an approval of the merger, whereas a merger resulting in an HHI of above 1,500 and a delta of more than 100 points is said to 'often warrant scrutiny', and a merger resulting in an HHI above 2,500 and with a delta of more than 200 points is presumed to be likely to enhance market power.[18]

Where market shares or concentration are found to be high, the next stage will be to consider whether entry or expansion opportunities are sufficient to constrain any future significant price rises. If entry barriers are sufficiently low, even a merged entity with a high market share will be constrained by the threat of entry. Chapter 3 sets out the categories of barriers to entry, including absolute barriers such as patents and licences, and strategic barriers such as economies of scale and reputation. The absence of any sunk costs of entry may potentially give rise to a degree of contestability of the market, meaning that even a very high or 100% post-merger market share might not constitute an SLC. The last potential constraint on a large firm's ability to raise prices is if it has sufficiently strong buyers. A context in which buyer power can be particularly strong is in bidding markets. An additional factor to consider in mergers involving companies producing homogeneous goods is whether there is scope for the merged entity to engage in price discrimination. We saw in Chapter 2 that such an ability may give rise to separate price discrimination markets according to types of buyer, but even if you do not split the market such differences between buyers still need to be considered. In these cases, having some strong buyers may not be sufficient to ensure no SLC. The concern is about adverse effects on targeted customers, even if such effects do not have an impact on other customers. In *Cott/Macaw*—the merger between two producers of PET-bottled carbonated soft drinks (CSD) discussed in Chapter 3—the CC examined evidence on whether smaller retailers were less able than the larger ones to extract good terms from the CSD suppliers:

> we set out the factors that contribute to retailers having significant bargaining power over suppliers of own-label PET-bottled CSDs. We considered that the combination of (a) the dissemination of the effects of the buyer power of large retailers to smaller retailers, and (b) the presence of . . . other factors that provide smaller retailers with effective bargaining

---

[17] Council Regulation (EC) 139/2004 of 20 January 2004, [32].

[18] Department of Justice and Federal Trade Commission (2010), 'Horizontal Merger Guidelines', 19 August, p 19.

power, support the view that smaller retailers do not have a significantly weaker bargaining position than large retailers with respect to suppliers of own-label PET-bottled CSDs.[19]

Finally, what is the prospect of an SLC arising from unilateral effects in an oligopolistic market? In Chapter 3 we discussed competing oligopolists in a Cournot-type market (few suppliers; homogeneous goods). They recognize their interdependence, in that the output decisions of one have a strong impact on the profitability of the others. We also saw that with this type of market structure, as the number of firms is reduced, the market price is predicted to rise. The extent of such a price rise will depend on the demand elasticity, the number of firms (ie, whether the merger is three to two, or six to five), and the ease of any likely entry or expansion response of rivals. The tele.ring acquisition discussed in section 7.2 provides an example of this type of effect. While the merged entity was not the largest player in the market post-merger, the European Commission considered that the reduction in rivalry arising from the removal of tele.ring as an independent competitor would be likely to lead to a unilateral price increase.

7.4.3 UNILATERAL EFFECTS IN DIFFERENTIATED PRODUCT MARKETS: WHY MARKET SHARES ARE NOT ENOUGH

How frequently do we see truly homogeneous products? In many markets, companies seek to find ways to differentiate their offerings in order to build customer loyalty and to find the scope to raise prices. Therefore, most merger cases need to consider the complexities that arise when products are differentiated. Two main types of product differentiation are observed in merger analysis: branding (eg, cola, tissues, pens, clothing) and location (eg, grocery stores, cinemas, hospitals). In these cases, unilateral effects analysis involves an assessment of expected post-merger prices—ie, would the merger lead to an added incentive for, and ability of, the merged entity to raise prices on one or more of its products, and, if so, would the magnitude of the price rises suggest an SLC?

With product differentiation, market shares are no longer necessarily a good reflection of the loss of rivalry from combining two companies. This is quite intuitive—if two companies produce the same basic product (such as apples), adding together their apple production gives you a meaningful idea of their combined force in the eyes of competitors and consumers. If two companies produce different types of fruit (apples and oranges), it is not so straightforward to add them together. Some consumers may consider oranges a good substitute for apples, but others may prefer bananas or peaches. To understand whether this latter merger will lead to adverse effects on either apple or orange consumers (or both), an approach that recognizes the differentiation will be necessary.

This is a theme addressed in Chapter 2 on market definition. The tools for market definition work best if products are homogeneous. However, even if products are differentiated to some extent, it can still be useful to group together those that are in

---

[19] Competition Commission (2006), 'Cott Beverages Ltd and Macaw (Holdings) Ltd merger inquiry: Final report', 28 March, at [5.46]. We advised the merging parties in this inquiry.

reasonably uniform categories (top-of-the-range sports cars, Italian designer shoes) and apply the hypothetical monopolist test to each of the groups as if they consisted of homogeneous goods. Many of the aspects of market definition discussed in Chapter 2 (eg, supply-side substitution, market aggregation, and chains of substitution) can be specifically tailored to deal with the challenges of product differentiation. We also explained how economists have recently developed tools to apply critical loss analysis to groups of differentiated products.[20] Yet there comes a point when the degree of production differentiation is so high that market definition becomes too difficult, artificial and potentially misleading. The question becomes more about which products are each other's closest substitutes than about which products are inside or outside the boundaries of the relevant market. In these situations you can skip the market definition stage altogether and focus on the analysis of unilateral effects.

In such cases, the aim is to capture the 'closeness' of competition between the parties and, from this, to understand the likely effect of the merger on the merged firm's incentives. This means understanding the dynamics of the market and the choices likely to be made by customers and competitors in response to changes in the pricing of one of the products. Rather than market shares, the key measure is diversion ratios. These represent the proportion of sales captured by substitute products when the price of one product is increased—ie, they capture the closeness of competition between products. Before examining the techniques for unilateral effects analysis, let's consider two examples that illustrate the main principles of closeness of competition. The first is in the market for baby food in the USA, with Heinz's proposed acquisition of Beech-Nut.[21] The second is from the UK, where LOVEFiLM, an online DVD and games subscription rental service, acquired the similar business line from Amazon (we considered this case in Chapter 2 as well).[22] The combined share of Heinz and Beech-Nut in baby food was around 30%–35% and the merger was blocked in 2000. The combined share of LOVEFiLM and Amazon in online DVD and games rentals was around 90% and yet the merger was cleared. This illustrates that market shares do not paint the full picture.

Heinz and Beech-Nut were the second- and third-largest suppliers in the US baby food market, significantly behind Gerber, which had around 65% of the market. The Court of Appeals upheld the FTC's injunction to halt the transaction. The FTC's rationale was that, although the merging parties were relatively small, with market shares of around 15%–20% each, they were each other's closest competitor. Competition between the parties mainly took place in vying for shelf space at retail outlets, including offering lower prices and promotions. Most retailers stocked two baby food product ranges— Gerber plus either Heinz or Beech-Nut. (In this regard, Gerber was a 'must stock' item for retailers; a theme we discussed in the context of loyalty rebates in Chapter 4.)

---

[20] See Farrell and Shapiro (2008), Daljord, Sørgard, and Thomassen (2008), and ten Kate and Niels (2010).

[21] *FTC v HJ Heinz Co* 246 F 3d 708 (US Ct of Apps (District of Colombia Cir.), 2001).

[22] Office of Fair Trading (2008), 'Anticipated acquisition of the online DVD rental subscription business of Amazon Inc. by LOVEFiLM International Limited', ME/3534/08, 8 May. We advised the acquiring party in this transaction.

The competition between the two smaller rivals led to pressure on Gerber's pricing as well. Post-merger, it would be removed, and entry by other parties was considered unlikely because barriers were high. The Court found that:

> the merger will eliminate competition between the two merging parties at the wholesale level, where they are currently the only competitors for what the district court described as the 'second position on the supermarket shelves.' [*HJ Heinz* 116 F Supp 2d at 196.] Heinz's own documents recognize the wholesale competition and anticipate that the merger will end it. Indeed, those documents disclose that Heinz considered three options to end the vigorous wholesale competition with Beech-Nut: two involved innovative measures while the third entailed the acquisition of Beech-Nut. Heinz chose the third, and least pro-competitive, of the options.[23]

Hence, an analysis of the nature of competition in the market highlighted the harmful unilateral effects that would arise if the merger were to proceed, despite the low market shares of the merging parties and the strength of the main competitor in the market.

The issue of the closest competing products also arose in *LOVEFiLM/Amazon* (2008). Online DVD rental involves customers paying a fixed monthly fee entitling them to select and receive DVDs. The number of DVDs rented is determined by the tariff package and the speed at which the customer returns each DVD (there is no limit on how long you can keep a DVD, but until you return it you won't receive the next one). This was a relatively new type of business model, having been launched only in 2004, and the merged entity would have a share of online DVD rentals of 92%. Despite this strong position, the OFT approved the merger with no undertakings required. The evidence showed that customers saw other methods of acquiring DVD content as close substitutes—including renting DVDs from 'bricks and mortar' rental shops and downloading films—and that both businesses regularly monitored activities in these other products, confirming the competitive constraint. This evidence was consistent with online DVD rentals forming part of a wider relevant market, and with the two merged businesses not being each other's closest competitors; either way, the conclusion was that no SLC would result from the merger.

These two cases tell us that merger assessment is more complicated than measuring the relative size of the merging parties. How do we assess the closeness of competition? The basic economic principles are the same as those discussed in Chapter 2 in the context of the SSNIP test. We next consider diversion ratios in greater detail and how to calculate them as an input to estimating the price effects of the merger.

7.4.4 UNILATERAL EFFECTS IN DIFFERENTIATED PRODUCT MARKETS: DIVERSION RATIOS

We explained diversion ratios in Chapter 2 in the context of finding the closest substitutes as part of market definition. Here we explore how diversion ratios can be used for

---

[23] *FTC v HJ Heinz Co* 246 F 3d 708 (US Ct of Apps (District of Colombia Cir.), 2001).

unilateral effects analysis of mergers. Diversion ratios measure the proportion of sales diverted to substitute products when the price of a particular product is increased. For example, suppose the sales of product A fall from 1,000 to 900 units when A's price increases by 5%, and 30 and 70 of the lost units are captured by products B and C, respectively. The diversion ratio from A to B is 30%, and the diversion ratio from A to C is 70%. This indicates that product C is the closest substitute for product A. As set out in Chapter 2, diversion ratios are related to own- and cross-price elasticities: the former determine the volume of sales lost after the price increase (here the 10% loss of sales after a 5% price increase implies that the elasticity was –2); the latter capture the degree of substitutability between products. In general, the higher the diversion ratio between products, the closer substitutes they are, and the more intense the competition is between them. As with market share calculations, you have a choice about whether to measure diversion in volume or value terms depending on the specifics of the products. Sales or customer diversion ratios measure the effects in volumes (as with the 30% and 70% in the example above) and revenue diversion ratios capture diversions in terms of value.

How can you obtain the necessary information on diversion ratios? Three avenues are commonly explored. First, there may be evidence on diversion ratios from data collected by the companies during their normal course of business (ie, not for the purpose of the merger investigation). Businesses sometimes ask existing customers who are leaving where they are switching to, or ask new customers where they formerly purchased the product. In such cases it may be possible to estimate diversion ratios based on this information, although in practice such information may not be representative of customer behaviour in general, or may not capture the full breadth of diversion options that are relevant for the competition inquiry.

Second, diversion ratios can be directly calculated from own- and cross-price elasticities. Sometimes relevant elasticity estimates may be available from existing analyses of demand—eg, elasticity estimates carried out in the context of a previous competition case or in published economic studies of the sector in question. More commonly, you may have to carry out your own elasticity estimations in the context of a demand system—using the techniques explained in Chapter 2 (unilateral effects analysis builds on the same demand system as the hypothetical monopolist test). The elasticity estimates and demand system can then be used to simulate the price effect of the merger. Industries where detailed price and quantity data is collected—eg, store scanner data—often lend themselves to such empirical elasticity modelling and merger simulation. The *Volvo/Scania* merger (2000) is an example of where this approach has been adopted—see below.

Third, diversion ratios can be gathered directly using consumer surveys. Given the difficulties with the above two approaches when insufficient data is available, a consumer survey tends to be the most common and practical method for obtaining diversion ratios in competition cases. This involves asking consumers directly which alternative product or supplier they would substitute to if they were to switch away from the currently chosen product following a small price increase or the removal of that product altogether (eg, 'if the shop you have just visited were closed, which shop would you use instead?'). In Chapter 2 we discussed best practice and potential pitfalls in designing consumer surveys. The 2010 US Horizontal Merger Guidelines confirm the suitability of these data sources:

> The Agencies consider any reasonably available and reliable information to evaluate the extent of direct competition between the products sold by the merging firms. This includes documentary and testimonial evidence, win/loss reports and evidence from discount approval processes, customer switching patterns, and customer surveys.[24]

A case where diversion ratio evidence from consumer surveys played an important role is the *Co-op/Somerfield* (2008) supermarket merger, which was cleared at phase one by the OFT.[25] The OFT based its decision on what it described as 'probably the largest consumer survey ever conducted in a merger case.'[26] More than 40,000 customers were surveyed in over 400 Co-op and Somerfield stores. Here, customers were asked where they would do their grocery shopping if the store where the survey was conducted were to close. In general, higher diversion ratios between merging stores imply more intense, or 'closer', competition between the stores pre-merger, and hence higher predicted post-merger price rises. This is because a high diversion ratio means that many customers would shop at the Co-op (acquiring) store if the Somerfield (target) store were closed (ie, customers view the merging stores to be close substitutes). A merger between the stores would remove the competitive constraints that they impose on each other and might therefore lead to price increases. Potential competition concerns were identified for 126 local markets, and divestment remedies were agreed for those markets.

7.4.5 UNILATERAL EFFECTS IN DIFFERENTIATED PRODUCT MARKETS: 'SIMPLE' SIMULATIONS OF THE PRICE EFFECTS OF A MERGER

While diversion ratios are useful, the question remains: when are close competitors too close? Diversion ratios are not enough on their own to draw conclusions about the prospect of an SLC because they do not tell you how the threat of this diversion will affect the pricing decisions of the merged company. To do this, we need to consider the diversion evidence within a framework of how prices will be set post-merger. To undertake this analysis, competition authorities have available a whole spectrum of tools of varying levels of complexity. At one end, very simple assumptions on company behaviour and demand can be used; at the other end, a full merger simulation could be undertaken, incorporating sophisticated demand system conditions and allowing for various forms of interaction among companies. Between these extremes there are tools

---

[24] Department of Justice and Federal Trade Commission (2010), 'Horizontal Merger Guidelines', August, p 20.

[25] Office of Fair Trading (2008), 'Anticipated Acquisition by Co-operative Group Limited of Somerfield Limited', November. We advised the acquiring party in this transaction.

[26] Office of Fair Trading (2008), 'OFT Considers Grocery Store Divestments in Co-op/Somerfield Merger', press release 120/08, 20 October.

which relax some of the assumptions of the simplest approaches without being as comprehensive (and time- and data-intensive) as a full merger simulation.

We set out these approaches below, but first we go through the basic economic framework. This begins with the pricing logic of a profit-maximizing company after it has acquired a similar, but differentiated, competitor product. The process is very similar to that set out in Chapter 2 for considering the behaviour of the hypothetical monopolist in the SSNIP test. The reason for this similarity is that product differentiation gives the supplier a position of monopoly power over its own brand. In essence, in unilateral effects analysis you have the same demand system as for the hypothetical monopolist test, except that every product (brand) is already a monopoly, so you can focus the analysis on competition between products (brands). With control over two products (brands) post-merger, the merged entity will consider its incentive to raise the price of the new product portfolio, in the same way that our hypothetical monopolist sets prices in the second iteration of the hypothetical monopolist test, where it controls the focal product and the nearest substitute. Pre-merger, if it raised the price of its existing product, it would earn higher profit margins on the sales it continued to make, but would lose the margins on sales that would be lost as a result of the price rise. Owning both products post-merger, the company will no longer be concerned about losing sales to the recently acquired product. Whether it is profitable to raise prices will therefore depend on the company's margins on the existing and new products and the diversion between the two. If it is rational to raise prices post-merger in this framework, the merger is more likely to result in an SLC. There are no clear-cut thresholds, but 5% is commonly used for judging a price increase to be sufficient to lead to an SLC.

Full merger simulation is not always practical as it is demanding in terms of data and modelling complexity. There are simpler models of competition that are less data-intensive and that can be—and indeed have been—applied in order to calculate 'indicative' or 'illustrative' price increases post-merger. The most common approach is to take the Bertrand oligopoly model of symmetric differentiated goods (see Chapter 3 for an explanation of this model). Bertrand competition means that companies compete on price and that capacity is not constrained. With homogeneous products, these assumptions mean that the Bertrand oligopolists behave as if the market were perfectly competitive and prices are in line with marginal costs. With differentiated products, raising the price of one product does not lead to the entire market switching to the cheapest supplier—customers have differing preferences for the various product characteristics and this gives each company some market power. In this model, price will be above marginal cost in equilibrium—by how much will largely depend on the degree of differentiation and the number of competitors. To 'simulate' the effect of the merger, you add two of the products together and you get a new equilibrium of prices and outputs. By comparing the pre- and post-merger outcomes, you get an indication of the price effect of the merger. All you need for this simulation exercise are estimates of the diversion ratios (eg, from your survey) and data on existing price–cost margins.

How does this work in practice? In the simplest situation, we consider two products, A and B, which are merged. They have the same price–cost margin (m; this is the same m as used in the critical loss formula in Chapter 2), and the diversion ratios (d) from A to B and from B to A are symmetric. A further assumption relates to the shape of the demand curve. The two most commonly used shapes are linear demand (as in the charts presented in Chapters 2 and 3) and isoelastic demand (where the own-price elasticity is equal along the whole of the demand curve; in Chapter 2 we explained that with linear and most other forms of demand the elasticity changes as you move along the curve). Based on all these assumptions, the Bertrand model generates a formula for the post-merger price increase, and this formula depends only on m and d. For linear demand the price increase equals $md / 2(1 - d)$. For isoelastic demand it is $md / (1 - m - d)$. Table 7.1 takes you through these calculations and shows the sensitivities of the simulated price rises to different demand assumptions and different values for m and d.

Some of the results of the sensitivity tests in Table 7.1 are intuitive. You can see that where margins are higher, the optimal price rise post-merger is significantly greater (particularly for the isoelastic demand curve specification, where the price increase changes from 20% to 60% as m changes from 40% to 60%, for the same level of diversion). The margin indicates the degree to which a company can set prices independently of its competitors—theoretically, the higher the margin, the weaker the competitive constraints faced by the company, and hence, the greater the ability to increase prices (we explained this Lerner relationship in Chapter 3). With higher margins pre-merger, the company will be reluctant to raise its prices further since every lost sale means a significant loss of margin. Post-merger, the fact that the company does not lose the margin on the sales that divert to the other product means that it is more willing to raise its price. In the last scenario—with low diversion—overall the price rises are lower. Low diversion means that consumers do not see the products as close substitutes, and therefore the unilateral effect of the merger is weaker.

Table 7.1 also demonstrates the sensitivity with respect to the demand assumptions. Across all three examples, the difference between isoelastic and linear is very marked. If the competition authority were to use a 5% threshold for the price rise, in one of these scenarios the merger would be cleared if the linear specification is used, but it would be

Table 7.1 Simulated price rises

Description	Moderate margin and diversion	High margin	Low diversion
Margin (m)	40% = 0.4	60% = 0.6	40% = 0.4
Diversion ratio (d)	20% = 0.2	20% = 0.2	10% = 0.1
m × d	0.08	0.12	0.04
1 − m − d	0.4	0.2	0.5
1 − d	0.8	0.8	0.9
Price rise, isoelastic demand: $md / (1 - m - d)$	0.2 = 20%	0.6 = 60%	0.08 = 8%
Price rise, linear demand: $md / 2(1 - d)$	0.05 = 5%	0.075 = 7.5%	0.022 = 2.2%

blocked in all three cases if the isoelastic specification is used. Why does the demand assumption matter so much? Recall our discussion in Chapter 2 of critical loss analysis and the difference between what a monopolist 'could' profitably do and what it 'would' do to maximize profits. Here we are focused on profit-maximizing choices—ie, what the merged entity would do—and therefore the particular shape of the demand curve matters. In addition to linear and isoelastic demand there are other possible specifications, such as logit demand and the almost ideal demand system (AIDS); we refer to these below, when discussing full merger simulation.

With all other assumptions remaining the same, the post-merger predicted price rise with isoelastic demand will be higher than that with linear demand (as Table 7.1 demonstrates). This is because linear demand reflects a realistic, self-correcting mechanism: as the price rises, demand becomes more elastic and therefore consumers become more likely to switch away (we explained this in Chapter 2). This makes the merged entity less keen to raise prices. By contrast, in the isoelastic formulation the responsiveness to prices does not alter regardless of the level. Figure 7.2 shows how the different demand functions will change the simulated price increase. Pre-merger, we are at point A and we want to estimate the profit-maximizing position for prices post-merger. Knowing the elasticity at point A and making different assumptions about the shape of the demand curve allows us to extrapolate the demand curve—this is shown as the four lines fanning out from point A. Given the evidence on how much of the lost demand will divert back to the commonly owned product, we can then determine the optimal price increase on the focal product. This is shown in the diagram as a dot on each of the lines. You can see that the price rises are higher along the isoelastic curve and that this effect becomes more marked as the optimal price rise gets larger. The AIDS and logit specifications sit somewhere in the middle.

So which demand specification should you use? This requires a deeper understanding of the market. Because the isoelastic demand function lacks a self-correction

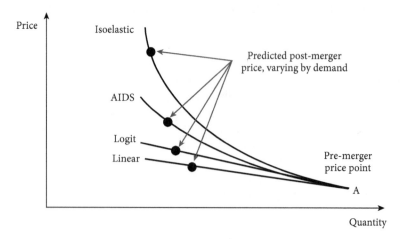

Fig. 7.2 Predictions of optimal rises in price for different demand functions
Source: Based on Crooke et al. (1999).

mechanism, it is less realistic and should be used with caution as it may predict very high and unrealistic price increases—in the *Somerfield/Morrisons* supermarket merger, the CC found price rises exceeding 1,000% based on the assumption of isoelastic demand.[27] Often it may be good practice to consider more than one formulation and then judge whether the evidence in the round is suggestive of a problematic price rise. This also highlights the attractiveness of a full merger simulation. By actually estimating the demand functions, there is no need to make these types of assumption; however, as we explain below, this is not an easy option and the level of complexity can lead to much uncertainty over the final price rise predictions.

7.4.6 EXTENSIONS TO 'SIMPLE' MODELS OF UNILATERAL EFFECTS— EFFICIENCIES AND ASYMMETRY OF DIVERSION

The indicative price rise method discussed above lies at the more simplistic end of the possible approaches to simulating merger price effects. It has the important advantage of being a straightforward and transparent tool. However, this comes at the expense of a number of restrictive assumptions, which do not allow it to incorporate certain features that may be relevant in any particular case, such as merger efficiencies and the possibility that the constraints the companies place on each other are asymmetric. In some cases you may relax some of these assumptions.

We discuss in section 7.6 how merger efficiencies in general can be incorporated into the analysis. Here we discuss the narrower point of how to incorporate any variable cost efficiencies into the price rise analysis. As we discuss in Chapter 10 (in the context of the pass-on of cartel overcharges), if the variable or unit cost of production decreases, even a profit-maximizing monopolist will have an incentive to pass on part of this cost reduction. Thus, if the merger delivers such cost efficiencies (for example, by giving the merged entity greater negotiating strength and therefore an ability to purchase inputs more cheaply), this will reduce the potential price rises—indeed, if large enough, it could even lead to price reductions post-merger (see also Figure 7.1). In the case of linear demand, there is a simple adjustment to the price-rise formula that takes into account such efficiencies: the price rise becomes $md / 2(1 - d) - \Delta m/2$, where, as above, m is the pre-merger margin and d is the diversion ratio. Δm reflects the increase in the product margin due to the cost reductions from efficiencies. In this linear demand formulation, half of the cost savings will be passed on in the form of a lower price increase. As an illustration, using the final scenario in Table 7.1 (40% margins, 10% diversion ratios), if merger efficiencies are forecast to deliver a 3% increase in variable margins then we would expect only a 0.7% price increase with linear demand, compared with 2.2% without efficiencies. If these efficiencies were as high as 5%, this would in fact lead to a predicted price *reduction* post-merger. A recent case where merger efficiencies were considered as part of the price-rise analysis was the South African Competition Tribunal

---

[27] Competition Commission (2005), 'Somerfield plc/Wm Morrison Supermarkets plc: A Report on the Acquisition by Somerfield plc of 115 Stores from Wm Morrison Supermarkets plc', September.

assessment of the *Masscash/Finro* merger in the groceries wholesale sector.[28] Assuming linear demand, the Tribunal found that a 1% efficiency assumption would lead to a reduction in the predicted price rises of half a percentage point.

The assumption made thus far that diversion is symmetric means that there is no significant difference in the choice set or preferences of customers whether they start at product A or B. Given that we are in a differentiated product environment, this may not be a realistic assumption. In practice, one company may constrain the other company's pricing more strongly than the other way round. For example, in a merger where location is key, it may be that one of the stores has a number of other competitors close to it, but that they are too far away to affect the other store. This is likely to lead to the diversions between the stores being different since customers at one store have more choice than customers at the other. The additional data requirements for calculating the price rise using this approach are relatively limited—you need data on the margins of both parties and the diversion ratios from the perspective of their products or locations.

The formula becomes a bit more complicated and rather than describing it here we show how the results in Table 7.1 may change.[29] Looking at the first column in Table 7.1, we assume that, instead of there being a symmetric 20% diversion between the two products, the diversion from A to B is 30% and the diversion from B to A is 10%. This means that B places more of a constraint on A than the other way round. With the symmetric diversion, the simulated price rise was 5%. With asymmetric diversion we predict that the price of A will rise by 6.7% and the price of B will rise by only 3.3%. The intuition is that since product B is more of a constraint pre-merger on product A than A is on B, post-merger the price of A will rise more as this constraint is removed.

7.4.7 FULL MERGER SIMULATION MODELS

A full merger simulation is the most comprehensive and complex approach to estimating the price effects of a merger, accommodating a variety of features such as asymmetries among companies, merger-specific efficiencies, and various forms of interaction among companies in the market. The approach involves specifying an appropriate industrial organization (IO) model that reasonably reflects the nature of competition in the market (this can be different from the differentiated-goods Bertrand model used in the 'simple' approach above), and a demand function reflecting consumer preferences and responses in the market. The model is then calibrated using actual market data on factors such as prices, quantities, and market shares. Some of the data used for this purpose, such as pre-merger prices and market shares, is often readily available (eg, from industry reports or the merging parties' own market intelligence), but parameters such as the elasticity of demand will usually need to be estimated. Whereas above we focused on linear or isoelastic demand specifications, in full demand-system

[28] *Masscash Holdings (Pty) v Finro Enterprises (Pty) Ltd t/a Finro Cash and Carry* (04/LM/Jan09) [2009] ZACT 66 (Competition Tribunal in South Africa). We assisted the South African Competition Commission in this case.
[29] See Oxera (2010b).

modelling, the logit and AIDS models are often preferred as they are more flexible demand specifications. The logit framework treats consumer demand decisions as a series of discrete choices (as in the *Kraft Foods/Cadbury* example discussed below). The AIDS framework is more flexible and assumes that consumers allocate their budget between products rather than making discrete choices. The use of full merger simulations has been limited because of their complexity and data requirements. The 2010 US Horizontal Merger Guidelines state that:

> Where sufficient data are available, the Agencies may construct economic models designed to quantify the unilateral price effects resulting from the merger . . . The Agencies do not treat merger simulation evidence as conclusive in itself, and they place more weight on whether their merger simulations consistently predict substantial price increases than on the precise prediction of any single simulation.[30]

Nonetheless, it is useful to consider a number of cases where such models have been used in the SLC assessment. One is *United States v Interstate Bakeries Corp and Continental Baking Co*, which involved a merger between two leading wholesalers of white pan bread in Chicago and Los Angeles.[31] The approach used a Bertrand oligopoly model to reflect the brand-level competition in the market, and a logit demand to represent the demand conditions. It accounted for the competitive constraints imposed by the closest competitors of the merging parties in the two areas. Under this approach, the predicted price increases were around 5%–10% for the merging parties and 3%–6% in the overall market. In the end, the merger simulation was not relied on in court as the parties reached an out-of-court settlement. A similar model was considered by the European Commission in the *Volvo/Scania* merger between two manufacturers of trucks, buses, and other industrial equipment.[32] The simulation employed a logit demand system and a Bertrand model of price competition, and predicted price increases in excess of 10% in most markets. It was criticized by the merging parties in relation to data measurement errors, and the mismatch between actual price–cost margins and those estimated by the model. In its final decision, the Commission did not rely on the results, stating that:

> Given the novelty of the approach and the level of disagreement, the Commission will not base its assessments on the results of the study.[33]

The Commission did, however, rely on a model of this kind in the *Lagardere/Natexis/VUP* merger between suppliers in the market for communication, media, and creative publishing. In this case the model and the simulated price rise were found to be robust and reliable.[34]

A very different simulation model, involving auctions, was considered by the European Commission in the *Oracle/Peoplesoft* merger between the second- and

---

[30] Department of Justice and Federal Trade Commission (2010), 'Horizontal Merger Guidelines', August, p 21.

[31] See Werden (2000).

[32] *Volvo/Scania* (Case COMP/M.1672) [2001] OJ L143/74. See also Ivaldi and Verboven (2005).

[33] Ibid., at [75].

[34] *Lagardere/Natexis/VUP* (Case COMP/M.2978) [2004] OJ L125/54. See also Budzinski and Ruhmer (2008).

third-largest vendors of service software products.[35] A sealed-bid auction model was used to represent the competition in procurement, along with possible efficiency gains. Although the model predicted price increases of 6.8%–30% for various products, it was later disregarded by the Commission in light of new evidence and subsequent doubts over the reliability of results. The Department of Justice, which was also assessing the merger, found similar price effects while using a different auction format (English auction with complete information). Nonetheless, the District Court rejected this model on the basis of the uncertainty of the predictions.[36]

A further example of the European Commission's reliance on merger simulation is seen in Kraft's acquisition of Cadbury, approved (with conditions) at phase one in 2010.[37] In this case a detailed econometric merger simulation was conducted by the merging parties. The chocolate sector was divided into three segments: countlines (chocolate bars), tablets, and pralines. In the UK and Ireland the merged entity would have high market shares of 30%–40% in countlines and pralines and 60%–70% in tablets, where both companies had a number of strong brands (Toblerone, Milka, and Côte D'Or for Kraft; Dairy Milk, Green & Blacks, and Bournville for Cadbury). The merging parties based their merger simulation analysis on a differentiated-goods Bertrand model of price competition and employed a nested logit demand system. This effectively allows for a two-stage ('nested') structure of consumers' choices: first, the choice between consuming a countline, tablet, or praline product and, second, the choice of the brand within the selected segment. The model predicted a price increase of less than 1% in the UK and Irish markets. The Commission requested further sensitivity analyses of these results, but concluded that 'this merger simulation provides further evidence that the proposed operation is unlikely to lead to significant price increases in the UK and Ireland.'[38]

7.4.8 RIVALS' REACTIONS—ENTRY AND REPOSITIONING

The merger simulation approaches discussed above—both the simple and more complex ones—assess what happens to prices in the market if two products or brands are joined together. They do so by taking the current degree of product differentiation as given—ie, products themselves do not change the way they are positioned in the market and relative to each other; all that changes is that two products that were previously independent are now brought under common ownership. In reality, however, other suppliers may reposition their products in response to the merger. Analysing such repositioning is complicated, and to a great extent speculative. The US Guidelines suggest that repositioning can be analysed in a similar way to entry:

> In some cases, non-merging firms may be able to reposition their products to offer close substitutes for the products offered by the merging firms. Repositioning is a supply-side

---

[35] *Oracle/Peoplesoft* (Case COMP/M.3216) [2005] OJ L218/6.
[36] *United States of America et al. v Oracle Corporation* 331 F 2d 1098 (ND Cal 2004).
[37] *Kraft Foods/Cadbury* (Case COMP/M.5644) [2010] OJ C29/4.
[38] Ibid., at [69].

response that is evaluated much like entry, with consideration given to timeliness, likelihood, and sufficiency.[39]

This means that the likelihood of repositioning will depend on the sunk costs associated with repositioning, as well as the length of time that any such response would take. Repositioning usually reduces any concern about an SLC—even if the merging parties are each other's closest competitors, other rivals may enter this part of the product-differentiation spectrum. Yet repositioning may also be done by the merged entity. One case that shows both effects is Heinz's acquisition of HP Foods UK in 2006.[40] This deal led to a potential overlap in a number of sauce products, baked beans, and other tinned food products. It was unconditionally cleared by the CC on the basis that the Heinz and HP brands were not close competitors in ketchup and baked beans, although barriers to entry were high for these products. For other sauce products, the CC found that there was a sufficient threat of entry. A 2009 review of past merger decisions of the UK government and competition authorities showed that products in this market were subsequently repositioned in a way that was not predicted by the CC at the time (Deloitte, 2009). There was successful entry into the baked beans segment, with the new entrant capturing 10% of the market (supporting the clearance of the merger). However, Heinz itself repositioned a number of its sauce brands and entered the brown sauce market, suggesting that it might now be more difficult for entrants to fill this space in the spectrum of differentiated products.

7.4.9 DIRECT ESTIMATES OF PRICE EFFECTS

So far in this section, we have presented some practical approaches to assessing the unilateral effects of a horizontal merger, all of which involve simulation of the likely increase in price. In homogeneous products, we use concentration analysis and an understanding of entry barriers to estimate the likely extent of price effects. For differentiated products, these estimates are based on extrapolating pre-merger demand conditions and information on diversion ratios. An alternative route is to look for a 'natural experiment' which gives a direct indication of how prices might be expected to change post-merger. The US Horizontal Merger Guidelines set out the relevant types of evidence in this category:

> The Agencies look for historical events, or 'natural experiments', that are informative regarding the competitive effects of the merger. For example, the Agencies may examine the impact of recent mergers, entry, expansion, or exit in the relevant market. Effects of analogous events in similar markets may also be informative.

Competition authorities also look for reliable evidence based on variations among similar markets. For example, if the merging firms compete in some locales but not others,

---

[39] Department of Justice and Federal Trade Commission (2010), 'Horizontal Merger Guidelines', August, p 22.

[40] Competition Commission (2006), 'HJ Heinz and HP Foods', 24 March.

comparisons of prices charged in regions where they do and do not compete may be informative regarding post-merger prices.[41]

One of the best-known examples of this technique is the *Staples/Office Depot* (1997) merger where the FTC looked at how the pricing of these two retail chains of large office supply stores differed pre-merger across local markets (we discussed this case in Chapter 1).[42] It found evidence in internal documents that the two chains saw each other as direct competitors and that they generally set lower prices in those cities in which both chains had a presence than in cities where only one of them had a store. The FTC's econometric analysis confirmed this, showing a statistically significant price difference of more than 5% between cities with just one of these stores and cities with both (after controlling for any other factors that may have contributed to the price difference). On this basis, the FTC concluded that the merger would lead to a price increase.

The European Commission pursued this type of econometric evidence in analysing Ryanair's acquisition of Aer Lingus in 2007.[43] It identified significant overlaps between the two airlines in 35 point-to-point markets. In 22 markets the merger would create a monopoly and in the other 13 markets it would lead to market shares above 60%. The Commission highlighted that this was an unusual airline merger case since it involved two airlines based at the same airport. Believing that there was a significant likelihood that the high market shares indicated dominance, it investigated whether the two airlines were each other's closest competitors and the extent to which Ryanair's prices were affected by the presence of Aer Lingus on a route. Both the Commission and Ryanair used econometric evidence to investigate the direct effect of the merger. Ryanair undertook a study of 313 city pairs on which it operated and systematically tested for any price differences between the routes depending on whether Aer Lingus was present on the route. The Commission estimated the impact of the entry of Ryanair on routes operated by Aer Lingus. It considered that the effect on competition of Ryanair's entry on a route in the past was a good natural experiment to understand the likely effect of the removal of this competitive constraint after the merger. The Commission used what is known as a 'difference-in-differences' regression technique (see Chapter 10 for more detail on this technique), which covers information both over time and across a number of different routes. Its study found that Aer Lingus's prices were 5%–8% lower when Ryanair was present on a route, and that the same effect was not observed when other carriers had entered a route. In contrast, Ryanair's approach (which had comparisons only across routes, not over time) found there to be no significant difference in its pricing depending on the presence of Aer Lingus. The Commission rejected Ryanair's approach on the grounds of a lack of robustness and also did not accept that it was a suitable natural experiment for judging the price effect. It undertook further analysis in order to understand the actual pricing behaviour of the two parties, the likelihood of

[41] Department of Justice and Federal Trade Commission (2010), 'Horizontal Merger Guidelines', August, p 3.

[42] *FTC v Staples Inc* 970 F Supp 1066 (DDC 1997). See also Baker (1999).

[43] *Ryanair/Aer Lingus* (Case COMP/M.4439), July 2007.

entry, and the scope for efficiencies to offset any identified SLC. It concluded that the result of the proposed merger would be the creation or strengthening of a dominant position on the overlap routes.

7.5 NON-HORIZONTAL MERGERS

7.5.1 A DIFFERENT CONCERN

Non-horizontal mergers involve companies that do not compete in the same market. They often involve the merger of complementary goods—a bottling plant is a complement to a water spring (a 'vertical complements' merger), and a gin factory is a complement to a tonic producer (a 'horizontal complements' merger). As we know from Chapter 2, bringing two complementary goods together under the control of one company has exactly the opposite effect of combining two substitutes: prices will fall rather than rise. The logic is that the merged entity is now actually concerned that raising prices by too much will have a negative impact on demand for both of the goods it controls. In a vertical merger context this is known as solving the problem of double marginalization—we explain this in Chapter 6 on vertical restraints. For this reason, non-horizontal mergers often lead to lower prices for consumers, and in the main do not raise significant competition concerns. Another reason for welcoming the combination of complementary goods is that it can eliminate inefficiencies in investment decisions, such as coordination problems and 'hold-ups' (again, see Chapter 6).

The concerns about non-horizontal mergers are different. The theories of harm put forward in this type of merger are similar to those we saw in Chapter 4 on abuse of dominance: the ability and incentive to harm rivals in upstream and downstream markets by raising their costs through some form of refusal to supply, bundling, or leveraging. In some sense non-horizontal merger control is trying to protect against these practices materializing post-merger. Indeed, a 2007 speech by a Commissioner at the FTC noted that, since 1979, the US federal agencies had not litigated to the point of conclusion a single merger challenge on a vertical theory, partly reflecting a preference to tackle these theories of harm ex post under the conduct rules in antitrust law, rather than ex ante at the time of the merger review (Rosch, 2007).[44]

In this section we discuss three types of non-horizontal merger—vertical, diagonal, and mergers with portfolio effects. A vertical merger is between different layers of the supply chain (eg, a water spring and a bottling plant), where the latter relies on an input (ie, water) from the former. A diagonal merger is between an upstream company and a downstream company that does not use that upstream company's input, but competes with other downstream companies that do use the input. A merger with portfolio and range effects is one between companies that supply goods that may be successfully bundled or tied together—eg, a merger of horizontal complements. All these non-horizontal

---

[44] The 1979 merger litigation was *Fruehauf Corp v FTC* 603 F 2d 345 (2d Cir. 1979).

combinations produce no immediate change in the level of concentration in any relevant market—and are therefore not caught by market share or HHI thresholds (although some mergers have both horizontal and non-horizontal aspects). The theories of harm to consumers are based on concerns about a merged company's ability to foreclose rivals post-merger. To assess this, the questions to ask are:

- Does the merged entity have the ability to foreclose rivals?
- Does it have the incentive to foreclose rivals?
- Is there a negative effect on competition?[45]

Only if all three conditions are met would there be serious concerns about the unilateral effects of the non-horizontal merger on competition. In particular, the ability and incentive to exclude certain competitors does not always equate to the ability to harm competition to the detriment of consumers—hence the final question as to whether competition, and consumers, will be harmed by the foreclosure, taking account of efficiencies and the extent of foreclosure of competitors (as we saw in Chapter 4, foreclosure is a matter of degree and only significant foreclosure would be of concern). Non-horizontal mergers are more likely than horizontal mergers to generate consumer benefits since, as noted above, the cost savings of eliminating double marginalization and investment hold-up can be passed on to consumers. Yet in the legal assessment, efficiencies remain a 'defence' (ie, the burden of proof is on the parties), just as is the case in horizontal mergers. Indeed, the very efficiencies created by a non-horizontal merger may be used against it—we discuss this 'efficiency offence' in section 7.6.

An alternative theory of harm for non-horizontal mergers is around coordinated effects (see Chapter 3)—the ability to foreclose rivals (or at least make their life difficult) that is brought about by some non-horizontal mergers can be an additional punishment mechanism to facilitate tacit collusion, and the possibility of profits from coordination might be sufficient to provide an incentive to foreclose.

The final general point to note on non-horizontal mergers is that all these theories of harm—refusal to supply, raising rivals' costs, and bundling—are similar or identical to the concerns raised in abuse of dominance and vertical restraint cases (as discussed in Chapters 4 and 6). The possible threat of action under Article 102 (or 101) is something the authorities can take into account when determining whether a particular theory of harm is likely to occur. This may to some extent require a policy choice between ex ante merger control and ex post competition enforcement. The merged entity itself may also weigh up the risk of being found dominant if it goes ahead with a certain foreclosure strategy and may adjust its behaviour accordingly; something which the competition authority in turn could take into account at the merger review stage.

---

[45] This approach is reflected in European Commission (2008), 'Guidelines on the assessment of non-horizontal mergers under the Council Regulation on the control of concentrations between undertakings' [2008] OJ C265/07, 18 October.

7.5.2 ASSESSING A VERTICAL MERGER

The *ability* to foreclose is a matter of whether the merged company controls an input that is sufficiently important to downstream rivals that a lack of access to it reduces their ability to compete in the downstream market. This will depend on the cost of that input as a proportion of the total costs of producing the downstream product—if the input is relatively unimportant, having to use a more expensive alternative will have little effect on downstream competition. It will also depend on what alternative inputs are available—if an input is essential and has no alternatives, the disadvantage to downstream rivals is absolute (but in this case the upstream company would probably also be constrained by Article 102, pre- and post-merger).

The economics of assessing a vertical merger are also a matter of looking at the *incentive* to foreclose. If the merged company stops selling its upstream product to rivals, it will forgo profits on those lost wholesale units, but may earn additional profits downstream as rivals find it more difficult to compete without that upstream input. This depends on some degree of imperfect competition downstream. Even an upstream monopolist that buys a downstream company will not automatically wish to foreclose downstream rivals since healthy competition downstream can contribute to expanded sales, which in turn expands demand for the input and enhances profits upstream.

Given some possibility of greater pricing power downstream (for example, if the downstream market is characterized by economies of scale or network effects), it is the balance of profits upstream and downstream that determines the incentive to foreclose. This is illustrated in Figure 7.3. Upstream firm 1 and downstream firm A merge, and the merged entity has the option of cutting off downstream firms B and C from the input supplied by upstream firm 1. If the merged entity does this, it will sacrifice profits upstream on those units formerly sold to B and C. However, at the same time it might earn higher profits downstream because B and C now struggle to compete when using the inferior or more expensive input supplied by upstream firm 2. Figure 7.3 illustrates

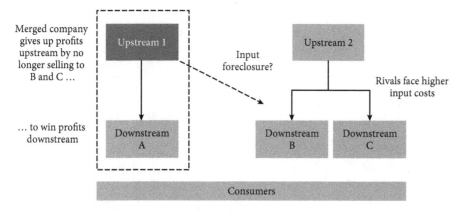

Fig. 7.3 Vertical merger: input foreclosure effect

a case of total input foreclosure, where upstream firm 1 simply stops selling to companies B and C. A variant on this is partial input foreclosure, where upstream firm 1 reduces the quality (or increases the price) of the input sold to B and C while keeping quality high (or prices low) for its new integrated downstream arm.

Thus, the profitability of an input foreclosure strategy reflects a trade-off between profits lost upstream and profits gained in the downstream market. You can analyse this by looking at the arithmetic of profit incentives. Working out the incentives can be a complex exercise since you need to know what drives profits upstream and downstream. For example, the ability to win significant profits downstream will depend on the profit margin downstream and the degree to which the merged firm can win additional sales when its rivals are disadvantaged by lack of access to its upstream product. This in turn depends on the extent of the disadvantage, the diversion from B's and C's products to that of A, and the price elasticity of demand for the downstream product. Table 7.2 looks at this in a simple example that isolates the effect of the substitutability of A with B and C. Producing 1 downstream unit requires exactly 1 upstream unit. Pre-merger, the upstream business sold 8 out of 10 units in the upstream market (ie, its market share was 80%), with profits per unit of €1.50 and hence total profits of €12.00. The downstream business A sold 5 out of 10 units in its market (ie, a downstream market share of 50%), with profits per unit of €1 and hence total profits of €5.00. What effect does the merger have on the incentive to foreclose (ie, to stop selling the upstream product to B and C)?

Assume that the merged firm does refuse to supply B and C with the input such that these rivals must rely on an alternative supplier. Say that this supplier's input is either inferior or more expensive. Accordingly, B and C pass this cost on to consumers, and the merged firm has an opportunity to raise prices and also increase its market share (it can raise prices but still undercut the price of B and C). If the merged firm's downstream sales rise from 5 to 7 (the middle column), the foreclosure strategy works: the merged firm forgoes €1.50 of profit upstream but gains €3.40 downstream, partly by selling more units downstream and partly through increased margins. However, if the

Table 7.2 Incentive to foreclose in a vertical merger

	Pre-foreclosure	High downstream switching post-foreclosure	Low downstream switching post-foreclosure
Upstream units	8	7	6
Upstream margin (€)	1.5	1.5	1.5
Upstream profits (€)	12.0	10.5 (down by €1.5)	9.0 (down by €3.0)
Downstream units	5	7	6
Downstream margin (€)	1.0	1.2	1.2
Downstream profits (€)	5.0	8.4 (up by €3.4)	7.2 (up by €2.2)
Total profit (€)	17.0	18.9 (up by €1.9)	16.2 (down by €0.8)

merged firm's sales rise only from 5 to 6 (the right column), the foreclosure strategy is pointless—it has lost 2 units of upstream sales, worth €3.00 in upstream profits, while gaining only €2.20 in downstream profits. In this example the parameter we vary is the extent of downstream switching to the merged firm in response to increased prices by B and C, but equally we could vary the profit margins, the market shares, or the pricing reactions. All these factors would influence the incentives outcome, and whether the merger is likely to lead to foreclosure.

This simple exercise is not dissimilar from the type of modelling that the European Commission undertook in *TomTom/Tele Atlas* (2008), a vertical merger of a satellite navigation equipment supplier with a producer of digital maps.[46] The main theory of harm in this case was input foreclosure, ie, that the merged entity would restrict access to Tele Atlas maps to TomTom's competitors in the sat nav market, thereby raising its downstream rivals' costs and increasing the price charged to consumers. In order to assess the profitability of an input foreclosure strategy, the Commission estimated how many sales TomTom would be able to capture downstream with such a strategy (which is similar to working out whether we are in the high or low switching scenario in Table 7.2). It found that the sales captured by the merged entity downstream by raising its rivals' costs would not be sufficient to compensate for the lost sales upstream.

The Commission also considered the efficiencies of the vertical integration between TomTom and Tele Atlas. Its model predicted a small decrease in average sat nav prices as a result of the elimination of double marginalization. The overall price effect depends on the balance of pricing power and merger efficiency—long-term, higher prices are likely if the foreclosure effect is substantial (and barriers to entry are high), and less likely if the merger leads to significant cost efficiencies. A potential outcome of these dynamics is that one vertical merger will prompt another, since rivals that are disadvantaged by foreclosure might make up that difference by seeking their own vertical partnership. Indeed, around the time of the TomTom/Tele Atlas transaction, downstream rival, Garmin, agreed a long-term contract with alternative map supplier NAVTEQ, and NAVTEQ itself merged with Nokia (which incorporates sat nav technology into certain types of mobile phone).[47]

A different type of foreclosure is 'customer foreclosure' as illustrated in Figure 7.4, where it is upstream firm 2's access to downstream firm A that is cut off or degraded by the merged entity. The analysis of customer foreclosure is similar to that of input foreclosure, but relies on the importance of economies of scale or scope at the upstream level. If downstream firm A is an important route to market for upstream firm 2, cutting off access may make upstream firm 2 a less effective competitor to upstream firm 1, and enhance the merged entity's upstream market power. This can arise if downstream firm A is such an important distributor or customer that upstream firm 2's business now falls below the minimum efficient scale. The merged entity will lose downstream customers

---

[46] *TomTom/Tele Atlas* (Case COMP/M.4854), Commission Decision of 14 May 2008.
[47] *Nokia/NAVTEQ* (Case COMP/M.4942), Commission Decision of 2 July 2008.

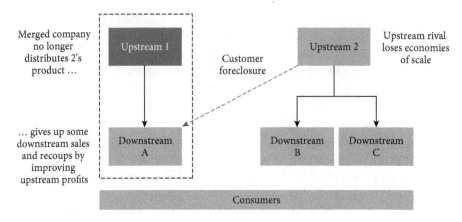

Fig. 7.4 Vertical merger: customer foreclosure effect

who still prefer upstream firm 2's product, but might offset this loss by increased sales and market power upstream.

Customer foreclosure can be accompanied by input foreclosure—a double whammy. Imagine that, in addition to the customer foreclosure in Figure 7.4, the merged entity refuses to sell upstream firm 1's product to firms B and C. Now B and C can buy only from upstream firm 2. If firm 2 is still below efficient scale at that point, the inputs bought by B and C would be inferior to those bought by firm A, and accordingly the merged entity might gain market power downstream as well. For the merged entity to have this incentive, downstream firm A has to be a very important distributor, and upstream economies of scale or scope must be significant. Whether this harms consumers still depends on the balance of merger efficiencies and market power accruing to the merged entity.

7.5.3 DIAGONAL MERGERS

A diagonal merger is between an upstream company and a downstream competitor to the customer of that upstream company. See Figure 7.5, where downstream firm A merges with upstream firm 2. This type of merger lacks the same efficiencies that arise in a vertical merger, since firm A does not actually use the products of upstream firm 2. The theory of harm is that the merged entity could harm downstream firm B by raising the prices it charges for the input used by firm B.

The usual analysis of ability, incentive and effect applies here. The merged firm has a greater ability to foreclose firm B if its upstream input is an important component of B's product, and if B lacks a good alternative for that input. The classic (hypothetical) example of where a diagonal merger produces a competition problem is in relation to steel and brass as the downstream products and iron and zinc as the upstream products. Steel is an alloy of iron and carbon, and brass of copper and zinc. But for a number of applications, steel and brass are substitutable, and compete in the same relevant market.

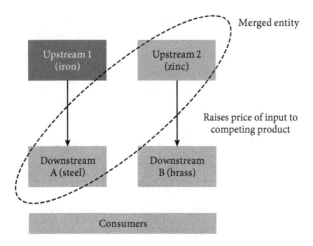

Fig. 7.5 Diagonal merger

What happens if the main producer of zinc is bought by a producer of steel? Although there is no obvious horizontal overlap, a merger between the steel and the zinc producer can have anti-competitive effects if the merged entity can raise the price of zinc and this feeds through to a higher price for brass. Subsequently, customers will switch to steel from brass, benefiting the steel business of the newly formed company. Thus, a price rise for zinc becomes more profitable than it was before the merger of zinc and steel. This conclusion relies on three conditions. First, the zinc supplier must have a very significant market position, otherwise brass manufacturers could simply source zinc from other suppliers in response to higher prices. Second, brass and steel need to be close competitors such that customers will rapidly switch to steel when the price of brass rises. Third, zinc has to be an essential or a significant input to the production of brass in terms of its share in total production costs. If not, the zinc price increase would be diluted in the total brass costs and therefore not significantly affect competition between steel and brass.

In *Google/DoubleClick* (2007) this theory of diagonal mergers was invoked to analyse the effects of the transaction.[48] As this was a complex merger, we stylize the facts here to focus on the diagonal theory of harm. Google is a supplier of text-based Internet advertising ('steel'), whereas DoubleClick provides services and technology used as an input ('zinc') for Internet display advertising ('brass'). Display advertising consists of images and other audiovisual content, and competes with text-based advertising. DoubleClick's technology is a necessary input for display advertising, but not for Google's text-based advertising. The theory of harm was that the merged company might raise DoubleClick's prices, which would result in higher input costs for display advertising and therefore ultimately generate more demand for Google's text-based adverts. The European Commission cleared the merger, arguing that the incentive and effect for a DoubleClick

[48] *Google/DoubleClick* (Case COMP/M.4731), Commission Decision of 11 March 2008.

price rise were not consistent with this theory of harm. It found that credible alternatives to DoubleClick's technology and services existed, which would enable display advertisers to substitute away from DoubleClick in response to higher prices charged by the merged entity (this is equivalent to our brass producers being able to switch to other options for their zinc). The Commission also investigated the dilution effect and found that the cost of DoubleClick's technology represented only a small proportion of the total costs of providing display advertising, and hence that a price rise would have little impact on downstream competition between display advertising and Google's text advertisements.

7.5.4 MERGERS WITH PORTFOLIO EFFECTS

This type of merger occurs when the merged company can offer bundled products against which competitors offering a smaller portfolio of products cannot effectively compete. The general idea behind portfolio and range effects is that a company active in various different, but related, relevant markets can exercise market power even without being dominant in the individual markets. In other words, having a portfolio of activities in different markets gives a degree of market power that is greater than the sum of its parts. The concept of portfolio power was applied in the Commission's assessment of the *Guinness/Grand Metropolitan* merger in 1998—a deal involving two producers of a wide range of alcoholic beverages. The authority stated that:

> The holder of a portfolio of leading spirit brands may enjoy a number of advantages. In particular, his position in relation to his customers is stronger since he is able to provide a range of products and will account for a greater proportion of their business, he will have greater flexibility to structure his prices, promotions and discounts, he will have greater potential for tying, and he will be able to realise economies of scale and scope in his sales and marketing activities. Finally the implicit (or explicit) threat of a refusal to supply is more potent.[49]

Is there really a concern here? A broad portfolio may allow a company to offer its customers product bundles or one-stop shopping, or to obtain economies of scope in production and distribution. All of this can be efficient and beneficial for consumers—we explained the efficiency benefits from bundling in Chapter 4. But imagine that the merged company produces two complementary products while all its potential rivals produce only one product (the merged entity has the greater portfolio). The theory of harm is that the merged entity will increase the price of one product when sold on a stand-alone basis, while keeping constant or lowering the bundled price of the two products. This would give customers an incentive to buy the second product from the merged entity as well, and potentially allow it to exclude competition in that second product. This is the same theory of harm as for bundling and tying as abuse of dominance. However, as with other non-horizontal mergers, the framework of ability, incentive and effect is useful to analyse portfolio effects. In particular, in the merger context,

---

[49] *Guinness/Grand Metropolitan* (Case IV/M. 938) [1998] OJ L288/24.

a portfolio effects theory of harm does not work unless consumers have preferences for buying the bundle and there are significant economies of scope in supplying that bundle (which gives the ability to foreclose), and unless rivals in the second market can be kept at a disadvantage (which gives the incentive to foreclose). If rivals have counterstrategies, such as entering the second market and thereby themselves generating the relevant economies of scope, competition will be 'bundle to bundle' and no concern is likely to arise. We return to portfolio and range effects in the next section in the context of the 'efficiency offence', and in particular the *General Electric/Honeywell* case.

7.6 MERGER EFFICIENCIES

7.6.1 A BALANCING ACT

Mergers may give rise to efficiencies that can at least offset the adverse effects of reduced competition. Merger efficiencies now form part of a standard merger assessment in the major jurisdictions (the EU Merger Regulation did not explicitly allow for an efficiency defence until 2004). Usually the burden of proof for showing efficiencies is on the merging companies rather than the competition authority, and the authority's role is to verify the claimed efficiencies and to evaluate whether they are sufficient to offset any price increases. The European Commission states that it may decide that the merger does not raise competition concerns when it:

> is in a position to conclude on the basis of sufficient evidence that the efficiencies generated by the merger are likely to enhance the ability and incentive of the merged entity to act pro-competitively for the benefit of consumers, thereby counteracting the adverse effects on competition which the merger might otherwise have.[50]

The concept of an efficiency defence exhibits some inherent tension. A merger may result in efficiencies, but if it also increases market power, it is not clear whether these efficiencies will be passed on to consumers. The assessment (and quantification) of the overall market impact of efficiencies resulting from a given merger therefore requires careful analysis. The framework within which such an assessment takes place is in essence the one in Figure 7.1. Chapter 9 contains a discussion of merger remedies, including how they seek to preserve merger efficiencies while remedying the competition concern.

7.6.2 SOURCES OF MERGER EFFICIENCIES

The most obvious merger efficiencies are supply-side efficiencies—be they in terms of fixed or variable cost savings. A merger can achieve cost reductions in a number of ways,

---

[50] European Commission (2004), 'Guidelines on the assessment of horizontal mergers under the Council Regulation on the control of concentrations between undertakings' [2004] OJ C31/03, at [77].

one being economies of scale. As the scale of the production is increased, total costs per unit fall. Another is economies of scope—joint production or marketing of different products leading to lower variable or fixed costs. Cost reductions can also be achieved through rationalization of production processes, such as improved capacity utilization, lower transport costs by optimizing production locations or distribution networks, and the shifting of production to facilities with lower costs. Finally, costs may fall through the elimination of double marginalization, as explained in section 7.5 and in Chapter 6.

In addition to cost reductions, there are other types of potential merger efficiencies, such as product repositioning post-merger which results in a greater variety and choice for customers. In the merger of Global Radio and GCap, two commercial radio stations in the London area, product repositioning was seen by the OFT as a relevant benefit of the merger.[51] The transaction combined largely complementary assets. In the counterfactual of no merger, the independent radio stations would each target a 'middle-of-the-road' music mix in order to appeal to a wide audience. The merged company would recognize the benefit of having more narrowly defined target audiences—eg, younger versus older people—which could be complementary audiences. Product repositioning would allow advertisers to reach their target audiences more effectively. As the OFT explained:

> Global will reposition its now commonly-owned stations to attract listeners, in a way designed to increase total audience size for all stations combined, and increase the demographic focus of the respective station audiences. While directly benefiting end-consumers—who are at no risk of price effects—advertisers also benefit: not only from the ability to reach a greater audience, but also to better target their advertising towards more focused demographics (because many product advertisements are targeted, to greater or lesser degree, towards certain age, gender and income groups), which means less wastage of the message and better value-for-money for the advertising customer. Both types of efficiencies, if realized, will improve the Global/GCap station offer to listeners and advertisers.[52]

Another example of demand-side merger efficiencies is 'one-stop shopping' for customers, which may reduce their transaction or search costs. This was also found in *Global Radio/GCap*. The OFT considered that bundles of radio airtime could be sold to advertisers more efficiently as a result of the merger since advertisers would have to purchase only one large bundle instead of several smaller bundles from independent radio stations.

Competition authorities also consider dynamic merger efficiencies. These concern innovation and R&D, and are typically considered over a longer time period than efficiencies resulting from cost reductions.[53] Dynamic merger efficiencies include the diffusion of know-how, more efficient use of IP, and increased or improved R&D. For instance, mergers may help develop new products or reduce costs by combining certain

---

[51] Office of Fair Trading (2008), 'Completed acquisition by Global Radio UK Limited of GCap Media plc', Case ME 3638/08, Decision, 27 August.

[52] Ibid., at [18].

[53] See Organisation for Economic Co-operation and Development (2007).

assets and expertise that are not easily transferred between separate companies. A merger could also result in elimination of the duplication of R&D efforts, or could facilitate obtaining finance for R&D projects. Dynamic merger efficiencies are often the main rationale for R&D joint ventures, which, depending on their exact form and the applicable legal rules, can be assessed by competition authorities in a similar way as full mergers or as agreements under Article 101 (we discuss such agreements in Chapter 5).

7.6.3 ASSESSING MERGER EFFICIENCIES

Competition authorities require that the claimed merger efficiencies meet a number of conditions before they are weighed against potential lessening of competition. The European Commission requires that merger efficiencies 'benefit consumers, be merger specific and be verifiable', with these three conditions being cumulative.[54] The US agencies have a similar approach, which is to:

consider whether cognizable efficiencies likely would be sufficient to reverse the merger's potential to harm customers . . .

credit only those efficiencies likely to be accomplished with the proposed merger and unlikely to be accomplished in the absence of either the proposed merger or another means having comparable anticompetitive effects . . .

verify by reasonable means the likelihood and magnitude of each asserted efficiency, how and when each would be achieved (and any costs of doing so), how each would enhance the merged firm's ability and incentive to compete, and why each would be merger-specific.[55]

Economic theory suggests that competition authorities should indeed be relatively sceptical of efficiency claims based on simple scale economies, as opposed to genuine synergies (Farrell and Shapiro, 1990). First, such scale economies can, at least in principle, be achieved unilaterally through organic growth, and consumers are likely to benefit more if companies *compete* to gain scale rather than buy it. These efficiencies may therefore not be merger-specific. Second, if efficiencies are specific to the merger, the authority must still assess whether they will be large enough and passed on to consumers. If a merger results in market power, cost savings will be passed on to consumers in part, not in full (see Figure 7.1). We explore the criteria of merger specificity, verifiability and consumer benefits in more detail below, but first we discuss a merger between two small hospitals in the Netherlands that illustrates the relevance of these criteria.

The transaction was approved by the Dutch competition authority (NMa) despite the combined market share of the two parties being in excess of 80% in the relevant markets (the regional markets for clinical general hospital care and non-clinical

---

[54] European Commission (2004), 'Guidelines on the assessment of horizontal mergers under the Council Regulation on the control of concentrations between undertakings', [2004] OJ C31/03, at [78].

[55] Department of Justice and Federal Trade Commission (2010), 'Horizontal Merger Guidelines', 19 August, p 30.

general hospital care).[56] Both hospitals had experienced problems and inefficiencies pre-merger; they had difficulties filling vacancies, and neither hospital had 'level-2' accidents & emergencies (A&E) facilities or adequate intensive-care units. These issues had led to patients in the region having to travel further afield for surgery or being treated in inadequate facilities. The problems were interrelated—on the one hand, the lack of intensive care facilities limited the types of surgery that could be performed; on the other hand, their small catchment areas (narrow geographic market) meant a relatively low demand for specialist procedures and intensive-care facilities. As a result, specialists were not being attracted to these hospitals with limited specializations and low complexity of procedures. In essence, this was an economic problem—the merging parties were operating below the minimum efficient scale for general hospitals. The aim of the merger was to achieve the required scale of operation by combining the catchment areas. This would allow both hospitals to attract larger teams of medics with greater specialization and thereby improve the quality of service to patients. Thus, the efficiency argument in this case was in terms of quality rather than costs. The NMa found that the merger would reduce competition (given the high market share), but that this would be outweighed by efficiencies. The efficiency defence for this merger passed the merger specificity test as well as satisfying the consumer benefit and verifiability conditions (subject to some remedies being implemented).

7.6.4 WHEN DO MERGER EFFICIENCIES BENEFIT CONSUMERS?

Competition authorities generally require that merger efficiencies be passed on to consumers to a sufficient degree and in a timely fashion. The analysis of when cost savings are passed on to consumers in mergers is similar to the analysis of when cost increases are passed on to consumers in a damages case—we discuss this in Chapter 10. Only a few additional remarks are warranted here. Two main factors influence whether efficiencies are passed on: the market structure post-merger, and the nature of the efficiencies. Mergers leading to a highly concentrated market are less likely to be cleared on efficiency grounds since the pass-on of any benefits resulting from merger efficiencies will be more limited when a company faces little competition in the market post-merger. However, even a merger to monopoly does not mean that efficiency gains are not passed on at all—it is normally profit-maximizing for a monopolist to pass on a substantial proportion of its cost savings (50% if demand is linear), as explained in Chapter 10. As to the nature of the efficiencies, variable cost reductions are more likely to benefit consumers in the form of lower prices than fixed cost reductions, since in theory prices are set with reference to variable (marginal) costs. However, fixed cost reductions (eg, resulting from innovation efforts) can also benefit consumers in the longer term. Furthermore, if complementary products are merged, it is profit-maximizing to sell these products at a lower price than the sum of their prices under separate ownership, regardless of the degree of competitive pressure.

---

[56] NMa (2009), *Walcheren Hospital—Oosterschelde Hospitals*, Case 6424.

The European Commission's assessment in 2004 of the proposed strategic alliance between Air France and Alitalia is one example where the efficiency defence was dismissed partly because the pass-on of efficiencies was not sufficiently established.[57] Air France and Alitalia sought to interconnect their worldwide aviation networks by creating a European multi-hub system at Paris, Rome, and Milan, and by coordinating their passenger service operations, including code-sharing, scheduled passenger networks, and sales. The Commission acknowledged that the proposed alliance could generate significant efficiencies in terms of creating a more extensive network (which would offer customers better services in the form of more direct and indirect flights), as well as cost reductions due to an increase in traffic throughout the network, better planning of frequencies, and other operational efficiencies. It also recognized that these efficiencies are merger-specific. However, the Commission was concerned that the expected cost reductions would not result in lower fares:

> The Parties have not, however, shown how such cost savings and synergies would be passed on to the customer and were not able to identify precisely on which routes (trunk routes, other routes within the France-Italy bundle, other routes) price decreases would be applied as a result of the Alliance. If their co-operation results in the elimination of competition in certain markets, there will be no incentive for them to pass on these efficiencies to local passengers.[58]

The Commission approved the alliance, but subject to remedies on particular routes where the parties faced little or no competition.

Cost reductions resulting from any anti-competitive reductions in output are not considered to be beneficial to consumers. In *FTC v Cardinal Health*,[59] two mergers would have replaced competition between the four largest drug wholesalers in the USA with a duopoly controlling nearly 80% of the market. The FTC was concerned that 'hospitals, pharmacies, and government purchasers will find themselves paying higher prices for drug wholesaling services'. The merging parties argued that the proposed acquisitions would result in significant efficiencies—the principal argument was that cost savings would result from the consolidation and closing of distribution centres. However, the FTC argued that this was instead 'the very anticompetitive effect flowing from the transaction'. It pointed out that the parties themselves had recognized that excess capacity drove down prices; hence the elimination of this capacity would increase prices to consumers. Furthermore, the FTC argued that the claimed efficiencies were not merger-specific.

The requirement for efficiencies to be realized in a timely manner is a complex issue, and competition authorities may differ in their assessment of this condition. In the EU, the further in the future the efficiencies are expected to materialize, the less weight is

---

[57] *Société Air France/Alitalia Linee Aeree Italiane SpA* (Case COMP/38.284/D2), Commission Decision of 7 April 2004.

[58] Ibid., at [137].

[59] *FTC v Cardinal Health, Inc et al.* 12 F Supp 2d 34, United States District Court for the District of Columbia (1998).

attached to them when assessing the effects of a merger. This has implications for the assessment of the dynamic efficiencies discussed above—since they may take a longer time to materialize than static efficiencies, the European Commission is likely to give them less weight.

7.6.5 EFFICIENCIES MUST BE MERGER-SPECIFIC

Competition authorities consider only those merger efficiencies that could not be achieved by other realistic and less anti-competitive means, such as contracts, licensing agreements, or joint ventures. A lack of merger specificity has been found in a large number of merger cases. For example, in the merger between Live Nation and Ticketmaster that we discussed in section 7.3, the CC considered the possible vertical merger efficiencies between the ownership and operation of live music venues and the business of selling tickets. However, it concluded that such efficiencies could also be achieved through long-term contracts between Ticketmaster and Live Nation, and therefore were not specific to the merger.[60]

Isn't it counterintuitive that merging parties find it difficult to prove merger-specific efficiencies? The main reason for this difficulty is the following. If achieving economies of scale is very attractive (ie, it leads to a significant cost advantage), it is more likely that a merged company would seek to do so, but it would also be more likely that individual companies would have a strong incentive to expand organically. In other words, the more significant the economies of scale, the more likely it is that they will eventually be achieved without a merger, by companies competing to grow their market share. A merger would be a quick way to achieve the minimum efficient scale, but it is not the most competition-friendly way. Consumers are more likely to benefit if companies compete to gain customers. Therefore, as regards economies of scale, the only merger-specific benefit is the speeding up of the process of realizing scale efficiencies, not the economies of scale in their own right. In the merger between AmeriSource Health Corporation and Bergen Brunswig Corporation, the third- and fourth-largest drug wholesalers in the USA, the FTC accepted the parties' merger efficiency arguments, partly because the merger would speed up the process of those companies achieving efficient scale relative to a counterfactual where they each sought scale independently (note that the *FTC v Cardinal Health* case discussed above also involved these two companies, when they tried to merge with the two market leaders but were unsuccessful):

> Based on our review, the proposed transaction likely will give the merged firm sufficient scale so that it can become cost-competitive with the two leading firms and can invest in value-added services desired by customers. Furthermore, we believe that the combined firm will be able to initiate these improvements more rapidly than either could do individually, and that this timing advantage will be significant enough to constitute a cognizable merger-specific efficiency. The resulting firm, operating in a market increasingly characterized by value-added

---

[60] Competition Commission (2010), 'Ticketmaster and Live Nation', 7 May, at [7.13]–[7.14].

services, likely will provide customers with greater choices among suppliers and therefore will give customers sufficient leverage to obtain competitive prices.[61]

Farrell and Shapiro (2001) distinguish between two types of efficiency arising from mergers: efficiencies without synergies (eg, economies of scale) and genuine synergies. A synergy arising from a merger requires the combination of assets that are owned by different companies. Synergies allow output or cost configurations that would not be feasible or practical without the merger and can therefore by definition not be achieved unilaterally. However, this does not yet make them merger-specific. There may be a means of combining the assets that is less restrictive. For example, if similar assets are readily traded then it seems unlikely that a merger is required to combine these assets (the parties can each buy such assets for themselves). Furthermore, there may be other merger candidates that have the required assets but trigger fewer competition concerns. Farrell and Shapiro conclude that, in general, the more difficult it is to find the assets, the more likely the synergies are merger-specific. However, the existence of highly specific assets is also likely to make entry or expansion by other companies more difficult since they may constitute an entry barrier in the form of sunk costs, and this may again raise the likelihood of finding an SLC.

7.6.6 THE 'EFFICIENCY OFFENCE'

In Chapter 1 we saw how US antitrust law in the 1960s was not very friendly toward big efficient companies. We gave the example of *FTC v Procter & Gamble* (1967), a merger concerning the household liquid bleach market.[62] The Supreme Court established the 'entrenchment doctrine', whereby mergers could be prohibited if they strengthened the position of the merging parties relative to rivals through efficiencies, broader product ranges, or greater financial resources. Becoming too efficient was deemed bad. This approach changed radically in the 1970s under the influence of the Chicago School. In competition regimes elsewhere, the 'efficiency offence' still plays a role from time to time.

The *General Electric/Honeywell* merger case of 2001 has been much discussed, largely because it illustrated the different approaches of the US and the EU competition authorities—while the former cleared the merger, the latter blocked it.[63] One of the main differences in the assessment of this merger was how efficiencies were treated. General Electric (GE) was a major supplier of large aircraft engines, while Honeywell supplied avionics and other components for commercial aircraft. Thus there were limited horizontal overlaps between the merging parties (there were some in certain products, such as US military helicopter engines). This was largely a so-called conglomerate merger. A rationale for such mergers can be improved efficiency, resulting from economies of scale and scope.

---

[61] 'Statement of the Federal Trade Commission: *AmeriSource Health Corporation/Bergen Brunswig Corporation*', File No 011-0122, 24 August 2001, pp 2–3.

[62] *FTC v Procter & Gamble* 386 US 568 (1967).

[63] Majoras (2001), and *General Electric/Honeywell* (Case COMP/M.2220) [2004] OJ L48/1.

The case in itself is complex and the differences between the US and the EU approach are not straightforward, but in essence the US authorities approved the merger (subject to some conditions in the markets where GE and Honeywell had horizontal overlaps) on the basis that it would enhance efficiency, and thus would foster competition, while the EU blocked the merger because it believed that the more efficient merged entity would have both the incentives and the market power to exclude competitors. The theory of harm in the EU was referred to as range effects, which are in essence similar to the portfolio effects discussed in section 7.5. A concern was that the merged entity would have the ability and incentive to offer low-priced bundles of aircraft engines and systems which its non-integrated competitors would be unable to match. Thus, the same efficiencies that were seen as desirable in the USA were seen as an unfair advantage in the EU—economies of scope yielding the ability to bundle products and sell them at a lower price. This case gave rise to extensive debate about whether EU merger control was seeking to protect competitors rather than competition, (Majoras, 2001; Kolasky, 2001; and Emch, 2004). These days the 'efficiency offence' has a diminished role in merger control.

8

STATE AID

8.1 STATE AID IN A WIDER CONTEXT

Article 107(1) TFEU states:

> Save as otherwise provided in the Treaties, any aid granted by a Member State or through State resources in any form whatsoever which distorts or threatens to distort competition by favouring certain undertakings or the production of certain goods shall, in so far as it affects trade between Member States, be incompatible with the internal market.

'State aid' therefore exists when there is a measure granted by the state and through state resources that has all of the following effects—it confers a benefit or advantage on the recipient, it is selective in favouring certain undertakings or the production of certain goods, and it is liable to distort competition and affect trade between Member States. With that definition in mind, you might think that free market economists would never approve of state aid—to quote popular economic opinion, 'why should any company that isn't run well, or doesn't sell products that are up to the mark, get bailed out by the government?' And in a way you would be right, since when governments provide support that is targeted at specific undertakings rather than available to all there is always some degree of distortion of the market process. As John Vickers, economist and at the time Chairman of the Office of Fair Trading (OFT), put it (2005b, p 2):

> The principal way in which subsidies can do harm by distorting competition is that if my firm or the goods that I produce get a subsidy and yours do not, then I will retain business, or take business from you, that you would serve more efficiently than me if competition had been undistorted. Inefficient though I may be, you do not get a fair opportunity to enter or grow in the marketplace. My incentives to become more efficient or innovative are dulled in the process, and so too are yours if you do not see a fair opportunity to compete. Inefficiency is perpetuated, dynamism, productivity and competitiveness are lost, the economy is poorer and the public are worse off.

Despite this, most economists, including Vickers and ourselves, would agree that markets do not always work perfectly. State aid can be a tool to correct market failures and to achieve goals of common interest, and the role of economics in explaining how and when markets fail is critical to a sensible policy on state aid. Output or investment subsidies may be the best response, for example, when companies generate positive externalities—a situation often thought to arise in technologically progressive industries. On the other hand, misdirected subsidies can cost the economy twice: first as a cost to taxpayers, then as a cost to consumers. This leads to some interesting questions that economics can help to answer. Should aid be granted to a large car manufacturer that runs into difficulty because of an economic recession? Should government support be used to fund green cars, or low-energy light bulbs, or lending to small businesses? How may it be judged whether a new tax distorts competition? And what does economics have to say about propping up failing banks during a financial crisis?

Before we go further, note that 'state aid' is not synonymous with 'subsidy'. It is a broader concept that can include other types of advantageous government treatments such as tax exemptions and preferential tariffs. The economic essence of state aid is that if the effect of a particular state measure is to benefit a particular undertaking or category of goods, then it might be regarded as an aid. State aid is in this sense a matter of substance and not form, as recognized in a 1961 judgment by the European Court of Justice:

> A subsidy is normally defined as a payment in cash or kind made in support of any undertaking other than the payment by the purchaser or the consumer for the goods or services which it produces. An aid is a very similar concept, which, however, places emphasis on its purpose and seems especially devised for a particular objective which cannot normally be made without outside help. The concept of an aid is nevertheless wider than that of a subsidy because it embraces not only positive benefits, such as subsidies themselves, but also interventions which, in various forms, mitigate the charges which are normally included in

the budget of an undertaking and which, without, therefore, being subsidies in the strict sense of the word, are similar in character and have the same effect.[1]

While state aid is a broad concept, clearly not all public spending amounts to state aid. To put it in perspective, public spending accounts for something like 50% of European GDP, whereas around 0.5%–0.6% of GDP is state aid (not an immaterial amount— around €67 billion in 2006).[2] During the financial crisis the amount of state aid rose to 2.2% of GDP in 2008, or €280 billion.[3] Still the great majority of public projects are not classified as state aid.

State aid control is a major part of EU competition law. It is meant to maintain a level playing field across Member States, which helps facilitate the creation of a single market. State aid control is unique to the EU—no other competition regime in the world has anything quite like it. There is a degree of control of government subsidy in the US federal system. Article I of the US Constitution assigns to Congress the power 'to regulate commerce with foreign nations' and also 'among the states'. In *West Lynn Creamery, Inc. v Healy*,[4] the state of Massachusetts imposed a uniform tax on all milk sold in the state regardless of its source. The proceeds of the tax were then used to provide payments to in-state dairy farmers. The Supreme Court determined that the scheme was the equivalent of discriminatory taxation and deemed it unconstitutional. From an economic perspective, the reasoning of the Supreme Court in this case shares some of the principles of EU state aid control about the promotion of fair competition and trade within a single market. But in general the USA has a much less elaborate approach to state aids than the EU. Closer to the EU rules are the subsidies rules of the World Trade Organization (WTO), but these apply mainly to the narrower topic of export subsidies. While we follow the European legal framework throughout this chapter, the core economics here should be applicable to non-EU jurisdictions where competition issues arise on the effects of government subsidies.

An important theme in this chapter is that an economics-based approach to state aid is possible, even if such an approach is not always used at present, as it is in merger control or abuse of dominance. (One potential reason why state aid lags behind is that the legal proceedings in state aid are between the Member State and the European Commission, whereas the aid beneficiary, which has the greatest interest in the outcome, often does not get directly involved. Another is that state aid is often politically

---

[1] *De Gezamenlijke Steenkolenmijnen in Limburg v High Authority of the European Coal and Steel Community* [1961] ECR 1, at [19]. See also Bacon (2009), [2.05].

[2] For example, in 2006 the overall level of state aid, including aid to the agriculture, fisheries, and transport sector, stood at €67 billion and accounted for 0.58% of GDP. This figure excludes subsidies to the railway sector (€37 billion in 2006) as well as aid for the compensation of services of general economic interest. See the European Commission's regular 'State Aid Scoreboard', available at: <http://ec.europa.eu/competition/state_aid/studies_reports/archive/scoreboard_arch.html>.

[3] European Commission (2009), 'Commission Staff Working Document Accompanying the Report from the Commission: State Aid Scoreboard—Autumn 2009 Update—Facts and Figures on State Aid in the EU Member States', SEC(2009) 1638, 12 December, p 8.

[4] 512 US 186 (1994).

sensitive, meaning that getting the economics right is not necessarily the first priority.) In line with EU state aid case practice, we focus on three areas of the legal framework where economics already plays a more influential role:

(1) the market economy investor principle (MEIP), which deals with the question of the existence and quantification of state aid;

(2) the assessment of compensation for services of general economic interest (SGEIs), which deals with the question of how much aid is necessary to meet an objective such as the provision of post office services throughout the country or of local bus services in rural areas; and

(3) the balancing test, which asks whether aid will address a market failure or other objective of common interest while limiting the distortions of competition, so that the overall balance is positive. The particular value of economic analysis is in identifying the market failure that state aid is meant to address, and in determining whether state aid is an efficient solution to the problem. As the Commission noted in its 2005 State Aid Action Plan, 'appreciating the compatibility of state aid is fundamentally about balancing the negative effects of aid on competition with its positive effects in terms of common interest.'[5]

In this chapter we focus less on certain other areas of state aid, such as the various sector-specific frameworks (eg, for coal, steel, or shipbuilding)—the underlying economics does not vary much across these but the details of the legal framework can be highly specific. Nor do we focus on regional aid or employment aid, since these are issues that have more to do with social considerations than competition economics. The end result is that this chapter is a reference point for the economics of state aid cases irrespective of the sector, but has rather less to say on types of state aid that are motivated by social policy considerations. The chapter follows the standard European legal framework for assessing state aid. The MEIP fits into Article 107(1), assessing SGEI compensation falls into Article 106, and the balancing test is a matter for Article 107(3). Sections 8.2 and 8.3 look at the basic economic principles of state aid, and at where economics can be used in a state aid case. Sections 8.4 to 8.6 consider the first stage question, 'is there state aid?'. Section 8.4 explains the MEIP. Section 8.5 deals with the potential distortion of competition and trade, and section 8.6 explains how to implement the *Altmark* criteria for the existence of aid with respect to SGEI. The second stage question, 'are there valid reasons to grant state aid?', is addressed in sections 8.7 on SGEI and 8.8 on market failures, plus a separate discussion of restructuring aid in section 8.9. The final stage question for state aid, 'on balance, should the measure be approved?', is examined in section 8.10, which deals with the balancing test. Section 8.11 considers remedies in state aid cases, and section 8.12 concludes with some comments on state aid enforcement.

---

[5] European Commission (2005), 'State Aid Action Plan: Less and Better Targeted State Aid—A Roadmap for State Aid Reform 2005–2009', COM(2005) 107, 7 June, [11].

8.2 THE BASIC ECONOMIC PRINCIPLES OF STATE AID

8.2.1 EFFICIENCY VERSUS EQUITY

State aid has two possible justifications from an economic perspective: it enhances efficiency or it enhances equity. As to the former, state aid can be an intervention aimed at fixing a market failure. An example is a subsidy to fund basic research. The market failure here is an inability to privately capture the positive spillover effects of innovation—that is, where the benefits of innovation cannot be entirely appropriated by the innovator (such as a technological breakthrough that is copied by other companies). This is an example of an externality, where decisions by one market participant do not take into account the impact on other market participants. As to equity, state aid can be aimed at achieving a social objective such as universal service provision or a subsidy to persuade a company to retrain workers who have been made redundant.

The efficiency-enhancing effect of state aid ought to expand economic output (a bigger cake), whereas the equity-enhancing effect redistributes economic output (dividing up the cake fairly). An equity-enhancing effect would be to transfer output from a rich region to a poor region. Rescuing jobs in one region often means sacrificing them in another region (whether inside or outside Europe). These are policy judgements. Economics generally has less to say about equity effects (it can only help identify them) than it does about efficiency gains. We therefore focus on efficiency effects in this chapter, that is, interventions aimed at fixing a market failure.

8.2.2 WHAT IS A MARKET FAILURE?

As discussed in Chapter 1, standard economic theory shows that under normal circumstances the operation of rivalry between companies that maximize profits can deliver an optimal outcome for the economy as a whole. At a 'micro' level, markets can keep price–cost margins low, deliver lower production costs and higher quality, and drive product innovation over the longer term. In turn, at a 'macro' level, this can lead to improved economic growth and productivity in the use of resources. However, there are also a number of circumstances in which the operation of markets—left to their own devices—may not deliver an optimal outcome from a societal perspective. In such circumstances, what is optimal behaviour for an individual agent in the economy at a particular point in time may not be optimal for the economy as a whole. Where this wedge exists between individually and collectively optimal behaviour, market failures are said to be present. There are many instances where state aid is a legitimate response to market failure. The most frequent causes of market failure are externalities (eg, with respect to innovation or the environment), information asymmetries, coordination problems, and market power. You will see all these explained later in the chapter. An example of a negative supply-side externality we noted in Chapter 1 was the factory upstream that freely dumps its waste into the river, thus affecting a fish farm further downstream.

8.2.3 WHAT SHOULD BE TREATED AS 'STATE AID'?

It is well established in economic theory that state intervention (of which state aid is only one form) may improve the allocation of resources where markets are affected by market failures. If done properly, government intervention can increase efficiency by correcting such market failures. To qualify as state aid, a measure must involve a potential distortion of competition and trade. (Hence there is always a cost attached to state aid, aside from the obvious point that a transfer of state resources places a liability on the taxpayer.) State aid rules are triggered only by measures which benefit economic undertakings rather than individuals, and only by selective measures, such as a tax break for one company, rather than general measures, such as a tax break for all capital investment. That is why the vast majority of government expenditure, fiscal policy, and public procurement (eg, on roads and schools) cannot be classed as state aid. For example, the European Commission stated during the financial crisis that began in 2007–08 that 'general measures open to all comparable market players' on equal terms were likely to be outside the scope of the state aid rules.[6] State aid rules apply in the same manner regardless of whether undertakings are private companies or owned by the state, since the principle of equal treatment is a condition of Article 345 TFEU. Provided that the undertaking carries on an economic activity, it may be subject to state aid control.[7]

State aid need not involve an actual transfer of state resources. The aid may be a contingent benefit such as a state guarantee (which is triggered only if a loan becomes nonperforming). From an economic perspective, even the informal promise of state involvement, such as where the state announces a willingness to be the lender of last resort, may confer an advantage. Aid may also involve forgoing extra revenue rather than transferring existing resources, such as where a new tax is created that is coupled with various exemptions from the tax.

State aid always involves conferring an advantage or benefit on an economic undertaking. If it induces the undertaking so favoured to lower its prices, the normal pricing signals for resource allocation may be distorted, and so more resources are used for the subsidized activity. State aid can also mean that less efficient companies are artificially kept afloat, thus making it more difficult for new and more efficient companies to enter the market. The productive efficiency of companies can also be impaired if attention is diverted to finding new ways to obtain government subsidies rather than serving customers. And companies have less incentive to produce efficiently and invest if they can assume that the state will come to their aid to save jobs if they are in financial difficulties. Finally, if state aid changes the profitability of an investment, companies may be induced to change the level, nature and timing of their investment.

---

[6] European Commission (2008), 'Communication from the Commission: The Application of State Aid Rules to Measures Taken in Relation to Financial Institutions in the Context of the Current Global Financial Crisis', 13 October, [51].

[7] See, for example, Cases C-34–38/01 *Enirisorse v Ministero delle Finanze* [2003] ECR I-14243, and Case C-237/04 *Enirisorse v Sotacarbo* [2006] ECR I-2843, at [32]–[33].

8.2.4 AN ECONOMIC INTERPRETATION OF THE WELFARE STANDARD APPLIED IN STATE AID LAW

In economic theory, consumer welfare is usually defined as consumer surplus in all markets, that is, the difference between the willingness to pay for a good and the price of that good (as explained in Chapter 1). Likewise, producer welfare is equivalent to producer surplus, ie, the amount that producers benefit by selling at a market price that is higher than the marginal cost of production. A weighted social welfare standard takes into account not only the sum of consumer and producer surpluses, but also how welfare is distributed across countries and citizens, using a weighting system to represent the importance attached to the utility of different individuals. Social welfare thus integrates efficiency elements (by looking at how much wealth is created by affecting consumer and/or producer surpluses) as well as equity elements (by looking at how this wealth is divided between Member States and citizens). This appears to be closest to how state aid policy operates in practice.

Since the welfare standard is not clearly defined in policy application, and because we focus on efficiency rather than equity concerns, we do not think it necessary to spend time debating exactly what is the right welfare standard. Rather, we stick to the more general formula that state aid is warranted only if its expected benefit, in terms of improving market outcomes, outweighs the expected cost of intervention, in terms of distortions of competition and trade (plus the cost of associated taxation). The consequence of this is that state aid control should block or apply remedies to state aid that leads to undue market distortions. In the words of the European Commission's State Aid Action Plan (2005):

> One important justification for state aid is . . . the existence of a market failure . . . However, it is not enough for state aid to target a market failure. Before resorting to state aid, which is in general only the 'second best' option to achieve optimal allocation of resources, it should be verified whether other less distortive measures could remedy the market failure. State aid should be the appropriate policy instrument and should be designed so that it effectively solves the market failure, by creating an incentive effect and being proportionate. In addition, state aid should not distort competition to an extent contrary to the common interest.

We describe below how you might go about measuring the costs and benefits of state aid.

8.3 WHERE DOES ECONOMICS FIT IN TO A STATE AID CASE?

Let's start with Article 107(1). The first question is whether an advantage is conferred through state intervention in the market. Here economics provides one relevant test, which is whether the funding from the state occurs on terms that are more favourable than those available from the private sector. This MEIP test applies in cases where the state acts as a market participant. The second question is whether the aid is selective.

This can be straightforward: is the aid available to some companies but not others? A measure is in principle selective if it produces advantages exclusively for certain undertakings or certain sectors. Here there is usually no great need for economics, although in some cases it will be helpful to have done some market definition work to understand the extent of selectivity (ie, who are the recipient company's competitors?). The final question is whether aid distorts or threatens to distort competition and trade. Perhaps surprisingly, economics also has a limited role here in terms of answering yes or no, since according to case law these conditions are typically fulfilled if the measure is selective in terms of granting an advantage—hence the question usually, but not always, reverts back to selectivity. If there is a selective element, this is assumed to be distortionary. This has certain parallels with the treatment of object cases under Article 101(1)—as discussed in Chapter 5. In state aid, the interpretation of Article 107(1) is contingent on a rather low threshold for distortions to competition and trade. In an Article 101(1) object case, competition law proceeds by assuming that any agreement of the form which is said to restrict competition 'by object' is anti-competitive and therefore illegal.

Next, consider Article 107(3). This provision may be implemented by the 'balancing test', as set out in the 2005 State Aid Action Plan. This test asks whether the aid: (i) addresses a market failure or other objective of common interest; (ii) has a sufficient incentive effect on the behaviour of the recipient to ensure that the aid achieves its objective; (iii) distorts competition and trade; and (iv) results in an overall positive balance, given the magnitude of the previous effects (positive on market failure, negative on competition).

Here the questions are certainly more economics-orientated. The legal framework can set out presumptions on what the relevant market failures are and at what point competition is distorted, but it cannot do so without being informed by economics. While the mere possibility of distortion of competition and trade was enough for Article 107(1), now the magnitude of these distortions needs to be assessed for Article 107(3).

Finally, regarding Article 106 on SGEIs, the main characteristic of these services is that they are not provided by the free market. An example of an SGEI approved by the Court of Justice is the obligation to supply electricity in a specified territory, such that all consumers receive uninterrupted supplies in sufficient quantities to meet demand at any time, at uniform tariff rates, and on non-discriminatory, objective terms.[8] Economics has a role in the question of whether SGEI funding constitutes aid (similar to its role in the MEIP), and in the question of appropriate compensation for an SGEI. If a measure meets the *Altmark* criteria, it is not characterized as state aid—these criteria are taken from a judgment involving a local bus service in Germany.[9] The bus operator had 18 licences to operate passenger services in a particular district, for which it received a subsidy from the public authorities. A competitor contested this subsidy,

[8] Case C-393/92 *Almelo* [1994] ECR I-1477, at [48].

[9] Judgment in Case C-280/00 *Altmark Trans GmbH and Regierungspräsidium Magdeburg v Nahverkehrsgesellschaft Altmark GmbH* ('*Altmark*') [2003] ECR I-7747.

and the German Federal Administrative Court referred to the European Court of Justice the question of whether the subsidy constituted state aid. In its judgment, the Court of Justice stated that compensation for public services does not contain aid when four conditions are met:

(1) The recipient undertaking must have public service obligations to discharge and those obligations must be clearly defined.

(2) The parameters on the basis of which the compensation is calculated must be established both in advance and in an objective and transparent manner.

(3) The compensation cannot exceed what is necessary to cover all or part of the costs incurred in the discharge of the public service obligations, taking into account the relevant receipts and a reasonable profit.

(4) Where the undertaking is not chosen in a public procurement procedure, the level of compensation must be determined by a comparison with an analysis of the costs that a typical undertaking would incur (taking into account the receipts and a reasonable profit from discharging the obligations).

Each of these four conditions has an economics component, as described in section 8.7. If an SGEI measure does not meet all four *Altmark* conditions, it may be state aid, depending on the usual criteria, in which case the question turns to whether it is *compatible* state aid. Compatibility is judged by the provisions of the SGEI Framework and its sector-specific variants.[10] The economic aspects of that framework are discussed in section 8.8 of this chapter.

8.4 IS THERE STATE AID? IF SO, HOW MUCH? THE MARKET ECONOMY INVESTOR PRINCIPLE

8.4.1 WHEN DOES THE MEIP APPLY?

The first principle embedded in Article 107 is that the issue of state aid arises only when an advantage is conferred through state intervention in the market. In cases where the state acts as a market participant, such an advantage emerges when the intervention is made on terms which could not have been obtained from a commercial ('market economy') operator acting with a view to obtaining a normal return.[11] Thus, if a public authority grants funding or guarantees to a company on terms which that company could have obtained by going to a bank or to the capital markets, there is no advantage conferred to the company. This is irrespective of whether the alleged aid recipient is a government-owned entity (eg, a state-owned airport) or a private company. The MEIP

---

[10] European Commission (2005), 'Community Framework for State Aid in the Form of Public Service Compensation' [2005] OJ C297, 29 November.

[11] For a legal definition see Bacon (2009), [2.34].

question is therefore how to assess whether the terms of the alleged aid measure are in fact compatible with terms acceptable to the commercial investor.

We are concerned here only with cases where the MEIP is engaged, ie, where the state acts as a market participant. The market economy investor test does not operate where the state exercises its sovereign or public functions. This is because wherever the state acts as a market participant, its activity can be compared with a private commercial participant in the market, whereas where the state exercises its functions in, for example, social security, there is no such market comparator. The legal principle was set out in the *Banks v Coal Authority* case (2001):

> The application in practice of these definitions of aid will vary according to whether the State or other public authority acts in the exercise of its sovereign or public functions or, on the other hand, acts simply as a market participant. This has given rise to two different notions of normality. In the former case, in areas such as tax, social security or insolvency, Community law has no a priori conception of what the normal level of charges or benefits should be . . . Hence, it is necessary to determine whether a given measure is general in nature, or is specific (and advantageous) to a particular undertaking or sector. This presupposes, inevitably, a degree of comparability between the respective circumstances of the favoured undertakings or sectors and of the others . . . benefit of certain among them may be construed as an aid to those treated more favourably.

> In the case of State commercial activity, in fields such as public investment and public disposal of assets, Community law does prescribe a standard (although it is one whose concrete application will be determined by the circumstances of any given case): that of the ordinary economic agent or the private commercial actor in a market economy. Thus, a dichotomy can be identified between, essentially, descriptive and prescriptive approaches to identifying normality according to the type of alleged aid being scrutinised.[12]

8.4.2 AN OVERVIEW OF THE MEIP

One of the earliest descriptions of the MEIP is set out in the 1998 *Van der Kooy* case:

> It is of the essence of a State aid that it is non-commercial in the sense that the State steps in where the market would not. The state may have its reasons for doing so but they are not commercial in the ordinary sense of the word. Thus the state may subscribe for shares in a company or lend money, but when it does so to an extent or on terms which would not be acceptable to the commercial investor, it is granting aid which falls within Article [107] if the tests of that provision are satisfied.[13]

To an economist, there is at first sight something inherently paradoxical in the MEIP. Doesn't the mere fact that the state spends money imply that no private party would do so? Or to put it another way, if you meet the MEIP, why did the state provide the funding in the first place? Indeed, some of the most publicized state aid cases have involved

---

[12] Opinion of Advocate General Fennelly in Case C-390/98 *Banks v Coal Authority* [2001] ECR I-6117, at [19]–[20].

[13] Cases 67, 68, and 70/85 *Van der Kooy v Commission* [1988] ECR 219.

government rescues of failing firms or banks, which almost by definition would not meet the MEIP. Yet there is more to it than that. Many state-owned entities engage in normal commercial activity, which is fully in line with the principle of 'no prejudice of the system of property ownership' established in Article 345 TFEU. In such a mixed economic landscape, it makes sense to ask the question whether a particular state action does indeed qualify as commercial, or whether an element of aid is involved. This application to state-owned companies operating in a commercial environment is one of the more straightforward uses of the MEIP. Incidentally, it also makes sense in terms of the efficient use of taxpayers' money that the state properly considers the profitability of the investments it makes—just as real private investors are accountable to their shareholders, governments are accountable to taxpayers. MEIP analysis can therefore be a by-product of seeking value for money for the taxpayer.

Many state-owned operations have both commercial activities (which are, or could be, run for profit) and other social, public policy activities (which require subsidization from the government). A seaport or airport owned by the local government undertakes commercial activities that private port operators would also undertake—for example, charging shippers for port and handling services—but may also perform public functions such as providing basic infrastructure and promoting local employment and business activity. This distinction is not always straightforward, as the operations may be set up under a complicated legal ownership or organizational structure that makes it difficult to identify exactly where the commercial operations end and social aspects come in. Yet from an economic perspective it is often feasible to ring-fence the commercial aspects of the operations, thus rendering them independent of the legal structure. It is the costs and benefits related to these commercial activities are relevant for the MEIP test. In *Ryanair Ltd v Commission*, the Court of First Instance (now the General Court) determined that whereas the Commission had applied the MEIP only to the airport operator, which set certain airport fees, the Commission ought to have also included commercial aspects of the activities of the Walloon Region, which set certain airport charges by political decree. This would have the effect of identifying all the commercial aspects, and separating them from public functions, in order to consider the airport as a single commercial entity for the purposes of applying the MEIP.[14]

A separate issue is how to measure whether the state intervention yields an advantage to the recipient. In the 'Helaba' cases, *Bundesverband deutscher Banken eV v European Commission*, the General Court stated that, in applying the MEIP, the Commission is obliged to:

> make a complete analysis of all factors that are relevant to the transaction at issue and its context, including the situation of the beneficiary undertaking and of the relevant market, in order to verify whether that undertaking is receiving an economic advantage which it would not have obtained under normal market conditions.[15]

---

[14] Judgment of the Court of First Instance in Case T-196/04 *Ryanair Ltd v Commission*, 17 December 2008.
[15] Judgment of the General Court (Fourth Chamber) (2010) in Case T-163/05 *Bundesverband deutscher Banken eV v European Commission (Helaba)* [2010] ECR 98.

What is the conceptually correct approach to assess the existence and extent of economic advantage? The test boils down to an analysis of future profitability and an estimation of the cost of capital. This estimation of whether an investment is commercially viable is a ubiquitous practice in the business world. You saw in Chapter 3 the main techniques for assessing profitability. The MEIP test draws on the same financial tools. If the expected profits are lower than the estimated cost of capital of the company then it can be concluded that the government is making a return on its capital injection that would not have been acceptable to a private investor under similar market conditions. The aid component is then equal to the difference between the cost of capital and the expected profits.

For example, if a state loan is provided at a 4% interest rate, but a private investor taking on the same risk would require interest at 7%, it is easy to see that the quantum of aid is the difference between the two rates and that the deal contains an element of state aid. There are two ways of finding out that a private investor would have accepted a rate of 7%—asking the question of whether comparable private sector projects have actually been financed at a rate of around 7%, or asking whether the appropriate cost of debt for the particular project, given its risk characteristics, is around 7%. Which of these is more appropriate in the circumstances of a given market we will see in a few moments.

8.4.3 WHO IS THE 'MARKET ECONOMY INVESTOR'?

The MEIP has two sides: the investor and the recipient. Is the test whether the public investor acted equivalently to a market economy investor, or whether the recipient's deal was no better than could have been obtained from the market? In the *Helaba* cases (there were two parallel cases), the General Court considered this question carefully, ultimately upholding the Commission's finding that the German state (*Land*) of Hessen acted as a private investor in transferring the €1.264 billion Housing and Future Investment Fund to the bank Landesbank Hessen-Thüringen Girozentrale (Helaba).[16] It explained that whether the *Land* of Hessen could have done better with its investment than place it with Helaba is immaterial. Rather, the question is whether Helaba could have obtained similar terms by going elsewhere:

> It must be held, first of all, that, as the applicant itself conceded at the hearing, the question as to what alternative investment opportunities might have been of interest to the *Land* is irrelevant in the present case. It is not a question of determining whether the *Land* could have obtained a better return on its special fund by investing it differently or in another undertaking, but whether, by investing that special fund in Helaba under the agreed conditions, the *Land* conferred an advantage on Helaba which it could not have obtained in any other way.[17]

This makes sense from an economic perspective. The MEIP is a test of economic advantage, and is therefore a question of whether a transfer is made on terms that could have

---

[16] Ibid.
[17] Ibid., at [58].

been obtained in the private sector; it is *not* a test of the economic rationality of the public body that transfers funds to the private sector. Even if the public body could have made better use of its funds elsewhere, this does not mean that the recipient has gained an advantage. The correct test is whether the terms offered to the recipient would be available from (and, therefore, acceptable to) a private investor.

When applying this test, it is possible to ask whether the recipient had private sector alternatives (ie, benchmarking) or whether a private investor would have done the deal (ie, calculating expected profits)—these are just two sides of the same coin. Sometimes the latter approach of asking whether an investor would have accepted the deal can be a more practical approach. In particular, whereas financial instruments such as the loan portfolios transferred to Helaba have an identifiable and specific rate of remuneration which may be benchmarked against alternatives available in the private sector (such as debt issued by listed companies), the same is not true of many investment projects. For example, what would be the rate to benchmark against comparators in the case of a deal between an airport and an airline? There is no single parameter that captures the combination of commercial benefits and costs, other than the overall expected rate of return on the project. Therefore, many applications of the MEIP involve calculating expected profit, which in turn can be compared with the hypothetical private investor's opportunity cost, namely, the appropriate cost of capital for the project.

In the *Helaba* cases, it appears that the *Land* as investor may have increased its risk, relative to holding a diversified portfolio, by concentrating a large amount of capital in Helaba. Thus the *Land* may have put itself into an economically suboptimal position of excessive risk exposure to Helaba. But this does not mean that aid was involved. The test is whether the contribution brought particular benefit to Helaba. In this case, according to the evidence of the Commission, the bank could have achieved its desired outcome by raising capital from a large number of investors, each of which may have held a diversified portfolio and thus not have exposed itself to excessive risk. As such, the Commission found no aid was involved. The message for other cases is that the private investor of the MEIP is appropriately characterized as the financial market in general (which would not face liquidity constraints) as opposed to one investor in particular.

8.4.4 WHAT EVIDENCE IS RELEVANT?

The profitability analysis in state aid cases is forward-looking, not backward-looking, and should be made on an ex ante basis, taking into account only the market situation and prevailing expectations at the time the measure was introduced, ignoring subsequent developments.[18] The MEIP test assesses whether the government could have expected to earn a normal rate of return at the time the state intervention was made, or, if the market price is used as a benchmark, whether contemporaneous market prices indicate that the beneficiary could have obtained the same deal from the private sector. In case practice, when the Commission is looking back at alleged aid already granted, this is inevitably

---

[18] Case T-16/96 *Cityflyer Express v Commission* [1998] ECR II-757, at [76].

somewhat artificial (one has to go back in time). But still, ex post information should not be used directly for the MEIP test. This principle was recognized in the 2002 *Stardust* case, where the European Court of Justice established that:

> In this case, it is undisputed between the parties that, in order to examine whether or not the State has adopted the conduct of a prudent investor operating in a market economy, it is necessary to place oneself in the context of the period during which the financial support measures were taken in order to assess the economic rationality of the State's conduct, and thus to refrain from any assessment based on a later situation.[19]

It is possible that an ex post analysis (ie, a few years after the capital injection was made) would show that the company has not made a sufficiently high rate of return on capital, but this would not necessarily mean that the capital injection by the government constituted state aid. The low return could be due to macroeconomic circumstances that were unexpected at the time of the capital injection, when the *expected* returns may have indeed been above the cost of capital. It would be incorrect, for example, to assess aid to a bank granted in 1998 and to rely for MEIP purposes on comparisons with other banks' performance between 1994 and 2004—the later period between 1998 and 2004 is only one outcome in a range of possible outcomes that could have been expected in 1998.[20] However, examining the ex post performance of the investment or the performance of similar companies can still serve a purpose as a sense-check of the ex ante assumptions, particularly where there are no unexpected changes in circumstances.

The analysis will not normally be limited to the short-term profitability of the company. In applying the MEIP, the correct analogy is a private company pursuing a structural policy and being guided by profitability perspectives in the longer term. If the company under investigation has made a loss during the first three years of an investment project, for example, this does not necessarily indicate that the capital injection constituted state aid. When a company launches a new product, it often incurs losses during the initial phase and is often able to make a return on its investment only in the medium or long run.

8.4.5 CHOICE OF COMPARATORS

Insofar as you are using a comparator approach to the MEIP (ie, benchmarking against the market) instead of, or as well as, profitability analysis, you face the task of observing what happens in the market and translating it to the case at hand. To illustrate, in the bank case *Helaba*, the Commission found that:

> Helaba could easily have covered its estimated capital requirement in the period from 1998 to 2002 by taking up, at intervals, several smaller silent partnership contributions from a number of different institutional investors . . .

---

[19] Case C-482/99 *France v Commission* [2002] ECR I-4387.

[20] See, for example, the discussion at [207] in Judgment of the General Court in Case T-163/05 *Bundesverband deutscher Banken eV v European Commission* [2010] ECR 00.

since the expense borne by Helaba on account of the contribution at issue is in the middle or upper part of the market range, there is no evidence of an advantage for Helaba or, therefore, of State aid.[21]

This satisfies the basic logic of the MEIP as a test of economic advantage. Thus Helaba had options to go to the market rather than deal with the *Land*, and these options were comparable in financial terms to the deal it made with the *Land*. But what counts as comparable? The *Land* had specific assets (portfolios of loans for investment and housing) which were encumbered with social objectives that would not be typical in the private sector. The assets could provide liability protection for Helaba (ie, to absorb losses in the event of the bank experiencing financial difficulty), and did assist in enhancing Helaba's capital adequacy ratio, but they were not a cash injection and could therefore not be used directly to make loans:

> the transfer of the special fund to Helaba does not mean an influx of liquidity or of revenue for the bank, since the payments relating to the construction of social housing are allocated to the special fund and must be used to provide assistance.[22]

The consequence is that finding a direct comparator in the private sector was bound to be a difficult task—at best the MEIP could be applied using private sector comparators with some, but not all, of the same features as the *Land–Helaba* deal. Given that the Court accepted that the Commission did not make a manifest error of assessment in the use of its comparator evidence, it would appear that the search for comparators can be defined as having a relatively broad scope. It is true that comparators must be carefully chosen, and a variety of 'benchmarking' techniques are available to pick out the most relevant private sector deals to use in the comparison (see section 8.7 on finding private sector comparators). But these techniques do not need to be perfect. As we see in *Helaba*, the General Court accepts that a permanent capital contribution by the state can be compared with time-limited private sector capital contributions: 'this is not a characteristic that precludes any comparison.'[23] Moreover, the Court did not object to the Commission's claim that the *Land* and Helaba were acting as 'market pioneers' in setting up the particular form of capital contribution, and it appeared to believe that the novel structure of the contribution did not vitiate the Commission's comparison with more standard investments.

The Court's conclusion was that the MEIP can appropriately adjust for economic differences between the measure at hand and the private sector comparators being used:

> In a case such as the present case, where the Land seeks to invest a particular type of asset, a transaction cannot be deemed to give rise to State aid where, following negotiations between the public authority wishing to invest and the undertaking, the terms which the latter is prepared to accept on account of the disadvantages facing that undertaking because of the nature of the capital transferred result in a remuneration that is lower than that agreed on

---

[21] Ibid., at [79] and [195].
[22] Ibid., at [272].
[23] Ibid., at [204].

the market for cash investments. In so far as those terms are not more advantageous for the undertaking than those which it could have obtained if the transaction related, as would normally be the case, to liquid capital, it does not gain an advantage which it would not have been able to obtain on the market. By contrast, it cannot be held that, for a transaction of that kind not to be regarded as giving rise to State aid, the public authority must always receive the same remuneration for its investment as an investor who is prepared to transfer liquid capital.[24]

It follows that the MEIP is not a rigid instrument that seeks to make a straight comparison between homogeneous private and public measures, and that fails whenever peculiarities or differences are found in the comparators. If necessary the MEIP can be an economically sophisticated and flexible tool by which a comparison can be made between heterogeneous private and public transactions, making the appropriate adjustments to take account of any differences between the measure at hand and the private sector comparators.

8.4.6 AN INCREMENTAL APPROACH

The MEIP should be applied on an incremental basis—ie, it should consider only the costs and revenues associated with the project at hand. The logic of this is as follows. Assume that a state-owned enterprise is losing €0.4 million per year before a deal is signed; after the deal is signed for a new project, the enterprise's losses are reduced to €0.2 million per year in the short run, and profits are anticipated for the long run. Although an assessment of the profitability of the state-owned enterprise as a whole will show that it is still loss-making at the time the project commences, the project itself is profitable and would therefore be likely to be undertaken by a private investor.

While the analysis is meant to be incremental, it should not ignore a context of previous state support. If the government's participation in a capital-raising exercise is 'polluted' by the effects of previously granted state guarantees or capital injections, you cannot be sure whether its latest capital injection is made on true market economy terms. This applies even if the government's latest participation is made on equal terms with private investors, since the private investors may also make their investment decisions according to the element of previously granted state aid (eg, a guarantee). You can see this reasoning in the Commission's 2009 decision on Lloyds Banking Group:

> In order to determine whether the measure is aid, it is also necessary to verify whether the State acted as a market economy investor. In this respect, the UK authorities and LBG claim that a private investor would have participated in the share offer in similar circumstances since the shares are offered to the existing shareholders at a deep discount to the stock market price. Not participating therefore means foregoing the possibility to purchase these shares at a discounted price. The Commission considers that these considerations advanced by the UK authorities and LBG do not mean that the participation in the share offer is not

---

[24] Ibid., at [277].

State aid. Rather, the Commission notes that the State's participation in the Seaview project follows other aid measures granted to LBG in recent months, in particular the £14.7 billion capital injection to LBG completed in January and June 2009, which resulted in the current 43.5% shareholding of HM Treasury in LBG. As established in the case-law of the Community courts, when assessing the support provided by the State the Commission should take into account any earlier aid measures provided by the State to the same beneficiary. The Commission considers that the State participation in the Seaview project, intended to avoid the loss of State resources which would result from foregoing the opportunity to buy shares at a deep discount to stock market price, cannot fulfil the market economy operator principle. It cannot be considered as free of aid, because the opportunity to buy shares at a deep discount price exclusively results from an aid measure granted in the prior months, ie, the £14.7 billion recapitalisation. Thus, the Commission considers that the State's participation in the Seaview project must be seen in the context of the earlier State aid granted to the bank. In other words, a private investor would not find itself in the situation of the State since it would not have granted the £14.7 billion recapitalisation.[25]

This makes sense from an economic perspective—in the case of a company that has some ongoing benefit from an earlier state aid measure and receives a new state grant, it is difficult to say whether the terms of the new intervention are affected by the earlier measure. If the state offers a loan at a rate of 7%, but has guaranteed some assets of the company, it may well be that private investors would also offer a loan at 7%, knowing that the default risk continues to be mitigated by the earlier guarantee scheme. What is very difficult to calculate is the counterfactual scenario whereby the new state intervention is made *without* the benefit of the earlier guarantee. In this counterfactual scenario, would private investors still offer a loan rate of 7%? Insofar as this counterfactual cannot be calculated, it is impossible to say that a private investor would agree to the terms of the new intervention in the absence of the earlier state aid, and there will usually be a presumption that aid exists. In *France Télécom*, the Commission considered that a successful recapitalization of the company was not sufficient to show that the MEIP test was satisfied, since the recapitalization was said to have been tainted by the earlier promise of state support (even though the state support was never in fact granted).[26]

A similar difficulty arises if all possible comparators for the MEIP benefit from some elements of state support—it may become impossible to find a true 'market economy' benchmark. This might occur, for example, in a sector such as defence, where government support is pervasive. In this case it may be more appropriate to test the MEIP by profitability analysis, since there is a lack of evidence on the true 'market price'.

---

[25] European Commission (2009), 'State Aid No. N 428/2009—*United Kingdom. Restructuring of Lloyds Banking Group*', Letter to the Member State, 18 November, [128].

[26] Commission Decision 2006/621/EC of 2 August 2004 on the State Aid implemented by France for France Télécom, [263].

8.4.7 PROFIT MEASURES AND DISCOUNT RATE

As we saw in Chapter 3, the internal rate of return (IRR) and net present value (NPV) are the correct methods for measuring economic profitability in competition analysis. Profitability can also be calculated in terms of accounting returns, where earnings are divided by book value of equity (ROE) or the book value of equity and debt (ROCE). However, as we saw in Chapter 3 these accounting returns should in general not be considered as the correct measure of an investor's expected average return. ROE and ROCE are calculated on an annual basis, whereas a rational investor will consider the return over the entire lifetime of the project. The Commission used the IRR and NPV in its decision on *NeoVal*.[27] NeoVal was a French programme to develop advanced driverless metro trains, and involved state support provided to a French subsidiary of Siemens AG. A question in the Commission's investigation was whether the €26.5 million NeoVal aid would have the correct incentive effect—a question answered using profitability analysis, where NPVs and IRRs were calculated in three scenarios: a base case where Siemens would undertake only basic R&D; a second scenario where Siemens would undertake the full NeoVal programme but without subsidy; and a third scenario where Siemens went ahead with NeoVal, part-funded by state aid. The Commission compared the profit measures to test whether the aid was necessary—ie, whether the full NeoVal project would be profitable only if state aid were granted—and concluded on this basis that the aid did indeed appear necessary.

A rational private investor will invest only if it expects to earn at least the opportunity cost of capital, defined as the return it could expect from other investments of similar risk profiles in the capital markets. Thus, the expected profits are to be compared with the cost of capital of the company under investigation. The cost of capital is an estimate of the price the company must pay to raise the capital that it has employed—ie, it is the return that private investors would require if they invested in the company. The standard measure of this is the weighted average cost of capital (WACC). As explained in Chapter 3, this is the average of expected rates of return to debt and equity, weighted by the relative proportions of debt and equity in a company's capital structure. This is easy to calculate for a company listed on a stock market and with debt that is publicly traded. For a non-listed company—such as one that is state-owned—the correct approach is to find a suitable set of listed comparators. For example, if the alleged aid beneficiary is a TV broadcaster, a sensible approach is to estimate the average rate of return that investors require for listed European broadcasters. Techniques for finding suitable comparators are set out in section 8.7.

The WACC formula is the return expected by equity holders, weighted by the proportion of equity in a company's capital structure, plus the return expected by debt holders, weighted by the proportion of debt in the capital structure (the latter is known

---

[27] European Commission (2007), 'State Aid: Commission Authorises €26.5 Million in Aid from the French Industrial Innovation Agency for the NeoVal R&D Programme', press release, 22 February. For details of the profitability analysis in *NeoVal*, see Neven (2007).

Table 8.1 Cost of capital calculation

	'Less risky' eg, power generator	'More risky' eg, airline
Cost of debt		
Risk-free rate (%)	3.00	3.00
Debt premium (%)	2.00	4.00
Cost of debt (%)	5.00	7.00
Cost of equity		
Risk-free rate (%)	3.00	3.00
Asset beta	0.30	1.00
Gearing (%)	60.0	60.0
Equity beta	0.75	2.50
Equity risk premium (%)	4.50	4.50
Corporate tax rate (%)	28.0	28.0
Cost of equity (%)	6.38	14.25
WACC		
Pre-tax WACC (%)	6.54	12.12

as the 'gearing' ratio). As such, the appropriately weighted average of the cost of debt and equity represents the aggregate cost of capital for the company. Table 8.1 shows the calculation of the cost of capital for a relatively low-risk firm, a power generator, and for a higher-risk firm, an airline. You can see that the cost of capital for the airline is considerably higher than for the power generator, a result which in this stylized example is driven purely by the differences in the debt premium (ie, the return demanded by creditors to the company over a risk-free rate), and by differences in the asset beta (which is a measure of the extent to which the company's returns follow the stock market). For a utility business, returns will be more stable through time than the market as a whole, yielding a low asset beta; for an airline, returns will be sensitive to wider trends in the economy, yielding a higher asset beta.

The risk-free rate represents a cost of 'risk-free' borrowing—no such thing exists, but the risk-free rate is usually approximated by redemption yields on government bonds (which normally, but not always, have very limited risk). As noted above, the debt premium and the asset beta capture the riskiness of the company's activities, while the equity risk premium (ERP) captures a premium that investors, on average, require from investing in equities as opposed to risk-free assets. With gearing at 60% (which means that the companies are 60% debt-funded and 40% equity-funded), the asset beta is 40% of the equity beta in this example. A multiple of the equity beta and the ERP captures the market risk premium of a particular company. The appropriate ERP can be estimated by considering historical data on equity and risk-free returns.[28] For state-owned and most other non-listed companies, the risk inherent in equity cannot be estimated directly. Instead, the standard approach is to identify relevant publicly listed comparator companies, and to estimate the equity beta for these as a proxy for the equity beta of the company in question. Similarly, the cost of debt can be obtained from yields on outstanding debt or credit default swaps of comparator companies. All this information is entered into the WACC formula, which is then worked out as follows:

cost of debt = risk-free rate + debt premium

equity beta = asset beta / (1 – gearing)

cost of equity = risk-free rate + (equity beta × equity risk premium)

pre-tax cost of equity = cost of equity / (1 – corporate tax rate)

pre-tax weighted average cost of capital = cost of debt × gearing + ((1 – gearing) × pre-tax cost of equity)

So, for the airline's cost of capital, we have the following calculation:

cost of debt = 3% risk-free rate + 4% debt premium = 7%

equity beta = 1.00 asset beta / (1 – 0.60 gearing) = 2.50

cost of equity = 3% risk-free rate + (2.50 equity beta × 4.5% equity risk premium) = 14.25%

pre-tax cost of equity = 14.25% cost of equity / (1 – corporate tax rate of 28%) = 19.79%

pre-tax weighted average cost of capital = 7% cost of debt × 0.60 gearing + 19.79% pre-tax cost of equity × (1 – 0.60 gearing) = 12.12%

If the state is an equity investor, the required rate of return is the cost of equity, rather than the WACC. Conversely, if the state provides guaranteed debt, the appropriate rate of return is the cost of debt. To satisfy the MEIP this would need to be the true market cost of debt excluding the state guarantee. It follows that you can quantify the value of a state guarantee as the difference between the true market cost of debt and the rates paid on a state-guaranteed loan. This presumes that the loan could have been obtained without the guarantee but at a less favourable rate. The analysis might be different if the loan could not have been obtained at all—that is, in circumstances where financial markets have little liquidity (ie, where the pool of potential investors dries up). Such an extreme liquidity situation arose during the financial crisis that began in 2007–08, which explains why the MEIP was exceptionally difficult to apply in the crisis-related state aid cases. Some case law indicates that where a state guarantee enables a borrower to obtain a loan which otherwise could not have been obtained at all, the entire loan might be regarded as aid.[29] This is not really sound economics—it is merely observed that a private loan

---

[28] Such information is widely cited in regulatory cost of capital determinations, or can be found in sources such as Dimson et al. (2010).

[29] Case C-288/96 *Germany v Commission* [2000] ECR I-8237, at [30]–[31] and [40]–[41].

was not obtained, not that it was unobtainable at any price—but is perhaps a practical necessity in some cases.

8.4.8 THE MEIP AS APPLIED TO DIFFERENT FORMS OF AID

The most intuitive application of the MEIP is to an investment decision by the state. Where the state is a guarantor or a creditor, or is selling or renting out an asset (such as land), things may seem less straightforward. However, the basic principle remains the same: the litmus test is whether the alleged aid measure would have been granted on the same terms by the private sector. For example, the question for loans is whether a private creditor would have provided the same facility, given the same set of circumstances.

For the sale or rental of a state asset it is convenient to consider the MEIP on the basis of whether the deal is done at a market price, rather than try to calculate the expected rate of return and compare this to a cost of capital. This yields two options for selling or renting out an asset. The first is to allow the market to determine the price (ie, hold a competitive tender and accept the best bid). The second is to orientate the price to market circumstances by looking for comparators (for example, renting out an office on the basis of rates achieved for similar properties in the private sector), or—possibly amounting to the same thing—by seeking an independent valuation by an asset valuer. The European Commission's Vademecum on state aid points to the role of a market price in determining whether a measure constitutes 'economic advantage':

> The aid should constitute an economic advantage that the undertaking would not have received in the normal course of business. Less obvious examples of transactions satisfying this condition are given below:
>
> – A firm buys/rents publicly owned land at less than the market price;
>
> – A company sells land to the state at higher than market price;
>
> – A company enjoys privileged access to infrastructure without paying a fee;
>
> – An enterprise obtains risk capital from the state on terms which are more favourable than it would obtain from a private investor.[30]

In risk capital state aid cases the 'market price', as determined by the participation of private investors, is central. According to the Risk Capital Guidelines no state aid is granted to the investor if the investment is effected *pari passu* between public and private investors. This is assumed to be the case if both public and private investors share the same risks and rewards and level of subordination, and normally if at least 50% of the funding of the measure is provided by private investors independent of the target company.[31] In other cases a market price is difficult to find—for instance, where the price to be

---

[30] European Commission (2007), 'Vademecum Community Rules on State Aid', 15 February, p 3.
[31] Community guidelines on state aid to promote risk capital investments in small and medium-sized enterprises ('Risk Capital Guidelines') [2006] OJ C194/2, s 3.2.

benchmarked is a fair transfer price between a network utility and its downstream subsidiary for access to the utility's network, or a transfer price between a public service broadcaster and its commercial arm for access to television rights. In both cases, the problem is a lack of good comparators—you don't see much duplication of utility networks within the same country, and one TV programme is not normally worth the same as another. Where there is a lack of reliable data on market prices, you might also need to look at cost-based prices. The *Chronopost* case is helpful in this respect.[32] Chronopost SA was a wholly owned subsidiary of La Poste, the French provider of universal postal services, and operated express delivery services, which is a competitive market in France. The case sets out the useful principle that there would be no state aid to Chronopost if it were established, first, that the price charged properly covers all the additional, variable costs incurred, plus an appropriate contribution to the fixed costs and an adequate return on capital investment; and second, that there is nothing to suggest that those elements have been underestimated or fixed in an arbitrary fashion. We return to the topic of cost-based prices in section 8.7.

8.4.9 THE MEIP AS A TOOL FOR AID QUANTIFICATION

In some situations, determining the size of the economic advantage is fairly straightforward, ie, for direct subsidies granted to companies. However, in many cases measuring the size of aid requires a more sophisticated approach, eg, comparing the terms of the aid measure with the terms that would have been provided by the market economy investor. The MEIP is particularly helpful for aid quantification in cases where the state intervenes with measures that are directly comparable to private investment decisions, for example, by making equity investments or providing loans or loan guarantees.

For example, in normal circumstances the aid element for a guarantee will be the difference between the appropriate market price for the guarantee and the actual price paid for it by the borrower. (In exceptional circumstances where markets suffer a liquidity crisis it may be difficult to observe a 'market price' as there may be no 'market' to speak of.) In the case of Banco Privado Português, the Commission found that a state guarantee on a €450 million loan constituted illegal and incompatible aid, and then ordered recovery of the difference between 'the price the bank should have paid for the guarantee and the lower fee actually paid', in order that 'the bank is not unduly advantaged compared to its competitors, who have to pay market rates for their funding.'[33] Where no market price for the guarantee is observable, the aid element can be calculated on the basis of comparable soft loans in the private sector (such as lending to a subsidiary where the subsidiary benefits from the guarantee of a parent company). Here the estimate of the

---

[32] See [82] and [100]–[114] of Judgments of Court of Justice of the European Communities No C-341/06 P, of 1 July 2008 in Joined Cases C-341/06 P and C-342/06 P.

[33] European Commission (2010), 'State Aid: Commission Orders Recovery of Illegal State Aid from Banco Privado Português', press release IP/10/972, 20 July.

guarantee value is the difference between the market interest rate for the subsidiary without the parent's guarantee and the interest rate obtained thanks to the parent's guarantee. The amount of aid is the difference between the guarantee value and any premium paid to the state.

Despite this simple logic, quantifying aid using the MEIP can be very difficult in certain cases. In *France Télécom*, referred to above, the issue was the value of a statement of government support (not a guarantee per se, but words implying that the state would step in if necessary). In the case of state support provided during the financial crisis to otherwise sound banks in around 2008–09, liquidity dried up from the market (the MEIP relies on the concept of liquid financial markets). Nonetheless the MEIP is still the correct conceptual framework and guide to quantifying aid. In a situation like *France Télécom*, the practical application of the MEIP does break down somewhat as you can neither conduct a profitability analysis nor find a direct private sector comparator. The guiding principle of the hypothetical private investor might lead you in this case to examine the closest private sector counterpart (a quasi-guarantee such as a comfort letter) and then calibrate its value according to the change in the price of France Télécom's debt which followed from the announcement by the state. Likewise, in financial crisis cases, the MEIP remains at least a useful thought framework, which would for instance narrow the analysis to examining evidence contemporaneous to the state measure (such as the capital raised privately by Barclays, an unsupported bank, in 2008), rather than ex post evidence.

8.5 IS THERE A DISTORTION OF COMPETITION OR TRADE?

8.5.1 TESTS FOR DISTORTION

The legal threshold for the presence of a distortion of competition appears to be very low. The language of Article 107 refers to aid being that which 'distorts or threatens to distort' competition. For the binary decision as to whether a particular measure either does or does not threaten to distort competition, the analysis tends to be quite limited. But for the purpose of the balancing test (see section 8.10), you also need to know how much distortion of competition a particular measure is likely to induce, which will require a more sophisticated analysis.

The underlying economics of determining competitive distortion are similar to those applied to Article 101, which prohibits agreements that prevent, restrict or distort competition (albeit with the stricter requirement that the distortion be appreciable or significant), as discussed in Chapters 5 and 6. In Article 101 cases, as with state aid, balancing positive and negative effects can be required. The following factors are relevant to the assessment of distortion under the state aid rules:

- Is there strong selectivity (ie, the aid is targeted at individual companies or specific industries)?

- What is the market position of the company? (The criteria for market power discussed in Chapter 3 are relevant here.)
- What price does the aided company charge?
- Is there much cross-border trade in the markets affected?
- Is the particular form of the aid prone to lead to distortions?
- What was the procedure for selecting beneficiaries?

It is worth remembering that state aid is intended to change market outcomes—the point of aid is to remedy a market failure or deliver an objective of common interest, providing something that the market does not provide when left to its own devices. That state aid distorts the outcomes of normal competition is therefore inevitable; if there were no distortion, the aid would not have achieved its intended effect. What is of concern in state aid is that subsidies are targeted at the market failure, and do not 'spill over' to affect other incentives. For example, you might wish to encourage the development of a more fuel-efficient engine, and therefore grant a subsidy to a large car manufacturer. The unintended consequence or 'spillover' effect might be that the small engineering company that has been developing a similar technology cannot now sell it to the large car manufacturer. Similarly, you might wish to encourage more lending to credit-constrained small businesses and therefore provide state guarantees on bank lending to such companies. The unwanted spillover effect might be that a foreign bank not covered by the guarantee now cancels its plans to enter the market for small business lending.

What is common to the spillover effects is that the competitive balance has changed—the small engineering company is disadvantaged relative to the large car manufacturer, and the foreign bank is disadvantaged relative to domestic banks. Hence the aim of looking at distortions of competition is to decide whether the aid creates (undue) distortions to a level playing field. This means that you cannot say: aid recipient X has increased its market share by Y%, and that is the distortion of competition. The fact that recipient X has increased production may well be exactly the intended effect of the aid. You would have to say: rivals to aid recipient X now find it difficult to compete, because they have no access to the funding available to company X. The nature of the inquiry into competitive distortion is therefore looking more towards competitive dynamics (cost structures, barriers to entry, and expansion) and less towards competitive outcomes (changes to market shares or prices). Observing short-run outcomes, you would tend to see that state aid benefits consumers via lower prices charged by the aided company; but in the long run, the disturbance to competitive dynamics can ultimately harm consumers. Hence, insofar as competitive outcomes (prices, market shares) are used to measure distortion, they need to be observed in light of the intended consequence of the aid.

8.5.2 STRONG SELECTIVITY

With regard to selectivity, the less selective an aid measure, the smaller the distortion of competition. During the global financial crisis that began in 2007–08, the European

Commission stated that 'general measures open to all comparable market players' on equal terms are likely to be outside the scope of the state aid rules.[34] If a measure is company-specific, such as restructuring aid to an airline, selectivity is obvious. If a measure is industry-specific, the selectivity question is whether access to public support is available to all in the industry, including new entrants, and whether it is limited according to the domicile of the company. For example, in 2008 the European Commission blocked a planned Irish scheme to guarantee the assets of only Irish-owned banks. This scheme, formulated in the context of the financial crisis that began in 2007–08, would have likely resulted in difficulties for any non-guaranteed bank in Ireland, as savers would have had an incentive to switch their deposits to Irish-owned banks, thereby distorting competition between banks in Europe.[35] To be a truly general measure, aid should not be restricted to the 'favoured circle of those with an established track record and good contacts with public decision-makers'.[36] Truly general measures are not aid by definition, since they harbour no element of selectivity. We note in passing that a lack of selectivity is not always a virtue: if the aim of aid is to change the incentives faced by a specific company or set of companies (eg, to fill a narrow funding gap), selectivity can be a positive feature in terms of its incentive effect and limiting aid to the minimum necessary.

8.5.3 WHAT IS THE MARKET POSITION OF THE COMPANY?

Market structure, or more particularly the market share of the aid recipient, matters because it affects whether that recipient is likely to be able to influence market outcomes. A small, capacity-constrained company which expands output as a consequence of a subsidy may remain below the threshold at which it has power to behave independently of competitive pressures. If the affected market is concentrated and the subsidy recipient is a major player then it is more likely that competitors will have to alter their business in response to the subsidy. This may reduce the efficiency of the market. It could also result in the exit of competitors, thus increasing the market share of the recipient further and enhancing the scope for anti-competitive behaviour. The criteria for market power discussed in Chapter 3 are of relevance here, as are the techniques of market definition in Chapter 2. The competitive effects of state aid will also depend on the degree of product differentiation, for the reasons we saw in Chapters 2 and 7—if one company has an advantage in a market with differentiated products, the competitive impact is less than if that same company faced closer, non-differentiated competitors,

---

[34] European Commission (2008), 'Communication from the Commission: The Application of State Aid Rules to Measures Taken in Relation to Financial Institutions in the Context of the Current Global Financial Crisis', 13 October, [51].

[35] The remedy was to extend the scheme to other banks with significant operations in Ireland. See Kroes (2008).

[36] Economic Advisory Group on Competition Policy (2006), 'The European Commission's Draft Community Framework for State Aid for Research, Development and Innovation: Commentary by the Economic Advisory Group on Competition Policy', 3 July, p 2.

since consumer switching to the aided company will be affected by the degree of product differentiation.

8.5.4 WHAT PRICE DOES THE AIDED COMPANY CHARGE?

If the aided company does not change its prices, or if it changes prices but has a negligible market share (both before and after the price change), the competitive impact of the subsidy is likely to be minimal in the short run. Whether or not prices change will be influenced by the structure of the aid measure (fixed or variable subsidy), as discussed below. The principle is that a subsidy to variable costs will lead to a change in the company's price, whereas a subsidy to fixed costs will typically not affect price. If you observe that the company's price, with and without the aid, is the same as the market price, there is less scope for distortion in the short run.

However, charging a market price does not necessarily preclude a distortion of long-run outcomes. In principle it may be sufficient for a 'distortion' that a state subsidy alters the recipient's costs or revenue prospects and so affects its decisions concerning entry, exit, or levels of output. Even when a company is charging a market price, a subsidy that reduces the company's marginal cost will lead it to produce more than it otherwise would have done (since each unit of output is more profitable than in the counterfactual of no subsidy), which might be considered a distortion of the market.

8.5.5 ARE THE MARKETS AFFECTED TRADE-INTENSIVE?

Regarding a distortion of trade, it is necessary to show that the aid strengthens the position of an undertaking compared with other undertakings competing in intra-EU trade.[37] This can occur even where an undertaking operates purely at a domestic level, since the prospects for companies in other Member States to compete with that company (eg, by exporting their products) may be affected where the subsidy expands the domestic company's output beyond the level which would be produced in the absence of aid. In *Heiser*, which concerned aid to medical practitioners in Austria, despite the generally local character of medical services, it was held to be 'not inconceivable' that Austrian medical practitioners might be in competition with those in other Member States, and as such an actual or potential effect on trade could not be excluded.[38]

There are some cases where no effect on inter-state trade is found, but Advocate General Jacobs indicated in *GEMO* that such cases are rare:

> In economic sectors with little competition in intra-Community trade such as car repairs, taxi services, or sectors with prohibitive transport costs, aid of a relatively small amount

[37] Bacon (2009), para 2.142, referring to Case 730/79 *Philip Morris v Commission* [1980] ECR 2671, at [11], and Cases C-393/04 and C-41/05 *Air Liquide Industries Belgium* [2006] ECR I-5293, at [35].
[38] Case C-172/03 *Heiser* [2005] ECR I-1627, at [33] and [35].

granted to small undertakings operating on essentially local markets might not affect trade between Member States.[39]

An example of such a market is found in a national court's judgment on a state aid case regarding car parking, in *P1 Holding BV v Municipality of Maastricht*.[40] The municipality of Maastricht had entered into an intention agreement with car park firm Q-Park NV in November 2002, in which Q-Park was granted the right to operate a number of car parks for a period of 30 years. The agreement was entered into without giving other market parties the opportunity to tender. P1 Holding, a competitor of Q-Park, argued that the agreement was contrary to state aid rules. The District Court considered that the claim by P1 Holding could succeed only if the agreement between the municipality of Maastricht and Q-Park adversely affected trade between Member States, and that it was up to P1 Holding to provide evidence of this. P1 Holding argued that from the geographical location of Maastricht (it is not far from Belgium and Germany), it followed that it is likely that market parties from other Member States would be interested in the municipality of Maastricht and that there were various foreign companies that were active in the car park business that would be capable of carrying out this assignment. To substantiate this, P1 Holding provided four attendance lists of public tenders in the Netherlands, showing the presence of foreign market parties.

However, the Court considered that P1 Holding failed to prove a distortion of the trade between Member States. The argument regarding the geographical location of Maastricht was said to be insufficient to substantiate a claim of distortion of trade between Member States. Furthermore, the attendance lists of public tenders dated from the years 2005, 2006, and 2007, whereas the agreement between the municipality of Maastricht and Q-Park was dated 27 November 2002. P1 Holding also did not provide evidence of the activities of the foreign parties cited in the four public tenders in other Member States at the time of the agreement. The District Court thus ruled that the agreement between the municipality of Maastricht and Q-Park did not affect trade between Member States and was therefore not in conflict with Article 107 TFEU.

In light of this judgment, as compared with the judgment in *Heiser*, the exact legal threshold for an effect on inter-state trade seems a little uncertain. Economics can at least assist by identifying the markets in which an effect on trade is more likely. From an economic perspective, the degree of the effect on trade is enhanced where markets are more trade-intensive—a key measure of trade intensity being the share of imports and exports in the particular sector. This is influenced by factors such as the transport costs for the good, whether it can indeed be easily traded (local travel and restaurant services, for example, cannot be traded), and the degree of differentiation between national markets (some products are attuned to national tastes, such as speciality foods). Another measure is the extent of cross-border participation in tenders for public service contracts,

---

[39] Case C-126/91 *GEMO* [2003] ECR I-13769, at [145].

[40] *P1 Holding BV v Municipality of Maastricht*, District Court Maastricht ('Rechtbank Maastricht'), 8 October 2008, LJN BF 7031.

as considered in the P1 Holding case. There is a commonality here with the tools of geographic market definition which we discussed in Chapter 2.

As to international markets, recall that it is necessary to show that the aid strengthens the position of an undertaking compared with other undertakings competing in intra-EU trade. What if the undertaking competes with companies in global markets? For example, in respect of support given to Airbus Industrie, the question was asked:

> What measures has [sic] the Commission taken to ensure that the launch aid proposed by the British, German, French and Spanish Governments for Airbus Industrie's A3XX aircraft does not distort competition for other segments of the EU civil aviation market?

The answer was:

> The fundamental position of the Commission is that the R&D aid for Airbus Industrie does not affect trade between Member States and so is not caught by Article 87(1) [now Article 107(1)].[41]

The rationale for this answer, we might suppose, is that competition and trade is not distorted if there is only one manufacturer in Europe that can undertake the investment—ie, if there is a monopoly firm and high barriers to entry, such that competition from other firms is impossible. This is a rather exceptional scenario, and even so there is still the question of which firm gets to be the single manufacturer. Picking a winner is itself distortive, even if afterwards it appears that no other firm is a potential candidate for state support.

In general, whether the measure in question has a significant effect on trade depends not only on trade intensity but also on the form of the measure. As such we now turn to the economics of different forms of aid.

8.5.6 THE FORM OF AID

The main economic difference in the form of aid is between a 'variable subsidy', which affects only variable costs, and a 'lump-sum subsidy', which affects only fixed costs. Lump-sum subsidies do not affect the marginal costs of the recipients, and therefore do not directly affect the pricing decisions either—basic economic principles (see Chapters 1 and 2) indicate that companies set prices with reference to their marginal costs, not their fixed costs (fixed costs do matter for the decision about whether to enter or exit a market, but not in the setting of prices). Lump-sum subsidies apply when the form of funding is fixed, regardless of the recipient's level of output produced or its revenues (or profits). Literally, they apply not to marginal output decisions but rather to 'lumpy' amounts of fixed cost. In the 2009 Royal Mail state aid case, the European Commission found that:

> deficit payments which Royal Mail is required to make to the pension scheme, once established following negotiations between the company and the pensions trustees, do not vary

---

[41] European Commission (2001), 'Written Question E-2718/00 by Christopher Huhne (ELDR) to the Commission. Subject: Launch aid for Airbus Industrie's A3XX aircraft' [2001] OJ C113 E/164, 18 April. Available at: <http://eur-lex.europa.eu/LexUriServ/LexUriServ.do?uri=OJ:C:2001:113E:0157:0158:EN:PDF>.

according to levels of output or input. Their reduction in the initial years by means of the measure does not therefore affect marginal costs and is not such as to affect Royal Mail's commercial decisions . . . [42]

The Royal Mail point is a general one—consider a lump-sum subsidy to a company in a competitive market. The effect of the transfer is to reduce the fixed cost of production, but marginal cost (the cost of producing each extra unit of output) is not altered and consequently there is no effect on the profit-maximizing level of output produced by the recipient. A lump-sum subsidy has no short-run effect on the market price under these circumstances and hence there is no immediate distortion of the competitive outcome (such as a jump in the market share of the aided company). A lump-sum subsidy is, in these conditions, a direct transfer from the state to the company receiving the aid.

Under such circumstances, if the objective of state aid is to encourage output expansion (eg, increase production of energy-saving light bulbs), government intervention would not achieve its objective, and public resources would be wasted. Furthermore, as a result of the lump-sum subsidies, the recipient's profits increase by an amount equal to the transfer. The same logic can be seen in the pass-on of cartel overcharges, discussed in Chapter 10, where we show that a change in fixed costs due to cartel overcharges may not be passed on in the same way as an overcharge that affects variable costs.

Fixed costs influence whether a firm can viably operate in the market—depending on the size of the government transfer, the extra profits might allow relatively inefficient companies to remain in the market, which in the longer term would change incentives and perpetuate market inefficiencies. You cannot therefore rule out competitive distortion from lump-sum subsidies, albeit that the effects will be felt mainly in the long run. Also, the incentives of the recipient to invest in developing or adopting more cost-efficient and innovative methods of delivering products may decrease as a result of the subsidies. Consequently, productive and dynamic efficiency may be diminished.

Variable subsidies can in general have a greater effect on market outcomes than lump-sum subsidies and hence are more likely to distort competition (but may also be more effective at achieving their intended aim—see below). Certainly the short-run effects will be greater. In the case of a unit subsidy where the total amount of aid is a function of the units of output produced by the recipient, marginal cost falls by the extent of the unit subsidy. This will encourage a previously efficient company to expand its production up to the point where the new marginal cost curve meets with the demand curve. At this point, the company will be producing too much output at an inefficiently high cost (see Figure 8.1). The effect is to distort competition, since the aided company gains market share at the expense of more efficient competitors. On the positive side, a variable subsidy directly changes a company's incentives—so if society wishes to have greater output of energy-saving light bulbs, shifting the energy-saving light bulb company's marginal costs will have this effect, whereas a lump-sum subsidy will not

---

[42] Commission Decision of 8 April 2009 on the measures C 7/07 (ex NN 82/06 and NN 83/06) implemented by the United Kingdom in favour of Royal Mail, 2009/613/EC, 15 August, [118].

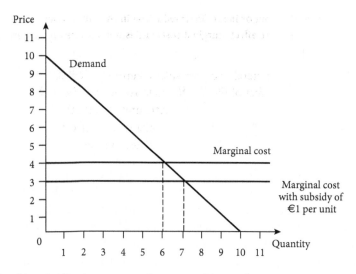

Fig. 8.1 Variable subsidies to a company in a competitive market: output expansion effect

have such a direct effect. We return to this in the discussion of the balancing test in section 8.10.

8.5.7 THE RELEVANCE OF THE PROCEDURE FOR SELECTING BENEFICIARIES

Insofar as beneficiaries are selected through a competitive tender, it is less likely that the measure involves state aid, since the element of 'selective advantage' is dissipated—all suppliers have an equal chance before the tender. When the state is procuring a service, an open tender process can be on market terms and as such will not involve state aid. In the context of SGEIs, it is of importance whether or not a competitive tender is held— this is covered in the next section.

8.6 SERVICES OF GENERAL ECONOMIC INTEREST: THE *ALTMARK* CRITERIA

8.6.1 TYPES OF SGEI

SGEIs are services purchased by the state that would not be provided by the market. They create obligations imposed by the state on companies to deliver social policy objectives, often with a goal of ensuring that all citizens have access to a given good or service (eg, local transport or postal services). For a genuine need to exist, it must be the case that in the absence of public support a certain group of citizens would be under-served—that is, they would be unable to buy the product at an 'affordable' or 'fair' price, or they would not be served at all because no private sector provider would find it economical to do so. Examples of SGEIs being defined include an obligation on airlines to operate routes which are not commercially viable, an obligation to distribute post across a national territory at a uniform tariff, and the provision of private medical insurance at an affordable price. Other SGEIs are found in sectors such as gas, electricity, and telecoms—services that may be 'essential' to all consumers. The obligation to serve all consumers on equal terms is also known as a universal service obligation (USO), or as a public service obligation (PSO). We use the term USO in what follows, but recognize that in many cases, such as local bus services, it is not *all* consumers who benefit— rather it is a certain subset of consumers defined by geography or income.

A further justification for SGEIs relates to other social policy goals. An example is the provision of public service broadcasting: TV programming with a 'higher purpose', providing types of programmes that would not be supplied by market forces alone. As recognized by the European Commission, state aid policy in the broadcasting sector has to take account of the functions performed beyond the normal provision of economic services:

> The broadcast media play a central role in the functioning of modern democratic societies, in particular in the development and transmission of social values. Therefore, the broadcasting sector has, since its inception, been subject to specific regulation in the general interest. This regulation has been based on common values, such as freedom of expression and the right of reply, pluralism, protection of copyright, promotion of cultural and linguistic diversity, protection of minors and of human dignity, consumer protection.[43]

8.6.2 THE *ALTMARK* CRITERIA

State aid policy in the SGEI area is defined by the assessment of how companies providing SGEIs can be compensated by the state without distorting competition. The SGEI equivalent of the MEIP and the starting point for state aid analysis in this area is the *Altmark* judgment, in which the European Court of Justice stated that compensation for public services does not constitute aid when four conditions are met:

(1) The Universal (or Public) Service Obligation is clearly defined.

(2) The parameters for the compensation are objective, transparent, and are established in advance.

(3) The compensation should not exceed costs plus a reasonable profit.

(4) The compensation is determined either through public procurement (that is, a public tender has taken place and it is the winning firm which is chosen to provide the USO) or, if no public tender has taken place, the firm should be compensated on the basis of the costs of a typical well-run company.[44]

---

[43] Communication from the Commission on Services of General Economic Interest in Europe [2001] OJ C17/4, 22.

[44] Judgment in Case C-280/00 *Altmark Trans GmbH and Regierungspräsidium Magdeburg v Nahverkehrsgesellschaft Altmark GmbH* ('*Altmark*') [2003] ECR I-7747.

These criteria work in a similar way to the MEIP test. If they are not met, there is state aid, and if they are all met there is no state aid. This makes economic sense because the criteria require that compensation for a public service is no more than is necessary *for an efficient operator*. In other words, where *Altmark* is met there is no reasonable prospect of deriving undue competitive advantage from the state subsidy, since the amount of state support is no more than sufficient to cover the undertaking's non-commercial SGEI obligation. You can see the parallel with the MEIP—the state transfer affords the undertaking no economic advantage, and therefore does not count as state aid.

Some state aid procedural guidance expresses doubt about whether the *Altmark* criteria can ever be met in practice. This example is taken from the 'State Aid Unit SGEI Guidance' of State Aid Scotland:

> These criteria are very difficult to meet and we are not aware of any instances in the UK where all conditions have been met. In practice most services would require a competitive tender to be held. There are examples of where the Commission believe that *Altmark* has been met. For example, the financing of a scheme promoting investments in order to ensure security of electricity supply in Ireland (N475/2003), the financing of general broadband in France (N381/2004). Most compensation given towards a SGEI is likely not to meet all of the *Altmark* criteria and will therefore be aid.[45]

This partly reflects the inherent difficulty in measuring efficiency, but it may also reflect the lack of cross-fertilization between the economics of regulation and the economics of state aid. If you consider any regulated sector, such as water, gas, electricity, or postal services, it is quite normal for a regulator to benchmark companies' costs and test their efficiency. It is somewhat surprising that this analysis does not seem to have been translated to state aid cases.

If the *Altmark* criteria are not met and state aid is present, the more general SGEI Framework—or one of its sector-specific variants (such as the one for public service broadcasting)—applies. The SGEI Framework states that aid is compatible provided that the following conditions are met:

(1) The public funding is provided for a genuine service of general economic interest.

(2) There is a clear specification of the public service obligations and the methods of calculating compensation.

(3) The amount of compensation does not exceed what is necessary to cover the costs incurred in discharging the public service obligations, taking into account the relevant receipts and reasonable profit for discharging those obligations.[46]

Since these criteria are substantively similar to the first three *Altmark* conditions, it makes sense to discuss their economic interpretation together in what follows. The final

[45] State Aid Scotland (2010), 'State Aid Unit Services of General Economic Interest (SGEI) Guidance', 23 February.

[46] European Commission (2005), 'Community Framework for State Aid in the Form of Public Service Compensation' [2005] OJ C297, 29 November.

Altmark condition, requiring either a competitive tender or knowledge of the costs of an efficient operator, is not part of the SGEI Framework and is discussed separately below.

Note that despite the overlap between the *Altmark* and SGEI Framework, the formal assessment proceeds first with the verification of the presence of state aid by applying the four criteria set out in the *Altmark* judgment, and then, if state aid exists, an examination of its compatibility with the internal market on the basis of the SGEI Framework. From an economic perspective, we simply note that if the second stage is reached, most of the relevant analysis will have been already conducted for the first, *Altmark*, stage.

8.6.3 THE FIRST *ALTMARK*/SGEI CRITERION: THE SERVICE OBLIGATION MUST BE CLEARLY DEFINED

Economics can help unpick what is being promised when a company (such as a postal operator or telephone network) is subject to an SGEI obligation, since the essence of an SGEI is that it is a service that the market would not otherwise supply. Member States have considerable discretion in defining their own SGEIs, but are subject to not making a 'manifest error' in that definition, such as defining as an SGEI a service that the market would supply anyway.

If the SGEI is of the USO type it will often involve two requirements: to offer universal coverage, ie, the obligation to provide the product at a reasonable price to all consumers; and to offer uniform pricing, that is, to supply at the same price to all consumers regardless of any cost differences in supplying different groups. Part of the policy motivation for these two obligations is social equity—for example, a belief that rural consumers need broadband at the same price and of the same standard as urban consumers because without it their participation in civic life may be diminished ('digital exclusion').

In principle, the policy motivation could also be efficiency-related, eg, where there is a market failure relating to network externalities (ie, adding the extra users to a telephone network will give existing users the benefit of being able to call whoever they wish, but the marginal users do not factor this into their decision to join the network—see also Chapters 2, 3, and 4). Another efficiency rationale relates to an SGEI being defined for public goods. These are goods where consumption is non-rivalrous—this means that more than one individual can consume the good without it affecting the consumption of others, eg, a firework display—and non-excludable—it is highly costly to prevent people from benefiting from the provision of the service, eg, street lighting. Consider the case of national defence. The fact that one person benefits from the services provided by armed forces does not affect other people's benefit from the same services, so access to national defence is non-rivalrous. In addition, no particular individual can be prevented from taking advantage of the protection provided, so national defence is non-excludable. The problem is that because public goods are non-rivalrous and non-excludable, consumers, when asked, tend to understate the benefits they receive from the public good in order to obtain them at a lower price or even for free—a form of free-rider problem which we also encountered in Chapter 6. Voluntary contributions by users will be low compared with the cost of providing public goods. As a result, if left to the market there will be under-provision (or no provision at all) of such goods. In areas in which the market cannot solve the free-rider problem, such as defence, there is a justification for more proactive government intervention. Specifically, the government might decide to procure the good directly, or subsidize companies to encourage them to provide it.

USO obligations frequently refer to SGEIs provided by former state-owned monopolies—the postal service is an example. As monopolies, internalizing the cross-subsidy to apply universal coverage and uniform pricing was not too much trouble for these companies, since those customers who effectively funded the cross-subsidy had no other option. But as privatized companies in liberalizing markets, these obligations may be an increasingly heavy burden and previous rich sources of funding will dry up as new entrants follow the logical strategy of cherry-picking. Entrants will seek to exploit the profitable difference between the uniform price charged by a USO incumbent and the cost of supplying the same service to low-cost consumers or low-cost areas, such as urban areas for a postal network. They would not serve the unprofitable customers. If the USO applies only to the incumbent and not any of its competitors, this drives a need to be very clear about the terms of the USO. From an economic perspective the important point is that the terms of compensation are linked to the losses incurred as a result of fulfilling the USO (note that losses are inherent, otherwise there is no real need to impose an *obligation* to provide universal service). For instance, a fixed telecoms network operator may be obliged to provide network access to users in isolated rural areas on the same terms as those offered to users located in a city area. The cost of linking an additional residential user to the network may be high in the former case, and very low in the latter. Without USO or other public interventions (such as direct subsidies to the users involved), users in isolated areas might not be served at all, or the market would charge a large premium for rural supply. The definition of the USO should therefore identify the service to be provided to isolated areas, with precise service parameters such that the associated costs are clear and the compensation can be calculated. In healthcare insurance, the same exercise might involve determining which companies have a disproportionate number of older customers—ie, those customers who might not be served in the absence of the USO. In the Irish electricity decision, the European Commission demonstrated the logic of defining an SGEI based on a clear distinction between what the market will and won't deliver:

> meeting security of supply via the setting up of sufficient reserve capacity generation can be considered in itself as a service of general economic interest, to the extent that:
>
> - A clear distinction is made between 'normal' capacity and 'reserve' capacity generation. The former being the capacity that the market would spontaneously provide to cover expected demand (or expected increases of demand) under normal market and regulatory conditions ...
>
> - The 'reserve' capacity is the additional capacity that would not be spontaneously provided by normal market forces but is considered necessary in order to meet peaks of demand.[47]

---

[47] European Commission (2003), 'State aid N 475/2003—Ireland—Public Service Obligation in respect of new electricity generation capacity for security of supply', Letter to the Member State, C(2003) 4488 final, 16 December, [35].

8.6.4 THE SECOND *ALTMARK*/SGEI CRITERION: PARAMETERS FOR THE COMPENSATION MUST BE OBJECTIVE, TRANSPARENT, AND ESTABLISHED IN ADVANCE

In practice it may be difficult to set out a detailed plan of costs when a company is engaged to provide an SGEI. Assuming that the SGEI is to be provided over the course of several years, there will be considerable uncertainty attached to cost estimates, and until the company has put in place accounting separation between the SGEI and its other commercial activities, questions of cost allocation may cause difficulties (we return to this below). Therefore, a realistic approach is to set out the main parameters for the future calculation of the SGEI compensation—for example, that the compensation will be determined according to the number of users, that it will meet all direct costs associated with each user, and that it will meet a proportion of the fixed costs that are common to the SGEI function and commercial activities. In its guidance on SGEI compensation, the Commission suggests that:

> The Decision [on SGEI compensation] only requires that the entrustment includes the basis for the future calculation of the compensation, for example that the compensation will be determined on the basis of a price per day, per meal, per care based on an estimation of the number of potential users . . . What is important is that there is clarity over the basis on which the funding body (the State, the local authority) will finance the provider. Such a transparency is also beneficial to taxpayers.[48]

Note that if compensation is awarded following a competitive tender, it is highly likely that the parameters will meet the substance of the second *Altmark*/SGEI criterion. If there were initially doubts as to the parameters for compensation, the companies bidding are likely to have demanded clarification before committing to the tender. Nonetheless, even if the parameters for compensation are established in advance, this does not guarantee that compensation will be appropriate. This takes us to the next step, which is how to set the appropriate compensation for an SGEI.

8.6.5 THE THIRD *ALTMARK*/SGEI CRITERION: COMPENSATION MUST NOT EXCEED COSTS PLUS A REASONABLE PROFIT

The third criterion requires that compensation for providing SGEIs does not exceed what is necessary to cover all or part of the costs incurred in the discharge of these services—taking into account the relevant revenues and a reasonable profit. Again, it is easier to fulfil this criterion in the context of a well-defined competitive tender, where effective competition should ensure that compensation to the winning bidder will not

---

[48] European Commission (2007), 'Commission Staff Working Document: Frequently Asked Questions in Relation with Commission Decision of 28 November 2005 on the Application of Article 86(2) of the EC Treaty to State Aid in the Form of Public Service Compensation Granted to Certain Undertakings Entrusted with the Operation of Services of General Economic Interest, and of the Community Framework for State Aid in the Form of Public Service Compensation', SEC(2007) 1516 final, 20 November.

be excessive. The difficulty arises in cases where a competitive tender cannot be held, such as where the undertaking in question is a long-standing SGEI provider, but now wishes to use some of its publicly funded assets for a commercial purpose. The Commission has provided the following explanation of the conditions under which the amount of compensation will be deemed appropriate:

1. The amount of compensation shall not exceed what is necessary to cover the costs incurred in discharging the public service obligations, taking into account the relevant receipts and a reasonable profit on any own capital necessary for discharging those obligations ...

2. The costs to be taken into consideration shall comprise all the costs incurred in the operation of the service of general economic interest. They shall be calculated . . . as follows:

   (a) where the activities of the undertaking in question are confined to the service of general economic interest, all its costs may be taken into consideration;

   (b) where the undertaking also carries out activities falling outside the scope of the service of general economic interest, only the costs associated with the service of general economic interest shall be taken into consideration;

   (c) the costs allocated to the service of general economic interest may cover all the variable costs incurred in providing the service of general economic interest, a proportionate contribution to fixed costs common to both service of general economic interest and other activities and a reasonable profit;

   (d) the costs linked with investments, notably concerning infrastructure, may be taken into account when necessary for the operation of the service of general economic interest.

3. The revenue to be taken into account shall include at least the entire revenue earned from the service of general economic interest ...

4. For the purposes of this Decision 'reasonable profit' means a rate of return on own capital that takes account of the risk, or absence of risk, incurred by the undertaking ... This rate shall not normally exceed the average rate for the sector concerned in recent years. In sectors where there is no undertaking comparable to the undertaking entrusted with the operation of the service of general economic interest, a comparison may be made with undertakings situated in other Member States, or if necessary, in other sectors, provided that the particular characteristics of each sector are taken into account ...

5. When a company carries out activities falling both inside and outside the scope of services of general economic interest, the internal accounts shall show separately the costs and receipts associated with the service of general economic interest and those of other services, as well as the parameters for allocating costs and revenues. The costs linked to any activities outside the scope of the service of general economic interest shall cover all the variable costs, an appropriate contribution to common fixed costs and an adequate return on capital. No compensation shall be granted in respect of those costs.[49]

---

[49] European Commission (2005), 'Decision of 28 November 2005 on the Application of Article 86(2) of the Treaty to State Aid in the Form of Public Service Compensation Granted to Certain Undertakings Entrusted with the Operation of Services of General Economic Interest', notified under document number C(2005) 2673.

Given that the Commission's guidance leaves some areas of uncertainty, we provide some economic guidance further below on the unresolved points. Consider the case of an SGEI provider that also engages in commercial activity. What is the right way to allocate fixed and common costs between the SGEI activity and the commercial activity? And what is a reasonable profit, and how do you measure it? We tackle these questions in section 8.7.

8.6.6 THE FOURTH *ALTMARK* CRITERION: COMPENSATION MUST BE DETERMINED THROUGH PUBLIC TENDER OR BASED ON THE COSTS OF A TYPICAL WELL-RUN (EFFICIENT) COMPANY

This efficiency criterion is unique to the *Altmark* test for determining the existence of state aid. An efficiency standard does make sense, since propping up inefficient companies (even those performing a public duty) has the character of aid, whereas procuring a service from an efficient company (ie, at minimum cost) does not. The principle is that compensation should not exceed the extra costs of PSOs, and thus that additional compensation should not be permitted for the bloated costs of an inefficient company. Checking for efficiency can be done in two ways: a competitive tender, or a benchmarking exercise on the costs of the incumbent. As we mentioned earlier, the very nature of SGEIs is that they are not services provided by the market, which means that finding a benchmark for the incumbent's costs can be tricky, but is not impossible (see below).

The *Altmark* criteria are easier to meet when a public procurement process or competitive tender is undertaken. The finance of the scheme promoting investments in order to ensure security of electricity supply in Ireland was not deemed to be state aid.[50] The Commission considered that the measures imposed genuine SGEI obligations on electricity generators—ie, bringing to the Irish electricity grid new reserve generation capacity in order to meet the electricity demand in the future at any time of the year, including in peak periods. The open, competitive procedure that took place helped ensure that the other three conditions laid down by the *Altmark* decision were met. The Commission stated that as 'the competition is open, transparent, and has attracted many bidders, the Commission considers that the bidders will minimise the capacity payments they request, that is, require no more than the repayment of their investment plus the standard profit margin which is expected in this sector of the industry.' This relates to the third criterion, ie, reasonable compensation. It concluded that as 'all four conditions of the *Altmark* Judgement are met, the scheme involves no State aid within the meaning of Article 87(1) of the EC Treaty [now 107(1) TFEU] to the generators.'[51]

---

[50] European Commission (2003), 'State aid N 475/2003—Ireland—Public Service Obligation in respect of new electricity generation capacity for security of supply', Letter to the Member State, C(2003) 4488 final, 16 December.

[51] Ibid., at [65].

Similarly, subsidies used to finance broadband infrastructure in France were not considered to be state aid based on an evaluation under the *Altmark* criteria.[52] The generalized access to broadband infrastructure for all the population was considered to be an SGEI. There was said to be no risk of over-compensation since the parameters for the calculation of the compensation were precisely defined within the business plans of the operators. Any risk of over-compensation was also mitigated by the fact that the public authority required the operators providing the service to set up a separate company for that service which would guarantee the neutrality of the service provider in question. The needs of the project and the offers of the candidates were analysed in detail. The procedure chosen permitted the selection of the most efficient candidate offering the service at the least cost to the community.

The Commission employed the *Altmark* criteria in its 2008 decision concerning alleged state aid granted in 2002 by the Tyrolean public transport authority to its publicly owned business, Postbus AG.[53] It concluded that the first two criteria were met since the service constituted an SGEI (first criterion met) and remuneration was paid on a fixed price/km basis as well as for a fixed number of kilometres driven (second criterion met, as the parameters were objective and set in advance). It also concluded that the compensation paid was 'fair and adequate given the average costs in the sector', and thus did not amount to over-compensation (third criterion met). However, determining compliance with the fourth criterion was more complex. While the Commission accepted that Postbus's costs were those of an average Austrian undertaking, it considered that this was not sufficient to demonstrate that the costs were those of a 'well-managed undertaking', since the Commission had noticed that Austrian bus operators rarely participated in competitive tenders, and hence there was no guarantee that any of the comparators was efficient (recall the quiet life of the monopolist in Chapter 1). It therefore decided that the fourth criterion—the efficiency criterion—was not met.

If the fourth *Altmark* criterion is to be satisfied in the absence of a tender process, the right approach is to benchmark the SGEI company's costs with those of efficient undertakings. Finding a comparator group for SGEIs can be a difficult task, since the nature of SGEIs is such that few companies perform SGEI-type functions.[54] Evidence from regulatory practice illustrates approaches to benchmarking that might be employed to overcome this problem. When only part of the business is engaged in the provision of SGEIs, internal comparisons between SGEI and non-SGEI operations could provide a plausible approach to assessing the efficiency of the SGEI operations, provided that you are confident that the non-SGEI (commercial) functions operate in competitive markets

---

[52] Commission Decision in case N 381/2004—France—Setting Up of a High Speed Infrastructure in Pyrénées-Atlantiques [2005] OJ C162/05, of 2 July.

[53] European Commission Decision of 26 November 2008 on State Aid Granted by Austria to the Company Postbus in the Lienz District C 16/07 (ex NN 55/06), 2009/845/EC.

[54] For a detailed discussion of the complexities of setting appropriate benchmarks, see Oxera (2008c).

and represent efficient costs.[55] Comparison with similar companies may be possible either within the sector itself in a particular country or region—if the structure of the sector is such that it provides comparators—or with similar companies in other countries. Functional or process benchmarking—using bottom-up, activity-based approaches—against companies outside the sector with similar processes could be another feasible technique.[56] Again, the starting point needs to be that comparators are regarded as efficient. Comparisons can also be made with companies that have won a series of competitive tenders in the sector—as the European Commission reasoned in *Postbus*, the case we saw above:

> The next question is whether the costs in Postbus also correspond to the costs in a well-managed undertaking. In the bus transport sector, which has been dominated by monopolies and in which contracts have been awarded without tenders for a long time, an undertaking operating in the market is not necessarily a well-managed undertaking.

> In this regard, it should firstly be noted that Austria has not explained how these parameters also represent the average in a well-managed undertaking. By way of example, the Commission considers that Austria could have taken as a basis the average costs in undertakings which have won a significant number of tenders in the sector in the last few years.[57]

The paucity of cases in which efficiency is proven for the fourth *Altmark* criterion, other than through a competitive tender, is an indication of the difficulties of applying this part of state aid law. There are many cases where the Commission has found this criterion *not* to be satisfied, and few where it has found measures to pass the test under this condition. However, as many SGEIs are found in regulated sectors, it is surprising that state aid law does not make use of existing regulatory practice on efficiency. Testing cost efficiency is common practice in the modern regulation of assets in the energy, water, transport, and communications sectors. The evidence to test the fourth *Altmark* criterion in the absence of a competitive tender might therefore be found by asking sectoral regulators for their views on efficiency, or in non-regulated sectors by transferring standard regulatory benchmarking techniques to a non-regulated context.

8.7 SERVICES OF GENERAL ECONOMIC INTEREST: MEASURING APPROPRIATE COMPENSATION

8.7.1 WHY BOTHER MEASURING COSTS?

Worrying about SGEI costs is driven by a concern about over-compensating companies entrusting with SGEIs, and the associated problem that over-compensation can lead to competitive distortion via a cross-subsidy to non-SGEI commercial activities.

---

[55] For an application of internal benchmarking, see Horncastle et al. (2006).

[56] See Oxera (2008b).

[57] European Commission Decision of 26 November 2008 on State Aid Granted by Austria to the Company Postbus in the Lienz District C 16/07 (ex NN 55/06), 2009/845/EC, [86].

The reason why this is a common concern is that it makes perfect economic sense, having invested in an expensive fixed-cost SGEI network (eg, rural post offices), to maximize output from that asset, for both the SGEI purpose and any commercial application that may be found. Rivals in those commercial applications that lack the subsidized SGEI asset may then struggle to compete at the resulting prices. It follows that there is a welfare trade-off in SGEI cases between making efficient use of the SGEI asset (and if usage is high, the required state subsidy to the asset might be lower), and distorting competition by pricing commercial access to the SGEI asset at low rates that are very difficult for rivals to match. The practical solution is to have a reasonable cost allocation between SGEI and non-SGEI activities and to check that pricing of commercial access to SGEI facilities is at a price in line with market practice.

8.7.2 THE PROBLEM: JOINT AND COMMON COSTS

One challenging issue that comes up in these cases is how to allocate costs that are common or joint between the company's SGEI and commercial activities (we also discussed the issue of cost allocation in Chapter 4). Where costs are truly joint, they are incurred irrespective of the proportions of SGEI and commercial activities undertaken. An example of a joint cost is in the production of petrol, which results in the joint production of such items as naphtha, kerosene and distillate fuel oils. Another example is in meat production, in which various cuts of meat and by-products are processed from one original carcass with one lump-sum cost. A common cost is a cost which is incurred simultaneously for two or more products or a whole organization, where it cannot be allocated directly to any particular product, but where indirect cost allocation is possible—eg, an access road which goes to two different business units will require maintenance according to the volume of traffic; insofar as you know the split of traffic between two uses of the road, it would be possible to allocate the cost of the maintenance between them. You can think of the difference between joint and common costs as being whether it is possible to just produce one product from the given cost: with a common cost (eg, a head office) this is possible; with a joint cost (eg, producing petrol from crude oil) it is not, since obtaining petrol from crude oil automatically results in by-products that are obtained in fixed proportions with the petrol.

In theory, there is no single correct method for cost allocation. The choice of method can depend on the circumstances of the sector in question and the underlying reasons for allocating costs. However, there are some economic principles underlying a good cost allocation system. One of these is that costs should be allocated in accordance with the activities that 'cause' them. In this respect, it is often the state's demand for the SGEI facilities that 'causes' these facilities to exist, and therefore the non-SGEI usage should bear only a limited proportion of the common costs of the facilities. For instance, national defence facilities exist for a public purpose, and if they can be exploited for a commercial purpose (eg, renting out a test facility), you would not expect the commercial rent to recover all the fixed costs incurred in developing that test facility for its public purpose. Another principle is that the allocation method should be transparent, practical to implement, and objectively verifiable.

8.7.3 OPTIONS FOR COST ALLOCATION

To consider different options for cost allocation, imagine a transport network used for SGEI and non-SGEI services. There is €100 million of fixed cost to allocate, and the task is to determine the right (ie, non-distortive) price for the SGEI transport product and the right price for the commercial transport product. Table 8.2 presents the outcomes of the cost allocation exercise according to three options: first, allocating the fixed cost in proportion to the share of direct cost; second, allocating according to share of total production; and third, allocating in proportion to revenue.

In this example, previous commercial prices were too low at €3, and should be raised to avoid the cross-subsidy from SGEI activity to commercial activity. But what is the best way to allocate costs, and therefore to decide the right price? As you can see, allocating by share of revenue tends to mimic pre-existing prices (the commercial price

Table 8.2 Cost allocation between SGEI and non-SGEI activities (€)

Fixed cost to be allocated	100,000,000	
	SGEI	**Commercial**
Units of production	10,000,000	10,000,000
Variable cost per unit	5.0	2.0
Pre-existing price	16.0	3.0
Pre-existing revenue	160,000,000	30,000,000
Allocation by share of direct cost		
Share of total direct cost	71%	29%
Allocated fixed cost (per unit)	7.1	2.9
Mark-up	12%	12%
Implied price	13.6	5.4
Allocation by share of production		
Share of production	50%	50%
Allocated fixed cost (per unit)	5.0	5.0
Mark-up	12%	12%
Implied price	11.2	7.8
Allocation by share of revenue		
Share of revenue	84%	16%
Allocated fixed cost (per unit)	8.4	1.6
Mark-up	12%	12%
Implied price	15.0	4.0

Note: In this example profits (mark-ups) are the same whichever cost allocation mechanism is chosen. This is because for simplicity the units of production have been held constant.

would only rise to €4). Revenue is often rejected as a cost allocation method precisely because it produces this circular result, ie, the 'correct' price is determined by whatever price structure was already in place. As to the other allocation methods, allocating fixed cost by share of direct cost has economic merit as it reflects the higher marginal costs on SGEIs (recall that prices should in principle reflect marginal costs). Allocating by share of production has the reasonable economic justification that the fixed cost allocation reflects the intensity of use of fixed assets—in this case 50:50 between the SGEI activity and the commercial activity. There is still some scope for debate about the correct price, but the firm in question now has a reasonable floor for its commercial price-setting (ie, in line with the allocation by share of direct costs).

Other cost allocation methods are activity-based costing (ABC) and equi-proportional mark-ups (EPMU). ABC is a form of input-based allocation where common costs are allocated according to the activities undertaken to produce the product. ABC methods rely on a concept of cost causality to reduce the number of non-attributable cost items that are assigned by a simple key (such as the output and revenue methods). For example, where the time of managing staff is split 70:30 between two products, the costs of those staff are allocated in the same proportion to the respective products. EPMU is a form of input-based allocation where non-attributable common costs are allocated in proportion to the attributable cost of the service.

8.7.4 ASSESSING OVER-COMPENSATION: 'REASONABLE PROFIT' IN ALTMARK AND THE SGEI FRAMEWORK

For the purpose of *Altmark* and the SGEI Framework, compensation should not exceed costs plus a 'reasonable profit'. How can this be assessed? The essential task is to first isolate the costs and revenues of the undertaking's SGEI provision—we tackled the most difficult issue above, which is allocating fixed costs between SGEI and non-SGEI activity—and second, measure the profitability of the undertaking's SGEI provision. So here we explain how to do that profitability analysis, for example, to assess whether the compensation for the SGEI provision of health insurance is at the right level. The same methods for profitability have been applied many times in other contexts, but state aid does have some specific guidance which is worth citing. The SGEI Framework provides that:

> The amount of compensation may not exceed what is necessary to cover the costs incurred in discharging the public service obligations, taking into account the relevant receipts and reasonable profit for discharging those obligations.[58]

The revenues to be included are defined as follows:

> The revenue to be taken into account must include at least the entire revenue earned from the service of general economic interest. If the undertaking in question holds special or exclusive rights linked to a service of general economic interest that generates profit in

---

[58] European Commission (2005), 'Community Framework for State Aid in the Form of Public Service Compensation' [2005] OJ C297, 29 November, at [14].

excess of the reasonable profit, or benefits from other advantages granted by the State, these must be taken into consideration.[59]

The costs to be included are defined as follows:

The costs allocated to the service of general economic interest may cover all the variable costs incurred in providing the service of general economic interest, an appropriate contribution to fixed costs common to both the service of general economic interest and other activities and an adequate return on the own capital assigned to the service of general economic interest.[60]

Reasonable profit is defined as follows:

'Reasonable profit' should be taken to mean a rate of return on own capital that takes account of the risk, or absence of risk, incurred by the undertaking by virtue of the intervention by the Member State, particularly if the latter grants exclusive or special rights. This rate must normally not exceed the average rate for the sector concerned in recent years.

This definition implies that there are two ways in which reasonable SGEI profit must be benchmarked. The first is with reference to the company's own cost of capital (an internal benchmark), and the second is in relation to the profitability observed in the industry (an external benchmark). This dual approach is similar to that relating to the MEIP in section 8.4, and as with the MEIP, the appropriate method can vary according to the case at hand—in a contested case it makes sense to try both internal and external benchmarks. The SGEI Framework states that external benchmarking can also be done with reference to companies in other countries or sectors.[61]

Using the measure of profitability and evaluation of internal and external benchmarks, the Member State is then under an obligation to ensure on an ex post basis that there has been no SGEI over-compensation:

Member States must check regularly, or arrange for checks to be made, to ensure that there has been no over-compensation. Since over-compensation is not necessary for the operation of the service of general economic interest, it constitutes incompatible State aid that must be repaid to the State.[62]

We now look at the economic tools for measuring profitability.

8.7.5 WHICH MEASURE OF PROFIT?

As we saw in Chapter 3 (and also in section 8.4 above), economic measures of profitability—in particular the IRR and NPV—are the most appropriate for assessing the returns on a company's investments in the context of a competition analysis. The same

[59] Ibid., at [17].
[60] Ibid., at [16].
[61] Ibid.
[62] Ibid., at [20].

logic applies in SGEI compensation. To analyse formally compensation for an SGEI is a matter of profitability analysis, involving the usual issues of cost allocation (as also discussed above) and benchmarking a 'reasonable' level of profit (we discussed the WACC in section 8.4). The IRR and NPV take into account the inflows and outflows of an activity over time, and reflect the economic principle of the time preference of money. The IRR methodology is normally applied over the entire life of a project. There are also ways to apply the IRR approach to discrete time periods—a method referred to as the truncated IRR. For this it is necessary to value the assets related to the performance of the SGEI at the start and end of the selected period, since these approximate the value of the 'investment' necessary to generate the cash flows.

The alternative is to use measures which make direct use of accounting data: ROCE and ROE. They are easy to understand and can be conveniently calculated, albeit that they may not give an accurate picture of economic profitability, as explained earlier in the MEIP section and in Chapter 3. Despite any shortcomings, given that the object here is a periodic check on SGEI compensation, ROCE and ROE considered over a number of years may be fit for purpose as a practical method.

8.7.6 RETURN ON CAPITAL EMPLOYED AND RETURN ON EQUITY

The ROCE is calculated by dividing earnings before interest and taxes (EBIT) by total capital (ie, debt and equity). The advantage of ROCE is that it is based on more readily available accounting data. The ROE is calculated by dividing net earnings after tax by equity-funded capital employed. Figure 8.2 shows these accounting relationships.

Both the ROE and the ROCE involve measuring equity capital, either in isolation or as a component of total capital. Where a business does not have equity capital, which is

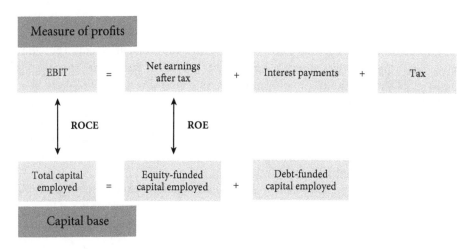

Fig. 8.2 ROCE and ROE

likely in the case of a state-owned entity, you have two options: first, a proxy for equity capital can be estimated from various items on the balance sheet, depending on which of the items are akin to equity capital and total capital in a privately owned company. Alternatively, a proxy for equity capital can be estimated by first considering the capital structure of comparator companies, and then applying this hypothetical capital structure to the SGEI state aid recipient.

8.7.7 INTERNAL BENCHMARK FOR DETERMINING APPROPRIATE SGEI COMPENSATION

Having obtained an estimate for the IRR, ROCE, or other profitability measures, the next task is to benchmark it. The own cost of capital approach (ie, the internal benchmark) analyses the presence, or indeed the degree, of over- or under-compensation by comparing the company's calculated profitability with the relevant cost of capital. The SGEI Framework suggests that the cost of capital benchmark should be company-specific, but not exceed the industry average:

> A rate of return on own capital that takes account of the risk, or absence of risk, incurred by the undertaking by virtue of the intervention by the Member State . . . must normally not exceed the average rate for the sector concerned in recent years.[63]

We saw in section 8.4 how to calculate the appropriate cost of capital benchmark. It remains only to ask whether the IRR or ROCE is in line with the cost of capital, in which case the rate of SGEI compensation is appropriate. If the IRR or ROCE is lower, there is under-compensation, and if higher, there is some degree of over-compensation.

8.7.8 THE USE OF COMPARATORS (SGEI AND MEIP)

As with the MEIP (see section 8.4), the external benchmark approach for SGEI compensation compares the IRR, ROCE, or other measures of economic profitability for the company against the equivalent profitability measures of its comparator companies. A comparator should have its primary business in the relevant activity (providing national transport services, health insurance, etc). The SGEI Framework specifies that comparators should ideally come from the same country, which makes sense given institutional and macroeconomic differences between different countries, but also note that they may come from other Member States. Appropriate comparators also need to be selected according to their risk exposure. The benchmarked returns should be those of companies that are exposed to a similar degree of risk, given that higher risk is reflected in higher required returns by investors.

Incidentally, the legal requirement that the comparators should be selected only from the same or other Member States doesn't make economic sense. It can be a significant limitation in markets such as healthcare, where US comparators (private sector

---

[63] European Commission (2005), 'Community Framework for State Aid in the Form of Public Service Compensation' [2005] OJ C297, 29 November, at [18].

companies with a stock market listing) may be amply available whereas EU comparators are difficult to find due to the structure of supply in EU healthcare markets.

Once a comparison is obtained, the question remains as to whether any excess profitability over and above the benchmark is 'reasonable'. From an economic perspective you would assess whether any differences observed between profits and benchmarks are *persistent* and *significant*—ie, differences between profits and benchmarks are observed over a sufficiently long period of time and they are material, given the scale of the undertaking. It follows that, from an economic perspective, 'reasonable' profits may encompass some variation from year to year. With that caveat in mind, the difference between the profits and the benchmark (internal or external) is the degree of over- or under-compensation for the SGEI. If the result is that over-compensation is present, it follows that there is an element of aid to be repaid, equal to the 'excess profit'. The current rule is that where over-compensation does not exceed 10% of the amount of the annual compensation (or 20% in the case of an undertaking in the social housing sector that operates only SGEIs), it may be carried forward to the next annual period and deducted from the amount of compensation payable in respect of that period.[64]

8.8 DOES THE STATE AID MEASURE ADDRESS A MARKET FAILURE?

8.8.1 MARKET FAILURES RELEVANT TO STATE AID

So far in this chapter we have identified whether aid exists (MEIP and *Altmark*) and then quantified it (MEIP and SGEI compensation). Now we ask whether aid can be justified from an economic perspective. As we saw in the introduction to this chapter, market failures are the main economic justification for providing state aid. State intervention might improve outcomes when markets deliver too much, or too little, of a particular product or service. It is not difficult to conceptualize the main market failures that are relevant to state aid, but it can be complex to specify when government intervention will deliver a better solution, given that governments are themselves not immune to failure in the allocation of resources. To this end, it is helpful to systematically identify the market failure at hand, why it occurs, and how it relates to a particular category of state aid. The classic market failures that state aid seeks to address are externalities, the provision of public goods (eg, for SGEIs), and information asymmetries.

8.8.2 EXTERNALITIES

Externalities occur when the decisions of one economic agent have consequences, positive or negative, for another agent, but these consequences are not taken into account

---

[64] Bacon (2009), para 3.77. See also Commission Decision of 28 November 2005 on the application of Article 86(2) of the EC Treaty to State aid in the form of public service compensation granted to certain undertakings entrusted with the operation of services of general economic interest, [2005] OJ L312, 29 November.

by the first agent. Positive externalities include the spillover effects of innovation. Classic examples of negative externalities include a factory which pollutes a river, thereby harming all those who rely upon clean water downstream. If the factory does not face a marginal cost for polluting equivalent to the harm it imposes on others, then an externality market failure exists—the market produces too much pollution and does not give sufficient incentive for the factory to invest in 'clean' production technology. Figure 8.3 illustrates the point—the marginal social cost of the factory's production, incorporating the cost of pollution, is always greater than the marginal private cost, which ignores the pollution externality. As such, the factory produces too much output from a social welfare perspective, such that total output is 7 units at a price of €3 per unit, whereas the socially optimal output is 6 units at a price of €4 per unit.

Government intervention can help solve the market failure. Some types of intervention may fall under the state aid rules, while others may not. The factory's incentives can be changed by an environmental subsidy (which would fall under the state aid rules), by taxation, or by a system of tradable emissions permits (the last two mechanisms would probably not require state aid scrutiny). Imposing a tax of €1 per unit on the factory's production would move the marginal private cost curve up by 1 unit such that it coincides with the marginal social cost curve, and in equilibrium the price would increase to €4 and so decrease the quantity demanded to the social optimum of 6 units. Subsidizing an environmentally friendly alternative factory, such that consumers face an artificially low price for the alternative good, could have a similar effect, ie, by shifting the (residual) demand curve faced by the polluting factory to the left, as illustrated in Figure 8.4. In this case, the quantity demanded of the polluting factory's output has also fallen to the social optimum of 6 units. The subsidy can therefore be said to resolve an externality market failure. In this analytical framework, subsidies (and taxes) can be used to shift either demand curves or

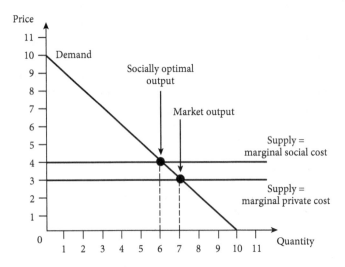

Fig. 8.3 Over-production of a polluting good with a negative externality

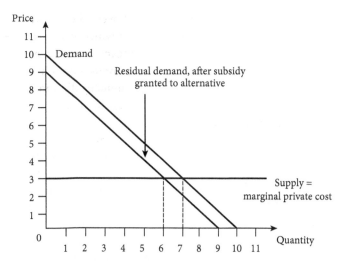

Fig. 8.4 Effect on production of a subsidy given to a non-polluting alternative

supply (cost) curves. Shifts in the supply curve are achieved when subsidies (taxes) target marginal costs directly. Interventions that change the per-unit costs of producers tend to be more effective in resolving the market failure than lump-sum transfers—although, as we discussed in section 8.5, by the same token, the potential distortions to competition that are created by such measures are also greater.

8.8.3 EXAMPLES OF POSITIVE EXTERNALITIES

An example of a positive externality is the knowledge spillover generated from investments in R&D, and especially basic research. By definition, basic research is undertaken mainly to acquire new scientific and technical knowledge not yet linked to any particular commercial application or use. As a result of its lack of specificity, the knowledge generated can have a number of potential applications and, therefore, benefit a wide range of companies undertaking different economic activities. For the investor, it might be difficult to exclude third-party companies from using the knowledge created and make them pay individually for the benefits they receive. This may discourage it from investing in non-company-specific basic research. Furthermore, because of the lack of direct applicability of basic research, its economic returns are likely to be relatively low. Indeed, the main way in which basic research is appropriated is via publication in scientific or academic journals, an activity that does not allow companies investing in basic research to extract rents from their investments. In contrast, the results of applied research, and particularly those of development activities, can be appropriated via patents, trademarks, and other forms of intellectual property rights.

Under these circumstances, the marginal private benefit of investing in basic research will be lower than the marginal social benefit—ie, there is a positive externality. In order to restore allocative efficiency, the government could intervene and grant companies a subsidy to reflect the social benefit of the knowledge spillovers. This subsidy could take the form of a direct grant to companies engaging in R&D, subsidized interest rates for loans that the companies might obtain, tax breaks, loan guarantees, government holdings of all or part of a company, or the provision of capital on preferential terms.

8.8.4 INFORMATION ASYMMETRIES

Information asymmetries arise when agents who come together in a transaction have different amounts of relevant information. As a result, the party with the better information may engage in opportunistic behaviour. Asymmetric information is a common type of market failure in financial markets (it is also relevant to market failures in innovation, as explained below). Financial institutions may be imperfectly informed about a number of factors, including the risks they might have to take when lending money or providing equity capital to companies, and the likelihood of funds being misused. In this type of situation, even if a project is commercially viable it may fail to get bank funding.

In particular, it can be difficult for a financial institution to distinguish 'low-risk' from 'high-risk' loans or investments, especially with regard to new products or new companies with no track record. The bank may therefore attribute 'average risk' to all small and medium-sized enterprise (SME) investments. The result is that low-risk projects that would otherwise be profitable cannot be financed, and this problem is likely to be worse for smaller and newer companies. In these circumstances, state intervention might be used to aid the provision of risk capital to SMEs, with the aim of restoring investment to a more optimal level.

In the case of a small company trying to raise capital to develop and commercialize a new product, problems of information may lead to sub-optimal investment. First, the company may have more information than a financial institution about the risks and opportunities of the product in question, which is to say that the bank (the principal) can only imperfectly observe the actions of the company (the agent). Second, the company's management could conceivably create hidden risks to the bank's investment—for example, by diverting the funds to more risky opportunities. Third, complete contracts covering all such eventualities for the investment might not be feasible or enforceable. In these circumstances the result may be that viable projects cannot raise sufficient private finance. As such, total financing in the economy may be sub-optimal, and state intervention may be an option to increase investment.

8.9 AID FOR THE RESCUE AND RESTRUCTURING OF COMPANIES IN DIFFICULTY

8.9.1 STATE AID POLICY ON RESCUE AND RESTRUCTURING AID

Rescue and restructuring aid is provided to an individual company that 'is unable, whether through its own resources or with the funds it is able to obtain from its owner/shareholders or creditors, to stem losses which without outside intervention by public authorities will almost certainly condemn it to go out of business in the short or medium term'.[65] Rescue and restructuring aid is mainly intended to help companies in financial difficulty that, because of their size, are considered to be important drivers of economic activity in a region. The Commission defines rescue aid as:

> temporary and reversible assistance. Its primary objective is to make it possible to keep an ailing firm afloat for the time needed to work out a restructuring or liquidation plan.[66]

Restructuring aid tends to follow from the provision of rescue aid. Its purpose is to finance the reorganization and rationalization of the company's activities onto a more efficient basis, thus restoring its long-term viability. The Commission's guidance puts forward various possible justifications for this type of aid:

> The provision of rescue or restructuring aid to firms in difficulty may only be regarded as legitimate subject to certain conditions. It may be justified, for instance, by social or regional policy considerations, by the need to take into account the beneficial role played by small and medium-sized enterprises (SMEs) in the economy or, exceptionally, by the desirability of maintaining a competitive market structure when the demise of firms could lead to a monopoly or to a tight oligopolistic situation. On the other hand, it would not be justified to keep a firm artificially alive in a sector with long-term structural overcapacity or when it can only survive as a result of repeated State interventions.[67]

The Commission generally employs three principles in its analysis of restructuring aid:

- Restoration of long-term viability—the aid should lead to the restoration of viability of the beneficiary in the longer term without state aid.

- Avoidance of undue distortions of competition—the aid should be accompanied, to the extent possible, by measures that minimise distortions of competition.

- Ensuring appropriate burden sharing—the aid should be limited to the minimum required and be accompanied by a substantial 'own contribution', ie, the company should contribute to the restructuring from its own resources (including raising money from shareholders and/or suspending dividend payments).

8.9.2 ECONOMIC CONCERNS WITH RESTRUCTURING AID

You can see that even with these three conditions for aid approval, state aid for the rescue and restructuring of companies is one of the most distortive forms of aid. There is a good chance that companies are in difficulty because they are less efficient than their rivals. By subsidizing them, state aid maintains companies which under normal market conditions would exit the market. Government funding might therefore perpetuate

---

[65] European Commission (2004), 'Community Guidelines on State Aid for Rescuing and Restructuring Firms in Difficulty' [2004] OJ C244, 1 October, at [9].
[66] Ibid., at [15].
[67] Ibid., at [8].

market inefficiencies by distorting entry and exit decisions and dampening the normal process of 'creative destruction' which selects only efficient companies to prosper in the market.

If it is considered desirable to have a policy of rescue and restructuring aid—a political decision—then from an economic perspective it would be advisable to at least identify clearly some of the market failures that the aid is addressing. First, the failure of a firm may result in a number of redundancies and, if the labour market is unable to reabsorb these workers readily, long-term unemployment may result, which could be harmful to the social fabric of a region. This is arguably akin to a labour market failure, driven by labour market inflexibility in terms of geographic mobility and a preponderance of workers who possess very specific rather than general skills. Second, if the company is sufficiently large, its failure could result in the breaking of a substantial chain of supply contracts, damaging other companies. This is akin to network effects in the market, meaning that the assisted company needs to remain in place over a period during which suppliers in the chain find alternative customers. Third, rescue and restructuring aid may have some justification when it maintains a competitive situation in a market (eg, if the failure of a company is likely to result in a monopolistic situation), thereby addressing a market power externality. However, supporting an inefficient company to prevent monopoly is not really an efficient solution. The long-term aim would be to encourage efficient entry or, if there were such scale advantages that only one company is efficient, to address market power through other regulatory tools (or competition law).

Ideally, rescue and restructuring aid would mimic the structured intervention processes that private liquidators invoke when a company goes into bankruptcy: incentivizing management to resolve the problems inherent to the business in the first instance, increasing the pressure to do so within a certain timeframe, and realizing residual company value through choosing between retaining the business as an ongoing concern, selling the company, or liquidating its assets. Whether rescue and restructuring aid is a superior alternative to the normal insolvency procedure depends on determining the counterfactual. If insolvency would lead to, for example, a serious problem of long-term unemployment in a region, whereas rescue and restructuring aid would smooth the restructuring process such that employment consequences are mitigated, there is more justification for aid. The task is therefore to understand the economic factors that determine the counterfactual, such as employment conditions in the region and industry in question, and to analyse how restructuring aid can make a significant difference to final outcomes for output and employment (Oxera, 2010a). There might be some justification for aid if the company concerned is a natural monopoly provider of essential services, in which case the social priority is to maintain the business as an ongoing concern rather than to maximize the value of assets per se (which could involve liquidation or sale) to creditors, following normal bankruptcy procedures. Utility businesses, such as rail network infrastructure companies or nuclear power companies, might fall into this category. A distinction should therefore be drawn between those companies which, if they were allowed to fail, might have a systemic impact on end-customers or the supply chain (eg, a natural-monopoly rail infrastructure company), and those which would be unlikely to (eg, an airline, where there are likely to be other more efficient competitors in the market to take over the failed operator's assets). In any event, the assessment of whether aid should be granted must always take account of the counterfactual of insolvency procedures, since the systemic impact can often also be mitigated by a well-designed insolvency regime—in particular one that takes special account of companies whose failure has more systemic impact (eg, banks).

8.9.3 RESTRUCTURING AID IN A FINANCIAL CRISIS

The financial crisis that began in 2007–08 provided an unprecedented and difficult environment not just for the global economy, but also for EU state aid law. State aid during that financial crisis was treated mainly under Article 107(3)(b) TFEU, and warrants separate consideration from ordinary rescue and restructuring aid.

In the crisis, banks and other financial institutions experienced an extreme combination of write-downs on their assets, dried-up liquidity in wholesale funding markets, and loss of consumer confidence. In response, national governments took various measures to support their banking sectors, including the provision of direct state aid to banks. The main objective of this was to avoid the considerable externality effects for the rest of the economy in the event of the failure of one or more systemically important banks. The measures taken are widely understood to have played an important role in avoiding meltdown of the financial markets, in restoring confidence in both the financial markets and in the economy more widely, and in supporting the flow of credit to the real economy. Starting in October 2008, the European Commission approved a large number of guarantee and recapitalization schemes. Over and above these guarantee and recapitalization measures, a number of Member States notified asset relief measures and direct lending.

The main economic rationale for granting state aid to financial institutions in crisis was to avoid the collapse of banks causing serious problems for the wider economy. The concern was the spread of contagion effects whereby customers, equity markets, and debt markets (including inter-bank lending) would lose confidence in all banks with a similar business model and cease to provide funding, with the consequence that normal flows of credit through banks to the real economy would be seriously disrupted. The market failures here relate to externalities (the creditors of the bank at risk don't take into account the wider costs of liquidation) and information asymmetries (in the heat of the moment investors don't know exactly which banks will fail, and so withdraw support indiscriminately). At the same time, support to banks in the EU needed to be provided within the confines of state aid law. As recognized by the Commission, in a crisis environment Member States could be tempted to pursue unilateral national interests, and they did indeed introduce a range of measures to support their financial services sectors.

First, governments supported the overall financial system. This support included, for example, the provision of exceptional liquidity facilities by the European Central Bank

with the goal of preventing shortages of liquidity. Although such measures clearly benefited the financial sector (as, in general, cheaper capital means higher profits, and some
weak banking institutions avoided failure), they do not generally count as state aid as they
were available to all banks and hence did not have the character of being 'selective'.

Second, governments recapitalized banks that were thought to be financially viable
but that, due to closed capital markets and adverse selection, could not raise capital at a
reasonable price. To achieve this, governments provided Tier 1 capital (ie, loss-bearing
equity), and temporarily or permanently acquired banks' assets. From the state aid perspective, such interventions are justified as they seek to remedy market failures, which
in this case relate to inefficiently functioning capital markets. The main consideration is
whether in such cases the aided banks benefit relative to non-aided banks due to the
potentially lower price of state capital—hence, the capital price of the state support is
key to minimizing competition distortions.

Third, governments aided some fundamentally non-viable banks—ie, banks that
could not cover losses over the business cycle—that were at risk of failing. From the
state aid perspective, supporting such banks could have a significant impact on market
structure and competition, and has less justification on the grounds of remedying
market failures. In principle, aid to non-viable banks must be accompanied by measures aimed at limiting distortions of competition, or should be granted only in order to
liquidate the bank in an orderly fashion (eg, the aid to Bradford & Bingley in the UK,
where the state provided a working capital facility to allow the liquidation of the bank's
assets to be conducted over a period of several years, in light of perceived risks of
'uncontrolled insolvency'[68]).

The Commission appears to have tried to capture the distinction between these cases
within the banking sector, as well as the difference between crisis aid to banks and
normal state aid issues, in the series of crisis-specific Communications that were introduced to assess state aid granted to financial institutions. In these Communications, the
Commission recognized that the severity of the crisis justified the granting of aid under
Article 107(3)(b), which allows aid 'to remedy a serious disturbance in the economy of
a Member State'. It also set out a framework for the provision of public guarantees,
recapitalization measures and impaired asset relief, whether granted by Member States
to individual banks or as part of a wider national scheme. Although issued specifically
in response to the crisis and only for aid granted to financial institutions, the
Communications were based on the same three general principles as for rescue and
restructuring aid, ie, restoration of long-term viability, avoidance of undue distortions
to competition, and ensuring appropriate burden sharing. While the Commission made
use of these principles designed for dealing with aid granted to failing firms, it also recognized that the problems faced by banks in the crisis were substantially different. For
one, the traditional Rescue and Restructuring Aid Guidelines address the problem

---

[68] European Commission (2010), 'State aid N 194/2009—United Kingdom Liquidation Aid to Bradford and
Bingley plc', C(2010) 350 final, Letter to the Member State, 25 January, [13].

of how to deal with a single failing firm, while the crisis-specific Communications attempted to deal with problems in an entire sector. Furthermore, the problems faced by particular banks in the crisis were not necessarily of their own making; a loss of general market confidence can make it impossible for a bank to raise money regardless of whether it is healthy. The Commission recognized that in the prevailing circumstances healthy ('fundamentally sound') banks could be affected as well as non-healthy banks, and therefore determined that healthy banks did not require such extensive restructuring, or to pay as much for the aid received (in terms of fees to the state or the interest rate on loans).

A bank that fails, regardless of whether it is sound, has the potential to create serious disruptions to the economy and create difficulties for other banks, including direct competitors. This is not dissimilar to the point discussed above in relation to the systemic risk of a utility company. Thus, in the case of the failure of a large bank, it would be less straightforward to argue that its competitors would have benefited from the removal from the market of their rival, as would be the case for 'traditional' failing firms. Indeed, banks may be better off with their systemically important rivals staying in the market, regardless of whether these rivals are efficient. If this were the case, so long as the winding-up of these banks cannot be accomplished without serious negative impacts, there would seem to be little role for restricting state aid to banks on the basis of short-run competitive distortions. The benefit of saving the economy and the banking system would outweigh the risk of distorting the market in the supply of banking services.

The trade-off between short-run stability and long-run healthy competition was not the only tension. Some aided banks faced lending commitments imposed by the Member States in exchange for the aid, which tended to preserve or expand their market share, when from a state aid perspective the aided banks ought to restrict growth or even shrink in size. What should a bank do when the requirements of the Commission to minimize the distortion are in conflict with the commitments made to its national government as part of the conditions for receiving the aid in the first place? Certain banks had a commitment to lend to SMEs in their domestic markets where they already had a high and static market share. Here any state aid remedies restricting the growth of the aided bank would have been in conflict with the commitment of the bank to the Member State. We turn to the more general subject of remedies below, and look at some of the remedies applied in bank cases that arose during the crisis.

8.10 THE BALANCING TEST

The 'balancing test' has found its way into nearly all of the Commission's recent guidelines on the assessment of the compatibility of state aid. The test is about weighing up the negative effects on trade and competition against the positive effects in terms of a contribution to solving market failures or other objectives of common interest. Balancing these effects is an exercise in the analysis of economic welfare. For that purpose, the European Commission has established a test which consists of the following questions:[69]

(1) Is the aid measure aimed at a well-defined objective of common interest?

(2) Is the aid designed to deliver the objective of common interest, ie, does the proposed aid address the market failure or other objectives?

   (i) Is the aid an appropriate policy instrument for addressing the policy objective concerned?

   (ii) Is there an incentive effect, ie, does the aid change the behaviour of the aid recipient?

   (iii) Is the aid measure proportionate to the problem tackled, ie, could the same change in behaviour be obtained with less aid?

(3) Are the distortions of competition and effect on trade limited, so that the overall balance is positive?

We concentrate here on the last part of the test, ie, the balancing itself, since previous sections have covered other parts of the balancing test (eg, regarding market failures).

8.10.1 QUANTIFYING THE POSITIVE AND NEGATIVE EFFECTS OF AID

The balancing exercise is not a precise numerical task, but a question of weighing one form of economic harm—distortion of competition—against a form of economic benefit—ameliorating a market failure. The latter comes in many forms, as we have seen. While it is reasonable to compare outcomes (price, quantity) of harm to competition with outcomes (price, quantity) of resolving an informational asymmetry (where you would expect output to increase), it is more difficult to compare outcomes where the benefit is in non-traded goods, such as air quality or other environmental goods, or where outcomes conflict. Think of aid to the coal industry which is intended to improve the security of energy supply—it may solve one market failure while creating another (excessive pollution). Where economics can help is in providing a more robust thought framework to consider these questions and trade-offs.

Where state aid has a particular efficiency objective, such as the promotion of R&D or the reduction of environmentally hazardous materials, the key question to ask is what is likely to occur in the counterfactual to aid, and to establish whether the aid has the right incentive properties to substantially change behaviour. We have seen examples of counterfactual scenarios in previous sections of this chapter. Without a proper incentive effect, company behaviour is not affected (eg, no more energy-saving light bulbs are produced compared with the counterfactual), and consumers therefore receive no benefit, since the aid is simply a transfer from the public purse to the aid beneficiary. This is

---

[69] European Commission (2009), 'Common Principles for an Economic Assessment of the Compatibility of State Aid under Article 87.3', DG Competition staff working paper, 15 May.

a clear detriment to consumers (as taxpayers). Tests of indispensability and proportionality are familiar from other parts of EU law. For example, one of the tests in the Article 101(3) prohibition of anti-competitive agreements is that there must be no restrictions on competition that are not indispensable to the attainment of benefits from the agreement.

Having established that aid will have a positive effect, it is appropriate to look at quantifying the effect in terms of consumer benefits (at least in the first instance). If state aid is expected to generate a reduction in marginal cost, the short-term impacts on price and output levels can be quantified using the standard tools that we saw used in Chapter 7 on merger effects. Non-price benefits, such as enhancements to choice and quality, are more difficult to quantify. Nonetheless, consumer surveys or market research can help put a price on these benefits—for example, by using conjoint analysis to determine consumers' willingness to pay for particular product attributes (see Chapter 2 for a description of how this works). This all results in benefits that are quantified using the same denominator, ie, consumer welfare expressed as consumer surplus in monetary terms.

Where state aid is expected to generate a reduction in fixed cost, economics tells us that there is no direct impact on price and output, but rather an impact on the entry and exit decisions of companies. As such, the benefit will either be in terms of reduced market concentration or in facilitating the launch of a new product, which would otherwise have been uneconomic to produce (fixed costs would not have been fully recoverable). The former benefit can be measured, albeit imprecisely, using the concentration measures outlined in Chapter 3, which show that reducing market concentration is a priority only in highly concentrated markets. The latter benefit, new product entry, can be assessed by looking at the amount of consumer surplus generated by the product. In practice, the data required to achieve this (in particular the demand curve and marginal costs) is unlikely to be available, and so the practical option is to look again at market research on what consumers value most (eg, a new train service may reduce commuting time, and one that runs at peak time is more valuable than an off-peak service). The end result may not be a precise quantification, but it may be that orders of magnitude can be attached to the positive effects of aid. The widespread use of cost–benefit analysis in policy-making demonstrates that in many cases non-monetary benefits are quantifiable—see the discussion in Chapter 9 about cost–benefit analysis being used in determining remedies in competition cases.

8.10.2 THE BALANCING EXERCISE

Having obtained an indication of the orders of magnitude of effects—positive and negative—a balancing exercise is required. This is an exercise in cost–benefit analysis, but one which will often encompass non-quantifiable effects (eg, damage to long-run competition). The way in which the Commission will approach this task is best understood by looking at its own guidance. A Commission staff working paper notes that 'it should also be considered that, as a general rule, State aid is prohibited and can be authorised only by derogation to this general principle. This implies that, in case of doubt, the

Table 8.3 The balancing exercise: main economic criteria

Aid more likely to be approved if...	Aid less likely to be approved if...
The positive effects are almost certain (eg, by the design of the aid), whereas the negative effects are less likely	The distortions of competition are almost certain and the state aid mostly benefits the recipient of the aid
The aid is necessary to generate positive effects that are very significant (and notably greatly exceed the aid amount), that benefit many Member States, and that have demonstrated strategic importance for the common European interest	The aid is a subsidy for variable costs that merely supports particular output or price levels
The aid is well targeted and the benefits are located in underdeveloped regions or go to socially underprivileged groups, and the Commission has found that the aid is limited to the net extra costs to compensate for social/regional handicaps	The aid amount is very significant and the positive effects are very limited compared with the cost of the aid
The aid results in important positive spillovers to product markets other than those directly concerned, so that competitors and consumers in these markets may also benefit from these spillovers	The positive effects are limited to the Member State granting the aid whereas substantial negative effects are felt in a number of Member States
The aid does not significantly distort the proper functioning of the internal market and does not produce significant disparities between undertakings established in different Member States and/or in the location of the production factors within the EU	The aid significantly increases social and/or regional disparities and/or leads to environmental damage or pollution
The aid results in clear positive effects for citizens, including in the long term, whereas negative effects are limited and do not significantly hamper competition	The aid generates significant and durable distortions of competition and the beneficiary is a dominant company, whose market position will be reinforced as a result

Source: Based on European Commission (2009), 'Common Principles for an Economic Assessment of the Compatibility of State Aid under Article 87.3', DG Competition staff working paper, 15 May.

Commission is more likely to prohibit the aid.[70] As such, it should be expected that aid approval would be contingent on the balance of effects being firmly tilted towards the positive, in a way that is obvious and verifiable, and that marginal cases would not receive approval.

[70] European Commission (2009), 'Common Principles for an Economic Assessment of the Compatibility of State Aid under Article 87.3', DG Competition staff working paper, 15 May, [70].

Table 8.3 summarizes the content of the Commission staff working paper, in terms of what it tells us about that balancing exercise and where aid is likely to be approved. You can see the themes of this chapter reflected throughout Table 8.3—such as the relevance of the market position of the beneficiary, the structure of the aid measure (whether it is a subsidy to variable cost), and the importance of positive spillover effects (such as the positive externalities associated with certain R&D activity).

8.11 REMEDIES TO MINIMIZE THE DISTORTION OF COMPETITION

The underlying principles for minimizing the distortion of competition in a state aid case are much the same as the principles for applying remedies to an ordinary competition law case—these are set out in Chapter 9. The Commission's general aim (at least in restructuring aid cases, where remedies, or 'compensatory measures' as they are called, are frequently observed) is that the extent of remedies in a state aid case should be linked to the extent of distortion of competition.[71] Before applying such measures, it may be possible to improve the design of the aid measure so as to reduce the distortion.

8.11.1 IMPROVING THE DESIGN OF AN AID MEASURE

Where the design of the aid measure is concerned, the Commission examines the following potential remedial changes (among others).[72] These changes are to ensure aid has the right incentive effect without causing unnecessary harm to competition. First, it is explored whether there is a case for a reduction of the aid amount, of the aid intensity, or the scope/target of the aid (activities or markets covered) to make the measure proportional. As we saw in section 8.5 on lump-sum versus variable subsidies, the financial structure of the aid measure should be aligned with the objective (eg, expanding output of a good with a positive externality). Aid intensity can be reduced to avoid problems of moral hazard, ie, the problem that a company may take greater risks, knowing that it can fall back on state aid. Also the scope of the aid can be reduced to fit the market failure—eg, supporting only SMEs engaged in innovative activity rather than all SMEs. Second, reduction of the selectivity of the measure is considered, for instance, by using an open selection procedure for the aid beneficiary or by opting for a general scheme, and avoiding any bias in favour of companies with market power. As we saw in section 8.6, following a proper public procurement procedure can in many cases avoid conferring advantage on a particular undertaking. The third possible change in

---

[71] European Commission (2004), 'Community Guidelines on State Aid for Rescuing and Restructuring Firms in Difficulty' [2004] OJ C244, 1 October, at [40].

[72] European Commission (2009), 'Common Principles for an Economic Assessment of the Compatibility of State Aid under Article 87.3', DG Competition staff working paper, 15 May, [74].

design of the aid is to limit the possibility for cross-subsidization through increased transparency and separation of accounts, or by separation of activities in different companies. Section 8.7 explained how to divide costs between aided and non-aided (commercial) activities, so as to avoid distortion of competition by cross-subsidizing commercial activities.

8.11.2 APPLYING REMEDIES TO REDUCE THE IMPACT ON COMPETITION AND TRADE

In applying remedies for the distortion of competition and trade, the Commission has suggested it will consider five main options: capacity reduction, divestments, behavioural commitments, market liberalisation, and open licensing of IP.[73]

The first option is a reduction in the production capacity of the aid beneficiary. This is to ensure that the company receiving state aid is not able to expand at the expense of competitors which have not received aid. An aided company which has a substantial market position or which is dominant is more likely to distort competition. As such, remedies aimed at reducing that market share may be an option. Note that in most circumstances, it is counterproductive (in terms of competitive distortion) to impose behavioural remedies such as a market share cap, since this will tend to reduce the intensity of competition. The most appropriate way to reduce production capacity is therefore likely to be divestments (see below), or restricting planned investments in production capacity by the aid recipient. Where the efficiency justification for the aid is to expand output to resolve a market failure, capacity-based remedies are generally not appropriate. An output cap may be counterproductive to the aim of the state aid.

The second option is divestiture of assets. This is a variant on reducing capacity with the aim of constraining market share. It is more common in restructuring aid cases, and so we return to this type of remedy below. Suffice it to say that divestments are generally preferred to behavioural constraints on market share, since the divested assets will continue to function under a new owner as competitive assets in the market whereas a market share cap would involve constraining the competitive behaviour of those same assets under the ownership of the aided company.

The third option is a behavioural commitment to prevent foreclosure (eg, guaranteed access to network or other essential facilities). Access remedies are discussed in Chapter 9, and have attractive properties as a remedy for competitive distortion since they lower barriers to the entry and expansion of competitors to the aided company. On the other hand they require proper monitoring by a regulator or monitoring trustee, which has costs attached—as described further in Chapter 9.

Occasionally, a behavioural commitment will be made in terms of pricing. For example, the behavioural commitment in *Commerzbank* was that the bank would not be permitted to do business (including deposit-taking) under more favourable price

---

[73] Ibid., at [75].

conditions than its top three competitors in markets/products where it had a market share above 5%.[74] Thus, the institution that has received state aid may be barred from offering products at more attractive prices than its competitors. This is to ensure that the company does not benefit from its reduced cost of capital due to a state aid injection at the expense of its competitors. A price-based remedy of this type tends not to be a good solution for consumers, for the obvious reason that it leads to higher prices.

The fourth option is a commitment by the Member State to open markets, eg, liberalization measures, easing of technical and non-technical barriers. This type of remedy has the same objective as an access remedy, ie, to lower entry barriers. Liberalization of markets may be desirable irrespective of state aid, but for political reasons a state aid investigation may provide the Commission with a particularly good lever to spur the Member State into action.

The final option is open licensing of IP or standards. This is another variant on an access remedy, but tends to be linked to aid involving research and innovation. An IP remedy is most appropriate when the positive spillover effects of innovation can be enhanced by removing licensing restrictions. For instance, in March 2010, the Commission approved French aid for 'green' fuel development, and applied IPR measures to limit distortions to competition:

> GDF Suez has undertaken to forego the exclusive rights that could be granted to it by its partners over their technologies. The distortions of competition caused by public support will therefore remain limited, in particular because the future demonstration plant will be open to other stakeholders in the sector. Finally, the presence of major European competitors and the fact that the project is different from other expected technologies will make it possible to maintain competitive pressure in energy markets in general, and in the biofuels market in particular.[75]

8.11.3 REMEDIES IN RESTRUCTURING AID

Remedies are common in restructuring aid cases since this type of aid is particularly likely to cause competitive distortion. In order to approve restructuring aid, the Commission requires measures to be introduced to limit distortion of competition caused by the aid (remedies may also be driven by a concern about burden sharing). In the narrow interpretation of the Commission's guidelines, such measures should address only competition concerns that may arise after restructuring as a direct result of the state aid given. It is possible, however, that the Commission may seek to address other pre-existing competition concerns through restructuring remedies. For instance, in the bank Restructuring Communication of 2009, the Commission referred to concerns over state aid that 'prolongs past distortions of competition created by excessive

---

[74] See Genner et al. (2009), p 85.
[75] European Commission (2010), 'Commission Clears French Aid Worth €18.9 Million for the GAYA Motor Biofuels Research Programme', press release, 24 March.

risk-taking and unsustainable business models by artificially supporting the market power of beneficiaries.'[76]

Recall the principles of restructuring aid as cited above in section 8.9—restoration of long-term viability, avoidance of undue distortions to competition, and ensuring appropriate burden sharing. In order for restructuring aid to be approved, the aided business needs to be viable in the long term. In this context, viability could be defined as earning the company's cost of capital in the base case. Restructuring and behavioural remedies could include constraints and guidance on how business activities need to be refocused away from risky activities and towards those activities that have generated stable returns in the past. The company may be required to abandon activities in which it has performed poorly in the past as a way of ensuring its long-term viability. To ensure appropriate burden sharing, the Commission requires that when receiving state aid, beneficiaries contribute to restructuring costs. The objective of these measures is to limit moral hazard. For example, the business may be required to sell off units engaged in more risky and volatile activities.

The combination of viability and burden sharing generates a new set of concerns for remedies to satisfy, over and above the remedies discussed in the previous section, for the simple reason that they are two objectives in conflict with one another—the more burden sharing that takes place, the greater the threat to viability. Remedies intended to reduce distortion of competition may also threaten viability, as the most effective competition remedies (eg, divestments in a concentrated market) would tend to strike at the most profitable activities of the aid beneficiary (since the market power in a concentrated market will be a source of high profits).

Other options seen in the context of bank-restructuring cases for burden sharing include controls on dividends and interest payments, bans on acquisitions, and divestments. Requiring suspension of dividend and interest payments to holders of hybrid capital (ie, capital with both debt and equity features, such as preference shares) tends to be motivated by factors relating to burden sharing. If the bank is prevented from paying coupons on hybrid capital, this is an 'own contribution' (in the sense that bondholders contribute) to restructuring and facilitates maintaining aid at the minimum level necessary. A ban on acquisitions is targeted at avoiding undue distortions of competition. By barring an institution which has received state aid from making acquisitions, the Commission may ensure that it does not use state financing as a source of cheap capital with which to acquire competitors. Regarding burden-sharing divestments, the sale of non-core assets may be required in order to generate funds for the bank's own contribution, and thereby to ensure that aid is kept to the minimum possible. On the other hand, divestiture of core assets may be influenced by a rationale of minimizing distortions to competition if the divestiture is in markets where the institution has a strong position. However, the Commission is constrained in requiring the

---

[76] European Commission (2009), 'Commission Communication on the Return to Viability and the Assessment of Restructuring Measures in the Financial Sector in the Current Crisis Under the State Aid Rules' [2009] OJ C195/9, 19 August, at [28].

divestment of core assets by the need to ensure an institution's long-term viability—a core asset is almost by definition a core source of viability. The sale of foreign subsidiaries, whether core or non-core, may be treated slightly differently, as the Commission would not wish to undermine competition in another Member State by facilitating consolidation, or to undermine the integration of European markets. In concentrated markets, whether foreign or domestic, divestment remedies will tend to come with conditions attached in terms of who is an acceptable purchaser—the same logic applies in merger control; see Chapters 7 and 9.

8.12 CONCLUSION: COMMENTS ON STATE AID ENFORCEMENT

In this chapter we have tried to follow the legal structure of the EU state aid regime and have indicated those parts of the structure where there is a role for economic principles and analysis. From an economic perspective, is there merit in having a set of rules to control state aid and subsidies? The answer is yes. The rules seek to preserve a level playing field within the EU single market, which is generally good for competition and efficient market outcomes. Effective competition across European markets can be compromised if governments support and promote inefficient 'national champions'. The rules also help to avoid wasteful 'beggar-thy-neighbour' subsidies, whereby one Member State's subsidy harms companies in another Member State, which then pays its own subsidy, cancelling out the impact of the first subsidy and wasting taxpayers' money in two countries. While Member States have an incentive to avoid distortions with their own national markets, they generally lack an incentive to avoid cross-border distortions.

The state aid rules, if based on sound economic principles, allow policy-makers to distinguish between 'good' and 'bad' interventions in the market, and thereby facilitate the use of the former. In a more laissez-faire political environment, there may be a tendency to tar all government measures with the same brush, and thereby reject many good ones that are meant to address harmful market failures. As EU Competition Commissioner, Joaquin Almunia (2010), noted:

> Ultimately, [rules on government subsidies] help governments assess the effectiveness of proposed subsidy measures, and help channel funds to where they are the most necessary and can deliver the most benefit to taxpayers.

There is still great scope for EU state aid law to make better use of competition law and economic tools in terms of defining what aid should or should not be prohibited. As we have seen in this chapter, only a relatively narrow subset of government subsidies will generate significant harm to competition and trade. Many measures that might be thought of as 'state aids' are no more harmful in terms of effects on competition and trade than other aspects of public policy (eg, planning decisions on the location of transport networks or other important public facilities). A prioritization of state aid control could be achieved by an economic evaluation of where state aid has had the most negative effects on competition and growth, and particularly where state aid in one Member State has had negative spillover effects on other Member States. In the current legal structure such economic considerations come into play at various stages (eg, in some of the SGEI criteria and the balancing test), but not always in a coherent way.

Another aspect to rational state aid control is the manner of enforcement. This issue falls outside the scope of this book, but a few concluding comments may be useful. The fact that proceedings in state aid do not always involve the aid beneficiaries themselves may limit the extent to which the Commission can obtain information relevant to its assessment of distortion of competition. Moving state aid procedure further in the direction of merger control (greater information-gathering powers, tighter timetables) may help efficient enforcement. Regarding deterrence and penalties, the Commission's main remedy against unlawful state aid that has already been paid is that it has to be refunded to the subsidizing Member State. We understand that the track record of enforcing refunds is imperfect. From an economic perspective, this remedy does not have very strong incentive or deterrence properties, as compared with the fines or damages awards in other areas of competition law (which we discuss in Chapters 9 and 10).

Another policy issue that is increasingly being debated is whether there is greater scope for private enforcement in state aid. As explained in Chapter 10, private enforcement is being promoted in agreement and abuse cases, where parties harmed by anticompetitive conduct in theory have the right incentives to sue their competitors or suppliers. In state aid, competitors of the aid beneficiaries may have insufficient interest in taking an original private action if the outcome is merely that aid is refunded to the subsidizing Member State. In terms of damages, state aid prohibitions are directed against Member States rather than at the aid beneficiaries, so claiming damages from those beneficiaries may be problematic. For example, in *Betws Anthracite*, a damages case relating to a Commission Decision which found that a German anthracite producer, Preussag, had misused aid, the English High Court ruled that there was no cause for action against a competitor even for unlawful misuse of aid:

> In my view there is no cause of action in Community Law for the claim advanced by Betws. Specifically, there is no cause of action by Betws against Preussag on the ground that Preussag has used unlawful State aid to the detriment of their competitors including Betws. The Aid Decision was directed not to Preussag but to the German State. At best, Betws would have a claim against Germany.[77]

Therefore, if private enforcement of state aid law is seen as a useful complement to public enforcement, economic logic requires that incentives to bring private actions need to become more effectively aligned than they are currently.

---

[77] *Betws Anthracite Ltd v DSK Anthrazit Ibbenburen GmbH* [2003] EWHC 2403 (Comm), 27 October 2003, at [30].

9

DESIGN OF REMEDIES

9.1 AFTER THE DIAGNOSIS, WHAT NEXT?

Most of the scholarly literature on competition law, and most of this book so far, have focused on the identification and analysis of competition problems. Much less attention has been paid to the design of remedies for these problems. As one commentator noted, 'Everybody likes to catch them, but nobody wants to clean them.'[1] This is clearly an important shortcoming and is increasingly recognized as such among competition officials and practitioners. Remedies matter a great deal for the effectiveness of competition law enforcement. If a competition authority spends a substantial amount of time and resources on an investigation and concludes that there is a competition problem, this is of little value to consumers if a suitable remedy cannot be found. We use the term remedy here in a wide sense—it includes not only remedial actions that directly alter the structure of the market or the behaviour of the parties under investigation, but also the imposition of fines on those parties, and the award of financial damages against them. Competition authorities and courts around the world use different combinations of these types of remedy.

There is an equally mixed picture in terms of the policy objectives that remedies seek to achieve.[2] Are the remedies aimed at punishing the perpetrators, at putting an end to the infringement, at restoring competition in the market, at deterring future infringements of the law, or at compensating the victims of the anti-competitive behaviour? This may depend on the type of competition case. In merger cases the simplest remedy is a prohibition of the merger. Not much else may be required, as competition in the market will continue as usual after the prohibition (unless the merger has already been completed and the two parties need to be separated again). However, there are many merger cases in which the authority does not wish to prohibit the merger outright, but rather approves it in exchange for certain commitments by the parties that are aimed at preserving competition. These commitments can be structural (the merging parties commit to divesting some of their activities or assets) or behavioural (the merged entity promises to engage or not engage in certain behaviour). Fines are rare in merger control (they may be handed out where parties complete a merger they should have notified, or where they refuse to cooperate with the authorities). For cases involving restrictive agreements and abuse of dominance the picture is more complicated. A simple prohibition may not be enough. Fines are often imposed, serving the dual purpose of punishing the perpetrators and, if set sufficiently high, discouraging future infringements. Some jurisdictions take punishment and deterrence a step further and impose prison sentences for hardcore cartel agreements. EU law has endorsed the objective of compensation for the victims of the infringements, be they competitors or customers, which can be sought through private damages actions before national courts—a topic discussed in Chapter 10. But ideally in agreement and abuse cases where competition has been harmed, remedies should also be aimed at restoring competition—imposing a fine, a prison sentence or a damages award may not be sufficient to repair the harm done to competition, or to change the competitive situation such that a repeat of the infringement can be avoided. This is where structural and behavioural remedies are required.

---

[1] Comment made by Tad Lipsky at the 2007 Federal Trade Commission hearings on s 2 of the Sherman Act (transcript of 28 March, p 47, at: <http://www.ftc.gov/os/sectiontwohearings/docs/transcripts/070328.pdf>). The quote is attributed to William Baxter, the Department of Justice Assistant Attorney General who in 1982 broke up AT&T, a case discussed in this chapter.

[2] See Organisation for Economic Co-operation and Development (2006).

This chapter discusses the economic principles that can assist in the design of remedies in merger, agreement, and abuse cases (in Chapter 8 we discussed remedies in the specific context of state aid). Optimal remedies are those that are effective at achieving the policy objectives, in a manner that is proportionate to the severity of the competition problem and at the same time not unnecessarily costly or time-consuming to implement. Merger control is the area in competition law where the design of remedies has received most attention. The market investigations regime, a competition law tool that is unique to the UK (under the Enterprise Act 2002) also offers useful lessons. These investigations typically deal with markets in which competition is not functioning effectively but for reasons other than abuse of dominance or restrictive agreements, and therefore the remedies proposed are often aimed at changing some of the structural or behavioural features of the market. Competition law can also learn from other disciplines, in particular the economic regulation of networks and utilities, which has developed extensive insight and sophisticated tools that can be of direct use in the design of competition law remedies, including vertical separation, access regulation, and price regulation. We discuss structural remedies in section 9.2 and behavioural remedies in section 9.3. In section 9.4 we deal with behavioural economics, a relatively new field that combines insights from economics and psychology, and that has a potential role to play in the design of remedies and regulations, particularly in consumer markets. In section 9.5 we return to the more traditional theory of incentives (including the incentives faced by criminal minds), which is relevant for the determination of optimal fines. The section also covers companies' ability to pay fines, a hotly debated topic that arises under the European Commission's fining guidelines. Finally, section 9.6 covers another area where competition law can learn from regulation and public policy in general, namely that of cost–benefit analysis (CBA). In recent years, competition policy has seen an increasing emphasis on the measurement of costs and benefits, not just of specific interventions and remedies, but also of having a competition regime in the first place.

9.2 STRUCTURAL REMEDIES

9.2.1 EXPERIENCE IN COMPETITION LAW: MERGERS

Structural remedies are those that directly alter the structure of the market, usually in the form of divestiture of assets. They can be horizontal or vertical. Horizontal separation involves the sale of assets that compete with each other in the same product or geographic market. Vertical separation means divesting assets in different layers of the supply chain—it is the opposite of vertical integration. Structural remedies can be used to restore competition in the market, or indeed to create more competition than there was before the intervention. The main theoretical attraction of structural remedies is that you only need to strike once: after you have dissolved a position of market power (or removed a bottleneck problem in the vertical supply chain), you can leave the newly created competitive structure to its own devices and not worry about the ongoing supervision that you would need if you imposed behavioural remedies. On the other hand, structural remedies are by nature rather intrusive—you are forcing a company to cut off some of its limbs—and may not always be proportionate to the competition problem at hand. Divestitures may create inefficiencies if the limbs that are cut off actually formed an efficiently integrated part of the company—we saw in Chapters 6 and 7 how vertical integration can be an efficient solution to coordination problems. Moreover, in practice, structural remedies may not always succeed in creating viable competition and may require a degree of ongoing supervision (thus diminishing one of the theoretical benefits of this type of remedy).

Structural remedies are common in merger cases. Many competition authorities have extensive experience with imposing such remedies, and have begun to systematically analyse past cases in order to learn lessons and develop best practice.[3] Many mergers and acquisitions are cleared on the condition that the parties divest certain assets that belonged to either the acquiring or the acquired party. These remedies are relatively straightforward where existing business units are sold off in their entirety, but even if the divestment requires some splitting of business units, the organizational difficulties of such an exercise will often pale in comparison with the complexity of making the merger itself work. Divestment is also relatively straightforward where the assets can be run with a high degree of independence. Going back to some of the examples of mergers we saw in Chapters 2 and 7, individual cinemas, holiday parks, and supermarkets are not difficult to separate from the rest of the chain they were part of. By the same token, they can be easily integrated into a competing chain which purchases them (sometimes not much more than a change in livery is required). The same sometimes holds for the divestment of brands. In mergers between spirits companies it is not uncommon for an entire brand of beverages to be divested if the competitive overlap with another merging brand is too large.[4] In other industries this may not be as effective. Two merging hospitals will find it difficult to divest activities that take place under the same roof. Bank branches, like supermarkets and cinemas, can be sold off relatively easily, but this may not solve the competition concerns in question if customers keep their current account with the original bank and use other branches or other channels (telephone, Internet, cash machines) to access their account.

Additional questions that need to be addressed when determining the appropriate divestments are how many assets must be sold off, and to whom—the underlying objective being to ensure viable competition in the market post-merger. As regards the first question—how many assets—the more the original market structure can be emulated the better. But even if the divested assets represent a smaller market share than that of the smaller of the two merging parties before the transaction, the remedy can be effective if the assets are particularly attractive or efficient ones, and if they are scooped up by

[3] The European Commission undertook a major study in 2005 into 40 past merger decisions involving a total of 96 remedies. European Commission (2005), 'Merger remedies study', October.

[4] For example, in *Pernod Ricard/Allied Domecq* (Case COMP/M.3779), Commission Decision of 24 June 2005.

a smaller rival with ambitions to grow in the market. This to some extent answers the second question, ie, who should be allowed to buy the assets. The market is generally best placed to decide on this (the keenest buyer with plans to use the assets productively will usually step forward in a sales process), but you want to avoid the assets being purchased by a competitor which already has a very large share of the market (such a purchase might trigger a merger inquiry of its own).

The *Fortis/ABN AMRO* merger case in 2007 is one where the structural remedy arguably went a step further than just the aim to restore competition to pre-merger levels.[5] A consortium of the Royal Bank of Scotland, Banco Santander Central Hispano, and Fortis acquired ABN AMRO for €72 billion (the largest ever bank merger in Europe). This raised competition concerns, mainly in the Netherlands where ABN AMRO was one of the traditional top three banks and Fortis (from Belgium) one of its more rapidly growing competitors. The main problem was in the provision of banking and factoring services to commercial customers (factoring is a form of financing where the bank takes over its client's invoices to third parties). The European Commission required the divestment of a significant commercial banking division that existed within ABN AMRO, together with a number of business advice centres and a factoring division. Altogether this divestment package was nearly twice the size of Fortis's activities in commercial banking before the merger, and it removed the overlap in factoring. The Commission was satisfied that this remedy would solve the competition concerns and that the divested assets were commercially viable if sold to the right purchaser. In addition, however, the Commission determined that the purchaser had to be a bank that was able to serve international corporate customers and that had a presence in the major world and European financial centres. This requirement effectively meant that the assets could not be acquired by one of the smaller Dutch banks, some of which had demonstrated ambitions to grow in the commercial banking market but lacked such international presence. The Commission probably saw the remedies negotiations as an opportunity to promote cross-border integration of European banking markets, a policy objective it has long sought to achieve through various means but with limited success. (In the event, both the deal and the execution of the remedies were delayed, and changed somewhat in nature, when the two banks had to be rescued from collapse in 2008 during the financial crisis.)

9.2.2 EXPERIENCE IN COMPETITION LAW: CONDUCT CASES

In agreement and abuse cases the use of structural remedies is rare. The two most famous corporate break-ups in the USA—Standard Oil (1911) and AT&T (1982)—took place in very different times and circumstances, but both cases usefully illustrate some of the economic principles that are of relevance when designing a structural remedy.

---

[5] *Fortis/ABN AMRO Assets* (Case COMP/M.4844), 3 October 2007. We advised the merging parties during this inquiry.

Following a lawsuit by the Department of Justice (DOJ), the Supreme Court ordered in 1911 that Standard Oil Company of New Jersey be dissolved and split into 34 companies.[6] For decades, Standard Oil—co-founded and majority-owned by John D Rockefeller—had been by far the dominant company in the refinement and shipment of oil in the USA, with a market share of 80%–90% (Scherer and Ross, 1990, pp 450–1). It had achieved this position through a combination of efficiency (nothing wrong with that of course), the acquisition of more than 120 rival companies (merger control did not exist at the time; a Standard Oil situation would be much less likely to arise today), and famously aggressive business practices. It was these practices that the DOJ attacked (as also discussed in Chapter 4), and for which the Supreme Court accepted dissolution of the company as the remedy. They included obtaining preferential treatment from railroad companies, unfair practices against competing pipelines, local price cutting at points where competition was to be suppressed, industrial espionage, and operation of bogus independent companies. Reference was also made to the 'enormous and unreasonable profits' earned by Standard Oil because of its monopoly power.

Interestingly, Standard Oil argued in its defence that the companies it controlled in different parts of the USA operated quite independently and competitively (it also argued that its control of the industry was, in the words of the court, 'the result of lawful competitive methods, guided by economic genius of the highest order'). While this argument was not accepted, it did perhaps point to the feasibility of making those companies independent for real. Indeed, more than just a single company, Standard Oil was a 'combination' or 'trust', controlling a host of other companies through shareholding arrangements—Standard Oil and its contemporaneous brethren gave rise to the term 'antitrust' when the Sherman Antitrust Act was passed in 1890. It was this 'combination' that the Supreme Court ruling ordered to be dissolved so as to 'neutralize' its unlawful monopoly power. It considered that the mere cessation of the above-mentioned practices would be insufficient, since the market was already effectively monopolized. The position of the DOJ had been that the existence of Standard Oil, 'with the vast accumulation of property which it owns or controls, because of the infinite potency for harm and the dangerous example which its continued existence affords, is an open and enduring menace to all freedom of trade, and is a byword and reproach to modern economic methods.' The Supreme Court agreed in the end. While there have been heated debates ever since the ruling about whether the structural remedy was appropriate or proportionate, the break-up did, with some delay, result in greater competition among the newly created oil companies—these included the likes of (predecessors of) Exxon, Mobil, Chevron, Amoco, and Conoco. As to John D Rockefeller, he is said to have done rather well out of the break-up, as the (minority) shares he kept in the resultant companies all increased significantly in value.

---

[6] *Standard Oil Co of New Jersey v United States* 221 US 1 (1911).

The break-up of AT&T was agreed in a settlement with the DOJ in 1982 and became effective from 1 January 1984.[7] AT&T operated the 'Bell System', which basically had a telephony monopoly in the USA from the early twentieth century, and consisted of entities delivering long-distance and local calls, equipment manufacturing, and R&D. In the 1960s and 1970s, new communications technologies began to compete with AT&T at the 'edges' of the Bell System—rival telephony equipment and wireless inter-city call services sought to establish a market presence, but were heavily reliant on AT&T for interconnection and compatibility with the rest of the system. AT&T responded to these competitive threats through a range of hostile actions, including refusals to interconnect and accept 'foreign' equipment, or to do so only at a high price and with delays. AT&T also heavily lobbied the sector regulator, the Federal Communications Commission (FCC), to help protect its monopoly status and thereby preserve the integrity of the telephone system. The DOJ filed a lawsuit against AT&T in 1974 and, after eight years of legal battles, a settlement was reached. The Bell System was to be broken up into a long-distance telephony arm—the new AT&T—which also kept the equipment-manufacturing and R&D entities, and seven separate incumbent local exchange carriers (known as the regional Bell operating companies, or 'Baby Bells'). This was therefore a combination of vertical and horizontal separation. You may find it paradoxical that such a radical intervention was made at a time when antitrust law in the USA tended more towards the laissez-faire (see Chapter 1). However, the DOJ's position was that a radical structural break-up would be the most effective way of intro-ducing competition once and for all, and of bringing to an end the persistent disputes and need for oversight of AT&T's behaviour. The court that reviewed the case had also considered the question of whether the FCC was realistically capable of efficiently regulating a company the size of AT&T (Scherer and Ross, 1990, pp 462–4).

What happened next? Competition certainly developed in the long-distance call market (Sprint and MCI were major challengers). Long-distance call rates fell sharply (local call rates increased, because they had previously been subsidized by the long-distance calls). The equipment and R&D entities were not as commercially successful as the new AT&T had hoped, again due to a large extent to competitive dynamics. As competition developed further in telephony markets over the years, consolidation took place among the Baby Bells, and in fact in 2005 AT&T was acquired by SBC Communications (keeping the name AT&T), which reunited it with three of the former Baby Bells. However, this partial reintegration was not seen as problematic given that competitive dynamics in the market had changed significantly since 1982. One thing that did not work so well after the break-up was that extensive legal and regulatory dis-putes continued. These related in particular to the behaviour of the Baby Bells, which had inherited local monopolies and were frequently accused of charging excessive access charges. The need for extensive oversight by the courts and the FCC therefore remained.

---

[7] *United States v AT&T Co* 552 F Supp 131 (DDC 1982).

Not many structural remedies have been imposed under competition law since the *AT&T* case. During the DOJ's investigation into Microsoft in the 1990s and early 2000s, there were suggestions at some point to split the company horizontally into several 'Baby Bills' as a structural remedy. In the UK there have been some structural remedies under the market investigations regime and its predecessor. In Chapter 6 we discussed how the UK authorities ordered vertical separation between brewery companies and pubs in 1989. A more recent example is the forced divestment of airports by BAA with the aim of increasing competition—the Competition Commission (CC) required BAA to sell both Gatwick and Stansted Airports (to different purchasers), leaving it with Heathrow and Southampton Airports in the south-east of England, and to sell one of Edinburgh or Glasgow Airports, leaving it with two airports in Scotland instead of three.[8] Across Europe, there has been extensive vertical separation in regulated network industries. Although (mostly) outside the field of competition law, this provides some useful economic insights for when you consider structural remedies in competition cases. We turn to this now.

9.2.3 ECONOMIC INSIGHTS FROM NETWORK REGULATION: VERTICAL SEPARATION

Vertical separation has been introduced in a number of network industries in Europe since the early 1990s, starting with the gas, electricity, and rail industries in the UK. The main aims were to facilitate entry in the potentially competitive layers of the supply chain, and to restrict the incumbents' incentives to discriminate against non-integrated competitors in the provision of network access. In network industries where the incumbents have remained vertically integrated, regulators often impose accounting separation, a much milder form of separation aimed at monitoring the pricing behaviour and financial performance of the network facility. In recent years, vertical separation seems to have come back into fashion in Europe and is increasingly being considered as a tool to address the persistent discrimination problems where 'lighter' forms of access regulation have failed to deliver the desired market outcomes. This includes the telecoms industry which, unlike its US counterpart, has kept its vertically integrated incumbents. Due in part to pressure from regulators, the incumbents in the UK (BT), Italy (Telecom Italia), and Sweden (TeliaSonera) have introduced 'functional' vertical separation in the past few years. This is not quite full vertical separation since the ownership remains the same, but the network business is set up as an independent unit that offers the same terms and conditions for access to all retail service providers downstream, including the incumbent's own retail business—a concept referred to as 'equivalence' (Oxera, 2009). More movement in this direction is expected following reforms to the EU regulatory framework for electronic communications in 2009.[9] In the energy sector, some

---

[8] Competition Commission (2009), 'BAA Airports Market Investigation', March.

[9] Directive 2009/140/EC of the European Parliament and of the Council of 25 November 2009 amending Directives 2002/21/EC on a common regulatory framework for electronic communications networks and

European countries have a degree of separation of different parts of the electricity value chain (generation, transmission, distribution, and supply), and the European Commission has been promoting further structural 'unbundling' of the large energy companies, in particular splitting the transmission networks for electricity and gas from the more competitive activities.[10] The Cave (2009) review of the water sector in England and Wales recommended the promotion of competition through the legal separation of the retail businesses of water companies from their network operations. In contrast, the Hooper et al. (2008) review of the UK postal sector considered that vertical separation would be disproportionate as there was no evidence of persistent non-price-discrimination problems and competition has developed in upstream markets.

Over the years, a large body of economic literature has explored the relative merits of separated and integrated structures in network industries. Experience has shown that it remains tempting for vertically integrated companies to engage in the vertical leveraging of market power and foreclosure of entrants downstream. Hence, the overarching question faced by regulators has been whether the efficiency-related benefits of integration (lower transaction costs, the elimination of double marginalization, improved coordination) outweigh these vertical foreclosure effects. In industries that have not been separated, foreclosure has typically been dealt with through access regulation—by mandating the incumbent to provide third parties with access to its bottleneck facilities and on non-discriminatory-price and non-price terms (see section 9.3). However, discrimination and margin squeeze disputes have been common in this model (we saw examples in Chapter 4), and it has proved particularly difficult for regulators to monitor cases of discrimination in non-price terms for access. In this regard, vertical separation between the upstream bottleneck and downstream competitive businesses has again come to be seen as a remedy of last resort, just as it was at the time of the AT&T break-up in the USA.

The downsides of vertical separation that are being considered in the current policy debates are the same as before. One is simply that the benefits of vertical integration are removed. A vertically integrated company with market power at both stages of supply (upstream and downstream) may, in principle, sell to more consumers at a lower price (while earning more profit) than its separated equivalent—this is the double-marginalization problem that we discussed in Chapter 6. Moreover, the process of separation itself comes at a cost. Separation entails a one-off direct cost, as well as the ongoing costs of maintaining the separated structure. These costs may include the reorganization of the company and, where ownership is still held in common, the prohibition of certain forms of information transfer within the business (eg, through the creation of 'Chinese walls') and of duplication of staff or the splitting of activities undertaken jointly before separation. Vertical separation may also reduce incentives to invest or to innovate, because the non-competitive (separated) network business would no longer derive any profits

services, 2002/19/EC on access to, and interconnection of, electronic communications networks and associated facilities, and 2002/20/EC on the authorisation of electronic communications networks and services, Art 16(6) of the amended Framework Directive.

[10] European Commission (2007), 'DG Competition Report on Energy Sector Inquiry', 10 January.

from such efforts in the downstream activities. A further argument put forward by opponents to separation is that it reduces the coordination of investment and production decisions, given that the upstream company would no longer have direct contact with
end-user demand. The divisional structures implemented as a result of vertical separation
may curb the flow of information used by the network division to determine its investment strategies and priorities. This may slow down the decision-making process within
the separated company, and may lead to sub-optimal levels and types of investment.

The experience of the rail sector in Great Britain demonstrates the complexity of the
coordination issues that can arise as a result of vertical separation. The split between the
network operator and the train operators (which also exists in several other EU Member
States) has proved to be an effective way of ensuring non-discrimination, but it has also
led to imperfectly coordinated investment and a lack of focus on user requirements due
to the reduced incentive alignment between the various parties along the supply chain.[11]
The energy sector also has certain features that may make vertical separation less attractive (there are equally features that make it attractive) (Oxera, 2007). Separation may
result in hold-up and contract renegotiation in relation to sunk investments. Integrated
companies may have greater incentives to construct interconnectors between national
energy markets, and may be more able to coordinate the operation and scheduling of
the various layers in the supply chain (balancing supply and demand at all times is an
overriding imperative in energy markets). In line with the theoretical points mentioned
above, there are indications that vertically integrated energy companies tend to spend
more on R&D investment—they can apply new innovations to a variety of activities,
and thus have a better chance of internalizing the benefits of this investment (Markard
et al., 2004).

Given the potential huge upsides and huge downsides of vertical separation, the
policy decision of whether to impose such a remedy is inherently complex. A proper
economic CBA can help inform this decision—we discuss some of the basics of CBA in
section 9.6. The CBA will depend on the specific features of the sector and the country
in question. Regulatory objectives of separation vary across sectors (and sometimes
countries)—as noted above, sectors such as rail and energy tend to place greater emphasis on investment as a regulatory objective in its own right, whereas in telecoms regulation the promotion of entry and competition is considered of central importance. As a
starting point of your assessment, it is critical to understand the current level of competition in the different network and retail markets that would be affected by vertical
separation. In addition to the quantitative metrics describing the existing market conditions (eg, prices, market share developments, investment), you may need to pay particular attention to issues relating to non-price discrimination, which tend to be the
least transparent and therefore the most difficult to address in the absence of vertical
separation. The significance of non-price discrimination may be gauged from the

---

[11] For an overview, see Department for Transport and Office of Rail Regulation (2010), 'Rail Value for Money: Scoping Study Report', March.

number of disputes with, and complaints from, third parties. The case for vertical separation is also stronger where foreclosure of entrants through margin squeeze has been prevalent, where the incumbent has privileged access to commercially sensitive information obtained by the network business that may be exploited in retail offerings, and where a vertically integrated incumbent discourages customer switching by not processing entrants' wholesale orders as accurately as the orders of its own retail business.

If you decide in favour of vertical separation, you need to select the right form of separation. Earlier we explained that there is a range of options, with relatively mild accounting separation at one end, and functional and then full ownership separation at the other end. You also have to determine where to separate. The point of separation should correspond to the products and assets that possess the characteristics of a natural monopoly. Technological change may render separation at a given point no longer appropriate, and thus the scope of assets and services included in the separated entity may need to be revisited. An example is the amendments to the separation remedies in the telecoms sector that are required as a consequence of the migration from existing telecoms networks to next-generation access networks. Local-loop unbundling, a structural remedy heavily promoted in the early 2000s, loses some of its relevance in these next-generation networks since the local exchanges are no longer the crucial interconnection points in the network. Another example, in the energy sector, is the introduction of competition within a sub-set of the distribution function—ie, in metering and connections—which was previously considered a non-competitive layer in its entirety and therefore separated from other functions.

9.3 BEHAVIOURAL REMEDIES: PRICE AND ACCESS REGULATION

9.3.1 EXPERIENCE IN COMPETITION LAW

Behavioural remedies are less common than structural remedies in merger cases, but more common in agreement and abuse cases. In the latter, the remedy often goes hand in hand with the intervention against the practice itself. A company that is found to have abused its dominant position by refusing to supply a downstream competitor or by granting selective loyalty rebates to a rival's main customers is effectively told to stop doing it and never do it again. A fine may help to reinforce the message and also to deter dominant companies in other markets from engaging in the same type of conduct (see section 9.5). The ruling itself, if it is published and the reasoning explained clearly, can then become a useful part of the case law which helps other companies understand the rules. If the practice has already ceased at the time of the verdict—say, the company has stopped offering selective loyalty rebates—not much else may be required from the authority. However, in many cases the competition authority will not only want to put an end to the anti-competitive behaviour but also to incentivize the dominant company to start behaving in the opposite way—eg, to supply downstream competitors on fair and non-discriminatory terms. Such behavioural remedies (in the USA they are referred to as affirmative-obligation remedies) require ongoing, or at least periodic, monitoring. They effectively create the need for a new supervisory structure, either administrative or judicial. This in itself is nothing new. Many network and utility industries—telecoms, gas, electricity, water, postal services, rail, airports—have extensive sector-specific regulatory structures in place precisely to monitor compliance with the behavioural restrictions imposed on the regulated companies. The economic principles behind price and access regulation are also relevant for the design of remedies in competition law. The boundaries between regulation and competition law are fluid and differ across jurisdictions—some countries and sectors rely more heavily on sector-specific regulation, others more on competition law. Moreover, competition law is often called upon to deal with quasi-monopoly and bottleneck facilities for which no sector-specific regulations exist (we saw a number of examples in Chapter 4). We discuss some of the basic regulation principles in the next sub-sections.

Perhaps the main lesson from regulation is that effective monitoring of behaviour with regard to pricing and access is by no means impossible—the tools and practical experience exist—but the supervisory structure can be costly to implement and maintain. In the USA there seems to be a degree of institutional or even ideological resistance to turning competition authorities or courts into de facto regulators—the Supreme Court has warned against remedies that require courts to 'assume the day-to-day controls characteristics of a regulatory agency'.[12] Others take a more pragmatic view. But whichever the position, at the end of the day, as with all remedies, a careful consideration of the costs and benefits of behavioural remedies is required (see section 9.6 on CBA).

9.3.2 ECONOMIC INSIGHTS FROM NETWORK REGULATION: PRICE REGULATION

The field of network and utility regulation has developed extensive theoretical and practical knowledge of price regulation.[13] Here we summarize some of the basic principles that could be relevant when considering a pricing remedy in a competition law context—eg, as a remedy for excessive pricing or for a merger that creates a strong market position but is allowed on efficiency grounds. We saw in Chapter 4 that while excessive pricing cases are rare, competition authorities have occasionally prohibited such practices or used Article 102 as a 'stick' to get dominant companies to commit to price undertakings.

There are two main mechanisms for price regulation: rate-of-return regulation and price-cap regulation. Under rate-of-return regulation (also referred to as 'cost-plus'

---

[12] *Verizon Communications Inc v Law Offices of Curtis V. Trinko, LLP* 540 US 398 (2004). The Supreme Court cited work by Phillip Areeda, a leading commentator on antitrust law.

[13] A classic, and very accessible, work on the economics of regulation is Kahn (1988) (first published in two separate volumes in 1970 and 1971). A leading textbook that economists often refer to is Laffont and Tirole (1993). A good overview of the different price regulation mechanisms and practical experience with them is provided in Armstrong et al. (1994).

regulation), prices are set at a level that reflects the cost of service, and the supplier is allowed a fixed return on its asset base. This asset base is the outstanding (net of depreciation) historical investment in fixed assets. Operating costs are typically passed through directly, along with a depreciation charge and a return to cover the cost of capital. For an agreed base period, often 12 months, the supplier calculates its operating costs, depreciation, capital employed, and cost of capital. The regulator audits these calculations and determines the fair return. The certainty of earning a fair return normally provides good incentives for suppliers to make sufficient investments in the service and thus guarantee security of supply. A drawback of rate-of-return regulation is that it provides limited incentives for efficiency. If a company's costs of service increase, it can simply raise its price and continue making the same rate of return. Companies may also have the incentive to over-invest in their asset base (often referred to as 'gold-plating').

Price-cap regulation involves setting either price or revenue caps for a fixed time period (usually three to five years), thereby providing an incentive to reduce costs during this period. The cap itself is set with reference to a reasonable profit level similar to that in rate-of-return regulation, but because the cap doesn't change over the period, the company retains the benefits of any cost reductions that are achieved. The regulator reviews the price (or revenue) cap at the end of each period. If the regulated company is making high returns, the regulator will normally reduce the prices or revenues allowed to the company in the next period. If returns are low (and if this is attributable to external cost or demand factors rather than inefficiency), prices are permitted to rise. A common form of price cap is the formula RPI – X. RPI refers to the retail price index, a measure of consumer price inflation. The X is a factor that captures efficiency targets derived from expected trajectories of capital and labour productivity gains. Under this form of regulation, prices (or revenues) are required to decrease by X% in real terms per annum. This mechanism incentivizes suppliers to improve their efficiency during the price-cap period. Incentives to over-invest (or gold-plate) do not arise as this would reduce the profitability of the company. This feature of the price cap may also mean, however, that suppliers have incentives to reduce investments or quality of service below optimal levels in order to save costs.

A variant of the price cap is the revenue cap. Under the former, a company's revenues will change in proportion to changes in volume (every unit is sold at the same price). It will therefore be incentivized to increase volumes in order to increase revenues through the course of a price control period. The downside is that the company is exposed to the risk of reduced profits due to an unanticipated reduction in volumes. This risk will be exacerbated when there are high fixed costs, as these costs will be incurred irrespective of the volumes sold. In contrast, under a revenue cap, the revenue that a company is permitted to generate remains constant irrespective of the volume of output. The company has no particular incentives to increase volumes (since price per unit would have to come down if the revenue cap is reached), but nor is it exposed to uncontrollable downward shocks in volume.

The regulatory burden is high under any of the above mechanisms. Detailed expertise and analysis are required to assess the companies' costs and asset base, compare these with efficient benchmarks, and determine the cost of capital or reasonable return. Experience with rate-of-return regulation in the USA suggests that extensive supervision is required to avoid the gold-plating of assets. In turn, price-cap regulation typically requires additional quality-of-service regulation to ensure that investments are not reduced beyond the point where quality is affected. An additional complexity arises where the market is not a natural monopoly but rather one where competition exists or is being promoted at the same time as prices of the dominant supplier are regulated. In natural monopoly, reasonable profits are determined with reference to what capital providers actually invested in the asset base. In potentially competitive markets, the assets of the dominant supplier may have to be valued based on what an entrant would have to invest to replace them. This way, prices are still regulated but not at such low levels as to discourage new entry. Sector-specific regulators have been created to address these institutional and practical challenges of price regulation. Competition authorities and courts have not. The additional cost of expertise and analysis that is required by the authority or court when implementing a price remedy should be considered in the CBA of such a remedy.

9.3.3 ECONOMIC INSIGHTS FROM NETWORK REGULATION: ACCESS REGULATION

Access regulation has been of central importance in network industries. The first step is to decide whether to impose an access obligation—the economic principles behind this decision are not very different from the assessment of essential facilities under Article 102 (see Chapter 4). In the field of regulation, the focus is mostly on access to bottleneck and natural monopoly facilities such as rail infrastructure, electricity transmission networks, and local telephony loops. With an access obligation invariably comes the need to regulate the access price as well (otherwise access can be notionally offered but made prohibitively expensive). Given the high degree of market power of the network, unregulated access prices may be set at inefficiently high levels. To prevent this, many of the general principles of price regulation (discussed in the previous sub-section) apply to access regulation as well—capping prices at competitive levels should at the same time ensure that the network is allowed to earn a reasonable return and has the right incentives to invest and provide high quality. But there are additional policy objectives that are specific to access pricing: to promote efficient levels of entry in downstream (retail) markets that are reliant on the network, and to prevent vertically integrated network operators from leveraging their market power.

A general principle to achieve these objectives is that access prices and other terms and conditions should be non-discriminatory between integrated and independent competitors (vertical separation, discussed in section 9.2, is another way of avoiding the problem). But the price level and structure also matter. As noted above, a main objective of the access-pricing mechanism is to make competition work effectively in the downstream market. This means stimulating entry, but only by companies that are efficient (note the similarity with the as-efficient competitor test for abuse of dominance cases, discussed in Chapter 4). Aligning efficient entry and profitable entry is generally achieved by ensuring that access prices are somehow cost-reflective. There are a number of different access-pricing mechanisms you can choose from, most of them incorporating the principles of cost-reflectivity. We discuss some of the main ones below. We note here that competition law sometimes, but not always, prescribes cost-reflective access pricing—this is often a matter of judgement, not economics. In Chapter 4 we saw the example of the *Attheraces* case, where a cost-plus approach to access pricing was rejected because the input (horseracing data) had significant 'economic value' to the purchaser's downstream operations (a broadcast service) that was greater than the supplier's cost of producing the input.[14]

A first set of access-pricing mechanisms uses marginal costs as the basis. As we noted before (eg, in Chapter 1), optimal pricing theory states that prices should equal marginal or incremental cost if efficient resource allocation is to be achieved. Marginal cost pricing also ensures that prices are neither excessive nor predatory. The question is what to take as the relevant increment—we addressed this in Chapter 4 in dealing with predatory pricing. Short-run marginal cost is one option. If train service operators face the actual marginal cost that their services impose on the rail network, they will be incentivized to utilize network capacity efficiently. A train service will be operated wherever the benefit of that service to the operator (in revenues) exceeds the cost that the service imposes on the network (up until the point where network capacity is fully utilized and marginal costs would be much larger, ie, include the costs of network expansion). If there is effective competition in the downstream market (train services), retail prices will reflect the network access charges, thereby providing efficient incentives for usage by end-consumers. The downside of this mechanism is that short-run marginal costs do not include fixed costs. In most network industries, fixed costs are substantial, and therefore the network operator may not recover its total costs. This could negatively affect investment incentives and ultimately lead to sub-optimal network capacity (in some industries, such as rail, sea ports, and airports, this problem is sometimes resolved by allowing the fixed infrastructure costs to be recovered through means other than direct user charges, eg, through a government subsidy—see Chapter 8).

A more frequently used variant in regulation is long-run incremental cost pricing. A competition case in which long-run incremental cost was used (among other methods) to determine whether access charges were excessive is the *Albion Water* judgment by the UK Competition Appeal Tribunal (CAT) in 2008, concerning access to non-potable water to supply a paper factory.[15] This allows for remuneration of the fixed or quasi-fixed cost of providing additional network capacity (recall from Chapter 4 that as the relevant increment becomes larger or is considered over the longer run, more costs become incremental). Although it deviates from short-run efficient price signals (if there is excess capacity, pricing at short-run marginal costs gives the right signals for

---

[14] *Attheraces v British Horseracing Board* [2007] EWCA Civ 38, 2 February 2007.
[15] *Albion Water Limited and ors v Water Services Regulation Authority and ors* [2008] CAT 31, Judgment on Unfair Pricing, 7 November 2008.

usage of the capacity), this is a more efficient methodology in the longer run since it takes into account both short-run marginal costs and the contribution to capital costs of marginal use of the network, thus preserving incentives to invest in efficient network provision. It also allows incremental investments to be directed to those parts of the network where there is an efficient need for them.

Fully allocated cost pricing is a top-down approach whereby total costs are identified and, for a given volume projection, the access charge is set such that total revenue is sufficient to cover total costs. The European Commission inquiry into excessive charges for access to Belgacom's subscriber data, discussed in Chapter 4, is one example where fully allocated pricing was used as reference in an abuse of dominance case.[16] This pricing mechanism is fundamentally different from the principle of marginal cost pricing. Total costs will include an appropriate return on capital and allowances for depreciation, so that this mechanism can provide for appropriate investment incentives (at an aggregate network level; it does not help identify which parts of the network need incremental investment). Key cost drivers are then identified and portions of total cost allocated (a practical difficulty is the treatment of joint and common costs, for which some means of allocation between cost drivers must be found—see also Chapters 3, 4, and 8). However, since charging is based on average rather than marginal cost, this mechanism does not provide appropriate usage incentives. One particular problem arises where the network capacity is under-utilized and hence its fixed costs are spread over fewer users. This increases the average costs and hence the access price, thus perversely reducing the number of users even further.

Two-part tariffs are a way of combining the efficient-usage property of marginal cost pricing and the cost-recovery property of fully allocated costs (in Chapter 6 we discussed two-part tariffs in the context of vertical restraints). A two-part tariff consists of a fixed and a variable component. By charging short-run marginal costs as the variable component, incentives for efficient use of the existing network can be maintained, while charging a fixed component over a particular time period means that the fixed cost of investing in new assets can be recovered by the network operator. However, two-part tariffs are not always an efficient solution. The fixed component must not distort demand. If the fixed charge is too high, it will no longer be profitable for the smallest users to consume the good. One possible solution is to vary the size of the fixed charge depending on the ability of the downstream operator to pay. However, this may raise concerns about discriminatory pricing.

The efficient component pricing rule is the final access pricing mechanism discussed here. It is also known as the Baumol–Willig rule, after the two economists who first proposed it (Baumol, 1983; Willig, 1979). Two competition cases where the rule was discussed at length (one in negative and the other in positive terms) in the context of an alleged abuse of dominance are the *Albion Water* case in the UK and the *Telecom*

---

[16] European Commission (1998), 'XXVIIth Report on Competition Policy (1997)', p 26.

New Zealand case.[17] The efficient component pricing rule is applied to situations in which there is a vertically integrated network provider. Its main objective is ensuring efficient entry downstream—the access price is set such that only companies that are as efficient as the incumbent in the downstream market enter that market. It takes as a starting point the downstream (retail) price charged by the incumbent—say this is €1.00 per unit. The access price is then equal to that retail price minus the incumbent's downstream marginal cost per unit—if this downstream marginal cost is €0.20, the access price is €0.80. At this access price, only entrants that have downstream marginal costs of €0.20 or lower get sufficient 'headroom' to make a profit at this access price of €0.80 (given that they can't set a higher retail price than the €1.00 charged by the verti-cally integrated company). This mechanism is therefore also known as 'retail-minus'. In general it is relatively straightforward to implement as only downstream costs need to be analysed in detail. It is less strict on the network operator than marginal cost pricing since the retail price is taken as given—ie, there is no scrutiny of whether the €1.00 retail price reflects competitive or monopoly levels. This may give the right incentives for network investment (the €0.80 access charge gives a sufficient return to the network provider), but does not provide for any means to control end-consumer prices if those are set inefficiently high to start with (eg, if the true long-run incremental cost of net-work access is €0.70, the competitive retail price would be €0.90 not €1.00).

9.3.4 FRAND REMEDIES (FAIR, REASONABLE, AND NON-DISCRIMINATORY)

A generic behavioural remedy is the obligation to supply products or services on FRAND terms. This remedy has been applied in a range of competition policy contexts. Two examples are BSkyB's obligation to supply access to its technical platform services in the UK pay-TV market, and Microsoft's obligation to make interface information available in order to allow rival servers to achieve full interoperability with its servers and PCs running on Windows.[18] These companies were not forced to give away their products for free, but rather to set terms and conditions in line with the principles of FRAND. Sometimes the concepts of 'fair', 'reasonable', and 'non-discriminatory' can be applied using the established price and access regulation principles discussed in the previous sub-sections. But sometimes it is more difficult. Below we discuss the eco-nomic principles behind FRAND in a specific context: the licensing of intellectual

---

[17] *Albion Water Limited and ors v Water Services Regulation Authority and ors* [2006] CAT 36, Judgment, 18 December 2006 (this was an earlier judgment in the same case we cited above in the discussion of long-run incremental cost pricing); and *Commerce Commission v Telecom Corporation of New Zealand Limited and Telecom New Zealand Limited* CIV 2004-404-1333, Judgment of 9 October 2009, High Court of New Zealand.

[18] Ofcom (2005), 'Provision of Technical Platform Services: A Consultation on Proposed Guidance as to How Ofcom May Interpret the Meaning of "Fair, Reasonable and Non-discriminatory" and Other Regulatory Conditions When Assessing Charges and Terms Offered by Regulated Providers of Technical Platform Services', November; and Court of First Instance (2007), Case T-201/04 *Microsoft v EC Commission* [2007] ECR II-3601.

property (IP) through standard-setting organizations (SSOs). This has become a hot topic in both US and EU competition law in recent years.

Many products in the high-tech and telecoms industries—mobile handsets, memory chips, and digital video equipment, for example—are based on common technology standards, which are often set by SSOs (we also discussed standard setting in Chapter 5). Standards usually incorporate a large number of patented technologies. Those patents that form part of the standard are very valuable—all users of the standard (including equipment manufacturers) pay royalty rates to the patent holder. Patents that are excluded from the standard tend to lose their value quickly. Before making a particular patent part of the standard, SSOs often require the patent holder to commit to license their IP on terms consistent with FRAND (or the American equivalent, RAND, without the 'fair'). SSOs began to incorporate FRAND principles in the 1970s and 1980s, when industries were becoming increasingly aware of the potential commercial value of technology standards and had to devise practical solutions to achieve standard setting and avoid problems of hold-up. The hold-up problem in this context occurs when the manufacturers in the SSO must select a particular technology for the standard, but are concerned that they are subsequently charged exploitative royalty rates for that technology and cannot switch anymore because it is has become part of the standard (Chapter 6 also discussed the hold-up problem). FRAND is designed to give IP holders a reasonable return so as to preserve their incentives to innovate, but at the same time prevent them from unreasonably benefiting from the additional value that accrues to them from being included in the standard. The use of the FRAND principle has facilitated the development and acceptance of new standards. However, SSOs that require licensing on FRAND terms, such as the European Telecommunications Standards Institute (ETSI) and the Joint Electronic Device Engineering Council (JEDEC) in the USA, have never really come up with a precise definition of the concept. For a long time this lack of definition was perhaps not a major problem because licensing disputes were relatively rare, but in recent years the FRAND rules have led to numerous legal challenges, with some ending up being considered by competition authorities.

In May 2008, a US Court of Appeal overturned a finding by the Federal Trade Commission (FTC) that Rambus, a technology licensing company, had breached section 2 of the Sherman Act.[19] The FTC considered that Rambus had unfairly 'ambushed' an SSO—the JEDEC, which worked on a cooperative basis with industry participants to develop standards for random access memory chips—by not declaring its intention to acquire and subsequently enforce patent rights covering technology that was essential to implement two particular standards. The FTC also concluded that as part of this 'ambush' Rambus had charged prices above the RAND levels that the SSO would have enforced. Assessing this behaviour under competition law, and taking

---

[19] *Rambus Inc v FTC* 522 F 3d 456 (US Ct of Apps (District of Colombia Circuit), 2008).

(F)RAND as the appropriate benchmark and remedy, was a previously untested approach. The court disagreed with the FTC and stated that:

> the [Federal Trade] Commission failed to sustain its allegation of monopolization. Its factual conclusion was that Rambus's alleged deception enabled it *either* to acquire a monopoly through the standardization of its patented technologies rather than possible alternatives, *or* to avoid limits on its patent licensing fees that the SSO would have imposed as part of its normal process of standardizing patented technologies. But the latter—deceit merely enabling a monopolist to charge higher prices than it otherwise could have charged—would not in itself constitute monopolization.[20]

The relationship between actual pricing levels and the level compliant with FRAND obligations was at the heart of the European Commission's investigation into Qualcomm under Article 102, which was opened in 2007 following complaints by mobile phone and chipset manufacturers such as Ericsson, Nokia, Texas Instruments, Broadcom, NEC, and Panasonic. The alleged abuse concerned the terms under which Qualcomm licensed its patents that are essential to the WCDMA standard, which forms part of the 3G standard for European mobile phone technology (also referred to as UMTS). The investigation was closed in 2009 after the complaints were withdrawn.[21]

Many questions therefore remain about how FRAND should be interpreted in the context of IP and whether it can be an appropriate benchmark and remedy under competition law. The economic principles of FRAND are also still under development. As a starting point, it is useful to assess how essential a patent is for the standard. The degree of essentiality affects the scope for technological substitution, which also feeds into any assessment of market definition and market power when a specific competition case arises. In this context, three groups of patents are relevant. There are those that are technically essential and formally declared essential under the relevant standards. It is, by definition, not feasible to produce products (eg, network equipment or consumer devices) that comply with the relevant standards without using the technology covered by these patents, and therefore there is no supply-side substitution that could widen the relevant market beyond the technology covered by these patents. The second group is formed by commercially essential patents that are not formally declared essential under the standard. While it is technically possible to produce standards-compliant products without using the technologies covered by these patents, it is not commercially viable to engineer around them. Third are the non-essential patents—it is technically and commercially feasible to engineer around these patents, and therefore they may form part of a wider relevant market with substitutable technologies. FRAND can apply to all three groups, but is more critical for the first two.

The next question is how to determine what is 'fair' and 'reasonable'. The nature of IP rights means that static cost-based pricing rules do not provide useful guidance for

---

[20] Ibid., at [5].

[21] European Commission (2007), 'Antitrust: Commission Initiates Formal Proceedings Against Qualcomm', press release, MEMO/07/389, 1 October; and European Commission (2009), 'Antitrust: Commission Closes Formal Proceedings Against Qualcomm', press release, MEMO/09/516, 24 November.

setting price ceilings. In particular, the typically low marginal cost of distributing IP means that setting price equal to marginal cost—which is normally considered the efficient price level—would not generate incentives for innovation. It is therefore necessary to look for alternatives. Economics has thus far identified four possible approaches to interpreting FRAND in the context of SSOs. The first of these is the non-interventionist approach of allowing unfettered market prices, accepting the principle of charging what each purchaser will bear (this is in essence what the US court ruling in *Rambus* implies). The second is to carry out a profitability analysis of the investments and returns over the lifetime of the patent. This is a more comprehensive analysis than the static cost-based pricing rules and uses the financial tools discussed in Chapters 3, 8, and 10. The aim is to assess the level of returns on investments that are reasonable in light of the risk taken, and to set the FRAND royalty rates on that basis. The third is the Swanson–Baumol approach, whereby the price that the IP holder would be able and willing to charge *prior* to the acceptance of the IP into the standard is taken as the fair price, as it reflects the value of the IP independently of the value of the standard (Swanson and Baumol, 2005). The fourth is the Shapley value approach, resulting in a FRAND price that awards each IP holder the value that represents its contribution to the standard.[22] We discuss the last two of these in more detail below.

The approach developed by Swanson and Baumol can be summarized as follows. To alleviate concerns about the exertion of ex post market power by an IP holder that has been accepted into a standard, this approach would involve prospective licensees negotiating licence terms *prior* to their acceptance into the standard, and hence at a point in time when there is still active competition between technologies. Licence terms set at that point would remove the ability of the IP holder to change its pricing in response to changes in the value of the standard at a later stage. This is broadly the model that two SSOs—the Institute of Electrical and Electronics Engineers and the VITA Standards Organization—have been exploring, whereby IP holders reveal in their applications to the SSO the maximum royalty rate that would apply for the lifetime of the standard, were they to be accepted (Treacy and Kostenko, 2007). The Swanson–Baumol approach can be characterized as an efficiency-based approach (it shares some underlying features with the efficient component pricing rule, or Baumol–Willig rule, for access pricing discussed in the previous sub-section). This is because it is auction-based, so the resulting licensing rates should in principle reflect the value that each patent brings to the standard over and above the value that the next-best solution could provide. This approach is intended to mitigate the risk of hold-up. While the Swanson–Baumol approach is appealing in relation to the *future* pricing of technology that is yet to be incorporated into a standard, its usefulness as a benchmark for making ex post assessments under competition law is more limited. A competition authority would have to assess the extent to which, at the time that the particular IP was included in the

---

[22] This option is described as the 'Shapley solution' in Layne-Farrar et al. (2007). The underlying thinking is derived from Shapley (1953).

standard, alternative technological solutions were available that could have been substituted for the IP in question.

The Shapley value approach is based on a theoretical form of patent selection rather than the actual selection process. It is therefore somewhat less intuitive than the other approaches:

> Suppose that there are n patent-owners, one for each patent involved . . . Suppose the patent-owners arrive at the SSO in random order each with her patent in her pocket, with all possible arrival sequences equally likely. Now suppose that in each sequence, each patent-owner receives the amount by which her patent increases the value of the best standard that can be built from the patents that are already at the SSO when she arrives . . . The Shapley value gives the average of such contributions over all possible arrival sequences—each patent thus receives the average (over arrival sequences) of its marginal contribution. (Layne-Farrar et al., 2007, p 24)

Consider a standard with two complementary technologies: one to enable a vehicle to turn left, and one to enable it to turn right. The end-product (say, a car) needs both in order to be of any use. While for most users these technologies will be of equal value, the payouts to the IP holders may not be the same under the Shapley value approach. If, for example, just one company develops the technology to turn left, while two companies work out alternative technologies to turn right, the payoffs would be two-thirds to the former, and one-sixth to each of the latter—this is shown in Table 9.1, which has all six arrival sequences and shows for each which technology (R1, R2, or L) renders the product valuable upon arrival, ie, once there is a left and right technology. Note that in this analysis both innovators of turning right receive a payoff, even though only one of them can ultimately be included in the standard.

Despite their fundamentally different approaches, the Swanson–Baumol and Shapley value methodologies share similarities in their outcomes. An IP holder that faces no competition from alternative technologies vying to be included in the standard will always earn greater returns than an IP holder for a technology for which there is competition. In practice, this could lead to the paradoxical outcome of a monopoly provider of a peripheral technology earning greater returns than a provider of a more fundamental element of the standard for which alternatives exist. However, economically, this outcome would still be considered efficient—scarce goods should be priced

Table 9.1 Illustration of FRAND pay-offs based on the Shapley value approach

Arrival sequence of the technologies	Which technology adds the value?	Final pay-off to each technology
R1, R2, L	L	R1: 1/6th
R1, L, R2	L	R2: 1/6th
R2, R1, L	L	L: 4/6ths
R2, L, R1	L	
L, R1, R2	R1	
L, R2, R1	R2	

more highly; this is what you get in well-functioning markets as well, even if it may not appear 'fair'. Both approaches bring significant operational challenges. For the Swanson–Baumol approach to be effective the auction design would need to overcome the fact that value from a standard is created by aggregating different technologies to form a single standard—the sum is greater than the parts. Each patent holder would therefore need to assess not only its position relative to competing patent holders, but also the value of the technological input it is providing relative to the cumulative value of the technology. In this context, as we discussed in Chapter 5, the application of Article 101 to SSOs can make it difficult for participants in the SSO to have discussions or reach agreements in relation to pricing. Rather than preventing anti-competitive price increases, too strict an application of Article 101 to SSOs may therefore, paradoxically, limit the ability of IP holders to collectively restrain the cumulative charges for the IP in a standard.

9.4 BEHAVIOURAL REMEDIES: NEW INSIGHTS FROM BEHAVIOURAL ECONOMICS

9.4.1 MARKETS HAVE CONSUMERS AS WELL AS PRODUCERS

Most discussions about remedies to date have focused on the supply side of markets—the side of the producers. The structural and behavioural remedies considered in the previous sections are introduced to enhance the viability of competition between these producers. Fines—which we deal with in section 9.5—are, again, a supply-side remedy, aimed at punishing past anti-competitive behaviour, and providing a signal to other companies that deviant behaviour will not be tolerated. Compensatory damages to victims of competition law infringements—the topic of Chapter 10—involve a one-off transfer of funds from the perpetrators (on the supply side) to the aggrieved (on the demand side). These damages payments are backward-looking, aimed at drawing a line under past episodes.

Few of these remedies directly (or completely) tackle the problem of how markets in future can be made to work better for *consumers*. Increasingly, policy-makers and competition authorities are realizing that in order to deliver competitive markets *both* the supply and the demand side of markets need to work well. On the supply side, competition between firms should deliver what consumers want—low prices, high quality, and choice. On the demand side, well-informed, confident, rational, and effective consumers play a key role in activating this competition. If, however, consumers suffer from systematic biases in their judgement and actions, and are neither able nor inclined to make informed, rational decisions, producers will have little incentive to supply consumers with what they want. Instead, producers may simply become increasingly inventive in exacerbating and exploiting these biases.

Recognizing the interdependence between consumers and producers in the functioning of markets has two main policy implications. First, it points to important interactions, and possibly a need for some convergence, between consumer protection (focused mainly on the demand side) and competition policy (focused mainly on the supply side). Second, as part of a competition investigation, the demand side should not be taken as 'a given'. Indeed, the source of competition problems in the market may be on the demand side rather than (as is usually assumed) the supply side—for example, biases in consumer behaviour that limit switching. If this is the case, remedy design should seek to tackle these biases directly or at least take them into account.

This section gives an overview of behavioural economics, focusing on how psychology has influenced the discipline and how this has led to questions regarding the traditional theory of consumer behaviour. We then explore what behavioural economics means for consumer biases and competition policy and, in particular, how certain types of competition problem might be tackled through demand-side remedies.

9.4.2 BEHAVIOURAL ECONOMICS: AN OVERVIEW

Behavioural economics involves applying psychological principles to explain observed behaviour that deviates from the predictions of traditional economic models. It is perhaps more accurately referred to as 'psychology and economics'. Behavioural economics itself is not especially new—some of it dates back to the 1950s and it became a field in its own right in the late 1970s with the work of psychologists Daniel Kahneman and Amos Tversky (1979) and the economist Richard Thaler (1980). What is more recent is the attention it has received by the public at large, helped by popular economics books such as *Freakonomics* (Levitt and Dubner, 2005) and *Nudge* (Thaler and Sunstein, 2008), and by Kahneman winning the Nobel Prize for Economics in 2002.

Policy-makers, regulators, and competition authorities are increasingly looking to the lessons from behavioural economics to help them determine whether markets are working in the interests of consumers. The literature provides a backbone for understanding why consumers may face a variety of problems in processing information and making decisions. So why is behavioural economics relevant for understanding consumer behaviour? Traditional 'neo-classical' economics makes several assumptions about the preferences, cognitive ability, and rationality of consumers, which provides a useful, tractable framework for explaining how consumers behave given their budget constraints and the prevailing prices in the market. However, over time, what has become clear is that in many circumstances these assumptions do not match psychological reality. Whilst the traditional approach to human behaviour has merit in that it simplifies the analysis, the problem is that it ignores one crucial factor—consumers are indeed *human*. In effect, there are a number of important differences between the 'homo economicus' of the traditional models and the 'homo sapiens' of the real world.[23]

---

[23] For a more comprehensive discussion of the assumptions of traditional economic theory on the one hand and psychology and behavioural economics on the other, see Camerer and Loewenstein (2003).

As regards individuals' preferences, the traditional models assume that people are purely self-interested, and that they seek to maximize their own absolute level of utility. My happiness does not depend on what others have—I do not care that my neighbour has just bought the same car as me. Furthermore, the way in which information is perceived, and hence how individuals' preferences are formed, is insensitive to the way in which external information is portrayed or 'framed'. Context does not matter; and irrelevant information will be ignored. I do not care about the order in which a price comparison search delivers its results; I always go for the product that will best satisfy my (stable, non-malleable) preferences.

Traditional economics further assumes that individuals use all available externally-provided information when making decisions—in fact, the more information, the better—and that they have perfect recall of this information and their past experiences. Using all of this information, individuals engage in rational and conscious reasoning, looking both backwards and into the future, to weigh up what the best course of action would be. They then act on this, behaving consistently in a way that maximizes their utility. When I buy a printer at the point of sale from a particular store, I weigh up the cost of the printer against that offered by competing stores. I also consider the cost and availability of other printers, and whether the model in front of me is best able to serve my needs. I consider in full my future consumption of ink, given a robust forecast of my future inclination to type this text and hence use the printer. I ignore the fact that the store is promoting the printer as being 'half price', since I know that the same printer is available elsewhere at 'full price', for exactly the same amount of money. I also do not purchase the recommended warranty for the printer, since I do not need it and, besides, better warranty deals are available elsewhere. In this framework, emotions or prior beliefs (if these are wrong) do not affect consumers' decisions. It also assumes that individuals, drawing upon their cognitive capacity, are good at forecasting—they know and can predict what will make them happy, and they will behave consistently over time such that they maximize their lifetime utility.

In contrast, behavioural economics seeks to provide reasons why anomalies are often observed between the predictions of the above standard economic models and actual consumer behaviour. It builds on a fundamental cornerstone of psychology—that people can be thought of as relying on two cognitive systems. System I processing is undertaken by the older parts of the human brain, which we share with other species. It involves sub-conscious, instinctive, and emotive processing. System II processing is undertaken by 'newer' parts of the human brain, which we do not share with other species. It deals with conscious, rules-based, objective processing—and is capable of projecting far into the future.[24]

Behavioural economics incorporates the notion in psychology that individuals' perception and preferences depend on the context in which information is presented—ie, that preferences are 'reference dependent'. This is driven heavily by System I (albeit in

---

[24] For a more detailed explanation, see Gilbert (2006) and Thaler and Sunstein (2008).

interaction with System II). You care about what others are doing and what others have (for example, you care whether payoffs are 'fair'). You also care about the order in which information is presented to you since, instinctively, this may convey further information. You may place more weight on a product that features higher on a list. You may view a €5 bottle of wine that was previously €10 somewhat differently to an (otherwise identical) bottle sold at €5 at 'full price'. Importantly, people are emotional about their possessions. They tend to dislike the risk of losing what they have much more than they like the prospect of gaining that which they do not have (this is referred to as loss aversion). In a market context, consumers may therefore place a higher value on what they already have compared with what they have yet to purchase. This is known as the endowment effect. It can, among other things, lead to default bias—a preference for the status quo endowment—and consumer inertia. Hence, preferences are more malleable than assumed in standard theory: they are susceptible to external influence, 'constructed' rather than 'given', influenced by emotion, and dependent on context.

Behavioural economics also incorporates lessons from psychology in terms of how people actually make decisions. Unlike homo economicus, people do not always—or indeed usually—assess all available information, weighing up all alternatives, to reach a decision. To do so would be cognitively exhausting, and may overly complicate the simplest of day-to-day tasks. Try to think consciously about the rate at which you should be breathing, or how you should tie your shoe laces. Rather, many day-to-day decisions are simply made without 'thinking' much at all—and it is System I that enables us to do this. System I deals with moderating the innate tasks that we are born with (eg, breathing, blinking, walking), and provides a means for us to perform the stock of activities that, over time, we learn to do (eg, tying shoe laces, riding a bicycle, reading this text). Relying on System I for these tasks then frees up the mental capacity for us to use System II, which requires more effort, in an efficient way—to weigh up various options, to plan ahead, and to make conscious decisions about the best course of action. Once we have consciously learned how to undertake new tasks (eg, through revising for an exam, or undertaking courtroom training), they become embedded within our System I.

Hence, the human brain has evolved in a way that makes efficient use of scarce mental resources. However, it is not infallible. Whilst natural instinct may lead to the correct course of action some of the time, it may not do so all of the time. Furthermore, in between conscious (System I) and subconscious (System II) decision-making lies a collection of shortcuts known as 'rules of thumb' or 'heuristics'. Instead of looking at all available information and weighing up all potential courses of action, individuals may make decisions based on a selection of the available information and recent experience, looking towards what others have done, or focusing on aspects perceived to be important. Again, this saves effort in having to employ System II. Whilst these 'availability' heuristics provide a useful shortcut to making quick decisions, which are often 'operationally rational' given the circumstances, they can also lead to flawed decision-making. For example, as suggested above, heuristics may be vulnerable to how information is framed, which will affect the perception of the problem in the first instance.

A commonly cited example—which you should consider answering quickly and instinctively—is as follows: 'A bat and a ball together cost €110. The bat costs €100 more than the ball. How much is the ball?'[25]

Heuristic decision-making is vulnerable to a number of other biases as well. People may be overconfident in their abilities, and may over-predict unlikely events such as winning the lottery (optimism bias). They may selectively remember recent positive experiences and forget bad experiences, which may lead them to conclude that they generally get things right; or they may associate a good outcome with their own behaviour or action when, in reality, they had little to do with the outcome (attribution and confirmation bias). People may also use others' behaviour as a rule of thumb for the correct course of action when, in reality, others are making mistakes (herd behaviour).

Psychology shows that where external information is poor or where cognitive processing is too demanding, people are more likely to leave aside System II, relying instead on internal information (memory), instinct, and heuristics to make decisions—all of which lean more towards System I. In addition, if presented with too much information, people may 'decide not to decide'. Consumers may make a purchase when only three types of insurance policy are offered (they can select the most attractive one), but may fail to make a purchase at all when forced to choose between 20 alternatives. Information overload makes perception difficult (there is little context to the information, which may as well be 'white noise'). Moreover, consciously processing the various options (using System II) is time-consuming and difficult, whilst instinct (System I) offers little by way of a resolution. For many people, the route of least resistance is to procrastinate, and to be inert. Similarly, when offered several alternatives, consumers may simply select the 'default' or the recommended option.

It should be noted that emotion plays a major role in virtually all decision-making. Indeed, this leads to a significant day-to-day conflict between us consciously deliberating the future (driven by System II), and our more primitive, age-old need for immediate gratification (System I). People may know that it would be good for them to sign up to a pension scheme, but may not do so and instead use the money to go on holiday or buy a new car. Consumers may be tempted to take on a loan that, in the longer term, they know they may not be able to afford. People may also be poor at predicting the utility that they will derive in future from adopting a particular course of action. Economists call this 'time-inconsistent' behaviour. However, it is possible for consumers to 'precommit' to not being driven by their desires for immediate gratification. People who take a shopping list to the supermarket will have deliberated over what they actually need, the prices of the products concerned, and their budget. Those who simply turn up at a supermarket and grab a large trolley are more likely to be guided by what each carefully laid-out aisle of the store has on offer. These shoppers may be driven more by their need

---

[25] Instinct would say that the ball costs €10. Conscious deliberation would involve solving a set of simultaneous equations: (1) bat + ball = €110; and (2) bat = €100 + ball; by substituting (2) into (1), you eventually get the result that ball = €5.

for immediate gratification, and may not consciously process the cumulative prices (or indeed fat or salt content) of the products that they are purchasing.

9.4.3 BEHAVIOURAL ECONOMICS, COMPETITION POLICY, AND REMEDY DESIGN

Behavioural economics is not just of academic or popular interest. Policy-makers are looking at what it means for making markets work better. The UK Office of Fair Trading (OFT, 2010), one of the more proactive competition authorities in this field, has identified four categories of bias that, in its view, are most relevant to competition policy. (Note that the exact categorization of the biases is somewhat different to that set out in the discussion above.) The first of these are the framing biases, including the relative utility (a consumer's utility is affected by reference points); default bias (consumers adopt default options); and placement bias (consumers may choose the option placed at the top of a list). The second category is that of processing-power biases, including choice overload (consumers make choices on sub-sets of information); representational bias (consumers use visible value as an indicator of hidden value); and rules of thumbs (eg, consumers imitate other consumers). The third category consists of time-inconsistency biases—projection bias (consumers expect to feel the same tomorrow as they do today); over-optimism (consumers overestimate how much they will use a product or underestimate how much it will cost); and hyperbolic discount bias (consumers value today disproportionately more than tomorrow). Finally there are the loss-aversion biases, including the endowment bias (consumers value something more after having owned it than before owning it).

The OFT notes that in order for consumers to make sound decisions they need to go through three stages: they need to *access* information about the various offers available in the market; *assess* these offers in a well-reasoned way; and *act* on this information and analysis by purchasing the good or service that offers the best value. The 'access stage' relates to the information search that consumers undertake—in effect the reliance that consumers place on internal information (memory) versus being provided with, or seeking out, further external information. To some extent this also covers the way in which information is framed. However, most of the behavioural biases discussed above, and listed by the OFT, would appear to be relevant to the 'assess stage'. Here consumers may be sensitive to framing effects, may be poor at assessing the future, have limits to their processing ability, look at limited sub-sets of information, and use heuristics to make decisions. At the 'act stage', individuals may be inert in the face of too much information, or lack self control in balancing the present and the future.

Companies may seek to take advantage of consumers' behavioural biases at each of the three stages. At the 'access stage', suppliers may make it more difficult for consumers to search. Because consumers may focus unduly on pricing terms provided up front, suppliers may exploit this by shifting more of the price into add-on services (we discussed after-markets in Chapter 2), or making price-searching harder by using 'drip pricing' (where consumers can observe only part of the full price up front, with price increments subsequently being 'drip fed' to them as they spend time completing their purchase—you may have come across this when purchasing a holiday on the Internet). Companies may also make it more difficult for consumers to compare offers by obfuscating prices, increasing complexity, or using price promotions and frames to distort decision-making. Knowing that consumers exhibit inertia, suppliers may reduce the likelihood of switching through such means as requiring customers to use registered post to cancel a live subscription, or using automatic re-subscription as the default option (eg, automatic direct-debit renewal of an annual insurance policy).

'Partitioned pricing'—such as charging separate prices for a product and for delivery, or for a flight and a fuel surcharge—is a business practice that can be better understood using behavioural economics. In theory, if consumers are fully informed and fully rational, they should take account of the full price of a product when making a purchase decision. It should not matter if this price is quoted as one price or is split into a primary price with add-ons. However, studies have found many real-life examples of where partitioned pricing has been shown to influence purchasing decisions, and have provided psychological explanations for this (Morwitz et al., 2009). Partitioned pricing can affect consumers' price perceptions, purchase intentions and demand. The OFT has commissioned experimental research to explore how various common pricing practices might exacerbate biases in consumer behaviour (we also discussed such experimental economics in Chapter 5 in the context of the leniency policy for cartel whistleblowers):

> The research uses a controlled economic experiment to test five pricing frames, whereby the true price is provided in a complex way. The pricing frames investigated are drip pricing, 'sales', complex pricing, bait pricing, and time limited offers . . . The report found that all of these pricing practices have some adverse effect on consumer choice and that most of them do significantly impact on consumer welfare. It suggests that the root of the errors can be found in the existence of the behavioural biases, largely the endowment effect and cognitive errors. (London Economics, 2010)

Such biases might then reduce competition *within* a particular market. The process of competition between suppliers may 'unwind' this consumer behaviour, with the 'good' driving out the 'bad', but there are also instances where the market may not self-correct. A theoretical study by Gabaix and Laibson (2006) suggests that if there is a sufficient proportion of 'myopic' (or 'naïve') customers, competition does not induce firms to 'unshroud' information about add-on prices. Rather, sophisticated consumers buy the main good and do not buy the add-on, and benefit from a cross-subsidy from the 'naïve' customers who do pay add-on fees.

The presence of consumer biases can affect competitive interactions *between* markets as well, providing additional credence to the notion that a company can lever market power from a market in which it is dominant into one in which it faces competition. For example, behavioural biases provide additional insights into how tying or bundling might be anti-competitive—in effect by raising the cost to competitors of competing in the bundled or tied market (we discussed bundling and tying in Chapter 4). Indeed, since behavioural economics suggests that in the presence of consumer inertia, endowment effects, and default bias, even small switching costs can have significant effects on consumer behaviour, foreclosure through tying and bundling may be more feasible than it would be in the absence of such behavioural effects.[26]

9.4.4 THE *MICROSOFT* REMEDIES

Cognitive biases played a role in the Media Player part of the EU *Microsoft* case, which focused on Microsoft's practice of bundling (by default and free of charge) Windows Media Player with its Windows operating system.[27] Microsoft was dominant in the operating system market, but competitors were vying to gain market share in the emerging media player market. By bundling Media Player as the default application through which all media would play when an individual purchased a PC, Microsoft was considered to have leveraged its dominance in the operating system market into the market for media players. If consumers are fully rational, this default may not matter— after all, consumers can quickly log onto the Internet, and download an alternative media player free of charge. However, as noted by the OFT (2010), 'when viewed through a behavioural lens, it becomes clear that consumers are significantly less likely to switch from the preloaded Microsoft programs than might otherwise be expected. In this context, a strategy to foreclose could move from being unlikely to being much more plausible'. Indeed, the European Commission found that the pre-installation of Media Player on Windows created the potential for leveraging since, on the demand side 'users who find WMP pre-installed on their client PCs are ... in general less likely to use alternative media players as they already have an application which delivers media streaming and playback functionality', whereas on the supply side 'an aspect to consider is that, while downloading is in itself a technically inexpensive way of distributing media players, vendors must expend resources to overcome end-users' inertia and persuade them to ignore the pre-installation of WMP'.[28] Hence the finding of abuse took account— albeit implicitly—of the behavioural biases that consumers face.

However, the remedy put forward in this case did not seem consistent with the competition problems identified. Part of the remedy adopted was that Microsoft should make available versions of Windows with and without Media Player installed. In the event, very few copies of the version without Media Player were sold.[29] This is perhaps not surprising, since both were offered at the same price. Consumers, when presented with the two options, would most likely choose the version with Media Player pre-installed. Perhaps a more effective remedy would have been to include a CD containing a random choice of media players for consumers to choose from. By forcing consumers to make a conscious

---

[26] See Office of Fair Trading (2010).

[27] See Commission Decision of 24 March 2004 relating to a proceeding under Art 82 of the EC Treaty (Case COMP/C-3/37.792 *Microsoft*).

[28] Ibid., at [845] and [870].

[29] See Ahlborn and Evans (2009), p 24.

choice in this way, and by not including a default option, consumers might have selected an option that was more suited to their needs.

Interestingly, in a subsequent—and apparently similar—case, the Commission investigated the bundling of the Microsoft Internet Explorer web browser with Windows.[30] Here, the Commission agreed a different remedy with Microsoft. Users of Windows-based PCs who have Internet Explorer set as their default web browser, and who also subscribe to Windows Update (which updates their operating system), would be taken to a screen providing, at random, Internet Explorer and a number of competing browsers such as Firefox and Safari. For these consumers, this remedy in effect removes the impact of the default option, and instead forces them to make an active choice of their preferred browser. This might therefore be more effective in cutting the tie between Windows and Internet Explorer. Hence, whilst the behavioural remedy in the Media Player case by itself achieved little in restoring competition in the bundled market, the behavioural remedy in the Internet Explorer case—even if it appeared to be more interventionist—sought to restore competition through forcing customers to make an active choice.

9.4.5 THE IMPACT OF BEHAVIOURAL ECONOMICS: THE JURY IS STILL OUT

The *Microsoft* remedies show how the insights from behavioural economics are of relevance in standard Article 101 and 102 competition cases. A step further would be for competition authorities and regulators to try to improve market functioning through demand-side remedies. Here Articles 101 and 102 may be less suited. A better tool would perhaps be the market investigations regime, which is unique to the UK (under the Enterprise Act 2002 and its predecessors). As noted by the OFT (2010):

> standard antitrust policy is not necessarily well designed to address the demand-side effect of consumer biases . . . that of distorting or weakening the virtuous circle of competition. However, antitrust enforcement is just one tool Other tools include consumer policy, market studies, investigations (in the UK at least), and even the potential for authorities to advocate legislation in a particular market. This choice requires consumer and competition policy to work closely together; picking the best tool to fix the problem and not simply thinking about which has traditionally been used. In this regard, the UK is in a relatively unique situation in having a third type of instrument that sits between pure antitrust instruments and consumer instruments—market studies and investigations. These are designed to examine features of the market that distort competition, arguably precisely the type of concerns that consumer behavioural biases may create.

This market investigations regime has dealt with several markets that are prime candidates for the presence of consumer biases, such as extended warranties on electrical goods,

---

[30] European Commission (2009), 'Summary of Commission Decision of 16 December 2009 relating to a proceeding under Art 102 of the Treaty on the Functioning of the European Union and Art 54 of the EEA Agreement', (Case COMP/39.530 *Microsoft* (Tying), notified under document C (2009) 10033)' [2010] OJ C36/7.

personal current accounts, store cards, home credit, and payment protection insurance (PPI). The OFT emphasizes that this does not necessarily mean more intervention but rather smarter intervention. It favours the 'liberal paternalist' approach, as popularized by Richard Thaler and Cass Sunstein in the book *Nudge*, referred to above. Such interventions work to some extent *with* consumers' flawed preferences and decision-making abilities, rather than necessarily trying to correct them. On the one hand, such remedies may encourage consumers to make a choice—a so called 'forced choice'—rather than letting them remain inert or simply opt for 'the default'. The remedy in the Microsoft Internet Explorer case provides an example. On the other hand, and again consistent with the liberal paternalist approach, where there is a clearly superior outcome for consumers, the policy might be to set as the default the superior outcome, without restricting consumers' ability to choose an alternative. An example of this is the use of automatic enrolment in pensions schemes to overcome inertia in pension savings, while preserving the choice for savers to opt out of the scheme.

There is a fine line between 'liberal paternalism' and just paternalism. The CC investigation into personal current accounts in Northern Ireland came close to it. One of the competition concerns identified by the CC was that consumers generally do not actively search for alternative personal current accounts. However, the CC also noted that 'customers are generally not particularly interested in personal current accounts', and that 80% of those surveyed who had not switched bank gave as a reason the fact that they had been with their current provider for a long time.[31] If consumers do not care about a product, should competition authorities? Perhaps a potential dividing line here is between whether it is quirks in consumers' preferences, or flaws in their information sets and decision-making abilities, that are driving switching outcomes. Some economists would argue that policy-makers should be more concerned with the latter, and somewhat less with the former.

Another note of caution is that the theory of behavioural economics needs to be complemented with empirical evidence. This came up in the PPI investigation by the CC.[32] Consumers may face behavioural biases at the point of sale in purchasing a primary product (for example, a loan) and in choosing whether or not to buy an add-on product when they are offered it, such as PPI. PPI offers protection to consumers who take out a loan against events that may prevent them from keeping up with their repayments, such as unemployment and illness. When they are sold the add-on product at the point of sale (eg, the bank branch where the consumer purchases the primary credit product), consumers may lack the cognitive capacity to assess the level of the premium and whether the add-on PPI suits their needs. They may instinctively opt to include the product in their overall purchase by default. They may also be over-optimistic about their inclination to cancel the

---

[31] Competition Commission (2006), 'Market investigation into personal current account banking services in Northern Ireland—Provisional findings', October, [8] and Appendix 4.3. We advised one of the banks in the inquiry.

[32] Competition Commission (2009), 'Market investigation into payment protection insurance', 29 January. We advised two of the parties in this inquiry.

add-on PPI at a later date, even when offered a cooling-off period. However, when intervening in such markets, it is important to have evidence both on the nature and extent of biases present and of the effects on consumers of any remedies put forward. The CC considered that providers of the product in effect had point-of-sale monopolies in PPI, and that this led to high prices. As such, part of the package of remedies proposed by the CC was to prohibit credit providers from selling PPI as an add-on at the point of sale of a primary product (the loan), and indeed for up to seven days afterwards. However, the CAT rejected this remedy, since the CC had provided insufficient evidence of how consumers would respond to the remedy, whether it would benefit them, and how this would weigh against the loss of convenience to consumers.[33] The CC subsequently undertook consumer surveys and a number of experiments to obtain such evidence (in section 9.6 we discuss cost–benefit analysis of remedies more generally).

The PPI case demonstrates that when designing demand-side remedies it is important to obtain empirical evidence of their likely effects on consumers—it is not enough to assert that biases exist, and that a specific remedy will correct them. In practice, such evidence might be obtained from the empirical literature, through undertaking experimental analysis, or by undertaking other forms of 'road testing' of remedies (see also section 9.6). The PPI, current accounts and *Microsoft* cases all demonstrate that there is ample scope for improving remedies by making better use of the insights from behavioural (and experimental) economics. This is a developing area.

9.5 FINES

9.5.1 SETTING OPTIMAL FINES

The hefty fines imposed by the European Commission in recent years have grabbed the headlines, raising awareness of competition law among business communities and the general public. In the whole of the 1990s, cartel fines imposed by the Commission totalled only around €615 million. In the years 2006 to 2009, total annual cartel fines were €1.9 billion, €3.3 billion, €2.3 billion, and €1.6 billion respectively.[34] In addition, Microsoft was fined €899 million in 2008 and Intel €1.1 billion in 2009, both for abuse of dominance.[35] These penalties have raised many policy questions: How do the Commission and other competition authorities determine the level of a fine? Is there any economic basis for the fine? Can companies afford these fines? This last question is addressed in the next sub-section. As regards the first question—how are fines calculated—some greater

---

[33] *Barclays Bank Plc v Competition Commission* [2009] CAT 27, Judgment of 16 October 2009.

[34] See the European Commission document 'Cartel Statistics', available at: <http://ec.europa.eu/competition/cartels/statistics/statistics.pdf>.

[35] European Commission (2008), 'Antitrust: Commission Imposes €899 Million Penalty on Microsoft for Non-compliance with March 2004 Decision', press release, IP/08/318, 27 February; and European Commission (2009), 'Antitrust: Commission Imposes Fine of €1.06 Bn on Intel for Abuse of Dominant Position; Orders Intel to Cease Illegal Practices', press release, IP/09/745, 13 May.

transparency has been achieved through the publication of the European Commission's Fining Guidelines and similar documents in other jurisdictions.[36] The Fining Guidelines set out the steps and criteria that the Commission follows in its calculations. They explain how the basic amount of a fine is arrived at, and how adjustments are made for factors such as whether the company has engaged in anti-competitive behaviour before (fine adjusted upwards if this is the case) or whether it was cooperative during the investigation (fine adjusted downwards, or even to zero in the case of leniency; see Chapter 5). However, even with greater clarity on process and the mechanics of setting fines, the second question above remains: is there an economic basis for the fines imposed under competition law, and should there be? We do not have a definitive answer to this question. Instead, this sub-section sets out some of the economic principles that are relevant when determining optimal fines, and indicates what role these principles might play in competition law.

Why do you park your car neatly between the white lines of a parking bay and put enough money in the parking meter? Economists have two answers to this. The first is: it's because you know that otherwise you'll get a fine. You respond to financial incentives. The second answer is more akin to the principles of behavioural economics that we discussed in the previous section: you may have an intrinsic motivation to be law-abiding, so you would pay the parking meter even if the chance of a fine were low. Economists have joined scholars of law and psychology in studying the mindset of those tempted to break the law. The traditional economic framework in essence sees would-be offenders making a rational trade-off between the rewards of the illegal activity and the risk of being caught.[37] Behavioural economics has introduced some further subtleties to this framework. We explain here how this decision framework can assist with determining optimal fines.

Fines function as a punishment, but more importantly they are also aimed at preventing crimes. Indeed, the main objective stated in the Fining Guidelines is to ensure that the fine has the necessary deterrent effect.[38] Two conditions must hold in order to achieve deterrence: the likelihood of being caught must be sufficiently high (in some places the chance of getting a parking ticket is rather higher than in others); and the fine must be sufficiently high. Economic theory identifies two possible reference points to determine the optimal level of fine: the harm to society caused by the crime, and the illicit gains made by the perpetrator. On the first basis, if the cost to society of a particular crime is €1,000, and the offender is caught with 100% certainty, the fine should be set at €1,000. The harm to society can then be repaired (provided that the authorities redistribute the collected fines to those who have suffered—not something that

---

[36] European Commission (2006), 'Guidelines on the Method of Setting Fines Pursuant to Article 23(2)(a) of Regulation No 1/2003' [2006] OJ C210/02. These guidelines partly followed those issued by the Dutch competition authority—NMa (2001), 'Richtsnoeren boetetoemeting met betrekking tot het opleggen van boetes ingevolge artikel 57 van de Mededingingswet', December.

[37] Leading works include Becker (1968), Landes (1983), and Polinsky and Shavell (2000).

[38] European Commission (2006), 'Guidelines on the Method of Setting Fines Pursuant to Article 23(2)(a) of Regulation No 1/2003' [2006] OJ C210/02, at [4].

happens often). In reality, very few crimes are punished with 100% certainty. If the probability of detection and enforcement is only, say, 20%, a fine of €1,000 is too low—only €200 is recovered on average for every crime costing €1,000. Instead, the optimal fine would be €5,000—one in five criminals is caught, and a total of €5,000 is collected in fines, covering the cost to society of the five crimes. This very simple framework can be easily expanded with additional features—for example, the cost of enforcement. Having a police force and a court (or a competition authority) comes at a cost, and this cost must be weighed against the benefits of fighting crime. As a result, the socially optimal degree of law enforcement is usually not to catch 100% of criminals but some lower percentage. It can be optimal to let some criminals get away with it. In this framework there is to some extent a trade-off between the probability of detection on the one hand, and the level of fine on the other. In theory, the same result can be achieved either through very active enforcement (leading to a high proportion of criminals being caught) and low fines, or through more limited enforcement and higher fines. The disadvantage of the former option is that enforcement costs are high. The disadvantage of the latter option is that the fines may be disproportionate for those few criminals who do get caught (in the above example, a justice system may frown upon a criminal having to pay a fine of €5,000 for a crime that cost society only €1,000).

One problem with setting fines with reference to the cost of the crime to society is that this may not have a deterrent effect if the fine is lower than the benefit obtained by the criminal. If you are in a real hurry to get to a client meeting on time, and the fine for speeding is only €30, you may well consider that a cost worth bearing (especially if there is a chance that you may not even get caught). In contrast, if the fine is €300, your rational calculation may lead you to behave differently (it will depend on many factors, such as how much the client is worth to you, or what your hourly rate is). A similar example (made famous in *Freakonomics*, the book we mentioned in section 9.4) is that of a number of private day-care centres in Haifa, Israel, which began to charge parents a penalty of 10 shekels per child every time they arrived more than ten minutes late to pick up their child (adding to their monthly bill of 1,400 shekels).[39] The result was the opposite of what was intended: instead of having a deterrent effect, the new fining system resulted in an increase in the number of late pick-ups, as parents were more than willing to pay the fine in exchange for the extra time their child was looked after. The fine effectively became like any other price in the consumers' rational calculations (to put the 10 shekel fine into context, a typical parking fine was 75 shekels, but with a lower probability of detection, and a babysitter cost around 15–20 shekels per hour). An additional explanation for the increase—and here behavioural economics is at work—is that the parents now felt less guilty about arriving late and taking advantage of the teachers' goodwill because they were paying for it.

These examples show that deterrence can best be achieved through fines that directly reflect the benefits obtained by offenders, especially if there is a chance that these

---

[39] Levitt and Dubner (2005), Ch 1. The original study was Gneezy and Rustichini (2000).

private gains from the crime exceed the social harm caused by it. If the cost to society of you speeding is €15, and the chance of being caught is 50%, proponents of the first economic approach (fines based on the harm to society) would say that a fine of €30 results in the socially optimal level of crime. The fact that at this level of fine there are some lawyers and other well-off motorists who can afford to 'pay off' the authorities for the right to speed is simply part of the optimum in this framework. However, you can also see that deterrence is not achieved. Some commentators therefore do not regard this as the optimal situation in the context of competition law and would rather set fines with reference to illicit gains so as to achieve greater deterrence (Wils, 2006). The calculation is similar to the one above. If the extra profit from entering a cartel is €1,000 and the cartel will be punished with 100% certainty, a fine of €1,000 achieves effective deterrence. If the chance of punishment is only 20%, a fine of €1,000 is insufficient as the would-be cartelist will take the 80% chance of receiving a positive pay-off from the crime—instead, as before, the optimal deterrent fine is €5,000 (but this time because €1,000 is the illicit gain, not the cost to society). Behavioural economics identifies two additional reasons why fines may have to be set even higher than that (we saw these in section 9.4). One is the 'availability bias'—people tend to forget past fines after a while and hence may still not be sufficiently deterred; regularly grabbing the headlines with high fines is one way competition authorities can avoid this cognitive bias. The other reason is optimism bias; criminals tend to underestimate the probability of something bad happening to them (ie, that they get caught), and hence an uplift in the fine would again be required to make deterrence effective.

However, in practice, the difference between the two economic approaches—fines set with reference to the harm to the economy and fines based on illicit gains—may not matter too much for competition law. This is for two reasons. First, the Commission's Fining Guidelines are only loosely based on these economic principles—fines are set with reference to the value of the sales in the relevant market and the duration of the infringement, which are seen as 'an appropriate proxy to reflect the economic importance of the infringement'.[40] The term 'economic importance' can be interpreted as the importance to either the economy as a whole or to the perpetrators. Both are positively correlated with the value of sales in the relevant market in question—larger companies do more harm and gain more by doing so, in absolute terms, than smaller companies. But the Guidelines stop short of actually trying to measure either the harm to the economy or the illicit gain. Instead, they apply a number of rules to 'approximate' these effects: the basic fine is taken as a proportion of the sales in the relevant market, which can be up to 30% for the more serious cartel infringements. The second reason why the difference between the two approaches does not matter too much in practice is that cases like the Israeli day-care centre problem are less likely to arise in competition law, particularly in relation to cartels. As explained in Chapter 10, the total harm to the economy from cartels is typically greater than the illicit gains made by the cartelists—the

---

[40] European Commission (2006), 'Guidelines on the Method of Setting Fines Pursuant to Article 23(2)(a) of Regulation No 1/2003' [2003] OJ C210/02, at [6].

extra cartel profits are equal to the cartel overcharge harm, but there are additional inefficiencies and volume harms caused to suppliers and purchasers of the cartel. Therefore, fines
based on harm to the economy would achieve at least as much deterrence as fines based on
illicit gains (at least in the case of cartels).

This last issue does point to an unresolved policy question about the interaction between
fines and damages awards. They are to some extent substitutes and complements at the
same time. As discussed in Chapter 10, in the EU the main policy objective of awarding
damages is to compensate victims of infringements. But damages, like fines, also play a
role in deterrence (in the USA, deterrence is a major reason why treble damages are typically awarded in successful antitrust actions). The simple decision framework presented
above can be easily expanded to include damages as well. In the last example the fine was
set at €5,000, reflecting a probability of detection of 20% and illicit gains of €1,000. Now
suppose that there is a follow-on damages claim for €1,000 from the cartel's customers
relating to the cartel overcharge, and that the probability of this claim succeeding is 25%
(as explained in Chapter 10, there are many legal obstacles to successful damages claims,
so the likelihood of success in this example is only 25%). This adds another €250 to the
expected costs to the cartel of infringing the law, and hence reinforces deterrence. But it
also shows that in theory the fine can be reduced from €5,000 to €3,750 without affecting
the deterrent effect: 20% of €3,750 equals an expected fine of €750, plus the expected damages payment of €250 equals €1,000, which is the same as the illicit gain. As yet, no such
explicit link between fines and subsequent damages awards has been made in EU policy.

9.5.2 ABILITY TO PAY FINES

It is a generally accepted principle that the infringing party's ability to pay can play a role in
determining the fine. In countries such as Finland and Switzerland, speeding tickets are set
with reference to not only the speed recorded, but also the income of the offender (headline-
grabbing fines of several hundreds of thousands of euros have been imposed under these
rules; some people are hard to deter). In competition law, the ability to pay fines has become
a topical issue in the specific context of the high fines imposed by the European Commission,
a particularly pertinent subject for debate in times of economic downturn. The Commission's
2006 Fining Guidelines relating to competition infringements take into account potential
situations of *in*ability to pay fines:

> In exceptional cases, the Commission may, upon request, take account of the undertaking's
> ability to pay in a specific social and economic context. It will not base any reduction granted
> for this reason in the fine on the mere finding of an adverse or loss-making financial situation.
> A reduction could be granted solely on the basis of objective evidence that imposition of the
> fine as provided for in these Guidelines would irretrievably jeopardise the economic viability
> of the undertaking concerned and cause its assets to lose all their value.[41]

---

[41] European Commission (2006), 'Guidelines on the Method of Setting Fines Pursuant to Article 23(2)(a) of
Regulation No 1/2003' [2006] OJ C210/02, at [35].

These are stringent conditions. The company must go well beyond demonstrating that it is currently loss-making, or indeed that it has been consistently loss-making over a period of time. In order to demonstrate that there is a strong possibility of financial failure as a direct result of the fine, financial and economic analysis of the position of the company will need to be undertaken. There is currently little guidance or case law relating to how exactly these conditions should be interpreted. How can financial economics be used to meet this requirement of 'objective evidence'?

The most direct route to demonstrating an inability to pay an antitrust fine is to show that the fine will leave the company insolvent (solvency refers to a company having enough assets to cover its liabilities). In general, the most serious problems in paying will emerge if the fine is greater than the market value of shareholders' equity. Since a company's liabilities must equal its assets, not only would shareholder equity be wiped out, but the value of its other liabilities (debt) would effectively be reduced to a level below their book value, leading to insolvency. For companies listed on a stock exchange, the insolvency condition could be reflected in the fine levied being greater than the market capitalization of a company, because the market capitalization would, in general, reflect the net present value of the future payments to shareholders. Solvency constraints may mean that companies with highly leveraged (ie, high debt) capital structures may have less capacity to pay fines than companies with lower gearing levels.

The Fining Guidelines appear to be grounded primarily in issues of solvency. However, liquidity issues may rapidly come to threaten the solvency of a company in difficulty (liquidity refers to the extent to which a company has the cash, or assets that can be quickly converted into cash, to meet its short-term obligations). There are a number of ways in which liquidity crunches can threaten a company's survival. For example, many companies will require a certain amount of working capital in order to operate effectively, and liquidity will be required to cover these needs. Similarly, many sectors experience cyclical demand, and it is important for companies to maintain a buffer of available cash or credit lines in order to be able to pay costs during downturns. In a solvent company, all of these points are essentially about timing. In principle, if a company is solvent but has insufficient liquidity to meet both a fine and all of the requirements set out above, financial markets should be willing to provide funding to the company so that it can meet its expenditure needs. However, in practice, companies may often face capital rationing, which means that they cannot finance existing or new assets, and they might be restricted in their ability to pay current liabilities from future revenue streams. It is this capital rationing that can make even solvent companies unable to raise funds (something you can expect to happen more frequently in a financial crisis).

There are therefore a number of reasons why, even if sufficient funds can be raised by a company to pay a fine, the result may be a liquidity crunch which imperils its survival. Hence, when interpreting its Fining Guidelines, the Commission should take into account liquidity effects as well as solvency. Demonstrating liquidity constraints is a more complex analytical task than assessing solvency constraints. The process of determining the maximum fine that the company would be able to pay in the short run (defined here as the period over which the company cannot access financial markets) could involve comparing, on the one hand, the amount of cash and credit lines a company has, with, on the other, the combined total of expected short-term losses, requirements for short-term debt repayment and taxes, and working capital requirements. This would then represent the maximum fine that could be paid without the company having to access the financial markets to obtain additional funding to cover the fine—that is, it represents the short-term sustainability of the fine. Maximum fines payable on the basis of short-term considerations will often be relatively low (compared with those based on long-run funding considerations, as outlined below), and will to a large extent depend on a company's capital and funding structure. Companies that retain large amounts of cash or liquid assets on their balance sheets will in general, other things being equal, be able to pay larger fines in the short run than those that have relatively low cash levels, particularly when combined with a significant need for working capital. In extreme cases, the maximum fine payable based on short-term considerations may be zero.

Short-term considerations provide only part of the overall picture of the extent of fine that is affordable. Many companies will have scope to raise finance in order to cope with paying fines, and hence there is a need to determine the extent of payable fines based on long-term considerations as well. Whereas short-term ability to pay is based on the company's free cash flow, without raising new finance or selling assets, long-term ability to pay considers the extent to which a company can raise capital in order to fund the fine. There are three main ways in which a company could raise funds to increase its long-term ability to pay a fine above its short-term ability to pay: divestments, raising equity, and raising debt. Of the three, raising debt may be the most attractive, since divesting or selling assets could affect the viability of the business in the longer term, and equity markets may not always be willing to provide additional funding. When assessing a company's ability to raise debt, its credit rating can be used as a guide (and hence as relevant evidence in a competition case). As well as determining the riskiness of tranches of existing debt, a company's credit rating acts as an important determinant of the cost of raising additional debt, and the recovery rate in the event of default. Raising debt is therefore often easier for companies with high credit ratings.

There will continue to be much debate about the level of fines for the infringement of competition law and the capacity of companies to pay those fines. Existing economic and financial criteria can be applied to produce the required 'objective evidence' on a company's ability to pay, although more case law would provide even greater clarity.

9.6 MEASURING THE COSTS AND BENEFITS OF REMEDIES, AND OF COMPETITION LAW

9.6.1 WHY MEASURE COSTS AND BENEFITS?

In this chapter we have mentioned a number of times that any remedy that is being considered would require a careful cost–benefit analysis (CBA). Economics has a role to play in this kind of analysis too. In recent years, competition authorities in Europe—led by the Dutch competition authority (NMa) and the OFT—have been placing great emphasis on measuring the effects of competition law enforcement, including remedies.[42] Carrying out a CBA is generally good policy practice, and is increasingly relied upon by, and required from, policy-makers and regulatory authorities across the EU. For example, the Impact Assessment Guidelines of the European Commission state that, when considered proportionate:

> selected impacts [of policies] are estimated using quantitative techniques varying from simple extrapolation—based for instance on previously derived coefficients (e.g. units of CO2 per unit of industrial activity)—through to proper quantitative modelling. Essentially, the aim is to understand the extent of the impacts on the policy options and to estimate the costs and benefits in monetary form when this is feasible.[43]

In the UK, a 2003 Treasury Green Book sets out the methodology for making any economic assessment of the social costs and benefits of all new policies, projects and programmes.[44] Individual sector regulators have also developed detailed guidelines on how to undertake CBAs in impact assessments of their interventions.[45] In competition law, CBA can be applied to specific interventions and remedies, or to the competition regime itself. A thorough ex ante CBA enables better policy decisions (eg, more effective remedy design). Ex post CBA allows for the evaluation of past remedies and lessons to be learned for future actions.

There is an additional reason why measuring costs and benefits is important for competition policy. We have seen a spectacular global proliferation of competition law. Awareness of competition policy has probably never been so widespread among businesses and the public at large. Proponents of competition policy would consider this growing awareness as a positive development. It makes life easier for competition authorities, and probably means that more businesses refrain from engaging in illegal anti-competitive behaviour in the first place (the deterrence effect). However, this proliferation, and the apparent increasingly proactive stance taken by competition authorities, is bound to lead to someone asking at some point: what's it all good for? This legitimate question might be asked not only by businesses that may have an interest in a less interventionist competition regime (some businesses are more positive about competition policy than others), but also by scholars, politicians, and even the intended main beneficiaries of competition law—consumers.

Competition policy needs a robust answer when it is held to account in this way. In recent years competition authorities have, quite successfully, played the 'consumer-welfare' card in justifying their actions. It is a popular message to the public that competition law is there to protect consumers against anti-competitive practices

---

[42] See Office of Fair Trading (2005), Don et al. (2008), and van Dijk and Niels (2008).
[43] European Commission (2005), 'Impact Assessment Guidelines', SEC(2005) 791, 15 June.
[44] HM Treasury (2003), 'The Green Book: Appraisal and Evaluation in Central Government', 16 January.
[45] See, for example, Ofcom (2005), 'Better Policy Making. Ofcom's Approach to Impact Assessment', 21 July; and Financial Services Authority (2000), 'Practical Cost–Benefit Analysis for Financial Regulators', version 1.1, June.

by companies. However, this consumer-welfare justification has some downsides as well, and should therefore be used with care. For one, it can create false expectations and hence place competition authorities under undue pressure to intervene whenever a company is seen to be 'ripping off' its customers. It is also misleading to some extent since, from an economic perspective, competition policy is more effective when targeted at enhancing economic efficiency than at consumer welfare (we discussed this in Chapter 1). Competition policy therefore requires more than the consumer-welfare argument to sustain political legitimacy, and this is where the measurement of the effects of competition law enforcement comes in.

9.6.2 A REMEDY IN DISPUTE: CBA IN THE UK GROCERY INQUIRY

An example of where competition law expressly requires a form of CBA of remedies by the authority is the market investigation regime under the UK Enterprise Act 2002. In essence, market investigations involve the CC undertaking a detailed, two-year inquiry into a particular competition concern in a particular market that cannot be dealt with under Article 101 or 102. Grocery retailing has been one such market (others include personal current accounts and PPI, as we saw in section 9.4). In a 2008 report the CC found that this market was too concentrated and had unnecessary barriers to entry.[46] It recommended that an additional 'competition test' be applied to retail planning applications relating to large grocery stores, as part of a package of remedies to address the perceived problem of concentration in local markets. The result would be that additional restrictions—indeed, possibly an effective ban—are imposed on the expansion of large supermarkets in certain locations. This remedy thus used a set of local authority regulations unrelated to competition law that had previously been more or less indifferent as to who owned the land or who would own and operate the building once it had been completed. The competition test would operate such that planning permission would be granted to a grocery store development within a particular local area if, in addition to satisfying the normal planning restrictions, the retailer intended to operate the developed store as a new entrant in the local area; or the total number of fascias (ie, grocery retailer brands) in the local area amounted to four or more; or there were three or fewer fascias in total, but the relevant retailer would have less than 60% of grocery sales within the local area. Under this test, it would be difficult for a retailer with more than a 60% (local) market share to expand an existing store or to build a new one, as it would not obtain planning permission. This remedy would effectively have structural features similar to merger control—the latter stops the growth of large retailers through the takeover of existing competitors; the competition test in planning applications would stop organic growth by large retailers that also resulted in very high local market shares.

---

[46] Competition Commission (2008), 'The Supply of Groceries in the UK', 30 April.

However, on appeal, the CAT found that there was insufficient evidence presented by the CC that the costs of applying the competition test would be worth incurring, or that the outcome would even be effective or reasonable. In particular, it noted that:

> there is a significant gap in the Commission's analysis in relation to the 'costs' of the competition test. The Report does not fully and properly assess and take account of the risk that the application of the test might have adverse effects for consumers as a result of their being denied the benefit of developments which would enhance their welfare, including by leaving demand 'unmet'.[47]

The CAT not only found that the CC had provided insufficient evidence for an assessment of the test's potential welfare costs, but also criticized its assessment of the likely benefits of such a test:

> the Commission seems simply to have based its proportionality assessment on an assumption that the whole of the estimated customer detriment would be remedied by the test, in combination with the other remedies ... There is in the Report no recognition or weighing of the non-acknowledged possibility that the existing AEC [adverse effects on competition] might not be satisfactorily remedied or mitigated for many years.[48]

The CAT's decision implies that, in order to both advance a legally sound remedy such as the competition test and establish its effectiveness and proportionality, it is necessary to undertake a comprehensive analysis of the costs and benefits of the remedy. Following the CAT ruling (which resulted in a remittal back to the CC in early 2009), the CC duly undertook further analysis on the likely effects of the competition test on market structure, its wider costs and benefits, and its effectiveness and proportionality. In its subsequent decision, published in October 2009, it concluded that the test would deliver positive value to consumers on the basis that any reduction in consumer welfare in the short run would be offset by the longer-term benefit of increased competition.[49] However, the CC also introduced a *de minimis* provision such that the test would be passed in cases where store extensions were small (less than 300 square metres), provided that the store had not been extended in the previous five years. The CC concluded that this new provision would not have a material impact on the effectiveness of the remedy, but would be a more proportionate response to the adverse effect on competition it had identified. This case illustrates the importance of undertaking the CBA as an integral part of the competition analysis—where you assess both the problem and the remedies in a particular case—rather than doing it almost as an afterthought to justify the remedy once it has been imposed. This applies to any type of competition case.

---

[47] [2009] CAT 6, Case No 1104/6/8/08, at [111].
[48] Ibid., at [162].
[49] Competition Commission (2009), 'Groceries Market Investigation: Remittal of the Competition Test by the Competition Appeal Tribunal: Decision', 2 October.

9.6.3 WHAT TO MEASURE: IDENTIFYING THE COUNTERFACTUAL

CBA can be undertaken at distinct levels, depending on the question at hand. An important initial step is therefore to identify the objective of the CBA and to be clear about the relevant counterfactual against which costs and benefits can be measured. CBAs can be applied to remedies in individual competition cases, or more broadly to the competition regime as a whole. To start with the latter, an important distinction to be made is between the effects of *competition policy* and the effects of *competition*. Sometimes the case for competition policy is made in terms of the benefits of the process of competition. This is inaccurate (as we explained in Chapter 1) and may give competition policy too much credit. There can be competition without competition policy. Worse, as we also explained in Chapter 1, competition authorities can act against the interests of competition in the case of false positives, where action is taken against a business practice that in reality is pro-competitive.

The next important distinction is between the costs and benefits of competition policy, or *competition legislation*, and the costs and benefits of the *competition authority*. Again, both are relevant, but distinct, policy questions. To take the example of the Netherlands, a CBA could be undertaken for the Competition Law 1998. The relevant counterfactual for this analysis would be a situation in which the Competition Law was not enacted and the NMa had not been created. This would basically be the situation pre-1998 when the Economic Competition Law 1956 was in place, enforced by the Ministry of Economic Affairs—a regime that was generally considered less strict and relatively inactive (the Netherlands used to be regarded as a 'cartel paradise'). In this counterfactual some reliance might also be placed on intervention by the European Commission under the EU competition rules, which would come into play in the counterfactual without the 1998 law (given that these rules apply in Member States as well).

A separate, and substantially different, CBA can be conducted for the competition authority itself. There can be a competition law without a competition authority enforcing it, so that would be the relevant counterfactual.[50] Thus, the costs and benefits of, say, the NMa would be assessed against a situation in which the Competition Law 1998 was not enforced by the competition authority but rather through private litigation. This would to some extent be comparable to the situation in the USA, where around 90% of all federal antitrust cases originate from private actions.[51] In several EU Member States there is already a strong tendency towards more private litigation, particularly where business-to-business disputes are concerned, and the European Commission has been

---

[50] The reverse situation—a competition authority without a competition law—seems less plausible. Yet, this was precisely the situation in Jersey for some time. The Jersey Competition Regulatory Authority (JCRA) was set up in 2001 but the Competition (Jersey) Law did not come into force until 2005 (in the intervening period the JCRA did have certain regulatory responsibilities in the telecoms sector). Source: <http://www.jcra.je>.

[51] Jones (1999). Part of these private cases (5%–10%) follow on from publicly enforced cases—ie, where affected private parties claim damages from a perpetrator which has previously been found guilty by one of the competition authorities. Therefore, the 90% figure to some extent understates the importance of public enforcement. The source for the 5%–10% figure is Roach and Trebilcock (1997).

actively promoting private enforcement—a topic we discuss further in Chapter 10. A relevant question to ask in such an analysis would be: which types of conduct and practice are effectively addressed under private litigation? The costs and benefits of these are not ascribed to the competition authority.

A final distinction—of most relevance for this chapter—can be made between the costs and benefits of the *competition authority* and the costs and benefits of *its individual decisions and remedies*. For the former, the absence of the authority is the counterfactual—in other words, this analysis determines the incremental costs and benefits of the authority, where the presence or creation of the authority is considered as the relevant increment. For the latter, the authority is assumed to be in place, and the incremental analysis refers to the costs and benefits that are attributable to the enforcement action or remedies in question. The analysis can be applied either to individual decisions or to a cumulative set of decisions (eg, all merger decisions, or all abuse of dominance decisions). Ultimately, the sum of the costs and benefits of each action should tend towards convergence with the costs and benefits of the competition authority in question. After all, in the long run, most costs and benefits become variable. In practice, the assessment of the incremental costs and benefits of specific decisions and remedies is often used to infer conclusions about the costs and benefits of the authority. For example, the orders of magnitude of the benefits of certain decisions—such as all cartel actions by the authority—may already be so high as to outweigh all the 'fixed' costs of the authority in the particular year (see below).

9.6.4 HOW TO MEASURE: CATEGORIES OF COSTS AND BENEFITS

The next question that arises is what costs and benefits should be included in the analysis, and how the various categories of costs and benefits should be compared against each other. Superficially, calculations like these can be kept very simple and straightforward. Take the cartel fines imposed by the European Commission in recent years: as noted in section 9.5, these amounted to around €2 billion–€3 billion annually. Compare this with the annual budget of DG Competition, which is in the range of €100 million–€200 million (precise figures are difficult to distil from the Commission's budget figures, but the rough order of magnitude is what matters here). In one sense, therefore, it might be said that through its cartel actions alone DG Competition has already provided substantially greater benefits to EU taxpayers than it has cost them (if the collected fines reduce the need for funding through taxation). However, an important guiding principle for CBA is that it should be performed from a total economic welfare perspective. This means that *all* costs and benefits to *all* the various participants in the economy—consumers, producers, government, taxpayers—should be included in the calculations. All costs and benefits are monetized (as far as possible), such that they can be compared. This way, money transfers between different participants (eg, from consumers to producers) are welfare-neutral—ie, they are not net costs or benefits to the economy as a whole. As noted in Chapter 1, economists generally have little to say about distributive effects. However, if considered appropriate from a policy perspective, different weights can be given to different groups—eg, consumer welfare may be given greater weight than producer welfare, or poor consumers may be given greater weight than rich consumers. Likewise, if the effects take place over a number of years (as often is the case), some weighting between the years is required by applying a 'social' discount rate to future money streams (discounting is explained in more detail in Chapter 10).

Table 9.2 provides an overview of the main categories of costs and benefits that must be assessed in CBA. These same categories are of relevance to any policy question—ie, whether the CBA refers to competition, competition legislation, the competition authority, or individual enforcement actions and remedies. The main difference will lie in the counterfactual or increment against which these specific categories of costs and benefits are measured. For example, to assess the costs and benefits of the competition authority, the category of 'direct costs of the authority' needs to cover its entire budget. To assess a specific remedy imposed by that authority, the category covers only the costs incurred by the authority in relation to that decision. Here we give a brief description of some of these categories of costs and benefits.[52] The direct administrative costs of the competition authority can generally be taken from annual reports. Direct-cost measurement may be somewhat more difficult in a CBA of individual enforcement actions and remedies. The relevant direct costs should be only the additional resources used for that remedy—for example, the amount of staff or IT resources used. The economic benefits of competition and (where this is the appropriate counterfactual) competition law enforcement can be measured in terms of productive and allocative efficiency, enhanced dynamic competition/innovation, enhanced market functioning, and macroeconomic effects. We discussed the various types of efficiency in Chapter 1. As regards the macroeconomic effects, note that allocative and productive efficiency are both partial-equilibrium concepts (ie, they refer only to the market in question), and there are usually further effects on other sectors in the economy, particularly if the market concerned is one for capital or intermediary goods. As to the category of economic costs (negative market impacts), we note that while the objective of competition policy is to improve market functioning, actions and remedies by competition authorities can have (probably unintended) adverse consequences for the market as well. The CAT raised a concern about a possible negative effect ('unmet' consumer demand) from a remedy in the grocery example we saw earlier. One indirect benefit that competition law may generate is making interventions consistent and providing clear guidance, such that regulatory certainty among businesses is enhanced. Another indirect benefit that is of particular importance to competition law is the deterrent effect.[53]

---

[52] A more detailed overview is provided in Oxera (2004).
[53] For an empirical study on this deterrent effect, see Office of Fair Trading (2007).

Table 9.2 Main categories of costs and benefits to be assessed in the CBA

Costs	Benefits
Direct (administrative) costs of the authority	
Direct costs of companies	
– Competition law compliance costs	
– Costs of specific competition proceedings	
Economic costs to the market in question (negative market impacts)	**Economic benefits to the market in question (positive market impacts)**
– Allocative inefficiency	– Allocative efficiency
– Productive inefficiency	– Productive efficiency
– Distortion of incentives (reduced dynamic competition/innovation)	– Enhanced dynamic competition/innovation
	– Increased product/service quality
– Reduced product/service quality	– Enhanced market functioning
– Restriction on market functioning	
Indirect regulatory costs	**Indirect regulatory benefits**
– Legal uncertainty	– Legal certainty
– Likelihood of regulatory capture	– Deterrent effects
	– Improved quality of competition regime
Social costs (if relevant)	**Social benefits (if relevant)**
– Distributive costs	– Distributive benefits
– Reduced security/quality of supply	– Enhanced security/quality of supply
– Negative effect on vulnerable customers	– Positive effect on vulnerable customers
– Other negative externalities on society	– Other positive externalities on society

Source: Based on Oxera (2004).

9.6.5 WHEN TO STOP MEASURING: PRECISION AND PRIORITIES

The economics literature has developed a range of quantitative techniques that can be applied to CBA.[54] It is important to take an approach that is robust and quantitative, and at the same time practical and easy to apply. This means that quantitative analysis should be undertaken where feasible in order to obtain robust results, but this analysis should establish rough orders of magnitude of the various costs and benefits rather than seek (often spurious) precision in the calculation. The optimal degree of quantification of the costs and benefits will depend on the circumstances. A limiting factor for quantitative analysis is data availability. Not all costs and benefits can be readily quantified, either because of a lack of data or because the effects depend on various indirect economic interactions which are difficult to measure. Nevertheless, in practice, the assessment of rough orders of magnitude can often be sufficient to gain insight into the costs and benefits of the policy decision or remedy in question. This is because there may be one

---

[54] See Sugden and Williams (1978), Boardman et al. (2001), and Oxera (2004).

particular category of benefit (or cost) that far outweighs any of the categories of costs (benefits). In this case, it will not be necessary to quantify those costs with a high degree of precision, and it may be sufficient to describe the other benefits in qualitative terms. We note that this conclusion on the importance of detailed quantification refers to the specific context of CBA of competition law—in the context of damages cases, discussed in Chapter 10, there are legal and economic reasons why the quantification may have to be more precise than for CBA. We also note that the quantification techniques for CBA and for damages overlap to a large extent—both are concerned with measuring effects. We therefore refer to Chapter 10 for an overview of the various methods and models.

In a CBA, you can often conclude that the static welfare benefits of intervening in price-fixing cartel cases—focusing on the total cartel overcharge paid by consumers—will be so great that they exceed the direct costs incurred by the competition authority by multiple orders of magnitude—Baker (2003) shows that rough estimates of the direct benefits of cartel actions in the USA far outweigh the estimates of the total costs of US antitrust enforcement (see Chapter 10 for more discussion of the range of overcharges that have been observed in past cartels). The additional indirect benefits of the interventions—in particular the enhancement of dynamic competition and the deterrent effects on other cartels—can be described in qualitative terms, because they work in the same direction and thus would reinforce the conclusion. One tentative policy conclusion that follows from the above logic is that there is merit in giving priority to cartel enforcement in larger markets, as there the welfare benefits will be greatest. However, a qualification to this conclusion is that intervention against cartels in smaller markets can still fulfil an important signalling function and hence assist in deterring cartels. A handful of such actions in smaller markets may be sufficient to achieve this deterrent effect. Another conclusion is that if the objective of measuring costs and benefits is to show that competition policy benefits the economy as a whole, the case can already successfully be made based just on rough approximations of the order of magnitude of the benefits of the actions against cartels.

The above approach to assessing the benefits of cartel actions cannot be readily applied to mergers, agreements other than cartels, or unilateral conduct. As noted throughout this book, remedial actions against these latter practices are not as unambiguously beneficial as actions against cartels. Mergers and these other practices usually produce some efficiency benefits as well as anti-competitive effects, so intervention by the authorities can produce negative market impacts. The extent to which a competition authority is able to strike the right balance between these two effects will depend on the quality of the underlying analysis in its investigations, and will also inherently involve a degree of judgement. It depends on policy-makers' and competition authorities' views on how much to trust market forces and on whether it is more desirable to avoid false positives or false negatives (false positives result in over-enforcement; false negatives in under-enforcement).

A specific action against a merger or business practice can therefore not automatically be presumed to be beneficial to social welfare (in our view, this statement would hold even for competition authority decisions that are upheld at subsequent appeals stages). Indeed, CBA of a merger or abuse of dominance case runs the risk of becoming circular if it starts from the premise that the intervention is beneficial. An example of such circularity can be found in an analysis by the OFT of the effects of intervention against predatory pricing.[55] This circularity potentially biases the estimated benefits of intervention upwards. The welfare loss of predation (and hence welfare benefit of intervention) is taken as the net present value of the low prices to consumers during the predation period (treated as a consumer welfare gain) and the high prices during the subsequent 'recoupment' period (treated as a consumer welfare loss). In calculating this, the OFT effectively assumed that, first, recoupment was indeed going to be feasible, and second, predation was about to become successful at the point of OFT intervention (ie, the predator would switch from low to high prices at that point). However, these are precisely the factors that make predatory pricing cases so complex (we discussed this in Chapter 4). The likelihood of recoupment is not currently a legal requirement in EU case law, so it cannot be assumed from the outset that every action against predation does indeed have the welfare benefits set out in the OFT's analysis.

9.6.6 CBA AT THE DESIGN STAGE OF REMEDIES?

There is increasing acceptance of the principle that assessing the costs and benefits of remedies before they are implemented is a good idea, even if full quantification is not feasible. The 2008 Department of Justice report on single-firm conduct contains an entire chapter on remedies, in recognition of the fact that, 'Without a proper remedy, winning a judgement of a [Sherman Act] section 2 violation is similar to winning a battle but losing the war.'[56] It quotes the former FTC Chairman William E Kovacic, who had stated in an earlier article (1999) that:

> Responsible prosecutorial practice dictates that government agencies begin an abuse of dominance case only after they first have defined their remedial aims clearly and devised a convincing strategy for achieving them if the defendant's liability is established.

The European Commission undertakes 'market tests' of commitments in competition cases, although these tests are confined to the invitation to third parties to submit their comments within a specified time limit, usually one month. In addition, the OFT has recently published research on the practicality of 'road testing' competition remedies before they are implemented (Office of Fair Trading, 2009). Testing remedies before they are imposed should improve the outcomes of competition authority interventions. We saw above that CBA of remedies relating to mergers, agreements other than cartels, and unilateral conduct is less straightforward than for cartels, but this is not to say that it is impossible or unimportant.

---

[55] Office of Fair Trading (2005).

[56] Department of Justice (2008), 'Competition and Monopoly: Single-firm Conduct Under Section 2 of the Sherman Act', September, Ch 9. The DOJ withdrew this report in 2009, but the chapter on remedies remains a useful contribution to the debate.

Should a formal CBA be required for every competition law remedy? This policy question would perhaps merit a CBA of its own. Too formal a requirement on competition authorities could make competition law enforcement more like economic regulation, where the possible effects of specific interventions are often argued over for a considerable length of time before they are finally implemented. The general lesson for competition law is that CBA can be a useful policy tool that helps competition authorities develop their thinking about a competition problem and how to solve it, even if not all costs and benefits are quantified with precision in every case.

10

QUANTIFICATION OF DAMAGES[1]

[1] This chapter is based on a study prepared for the European Commission by Oxera and a multi-jurisdictional team of lawyers led by Dr Assimakis Komninos, entitled 'Quantifying antitrust damages: Towards non-binding guidance for courts', dated December 2009, copyright European Union, published at <http://ec.europa.eu/competition/antitrust/actionsdamages/>. The responsibility for any modifications lies with us.

10.1 DAMAGES CLAIMS, ECONOMICS, AND THE LAW

10.1.1 WHAT IS SPECIAL ABOUT THE ECONOMICS IN DAMAGES CLAIMS?

You have seen in this book how economics can help you understand the effects of business practices on competition, and how this in turn may help in determining whether competition law has been infringed. The use of economics does not need to stop there, however. In Chapter 9 we showed the economic principles on which competition authorities may base remedies for competition law infringements. In this chapter we deal with the economics of quantifying damages from infringements. After a competition authority has found an infringement and imposed a remedy (often a fine), parties that have been harmed by the infringement may file a claim for damages against the infringer. For example, manufacturers of car tyres may initiate a damages action against the members of a cartel among synthetic-rubber producers.[2] Or a small airline may claim damages after its dominant rival has been found guilty of making anti-competitive loyalty payments to travel agents.[3] Such 'follow-on' damages claims under competition law are increasingly common in many jurisdictions.

In principle, the same economic analysis of effects that is used to assess the existence of an infringement can be used to determine damages. After all, the main effect that is of interest during the competition investigation is harm to competition and consumers, and this harm is in essence what represents the damage caused by the infringement. An effects-based assessment of the dominant airline's loyalty payments would focus on whether these payments significantly foreclose distribution channels to smaller airlines, thus preventing those airlines from entering the market or gaining market share. If foreclosure is significant, this may harm competition and consumers generally but it also harms the individual rival airlines. The economic principles discussed in Chapters 4 to 6 (on abuse of dominance, cartels and horizontal agreements, and vertical restraints, respectively) are therefore of direct relevance to damages claims as well. However, there are some important differences too. Quantifying damages can be considered a 'discipline' in its own right within economics for competition lawyers, and hence merits a separate chapter in this book. This is for three main reasons.

First, a significant proportion of damages claims relate to cartel cases—in Europe alone in the last ten years, there have been damages actions (some of which are ongoing) against cartels in vitamins, sugar, gas-insulated switchgear, cement, lysine, car insurance,

---

[2] A cartel among five oil and chemical companies to fix the price of synthetic rubber was fined by the European Commission in 2006. European Commission (2006), 'Commission fines producers and traders of synthetic rubber €519 million for price fixing cartel', press release, IP/06/1647, 29 November.

[3] The Competition Tribunal in South Africa found South African Airways to have engaged in anti-competitive loyalty payments in *Nationwide Airlines (Pty) Ltd and Another v South African Airways (Pty) Ltd* (Case 80/CR/Sep06) [2010] ZACT 13 (Competition Tribunal in South Africa). We advised one of the two claimants in this case.

driving schools, liquid crystal displays (LCDs), cathode ray tubes, methionine, synthetic rubber, carbon and graphite products, air cargo services, hydrogen peroxide, industrial copper tubes, lifts and escalators, and football shirts. Price fixing and other hardcore cartel arrangements are usually the only category of anti-competitive practice that is prohibited per se, such that there is little need for an analysis of economic effects during the investigation (see also Chapter 5). This means that much of the economic analysis of the actual harm caused by cartels has to be undertaken in the context of follow-on damages claims. This analysis—presented in this chapter—relates mainly to the overcharge during the cartel period (how much more did the tyre manufacturers pay for synthetic rubber because of the cartel?); the degree to which customers of the cartel have passed this overcharge on to their own customers (have the tyre manufacturers increased the price of tyres to reflect the higher rubber cost?); and any effect the cartel may have had on volumes purchased and sold by customers (did tyre manufacturers purchase less rubber and sell fewer tyres?).

Second, it is commonly accepted that effects-based analyses at the infringement stage focus on harm to competition—where competition stands for the competitive process, not individual competitors. In contrast, damages claims are filed by individual competitors (or customers) who believe that they have suffered harm—nobody files a claim on behalf of the competitive process (several jurisdictions allow certain forms of class action on behalf of multiple competitors or customers, but that is still because those parties have been harmed individually). The economic analysis in damages claims must therefore focus on the harm to those specific competitors or customers. The damages question is: how much market share did the claimant airline lose as a result of the loyalty payments? While at the infringement stage the question is: did the loyalty payments significantly foreclose distribution channels to rival airlines, such that competition generally was harmed? You can see that there is some potential risk here of re-opening the debate on 'harm to competition versus harm to competitors'—see Chapter 4, where we pointed out that, from an economic perspective, harm to individual competitors is not in itself sufficient for there to be competition concerns. The distinction is clearer in follow-on damages cases—the competition authority has already found an infringement (presumably on the basis of harm to competition more widely), and now the competitor must show that it has actually suffered from that infringement. In original actions—where a competitor brings the case directly before a court—the infringement and harm must both be established, and the court must consider whether evidence of harm to the competitor also constitutes evidence of harm to competition.

Third, damages claims normally go further in actually quantifying the harm than analyses at the infringement stage. This is because a court must ultimately determine a precise monetary amount for the damages award (if any)—whereas a competition authority can limit itself to statements that such harmful effects are significant without quantifying them further. We show in this chapter how economics provides a toolkit of methods and models that can be, and have been, used by courts in damages cases, ranging from relatively simple approaches to more sophisticated ones. We introduce you to some of the basic principles of statistical and econometrics techniques that are used in damages cases (as well as in other types of competition case), and help you identify the critical questions to ask when confronted with such quantitative analyses.

10.1.2 POLICY PRINCIPLES BEHIND DAMAGES CLAIMS

Damages actions brought before courts by harmed parties are a form of private enforcement of competition law. This complements public enforcement of the law by competition authorities. In the USA, more than 90% of antitrust cases have been private actions (see Chapter 9). Elsewhere, the majority of cases tend to be taken on by competition authorities, but the importance of private actions has grown. As mentioned above, there is a distinction between original (or stand-alone) private actions—where infringement and damages must both be established by the court—and follow-on private damages actions that are brought before a court after an infringement decision by a competition authority.

There are various reasons why policy-makers find private actions attractive, and hence have sought to facilitate them. One is that they save taxpayers' money. Competition authorities have limited budgets, and must prioritize their enforcement actions. As economists would say, there is scope for an efficient division of labour here: business-to-business disputes on vertical and horizontal agreements and exclusionary behaviour seem to lend themselves to being effectively dealt with through private actions (businesses will be willing to pay for litigation if the stakes are sufficiently high). In the USA, treble damages are awarded to parties harmed by antitrust infringements, providing an extra incentive to bring private actions. Competition authorities can then deal with the rest—in particular, cases involving end-consumers, or cartel cases, where private parties are less likely to initiate a lawsuit as they lack the investigative powers that competition authorities have.

Another reason for policy-makers to encourage private damages actions is that they contribute to the deterrence of anti-competitive practices. Effective deterrence enhances competition without costing taxpayers much money. Nowadays, hefty fines, and possible prison sentences for individuals, already constitute a strong deterrent (though apparently still not sufficiently strong, judging by the number of cartels still being uncovered every year—see Chapter 9). The prospect of having to pay damages on top of the fines may further dampen any enthusiasm to form cartels. A curious finding from economic theory is that follow-on damages actions may actually be redundant from a deterrence perspective—the same deterrent effect can in theory be achieved by raising the fine itself up to the level at which the damage would ultimately be determined. That might save a lot of private litigation costs. However, it pre-supposes that public enforcement is sufficient to catch all competition law infringements, that there is some mechanism to distribute the money from the fines to the victims, and that competition authorities have as much information at the infringement and fining stages as would become available in a private damages action.

A third policy principle behind damages actions, and one that is embedded in EU law, is that of compensation. As stated in the European Commission's 'White Paper on

Damages Actions for Breach of the EC Antitrust Rules' and its accompanying Commission staff working paper, published in April 2008:

> Any citizen or business who suffered harm as a result of a breach of EC antitrust rules (Articles 81 and 82 of the EC Treaty [now Articles 101 and 102 TFEU]) must be able to claim reparation from the party who caused the damage. This right of victims to compensation is guaranteed by Community law, as the European Court of Justice recalled in 2001 and 2006.

> Victims of an EC competition law infringement are entitled to full compensation of the harm caused. That means compensation for actual loss (*damnum emergens*) and for loss of profit (*lucrum cessans*), plus interest from the time the damage occurred until the capital sum awarded is actually paid.[4]

We discuss in this chapter how the compensation principle can be made to work in practice. If followed to the letter it would imply a certain degree of precision in the determination of the harm—there should be neither under-compensation nor over-compensation. It would also mean that compensation should reach the victims of an infringement regardless of where they operate in the supply chain. If the cartel's direct customers have passed on the cartel overcharge, their own customers are the ones who should be compensated (unless those customers have also passed it on further downstream). We show how economics can help with these legal principles.

10.1.3 SEARCHING FOR THE RIGHT ANSWER, WITHIN PRACTICAL AND LEGAL BOUNDS

Any damages assessment needs to strike a balance between two objectives: first, finding the most accurate answer possible—the desire to determine the real damage value as closely as possible, which is how an economist would naturally seek to approach quantification problems; and second, using approaches that are clear and easy to apply and that fit within the existing legal frameworks.

Calculating the exact damage arising from an infringement of competition law requires complete information about what would have happened in a parallel world where the infringement did not take place. This is commonly referred to as the 'but for' or counterfactual situation (we encountered counterfactual analysis in different contexts in Chapters 5 and 6 on restrictive agreements, Chapter 7 on mergers, and Chapter 8 on state aid). Such complete information does not exist. Therefore, you have to describe this counterfactual scenario with a model using simplifying assumptions (when we say 'model', don't think immediately of complicated equations; any abstract projection of a counterfactual world would be considered a 'model' in economics). The aim of the model should be to produce an estimate of what would have happened 'but

---

[4] The Court of Justice judgments referred to are Case C-453/99 *Courage Ltd v Bernard Crehan* [2001] ECR I-6297, and Joined Cases C-295/04 to C-298/04 *Vincenzo Manfredi and others v Lloyd Adriatico Assicurazioni SpA and others* [2006] ECR I-6619.

for' the infringement. All models are necessarily simplifications of the real world. They can vary in the degree to which they take into account all possible factors that may influence the counterfactual; this variation is often driven by data or time (or budgetary) constraints. Nonetheless, despite the 'unknowability' of the exact damages value, the aim will be to approximate the answer as accurately as possible. This will normally require the use of established economic and financial methods (as described in this chapter), and therefore introduces an element of complexity to the legal analysis. Perhaps to the dismay of some competition lawyers, a degree complexity in the quantification of damages is inevitable because the way that markets and businesses work is complex—as we said in Chapter 1, don't blame economists for this.

At the same time, any area of law benefits from simple approaches that are easy to understand and apply. In this regard, many jurisdictions have developed rules addressing matters such as the distribution of burden of proof and the required level of proof. Several EU Member States have in place rules dealing with the degree of freedom that judges have in calculating damages in special cases or, more generally, when exact quantification is impossible or very difficult. Such rules may reflect to a lesser or greater extent principles of equity, justice, and procedural efficiency. For example, the Italian Supreme Court, in a follow-on damages claim regarding a car insurance cartel, confirmed that when the exact harm is difficult to prove, the Italian courts can rely on Article 1226 of the Italian Civil Code and award an equitable amount of damages (*ex aequo et bono*).[5] In that regard, the Supreme Court considered this case as 'a textbook example' of where the Italian courts should make use of such a power, due to the fact that it was difficult for the claimant to prove the precise value of the actual loss (essentially the cartel overcharge) that it had suffered. Another example of such a rule is section 287 of the German Code of Civil Procedure, which provides that a court has a degree of discretion to establish the amount of loss based on its best judgement and by assessing all the circumstances of the individual case. In Finland, Chapter 17, section 6 of the Code of Judicial Procedure provides that when no evidence is available, or when it is too burdensome to present such evidence, it is left to the discretion of the court to calculate the amount of damages within the limits of reason. All these rules mean that the amount of damages does not have to be proven to the last cent, thus giving courts a more efficient and feasible means of awarding damages.

Courts have long recognized that the counterfactual is 'unknowable'. And yet this has not deterred them from setting damages awards (both in competition law and other fields of law), nor from relying on economic analysis. One US court stated that 'The antitrust cases are legion which reiterate the proposition that, if the fact of damages is proven, the actual computation of damages may suffer from minor imperfections'.[6] Another US court held that 'The vagaries of the marketplace usually deny us sure

---

[5] *Fondiaria SAI SpA v Nigriello* (Italian Supreme Court, 17 February 2007).
[6] *South-East Coal Co v Consolidation Coal Co* 434 F 2d 767, 794 (6th Cir. 1970).

knowledge of what plaintiff's situation would have been in the absence of the defendant's antitrust violation.[7] According to the Patent Court in the UK:

> The role of the court in making an assessment of damages which depends upon its view as to what will be and what would have been is to be contrasted with its ordinary function in civil action of determining what was . . . In short one cannot expect much in the way of accuracy when the court is asked to re-write history. I would only add one general comment: quantification of damage in a case such as the present (of a patentee manufacturer) is a much harder, and less certain, task than I had hitherto thought. Although I have had to reach an answer I do not pretend it is an accurate measure of the damage, of what would have been. It is just the best assessment I can make. Moreover a number of aspects of the claim show that damage can potentially be large even if an infringer's sales are comparatively low. I have in mind particularly the effect of price depression on the patentee's sales, lost profits when lost sales affect marginal profits, and the loss of sales of articles or services associated with the patented goods. And of course all these heads have their own uncertainties of quantification.[8]

In addition to the issue of precision of the damages estimate, there is the question of who can show that they have been harmed. To an economist, an infringement anywhere in the supply chain can cause ripples along the whole chain such that various parties may potentially be harmed. However, legal principles such as causality, remoteness and foreseeability tend to put a limit on who can successfully claim for damages in practice. Direct competitors and direct customers of the infringing party are relatively close to the effects of the infringement—tyre manufacturers have made actual purchases from the rubber cartel members, so can be expected to claim for cartel overcharges; the small airline was actually competing with the dominant airline during the period of abuse, and hence can be expected to claim harm from the anti-competitive loyalty payments to travel agents. In contrast, an airline that was not in the market, but claims it would have entered were it not for the loyalty payments, would find it more difficult to pass the causality principle (there could be other reasons why entry did not occur). Likewise, indirect purchasers (the customers of the cartel's customers) are a step removed from the infringer, and would have to show that their suppliers had passed on the cartel overcharge to them.

Suppliers to the infringing parties may also have suffered harm, since cartels usually result in lower levels of output owing to the higher prices they fix. This may mean that fewer inputs are required, thereby reducing the volumes sold by suppliers. Firms in connected markets can equally be affected. This holds in particular for suppliers of complementary goods—for example, if a brick cartel has raised costs to the construction industry such that there is less construction activity, other suppliers to the industry are potentially harmed as well since their sales volumes may fall. Or take the example of a hot dog stand outside the brick factory—the brick cartel agreement leads to an output restriction, hence lower production in the factory, fewer workers buying hot dogs

---

[7] *J Truett Payne Co v Chrysler Motors Corp* 451 US 557, 565; 101 S Ct 1923; 68 L Ed 2d 442 (1981).
[8] *Gerber Garment Technology Inc v Lectra Systems Ltd* [1995] RPC 383, 20 March 1995.

during the lunch break, and the hot dog stand suffering harm. Economically, these are all forms of harm that would fall within the compensation principle, but courts have their reasons to draw the 'remoteness line' closer to where the infringement has taken place.

10.1.4 THE REMAINDER OF THIS CHAPTER

The aim of this chapter is to take you through the economic principles and methods that are of relevance to quantifying damages. Section 10.2 provides a brief description of the main stages in any damages estimation. Section 10.3 sets out a conceptual framework for estimating the harm from hardcore cartel agreements, while section 10.4 does this in relation to exclusionary practices. Section 10.5 presents a classification of methods and models that can be used for quantifying damages, and contains a general discussion on what you should look for in a method or model. The next sections explore each of the main classes of approach—section 10.6 deals with cross-sectional comparisons; section 10.7 with time-series comparisons; section 10.8 with difference-in-differences comparisons; section 10.9 with financial-analysis-based approaches; and section 10.10 with market-structure-based approaches. Section 10.11 addresses the economics of pass-on of overcharges. Section 10.12 concludes with an explanation of the principles behind interest and discounting, which are relevant to proceed from the counterfactual stage to a final damages value.

10.2 MAIN STAGES IN THE DAMAGES ESTIMATION

Compensatory damages awards seek to put a claimant back into the financial position that it would have been in but for the breach of competition law. Tyre manufacturers are entitled to be compensated for the cartel overcharge they paid on rubber. The small airline is entitled to compensation for the harm caused to it by the anticompetitive loyalty payments by the dominant airline. Any damages estimation has two main stages.

The first stage involves determining the counterfactual scenario. What would the price of rubber have been in the absence of the cartel? What market position and profits would the small airline have achieved in the absence of the exclusionary conduct? This is often the central stage in any damages estimation, and certainly the one that tends to attract most attention (and disagreement between parties) in these cases. Developing an accurate counterfactual requires a review of the following questions, as addressed further in this chapter. What type of competition law infringement is causing what type of harm? For example, is it a cartel causing an overcharge harm, or exclusionary conduct causing a fall in sales or lack of market access? The nature of the damages estimation will vary depending on the type of harm. What types of claimant have been harmed? Are they end-consumers or intermediate producers who purchased goods from the cartel, or are they competitors of the infringing party? What is the market and industry context in which the harm has arisen, and what impact does this have on the counterfactual analysis? For example, is this a mature or new market?

The second stage involves moving from the factual–counterfactual comparison to a final damages value. One step within this is to ensure that the damages estimate covers the relevant time period. If the counterfactual analysis has estimated the average annual overcharge of the synthetic-rubber cartel, and the cartel infringement lasted five years, the estimate needs to be aggregated over those five years. The analysis will usually require converting the aggregated figures (cash flows) over time into one value, expressed as the current value of all those cash flows combined. This requires cash-flow discounting and uprating, a standard method in financial analysis. The question of applying interest (which is a standard component of compensatory damages in Europe, as mentioned in the quote from the European Commission above) would be addressed as part of this stage. As we show in section 10.12, this final stage has received relatively little attention in the debates about quantifying damages, and is an area where the economics and the law are not always well aligned. The application of interest can make a substantial difference to the damages estimate, especially when long time periods are involved.

10.3 HARM FROM HARDCORE CARTEL AGREEMENTS: CONCEPTUAL FRAMEWORK

10.3.1 THE MAIN EFFECTS ILLUSTRATED

The archetypal cartel agreement is one in which firms collectively fix higher prices (see Chapter 5). The harm arising from this type of competition law infringement is that parties further down the supply chain pay more for the product than they would have in a non-cartelized market. The higher price would normally also result in existing customers purchasing lower volumes or in customers who would have purchased the product at the non-cartelized price not purchasing at all. Price increases and output decreases typically go hand in hand, as you will recall from the description of the downward-sloping demand curve in Chapter 1. (This is also why price-fixing cartels and output-fixing cartels usually have equivalent effects.) This reduction in volume harms those would-be purchasers, since they would have been willing to buy at the counterfactual price but not at the cartel price. However, it is often difficult to identify precisely who these would-be purchasers are, which is why claiming damages for this volume reduction tends to be more difficult.

Figure 10.1—which you will recognize from the charts in Chapter 2—shows the overcharge paid on all the units actually sold (rectangle A), and the reduction in volume (triangle B). Triangle C represents consumer surplus in this market (the difference between what consumers are willing to pay for each of the units bought, and what

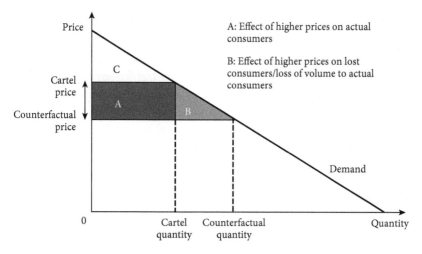

Fig. 10.1 Stylized illustration of the main effects of a price-fixing cartel

they actually pay). While this chart is similar to those in Chapter 2, note that the counterfactual price here is not necessarily the same as the price in perfect competition (markets are rarely perfectly competitive), and the cartel price is not necessarily the same as the monopoly price (not all cartels manage to set price at the profit-maximizing monopoly level).

10.3.2 THE CARTEL OVERCHARGE HARM

The overcharge, A, is the quantity of actual unit sales by the cartel multiplied by the difference between the actual cartel price and the counterfactual price (ie, the price that would have been charged in the absence of the cartel). It is convenient to express the overcharge A as a percentage of the actual price or revenue of the cartel. If the cartel price is €125, and the counterfactual price is €100, the overcharge would be 20% (€25 is 20% of €125). The overcharge is sometimes expressed as a percentage of the counterfactual price (in this case 25%). This is equally valid, but it is important to be clear about which basis for the percentage calculation is used. Expressing the overcharge as a percentage of the actual price makes it easy (and intuitive) to calculate the total amount of overcharge by applying the percentage to the amount that the buyer actually paid for its purchases. For example, if the cartel sold 1 million units at a price of €125 each, the total overcharge would be €25 million. If one specific claimant filed a successful damages action, and it could demonstrate that its total purchases from the cartel amounted to, say, €15 million over the relevant period, the amount it was overcharged is 20% of €15 million—ie, €3 million.

10.3.3 REDUCTION IN VOLUME AND OTHER TYPES OF HARM CAUSED BY CARTELS

The lost-volume effect (as represented by triangle B above) is known in economic theory as a deadweight welfare loss; it represents an inefficiency to the economy as a whole, as we explained in Chapter 1. This deadweight loss is greatest if the counterfactual price is equal to the price under perfect competition, but also arises if the counterfactual represents some other form of competitive, non-cartel interaction, such as oligopoly (where price is higher than under perfect competition). From an economic perspective, this is inefficient as the cartel does not serve those customers who would be willing to pay the price under more competitive conditions.

As discussed earlier, in practice, follow-on actions for damages in cartel cases are typically brought by parties that were actual (direct or indirect) purchasers of the cartel during the infringement period, and will most frequently focus on the harm caused to them by the overcharge (area A in Figure 10.1). Damages for different types of harm caused by the cartel, including the volume reduction (area B), negative effects on quality and choice, and possible other effects on cost levels, are generally more difficult to prove than the overcharge harm.

As regards damages from volume reduction, it may be difficult to identify the harmed parties. This may be less of a problem in the case of an existing customer purchasing lower volumes, but particularly applies to potential customers who did not purchase at all during the infringement period and yet would have purchased the product at the non-cartelized price. To take a hypothetical example based on a real case, in the private schools cartel case in the UK, those who could no longer afford to send their children to private schools at the inflated school fees may have been more harmed than those who paid the higher fees and did send their children to those schools.[9]

Those direct purchasers that are themselves producers or distributors may seek to link the reduction in volume of purchases from the cartel to a reduction in their own sales (and hence reduced profit) in a market downstream, and claim this as a separate type of harm from the cartel overcharge. In the example of the synthetic-rubber cartel, tyre manufacturers would in the first instance claim for a cartel overcharge harm. However, to the extent that they have passed this overcharge on through their tyre prices (and hence passed the harm on to their customers), they may still, in theory, have suffered harm from lost sales of tyres, as customers buy fewer tyres at the higher price.

10.3.4 QUANTITY-FIXING, CUSTOMER-ALLOCATION, AND BID-RIGGING CARTELS

Other forms of hardcore cartel agreement may cause the same types of harm as a price-fixing cartel (see also Chapter 5). Some hardcore cartels target quantities directly, rather

---

[9] Office of Fair Trading (2006), 'Independent Schools Agree Settlement: Competition Investigation Resolved', press release, 19 May.

than prices. For example, certain industries find it easier to monitor outputs, and thereby agree volume quotas rather than prices. The OPEC cartel is a notorious example. However, restrictions in output will normally result in a corresponding rise in the price paid and thus cause a similar harm to that caused by price-fixing cartels. Likewise, customer-allocation cartels give each cartel member a degree of monopoly power over its allocated customers, which allows it to restrict output and increase price.

Bid rigging is a specific type of cartel agreement that shares many similarities with price- and quantity-fixing cartels. If all cartel members agree on bid prices in relation to a specific project, the effect may be similar to that of a direct price-fixing cartel. Yet the assessment of the harm caused by a bid-rigging cartel also needs to take into account the fact that competition may be taking place within an auction framework, rather than within a more traditional market framework. In certain circumstances, if the bid-rigging cartel fails to include one of the firms, it is possible that this would undermine the bid-rigging behaviour in the auctions, bringing prices closer to competitive levels. At the same time, the clear rules of the game in such auctions (compared to normal markets) may make it more straightforward for economists to model how competition would function in the absence of the bid-rigging cartel.

10.3.5 DYNAMIC CARTEL EFFECTS

In addition to the price and quantity effects illustrated in Figure 10.1, cartels can have longer-term effects on the structure and functioning of the market. The reduction in rivalry between firms can result in lower levels of innovation and a slowing of the rate at which improvements in efficiency are achieved, or at which inefficient firms exit the market. Higher cartel prices may also have a distortive effect in downstream markets—for example, if certain purchasers can no longer afford high input prices and downstream concentration consequently increases.

To an economist, all of these longer-term effects should ideally be taken into account in the damages estimation, since they may affect the counterfactual price. For example, the counterfactual price might have been even lower (and hence the overcharge even higher) if the market would have seen cost-reducing innovations in the absence of the cartel. However, such factors can be taken into account only in circumstances where estimating these effects is really feasible, and where it is legally possible to include them, since it may be difficult to demonstrate a causal link between the infringement and the alleged longer-term harm.

10.3.6 THE ISSUE OF PASS-ON OF THE CARTEL OVERCHARGE

Figure 10.1 above shows the overcharge and lost-volume effect of a cartel on direct purchasers. These can be either sellers themselves (intermediate producers or distributors located one level further downstream in the supply chain) or end-consumers. However, the ultimate harm caused to particular direct and indirect customers by the overcharge (and also the volume effect) will depend on the extent to which the price increase caused by the cartel is passed along the supply chain. This is a significant and complex issue with any damages claim. The question of pass-on does not affect the calculation of the overcharge in itself, only the distribution of that harm along the supply chain. The issue of whether the passing-on defence—whereby a defendant can dispute a damages claim by a direct purchaser on the basis that the latter has passed on any cost increases further downstream—should be allowed has been the subject of much policy debate both in the USA and Europe.[10] The economics of how to determine pass-on rates has received less attention in the context of competition law damages. We explore this further in section 10.11.

10.3.7 THEORETICAL INSIGHTS INTO THE EXISTENCE OF CARTEL OVERCHARGES

Following a competition authority decision (or court ruling) that a cartel existed and was operational in the market, you might expect the overcharge of that cartel to have been greater than zero. As you have seen in Chapter 1, economic theory indicates that competition typically results in lower prices than monopoly. At its most effective, a cartel means that competitors act jointly as a monopolist, but even if less effective it leads to some competition between rivals being eliminated. There have been significant enforcement efforts against cartels by competition authorities worldwide in the last decade, and substantial fines and other penalties have been imposed (see Chapters 5 and 9). Where hardcore cartels have nonetheless been formed, using sophisticated methods to circumvent detection, it is not unreasonable to infer that the mere fact that the cartel members took such actions and risks would indicate that they considered it worthwhile.

As discussed in Chapter 9, the decision of whether a company or individual engages in cartel activity can be thought of as a calculation of whether it is profitable to do so. In a simple model, the company would be expected to commit the infringement if the expected additional profit from being part of the cartel (ie, above the profit earned when not being part of the cartel) is higher than the sum of the expected fine if the cartel is detected and the expected damages payout of a subsequent successful private action. According to this logic, and on the assumption that cartelists are rational companies (and not all companies are always rational), they would not be taking on the risk of being prosecuted for participating in a cartel if they did not expect to achieve significant extra profits through price increases from this activity.

This basic logic is sometimes (implicitly or explicitly) followed by courts. Two recent cases in Germany and one in Spain considered whether it is appropriate to assume that a cartel overcharge is greater than zero. In a vitamins cartel damages action, the

---

[10] See Antitrust Modernization Commission (2007) for an overview of the recent debates in the USA; and European Commission (2008), 'White Paper on Damages Actions for Breach of the EC Antitrust Rules', COM(2008) 165, April.

Dortmund Regional Court applied the prima facie rule that a market price is generally lower than a cartel price:

> The damage of a price cartel consists of the difference between the cartel price and the hypothetical competitive price in the absence of the cartel. According to the experience of life (*Lebenserfahrung*), it can be assumed that a competitive price is lower than a cartel price. The defendant did not show that it would have been different in this case and why. The difference between the competitive price and the cartel price represents a financial damage in the sense of lost wealth.[11]

The court found that the fact that prices increased or remained stable during the cartel, but declined as the cartel ceased to operate, supported this proposition. The evidence presented by the defendant did not convince the court that higher input prices led to a proportionate increase in the end-consumers' prices. Similarly, in a cement cartel case, a higher court in Germany stated that:

> The longer and more sustainable a cartel was practised, and the wider the area it was designed to cover, the higher the requirements that have to be imposed on a court if it wants to deny that the cartel agreement produced any economic benefits.[12]

The court emphasized that market mechanisms were unlikely to function properly due to the imposition of cartel quotas. It thus concluded that prices in the cartel were likely to be higher than in a competitive market. In a damages action against a member of a sugar cartel in Spain, the Provincial Court of Valladolid relied on the competition authority's statement that the agreement on prices had caused serious harm, and therefore rejected outright the defendant's expert report which had calculated the damage as zero.[13]

10.3.8 EMPIRICAL INSIGHTS INTO THE POSSIBLE MAGNITUDE OF CARTEL OVERCHARGES

Economists have carried out many empirical studies on overcharges in past cartels, and competition lawyers involved in damages actions have shown great interest in the results of these studies, in order to get a feel for what sort of orders of magnitude of overcharge are typically involved in such cases. We note from the outset that some care is required when interpreting this empirical data. Not all studies on cartel overcharges would qualify as sufficiently robust. It may also be that empirical studies tend to focus on cartels that are most likely to have had an impact on the market, in which case many cartels with no effect will not have been captured in these studies (although, as shown below, a small but significant proportion of the cartels studied resulted in no overcharges).

A study by Posner (2001) presents the overcharges for 12 cartel cases, with a median value of 28% of the cartel price (the median is the middle value if you rank all observations in a sample from lowest to highest). We note here that, like many other studies,

---

[11] LG Dortmund AZ 13 0 55/02 Kart *Vitaminkartell III* [2004] (Dortmund Regional Court, 1 April 2004).
[12] Oberlandesgericht Düsseldorf, *Berliner Transportbeton I*, KRB 2/05.
[13] Audiencia Provincial de Valladolid, Sentencia num. 261/2009, judgment of 9 October 2009.

Posner presents the overcharge as a percentage of the counterfactual price (38%, which is equivalent to 28% of the actual cartel price). As explained above, it is convenient to express the overcharge as a percentage of the actual cartel price, as this makes it easier to calculate the total amount of overcharge by applying the percentage to the amount that the buyer of the cartel actually paid for its purchases. It is straightforward to go from one to the other—to get the overcharge as a percentage of the actual price you divide the overcharge as a percentage of the counterfactual price by 1 + the overcharge as a percentage of the counterfactual price (so 0.38 / 1.38 = 0.28). Based on a survey of cartel cases between 1996 and 2000, the Organisation for Co-operation and Development (2002) finds that the median overcharge was between 13% and 16% of the cartel price (with a variation from 3% to 40%). Werden (2003) reviews 13 other studies, and arrives at a median overcharge of 15% of the cartel price.

A more recent study by Connor and Lande (2008) uses the most comprehensive dataset on cartel overcharges currently available, and is also currently the most widely cited study on this topic.[14] It contains 674 observations of average overcharges from 200 social science studies of cartels from the eighteenth century onwards—for example, it covers a British coal cartel that started in the 1770s and a Canadian petroleum lamp oil cartel in the 1870s—and finds that the median cartel overcharge for all types of cartel was 20% of the cartel price. An earlier study by Connor and Lande (2005) suggests that in around 7% of cartel cases there was no overcharge. As part of the 2009 study for the European Commission referred to above, Oxera examined the dataset underlying the 2008 Connor and Lande study, as well as an additional 350 observations provided by Connor and Lande (thus totalling more than 1,000 observations), and tested the sensitivity of the overcharge median and other results by limiting the sample to cartels that started after 1960 and to overcharge estimates obtained from peer-reviewed academic articles and chapters in published books (this reduced the sample size from over 1,000 to 114).

Figure 10.2 illustrates the distribution of cartel overcharges across this new dataset of 114 observations. The range with the greatest number of observations is 10%–20%. Oxera found that in this dataset the median overcharge is 18% of the cartel price—not far from the 20% found by Connor and Lande. The average overcharge is around 20%, compared with 23% in Connor and Lande. However, since the variation in observed overcharges is large, it is informative to consider the distribution of overcharges as well as the median or average overcharge.

In 93% of the cases the overcharge as a percentage of the cartel price is above zero (as in Connor and Lande, 2005). This supports the theory that in most cases the cartel overcharge may be expected to be positive, although it also indicates that there is a small but significant proportion of cartels where there is no overcharge. Whether any particular cartel falls into this category would need to be explored on a case-by-case basis.

---

[14] Professor Connor has previously published a number of articles using this dataset. Some cases in the dataset refer to purchaser cartels, and the 'undercharge' is expressed as an overcharge for those cases.

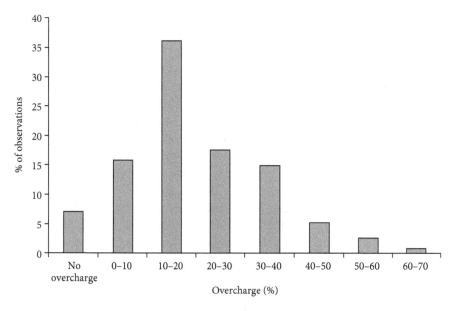

Fig. 10.2 Distribution of cartel overcharges in empirical studies of past cartels

Source: Oxera et al. (2009), based on underlying Connor and Lande data described above and selection criteria applied by Oxera.

Another interesting finding is that the sample includes 52 international and 62 national cartels, and the former have a larger mean overcharge (26%) than the latter (16%).

The important policy question is what you do with the results of this empirical litera-ture. Do you consider them merely interesting background information? Do you use them to inform your calculation of the possible order of magnitude of the damage at a very early stage in the case? Or do you go as far as using a presumption that the overcharge in the case you are considering is somewhere between 10% and 20%, as that is what most cartels in the past seem to have had as the overcharge? We would not advocate such presumptions. Yet they are sometimes made in practice. A prominent example is the Hungarian Competition Act, which provides that injured parties bring-ing claims against members of price-fixing cartels can rely on the rebuttable presump-tion that 'it shall be deemed that the infringement affected the price by 10% unless the contrary is evidenced'.[15] In a separate but related area of competition law, the cartel fin-ing guidelines issued by the United States Sentencing Commission are based on the assumption that cartels impose an overcharge of 10%.[16] We consider that the amount of the overcharge in any particular damages case would ultimately need to be determined according to the facts of the case.

---

[15] Competition Act (as amended, 2008), Hungary, s 88/C; applicable to damages arising after September 2008.
[16] Chapter 2R1.1, Bid-rigging, Price-fixing or Market-allocation Agreements Among Competitors, Application Note 3.

10.4 HARM FROM EXCLUSIONARY CONDUCT: CONCEPTUAL FRAMEWORK

As we saw in Chapter 4, exclusionary conduct can have the effect of stifling the competitive process. Apart from the broader negative impact that this may have on the economy as a whole—eg, dampening of competitive dynamics; reduction in efficiency and innovation—it can lead to various kinds of harm to specific parties. Existing competitors may be prevented from competing effectively in the market or be forced to exit altogether, while potential competitors may be prevented from entering the market (or be restricted to small-scale entry). This can affect their profits or value relative to the situation in which there is no exclusionary conduct. Buyers in the market (be they end-consumers, or intermediate downstream producers or distributors) may be harmed by exclusionary conduct if the reduction in competition leads to higher prices, a reduction in choice, or a reduction in quality.

The harm to buyers from exclusionary conduct may sometimes be difficult to identify or may not yet have manifested itself—for example, where an infringement is established before competitors are weakened or forced to exit the market, such that buyers have not suffered the full consequences of diminished competition. The harm caused by exclusionary practices will therefore usually be suffered most directly by competitors of the infringer. Indeed, it is our understanding that the majority of damages actions in Europe following exclusionary conduct have thus far been brought by competitors rather than buyers.

10.4.1 THE CONCEPT OF LOST PROFIT: THE LEGAL PRINCIPLES THAT DETERMINE WHICH ECONOMIC QUESTIONS ARE MOST RELEVANT

We noted in section 10.1 that certain legal principles limit the inherent chance of success for certain types of damages claim. This is important for economists, and lawyers using economists, to be aware of—to economists there is a broad set of damages that may arise from a competition infringement, and each type might in principle be quantifiable; to lawyers the set is narrower. This is perhaps most notable in the context of lost profit caused by exclusionary conduct. We therefore set out here our understanding of what would be the economic questions that are of most interest according to the relevant legal principles.

Companies that are already in the market affected by exclusionary conduct are, in legal terms, relatively close to the conduct, meaning that it is usually easier for them to substantiate a damages claim. A damage estimation in this situation would seek to identify what profit the victim would have made in the absence of the infringement in the 'normal' course of business. Companies that were not already in the market, but that were nonetheless excluded from it, may still be relatively close to the conduct, but they would need to be able to show that they were indeed excluded by this conduct and that there is a sufficient causal link between the exclusion and the harm they have suffered.

From an economic perspective, harm to competitors from an exclusionary infringement may arise in two ways. First, it may be in the form of increased costs (where costs include both cash cost items, such as input goods, and other more general items, such as the cost of financing the business). Second, it may be in the form of reduced revenue (where the infringing conduct affects the price or sales volume). The effect of both increased costs and reduced revenue is a reduction in profit. From a legal perspective, it is important (we understand from lawyers) to make explicit in each case whether this effect falls under actual loss (*damnum emergens*) or lost profit (*lucrum cessans*). To an economist there is not much difference, and the economic framework presented in this chapter can be used for both categories. However, in legal terms, the evidentiary requirements are different. Actual loss is generally easier to prove—for example, an airline whose access to distribution channels was foreclosed by a dominant rival and which had to find alternative, more expensive, distribution channels instead, should in principle be able to demonstrate the harm based on the actual additional expenditure incurred (it can show the actual invoices). In contrast, the airline may not always be able to prove the quantum of the alleged lost profit—eg, loss of market share or a fall in sales growth—or a causal link between the unlawful conduct and that lost profit. This is because of difficulties in establishing whether such losses were due to the anticompetitive practice or to other factors (eg, incompetence, lack of resources, luck, or external economic factors).

Most legal systems seem to take a relatively conservative approach when assessing lost profit—or related concepts, such as loss of chance and loss of opportunity—in damages actions following exclusionary conduct. In many cases across Europe the damages awarded are limited to actual losses or a narrow interpretation of lost profits. The following three cases—from France, Italy, and the UK—illustrate this conservative approach.

The Paris Court of Appeal ruled on an exclusionary damages case in 1998 after it had found in an initial 1993 judgment that the defendant, Labinal, had infringed Article 101(1) and Article 102 with the sole purpose of eliminating its only competitor, Mors, from a tender to supply tyre pressure measuring equipment to British Aerospace.[17] The court awarded Mors FF34.2 million for the losses caused by Labinal's infringements. The calculation of damages was based exclusively on the report of a court-appointed expert, with the court confining itself to assessing whether the expert's conclusions were reasonable and supported by statements made, or documents supplied, by the parties. The expert considered that Mors had incurred harm in the form of: (i) additional administrative and commercial costs; (ii) loss of opportunity to participate in other tenders; and (iii) the inability to recover one-off costs. However, the expert

[17] *Mors SA v Labinal SA*, Cour d'Appel de Paris, 1ère chambre, section A, arrêt no 334 (Paris Court of Appeal, 30 September 1998).

did not consider that Mors should be awarded damages for loss of opportunity to enter adjacent markets since it had failed to prove that it would have entered these other markets had Labinal's anti-competitive practices not taken place.

An exclusionary damages case before the Court of Appeal of Milan followed on from an earlier decision by the Italian competition authority, which considered that the collective boycott of the claimant's software packages by the members of the National Association of Employment Consultants constituted a violation of the Italian equivalent of Article 101.[18] The court compared the average number of contracts with the claimant that were terminated by the Association's members in the two years of the collective boycott (1997–98) with the average number of contracts terminated in the years prior to the boycott. On that basis, the court awarded €148,200 in damages. The next question was whether the claimant was entitled to recover damages for the slower growth of its business due to the boycott (a form of lost profit). While it was able to show that, prior to the boycott, its business was growing at a rate of more than 10% per annum and that this increase had suddenly ceased at the time of the boycott, the court considered that it could not be sure that this growth would have continued at a similar rate. The past evidence could not be used to support a presumption that this growth rate would have been maintained. The judgment was confirmed on appeal by the Italian Supreme Court.

Various English courts (and at some stage the European Court of Justice as well—see section 10.1) ruled on the famous *Crehan* damages case.[19] The claimant was a public house landlord who, in 1991, entered into an exclusive contract with Inntrepreneur to lease two public houses on condition that he stocked only its beers. After two unsuccessful years, Inntrepreneur terminated his tenancy and sought to recover money owed to it. Mr Crehan counterclaimed that the beer tie agreement infringed Article 101 and sought to recover three heads of damages: (i) losses that he suffered during the period of the lease between 1991 and 1993; (ii) future profits he would have made in the period between 1993 and 2003 in the absence of the beer tie; and (iii) the value in 2003 of the untied leases had he wished to sell these on. Both the High Court and the Court of Appeal accepted that if liability were established, the claimant would have been entitled to recover in full the losses suffered during the period of the two-year lease. However, the Court of Appeal took a more restrictive approach than the High Court in relation to the recoverability of future profits that the claimant would have made between 1993 and 2003 (ie, up until the date of the High Court's judgment). The High Court (albeit hypothetically as it dismissed the case on other grounds) calculated the total lost profit due to the claimant as £1,311,500. The lost profit figure included all three heads of damages listed above. In contrast, the Court of Appeal held that the claimant would have been entitled to only £131,336 in damages (ie, just over one tenth of the

---

[18] *INAZ Paghe srl v Associazione Nazionale dei Consulenti del Lavoro* (Corte d'Appello di Milano (Court of Appeal of Milan), 10 December 2004).

[19] *Crehan v Inntrepreneur Pub Company (CPC) & Anor* [2003] EWHC 1510 (Ch); [2004] EWCA Civ 637; [2006] UKHL 38.

damages calculated by the first court). It considered that the lost profit between 1993 and 2003 was too speculative. The case was subsequently appealed to the House of Lords, which overturned the Court of Appeal's finding that the beer tie agreement infringed Article 101 (as such, the issue of the quantum of damage did not need to be addressed in this last ruling).

10.4.2 THE CONCEPT OF LOST PROFIT: AN ECONOMIC FRAMEWORK

The basic economic framework to determine harm from exclusionary practices—encompassing both actual loss and lost profit in the legal sense—is illustrated in Figure 10.3. The damages are calculated as the difference between the factual and the counterfactual profit of the company. To take a simple example, if the victim of the infringement—say, the small competitor airline that was harmed by the dominant airline's exclusionary conduct—had actual revenues of €10 million and actual costs of €8 million, its actual profit would be €2 million. If its counterfactual revenues in the absence of the infringement would have been €15 million and its counterfactual costs €12 million then its counterfactual profit is €3 million and the lost profit €1 million. This framework can be used directly to quantify damages (it does not specify which party legally bears the burden of proof at each step of the quantification).

The framework can be rearranged as illustrated in Figure 10.4, which shows a simpler expression for the fall in profit for a company that has suffered reduced volumes due to being partially or fully excluded from a market. The lost revenue in Figure 10.4 is calculated as the difference between the counterfactual and factual revenues. The costs avoided due to the infringement are then deducted from the lost revenue to obtain the fall in profit. For example, if volume falls, certain costs that vary with volume (eg, fuel

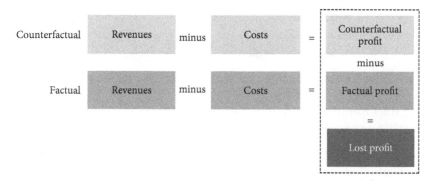

Fig. 10.3 Economic framework for calculating the effect of the infringement on profits

Note: As explained in the text, the term 'lost profit' as used in this economic framework can in principle comprise both the legal concepts of actual loss (*damnum emergens*) and lost profit (*lucrum cessans*).

Source: Oxera et al. (2009).

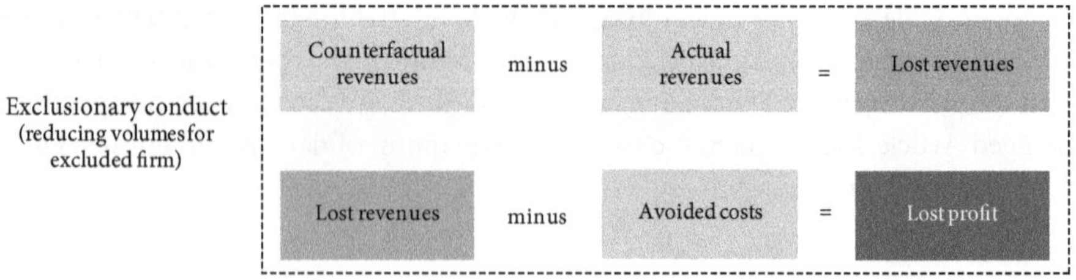

Fig. 10.4 Rearranged economic framework for calculating harm from exclusionary conduct (equivalent to Fig. 10.3)

Source: Oxera et al. (2009).

or input materials) will fall. A company that experiences a reduction in sales due to exclusionary conduct by a rival will in this sense have an offsetting benefit from a cost reduction, and this cost saving should, in theory, therefore be deducted from the lost revenue to obtain the lost profit, as illustrated in Figure 10.4. This rearranged expression has the advantage (compared with Figure 10.3) of requiring less detailed knowledge of the company's cost structure. This is because it is not necessary to calculate all the costs that the company would have incurred in the relevant period; instead, the focus is on the costs that the company did not incur because of the infringement—ie, the avoided costs. Following the above simple numerical example, lost revenues would be €5 million (€15 million of revenue in the counterfactual minus €10 million in the factual), and avoided costs €4 million (€12 million of cost in the counterfactual minus €8 million in the factual), giving a fall in profit of €1 million.

The effect on profits (whether actual loss or lost profit in the legal sense) is often approximated by reference to variables such as lost volumes, lost customers, or lost market share. These quantifications are (or should be) implicitly consistent with the conceptual framework in the figures above. For example, damages claims based on an estimation of lost sales volume can be translated into a negative effect on profits by applying some average counterfactual profit margin to each unit of sales lost. If the airline demonstrates that it sold 50,000 fewer tickets because of the abuse by its dominant rival, and it made a profit margin on tickets of, on average, €20, then its lost profit is €1 million.

10.4.3 THE EFFECT ON PROFIT FROM INFRINGEMENTS THAT INCREASE INPUT PRICES

Figure 10.3 can also be rearranged to capture the effect on profit from infringements that increase input prices—see Figure 10.5. This applies to exclusionary conduct that has, at some stage, the effect of raising prices to buyers, and to exclusionary conduct that has the effect of raising rivals' costs in downstream markets—a common theory of harm in abuse of dominance cases. The logic of Figure 10.5 also applies to the effect on the profits of the downstream purchasers of a cartel.

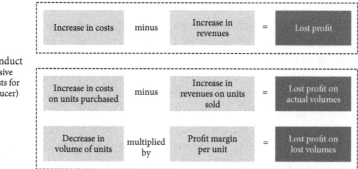

Price-increasing conduct
(eg, a cartel or excessive
pricing increasing costs for
an intermediate producer)

Fig. 10.5 Rearranged economic framework for calculating harm from price-increasing conduct (equivalent to Fig. 10.3)

Source: Oxera et al. (2009).

In the top section of Figure 10.5, the fall in profit of the company is calculated as the increase in its costs minus the increase in its revenues. In the case of a cartel or anti-competitive increase in an input price, the increase in costs to the downstream purchaser (the box to the left) will often be equal to the overcharge. The increase in revenues (the middle box) will include the pass-on of this overcharge to the victim's own customers. Pass-on is achieved through raising price, and in the damages estimation the higher revenues thus achieved may have to be offset against the higher costs caused by the infringement in question. The lower part of Figure 10.5 is equivalent but splits the profit effect from a higher price into three components: the increase in costs on units actually purchased (the overcharge effect); the increase in revenues on units actually sold downstream (which covers the pass-on effect); and the effect of lost volumes of sales downstream due to the price increase upstream. Within this framework, the total profit effect would equal the sum of the fall in profit from actual volumes and the fall in profit on lost volumes.

10.4.4 OTHER HARMED PARTIES

Finally, exclusionary conduct may have effects on other parties besides buyers and competitors. Suppliers upstream of the conduct may suffer lost sales (and thus reduced profits) to firms excluded from the market. These excluded firms would have purchased more from those suppliers in the absence of the abuse or agreement. However, it may be difficult in practice for parties that are not purchasers or competitors of the infringers to bring successful damages claims due to causation or remoteness problems, depending on the legal system concerned.

One example of a claim by a different type of party is a case in Lithuania where the claim was made by a competitor to the customers of the infringing party.[20] This damages

---

[20] *UAB Siauliu tara v AB Stumbras* (Lithuanian Court of Appeal, 26 May 2006).

claim followed on from a 2002 decision by the Lithuanian competition authority, which found that the defendant had abused its dominant position in the market for the supply of strong alcoholic beverages by making marketing payments to wholesalers in return for them favouring its products. The claimant, a wholesaler that did not receive any such marketing payments, sought to recover three heads of loss: (i) unpaid marketing fees in relation to products that the claimant had actually purchased from the defendant during the period of the infringement; (ii) lost profit due to lower purchases and sales of the defendant's products; and (iii) unpaid marketing fees in relation to products that the claimant would have purchased but for the infringement. When quantifying the harm, the expert appointed by the first-instance court concluded that the claimant was entitled to recover damages only in relation to the unpaid marketing fees for products that it had actually purchased from the defendant during the period of the infringement. However, the court chose not to follow its expert's opinion and awarded damages under all three heads of loss, albeit that the amount was reduced in light of the original fine imposed on the defendant by the Lithuanian competition authority and the hypothetical nature of lost-profit claims. The Lithuanian Court of Appeal subsequently reduced the amount of damages awarded to the claimant since it considered that the expert had been right to conclude that the claimant was entitled to recover damages only in relation to the unpaid marketing fees for products that it had actually purchased from the defendant during the period of the infringement. It held that the first-instance court's decision to disregard the expert's findings was unjustified, and that the claimant had failed to prove the losses it was seeking to recover under the last two heads of damages set out above.

10.5 A CLASSIFICATION OF METHODS AND MODELS FOR THE QUANTIFICATION OF DAMAGES

The economics and finance literature has developed a wide array of methods and models for quantifying damages. We use the terms 'methods and models' in a broad sense here, with the intention to encompass all possible methods, models, tools, techniques, frameworks, and approaches. These terms frequently have different meanings to different professions or academic fields, so using one single term here would not be appropriate. Because the economics literature uses the term 'model' more commonly, this chapter also uses this term more often, but it should be interpreted in the same comprehensive manner.

This section presents a classification of the methods and models into three broad groups: comparator-based, financial-analysis-based, and market-structure-based. This is taken from the 2009 report on quantifying damages by Oxera et al. for the European Commission. The classification encapsulates previous classifications, most notably those by the Ashurst (2004) study on antitrust damages for the European Commission, which offered five categories—before and after, yardstick, cost-based, price prediction using regression analysis, and theoretical modelling of oligopoly—and by US case law, which has explicitly identified three 'common approaches to measuring antitrust damages': the before-and-after approach, a yardstick or benchmark approach, and regression analysis.[21] (Regression analysis is a generic term for statistical methods that can be used for explaining the variation in data using other factors. Econometrics is the application of regression to economic data—see also Chapter 2.) The classification here draws clearer distinctions between what is being used as the counterfactual in each method, and the precise estimation technique. For example, before-and-after and yardstick are in reality two different types of comparator-based approach; the former involves making comparisons over time, the latter across product or geographic markets. Both can use the same or similar estimation techniques, such as comparison of averages and regression. Using the term 'yardstick' or 'benchmark' for comparisons across markets only and not over time is inaccurate. Similarly, the regression analysis grouping does not in itself clarify the basis for the counterfactual it can be used with. Since it uses data both over time and across markets or countries (as well as more generally), it cuts across the before-and-after and yardstick groupings.

10.5.1 THE CLASSIFICATION

The classification presented in Figure 10.6 is divided into three levels. The first identifies the approach. The second level identifies the basis for the counterfactual that underlies each of the approaches. The third level then summarizes the estimation techniques that can be used within each approach. In principle, each of these approaches can be used for quantifying damages for any type of antitrust infringement (cartels, other restrictive agreements, and abuse of dominance). They are not mutually exclusive and in fact often complement each other, as discussed below.

Comparator-based approaches use data from sources that are external to the infringement to estimate the counterfactual. This can be done in three ways: by cross-sectional comparisons (comparing different geographic or product markets); time-series comparisons (analysing prices before, during, and/or after an infringement); and combining the above two in 'difference-in-differences' models (eg, analysing the change in price for a cartelized market over time, and comparing that against the change in price in a non-cartelized market over the same timeframe). Various techniques can be used to analyse this comparator data, ranging from the simple such as comparing averages, to the more sophisticated such as panel data regression.

Financial-analysis-based approaches have been developed in finance theory and practice. They use financial information on comparator companies and industries, benchmarks for rates of return, and cost information on defendants and claimants to estimate the counterfactual. There are two types of approach that use this information. First are those that examine financial performance. These include assessing the profitability of defendants or claimants and comparing this against a benchmark, and

---

[21] *Conwood Co LP v US Tobacco Co* 290 F 3d 768, 793 (6th Cir. 2002).

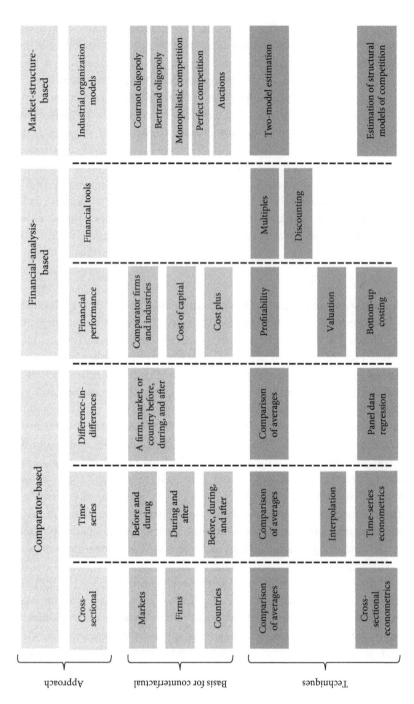

Fig. 10.6 Classification of methods and models

Note: The categories from previous classifications fit into this classification as follows. Before and after falls under 'time series'; yardstick or benchmark falls under 'cross-sectional'; cost-based approach falls under 'financial performance'; regression analysis falls largely under the 'comparator-based approaches', but can also be used for the 'financial-analysis-based approaches' and 'market-structure-based approaches'; oligopoly modelling falls under 'market-structure-based approaches'.

Source: Oxera et al. (2009).

bottom-up costing of products to estimate a counterfactual price for them. The second type is a group of more general financial tools, such as discounting and multiples, which can be used alongside the other categories of methods and models.

Market-structure-based approaches are derived from industrial organization (IO) theory and use a combination of theoretical models, assumptions, and empirical estimation (rather than comparisons across markets or over time) to arrive at an assessment of the counterfactual. These approaches involve identifying models of competition that best fit the relevant market, and using them to provide insight into how competition works in the market concerned and to estimate prices or volumes in the absence of the anti-competitive conduct.

10.5.2 SOME NOTES ON THE USE OF MODELS GENERALLY

No model can fully describe and predict the complete range of complex interactions that occur between individuals and firms, but nor is it intended to do so. Instead, models can be thought of as maps that make simplifications of the real world to make it understandable and interpretable. The simplifications made will depend on the intended use of the map. A geological map will make very different simplifications to a road atlas, despite both describing the same piece of land, because they are being used for different purposes.

Models typically make simplifying assumptions based on theory about how individuals and companies interact in markets. Some of these assumptions can then be tested using the input data relevant to the case. If the assumptions and data match those of the real world sufficiently, the model's predictions about the counterfactual (eg, on what the counterfactual price or market share would have been) are likely to represent unbiased estimates of the outcomes observed in the real world. To understand how robust a model is and how it can be used, there are three important issues to consider: the data used; the assumptions made; and the inference that can be drawn from the outputs.

Most models need to be calibrated (ie, populated with actual data and parameters) using some form of input data so that they reasonably represent the reality of the world they are describing and about which they are making predictions. The data can relate to transactions, individuals, companies, or markets. Different models will require different data, and in some cases assumptions can be substituted for data if it is not available. A model will only be as good as the quality of the input data used to populate it. Thus, it is important to ensure that the sourcing of data is free from potential biases and that the data used is consistent over time and over units (companies, business units, or individuals). Data will be biased if the sample is drawn in a way that is not representative of the 'population' it is meant to represent (see also Chapter 2 where we made this point in the context of survey evidence).

A sophisticated model based on unreliable or biased data is likely to be less robust than a simpler model based on better data. A critical question for you, or a court, to ask when presented with a model is therefore whether the data used is of sufficient quality and reliability, and whether a simpler model could be used. An example of a court rejecting a model on the basis of the quality of the data can be found in a US case on price discrimination with alleged anti-competitive harm to a competitor downstream.[22] The court found that the damages calculations by the plaintiff's expert 'are not based on authoritative industry data or recognized financial data. The very foundation of his calculation is based on the deposition testimony, estimates, feelings and beliefs of [a representative of the plaintiff] who will be a principal beneficiary of the trebled damages sum of $5,187,573.'

To understand what can be robustly inferred from the estimates based on the data and assumptions, models can be tested against the following two criteria. First, does the model generate unbiased estimates of what would have happened without the infringement? Second, do the estimates have the lowest possible level of uncertainty surrounding them? An unbiased estimate is one where the expected value is not materially different to the actual harm. The estimated value using any particular dataset or assumption may vary, but if (hypothetically) the procedure is undertaken many times, the average difference between the estimated and actual harm should be small. Depending on the method or model used, there may be additional conditions that need to be met, but all models should at a minimum be able to show that the estimation results are unbiased and not overly sensitive to the assumptions applied. When examining a particular econometric model, there is a suite of diagnostic tests that can be used to evaluate whether the model is likely to provide unbiased estimates. In addition, statistical models can give further information, known as confidence intervals, indicating the range which covers the actual value (as opposed to the estimated value) with a given degree of certainty (eg, a 95% confidence interval is often used, indicating that there is a 5% probability of the range not covering the actual value). When presented with an empirical study, you are entitled to require it to show the basic diagnostic tests—the threat of you asking another economist to scrutinize the results provides a good incentive on the first economist to deliver a transparent and robust analysis (a theme to which we return in Chapter 11).

The inference that can be drawn from a model also depends on the variables included. If an important variable that influences the process has been omitted, the estimates may be inconsistent and biased. For example, if, when predicting the counterfactual price of cement in a cartel damages case, the effect of a boom in the construction industry was not accounted for, the model might incorrectly ascribe the whole price increase of cement to the cartel. A properly constructed econometric model would take account of both explanatory factors and would be able to isolate the cartel effect on price from the boom effect on price. Sometimes, variables that are known to be of some potential relevance may not be included in the model because the data is not available

---

[22] *Vernon Walden Inc et al. v Lipoid GmbH et al.* (Civil No 01-4826 (DRD)) United States District Court for the District of New Jersey, 15 November 2005.

or because the variable has such a small impact on the outcome that it is not necessary. However, the aim of the model should be to produce an estimate of the counterfactual where the omission of certain factors is not likely to significantly bias the result. This brings us to the issue of causation, discussed below.

10.5.3 WHAT CAN ECONOMIC METHODS AND MODELS SAY ABOUT CAUSATION?

Quantifying the harm and showing a causal link between the harm and the infringement are essential parts of any damages action. They are therefore often closely linked, even if conceptually they can be seen as separate steps. What, if anything, can economic methods and models used for quantifying damages say about causation?

Econometric analysis seeks to identify statistically significant relationships between a 'dependent' variable—the variable that is to be explained (eg, demand for a product)—and various explanatory variables (eg, the price of the product and consumer income). The fact that one variable is dependent and the others are explanatory is a result of model construction, which is usually based on theory (ie, theory suggests that demand for a product depends on price). The econometric analysis itself does not prove causality as such; it tests whether the relationship between the variables is statistically significant. If the model is constructed with two completely unrelated variables that happen to have a high correlation (ie, they move similarly over time—eg, inflation and accumulated rainfall), then the model may still identify a statistically significant relationship but one that is economically meaningless (see also Chapter 2).

Nevertheless, econometrics can help address the issue of causation because it can take into account many possible explanatory factors (subject to data availability). This is important for damages actions since the difficulties in proving causation frequently arise when a model purports to show a relationship between two variables but ignores other explanatory variables. For example, a model may show that a competitor's sales have fallen during the period of an exclusionary abuse, but fail to address other possible explanations for that fall in sales, such as a general drop in sales in the market during the period, the entry of a new competitor, or managerial incompetence. A good econometric model would seek to 'control' for those other explanations—ie, incorporate them into the model as additional explanatory variables. That way, the various effects can be isolated from one another, and the model may well show that, while the other factors explain some of the sales loss, the remainder of the loss is still explained by the infringement. This applies irrespective of which party bears the burden of proof of causation under the relevant legal framework.

In US antitrust damages cases, where the use of econometrics is more common than in Europe, the issue of causation is often dealt with in this way. The US courts sometimes actually expect to see a regression analysis in order to have robust estimates and to isolate the effects of the infringement from other effects. In one case the court stated that the 'prudent economist must account for differences and would perform minimum regression analysis when comparing price before relevant period to prices during damage period'.[23] In various US cases, economic evidence has been rejected on the grounds that it did not sufficiently account for other possible explanations for the harm. In *Stelwagon v Tarmac Roofing*, the expert's opinion was not accepted since it 'failed to sufficiently link any decline in Stelwagon's MAPs sales to price discrimination. The sales may have been lost for reasons apart from price discrimination—reasons that [the expert]'s analysis apparently did not take into account'.[24] On a more positive note, a number of judgments accepted the evidence because the models used did sufficiently account for other explanations in addition to the infringement. In *Conwood v US Tobacco*, a case of alleged monopolization, the court accepted that the expert, in his regression analysis, had tested for 'all plausible explanations' for the claimant's low market share, thus allowing the court to isolate the effect of the infringement itself.[25] In Chapter 11 we return to the topic of admissibility of economic expert evidence in court proceedings.

10.5.4 SELECTING WHICH METHODS OR MODELS TO USE

Two main factors will typically influence the economist's choice: the availability and quality of data and information—more data usually makes a greater range of approaches possible—and the availability and quality of the counterfactual—in some cases a high-quality cross-sectional comparator may be available (such as a closely matching cross-country comparator for a cartelized market, where it is likely that there is no similar infringement in that comparator country), while in other cases it may not (eg, a close match is available, but there is some evidence of a similar infringement in the comparator country, potentially 'contaminating' the data).

The sources of data are potentially broad. Various elements are typically available in the public domain (eg, interest rates, which can be used to calculate an appropriate discount rate); others may be in the possession of a claimant (eg, invoices detailing prices paid and volumes purchased); and some may be available only from defendants (eg, revenues, costs, and volumes sold for a particular product line). Table 10.1 summarizes the typical sources of various types of data.

All the methods and models discussed here have a basis on which the counterfactual is constructed. For example, in the cross-sectional comparator-based approaches, the basis for the counterfactual is making comparisons across firms, product markets, or geographic markets. In the market-structure-based approaches the counterfactual is based on models of competitive interaction such as Bertrand or Cournot oligopoly

---

[23] *Re Aluminum Phosphide Antitrust Litig* 893 F Supp 1497, 1507 (D. Kan. 1995).

[24] *Stelwagon Mfg Co v Tarmac Roofing* 63 F 3d 1267 (3d Cir. 1995). A related legal issue in this context is that damages can be claimed only to the extent that they are caused by the infringer's illegal conduct, not by the infringer's legal conduct. Models quantifying damages should also separate those effects. One of the reasons a US court excluded the damages expert's testimony in *Concord Boat Corp v Brunswick Corp* 207 F 3d 1039 (8th Cir. 2000), a case involving exclusionary practices, was because 'it did not separate lawful from unlawful conduct'.

[25] *Conwood Co v US Tobacco Co* 290 F 3d 768 (6th Cir. 2002).

Table 10.1 Typical data sources used for damages estimations

Source	Typical data	Typical documents
Competition authority	Dates for the infringement, which parties were involved, how the infringement operated	Press releases, official decision documents
Public domain	Public domain pricing information, observable counterfactual market, demand elasticity estimates, inflation rate	Industry studies, industry/government statistical publications, price comparison websites, commercial databases specific to an industry, statutory accounts[1]
Claimants	Intermediate producer: payments, volumes purchased, cost structure (eg, proportions of fixed and variable costs), how the market and commercial interactions operate	Management accounts, sales databases, invoices
	End-consumers: payments, volumes purchased, willingness to pay/elasticity (eg, via survey)	Invoices, surveys, sworn statements
Defendants	Revenue, volumes, market share, prices, input costs, cost structure, how the market and commercial interactions operate	Management accounts, sales databases, customer relationship management systems
Other parties in the supply chain	Payments, volumes purchased, cost structure	Management accounts
Statutory sources	Statutory interest rates, corporate tax rates and rules, sales tax rates and rules, other taxes	Government departments or courts that determine the statutory interest rates, tax authorities

[1] Subscription services such as Datastream and Bloomberg provide access to company accounts data, and various statistical and financial markets data. Other sources such as Eurostat and various government statistical offices also provide data of varying types about industries.

Source: Oxera et al. (2009).

(see Chapter 3). The more of these bases for the counterfactual that are available, the more methods and models there will be to explore and use. As the quality of these bases improves (in terms of their usefulness, comprehensiveness, and accuracy), the estimates produced are more likely to be robust and reliable. For example, the quality of a cross-sectional comparator market for use as a basis for a counterfactual price in a cartelized market might be determined by factors such as whether that comparator market has itself been affected by cartel behaviour; the similarity of the product in that market; and the similarity of the exogenous shocks (eg, changes in input costs) faced by the cartelized and comparator markets.

The simpler techniques, such as comparisons of averages, which are straightforward to understand and calculate, are useful when the basis for the counterfactual is of a high quality. When there are important factors that mean that the comparator may not mirror the counterfactual, these simple approaches should be employed with care. Factors such as differences in size (eg, different-sized firms), macroeconomic conditions (eg, differences in inflation and growth), market characteristics (eg, how mature markets are), and exogenous shocks (eg, changes in regulations) may need to be controlled for in order to improve the comparability of the basis for the counterfactual and, consequently, the estimate of the damage. In such situations the more complex regression techniques may allow a more precise estimation of the counterfactual than the simpler models.

10.5.5 CHOOSING A SINGLE DAMAGES VALUE

In any given case it may be possible to apply more than one approach, using different models—and different assumptions within those models—and taking advantage of different available information. Furthermore, both claimants and defendants may offer differing estimates, perhaps using different approaches. However, ultimately, a court needs to decide on the specific amount of damages (if any) to be awarded. Methods and models cannot be ranked *a priori*. The main question in any particular case would normally be whether specific methods or models have been applied reasonably and robustly to the case at hand, not whether one approach is inherently superior to another.

The economics literature has identified that when presented with multiple estimates of the same variable, two main solutions are available for selecting a single value: identify a preferred approach (eg, one unique combination of modelling and data), or 'pool' a selection of reasonable approaches (see, for example, Timmerman, 2006).

First, identifying a single method or model for the case at hand essentially means focusing on the most appropriate one. The output from this model is then used as the best estimate of the harm. This has some potential advantages. It can provide more clarity for the court in terms of where each party stands if both choose a single model, since each is presenting a single construction of the counterfactual. This clarity means that the court has to choose between only two models. Where one model is a sub-set of the other (eg, the first model contains all the same features as the second, but the second model contains additional features), whether one model better fits the data can be tested statistically. For example, if two models use a similar approach to estimate a variable (eg, volumes), but one model includes an extra explanatory input (eg, the price of alternative goods), it is possible to test whether the additional explanatory input is improving the robustness of the estimate.

Second, the pooling of model results involves combining the results of two or more of the methods and models into a single value. One approach—which, according to the empirical economics literature, has been shown to work quite well—is that of simply taking the mean average of the available forecasts.[26] This is often used for macroeconomic forecasts. For example, if three robust models predict that the damages award should be €10.1 million, €11.2 million, and €12.0 million, the pooled model result, using a simple mean average, would be €11.1 million. This combined value can then be used as the best estimate of the actual harm. It is not always appropriate to use estimates of the damages in such an averaging process, particularly if there are reasons to prefer one group of estimates over another. Indeed, when pooling modelling results, it is standard practice to remove approaches that have significant weaknesses (a process sometimes referred to as 'trimming'), and also to take steps to avoid double-counting of similar approaches.

There are significant potential advantages to the pooling approach. When the models rely on different sub-sets of available data, combining the forecasts means that the final value reflects more of the underlying data (and hence more of the available information) than a single model alone. While it is theoretically possible to conceive of a 'unified' model that incorporates all the data sources of the individual models, it is often difficult to implement this in practice. Instead, pooling of different model results does create a form of 'unified' model, since it draws on all the approaches undertaken. In addition, even when care is taken during the model estimation, there may be biases in the individual models due to the particular assumptions and model structure employed. Pooling the results is likely to help reduce these, as positive and negative biases tend to cancel one another out, at least to some extent.[27] Furthermore, the direction and size of the biases may change over time in unpredictable ways, which can make it difficult to identify a single 'best' model; pooling the results of multiple models helps mitigate this problem.

While pooling has several advantages, it does need to be applied with care. It is most frequently used in cases where a single forecaster is attempting multiple approaches (eg, an expert in a damages action pooling across all estimates), or where multiple forecasters are attempting to estimate the same value for the same purpose (eg, a group of court-appointed experts). Pooling the results from different experts on opposing sides can also work, but only if their approaches start from similar premises and data-sets, and if any approaches with significant weaknesses are excluded from the pooling exercise.

Overall, the conclusion is that a range of methods and models can be used for estimating the various types of damage that might result from antitrust infringements. The choice of approach will depend on the details of each case, and particularly on the

---

[26] See, for example, Hendry and Clements (2004), which notes that 'the combination of individual forecasts of the same event has often been found to outperform the individual forecasts' (p 1).

[27] If the biases are all in the same direction, combining forecasts would not eliminate them, but nor would it exacerbate it them. Thus, combining forecasts can be expected to reduce biases in general, since at least some elements of the biases across models are likely to be in different directions.

availability and quality of data and information, and the basis of the counterfactual. In any given case, it may well be possible to apply more than one approach. The primary focus in any particular case would normally be on whether specific methods or models have been applied appropriately. The court can then either identify a preferred model for the case, or 'pool' a selection of reasonable and robust model results to arrive at a final damages value.

10.5.6 METHODS AND MODELS TO QUANTIFY OTHER FORMS OF HARM

Other forms of harm from antitrust infringements, such as loss of quality or choice, can also be quantified, although this is often more complex than estimating the overcharge, lost volumes, or lost profits. In many cases the methods and models described in this chapter can be used, but in others different types may be required. For example, evidence from surveys can be used to estimate consumers' willingness to pay for certain product attributes, such as enhanced features or quality of service, which may have been affected by an infringement (see also Chapter 2). In such cases, evidence from questions about what consumers would do if offered certain choices is combined with data on what they actually do, in order to produce estimates of consumers' valuation of product attributes.[28] This may even be undertaken for product attributes that do not actually exist in the marketplace, but that may have existed in the counterfactual. In this way, the effect of the infringement on product attributes such as quality may be quantified. An example of where this has been applied (outside the context of damages actions) is in estimating how much consumers are willing to pay for the different attributes of a taxi service, such as driver quality and vehicle type and cleanliness, in assessing the impact on consumer welfare of taxi regulation (Oxera, 2003b).

10.6 COMPARATOR-BASED APPROACHES: CROSS-SECTIONAL

10.6.1 MAIN FEATURES OF CROSS-SECTIONAL COMPARISONS

Comparator-based approaches estimate the counterfactual using data from sources that are not affected by the specific infringement or any other similar infringement. There are three sources of comparison: cross-sectional comparisons across product or geographic markets; comparisons over time (eg, prices in the same market but before or after the infringement period); and comparisons over both time and cross-sections, known as difference-in-differences. This comparator class of models is intuitively appealing in that they use information from actual transactions in markets where there

---

[28] See, for example, Hensher et al. (2005).

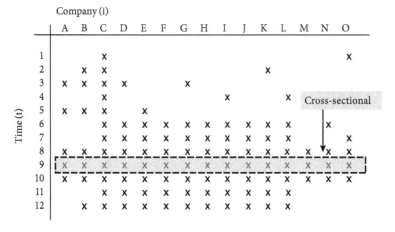

Fig. 10.7 Example of cross-sectional data

Note: The Xs represent data observations. The cross-sectional dataset highlighted here contains data observations across companies A to O for one period only—period 9.

Source: Oxera et al. (2009).

is no infringement. A possible problem with comparator models is that they effectively assume that all of the difference between the factual and estimated counterfactual relates to the presence of the infringement. This assumption might bias the estimated effect of the infringement if there are other factors that coincide with the presence of the infringement but that are not accounted for. This bias can be mitigated by including those other causes as additional explanatory variables in the model.

Cross-sectional models aim to estimate the effect of the infringement by comparing data in the relevant market with data from other markets not affected by the infringement. Pure cross-sectional models do not take into account the effects of data over time and are ideally based on data which is all from the same time period (eg, a specific month or year), such as the data in Figure 10.7.

Once appropriate comparators have been selected, a comparison can be made between the factual (ie, data from the market involved in the infringement) and the counterfactual (data from unaffected markets). Figure 10.8 provides an example— the price in the cartelized market is €12 while the average price in comparator markets is €10, implying that the overcharge is around €2.

10.6.2 CHOICE OF COMPARATOR

As noted before, cross-section comparisons can be made between companies, between product markets or between geographic areas. In *Conwood v US Tobacco*, a monopolization case in moist snuff (dipping tobacco), the plaintiff's expert compared market

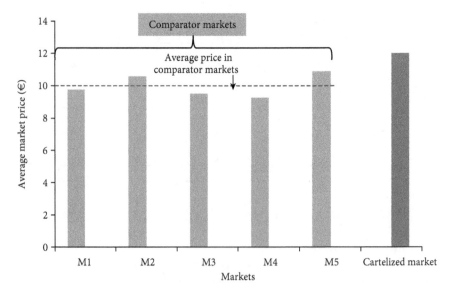

Fig. 10.8 Example of a cross-sectional comparison
Source: Oxera et al. (2009).

shares in different US states where no exclusionary practices had taken place, and in the related market for loose-leaf tobacco, in which the defendant was not active.[29] In *Apollo Theater Foundation v Western International*, an expert for the plaintiff used a range of past exclusive trademark licence fees from other firms and markets to estimate reasonable royalty rates in patent disputes, which were then used to calculate the counterfactual licence fees.[30] The ideal cross-sectional comparison includes data from only the relevant market and data from unaffected groups that are otherwise similar. If a regional infringement had the effect of increasing prices nationally, comparing data from two regional markets within the country would give a biased estimate of the damage since the comparator groups would be 'contaminated' by the effect of the infringement. In a case relating to a German paper wholesales cartel, both the higher regional court and the German Federal Court of Justice felt unable to use cross-sectional comparisons between cartelized and other regional markets for paper wholesaling for the purposes of estimating the overcharge because they were concerned that there was some evidence of cartels existing in all or most of the regional markets, and that these markets were therefore possibly affected by the cartel as well.[31]

The strength of a cross-sectional comparison lies in how like-for-like the comparison is and how many of the differentiating factors have been controlled for in the modelling.

---

[29] *Conwood Co v US Tobacco Co* 290 F 3d 768 (6th Cir. 2002).

[30] *Apollo Theater Foundation Inc v Western International* (02 Civ 10037 (DLC)), United States District Court of New York, 5 May 2005.

[31] *German Paper Wholesale Cartel* (German Federal Court of Justice, 19 June 2007).

In a US case concerning a refusal to deal with a prospective purchaser of the Chicago Bulls basketball franchise by the Chicago stadium owner, the claimant's expert calculated the counterfactual fair market value of the Chicago Bulls franchise using the recent sales prices of comparable National Basketball Association franchises.[32] Factors considered in the comparability of the franchises, and ultimately accepted by the court, included the size of the home city, the degree of population growth in the home city, the city's interest in basketball, and whether the franchise was an 'expansion' franchise. Likewise, in the *Conduit* case in Spain involving exclusionary practices by the telephony incumbent, the court considered it acceptable to take the UK market as a reference in calculating the claimant's lost market share in Spain, given the similarities between the two markets (although the damage estimate itself was not accepted by the court).[33]

10.6.3 TECHNIQUES USED IN CROSS-SECTIONAL COMPARISONS

Several estimation techniques can be employed to derive the counterfactual price using cross-sectional comparators, ranging from the simple to the more sophisticated.

A relatively simple comparison of averages uses the average price in an unaffected comparator group as an estimate for the counterfactual price. If there are five comparator markets with an average price of €10 (as in Figure 10.8), €10 is a simple estimate of the price that would have prevailed in the relevant market in the absence of the infringement. This price can then be compared with the actual price charged in the relevant market—eg, €12—to estimate the overcharge (€2, or 16.7% of the cartel price in this example). The measure of the average price could be the arithmetic mean, median or the modal price in the comparator market. The arithmetic mean is calculated by dividing the sum of all observations (here price points) by the number of observations. The median price is identified such that 50% of the companies in the comparator group charge a price below this median price and 50% charge above it. In other words, it is the price charged by the middle-ranked company. The modal price is one that is observed the most in the comparator group, and hence is the 'most common' price in the market. The choice among the three measures would depend on the nature of the market and the pricing pattern (ie, the distribution). In a market with ten companies, if nine companies charge €10 and one charges €25, the modal (or median, as they are the same in this example) price of €10 might be a more accurate representation of the market price than the mean price of €11.50.

Whichever metric is used, the counterfactual price can then be compared with the actual price charged in the market with the infringement in order to calculate the overcharge. If there is sufficient data on prices, a statistical test can be undertaken to check whether the counterfactual price is significantly different (in the statistical sense) from the actual price charged. Testing for statistical significance—and making the

---

[32] *Fishman v Estate of Wirtz* 807 F 2d 520 (7th Cir. 1986).
[33] *Conduit Europe SA v Telefónica de España SAU* (Madrid Commercial Court, judgment of 11 November 2005).

results of the tests transparent—is good practice in economics and statistics. It helps in understanding the uncertainty surrounding an estimate and informs about how much weight should be placed on the analysis. A statistical test accounts for the variation in the prices in the comparator group while testing whether the actual price in the market in which the infringement occurred is similar to the average price in the comparator group. One such test is the t-test, which is a standard test for statistical significance. If the variance of prices in the comparator group is large, even if the factual price in the market concerned is greater than the average price in the comparator market, the difference may not be statistically significant, in which case it cannot be treated as a robust finding. To continue with the above illustration, if the factual price was €12 and the average of the comparator markets was €10 then the overcharge may be estimated to be €2. However, the weight placed on this estimate of the overcharge may depend on the uncertainty surrounding the estimate of the counterfactual. If the confidence interval (which is determined through the t-test and indicates the range that contains the true value with, for example, 95% certainty) ranges from €5 to €15, less weight might be placed on the analysis than if the confidence interval suggests a range of €9 to €11.

Regression (econometrics) techniques are a more sophisticated statistical method that can explain the variation in data using other factors (we discussed some of the basic principles of regression in Chapter 2). These techniques address one of the main short-comings of simple comparisons of averages by controlling for differences in market or firm characteristics in the relevant and comparator markets. Among the possible models, ordinary least squares (OLS) regression is widely used for such purposes. OLS draws a 'line of best fit' across a chart with all observations, which minimizes the squared distance between the actual observation and the predicted value (see Figure 2.8 in Chapter 2 for an illustration).

When a regression technique is used for the estimation of damages, the analysis will be based on an implicit or explicit equation such as the stylized example below, which uses firm-level data from the infringement market and the comparator market. On the left-hand side of the equation is the variable to be explained, in this case price—thus, the variable Y_i represents the price of firm i. On the right-hand side are all the variables that can explain price. Thus, X_i includes characteristics of the firm or its market, such as input costs, product quality, and size—these are factors other than the infringe-ment that may influence price, and hence should be controlled for. D_i is the 'dummy' variable which is equal to one if firm i belongs to the market where the infringement takes place, and is equal to zero if the firm belongs to the comparator market—this is the variable of main interest to the analysis—and e_i is the error term we explained in Chapter 2.

$$Y_i = \alpha + \beta X_i + \delta D_i + e_i$$

The model can be estimated when sufficient datapoints are available for all the Y and X variables (the D values are taken directly from what is known about the infringe-ment). The regression analysis seeks to identify the statistical relationship between these variables. The parameters estimated in the model are an intercept term (α),[34] the relationship between the characteristics of the firms in the market (X_i) and the price (β), and the estimated size of the overcharge effect (δ). The coefficient of main interest in this regression is δ (linked to the variable of concern D_i), which represents the average change in price due to the fact that a firm belongs to the market where the infringement has taken place. This technique then assumes that any difference between the markets, given other factors X_i, is due to the infringement. The main (technical) assumptions behind this model specification are that the relationship between Y and X is linear; that the impact of the infringement is a constant amount across all firms (i); and that the errors (e_i) are uncorrelated with X_i or D_i with a mean of zero.

In essence, this approach is similar to a simple comparison of average prices, but it allows, at least in part, the isolation of that element of the difference in prices which is due to the anti-competitive conduct and not due to other factors, such as differences in firm size or product quality. Regression analysis, where it is feasible, generally leads to more robust results than simple price comparisons.

10.7 COMPARATOR-BASED APPROACHES: TIME SERIES

10.7.1 MAIN FEATURES OF TIME-SERIES COMPARISONS

The alternative—and perhaps most commonly used—source of a comparator is data over time. Although this approach is often described generically as 'before and after', it is appropriate to make an explicit distinction between three types of comparison that can be made using time-series data. First, before and during—an unaffected period before the infringement can be compared with the period of the infringement. Second, during and after—an unaffected period after the infringement can be compared with the period during which the infringement took place. Third, before, during and after— both comparisons can be made if data before and after the infringement is available. These variants have been used in many damages cases. In two German cases, the courts used the price after the termination of the cartels to estimate the overcharge and the consequent loss incurred by the claimants.[35] In *Apollo Theater Foundation v Western International*, a US case, the costs and advertising revenue trends from a period before the infringement were used to calculate projected revenues and costs for the infringement period, in order to estimate damages for lost profits (this case also used cross-section comparisons, as discussed in section 10.6).[36]

---

[34] If all the other variables on the right-hand side of the equation are zero, the variable on the left-hand side takes the value of this intercept term. This should not be interpreted as a base price, since any systematic error in the data or modelling across all observations will end up in this term.

[35] LG Dortmund 0 55/02 Kart *Vitaminkartell III*, 1 April 2004, and Oberlandesgericht Düsseldorf, *Berliner Transportbeton I*, KRB 2/05, 28 June 2005.

[36] *Apollo Theater Foundation Inc v Western International* (02 Civ 10037 (DLC)), United States District Court of New York, 5 May 2005.

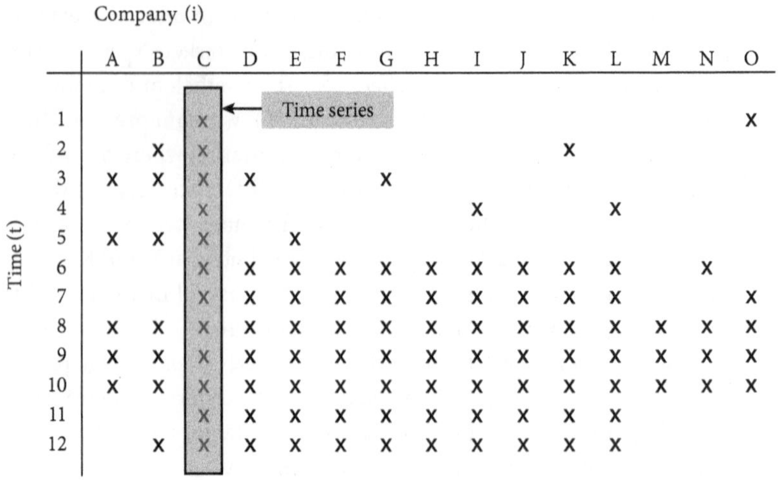

Company (i)

Time (t)	A	B	C	D	E	F	G	H	I	J	K	L	M	N	O
1			X												X
2		X	X									X			
3	X	X	X	X			X								
4			X					X				X			
5	X	X	X		X										
6			X	X	X	X	X	X	X	X	X		X		
7			X	X	X	X	X	X	X	X	X				X
8	X	X	X	X	X	X	X	X	X	X	X	X	X	X	X
9	X	X	X	X	X	X	X	X	X	X	X	X	X	X	X
10	X	X	X	X	X	X	X	X	X	X	X	X	X	X	X
11			X	X	X	X	X	X	X	X	X				
12		X	X	X	X	X	X	X	X	X	X				

(Row 1, Company C: "Time series" ← arrow)

Fig. 10.9 Example of time-series data

Note: As in Fig. 10.7, the Xs represent data observations. The time-series dataset highlighted here contains data observations across all periods 1 to 12 for only one company—company C.

Source: Oxera et al. (2009).

Figure 10.9 shows what time-series data might look like for a company (C) that is the subject of a damages claim.

10.7.2 CHOICE OF COMPARATOR

Ideally, time-series comparisons should be made using information from both pre- and post-infringement periods so that more information is used (which increases the likelihood of robust findings), and the model has to fill in the gap only for the period in between. Having data for the periods both before and after the infringement is advantageous in 'anchoring' the predicted prices for the infringement period with known data points. Both pre- and post-infringement data have advantages and disadvantages. One of the advantages of post-infringement data is that it covers a more recent period (at the time of the analysis), and is therefore more likely to be available. Another advantage is that it may be easier to identify a reasonably precise date at which the infringement ended—for example, dates cited in the competition authority's infringement decision. Using post-infringement data may have some drawbacks, however. It may take some time for the cartel behaviour to unwind fully and for the market to return to competitive pricing (eg, knowledge of business secrets revealed during the cartel period may persist). One of the advantages of pre-infringement data is that the market equilibrium that it represents is not contaminated by the existence of the cartel. However, it may be difficult to ascertain when the infringement began, and indeed there may not have been a clear-cut starting point. A further disadvantage is that the pre-infringement period is, by definition, historical, and it may therefore be more difficult to obtain data or the data that is available may be of poor quality compared with post-infringement data.

Time-series data has the advantage that the comparison involves like-for-like companies or markets since it refers to the same companies or markets in both the factual and counterfactual cases. A possible problem with time-series models is that they effectively assume that all of the unexplained differences between the time periods can be attributed to the infringement. As far as possible (and as with the cross-sectional comparators discussed in section 10.6), other drivers of the variable under consideration should be controlled for to ensure that the difference between the periods is not biased by any external factors (see below).

Data over time often displays characteristics not seen in cross-sectional data. For example, there may be a seasonal trend or serial dependence (autocorrelation) in time-series data, which means that a high value now (at time = t) is likely to be associated with a high value tomorrow (t+1). This is a potential problem since such patterns may be associated with the difference between the factual and counterfactual. More advanced time-series models can control for such patterns.

Time-series comparisons can sometimes be used by claimants to provide support for their argument on causation where a clear pattern is observed. For example, in the *LePage's* monopolization case in the USA, the court found that the 'impact of 3M's discounts was apparent from the chart introduced by LePage's showing that LePage's earnings as a percentage of sales plummeted to below zero—to negative 10%—during 3M's rebate program', and was satisfied that LePage's had 'introduced substantial evidence that the anti-competitive effects of 3M's rebate programs caused LePage's losses'.[37] Another relatively simple during-and-after comparison was made in a damages action before the Regional Civil Court of Graz in Austria that had followed on from a 2005 judgment by the Austrian Cartel Court, which imposed fines of €75,000 on five driving schools for price fixing.[38] The Cartel Court found that, for a period of two months, the schools had charged identical prices for the most popular driving courses, which was an infringement of the Austrian Cartel Act. The claim was brought by the Bundes-arbeitskammer (the Federal Chamber of Workers) on behalf of customers of the driving schools who had suffered damage as a result of the cartel. The Bundes-arbeitskammer argued that the loss suffered by customers could be quantified as the 22% difference between the price charged by the driving schools for the two months of the cartel's duration (which was identical for the cartel members) and the lower price once the cartel had ended (based on an average price calculated at that time). The court accepted this calculation.

---

[37] *LePage's Inc v 3M* 324 F 3d (3d Cir. 2003).

[38] *Bundesarbeitskammer v Powerdrive Fahrschule Andritz GmbH*, Landesgericht für Zivilrechtssachen Graz (Regional Civil Court of Graz), 17 August 2007.

10.7.3 TECHNIQUES USED IN TIME-SERIES COMPARISONS

Time-series models can be univariate ('pure') or multivariate. A univariate time-series model does not attempt to formulate a behavioural relationship between the variable under consideration (eg, price) and other potential explanatory variables (eg, costs). Instead, the historical pattern of the relevant variable itself is used as a predictor of its own future values. A multivariate time-series model, on the other hand, includes other explanatory variables and assesses the relationship between them to predict the relevant variable. Some of the main techniques for this group of comparators, from the simplest to the increasingly sophisticated, are the following.

Comparisons of averages are similar to those described under cross-sectional comparisons. The average price in the market concerned during the infringement period is compared with that in a period without the infringement, which is taken as an approximation for the counterfactual price (the Austrian driving school cartel is an example). This counterfactual price can be the average price from before or after the infringement period. As before, a statistical test (eg, a t-test) can be conducted to determine whether the difference is statistically significant and, if so, the difference can be interpreted as representing the overcharge.

Interpolation involves joining the price points before and after the relevant period to indicate what the prices would have been in the intervening period. In its simplest form the connecting line will be linear, as in the example in Figure 10.10, which is (loosely) based on a cartel damages case we have worked on. The top line shows the development of actual prices paid by the claimant. The starting point of the cartel is the date when, according to the European Commission's infringement decision, the first meeting between cartel members was held. The starting price for the interpolation is based on an average actual price in the months before this start date. The end price is an average actual price in the months after the Commission's dawn raids took place and the cartel broke down (the actual price plummets at about that time). The dashed line between these points shows the counterfactual price according to the interpolation exercise. More sophisticated versions of interpolation can incorporate seasonal patterns if that is a feature of the market. Figure 10.10 incorporates a different adjustment, namely one for exchange rate movements, since in this case the cartel fixed prices in one European currency and the claim related to prices in another currency which had devalued during the cartel period. This results in a new counterfactual line, as shown in the figure. It can be seen that the price increase (and later decrease) due to the exchange rate movement explains a small part of the price increase that took place at the start of the cartel, but there is still a significant overcharge effect.

ARIMA (autoregressive integrated moving average) is a widely used pure time-series technique. Rather than simple interpolation it uses the pattern of past values of the variable under investigation to forecast its future values. Figure 10.11 illustrates this technique with an example based on an exclusionary conduct case we have worked on. Historical sales volumes of the claimant (a competitor to the infringing party) are modelled using ARIMA, the results of which are then used to forecast volumes during the period of the infringement—October 2002 to January 2007 in this example.

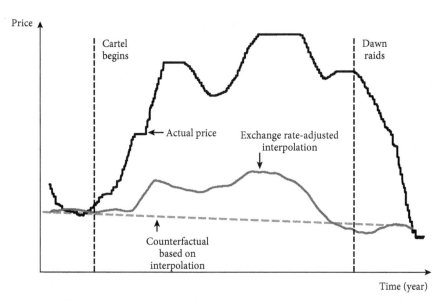

Fig. 10.10 Example of interpolation to determine the counterfactual (prices before, during, and after the cartel)

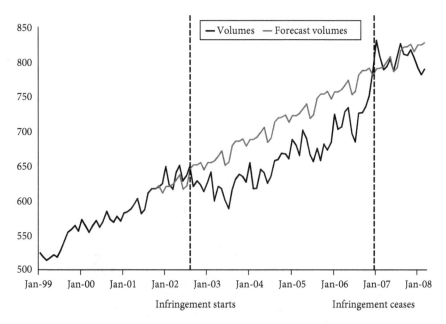

Fig. 10.11 Example of forecasting using an ARIMA model (sales volumes of a competitor before, during, and after an exclusionary abuse)

Note: The forecast volumes can be interpreted as the counterfactual volumes.

Source: Oxera et al. (2009).

The forecasts act as estimates of the counterfactual volumes, which can then be compared with actual volumes to estimate the harm resulting from the infringement (if lost volumes are estimated in this way, they would have to be multiplied by the relevant profit margin per unit in order to determine the lost profit of the claimant). If the comparison is between a period during the infringement and a period after, the process can be reversed such that the model backcasts (as opposed to forecasts) to the start of the infringement (in this example, the ARIMA modelling was on past data, but the figure also shows what happened after the infringement, which served as a cross-check of the results).

10.8 COMPARATOR-BASED APPROACHES: DIFFERENCE-IN-DIFFERENCES

The difference-in-differences technique aims to avoid some of the shortcomings of cross-sectional and time-series approaches, in particular the assumption that any unexplained difference is due solely to the infringement. Difference-in-differences estimators assess what would have happened without the infringement by examining what changed over time for the infringement and non-infringement markets, followed by a comparison of those differences. This technique requires data both over time and across infringement and non-infringement markets. Figure 10.12 illustrates the type of data required, often referred to as panel data.

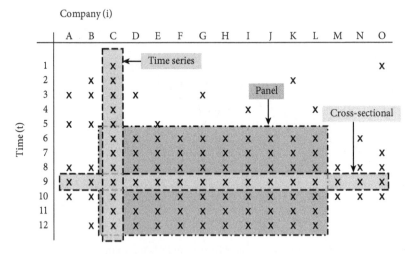

Fig. 10.12 Example of panel data used for difference-in-differences analysis

Note: As in Figs 10.7 and 10.9, the Xs represent data observations. The panel highlighted here contains data observations across periods 6 to 12 and companies C to L.

Source: Oxera et al. (2009).

The estimation techniques for panel data are similar to those often used for evaluating clinical trials and the effect of policy choices, in that one group has a 'treatment' applied to it (the infringement) while another that is not treated is used as a control group.[39] The difference-in-differences analysis then compares what happens to each group before, during and after the treatment. By using the control group, the analysis removes the impact of any changes that affect both treatment and control groups. Such changes would have introduced a bias in the time-series-based damages estimate.

Figure 10.13 illustrates how the difference-in-differences estimator can be determined. This technique uses the average price in the treatment group (ie, the infringement market, A) in the period before the infringement, and the corresponding averages for B (infringement market during the infringement), C (non-infringement market before), and D (non-infringement market during). The difference (B − A) reflects the change in prices in the market concerned before and during the infringement, while (D − C) reflects that in the comparator market. Not all of (B − A) may be due to the infringement, since the prices may have changed even without the infringement. This change can be assumed to be equal to that in the comparator market as reflected by (D − C). The difference in the differences in the average prices, ie, (B − A) − (D − C), is therefore used to identify separately the change in prices in the relevant market that is due to the infringement.

Conceptually, the difference-in-differences technique is an improvement on pure cross-sectional and time-series models since it exploits the variations over time as well as across firms. This increased variability helps in the estimation of the effect of the infringement, and can also account for certain factors that might affect prices in the

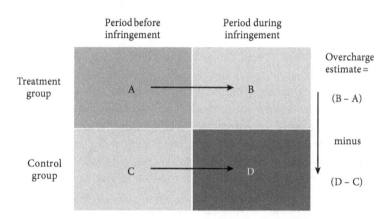

Fig. 10.13 Example of difference-in-differences model (prices for the treatment and control groups, before and during the cartel)

Source: Oxera et al. (2009).

---

[39] See, for example, Krum et al. (1994), and Card and Krueger (1994).

two markets. The data requirement for a difference-in-differences model is greater than that for an equivalent cross-sectional or time-series model since it effectively combines the two approaches.

10.9 APPROACHES BASED ON FINANCIAL ANALYSIS

10.9.1 THE DATA IS THERE; THE TOOLS ARE THERE

A lot of financial data exists, and is used on a daily basis by companies and investors to make business and investment decisions. Companies listed on a stock exchange produce statutory accounts and other periodic financial reports (unlisted ones may also have public accounts). Such accounts are normally audited, which makes the information less likely to be challenged on a factual basis in the context of a damages action. At the very least, data from public accounts can serve as a starting point or cross-check of more detailed analyses. Data from public accounts is not always immediately usable (eg, it may refer to a company as a whole, while the damages action refers only to one product or division within the company). However, most companies will use management accounts of some form for internal purposes, and those accounts will often contain more detailed and directly relevant financial information. Finally, financial markets generate a wealth of data on company share prices and other prices that can be of relevance for financial analysis of damages, such as interest rates and yields on debt securities. It is good practice to use all this financial data in a damages action where it is available and relevant.

The economics and finance literature has developed a range of tools and techniques for analysing this data, and these can be used for damages estimations. In damages cases there is not always a clear-cut distinction between finance and non-finance methods, since a form of financial analysis is often involved at some stage. In some cases, finance methods provide the core of the analytical approach employed in the counterfactual—for example, when using profitability analysis, which involves comparing factual returns (of claimants or defendants) with an appropriate counterfactual benchmark (eg, returns of comparators), to estimate the damage directly. In other cases, financial analysis tools can be used to address specific issues such as discounting to convert the factual–counterfactual comparisons over time into a final estimate of the damage.

Some of the financial-analysis-based approaches can be seen as one form of application of comparator-based approaches as described above, as counterfactual values are also often derived from comparator markets or time periods. The key feature of financial-analysis-based approaches is the choice of the indicator for which the counterfactual scenario is estimated. While the comparator-based approaches discussed previously are used to estimate a specific counterfactual parameter such as price, volume, or market share, the financial-analysis-based approaches are concerned with estimating indicators of financial performance, such as profitability, which can then be translated into the value of the damage.

Financial methods can also be used to construct counterfactual prices or profits by assessing information on the cost of production, cost of capital, and profit margins of the relevant market participants. This application of financial methods is different from the methods discussed thus far as it does not use comparators from other markets or over time, but rather derives the counterfactual according to a combination of theory, assumptions, and empirical information on the market itself. The market-structure-based approaches discussed in section 10.10 share this methodological feature.

10.9.2 THE ROLE OF FINANCIAL ANALYSIS IN THE COUNTERFACTUAL STAGE OF DAMAGES ESTIMATION

Financial analysis can be used in several ways. First, the deterioration in the financial performance of claimants as a result of the infringement can provide an estimate of the harm caused to them. Second, the improvement in the financial performance of the defendant as a result of the infringement can provide an estimate of the benefits derived from the infringement. From a legal perspective, this is not a direct basis for determining compensatory damages, but in certain circumstances it may be used to inform the valuation of the damage suffered by the victims of the infringement (eg, in cartel cases). Various techniques can be used for both types of analysis of financial performance—in particular, profitability analysis and valuation. A relevant benchmark would need to be identified for both, reflecting the profitability in the counterfactual. Finally, the counterfactual price level can be estimated by assessing the cost of production of the infringing parties, and combining this with information and assumptions on counterfactual profit margins. The approach generates a counterfactual price per unit by estimating the cost that a company operating in the counterfactual market would incur and adding to this a return that reflects the degree of competition in the counterfactual.

10.9.3 FINANCIAL PERFORMANCE OF CLAIMANTS

The damage incurred as a result of the infringement will in many cases be reflected in the observed financial performance of the claimant. The financial performance of a company would be expected to be adversely affected in the event that it is exposed to an overcharge from its suppliers or to an exclusionary abuse from a competitor. Hence, a comparison of the claimant's actual financial performance with the financial performance that would be expected in the absence of the infringement can be used to provide an estimate of the damage. Financial performance is usually measured in terms of either profitability—using a measure that relates the absolute profit (revenue minus cost) to the level of investment, assets, or sales of the business—or company valuation. Valuation is closely related to profitability, since valuations of assets are usually based on the expected profits that can be achieved with those assets.

In Chapter 3 we discussed the various measures of profitability that can be used for analysis of market power, and the same principles apply to using profitability in the context of quantifying damages. In short, these measures include: the net present value

(NPV), internal rate of return (IRR), return on capital employed (ROCE), return on sales (ROS), gross margins, and industry-specific measures (eg, in the case of credit institutions, margins over cost of debt). The NPV technique involves discounting the cash flows for a business or activity that are spread out over time in order to obtain the NPV. The IRR is the discount rate that results in a zero NPV. In theory, it is appropriate to use the NPV and IRR to measure profitability because these techniques reflect the principles of investment valuation that underpin investment decisions. Specifically, economic activities typically show a pattern of initial investment followed by a stream of net revenues or cash inflows. Profitability of an activity can be described as the net increase in value due to that activity, realized over time. The IRR and NPV take into account the cash inflows and outflows of an economic activity over time and the time preference of money (see also section 10.12).

As explained in section 10.3, from a legal perspective it is not always necessary for a claimant that has suffered from an overcharge to explicitly make the link between the overcharge and its own financial performance. Therefore, the approach of using the financial performance of the claimant to estimate damages is in practice more likely to be employed in exclusionary infringement cases where claimants have suffered a negative effect on profit.

One example is the (partly successful) damages action before the Versailles Court of Appeal in France, where an excluded competitor claimed damages for lost profit based on its financial performance.[40] This followed on from a July 1998 decision by the French Competition Council, which found that the defendants had deliberately delayed the communication of information to the claimant necessary for it to conduct its activities in the market for media services. Since this information could not be obtained from any other source, the Competition Council concluded that the defendants' conduct contributed to raising barriers to entry, thus constituting a breach of the French law equivalent to Article 101. The claimant sought to recover damages as a result of loss of clientele (€828,103) and damages resulting from the difference between the business plan and its actual financial results (€2,027,571). The court considered that while the claimant was entitled to recover damages as a result of its loss of clientele, the quantum of those damages should be reduced due to the claimant's lack of knowledge of the business area in which it was starting up. The court therefore awarded only €100,000 to compensate the claimant for the lost opportunity to penetrate the market more quickly (it provided no explanation as to how it arrived at this figure). Moreover, it rejected the claim for damages resulting from the difference between the claimant's expected business plan and its actual financial results, considering that since loss of clientele and the non-attainment of expected profits are one and the same loss, they can be compensated only once.

Another example is the exclusionary conduct case before the Court of Appeal of Milan, where the Italian competition authority had concluded that Telecom Italia

---

[40] *SA Verimedia v SA Mediametrie, SA Secodip, GIE Audipub*, Cour d'Appel de Versailles, 12ème chambre, section 2, arrêt no 319, 24 June 2004.

abused its dominant position by preventing the claimant from entering the market for services for closed user groups.[41] The claimant wished to provide a service that would have linked the telephone exchanges between its customers' offices using a network infrastructure exclusively composed of switching nodes and dedicated lines leased from the defendant. The claimant was to pay the defendant a fixed charge for the lease of dedicated local and trunk lines, while its own customers would pay for the use they actually made of the lines. However, it was found that the defendant refused to lease the lines required to link the offices of the claimant's customers. In order to quantify the claimant's actual losses, lost profits, and loss of opportunity, the court appointed an independent group of experts. The experts were able to calculate the claimant's actual losses on the basis of documented costs that the claimant had incurred. In relation to lost profits, the experts took into account a business plan drawn up by the claimant, but considered the projected figures relating to the acquisition of new customers to be too high. Moreover, they considered that the claimant's future expansion would have been limited by the fact that it had not made sufficient investments in publicity and other promotional activities, by the lack of sales staff, and by the significant delays between the signing of new contracts and the activation of the service. Similarly, as regards loss of opportunity, the damages sought by the claimant were significantly reduced as the experts considered that the claimant's argument that it would have availed itself of significant first-mover advantages was doubtful, because there were no barriers to entry into that market and because it would have been difficult for the claimant to ensure customer fidelity and thus substantial profit margins.

10.9.4 FINANCIAL PERFORMANCE OF DEFENDANTS

Similar types of analysis can be applied to value damages on the basis of the financial performance of the defendant, given that the benefits of infringement may be expected to be reflected in this performance. For example, an excessive price charged by a producer engaged in a cartel or an exploitative abuse would be paid by the buyer of the products. Hence, compared with the counterfactual, a certain cash flow would be transferred from the buyer (claimant) to the producer (defendant). Therefore, the financial performance of the producer would be expected to be better than in the absence of the overcharge. The value of the transferred cash flows may provide an estimate of the damage suffered by the claimant (see also section 10.10 on the relationship between the illicit gains and the cartel overcharge).

Although in the case of exclusionary abuses the same direct relationship between the profits of the claimant and those of the defendant does not usually exist, the financial performance of the defendant can still be used to value the damage in some cases. Specifically, it can be used to value the business opportunity exploited by the defendant from which a competitor claimant was excluded. In this context, it is useful to consider

---

[41] *Telystem SpA v SIP SpA* (now Telecom Italia SpA) (Milan Court of Appeal, December 1996).

the US Chicago Bulls franchise case again, as referred to earlier (*Fishman and Illinois Basketball v Wirtz*), where the defendant excluded the claimant from the ability to acquire an asset by refusing to enter into a contract for provision of supplementary services. Fishman and Illinois Basketball Inc. (the unsuccessful bidders for the franchise) brought an action against the Chicago Professional Sports Corporation (the successful bidder), its shareholders, William Wirtz (the owner of the Chicago stadium), and others for refusing to contract with Illinois Basketball Inc. for the lease of the stadium and hence foreclosing competition in the market for the franchise. In this case, the actual financial performance of the defendant was considered in the damages quantification. The value of the damage to the claimant was calculated as the value of cash flows generated by the defendant from the Chicago Bulls franchise over a given period.

Another example is the action before the Danish Supreme Court in relation to an exclusion case where the financial performance of the defendant was considered in the determination of the harm caused to the competitor claimant.[42] De Danske Statsbaner (DSB) is the state-owned train and ferry operator which owns Gedser Harbour and operated ferry transport services to Germany. As the owner of the harbour, DSB collected harbour fees from another ferry operator, GT Linien, for the use of the harbour. However, it did not collect fees for the use of the harbour by its own vessels since these were exempt from this duty under Danish law. On appeal, the Danish Supreme Court upheld an earlier Eastern High Court judgment, which found that DSB had abused its dominant position in the market for ferry transport between Denmark and Germany by collecting harbour fees from GT Linien without charging such fees to its own vessels, and that GT Linien was entitled to recover damages. In quantifying the damages, the court based its estimate in part on reconstructed accounts of Gedser Harbour prepared on the claimant's behalf, since the defendant was an integrated port authority and did not produce separate accounts. The case then involved a detailed consideration by the court of the financial evidence. While the claimant argued that it should be entitled to recover DKK25 million (around €3.3 million), the court agreed with the defendant that the reconstructed accounts did not sufficiently take into account depreciations, reserves set aside for investments by the port, and interest on its invested capital. The court therefore awarded the claimant only DKK10 million (€1.3 million) in damages.

10.9.5 IDENTIFYING THE RELEVANT COUNTERFACTUAL BENCHMARK FOR PROFITABILITY ANALYSIS

Where the damage is estimated using the claimant's profitability, it is necessary to identify and estimate the appropriate counterfactual returns in order to derive the effect on profitability. Where the defendant's profitability is assessed to provide information on

---

[42] *GT Linien A/S (under bankruptcy—subsequently GT Link A/S) v De Danske Statsbaner DSB and Scandlines A/Sn (formerly DSB Rederi A/S)* UFR 2005.2171H (Danish Supreme Court).

the harm to the claimant in a cartel overcharge case, it is equally necessary to identify and estimate the appropriate counterfactual returns. (In exclusion cases, such as the US and Danish examples given above, the defendant's profitability may in itself form the basis for the counterfactual, ie, the profitability that would have been achieved by the claimant.)

There are a number of candidates for an appropriate counterfactual benchmark. In the context of profitability analysis, one potential counterfactual benchmark is the cost of capital (ie, the minimum returns required by providers of capital to a business). This benchmark assumes that in the absence of the infringement the claimant or defendant would earn the cost of capital. In theory, the cost of capital reflects a rate of return that a company would be expected to earn in competitive markets; if the company fails to earn this rate of return, investors will not commit capital to it. Hence, the cost of capital may in certain circumstances be used as a basis for the counterfactual minimum profitability of a claimant in exclusion cases. If the claimant's factual profitability is below the cost of capital (or if it is zero because the claimant has been excluded from the market completely), and it is demonstrated that this is due to the exclusionary infringement, it may be determined that in the absence of the infringement the claimant would have earned (at least) the cost of capital, and hence the harm is estimated as the difference between the factual returns and the cost of capital.

On the other hand, if companies earn more than the cost of capital, this would in the longer run be expected to encourage new entry into the market, thus reducing returns to the cost of capital. However, this is not to say that the cost of capital necessarily represents the counterfactual in cases where the concern is about excessively high returns (eg, where the high returns of defendants are used to quantify harm to victims in a cartel overcharge case). First, the counterfactual market structure can be different from perfect competition, and hence companies can be expected to earn a return above the cost of capital even in the absence of the infringement. The market-structure-based approaches described in section 10.10 show how different economic models of competition may be used instead of the perfect competition model to determine the counterfactual. Second, the description above of how companies' returns tend towards the cost of capital in competitive markets usually applies over a longer-term period; counterfactual returns can be above the cost of capital in competitive markets if a short time period is considered (eg, there may be windfall gains due to macroeconomic factors, or profits may be temporarily high in innovative markets)—we also saw this in Chapter 3, which discusses the use of profitability as an indicator of market power.

Instead of using the cost of capital, counterfactual profitability can be determined on the basis of returns earned by comparator companies. Comparators may be drawn from the same industry in which the claimant or defendant operates (but this may have to be from the industry in a different geographic market if there is a possibility that the comparator information is 'contaminated' by the infringement), or from other industries with similar risk characteristics and market structure. The use of comparators as a benchmark for profitability is common in financial analysis. In the context of competition law damages, a hypothetical example would be a cartel in a minerals industry in which four companies operate globally. The profitability of the cartel members over the cartel period can be measured and then compared with the returns made by companies in another minerals industry that has similar risk characteristics and a similar number of competitors. The difference in profitability can then be taken as one approximation of the excess returns made as a result of the cartel.

10.9.6 BOTTOM-UP COSTING ANALYSIS TO ESTIMATE THE COUNTERFACTUAL PRICE

This technique involves estimating the counterfactual price on the basis of bottom-up analysis of the costs and required returns of the claimant or defendant. Typically, it uses an accounting approach that involves adding a mark-up to the unit cost of the product to obtain a counterfactual price. This mark-up could be measured as an absolute increase or a percentage profit margin on the costs. The resulting counterfactual price is compared with the factual price to obtain the per-unit value of the overcharge by the defendant, or undercharge by the claimant.

An example of where this approach was used is the exclusionary conduct case before the Düsseldorf Higher Regional Court.[43] This stand-alone damages claim was brought by a direct competitor of the defendant who had been bidding for the supply of gas to a particular client. Despite having offered the lowest price for the supply of gas, the claimant lost the bid because the defendant had threatened the client with an increase in its district heating price if it were to source gas or electricity from other suppliers. The court considered that the defendant's conduct constituted an abuse of a dominant position in the district heating market and ordered it to cease this practice. It also awarded damages corresponding to the claimant's lost profits in relation to this particular contract, amounting to around 5% of supply costs. The court stated that the claimant provided detailed information about its own supply costs; that it was able to prove that at that time it would have been able to supply the contracted amount of gas; and that under normal circumstances a 5% profit margin would have been expected.

Several practical issues come up when carrying out a bottom-up costing analysis, and may be overcome through pragmatic means. One relates to the averaging of costs over ranges of output. It is often reasonable to estimate the per-unit cost of the product by dividing the total costs of the relevant business activity of the defendant or claimant by the total volume sold. A mark-up is then applied to the estimated cost to obtain the counterfactual price. To give a stylized example, if a company sold 1,000 units of its product in one year, and its total cost for the year was €300,000, the per-unit cost would be €300. If these were sold with a gross margin of 10% (reflecting, for example, the profit margins made in comparable competitive markets), this would result in a counterfactual price of €330. This price can then be compared with the factual price.

---

[43] OLG Düsseldorf, urteil vom 16.4.2008 VI-2 U(Kart) 8/06—*Stadtwerk* (Higher Regional Court of Düsseldorf).

Another practical issue arises where the infringing party's costs may be 'too high', ie, the actual costs incurred by the defendant may be different from the counterfactual costs incurred by a firm operating in a more competitive market. The defendant may generate costs inefficiently due to a lack of effective competition in the market. Likewise, the defendant may restrict output below that which would be expected in a competitive market, and may therefore not benefit from any economies of scale that are present in the industry (ie, per-unit costs would fall if production were expanded to the competitive level). It may therefore be necessary to make an adjustment to the defendant's cost data when undertaking cost-plus analysis in order to deal with these problems. For example, by making comparisons with the costs incurred by a comparator firm (at either a disaggregated or aggregated cost level), it would be possible to identify the level of inefficiency present in the defendant's business. A downward efficiency adjustment may then be made to the per-unit costs estimated for the defendant. Alternatively, the extent of economies of scale in the industry may be estimated and an adjustment made to the per-unit cost estimates to account for the economies of scale that the defendant company has not exploited. However, using unadjusted costs will still usually provide a lower limit for the value of the damage since the adjustment would typically make costs lower, and hence damages higher (in cases where defendants' overcharges are estimated in this way).

10.9.7 FINANCIAL MULTIPLES

Another example of comparator-based approaches for quantifying damages based on financial analysis is the application of financial multiples to estimate the counterfactual value of the business. Value drivers such as revenue, units of production, book value of assets, and cash flows can be used to calculate the multiple for comparable firms or for the industry in question. This multiple can then be applied to the claimant or the defendant to obtain the counterfactual value of the firm and the lost value (ie, damage). Multiples are widely used for valuation by a range of financial practitioners. For example, most valuation reports by brokerage firms contain a separate section on the valuation of companies based on multiples. Financial covenants on debt are also often linked to multiples, and there are a number of antitrust damages cases where valuation of the damage involved a version of multiples analysis.

One example of the application of multiples analysis is to value the damage as a multiple of the reduction in revenues. This involves estimating a ratio of value to revenues for suitable comparator companies (or that ratio observed historically before the infringement) and applying it to the estimated reduction in revenues. Thus, if the estimated reduction in revenues in one period is €100, this can be converted into the value of the damage by multiplying it by the ratio of 'value to revenues' observed for similar companies—if this multiple is 15, the resulting estimate of the damage would be €1,500. This example assumes that the infringement has a permanent effect—ie, the revenues of €100 are lost every year over a very long time period. In many cases the effect of infringements will diminish over time, and this would need to be accounted for.

An advantage of multiples analysis is its ease of application. It requires only a single period's (eg, one year) revenues or profits lost due to the infringement and the appropriate revenue or profit multiple (an appropriate discount rate is implied in the multiple for comparators). The value of the multiple can be estimated according to market data for listed companies with similar risk exposures and growth prospects.

10.9.8 CONSISTENT TREATMENT OF TAXATION AND INFLATION

An important aspect in applying financial analysis is the consistent treatment of different components of the quantification such as taxation and inflation. The appropriate treatment of taxation of compensation for damages will depend on the applicable legal rules in the relevant jurisdiction. There are two general considerations in this respect. First, the approach to damages quantification—should quantification be undertaken on a pre-tax or post-tax basis? Second, taxation of the compensation for damages—should compensation be awarded net or gross of potential taxes that a claimant might pay once it receives the compensation?

The damage can be quantified on a pre- or post-tax basis. Under the former, pre-tax lost profits should be discounted at the appropriate pre-tax discount rate. Under the latter, post-tax lost profits should be discounted at the post-tax discount rate. In the absence of the infringement, the claimant would have to pay taxes on the profit it would have made. Hence, if the objective of the award of damages is to return claimants to the position they would have been in on a post-tax basis, the quantification of damages should be undertaken on a post-tax basis. Alternatively, if the award of damage compensates the claimant on a pre-tax basis (ie, without taking into account the avoided taxes on the profits that would have been made), damages should be quantified on a pre-tax basis.

Once the appropriate compensation for damages is estimated and awarded to the claimant, it may be taxed by the respective authorities. Hence, the question arises of whether the compensation for damages should take into account the impact of this subsequent taxation. Again, the exact treatment of tax will depend on the specific legal framework concerned.

In relation to the treatment of inflation, the financial analysis can be developed in either real (ie, adjusted for inflation) or nominal terms. Under the first approach, real lost profits should be discounted at the real discount rate; under the second approach, nominal cash flows should be discounted at the nominal discount rate. The resulting estimate of the damage should be the same under both approaches, provided that the underlying assumptions are consistent. Real and nominal values can usually be transformed from one to the other by applying appropriate inflation indices—either general price indices or more sector- or product-specific indices. From a practical perspective, it may be useful in this context to consider past effects on profits separately from expected future effects on profits. Past reductions in profits are typically estimated in nominal terms because the factual scenario is observed in nominal terms; therefore, it may be more practical to apply the quantification approach for past profits in nominal terms. Future effects on profits could be projected in both real and nominal terms.

10.9.9 WHICH PROFIT MARGIN SHOULD BE USED WHEN ESTIMATING DAMAGES?

Profit margins are often an important input into the quantification of damages. For example, they are relevant in lost-profit claims based on lost-sales estimations—the lost sales need to be multiplied by some average counterfactual profit margin per unit in order to get to the lost profit. As discussed above, bottom-up costing approaches to estimating the counterfactual price also require adding a 'reasonable' margin to the costs. Moreover, the market-structure-based approaches—discussed in section 10.10— rely on price–cost margins as an important parameter.

Conceptually, margins aim to reflect the profitability of the business and are usually expressed as the percentage of revenue available after accounting for various measures of marginal costs. They can also be expressed as a ratio of profits to the total revenue of the business. Another important conceptual issue here is the choice of timeframe of the analysis. In the short run, the profit margin earned by a firm on each additional sale is typically higher as a larger proportion of costs are fixed and invariant to extra output—we also saw this in Chapter 4. In the longer run, more costs become variable (eg, additional production facilities could be built, or existing ones closed), meaning that longer-run margins are typically lower than short-run margins.

In general, statutory accounts, which consist of a profit and loss statement and a balance sheet, can be used to obtain data for estimating a selection of useful margin figures. Similarly, management accounts, which normally provide a more detailed breakdown of various accounting measures by region and division, can be used to obtain margins for specific parts of the business. Figure 10.14 presents a stylized profit and loss statement from statutory accounts, along with an illustrative example, and describes some of the types of margins that could be useful to quantify damages.

Profit margins can typically be classified into three broad categories—gross margin, operating margin, and net margin—as shown in the figure and also in Table 10.2. The choice of margin often depends on the specific variable that you are interested in. In a cost-plus analysis, the margin used depends on the nature of costs being analysed. If the counterfactual cost of goods sold is being measured or estimated, gross margin is often added to these costs to obtain the relevant price, whereas if all operating expenses and non-operating costs are cumulatively estimated, net operating margin is generally used. The choice of margin also depends on the nature of the business. To identify relevant comparators for a business in a capital-intensive industry, it might be more appropriate to focus on the gross margin since the net profit could vary substantially according to the treatment of depreciation. Similarly, in an industry where businesses are particularly labour-intensive, pensions may be an important form of cost and may be treated as a non-operating expense. To capture the effect of

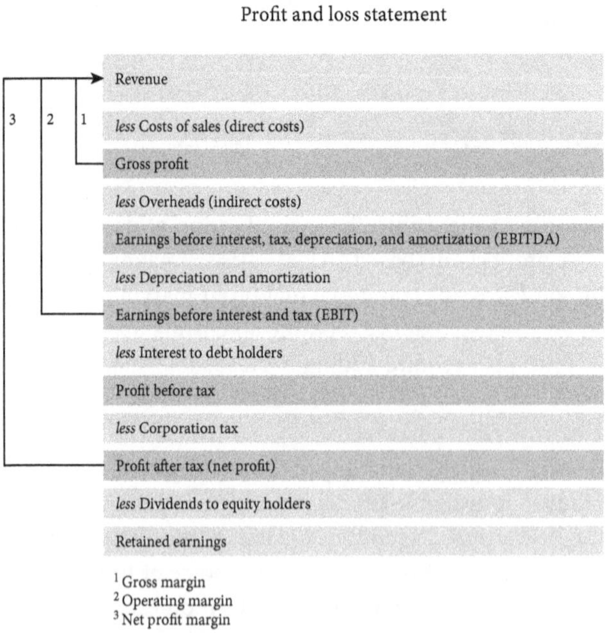

Profit and loss statement		Numerical example	
			€
Revenue		Revenue	100
less Costs of sales (direct costs)		Cost of sales	−40
Gross profit		Gross profit	60
less Overheads (indirect costs)		Overheads	−20
Earnings before interest, tax, depreciation, and amortization (EBITDA)		EBITDA	40
less Depreciation and amortization		Depreciation	−5
Earnings before interest and tax (EBIT)		EBIT	35
less Interest to debt holders		Interest	−10
Profit before tax		Profit before tax	25
less Corporation tax		Tax	−5
Profit after tax (net profit)		Profit after tax	20
less Dividends to equity holders		Dividends	−10
Retained earnings		Retained earnings	10

[1] Gross margin
[2] Operating margin
[3] Net profit margin

Fig. 10.14 Stylized example of margin information in statutory and management accounts

Note: Retained earnings are the part of net profits that is held back by the company rather than being distributed to the owners as dividends.

Source: Oxera et al. (2009).

such costs on profitability, the net operating margin will often be considered, since gross margins may fail to account for such costs.

10.10 APPROACHES BASED ON MARKET STRUCTURE AND INDUSTRIAL ORGANIZATION THEORY

10.10.1 WHAT ARE MARKET-STRUCTURE-BASED APPROACHES?

As you have seen in various places in this book, IO theory has developed a range of models of competitive interaction and firm behaviour that predict a variety of outcomes, from the least competitive (monopoly) to the most competitive (perfect competition). As explained in this section, these models can be used to estimate or simulate market outcomes (prices and volumes) in either the factual or the counterfactual scenario, or both. The use of IO models in damages estimations can range from the purely theoretical—where models are used to understand certain market dynamics conceptually—to the empirical—where they are calibrated for the actual market in question in order to estimate counterfactual values of the relevant variables. As with some of the

Table 10.2 Types of margin and their relevance (examples linked to Fig. 10.14)

Formula	Numerical example	Description
Gross profit margin		
(revenue – direct costs) / revenue	(100 – 40) / 100 = 60%	Illustrates the profit that a company generates from its core activities, per unit of revenue—eg, in the IO two-model approach, a gross profit margin is often used to estimate the cartel overcharge (see section 10.10)
Operating profit margin		
(revenue – direct costs – indirect costs) / revenue	(100 – 40 – 20 – 5) / 100 = 35%	Represents the proportion of the company's revenue that remains after accounting for direct and indirect costs, but before accounting for taxes and interest payments. For example, in the cost-plus approach, if both direct and indirect costs are estimated, the operating profit margin could be added to these costs to estimate the counterfactual price
Net profit margin		
(revenue – direct costs – indirect costs – interest payments – tax) / revenue	(100 – 40 – 20 – 5 – 10 – 5) / 100 = 20%	Reflects the proportion of revenue that is available to the investors or equity holders as dividends or for retention of earnings—eg, net profit margin is useful for cost-plus analysis when all forms of costs (direct, indirect, depreciation, interest payments, and tax) are estimated. A net profit margin could be added to this sum to obtain the counterfactual price

Source: Oxera et al. (2009).

financial-analysis-based approaches discussed in section 10.9, these market-structure-based approaches differ from the comparator-based ones (sections 10.6 to 10.8) in that they employ a combination of theoretical models, assumptions, and empirical estimation (rather than comparisons across markets or over time) to arrive at an assessment of the counterfactual. IO models also provide useful theoretical insights into the issue of pass-on of overcharges, as discussed in section 10.11.

In between perfect competition and monopoly—which we discussed in Chapter 1—the most common IO models are those of monopolistic competition, Bertrand oligopoly, and Cournot oligopoly (we discussed these in Chapter 3 as well). In monopolistic competition a large number of producers sell differentiated (rather than homogeneous) goods, so that they compete on product characteristics in addition to price.

The differentiation from rivals gives producers some ability to set their own price above marginal cost (hence the term 'monopolistic', which in this respect may be somewhat misleading as there are many competitors). Oligopoly models represent rivalry among the few—ie, markets where the number of competitors is sufficiently low that they recognize the mutual interdependence of their actions. In the homogeneous Bertrand model, firms set price (as opposed to quantity), and assume that the price of the other firms remains unchanged. An important assumption of the model is that each competitor can capture the entire market if it sets prices below those of its competitors (there are assumed to be no capacity constraints). This produces the outcome that all firms price at marginal cost (which is the outcome achieved in perfect competition) since any price above marginal cost will be undercut. In contrast, in Bertrand oligopoly with differentiated goods, when a firm increases its price it does not lose its entire sales since some buyers will have a preference for the characteristics of the good. Similarly, when a firm reduces its price, it does not gain the entire market. As a result, price will be above marginal cost.

The standard Cournot oligopoly is a market with homogeneous goods and a relatively small number of firms that set their quantity (or capacity) before making the pricing decision. Each competitor assumes that the quantity produced by competitors will remain constant, and will set its own quantity as a monopolist of the residual demand. This results in prices above marginal costs—by how much will depend on the number of competitors (the more firms there are, the lower the price, which is intuitive). The assumption about what firms expect their rivals to do can be varied in this model (this is known as 'conjectural variation'). The standard assumption as described above is that firms do not respond to quantity changes by others. This can be changed to expectations that quantity changes will be fully met by rivals at one extreme (which will result in a monopoly outcome since firms are reluctant to raise output) or, at the other extreme, that changes will be fully offset by rivals (ie, if one firm increases its quantity, it expects others to reduce their quantities proportionately; this results in an outcome resembling perfect competition as firms keep increasing output in the mistaken belief that the others will back off). Another variation on the standard Cournot model is to assume that products are differentiated rather than homogeneous.

The highest prices and the lowest quantities result if a market is monopolized. In contrast, perfect competition and Bertrand price competition in a market with homogeneous goods lead to the lowest prices and the highest quantities. Cournot oligopoly leads to prices and quantities in between perfect competition and monopoly levels. Similarly, Bertrand price competition in a market with differentiated goods leads to an intermediate outcome in terms of prices and quantities, and largely depends on the number of firms or products in the market and the degree of differentiation between them. For the purpose of quantifying damages, these theoretical results already provide some relevant insight for damages estimations—if the counterfactual for a cartel damages case is assumed to be Cournot competition between the cartel members, the counterfactual price will be higher (and hence the estimated overcharge lower) than if the counterfactual is assumed to be homogeneous Bertrand competition.

10.10.2 SELECTING THE MOST SUITABLE IO MODEL

The choice of model is important, given that the outcomes can vary significantly depending on the assumptions adopted. As noted previously, for any given factual situation where a cartel or other infringement has led to an increase in price, the more intense the competition is assumed to be in the counterfactual, the higher the estimated damage from the infringement (as the counterfactual price is lower when competition in the counterfactual is fiercer). The basis for the choice of model should be a consideration of how closely the market type and features of the affected market compare with the structure of, and assumptions behind, each model. If companies compete on price, the most relevant models of competition may be perfect competition, Bertrand oligopoly, or monopolistic competition, since in these models firms compete on price. If companies compete by setting quantities or pre-commit to a certain capacity, Cournot oligopoly would be more appropriate. If prices are formed via auctions, an appropriate model of auctions may be most relevant.

Legal precedent on the use of oligopoly models in damages actions is relatively limited, but highlights the importance of careful model choice for damages claims. In *Concord Boat Corporation v Brunswick Corporation*, a US case that we also discussed in Chapter 4, the expert on the plaintiff's side applied the Cournot model to determine the counterfactual.[44] Under the standard Cournot model with two identical firms in the market, the model predicts that each firm will have a 50% market share. The expert used this as the counterfactual and calculated damages for all periods when the defendant possessed more than 50% market share. This particular use of the Cournot model was criticized by the court on the basis that the model had not been adjusted to take into account differences between the quality of the two suppliers' products, or external shocks that could have led to the defendant possessing a market share of more than 50% in the counterfactual.

Another example is the European lysine cartel case (not a damages action before a court but an infringement decision by the European Commission), where one of the companies subject to investigation had used a simulation of a simple Cournot model for the counterfactual.[45] It then estimated the counterfactual price using cost and elasticity estimates from existing studies. The company also relied on a dynamic model, suggesting that the entry of a new competitor in the market had undermined the stability of the cartel. The European Commission considered the conclusions of the Cournot model results to be sensitive to the assumptions made—in particular, those on cost structures and elasticities of demand. The Commission also rejected the arguments of the cartelist based on the dynamic oligopoly model, stating that cartels can be stable with many more competitors.

---

[44] *Concord Boat Corporation v Brunswick Corporation* 207 F 3d 1039 (8th Cir. 2000), 24 March 2000.
[45] *Amino acids* (Case COMP/36.545/F32001/418/EC), 7 June 2000.

10.10.3 IS THE CARTEL OUTCOME CLOSE TO MONOPOLY?

In cartels, a monopoly assumption may sometimes be adopted to represent the factual scenario, the rationale being that firms in a market typically aim to maximize profits. When they join a cartel the companies effectively coordinate output and prices to try to jointly maximize profits. The highest profit that can be made is the monopoly profit. Thus, well-organized and effective cartels may be able to approach the optimum price and output levels consistent with this maximum profit level.

Yet there are several reasons why joint profit maximization by a cartel may not succeed and therefore not lead to monopoly profits, prices, and output levels. Cheating within the cartel may lead to higher overall output levels and lower prices compared with the joint profit-maximizing target. Coordination problems could prevent the companies from making monopoly profits. Moreover, actions by suppliers outside the cartel and variable demand conditions may destabilize the cartel's coordination efforts. Empirical studies show that these factors are often responsible for the breakdown of a cartel (Levenstein and Suslow, 2004).

Another question in this regard is: are prices seen during the periodic price wars that occur in some cartels close to the counterfactual competitive outcome? An important finding in economic theory is that periodic bouts of deviation and punishment, taking the form of sharp falls in prices, can be expected even in well-functioning cartels (Green and Porter, 1984). The answer to the question is not clear-cut. At the very least, the level of prices in those periods gives an indication of how low competitors in the market are prepared to go, but such prices may not necessarily be sustainable in a competitive situation in the absence of the cartel, or may exceed the competitive price.

This question was addressed in the paper wholesalers cartel case before the German Federal Court of Justice.[46] This judgment did not concern the quantification of damages, but rather related to the estimation of an overcharge by a cartel in the paper wholesale sector. At that time, German competition law required fines to be based on an estimate of actual overcharges, which were usually reviewed by courts. Following a finding of illegal price agreements and infringement of Article 101, wholesalers involved in the cartel were fined €57.6 million by the German competition authority in 2004. The cartels spanned ten regions in Germany from 1995 to 2000 and charged higher prices to smaller customers. The Federal Court of Justice disagreed with the method used by a lower court to estimate the overcharge in this case, which consisted of comparing the cartel price with the price charged by parties which were attempting to undercut the cartel price. The court found that such undercut prices could not serve as a reference for the competitive market price since they were still dependent on the cartel price. It considered that the prevailing price after the price cuts was likely to be much higher than the competitive price, and therefore that this method would underestimate the overcharge. In the absence of comparable reference markets, the court was of the view that the counterfactual price for estimating the overcharge should be

---

[46] *German Paper Wholesale Cartel* (German Federal Court of Justice, 19 June 2007).

established by way of an overall economic analysis, preferably with the help of an independent expert. The judgment suggested a bottom-up costing approach (in line with the method described in section 10.9), whereby an average profit margin—informed by comparator markets—is added to costs and adjustments are made for buyer power and market structure. The judgment also stressed the importance of cross-checking the results of an analysis by using other methods such as a comparison with a non-affected market segment or product market (in this case, the market segment of large customers), or the pricing behaviour in the relevant market after the end of the infringement.

10.10.4 USE OF IO MODELS IN DAMAGES ESTIMATION

As discussed in Chapter 7, competition authorities use IO models in merger control to simulate post-merger outcomes which, like damages counterfactuals, are unknown. In damages cases, IO models are combined with market data—the factual—to estimate demand and supply, which can then be used to determine market outcomes in the counterfactual (in a way, this is like merger simulation in reverse; in damages cases the counterfactual has more competition than the factual, while for merger cases the opposite is true).

In practice, the degree to which the theoretical IO models are calibrated can vary. At one extreme, very little actual data is used and the analysis relies mainly on the theoretical models to simulate or predict market outcomes in terms of prices or volumes. At the other extreme, all main parameters of the theoretical model are estimated using actual data. In practice, the analysis will normally try to estimate some of the key parameters of the model (such as the sensitivity of demand to price), and rely on assumptions for the other parameters. Modelling of the factual supply and demand, and making use of data on the factual market outcomes (such as prices and quantities), enables the estimation of (the relevant part of) the demand curve. Combining this knowledge with an IO model for the counterfactual supply, such as perfect competition or Cournot oligopoly, enables the simulation of the counterfactual price and quantity. The resulting damages estimate will be influenced to a large extent by the choice of the counterfactual model, which determines the counterfactual supply curve, as well as the shape of the demand curve. In particular, as noted above, the more competitive the model adopted for the counterfactual, the further apart the factual and counterfactual supply curves, and the greater the difference between the factual and counterfactual prices and volumes.

IO models can also provide the basis for sense checks of the results obtained through another quantification method. If there is evidence to suggest that the counterfactual market structure has the characteristics of perfect competition or Bertrand oligopoly with homogeneous goods, the theory suggests that the cartel overcharge can be expected to equal the cartel members' price–cost margin (since in competitive markets firms would set prices close to cost). If the counterfactual market structure is more like standard Cournot oligopoly, the overcharge can be approximated by reference to the cartel members' price–cost margin and the number of firms in the market.

Take the example of a cartelized four-firm market. The factual might be a monopoly model and the counterfactual might be modelled using Cournot oligopoly. A comparison of price outcomes under the two IO models enables a rough approximation of the possible overcharge. If the cartel price–cost margin was 20%, the cartel overcharge would theoretically have been 12%; if the cartel margin was 40%, the overcharge would have been 24%. These results are derived from a formula for the cartel overcharge where the factual is monopoly and the counterfactual an N-firm Cournot oligopoly—the formula is m times (N – 1) divided by (N + 1), where m is the cartel margin (this formula assumes linear demand and symmetric, constant marginal costs). So with four firms, N is 4, and with a margin of 20%, the result is 0.2 times (4 – 1 = 3) divided by (4 + 1 = 5), which equals 0.12 or 12%. According to this formula, the overcharge increases as the number of firms in the counterfactual increases (because more firms implies a more competitive counterfactual), and as the cartel profit margin increases (because there is more profit margin to be 'competed away' in the absence of the cartel). These results are based on a comparison with a factual characterized as a monopoly. As noted above, cartels may not be as effective at raising prices as a monopoly. If this is the case, the above formula will tend to overestimate the size of the overcharge, but can still be used as an upper bound when sense-checking the results from other approaches.

10.10.5 IS THERE A RELATIONSHIP BETWEEN ILLICIT GAINS AND THE CARTEL OVERCHARGE?

Another theoretical insight that has some practical use in damages cases concerns the relationship between illicit gains and the cartel overcharge. Overcharge harm is the additional payment (ie, the increase in price resulting from the cartel) made by the cartel's customers to cartel members. Therefore, if the formation of a cartel does not lead to a cost increase among cartel members, these additional payments result in an increase in the cartel members' profits, which is in theory equal to the additional payments made by all customers. Hence, when a cartel includes all industry members, the total illicit gain (ie, the additional profit resulting from the cartel overcharge) is equal to the total additional payments made by direct customers. This is represented as area A in Figure 10.1 at the beginning of this chapter.

It is important to establish the correct counterfactual when calculating the illicit gain. Although the comparator-based models do not require a specific assumption about the type of competition in the counterfactual market (they do assume that the comparator is not cartelized), the financial-analysis-based and market-structure-based models do. As discussed earlier, the choice of the counterfactual may have a substantial impact on the damages estimate. In particular, assuming a more competitive market than that which would have existed in the counterfactual can lead to overestimation of the illicit gains and hence overcharge harm, just as assuming a less competitive market can result in an underestimate. It should also be borne in mind that the cartel may have resulted in inefficiencies (such as overinvestment). This may be reflected in lower cartel profits, but would not imply that the overcharge harm is any lower than in the case of cartelists achieving full illicit profits. (This is a separate argument from that of cartelists failing to earn full illicit profits due to being unsuccessful in raising prices—in this latter case there is no overcharge harm.)

While this approach involves estimating the illicit gain earned by the cartelists, from a legal perspective it is not equivalent to awarding restitutionary damages (ie, an award assessed by reference to the defendant's gain rather than the claimant's loss). Instead, this approach is designed to result in compensatory damages (ie, damages that compensate a claimant for loss suffered as a result of wrongdoing) by taking advantage of the fact that the overcharge gain of the cartelist may in many ways be equal to the overcharge loss of the direct buyers. Various EU Member States explicitly or implicitly allow for the gains of the party infringing competition law to be used in the assessment of the compensation due to the harmed party. In the *Devenish* case in the English High Court, the claimant's expert noted that, in this case, 'compensatory and restitutionary damages are likely to be identical'.[47] German law explicitly states that the illicit gain may be used as an element of estimating the overcharge—indeed, it also gives guidance on how the illicit gain should be calculated:

> The profit is basically calculated by subtracting the cost of services rendered and the net operating costs incurred from the revenue of sales. Overhead or other operating expenses, which would have been incurred even in the absence of anti-competitive behaviour, are not deductible. When there are multiple harmed parties only the proportional gains are taken into account. The proportion shall be determined by the gain from the antitrust violation against the harmed party or from the subsequent contracts with the victim.[48]

In Denmark lost profits may also be established by considering the infringing party's 'improvement of business volume', as well as the decline in the harmed party's business. Similarly, in Sweden, it has been stated that the level of profit made by the infringing party may serve as a guide to the calculation of compensatory damages (Möllers and Heinemann, 2007).

10.11 INSIGHT INTO THE PASS-ON OF OVERCHARGES

10.11.1 THE PASSING-ON DEBATE

This section focuses on how to quantify pass-on. It does not go into detail on the extensive policy debate about whether the passing-on defence should be allowed—this defence means that purchasers or competitors who have suffered harm in the form of higher costs are not entitled to damages if they have passed the higher costs on to their

---

[47] *Devenish Nutrition Limited & Ors v Sanofi Aventis SA & Ors* [2007] EWHC 2394 at [76].
[48] Deutscher Bundestag (2004), 'Entwurf eines Siebten Gesetzes zur Änderung des Gesetzes gegen Wettbewerbsbeschränkungen', Bundestagsdrucksache 2004, 15/3640, relating to s 33(3) of the German Competition Act (GWB).

own customers in the form of higher prices. In the USA, where case law on antitrust damages is more developed than in other jurisdictions, relatively few cases have dealt with the issue of quantifying pass-on, since this has been ruled out as a defence by the federal courts, and only direct purchasers can claim cartel damages (although a number of US states do allow indirect purchasers to claim damages).[49] Economic incentives have played a role in this policy decision—it is perceived that direct purchasers are best placed to file a claim as they will generally have the best information available and may also be more likely to have the resources to make a claim (at least compared with end-consumers), so ruling out the passing-on defence gives direct purchasers better incentives to file claims.

In Europe, the general view is that, in line with the compensation principle, the passing-on defence should be allowed and indirect purchasers are allowed to claim for damages as well. Damages may arise anywhere along the supply chain, potentially all the way down to end-consumers. One theoretical insight is that, in most circumstances (see exceptions below), the sum of harms from the total overcharge at the cartel layer of the chain—area A in Figure 10.1—that is suffered at each layer of the supply chain cannot exceed A. There can be no double-counting of the harm (which in legal terms would result in a form of unjust enrichment by some parties in the chain). For example, if it is found that direct purchasers of the cartel have passed on 75% of A, and their respective customers have passed on 90% of their price increase to end-consumers, the direct purchasers have suffered a harm equal to 25% of A, their customers a harm of 7.5% of A (75% of A but with 90% of that passed on), and end-consumers 67.5% (90% of 75% of A), such that the total along the supply chain adds up to 100% of A. By the same token, however, the total overcharge harm caused to the rest of the chain is still area A, so if, legally, all parties at different layers further down the chain found some way of making a joint claim or distributing the damages amongst themselves, theoretically area A is still the right amount to claim for.

10.11.2 PASS-ON IN THEORY—THE RELATIONSHIP BETWEEN PRICES AND COSTS IN VARIOUS MODELS

Economic theory has identified relatively straightforward relationships between cost changes (such as changes in input costs) and price changes. In essence these relationships follow from the standard models of competition, oligopoly and monopoly, in which there is a certain relationship between price and marginal cost. In all these models, companies are assumed to maximize their profit given a certain level of marginal costs and the degree and nature of competition they face. The resulting equilibrium prices in these models can be expressed as a function of marginal cost (eg, in perfect

---

[49] *Illinois Brick Co v Illinois* 431 US 720 (1977); and *Hanover Shoe Inc v United Shoe Machinery Corp* 392 US 481 (1968).

competition, price equals marginal cost). These results can then be used to infer what happens to price if costs change.

Cost pass-on refers to the proportion of a cost change that is translated into a change in the final price. It can be represented by two measures. First, the percentage pass-on rate, which measures the absolute change in price expressed as a percentage of the absolute change in the marginal cost—if costs increase by 10 units and the price increases by 5 units, the pass-on rate would be 50%. Second, the pass-on elasticity, which gives the percentage change in price divided by the percentage change in marginal cost—if costs increase by 20% and the price increases by 15%, pass-on elasticity would be 0.75. Both measures have the same theoretical basis and are closely related. However, the percentage pass-on rate is more straightforward to determine and interpret. It fits together with the conceptual framework for determining the overcharge harm, as set out in section 10.4 (and in particular Figure 10.1). The percentage pass-on rate can be applied directly to the total overcharge A, which is determined in line with that conceptual framework. For example, if the overcharge is €3 million, and the pass-on rate is 50%, €1.5 million of the overcharge has been passed on.

A distinction must be made between firm-specific and industry-wide cost increases. Under the conditions of perfect competition, an overcharge that affects all competitors in a downstream market (industry-wide) would be passed on in full. If you find this result counterintuitive, you are not alone—most lawyers and business people would agree with you: 'my market is highly competitive, surely I cannot pass on any cost increase?' But it simply follows from the fact that, under perfect competition, prices equal marginal costs. All downstream firms that remain in the market therefore see no change in profit level—economic profit remains zero as prices equal marginal costs. (The cost increase could of course lead to a reduction in downstream output or to the exit of a number of downstream suppliers, which may give rise to a different kind of damages claim from the overcharge effect.) In contrast, for a cost increase that affects only one, or some, of the competitors in those markets, the expected pass-on rate would be 0%, since those competitors that do not face the increase can leave their prices unchanged. This may also be the case if, for example, an entire industry is affected by the overcharge, but that industry competes with another industry that uses a different upstream input not subject to the overcharge and that can therefore leave its prices unchanged. For example, sugar and high-fructose corn syrup compete in many downstream markets but use different inputs, so may be affected by upstream cartels in different ways. Likewise, an upstream cartel operating only in Europe may distort downstream competition if European purchasers compete with non-European producers unaffected by the cartel, and therefore cannot pass on the cartel input price. This step in the damages analysis will therefore often require a careful definition of the downstream product and geographic markets and an assessment of competition in the market.

Another well-known theoretical finding is that a monopolist with linear demand and constant marginal cost passes on exactly 50% of the cost increase. You may also find this result counterintuitive, since the monopolist would seem to have obvious reasons to pass on cost increases in full (or to not pass on any cost decreases). The reason, however, is related to the notion of profit maximization—if costs change, so does the profit-maximizing price.

Figure 10.15 illustrates the logic of pass-on in perfect competition and monopoly. It is based on the same demand and marginal cost curves as you saw in Chapter 2 (where it related to women's designer shoes; let's say this figure represents demand and costs for car tyres now). Marginal cost per unit equals 2. If tyre manufacturing were perfectly competitive, the price would be 2 and output 8. If there were a monopolist, the price would be 6 and output 4. Now a cartel in synthetic rubber causes the marginal costs of tyres to rise from 2 to 4. You can see that in perfect competition, the new price is 4 and output 6. So the cost increase resulting from the cartel is fully passed on to the price of tyres—hence no overcharge harm to tyre manufacturers that have purchased from the cartel (the tyre output decrease from 8 to 6 constitutes a different type of harm—a volume loss—which may have been reflected in certain tyre manufacturers going out of business or simply selling less, but is generally more difficult to claim in practice). In monopoly, marginal costs now equal marginal revenue where output is 3. The new price is 7. So the cost increase of 2 units has resulted in a 1-unit price increase from 6 to 7—a 50% pass-on.

Results that are in between perfect competition and monopoly are typically obtained in oligopolistic markets. In the standard Cournot oligopoly model (with constant marginal cost and linear demand), the pass-on rate for an (average) industry-wide cost change can be expressed as N divided by N+1, where N is the number of firms.

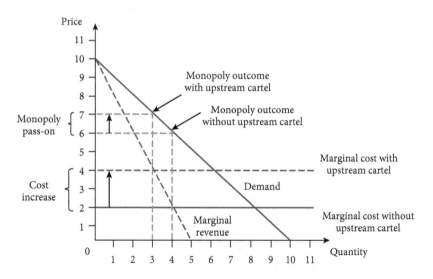

Fig. 10.15 Pass-on of cost increase

Therefore, for two firms the pass-on rate is two-thirds, while for seven firms it would be seven-eighths. The pass-on rate increases with the number of firms, which is consistent with the 50%–100% range identified above. The standard Bertrand oligopoly model with homogeneous goods has the same outcome as perfect competition, and pass-on is 100%. In the Bertrand model with differentiated goods, and in monopolistic competition, firms behave like monopolists for their own product, so with linear demand and constant marginal cost the pass-on rate would be 50%. Pass-on of cost increases that do not affect all competitors in an oligopolistic market gives rise to greater theoretical complications (ten Kate and Niels, 2005). In the Cournot model, a supplier facing a firm-specific cost increase would still remain in the market and partly pass on its higher costs, but would lose market share as a result (hence the damage it suffers is of a different nature from the overcharge; it is a form of lost profit).

10.11.3 PASS-ON IN THEORY—FURTHER INSIGHTS

In some cases the overcharge may have caused significant changes in the dynamics of competition in the downstream market—eg, smaller operators may have been forced to exit. In theory, this may give rise to a pass-on rate of greater than 100%, as increased downstream concentration may have led to higher downstream prices (although the term pass-on is not accurate in such a situation, as, in reality, a chain of events has taken place). Such factors would need to be assessed on a case-by-case basis.

In the theoretical models of competition, companies set their profit-maximizing price with reference to marginal costs. Fixed costs do not directly determine price in the same way as marginal costs, at least in the short run (in the longer run, many fixed costs tend to become variable). Therefore, a change in fixed costs due to an infringement may not be passed on in the same way. For example, if a cartel of copyright owners were to illegally fix an annual licence fee for access to the rights, downstream users of those rights may not pass on the fixed annual fee in the prices to their respective customers as this fee does not represent a marginal cost to them. However, fixed costs can influence whether a firm can viably operate in the market in the first place—ie, the margins between price and marginal cost need to be at least sufficient to recover fixed costs. An increase in fixed costs may, in the longer term, induce exit and lead the remaining firms to increase price, in which case there may be full pass-on eventually. The effect of changes in fixed costs should therefore be assessed on a case-by-case basis, and the duration of the infringement becomes an important factor to consider.

Finally, buyer power of downstream customers can influence the ability of downstream suppliers to pass on the overcharge for the upstream input. If strong buyers can credibly switch to alternatives, this may limit the ability to pass on cost increases, in line with the theoretical insights presented above. However, if buyer power has already been exercised and has meant that prices equal marginal costs, the situation may be similar to that in a competitive market where pass-on is near 100%. Again, in this situation, there may also be a volume effect that can give rise to a different type of damage from the overcharge.

10.11.4 EMPIRICAL EVIDENCE ON PASS-ON

Empirical studies on pass-on rates in antitrust damages cases are relatively rare. Other fields in the economic literature where pass-on has been studied empirically include tax incidence, exchange rate movements, and transmission of prices of intermediate goods. These fields provide some support for the insights presented here. For example, various studies have found that virtually 100% of changes in the price of intermediate inputs are passed on to the downstream price where the downstream market is highly competitive. These studies have covered, for example, petrol retailing and various agricultural products.[50] The 100% pass-on is sometimes achieved only after a lag of up to four months—ie, not immediately (which may or may not affect the damages estimate, depending on the length of the period considered—often, the longer the period, the greater the pass-on). In addition, some studies have found that the pass-on rate is higher for price increases than for price decreases. (In the standard IO pricing theory, such asymmetry does not exist, but for practical reasons prices may sometimes be 'sticky' downwards.) One US-based study found that the pass-on rate for an industry-wide cost shock in raw milk was 92%–94% in wholesale prices and 85%–87% in retail prices (Dhar and Cotterill, 1999). The study also tested separately for the effects of firm-specific cost shocks. It found that one supplier with significant market power had a firm-specific pass-on rate of 50%–60% (in line with the assumption for the monopoly level), while other suppliers with limited market power had a pass-on rate of 13%–19% (in line with the theoretical result where cost changes are firm-specific). Another US-based study on the cheese market found that pass-on rates were 73%–103% where the downstream industry competes according to the Bertrand oligopoly model (similar to the competitive outcome), and 21%–31% where the downstream industry engages in collusive pricing (similar to monopoly) (Kim and Cotterill, 2008).

Some (but not all) studies on exchange rate pass-on provide further support for the assumption regarding high pass-on rates where downstream markets are competitive. Exchange rate pass-on is conventionally defined as the percentage change in an imported good's local-currency price for a given percentage change in the nominal exchange rate. One study on the US automobile market found that the pass-on rate for Japanese cars was 15%–30% when an exchange rate shock occurred, while for German cars it was 65%–102% (Goldberg, 1995). During the period in question Japanese car manufacturers competed mainly in the small-car segment, and therefore were constrained by domestic competitors that were not subject to the exchange rate shock. Their pass-on rate was relatively low. In contrast, German car manufacturers mainly served the luxury-car segment, where there tended to be fewer competitors (and indeed this may constitute a separate market). Their pass-on rate was high.

So far, relatively few cartel damages judgments in Europe have covered the issue of quantifying pass-on. One is where a direct purchaser brought a damages action against

---

[50] See, for example, Bacon (1991).

a member of the vitamins cartel before a French court.[51] In relation to pass-on, the court held that the earlier European Commission decision and press release had stated that the cartel affected end-consumers and therefore that direct purchasers were able to pass on their cost increase. This judgment highlights the importance of pass-on, and that, logically, direct purchasers cannot have been harmed (other than through the volume effect) if it is established that end-consumers have faced 100% of the overcharge—ie, the overcharge harm must not be double-counted. However, in this particular case, it is open to question whether the Commission's statement about end-consumers being harmed was simply a general statement, and whether it was meant to imply that consumers suffered 100% of the overcharge (if not 100%, direct purchasers have presumably suffered part of the harm). In a separate damages action, another French court also rejected the claim on the basis that the overcharge on vitamins had been passed on, but for different reasons.[52] The court considered vitamins to be a small part of the finished good and that a small price increase would be sufficient to offset the overcharge. It also noted that the price of the claimant's finished good had increased by more than the prices of the vitamins, and that its sales volumes had also grown. Another damages action against the vitamins cartel was the *Devenish* case in the UK.[53] This also addressed the appropriateness of the passing-on defence, and the importance of avoiding double-counting of damages suffered by purchasers along different levels of the supply chain. One of the claimants, an indirect purchaser of vitamins, argued that its own pass-on rate was close to zero because of the purchasing power of its customers (mainly supermarkets). The courts did not conclude on the level of pass-on in this case.

Finally, in a damages action against a participant in a sugar cartel in Spain, the Provincial Court in Valladolid considered that biscuit producers in the country were affected because they compete in European markets with foreign producers who did not purchase from the cartel.[54] By implication the Spanish producers had to absorb the overcharge on sugar or else lose market share. This is consistent with the theoretical point we explained earlier in this section that if a cost increase affects only some of the competitors in the market, the expected pass-on rate would be 0%, since those competitors that do not face the increase can leave their prices unchanged.

10.11.5 THE EFFECT OF PRICING PRACTICES AND PRICE FRICTION

Certain pricing practices in the real world may mean that the theoretical pricing outcome driven by profit maximization does not apply, at least in the short run. Some companies price on a cost-plus basis, while others may have explicit contracts through

---

[51] *Arkopharma v Roche and Hoffmann-La Roche*, no RG2004F02643, Tribunal de Commerce de Nanterre (Nanterre Commercial Court, 11 May 2006).

[52] *Juva v Hoffmann-La Roche* (Paris Commercial Court, 26 January 2007).

[53] The case was heard by the High Court and subsequently appealed to the Court of Appeal. *Devenish Nutrition Limited & Ors v Sanofi Aventis SA & Ors* [2007] EWHC 2394 (Ch); and *Devenish Nutrition Limited v Sanofi Aventis SA & Ors* [2008] EWCA Civ 1086.

[54] Audiencia Provincial de Valladolid, Sentencia num. 261/2009, judgment of 9 October 2009.

which increases in input costs are agreed to be passed on in full to purchasers. On the other hand, there are industries where prices tend to be changed on an annual (or other periodic) basis, and not continually in response to cost changes. This would have to be assessed for each specific case at hand.

The extent to which a change in the cost of a particular cartelized input affects the total final-product cost and price depends on the relative size of the input cost. If pass-on is 100% and the overcharge is 20%, the final-product price increases by 10% if the input cost represents 50% of the final-product price, but only by 2% if it represents 10% of the final-product price. In other words, if the final-product price is €100, the initial input cost is €50 before the cartel and €60 during the cartel, the price increases to €110, which is 10% higher; if the input cost is only €10, the final price increases to €102. This will also have a bearing on the possible lost-volume harm suffered by the purchasers of the cartel (which will be higher the greater the importance of the cartelized input cost).

Even though in the standard theoretical models discussed above it does not matter, the magnitude of input cost may in practice influence the rate of pass-on. A variety of factors can determine this, and will typically have to be considered on a case-by-case basis. If the affected input cost makes up only a very small proportion of the final-product price, zero pass-on may occur if the affected business chooses not to reset prices. This may occur where downstream prices are set with respect to only major and more visible input costs, or where there are 'menu' costs associated with resetting and communicating the final-product price (most restaurants do not print a new menu every time the price of meat, fish, or potatoes changes). Alternatively, small changes in the input price may well be fully passed on in some circumstances if their magnitude is sufficiently small to avoid any significant demand reduction. This reasoning was used by the French court in the second vitamins case discussed above (*Juva v Hoffmann-La Roche*).

In principle, it is possible to estimate empirically the actual pass-on rates of relevance. This would require access to data on actual prices and costs at the relevant layers of the supply chain, and would usually involve econometrics techniques. Obtaining reliable results will not always be possible due to data difficulties. An alternative approach would be to empirically estimate a 'typical' pass-on rate for the industry at hand, similar to the empirical studies on pass-on described above. These 'typical' results could then be used as an approximation for pass-on in a specific case. A 'hybrid' approach would be to estimate a number of key structural parameters for the industry (in line with the structural IO approaches discussed above) and use these to populate a theoretical pass-on framework and obtain the pass-on rate that way. If, in any specific case, the above empirical approaches are not feasible due to practical reasons, the theoretical insights into pass-on presented in this section may still be useful in approximating likely pass-on effects for that case.

10.11.6 PASS-ON AND VOLUME EFFECTS

Where a purchaser has passed on (a proportion of) the overcharge it may still have suffered a volume harm resulting from that pass-on, which legally is a separate type of harm. As noted above, this harm is more likely to arise the greater is the significance of the cartelized input in the final-product price. In the USA this harm is rarely claimed for in cartel damages actions. The European Court of Justice acknowledged the possibility of such a loss-of-volume harm in the presence of complete pass-on in a 1997 judgment on port fees that were illegally levied in the French territory (this was not a competition law ruling).[55] Perhaps as a result of the passing-on defence being allowed, and used, in Europe, we are observing an increasing number of cartel damages claims that are not restricted to the overcharge but also cover harm from lost volumes.

10.12 FROM THE COUNTERFACTUAL STAGE TO A FINAL DAMAGES VALUE: INTEREST AND DISCOUNTING

A competition law infringement may have lasted many years. The counterfactual analysis may have generated an overcharge estimate in monetary terms for each year, and the yearly cash flows would have to be added up. From an economic perspective, this involves uprating and discounting cash flows to take into account the time value of money. For this you use a discount rate. Furthermore, part of the harm may be suffered even after the anti-competitive practice has ceased. Depending on the legal rules and the facts of each case, those future losses may need to be included in the damages calculation, again using discounting.

From a legal perspective, the uprating of cash flows is closely related to the application of interest to damages estimates. As noted at the start of this chapter, the compensation principle in EU law means that damages awards should also include interest. This requires moving cash flows between time periods in accordance with the legal rules (for example, from the year in which a harm occurred to the year in which the damage is paid), which in essence is a form of uprating. The principles of uprating and discounting, as set out here, also capture the application of interest, and are therefore in line with the compensation principle.

Legal rules and practices regarding the award and calculation of interest vary significantly across jurisdictions and across cases within jurisdictions. They also tend to be somewhat at odds with economic principles. One specific issue is whether the interest is simple or compound (interest on interest). Another is that various jurisdictions require statutory rates of interest rather than market rates to be used for certain periods of uprating. Some jurisdictions give greater weight to the economic principles of uprating and discounting than others. In this section we first set out those principles and then explore some of the differences between the law and the economics.

---

[55] Joined Cases C-192/95 to C-218/95 *Société Comateb and others v Directeur Général des Douanes et Droits Indirects* [1997] OJ C74/3. See, also, Joined Cases C-441/98 and C-441/98 *Kapniki Michailidis v IKA* [2000] ECR I-7145; and Case C-147/01 *Weber's Wine World Handels-Gmbh v Abgabenberufungskommission Wien* [2003] ECR I-11365 at [94].

10.12.1 UPRATING AND DISCOUNTING CASH FLOWS AND DETERMINING INTEREST

From an economic perspective, any summation or movement of cash flows over time needs to take account of the time value of money—€1 today is worth more than €1 tomorrow. This is a fairly standard approach to valuation and investment appraisal, and requires the use of an appropriate discount rate—as explained in any standard text on corporate finance.[56] Conceptually, the discount rate should take into account the time value of money, inflation, and risk. Inflation means that prices rise over time and hence the same nominal amount of money decreases in value. Future expected profits are uncertain. When calculating the value of the damage today for expected lost profits in the future, this uncertainty needs to be accounted for through the risk component of the discount rate (at least according to economic principles).

The logic of the time value of money is also captured in the legal principle of compensation. As noted by the European Commission:

> With regard to the payment of interest, the Court refers to its earlier judgment in the 1993 Marshall case. In that judgment, the Court stated that 'full compensation for the loss and damage sustained . . . cannot leave out of account factors, such as the effluxion of time, which may in fact reduce its value. The award of interest, in accordance with the applicable national rules, must therefore be regarded as an essential component of compensation'. The Court's objective is thus clearly to ensure that the victim is given the real value of the loss suffered. The reference in Manfredi to the payment of interest should therefore be understood as covering the whole period from the time the damage occurred until the capital sum awarded is actually paid.[57]

Applying interest on damages is one form of uprating cash flows in the quantification of damages. In simple terms, if an infringement has caused the victim a loss of €100 during each of the past five years, each year's loss needs to be uprated using the discount rate to determine the current value of this harm suffered. Suppose that the discount rate is 10% per year. The harm from the first of the five years (ie, the first €100) needs to be uprated five times, which is comparable to paying cumulative interest on that amount for five years. The current value of that amount is €161.05 (€100 times 1.10 to the power of 5). The harm from the second year needs to be uprated for four years (€100 times 1.10 to the power of 4, which equals €146.41), and so on. The present value of the total harm over the five years is €671.56. For simplicity, this example assumes that the cash flows occur on 1 January of each year. Another assumption is that the interest rate is compounded—ie, the calculation includes interest on accumulated interest from prior periods (see below).

---

[56] For example, Brealey et al. (2008).

[57] European Commission (2008), 'Staff Working Paper Accompanying the White Paper on Damages Actions for Breach of the EC Antitrust Rules', SEC(2008) 404, April, [187]. The cases referred to in this quote are Case C-271/91 *Marshall v Southampton and South West Hampshire Area Health Authority* [1993] ECR I-4367, at [31], and Joined Cases C-295/04 to C-298/04 *Vincenzo Manfredi and others v Lloyd Adriatico Assicurazioni SpA and others* [2006] ECR I-6619.

If it is demonstrated, and accepted by the court, that the infringement, even if it has ceased, will still cause losses to the victim in the subsequent three years (eg, because the victim cannot immediately recover the market position it would have had in the absence of the infringement), those future losses form part of the harm suffered. They need to be added to the present value of the harm over the first five years. Suppose the losses are €75, €50, and €25, and the same discount rate applies. The €75 occurs in the current year, so does not require uprating or discounting. The €50 occurs in the next year, so needs to be discounted once, and is worth €45.45 in present terms (€50 divided by 1.10). The €25 in two years' time is worth €20.66 in present terms (€25 divided by 1.10 to the power of 2). The present value of the total harm over the whole eight years (five past years, the current year, and the two future years) is now €812.68.

From the above example it follows that the choice of discount rate can have a significant influence on the damage value. If the discount rate was 5% instead of 10%, the present value of the damage from the five past years would be €580.19 instead of €671.56. If it was 15% the value would be €775.37. The higher the discount rate, the greater the present value of the past losses when uprated at the discount rate, but the smaller the present value of the future losses when discounted at this rate.

The point in time at which the damages value is measured can also have a significant impact—for different legal and economic reasons, the most appropriate point in time may be the end of the infringement, the filing of the claim, the start or end of the trial, the award of the damages, or the payment of the damages. There has been some debate in the US courts regarding the date on which a value must be measured in exclusionary cases. For example, in *Farmington Dowel Products v Forster*, an antitrust case in which the claimant's business was harmed and ceased to exist due to discriminatory pricing, the court accepted the going-concern value as at the day prior to the company being dissolved.[58] The court did not allow the claim of the going-concern value as at the day of trial, which was more than ten years after the company was dissolved. Its reasoning was that the profit projections for the ten years would be too speculative in nature. In contrast, in *Coastal Fuels v Caribbean Petroleum*, another price discrimination case, the claimant argued that the time period between the date when it was forced out of business and the date of the trial was not sufficiently long to make the estimate of the projected lost profits excessively speculative, and the court awarded damages that included the going-concern value as at the day of trial.[59]

10.12.2 CHOICE OF DISCOUNT OR INTEREST RATE

Various jurisdictions require statutory rates of interest—generally prescribed by civil or contract/tort law provisions—to be used for certain periods of uprating, ie, moving a sum of money from an earlier period to a later period, such as for late payment of

---

[58] *Farmington Dowel Products Co v Forster Mfg Co* 421 F 2d 61 (1st Cir. 1969).
[59] *Coastal Fuels v Caribbean Petroleum Corp* 175 F 3d 18 (1st Cir. 1999).

the damages. The date from which interest can be claimed varies across EU Member States, and can refer to the start of the infringement, the start of the legal action, or the date of the award. The legal framework concerned will determine which part of the cash flows in the damages valuation should be uprated by the statutory interest rate, and for which cash flows (if any) a discount rate can be chosen based on economic criteria.

Economic and finance theories have developed a range of principles on how to determine the discount rate (see also Chapter 3 and section 10.9). In the context of damages valuation, it may be appropriate to use the cost of capital for the claimant as the discount rate for future expected losses. This discount rate takes into account the time value of money and the business risk of the claimant (ie, the fact that future factual and counterfactual scenarios, and hence estimates of losses, are uncertain). Discounting expected future losses would provide an estimate of their value as at the award date.

Although the concept of the cost of capital is less well defined in the case of individual consumers (as opposed to companies), the principles underpinning the choice of the discount rate remain the same. Therefore, the appropriate discount rate should reflect consumers' rate of intertemporal substitution (ie, how they trade off having one particular amount of money at present with having some other amount in the future). One possibility is to use the social time preference rate. This is a commonly used concept in public policy cost–benefit analysis, involving the evaluation of alternative time profiles of consumption. It is the rate at which individuals are willing to trade off consumption over time.[60]

There are several possible approaches to uprating past losses, as detailed below. First, the cost of capital of the claimant—during the period in which the damages were incurred, a claimant earning 'normal' returns would have earned profit consistent in the long run with the cost of capital. Thus, damages uprated at the cost of capital would capture the expected return that the claimant could have earned on the amounts lost had they been available for investment—ie, it compensates investors for the use of their capital. Second, the risk-free rate—this is usually approximated by the rate on a virtually risk-free investment such as a government bond. The rationale for this is that the repayment of damages is certain once awarded (subject to an inability to pay by the defendant), thus ensuring that the claimant is compensated for the time value of money without risk component, which is conceptually equivalent to paying interest.

An example of where a court preferred one discount rate over another is the Chicago Bulls franchise case that we referred to in sections 10.6 and 10.9 (*Fishman and Illinois Basketball v Wirtz*). The original claim uprated historical cash flows at the risk-free rate (in this case they were negative as the claimant had to commit additional equity to the business in the counterfactual scenario). The Court of Appeal agreed with most aspects of the valuation analysis (multiples and comparators), but not with the uprating approach. It held that historical cash flows (which in this case

---

[60] See, for example, Sugden and Williams (1978); and HM Treasury (2003), 'The Green Book: Appraisal and Evaluation in Central Government', 16 January.

reflected equity contributions) needed to be uprated at the cost of equity capital to reflect the fact that the claimant would have incurred an opportunity cost of capital on the committed equity.

10.12.3 ECONOMICS AND LAW ON INTEREST: WHY THINGS ARE NOT ALWAYS SO SIMPLE

Interest (and discount) rates can be applied as simple interest or compound interest. When the interest rate is compounded, the calculation includes interest on accumulated interest from prior periods. For example, 10% is applied to €100 in the first year, giving €110, and in the second year the 10% is applied to that €110 from the first year, giving €121. From an economic perspective, compounding interest is the usual, and conceptually correct, approach to discounting. When you put your money in the bank, you expect interest to be paid on the whole balance, so on past interest too. And yet there are many instances where the legal framework requires the simple interest to be applied (ie, interest calculated solely as a percentage of the principal sum). For example, 10% is applied to €100 in the first year, giving €110, and in the second year the 10% is again applied to the €100, giving a total of €120. In this example the difference between the two methods is only €1. However, for longer time periods and higher interest rates the differences become substantially greater.

EU case law seems to have used both approaches, depending on the specifics of the case. In 2001 the General Court stated that:

> Regarding the rate of interest, it should be pointed out that, according to a principle generally accepted in the domestic law of the Member States, in an action for the recovery of a sum unduly paid based on the principle prohibiting unjust enrichment, the claimant is normally entitled to the lower of the two amounts corresponding to the enrichment and the loss. Furthermore, where the loss consists of the loss of use of a sum of money over a period of time, the amount recoverable is generally calculated by reference to the statutory or judicial rate of interest, without compounding.[61]

However, the General Court also found that, in that particular case, the actual amount to be calculated would be better reflected by applying a compound interest rate, and therefore applied the latter approach. A more recent UK House of Lords ruling, in *Sempra Metals*, contains a useful discussion of these points.[62] It notes some comments made by legal representative bodies that 'the obvious reason for awarding compound interest is that it reflects economic reality', and that 'computation of the time value of the enrichment on the basis of simple interest will inevitably fall short of its true value', but also that 'The virtue of simple interest is its simplicity. That cannot be said of compound interest, which can be calculated in different ways leading to different results.'

---

[61] Case T-171/99 *Corus UK Ltd v EC Commission* [2002] OJ C3/23.
[62] *Sempra Metals Ltd v Revenue & Anor* [2007] UKHL 34, 18 July 2007.

Case law in the UK also seems to increasingly recognize that the use of the statutory interest rate as opposed to a commercial interest rate is not necessarily aligned with business reality. In a case outside competition law the court held that:

> The Judgments Act [statutory] rate is fixed for the benefit of unpaid judgment creditors. It is not normally an appropriate rate of interest to award in the context of a dispute between two businesses . . . If Claymore or a company such as Claymore, had sought to borrow £750,000.00 over the period since June 2004, Claymore would have had to pay interest at more than 1% over base rate.[63]

Once the principle is acknowledged that the interest rate should reflect the commercial opportunity costs of borrowing, and hence that commercial interest rates should be used, it is a relatively small step to move towards using the cost of capital. Companies do not finance themselves by borrowing only—they have debt and equity capital, and hence the opportunity cost of raising capital contains both the cost of debt (interest) and cost of equity. In all, there is plenty of scope for the economics and the law to come closer together in the area of discounting and interest in damages cases.

---

[63] *Claymore v Nautilus* [2007] EWHC 805 (TCC).

11

THE USE OF ECONOMIC EVIDENCE IN COMPETITION CASES

11.1 SMOKESCREENS AND MUD-SLINGERS?

As we mentioned in Chapter 1, whether you are a practising competition lawyer, a competition official, a member of the judiciary, or a legal scholar, economics matters to you, because it matters to competition law. Legal provisions have economic concepts embedded in them—indeed, the very essence of competition law is based on the economic notion that competition is 'good' and monopoly is 'bad'. Competition authorities refer to economic principles and analysis in their decisions, and parties on either side of a competition dispute use economic arguments and evidence to support their case. Economics has developed a number of practical tests and criteria that make the application of the law more workable, and a range of statistical and econometric techniques that enable the gathering of robust evidence to back up theories and arguments. Throughout this book we have sought to give you a feel for what economics can contribute to competition law, and what its limitations are.

We conclude by looking at the use of *economic evidence*, and of *economists*, in competition cases. Usage of both has grown substantially in the past decade, and most competition lawyers and economists are now quite accustomed to working alongside each other as complements (not substitutes). However, we believe that much still needs to be done to extend good practice in the use of economic evidence and economic experts. By this, to be clear, we do not mean that economics should necessarily be used more than currently, but that it should be used more effectively. It is not helpful when economic experts appear to be slinging mud at each other's analysis instead of providing insight into the complicated economics of a competition case. Nor is the reputation of economists enhanced by the fact that often they do not explain their analysis and results very well, or worse, they throw up smokescreens of unnecessarily complicated theories and equations. That competition law is a complex field (in Chapter 1 we quoted one specialized court as saying that 'competition law is not an area of law in which there is much scope for absolute concepts or sharp edges'[1]) is not the fault of economics, but economists can do a lot more to help lawyers navigate through the application of the law to real-world markets. This begins with explaining economic principles and concepts clearly—something we have sought to do in this book.

In what follows, section 11.2 explores best practice in presenting economic evidence. Various competition authorities have issued guidance on this in recent years, which we consider to be a valuable step towards improving the contribution of economics to competition law. In section 11.3 we address the question of how courts and other decision-making bodies can assess what weight and credibility to attach to the evidence of economic experts, especially in situations where two experts reach different conclusions. Useful criteria for dealing with these situations have been developed in courts in the USA (the *Daubert* test) and the UK (the 'duty to help the court'). Section 11.4 concludes with some comments about future trends in the use of economics in competition law.

11.2 BEST PRACTICE IN PRESENTING ECONOMIC EVIDENCE

Academic economists may have a reputation for observing the world from ivory towers. But even practising competition economists sometimes carry out their analyses quite separately from the legal case they are supposed to enlighten. In our experience, the most effective legal cases are made when the legal advisers, the business people, and the economists work closely together on an integrated legal submission that reflects both the business reality and sound economic reasoning. This may then be complemented by separate, probably more technical, economic submissions containing empirical evidence to support the arguments put forward in the legal submission.

---

[1] Judgment in Cases 1035/1/1/04 and 1041/2/1/04 *The Racecourse Association and the British Horseracing Board v OFT* [2005] CAT 29, 2 August, at [167].

Competition authorities and lawyers must take a view on how much weight to attach to this evidence. This is inherently difficult. In Chapters 2 and 10, where we described some empirical techniques commonly used in market definition and damages actions, we gave some tips for critical questions that non-economists may ask of the quantitative results they are presented with. We used the analogy of the black box, which you may look into and shake and rattle, to see if it still holds together or starts to fall apart under scrutiny. But even for an economist it can be difficult to assess the robustness and credibility of another economist's empirical results if they are not presented clearly. This can work only if economists are able to properly 'peer-review' each other's work. Despite the old joke that when you ask two economists a question you get three different answers, we believe that experienced academic and practising economists actually do have a common understanding as to what constitutes a 'good piece of economic analysis' and what doesn't. Analysis based on established theory, using good data and carrying out a robustness check of the results are all elements of this common understanding. If it passes peer review by other economists, it is probably a good analysis. (This is not to say that the standard of robustness should be the same as that for peer-reviewed academic journals—empirical work in competition cases is usually carried out within much tighter timescales and with less data available than for academic work.) Economic evidence needs to be presented in such a way that it allows for a proper peer review by the economists at the competition authority or on the other side of the dispute. In this regard, we agree with the various guidance documents on best practice for submissions of technical economic analysis that have been issued in recent years by competition authorities, including the European Commission and the UK Competition Commission (CC). These documents follow a number of common principles, which have been expressed by the CC as follows:

Clarity and transparency: Submissions should not only present clearly the results and conclusions of the economic analysis undertaken, but they should also clearly state the methodology used, the assumptions made in reaching results, the justification for the methodology and the assumptions, and the robustness of the results to any assumptions made. Submissions should be understandable to non-economists, and CC economists should be able to determine how the analysis enables parties' economic experts to reach the submitted conclusions.

Completeness: Submissions should contain a complete description of the analysis undertaken. All relevant assumptions should be discussed and the choice of techniques explained. Relevant econometric output, diagnostic tests and checks for robustness should be included . . .

Replication of results: In a number of cases, the CC will want to replicate the results of the analysis that has been submitted. This means that parties should be prepared to respond to a CC request, at very short notice, for all relevant computer code and data files necessary for the CC's economists to reproduce the result presented in parties' submission. This will include the raw and the cleaned data and the programs for obtaining the latter from the former.[2]

---

[2] Competition Commission (2009), 'Suggested Best Practice for Submission of Technical Economic Analysis from Parties to the Competition Commission', 24 February, pp 1–2.

The European Commission guidance contains some useful additional points on presentation and interpretation of the results.[3] It states that the results of an empirical analysis should be reported in 'the standard format found in academic papers'. This includes reporting on statistical significance (did the result occur by chance?) and other diagnostic tests, and emphasizing those results that are statistically significant at the 5% level (a cut-off point often used in statistics, as discussed in Chapter 2, which means that you can be 95% confident that your results did not occur by chance). The Commission also emphasizes the importance of making the link between the results of econometric analysis and the underlying market reality. In line with our discussion in Chapter 10 about the use of economic models, it states that 'by their very nature, economic models and arguments are based on simplifications of reality', and that 'it is therefore normally not sufficient to disprove a particular argument or model, to point out that it is based on seemingly unrealistic assumptions'.[4] Instead, the Commission expects the analysis—or any critique of it—to explicitly identify which aspects of reality should be better reflected in the model or argumentation, and to indicate why this would or would not alter the conclusions. The analysis should also contain some general discussion on the practical relevance of the results, and on whether they are sensitive to changes in the data, the choice of empirical method, or the precise modelling assumptions. Another important point made in the European Commission guidance is that:

> The credibility of an economic submission is enhanced when the limitations with regards to accuracy or explanatory power of the underlying data and methodology are explicitly acknowledged. In this regard it is often advisable to address rather than minimize uncertainty.[5]

Again, clarity and transparency are the key words in this best practice—if the analysis has certain shortcomings, it is more credible to signal them up front rather than sweep them under the carpet and hope no one notices. It will not come as a surprise to you that even after a peer review there may be points of disagreement between the economists. Courts in the USA and UK have developed useful mechanisms to deal with such situations, as discussed below.

11.3 WHEN CAN COURTS RELY ON ECONOMIC EXPERTS?

Most competition authorities have economists among their staff—indeed, many now have a Chief Economist. Provided that the best-practice guidance discussed above is followed, the submission of empirical economic evidence in proceedings before competition authorities will allow for a more in-depth debate of the issues between

---

[3] European Commission (2010), 'Best practices for the submission of economic evidence and data collection in cases concerning the application of Articles 101 and 102 TFEU and in merger cases', January.

[4] Ibid., at [12].

[5] Ibid., at [41].

the parties and better decision-making. In competition cases before courts, however—which are increasingly common, now also outside the USA—there is the complication that many judges have not had extensive economics training. Courts are less well equipped than competition authorities to deal with technical economic evidence. They cannot peer-review the evidence themselves. Hence, when presented with such evidence, should they limit themselves to putting some critical questions to the expert, and if these are answered satisfactorily, regard the expert's conclusions as reliable? Should they rely on the other side's expert to provide the required peer review? Or should they appoint their own expert? Different jurisdictions deal with these challenges in different ways. The principles developed in the US and UK courts are particularly useful—together with the best practice guidance discussed above, they can make economics a more helpful discipline in competition law.

11.3.1 THE *DAUBERT* PRINCIPLE

US case law has developed the '*Daubert* test' on the admissibility of scientific evidence, which also applies to economic evidence in antitrust cases. Based on a 1993 Supreme Court ruling, the test has been refined through a number of subsequent judgments and is reflected in Rule 702 of the Federal Rules of Evidence.[6] It is intended to prevent testimony based on untested and unreliable theories. The main relevant aspects of the test are whether: (i) the testimony is based on sufficient facts or data; (ii) the testimony is the product of reliable principles and methods; and (iii) the expert has applied the principles and methods reliably to the facts of the case. Only if these criteria are met is the expert evidence admitted—note that admission is just the first hurdle; it does not necessarily mean that the evidence is given much weight. The *Daubert* test has been used to great effect in many antitrust cases in the last 15 years. Indeed, quite a few economists have seen their evidence not being admitted—prominent ones include a winner of the Nobel Prize for Economics, and the author of a leading guide to using economic evidence in antitrust court cases. Some common themes in the application of the *Daubert* test are described below.

The US courts frequently encounter expert evidence containing quantitative analysis in private damages actions (as we have mentioned in Chapters 9 and 10, such cases represent a large proportion of all antitrust cases in the USA). Such evidence is more likely to be admitted if it falls within one of the three 'common approaches to measuring antitrust damages' that US case law has recognized—the before-and-after approach, a yardstick or benchmark approach, and regression analysis (see also Chapter 10).[7] US courts have accepted the usefulness of regression analysis. In one case it was stated that 'if performed properly multiple regression analysis is a reliable means by which

---

[6] *Daubert v Merrell Dow Pharma Inc* 509 US 579 (1993). For a more detailed discussion of the test, see Berger (2000) and Cwik and North (2003).
[7] *Conwood Co LP v US Tobacco Co* 290 F 3d 768, 793 (6th Cir. 2002).

economists may prove antitrust damages.'[8] Indeed, courts to some extent appear to expect experts to conduct a regression analysis in order to produce robust estimates:

> [The] prudent economist must account for differences and would perform minimum regression analysis when comparing price before relevant period to prices during damage period.[9]

US courts have also considered the question of how much of an expert the expert needs to be. In one antitrust case involving a clinic's refusal to continue to treat two patients, the plaintiffs' expert had a PhD in economics, but no expertise in competition economics— the court duly dismissed him:

> The district court's and the plaintiffs' difficulty in describing the relevant market was to a great measure the result of the plaintiffs' reliance on [the expert] as their sole economic analyst/ expert. Dr. [expert] is the sole qualified source cited by the plaintiffs supporting their allegation of the Clinic's market power. Yet, Dr. [expert] conceded that he was 'not an expert,' that he had no background in antitrust markets, either geographic or product, and that he had no background in 'primary care' markets. Dr. [expert] further stated that he was not a member of any associations or industrial organization groups which form the bulwark of economists specializing in antitrust law and economics. Where supposed experts have admitted that they are 'not experts,' courts have had little difficulty in excluding their testimony.[10]

The English High Court faced a similar question in an abuse of dominance case where the expert was not an economist, but did have extensive business experience in the industry. The judge expressed a (slightly) more subtle view on this than his US counterparts:

> Whilst the concepts required to be investigated in a competition law case are no doubt most easily grasped, explained and opined upon by trained economists, they are concepts drawn from and related to the operation of the markets of the real world; and I regard it as unreal the thought that it is only trained economists with a list of learned articles to their name who have the expertise necessary to understand them and to help the court on their application to a particular case.[11]

Conversely, the question has arisen as to whether experts need to have had experience in the industry in question. In a case involving a horizontal group boycott under section 1 of the Sherman Act, the court noted the expert's (an accountant) extensive experience in business valuation, and was satisfied that while the expert had no prior experience in the industry concerned, he had made substantial efforts to acquaint himself with the industry for the purpose of the case.[12] This seems a sensible approach, since competition economists, like competition lawyers, can effectively work across a wide range of industries, and may often not be familiar with the industry in question at the start of a case. In this particular case, the expert's evidence was rejected for another reason— it was not based on any identifiable theory or technique, but rather on the expert's own

---

[8] *Petruzzi's IGA Supermarkets Inc v Darling-Delaware Co* 998 F 2d 1224, 1238 (3d Cir. 1993).
[9] *In re Aluminum Phosphide Antitrust Litig* 893 F Supp 1497, 1507 (D. Kan. 1995).
[10] *Nelson v Monroe Regional Medical Center* 925 F 2d 1555 (7th Cir. 1991).
[11] *Chester City Council v Arriva* [2007] EWHC 1373 (Ch).
[12] *Champagne Metals v Ken-Mac Metals Inc* 458 F 3d 1073, 1088 (10th Cir. 2006).

assumptions and judgement, such that the analysis could not be objectively tested or verified by others (which is another of the *Daubert* criteria).

Experts clearly cannot rely only on their past expertise. They are also expected to engage with the details and facts of the case, and ensure that their analysis fits the facts. In an antitrust dispute between boat builders and an engine manufacturer, the appeal court rejected the plaintiff's expert because his Cournot oligopoly model 'did not incorporate all aspects of the economic reality' of the market in question, and it 'ignored inconvenient evidence'.[13] The Cournot model itself was not challenged—this is after all a well-accepted model—but two experts on the other side criticized the way it had been applied in the case at hand, and the court considered that there was 'simply too great an analytic gap between the data and the opinion proffered' (we also discussed this case in Chapter 10). In another case, concerning price discrimination, the plaintiff's expert was rejected because his analysis was not based on authoritative industry data or recognized financial data, but rather on the 'deposition testimony, estimates, feelings and beliefs' of one of the plaintiff's executives.[14] This executive would have been the main beneficiary of the damages claim (so might have been biased), and in addition, the court considered him not sufficiently qualified to provide the general opinions upon which the expert relied in calculating the damages, as he had no specialized education and was neither an economist nor an accountant. The court also stated that the expert had not made any effort to verify the executive's estimates, either through consultation with industry experts or the relevant literature. That experts must do their homework is also a theme that has come up in the UK courts. In a recent damages action (outside competition law), where economic and business experts commented on the effect of a failed customer relationship management (CRM) system on the claimants' number of pay-TV subscribers, the judge stated that:

> It is clear that [the expert] is a person who has a great deal of relevant experience in this field and could provide a valuable opinion on the effect of the CRM System on Sky's customers. However, I found that his evidence failed to live up to expectations. It seemed that he had little grasp of the detailed facts and had not properly understood some features which were necessary to make churn predictions for Sky.[15]

11.3.2 DUTY TO HELP THE COURT

There are various ways to involve experts in court proceedings, and the rules differ across jurisdictions. Parties can each appoint their own expert, or they can appoint one

---

[13] *Concord Boat Corp v Brunswick Corp* 207 F 3d 1039 (8th Cir. 2000). This expert was the one who had written a leading guide on the use of economic expert evidence in antitrust damages court cases.

[14] *Vernon Walden, Inc v Lipoid GmbH and Lipoid USA LLC* (Civ No 01-4826 (DRD)), United States District Court for the District of New Jersey.

[15] *BSkyB Limited and Sky Subscribers Services Limited v HP Enterprise Services UK Limited (formerly Electronic Data Systems Limited) and Electronic Data systems LLC (Formerly Electronic Data Systems Corporation* [2010] EWHC 86 (TCC) at [288].

expert jointly. Courts may themselves appoint an expert, either as the main expert in the case or as the arbiter resolving any differences between the party-appointed experts. On the face of it, you might think that having a court-appointed expert is always preferable—this expert can assess the merits of the technical evidence as independently as the judge can. Indeed, if the theoretical optimum—the judge and the expert being one and the same person—is not feasible, then the closest you might get to that optimum is through a court-appointed expert who directly assists the judge in making the decision. However, we are supporters of another system—one which, in our own experience, and based on what several judges have said about it, can be highly effective in bringing out the best in economic experts. This is the system used in the English courts, where experts are usually party-appointed, and which combines a number of powerful mechanisms that provide the right incentives for experts to do the job properly: (i) a duty on the experts to help the court; (ii) a requirement on the experts to produce a joint statement of points of agreement and disagreement; and (iii) robust cross-examination of the experts by a barrister if the case goes to trial.

Part 35 of the Civil Procedure Rules (and the accompanying Practice Direction) determines that experts have a duty to help the court on matters within their expertise.[16] This duty overrides any obligation to the parties from whom experts have received instructions or by whom they are paid. Experts are expected to provide objective, unbiased opinions on matters within their expertise, and not to assume the role of an advocate. Under these rules, they should also make it clear when a question or issue falls outside their expertise, and when they are not able to reach a definite opinion, for example, because they have insufficient information. In our experience, this duty to help the court in itself provides a powerful incentive on the expert to carry out the analysis objectively and reliably—and indeed it also provides incentives on the instructing solicitors not to place undue pressure on the expert to say one thing or another. Judges tend to rapidly dismiss the evidence of an expert who does not appear to want to be helpful to the court—for example, when the expert gives the impression of behaving like an advocate, seems unwilling to comment on a matter from the other side's perspective when asked to do so, or appears to be hiding behind narrow instructions. This can be seen in the quote below, which is from a 1995 judgment that was influential in the development of the duty to the court principle (the expert evidence here did not relate to economics but to architecture, as the case involved a property rights dispute over the copying of a house design):

> That some witnesses of fact, driven by a desire to achieve a particular outcome to the litigation, feel it necessary to sacrifice truth in pursuit of victory is a fact of life. The court tries to discover it when it happens. But in the case of expert witnesses the court is likely to lower its guard. Of course the court will be aware that a party is likely to choose as its expert someone whose view is most sympathetic to its position. Subject to that caveat, the court is

---

[16] These rules are updated from time to time and are available on the Ministry of Justice website: <http://www.justice.gov.uk/civil/procrules_fin/index.htm>.

likely to assume that the expert witness is more interested in being honest and right than in ensuring that one side or another wins. An expert should not consider that it is his job to stand shoulder-to-shoulder through thick and thin with the side which is paying his bill. 'Pragmatic flexibility' as used by Mr. [expert] is a euphemism for 'misleading selectivity'.[17]

There have been several judgments in which courts have explicitly stated that they found an economic expert's evidence to be credible, persuasive or authoritative, and that they felt they could rely on the expert. Equally, courts have indicated where there were some doubts in this respect. This confirms to us that the duty to the court principle works effectively. The following extracts from recent court judgments illustrate the point. In an Article 101 case before the Court of Session in Edinburgh, the judge observed:

> I noted the considered and thoughtful way in which Mr [expert] gave his evidence. I am entirely satisfied that he acted throughout as an independent expert offering his opinions to assist the court . . . His credentials to give expert evidence on this subject are impressive. On the material issues, I accept all of Mr [expert]'s evidence and his conclusions.[18]

In a High Court ruling on an Article 102 case, the judge made the following comment about the claimants' expert:

> I was satisfied that Mr [expert] was giving his evidence honestly and was doing so in proper recognition of his duties to the court. I recognise, however, that he has been close to the action on the claimants' side of the record, and that there is therefore a risk that his opinion may perhaps have become unconsciously coloured by the claimants' interests.[19]

Under the Civil Procedure Rules, the experts from both sides of the dispute are normally expected to hold discussions and to produce a joint statement setting out the issues on which they agree and disagree (and the reasons for disagreeing). This may also involve the experts sharing their data and calculations with each other, in line with the best-practice principles set out in section 11.2. Together with the duty to the court, this requirement on experts to narrow the issues in dispute can be a powerful mechanism to help courts understand the economics of the case. Indeed it is a mechanism that arguably ought to apply in any type of competition proceeding—it would be equally helpful in administrative merger and abuse of dominance inquiries if the economists at the competition authority and those advising the parties could agree in advance what the relevant economic questions are, discuss which bits of the other side's analysis and conclusions they agree with and which bits they don't, and clearly state the reasons why. The Civil Procedure Rules state that 'the purpose of discussions between experts is not for experts to settle cases but to agree and narrow issues', and they also prescribe that the agenda for the expert meeting 'must not be in the form of leading questions or hostile in tone' and that—reader take note—'neither the parties nor their legal representatives may attend experts discussions' (unless ordered by the court, or agreed by all parties,

---

[17] *Cala Homes v Alfred McAlpine Homes East* [1995] FSR 818.
[18] *Calor Gas v Express Fuels and D Jamieson* [2008] CSOH 13, Court of Session.
[19] *Chester City Council v Arriva* [2007] EWHC 1373 (Ch).

and the experts). In our experience, these expert discussions may not always bring the parties' cases much closer together, but it is already helpful if there is agreement on basic principles, and the discussions do contribute to narrowing and clarifying the economic issues for the court. In one, possibly rare, case that we worked on (an arbitration involving an Article 102 allegation), the two experts agreed on *all* the economic criteria under which the case should be resolved, and considered that the rest was a matter of interpreting the factual evidence, such that there was no longer a need to cross-examine the experts at the hearing. The theory that the mechanism of the expert meeting and expert agreement can work satisfactorily is also borne out by the following statement by the judge in a recent damages case (outside competition law):

> The quantum experts have managed to make very good progress in agreeing figures. This meant that the issues between them were more limited. Both [expert 1 and expert 2] were impressive witnesses and although their approaches on particular issues differed, this was the result of opinion on such matters as validation of costs. I have therefore been able to see clearly what their views are and decide which view I prefer on particular issues.[20]

Finally, in addition to the duty to the court and the requirement to meet with the other expert, an economist involved in these proceedings faces the prospect of cross-examination by a barrister representing the other side—not always the friendliest of encounters. Applying some economic logic, the most powerful incentive on the party-appointed expert to produce a robust and carefully thought-through economic analysis is provided by the combination of the prospect of close scrutiny by the other expert and cross-examination by the barrister, and the desire to avoid a damning quote in the final judgment if your analysis is shown to be unreliable or unhelpful to the court. Indeed, these incentives are probably stronger than those faced by a court-appointed expert, who normally faces a lower degree of scrutiny or peer review.

11.3.3 ARE ECONOMIC EXPERTS GUILTY OF EX POST RATIONALIZATION?

The Competition Appeal Tribunal (CAT) in the UK has regularly pondered over what to make of the evidence and arguments presented by economic experts. Two related themes have come up in a number of cases. The first is the extent to which the economic reasoning by the experts actually matches the business reality (a theme also explored under the *Daubert* criteria in the USA)—does the theory fit the facts? The second is whether economic experts are guilty of ex post rationalization—when the economist comes up with a theory of how businesses behave, do you need evidence to show that businesses see themselves behaving in that way?

---

[20] *BSkyB Limited and Sky Subscribers Services Limited v HP Enterprise Services UK Limited (formerly Electronic Data Systems Limited) and Electronic Data systems LLC (Formerly Electronic Data Systems Corporation)* [2010] EWHC 86 (TCC), at [303].

In *RCA and BHB v OFT* (2005), a large group of British racecourses sold media rights collectively to a new venture for interactive TV and Internet betting on horseracing.[21] The question arose as to whether this collective selling constituted a restriction of competition under Article 101(1), or whether it was objectively necessary for the launch of the new venture. There was consensus during the proceedings that such a new venture required a 'critical mass' of horseracing content for a successful launch (in the end, the launch never actually happened). However, the Office of Fair Trading (OFT) had found there to be an infringement because it considered that, in a counterfactual without the agreement, the venture could have assembled a critical mass of rights by negotiating individually with each racecourse. Such separate contracts could have been made conditional on obtaining sufficient rights from other courses, so the OFT reasoned. The venture and the racecourses, in contrast, claimed that, from a practical point of view, collective selling was the only realistic way to achieve a sale and purchase of the rights, which had never been sold before (interactive betting was a new service at the time). The CAT agreed with the parties:

> The suggestion that the acquisition of the necessary critical mass by individual negotiation with up to 37 course owners either could have been done, might have been done, or was ever contemplated as something which could or might have been done, appears to us to represent a triumph of theory over commercial reality and to ignore the evidence of the events leading up to the [agreement].[22]

Another such 'triumph of theory over commercial reality' was encountered in *Enron v EWS* (2009), a damages case following an abuse of dominance finding by the Office of Rail Regulation.[23] The question that arose was whether in the counterfactual—in the absence of the abuse—the claimant would have secured a major four-year contract to supply coal to a coal-fired power station (a 'loss of chance' claim—see Chapter 10). The economic expert for the claimant argued that the operator of the power station, as a rational economic decision-maker, would have been likely to select the claimant's bid in the counterfactual. However, neither the facts nor the executive at the power company who was responsible for the coal supply contract at the time supported this argument. The executive gave various business reasons why he would probably not have granted the contract to the claimant in the counterfactual. The CAT found that the executive gave his evidence 'candidly and in a straightforward manner', and was 'impressed by his overall consistency on key points'.[24] In the end it placed greater weight on this evidence from the actual decision-maker than on what the economic expert said a hypothetical rational decision-maker would have done.

Nonetheless, attempts by economic experts to 'rationalize' certain business behaviour—whether actual or counterfactual—should not be dismissed outright

---

[21] *The Racecourse Association and the British Horseracing Board v Office of Fair Trading* [2005] CAT 29, 2 August.

[22] Ibid., at [170].

[23] *Enron Coal Services Limited (in liquidation) v English Welsh & Scottish Railway Limited* [2009] CAT 36, 21, December.

[24] Ibid., at [70(a)].

every time the business reality is slightly different from the theory. This brings us to the second, related theme that has come up in cases before the CAT. *Napp*, its very first judgment in an appeal under the Competition Act 1998, concerned an accusation of predation in one market and excessive pricing in another.[25] The economists acting for the defendant were effectively accused of ex post rationalization of the company's behaviour. The CAT stated that the defendant's justification for its behaviour did not flow from its internal documents, but from the work done by its economic advisers for the purpose of that particular case. It did not consider such work to be helpful in the absence of evidence that the company's behaviour had indeed taken into account the theory put forward later on by its economic consultants:

> Napp does not strike us as a naïve or badly managed company. If its pricing policy had in fact been set by Napp in the way that its economic consultants suggest, we would have expected the company's internal documents to demonstrate that.[26]

What can economists say to this in their defence? We have to go right back to the beginning. Economics emerged in the late eighteenth century. Commerce as we know it has existed for thousands of years. So it is almost inevitable that much of what economists have done is to provide explanations of business behaviour and market mechanisms that have existed for ages. And even though many prominent industrial organization (IO) economists now teach strategy at business schools, so there may be some cross-fertilization, we think that business practices will continue to precede economic theories about them. But even ex post, economics can provide critical insights into the effects of business practices on competition and economic welfare. The *Napp* case (as also discussed in Chapter 10) involved alleged predatory pricing of a pharmaceutical product in the hospital sector, combined with excessive pricing of the same product in the pharmacy ('community') sector. The economists presented the theory that Napp's pricing policy incorporated a 'follow-on effect', which basically means setting low prices for the drug in the hospital sector in order to enhance subsequent sales in the community sector. The economists described this effect in a rather narrow sense, in that more hospital sales would almost mechanistically lead to more community sales. There was no evidence that this was actually how Napp set its prices—the CAT stated that the term 'follow-on effect' was not used in the industry but rather 'coined by Napp's advisers for the purposes of this case'.[27] The managing director of Napp admitted that he had first come across the term when reading the papers for that case. Yet, apart from the fact that it is not uncommon for pharmaceutical companies to set low prices for the hospital sector in order to gain more business in the community sector, just like Napp did (even it if isn't widely referred to as a 'follow-on effect'), is it really the case that economic theories about how companies behave must always be reflected in internal company documents? Consider the insight first provided by Adam Smith. In his work *Wealth of Nations*, he explained that if economic agents, such as the butcher and the baker, all pursue their own self-interest (making money), this is actually a good thing, because there is an 'invisible hand' that ensures that, in the economy as a whole, the right business decisions and opportunities are taken such that markets work efficiently by themselves, making us all better off. Importantly, Adam Smith made it clear that such efficient market functioning arises *despite* the fact that the butcher and the baker are neither intending to achieve that efficiency nor even conscious of the fact that they are doing this (to be clear, the invisible hand has nothing to do with divinity, as some people seem to think—it is a metaphor for a simple but powerful force that operates in the economy):

> It is not from the benevolence of the butcher, the brewer, or the baker that we expect our dinner, but from their regard to their own interest. We address ourselves, not to their humanity but to their self-love, and never talk to them of our own necessities but of their advantages... As every individual, therefore, endeavours as much as he can both to employ his capital in the support of domestic industry, and so to direct that industry that its produce may be of the greatest value; every individual necessarily labours to render the annual value of society as great as he can. He generally, indeed, neither intends to promote the public interest, nor knows how much he is promoting it... And by directing that industry in such a manner as its produce may be of the greatest value, he intends only his own gain, and he is in this, as in many other cases, led by an invisible hand to promote an end which was no part of his intention. Nor is it always the worse for the society that it was no part of it. By pursuing his own interest he frequently promotes that of society more effectually than when he really intends to promote it.[28]

This eighteenth-century insight still underpins the way economists think about markets today. Applying it to *Napp*, whether any internal documents of the defendant confirm the theory put forward by the economist is to some extent irrelevant. The fact that the defendant's commercial staff are not aware of the economic theory according to which they behave does not mean that this economic theory should be dismissed. Companies involved in competition proceedings are like the butcher and the baker, seeking their own self-interest (profit maximization), and economists do have things to say about the consequences of such behaviour. To use a sports analogy, just because a snooker player does not sit there with a protractor, calculator, and a list of formulae before playing every shot doesn't mean that the laws of physics don't apply to the shots played. Likewise, many in business may have mastered the art of trading without being aware of the broader market mechanisms they are part of. Thus, ex post rationalization in itself is perhaps not such a terrible crime. But the other theme discussed in this sub-section is of prime importance: economic experts in court cases should ensure that the theories and empirical evidence they put forward contain a good dose of realism and are aligned with the facts of the case. The CAT's rejection of triumphs of theory over commercial reality is not without foundation.

---

[28] Smith (1776), Book I, Ch II.

11.4 THE USE OF ECONOMICS: A PROMISING FUTURE?

11.4.1 CURRENT TRENDS AND ADD-ONS TO THE EXISTING FRAMEWORK

For a long time it was restricted to antitrust law in the USA, but the use of economics has now spread to competition regimes in Europe and other parts of the world. It has permeated all the various areas of competition law that we have discussed in this book—abuse of dominance, horizontal and vertical agreements, mergers, and, more recently, state aid and damages. Economics has provided competition law with a better understanding of the effects of business practices, with practical concepts and criteria, and with quantitative tools that can generate empirical evidence to support theories and arguments. We have no reason to believe that this trend will change any time soon. If best practice in presenting economic evidence is adhered to more often, and courts become more familiar with such evidence, you can expect economics to continue to make significant contributions to competition law.

The 'mainstream' economic framework within which competition economists operate has, by and large, remained the same over the past decades. As discussed in Chapter 1, this framework is based around the influential insights of the Chicago School in the 1960s and 1970s on the efficiency benefits of many business practices that seemed restrictive, supplemented by more modern economic theories of IO that have deepened economists' understanding of those business practices. Many of the economic principles we have set out in this book originate from IO, which is concerned with how markets work, how demand and supply interact, and how rivals react strategically to each other's actions.

This basic competition economics framework is a flexible one. Throughout the book we have seen several examples of how it can be adapted to deal with new challenges, and how it can generate new ideas and concepts (some of which have proved very useful; some have more in common with management fads; and many are rehashes of older theories). In Chapter 2 we discussed the hypothetical monopolist test for market definition, and how some modifications to it have been proposed recently to deal with the issue of differentiated product markets (as also covered in Chapter 7). We also saw how economics can be used in dealing with the complex interactions between competition and IP law—Chapters 2 and 3 explored how innovation and market dynamics influence the assessment of market definition and market power; Chapter 4 showed how practices such as parallel trade, bundling and refusal to supply can be more difficult to analyse when IP rights are involved; Chapters 5 and 8 discussed how agreements between competitors and state support are often used to address market failures in innovation and R&D, and how this can be balanced against the competition and state aid rules; and Chapter 9 dealt with FRAND remedies in the area of access to IP licensing.

In various chapters we came across the concept of two-sided markets, which became something of a buzzword in competition law following the credit card interchange fee cases (see Chapters 2 and 5). Other 'new' concepts of recent times are hub-and-spoke collusion (Chapter 5) and diagonal mergers (Chapter 7). In addition to developing new theories and concepts, economists have become increasingly confident at empirical analysis—the statistical tools and the availability of data have both got better and better. We have discussed the empirical estimation of concepts such as demand elasticities (Chapter 2), unilateral effects of mergers (Chapter 7), and damages (Chapter 10).

11.4.2 NEW FIELDS OF APPLICATION

The economic concepts and tools described in this book have relevance to areas of policy and law outside competition law. Utility regulation is one of these areas. Ever since network industries such as electricity, gas, water, postal services, telecoms, rail, and airports were privatized and/or liberalized, policy-makers and regulators have been trying to find the optimal balance between competition and regulation. Some activities in these industries may always be natural monopolies, while in others you may get effective competition—so how should you identify and then regulate the natural monopoly activities, and at what point in the liberalization process can you withdraw regulation from the potentially competitive activities? Tools from competition economics can be of assistance in tackling these regulatory policy questions (in the same way that tools from regulation can be of assistance in competition law, particularly in the design of remedies, as discussed in Chapter 9). Market definition and market power assessments (dealt with in Chapters 2 and 3) can be used to distinguish the competitive from the not-so-competitive areas—the EU regulatory framework for telecommunications has gone furthest in incorporating these competition concepts into the decision-making process,[29] but regulations in the other network industries are also taking steps in that direction. Where ex ante economic regulation of an activity is withdrawn, 'ex post regulation' through the application of competition law can still be relied upon. We saw in Chapter 4 that some of the most interesting and challenging abuse of dominance cases arise in these network industries since the natural monopoly activities interact with other competitive layers in the supply chain.

Competition economics principles are also increasingly being applied to sectors that traditionally have not relied much on market functioning at all but are now beginning to do so. One such sector is the provision of healthcare services—many countries are introducing market mechanisms to complement or replace public sector activities, and have tasked competition authorities or specialist regulators with overseeing this new competition.[30] In Chapter 2 we mentioned some examples of how healthcare mergers have been dealt with under competition law. The economics of horizontal and vertical

---

[29] Directive (EC) 2009/140 of the European Parliament and of the Council of 25 November 2009 amending Directives (EC) 2002/21 on a common regulatory framework for electronic communications networks and services, 2002/19 on access to, and interconnection of, electronic communications networks and associated facilities, and 2002/20 on the authorization of electronic communications networks and services, Art 16(6) of the amended Framework Directive.

[30] Much has been written on competition in healthcare services. For an overview of recent developments in a number of countries, see Organisation for Economic Co-operation and Development (2005), and Leibowitz (2010).

agreements (Chapters 5 and 6) and of state aid and subsidies (Chapter 8) are also of relevance to this sector. Another sector where competition is a more recent phenomenon is the provision of public sector information services. Various types of government agency have statutory functions through which they gather certain valuable information—such as property registers, company registers, geological and geographic data, and weather statistics. These agencies often hold a statutory monopoly on the function in question, but the information has commercial value and applications outside their statutory functions. Competition concerns about access to this essential information are becoming increasingly common, in particular where an agency itself moves into the provision of commercial activities and competes with private sector companies. The economic tools for analysing market definition, market power, and abuse of dominance (Chapters 2 to 4) and state aid (Chapter 8) are of relevance to this area.[31]

Trade law is another area where competition economics principles have an obvious (but not yet accepted) application, in particular the rules on anti-dumping (as currently embedded in Article VI of the General Agreement on Tariffs and Trade 1994 and the accompanying World Trade Organization Anti-dumping Agreement). These rules allow countries to impose duties on imports that are sold below their 'normal' or 'fair' value, defined as either the price charged in the home country or a third country, or the (fully allocated) cost of production. If you think that the description of 'dumping' sounds just like price discrimination and predatory pricing, you are correct, but the way trade law deals with it differs dramatically from the way competition law treats price discrimination and below-cost pricing (as discussed in Chapter 4). Economic studies have shown that if competition law standards were applied to dumping practices, only a tiny fraction of all anti-dumping cases would actually result in intervention. To date, the anti-dumping rules have functioned mainly as a protectionist tool, and do not share the objectives of competition law (promoting efficiency and consumer welfare). Another sharp contrast with competition law is that anti-dumping policy has successfully resisted any influence from modern economic thinking throughout its 110 years of existence, despite having generated a good deal of (mostly highly critical) economic literature.[32] There are indications that this might be slowly changing: some jurisdictions, including the EU, now seem to be giving somewhat greater weight than they previously did to the interests of domestic user industries and end-consumers, who are typically most affected by anti-dumping duties as they end up paying higher prices for their imports.

11.4.3 NEW THEORIES

As we mentioned earlier, competition economics is mostly derived from IO theory, supplemented by quantitative and econometric techniques. In this book you have seen

---

[31] The OFT undertook an extensive analysis of competition issues in the provision of public sector information in 2006. Office of Fair Trading (2006), 'The commercial use of public information (CUPI)', December.

[32] For an overview of these debates, see Nelson (2006), Blonigen and Prusa (2003), and Niels and ten Kate (1997).

that two other strands of economics can also provide useful insights and concepts: financial economics and behavioural economics. The application of financial analysis in competition policy has long been controversial—the use of profitability as a measure of market power has been met with outright hostility from some competition economists (we showed in Chapter 3 that this hostility is rather misguided). While the gap between the fields of IO and finance remains huge—both in academia and among practising economists—the controversy has to some extent been overtaken by events. Financial analyses, such as valuations, business plan reviews, financial ratio analyses, and cost determinations, are now commonly used in several areas of competition law: revenue–cost comparisons in abuse of dominance cases (Chapter 4), the failing-firm defence in merger cases (Chapter 7), the market economy investor principle and the SGEI criteria under the state aid rules (Chapter 8), the design of pricing remedies, the setting of fines, and the ability of companies to pay fines (Chapter 9), and the quantification of damages (Chapter 10). Competition economists must accept that financial analysis is simply an integral part of the economics toolbox to be used in competition law.

The other field that has begun to make an impact on competition law is that of behavioural economics. This involves applying psychological principles to explain observed consumer behaviour that deviates from the predictions of traditional economic models—there are some differences between the 'homo economicus' of the traditional models and the 'homo sapiens' of the real world. While competition cases mostly focus on structure and behaviour of the supply side of markets, for competition to do its job you need to have a well-functioning demand side as well. As we saw in Chapter 9, behavioural economics provides useful insight into competition problems that may arise through cognitive biases in consumers, even in markets where the supply side seems reasonably competitive—default bias, choice overload, optimism bias, and loss-aversion bias are but a few. It also provides a tool for understanding how consumers may respond to remedies—recent (not so good) experiences with remedies in *Microsoft* and other cases suggest that there is plenty of scope for improvement, and for behavioural economics to play a bigger role in the design of remedies. A related field that we briefly touched upon is that of experimental economics. This may increasingly be used as a tool for testing remedies in a controlled environment (which is useful if testing them in the real marketplace is not feasible). In Chapter 5 we showed how experiments have also been used in analysing the effects of leniency policy.

11.4.4 QUESTIONING THE COMPETITION PARADIGM

The growing importance of competition economics is due in no small part to the rise of competition law itself. More and more countries are adopting competition regimes—China is a relatively recent, high-profile addition to the list, which also includes countries as diverse as Azerbaijan, Fiji, and Zambia. Equally importantly, enforcement of the competition rules has become more active, and more visible, across Europe and other parts of the world—witness the regularity with which competition cases make the headlines in the papers (and the relative ease with which you can now explain to friends and relatives what you do for a living). Competition law is seen as an important tool for supporting economic policies based on open markets and liberalization. A lot of the impetus towards the reliance on competitive markets has come from changes in economic policy and ideology in the late 1970s and early 1980s (Thatcherism and Reaganomics were part of this pro-market thinking, though they did not necessarily favour interventionist competition law). Can we take for granted the assumption that the political winds will always favour free markets and competition, supported by strong competition law? The answer is no. Even before the financial crisis that began in 2007–08, some discontent with the promotion of competition had begun to surface. In 2007, with political debates about the new European Treaty (or even Constitution) in full swing, there was pressure from some corners—mainly Paris—to downgrade the importance of competition in the central objectives of the EU. The new Treaty on the Functioning of the European Union (TFEU), which came into force on 1 December 2009, no longer contains the text of Article 3(1)(g) of the EC Treaty it replaced, which had obliged the European Community to establish 'a system ensuring that competition in the internal market is not distorted'. This caused something of a scare among the competition community since many European court decisions refer to that particular text. However, the TFEU makes several other references to the term 'competition'— some of them newly introduced—and, most importantly, it still contains the same core competition provisions on restrictive agreements, abuse of dominance and state aid (only the article numbers changed, fortunately following a simple rule of adding 20 to the old number). The then European Commissioner for Competition, Neelie Kroes, was also quick to reassure everyone (2007):

> An Internal Market without competition rules would be an empty shell—nice words, but no concrete results. The Protocol on Internal Market and Competition agreed at the European Council clearly repeats that competition policy is fundamental to the Internal Market. It retains the existing competition rules which have served us so well for 50 years. It re-confirms the European Commission's duties as the independent competition enforcement authority for Europe.

Another big challenge to the general confidence in markets—and indeed in economics as a profession—came with the financial crisis. Financial institutions ran into difficulties as financial markets dried up, and the impact was felt across the economy. Some have blamed the excessive freedom of financial markets, encouraging unhealthy risk-taking, with insufficient oversight by regulators. And some have blamed economists— for having devised the most complex mathematical formulae for derivative products that no one could really understand, and for failing to predict the financial crisis. While it is too early to assess the longer-term reputational damage caused by these events, competition law, and with it competition economics, has arguably maintained a greater degree of political support throughout the crisis than some had feared. Indeed, competition law has proved to be a tool that can adapt to new circumstances and even contribute to an effective policy response to the economic downturn. In Chapter 8 we discussed how the European Commission applied the state aid rules to the banks and other sectors that received financial support from governments. In Chapter 7 we saw how the merger control rules can address the issue of the failing-firm defence—helpful in an environment with many business restructurings and distress sales. Chapter 9 showed what analysis can be undertaken in order to assess whether a company under investigation has the ability to pay a fine (a defence increasingly invoked by companies in financial difficulties). All these are existing mechanisms under competition law that rely on economic principles and that have proved to be very effective in the economic downturn. As regards the reputation of economics, it has perhaps helped our cause that most of the criticism has, rightly or wrongly, been directed at macroeconomics and (part of) financial economics, not microeconomics and IO.

Economics has an important role to play in maintaining and promoting the legitimacy of competition and competition policy, not just in times of crisis. It can help not only in improving the application of competition law, but also in communicating the message that competitive markets generally perform well for consumers and the economy as a whole, and that competition law is a worthwhile policy tool. The economic notion that competition is 'good' and monopoly is 'bad' on the face of it seems an easy one to convey to the wider public, but not when there are so many visible 'victims' of free markets— bankrupt companies and unemployed workers. In these circumstances it often falls to economists to keep reminding the public that the alternatives—such as protection from imports or bail-outs of failed companies—may not be very wise or sustainable. As to the public legitimacy of competition policy (which, as we noted in Chapter 1, is subtly different from *competition*), economics can contribute by helping policy-makers quantify the costs and benefits of competition regimes and interventions and show that, usually, the benefits greatly outweigh the costs—we discussed this in Chapter 9.

11.4.5 THE POWER OF IDEAS

Finally, a major reason for us to be optimistic about the positive contributions that economics will make to competition law in years to come is that we believe in the power of ideas. This is based on an insight by John Maynard Keynes. Good ideas will eventually gain prominence among policy-makers and the public, even if they meet strong resistance to start with. Take the following statements:

> I like aggressive competition—including by dominant companies—and I don't care if it may hurt competitors—as long as it ultimately benefits consumers . . .

> Dominant companies should be allowed to compete effectively.

These quotes could have been taken from an average antitrust treatise or commentary in the USA in 1970s, when the Chicago School was in full swing. The second quote echoes a much older US antitrust judgment, by Judge Learned Hand in 1945, that 'The successful competitor, having been urged to compete, must not be turned upon when he wins.'[33] In fact, these are statements made by Neelie Kroes at the end of 2005, when

---

[33] *US v Aluminum Co of America* 148 F 2d 416, 430 (2nd Cir, 1945).

her Directorate General introduced the review of the policy on abuse of dominance.[34] Such statements had been rare in Europe before then, and would typically have been dismissed as 'Chicago ideas' or simply as 'American'. What caused such a change in mindset among the European competition community? We believe that Keynes's concept of the power of ideas is at work here. His highly influential work, *The General Theory of Employment, Interest and Money*, published in 1936, developed a new theory of how economy-wide demand and supply might not naturally tend towards equilibrium, leading to unemployment (it was the time of the Great Depression), and what governments could do about this. This represented quite a strong challenge to the prevailing orthodoxy in economics of 'classical' demand–supply theory. Keynes realized that his proposed policies (basically amounting to greater government spending) might, superficially at least, be seen as more suited to totalitarian states than to free-market economies. It was perhaps with these adverse (academic and political) circumstances in mind that Keynes ended his *General Theory* with a hopeful note that, if his ideas were, as he believed, correct, in the longer term they would be influential, even if they weren't immediately. Hence followed this passage:

> But apart from this contemporary mood, the ideas of economists and political philosophers, both when they are right and when they are wrong, are more powerful than is commonly understood. Indeed the world is ruled by little else. Practical men, who believe themselves to be quite exempt from any intellectual influences, are usually the slaves of some defunct economist. Madmen in authority, who hear voices in the air, are distilling their frenzy from some academic scribbler of a few years back. I am sure that the power of vested interests is vastly exaggerated compared with the gradual encroachment of ideas. Not, indeed, immediately, but after a certain interval; for in the field of economic and political philosophy there are not many who are influenced by new theories after they are twenty-five or thirty years of age, so that the ideas which civil servants and politicians and even agitators apply to current events are not likely to be the newest. But, soon or late, it is ideas, not vested interests, which are dangerous for good or evil.

If Keynes's insight is correct, economic ideas and theories will continue to have a useful role to play in competition law in decades to come.

---

[34] See Kroes (2005), and the DG Competition website at: <http://ec.europa.eu/competition/antitrust/art82/index.html>.

BIBLIOGRAPHY

ADAMS, W.J. and YELLEN, J.L. (1976), 'Commodity Bundling and the Burden of Monopoly', *Quarterly Journal of Economics*, 90, August, 475–98.

AGHION, P., BLOOM, N., BLUNDELL, R., GRIFFITH, R. and HOWITT, P. (2005), 'Competition and Innovation: An Inverted-U Relationship', *Quarterly Journal of Economics*, 120:2, 701–28.

AHLBORN, C. and EVANS, S. (2009), 'The Microsoft Judgment and its Implications for Competition Policy towards Dominant Firms in Europe', *Antitrust Law Journal*, 75:3.

AKERLOF, G.A. (1970), 'The Market for "Lemons": Quality Uncertainty and the Market Mechanism', *Quarterly Journal of Economics*, 84:3, 488–500.

ALLEN, K. and ECONOMY, P. (2000), *The Complete MBA for Dummies*, New York: IDG Books Worldwide.

ALMUNIA, J. (2010), 'Competition, State Aid and Subsidies in the European Union', speech to the 9th Global Forum on Competition, Paris, 18 February.

ALTMAN, E. and NARAYANAN, P. (1997), 'An International Survey of Business Failure Classification Models', *Financial Markets, Institutions and Instruments*, May, 1–57.

ANTITRUST MODERNIZATION COMMISSION (2007), 'Report and Recommendations', April.

APESTEGUIA, J., DUFWENBERG, M. and SELTEN, R. (2006), 'Blowing the Whistle', *Economic Theory*, 31, 143–66.

AREEDA, P. and HOVENKAMP, H. (2007), *Antitrust Law*, 3rd edn, Aspen Law & Business, vol. 1.

—— and TURNER, P.F. (1975), 'Predatory Pricing and Related Practices under Section 2 of the Sherman Act', *Harvard Law Review*, 88, 697–733.

ARMSTRONG, M., COWAN, S. and VICKERS, J. (1994), *Regulatory Reform: Economic Analysis and British Experience*, MIT.

ARROW, K. (1962), 'Economic Welfare and the Allocation of Resources for Invention', in R. Nelson, (ed.), *The Rate and Direction of Inventive Activity: Economic and Social Factors*, Princeton University Press.

ASHURST (2004), 'Study on the Conditions of Claims for Damages in Case of Infringement of EC Competition Rules: Analysis of Economic Models for the Calculation of Damages', Report prepared for the European Commission, 31 August.

BACON, K. (2009), *European Community Law of State Aid*, Oxford: Oxford University Press.

BACON, R.W. (1991), 'Rockets and Feathers: The Asymmetric Speed of Adjustment of UK Retail Gasoline Prices to Cost Changes', *Energy Economics*, July, 211–18.

BAIN, J. (1956), *Barriers to New Competition*, Cambridge, Massachusetts: Harvard University Press.

BAKER, J. (1999), 'Econometric Analysis in FTC v Staples', *Journal of Public Policy and Marketing*, 18, Spring, 11–21.

——(2003), 'The Case for Antitrust Enforcement', *Journal of Economic Perspectives*, 17:4, 27–50.

BAKOS, Y. and BRYNJOLFSSON, E. (1999), 'Bundling Information Goods: Pricing, Profits, and Efficiency', *Management Science*, December.

BALDWIN, L.H., MARSHALL, R.C. and RICHARD, J.F. (1997), 'Bidder Collusion at

Forest Service Timber Auctions', *Journal of Political Economy*, 105, 657–99.

BANERJI, A. and MEENAKSHI, J.V. (2004), 'Buyer Collusion and Efficiency of Government Intervention in Wheat Markets in Northern India: An Asymmetric Structural Auctions Analysis', *American Journal of Agricultural Economics*, 86, 236–53.

BAUMOL, W. (1982), 'Contestable Markets: An Uprising in the Theory of Industrial Structure', *American Economic Review*, 72, 1–15.

—— (1983), 'Some Subtle Pricing Issue in Railroad Regulation', *International Journal of Transport Economics*, 10, 341–55.

—— and BRADFORD, D.F. (1970), 'Optimal Departures from Marginal Cost Pricing', *American Economic Review*, 60, June, 265–83.

BAXTER, W.F. (1983), 'Bank Interchange of Transactional Paper: Legal and Economic Perspectives', *Journal of Law and Economics*, 26, 541–88.

BECKER, G. (1968), 'Crime and Punishment: An Economic Approach', *Journal of Political Economy*, 76, 169–217.

—— and MURPHY, K.M. (1993), 'A Simple Theory of Advertising as a Good or Bad', *Quarterly Journal of Economics*, 108, 941–64.

BERGER, M. (2000), 'The Supreme Court's Trilogy on the Admissibility of Expert Testimony', in Federal Judicial Center, *Reference Manual on Scientific Evidence*, 2nd edn.

BERTRAND, J. (1883), 'Review of "Recherches sur les Principes Mathématiques de la Théorie des Richesses"', *Journal des Savants*, 499–508.

BISHOP, S. and WALKER, M. (2010), *The Economics of EC Competition Law: Concepts, Application and Measurement*, 3rd edn, Sweet & Maxwell.

BLAIR, R.D. and HARRISON, J.L. (1993), *Monopsony: Antitrust Law and Economics*, Princeton University Press.

BLONIGEN, B.A. and PRUSA, T.J. (2003), 'Antidumping', in E. Kwan Choi and J. Harrigan (eds), *Handbook of International Trade*, Oxford: Blackwell Publishing.

BOARDMAN, A.E., GREENBERG, D.H., VINING, A.R. and WEIMER, D.L. (2001), *Cost–Benefit Analysis: Concepts and Practice*, New Jersey: Prentice Hall.

BORK, R.H. (1978), *The Antitrust Paradox*, New York: The Free Press.

BREALEY, R.A., MYERS, S.C. and ALLEN, F. (2008), *Principles of Corporate Finance*, 9th edn, McGraw Hill.

BRENNER, S. (2009), 'An Empirical Study of the European Corporate Leniency Program', *International Journal of Industrial Organization*, 27:6, 639–45.

BUDZINSKI, O. and RUHMER, I. (2008), 'Merger Simulation in Competition Policy: A Survey', MAGKS Papers on Economics, 20 August.

BUTTON, K.J. (1993), *Transport Economics*, 2nd edn, Cheltenham: Edward Elgar.

CAMERER, C. and LOEWENSTEIN, G. (2003), 'Behavioral Economics: Past, Present, Future', in C. Camerer, G. Loewenstein and M. Rabin (eds), *Advances in Behavioral Economics*, Princeton University Press.

CAPPS, C., DRANOVE, D., GREENSTEIN, S. and SATTERTHWAITHE, M. (2001), 'The Silent Majority Fallacy of the Elzinga–Hogarty Criteria: A Critique and New Approach to Analyzing Hospital Mergers', NBER Working Paper No 8216, April.

CARD, D. and KRUEGER, A.B. (1994), 'Minimum Wages and Employment: A Case Study of the Fast-food Industry in New Jersey and Pennsylvania', *American Economic Review*, 84:4, 772–93.

CAVE, M. (2009), 'Independent Review of Competition and Innovation in Water Markets: Final report', April.

CHEMLA, G. (2003), 'Downstream Competition, Foreclosure and Vertical Integration', *Journal of Economics and Management Strategy*, 12, 261–89.

COLLINS, A. and OUSTAPASSIDIS, K. (1997), 'Below Cost Legislation and Retail Performance', Agribusiness Discussion Paper No 15, April.

COMANOR, W.S. and WILSON, T.A. (1979), 'Advertising and Competition: A Survey', *Journal of Economic Literature*, 17, June, 453–76.

CONNOR, J.M. and LANDE, R.H. (2005), 'How High Do Cartels Raise Prices? Implications for Reform of the Antitrust Sentencing Guidelines', working paper, April.

—— and —— (2008), 'Cartel Overcharges and Optimal Cartel Fines', in S.W. Waller (ed.), *Issues in Competition Law and Policy*, vol. 3, ABA Section of Antitrust Law.

COURNOT, A.A. (1838), *Recherches sur les Principes Mathématiques de la Théorie des Richesses*.

CROOKE, P., FROEB, L., TSCHANTZ, S. and WERDEN, G. (1999), 'Effects of Assumed Demand Form on Simulated Postmerger Equilibria', *Review of Industrial Organisation*, 15, 205–17.

CWIK, C. and NORTH, J. (2003), 'Scientific Evidence Review: Admissibility and Use of Expert Evidence in the Courtroom', monograph no 4, American Bar Association.

DALJORD, Ø., SØRGARD, L. and THOMASSEN, Ø. (2008), 'The SSNIP Test and Market Definition with the Aggregate Diversion Ratio: A Reply to Katz and Shapiro', *Journal of Competition Law and Economics*, 4:2, 263–70.

DAVIS, P. and GARCÉS, E. (2009), *Quantitative Techniques for Competition and Antitrust Analysis*, Woodstock, UK: Princeton University Press.

DELOITTE (2009), 'Review of Merger Decisions under the Enterprise Act 2002', report prepared for the Competition Commission, Office of Fair Trading and the Department for Business, Enterprise and Regulatory Reform, 18 March.

DEMSETZ, H. (1974), 'Two Systems of Belief about Monopoly', in H. Goldschmid, H.M. Mann and J.F. Weston (eds), *Industrial Concentration: The New Learning*, Boston: Little, Brown.

DHAR, T.P. and COTTERILL, R.W. (1999), 'Cost Pass-through in the Case of Sequential Oligopoly: An Empirical Study of the Fluid Milk Market', University of Connecticut.

DIJK, R. van and NIELS, G. (2008), 'Competition Policy: What are the Costs and Benefits of Measuring its Costs and Benefits?', *De Economist*, 156, 349–64.

DIMSON, E., MARSH, P. and STAUNTON, M. (2010), *Credit Suisse Global Investment Returns Sourcebook 2010*.

DINNAGE, J.D. (1998), 'Joint Activities Among Gas Producers: The Competition Man Cometh', *Journal of Energy and Natural Resources Law*, 16:3, 249–85.

DON, H., KEMP, R. and SINDEREN, J. van (2008), 'Measuring the Economic Effects of Competition Law Enforcement', *De Economist*, 156, 341–8.

DOYLE, C and INDERST, R. (2007), 'Some Economics on the Treatment of Buyer Power in Antitrust', *European Competition Law Review*, 28:3.

DUGGAN, M. and LEVITT, S.D. (2002), 'Winning isn't Everything: Corruption in Sumo Wrestling', *American Economic Review*, 95:5, 1594–605.

EDWARDS, J., KAY, J. and MAYER, C. (1987), *The Economic Analysis of Accounting Profitability*, Oxford: Clarendon Press.

ELHAUGE, E. (2003), 'Defining Better Monopolization Standards', *Stanford Law Review*, 56, 253–344.

ELZINGA, K. and HOGARTY, T. (1973), 'The Problem of Geographic Market Delineation in Antitrust Suits', *Antitrust Bulletin*, 18:1, 45–81.

—— and MILLS, D.E. (1989), 'Testing for Predation: Is Recoupment Feasible?', *Antitrust Bulletin*, 34, 869–93.

EMCH, E.R. (2004), '"Portfolio Effects" in Merger Analysis: Differences between EU and U.S. Practice and Recommendations for the Future', *Antitrust Bulletin*, 49:1–2, 55–100.

EUROPEAN FEDERATION OF PHARMACEUTICAL INDUSTRIES AND ASSOCIATIONS (2008), 'The Pharmaceutical Industry in Figures'.

FARRELL, J. and SHAPIRO, C. (1990), 'Horizontal Mergers: An Equilibrium Analysis', *American Economic Review*, 80, 107–26.

—— and —— (2001), 'Scale Economies and Synergies in Horizontal Merger Analysis', *Antitrust Law Journal*, 68:3.

—— and —— (2008), 'Improving Critical Loss Analysis', *The Antitrust Source*, 7:3.

FRANK, R.H. (2007), *The Economic Naturalist: Why Economics Explains Almost Everything*, London: Virgin Books.

FREEMAN, P. (2004), 'The Enterprise Act and Innovation', speech at the CBI Competition Conference, 5 March.

GABAIX, X. and LAIBSON, D. (2006), 'Shrouded Attributes, Consumer Myopia, and Information Suppression in Competitive Markets', *Quarterly Journal of Economics*, 121:2, 505–40.

GALBRAITH, J.K. (1952), *American Capitalism: The Concept of Countervailing Buyer Power*, Boston: Houghton Mifflin.

GENNER, J., LIENEMEYER, M. and WALKNER, C. (2009), 'The Commerzbank Recapitalisation Decision: Providing Legal Certainty in Times of Crisis and Guidance for Future Restructuring', *Competition Policy Newsletter*, 2.

GILBERT, D. (2006), *Stumbling on Happiness*, Knopf.

GNEEZY, U. and RUSTICHINI, A. (2000), 'A Fine is a Price', *Journal of Legal Studies*, 1, 1–17.

GOLDBERG, P. (1995), 'Product Differentiation and Oligopoly in International Markets: The Case of the U.S. Automobile Industry', *Econometrica*, 63.

GRAHAM, J.R. and HARVEY, C.R. (2001), 'The Theory and Practice of Corporate Finance: Evidence from the Field', *Journal of Financial Economics*, 60, 187–243.

GREEN, E.J. and PORTER, R.H. (1984), 'Noncooperative Collusion under Imperfect Price Information', *Econometrica*, 52:1.

GUJARATI, D.N. (2009), *Basic Econometrics*, 5th revised edn, New York: McGraw Hill Higher Education.

HALE, G.E. and HALE, R.D. (1966), 'A Line of Commerce: Market Definition in Antimerger Cases', *Iowa Law Review*, 52.

HALL, G.R. and PHILLIPS, C.F. (1964), 'Antimerger Criteria: Power, Concentration, Foreclosure and Size', *Villanova Law Review*, 9.

HAMAGUCHI, Y. and KAWAGOE, T. (2005), 'An Experimental Study of Leniency Programs', RIETI discussion paper.

HARRINGTON Jr., J.E. (2008), 'Detecting Cartels', in P. Buccirossi (ed.), *Handbook of Antitrust Economics*, MIT Press.

HARRIS, B.C. and SIMONS, J.J. (1989), 'Focusing Market Definition: How Much Substitution is Necessary?', *Research in Law and Economics*, 12, 207–26.

HENDRY, D.F. and CLEMENTS, M.P. (2004), 'Pooling of Forecasts', *Econometrics Journal*, 7, 1–31.

HENSHER, D.A., ROSE, J.M. and GREENE, W.H. (2005), *Applied Choice Analysis: A Primer*, Cambridge: Cambridge University Press.

HICKS, J.R. (1935), 'Annual Survey of Economic Theory: The Theory of Monopoly', *Econometrica*, 3:1, 1–20.

HINLOOPEN, J. and SOETEVENT, R. (2006), 'Trust and Recidivism: The Partial Success of Corporate Leniency Programmes in the Laboratory', Tinbergen Institute Discussion Paper.

HOOPER, R., HUTTON, D. and SMITH, I. (2008), 'Modernise or Decline: Policies to Maintain the Universal Postal Service in the United Kingdom', December.

HORNCASTLE, A., JEVONS, D., DUDLEY, P. and THANASSOULIS, E. (2006), 'Efficiency Analysis of Delivery Offices in the Postal Sector Using Stochastic Frontier and Data Envelopment Analyses', in M. Crew and P. Kleindorfer (eds), *Liberalization of the Postal and Delivery Sector*, Edward Elgar Publishing.

HOTELLING, H. (1929), 'Stability in Competition', *Economic Journal*, 39: 41–57.

HOVENKAMP, H. (2001), 'Post-Chicago Antitrust: A Review and Critique', *Columbia Business Law Review*, 2, 257–337.

IVALDI, M. and VERBOVEN, F. (2005), 'Quantifying the Effects from Horizontal Mergers in European Competition Policy', *International Journal of Industrial Organisation*, 23, 669–91.

JACOB, B.A. and LEVITT, S.D. (2003), 'Rotten Apples: An Investigation of the Prevalence and Predictors of Teacher Cheating', *Quarterly Journal of Economics*, 118:3, 843–77.

JONES, C.A. (1999), *Private Enforcement of Antitrust Law in the EU, UK and USA*, Oxford: Oxford University Press.

KAHN, A.E. (1988), *The Economics of Regulation: Principles and Institutions*, MIT (first published in two separate volumes in 1970 and 1971).

KAHNEMAN, D. and TVERSKY, A. (1979), 'Prospect Theory: An Analysis of Decisions Under Risk', *Econometrica*, 47, 263–91.

KATE, A. TEN and NIELS, G. (2002), 'On the Rationality of Predatory Pricing; The Debate between Chicago and Post-Chicago', *Antitrust Bulletin*, Spring, 1–24.

—— and —— (2005), 'To what Extent are Cost Savings Passed on to Consumers? An Oligopoly Approach', *European Journal of Law and Economics*, 20, 323–37.

—— and —— (2006), 'Mexico's Competition Law: North American Origins, European Practice', in P. Marsden (ed.), *Handbook of Research in Trans-Atlantic Antitrust*, Cheltenham: Edward Elgar.

—— and —— (2009), 'The Relevant Market: A Concept Still in Search of a Definition', *Journal of Competition Law and Economics*, 5:2, 297–333.

—— and —— (2010), 'The Concept of Critical Loss for a Group of Differentiated Products', *Journal of Competition Law and Economics*, 6:2, 321–33.

KATZ, M.L. and SHAPIRO, C. (2003), 'Critical Loss: Let's Tell the Whole Story', *Antitrust*, Spring.

KAY, J.A. (1976), 'Accountants Too, Could be Happy in a Golden Age: The Accountant's Rate of Profit and the Internal Rate of Return', *Oxford Economic Papers*, 28, 447–60.

KIM, D. and COTTERILL, R.W. (2008), 'Cost Pass-through in Differentiated Product Markets: The Case of U.S. Processed Cheese', *Journal of Industrial Economics*, 56:1, 32–48.

KLEMPERER, P. (2005), 'Bidding Markets', Competition Commission discussion paper.

KOLASKY, W.J. (2001), 'Conglomerate Mergers and Range Effects: It's a Long Way to go from Chicago to Brussels', speech by the Deputy Assistant Attorney General, Antitrust Division, US Department of Justice, before the George Mason University Symposium, 21 November.

KOVACIC, W. (1999), 'Designing Antitrust Remedies for Dominant Firm Misconduct', *Connecticut Law Review*, 31, 1285.

—— (2007), 'The Intellectual DNA of Modern U.S. Competition Law for Dominant Firm Conduct: The Chicago/Harvard Double Helix', *Columbia Business Law Review*, 1, 1–82.

—— and SHAPIRO, C. (2000), 'Antitrust Policy: A Century of Economic and Legal Thinking', *Journal of Economic Perspectives*, 14:1, 43–60.

KREPS, D.M. and WILSON, R. (1982), 'Reputation and Imperfect Information', *Journal of Economic Theory*, 27, 253–79.

KROES, N. (2005), 'Preliminary Thoughts on Policy Review of Article 82', Speech at the Fordham Corporate Law Institute, New York, 23 September.

—— (2007), 'Statement by European Commissioner for Competition Neelie Kroes on Results of 21–22 June European Council—Protocol on Internal Market and Competition', MEMO/07/250, 23 June.

—— (2008), 'Dealing with the Current Financial Crisis', speech to the Economic and Monetary Affairs Committee, European Parliament, Brussels, SPEECH/08/498, 6 October.

—— (2009), 'Many Achievements, More To Do', speech to the International Bar Association conference on private and public enforcement of EU competition law, Brussels, 12 March.

KRUM, H., CONWAY, E.L., BROADBEAR, J.H., HOWES, L.G. and LOUIS, W.J. (1994), 'Postural Hypotension in Elderly Patients Given Carvedilol', *British Medical Journal*, 309, 775–76.

LAFFONT, J.J. and TIROLE, J. (1993), *A Theory of Incentives in Regulation and Procurement*, MIT.

LAFONTAINE, F. and SLADE, M. (2008), 'Exclusive Contracts and Vertical Restraints:

Empirical Evidence and Public Policy', in P. Buccirossi (ed.), *Handbook of Antitrust Economics*, MIT Press.

LANDES, W.M. (1983), 'Optimal Sanctions for Antitrust Violations', *University of Chicago Law Review*, 50.

LANE, F.C. (1968), 'Pepper Prices before da Gama', *Journal of Economic History*, 28:4, 590–7.

LAYNE-FARRAR, A., PADILLA, A.J. and SCHMALENSEE, R. (2007), 'Pricing Patents for Licensing in Standard Setting Organizations: Making Sense of FRAND Commitments', CEMFI Working Paper No 0702, January.

LEIBENSTEIN, H. (1950), 'Bandwagon, Snob, and Veblen Effects in the Theory of Consumers' Demand', *Quarterly Journal of Economics*, 64:2, 183–207.

LEIBOWITZ, J. (2010), 'A Doctor and a Lawyer Walk into a Bar: Moving Beyond Stereotypes', Remarks by the FTC Chairman to the American Medical Association House of Delegates, available at: <http://www.ftc.gov/speeches/leibowitz. shtm>.

LERNER, A.P. (1934), 'The Concept of Monopoly and Measurement of Monopoly Power', *The Review of Economic Studies*, 1:3, 157–75.

LEVENSTEIN, M.C. and SUSLOW, V.Y. (2004), 'Studies of Cartel Stability: A Comparison of Methodological Approaches', in P.Z. Grossman (ed.), *How Cartels Endure and How they Fail: Studies of Industrial Collusion*, Edward Elgar.

LEVITT, S.D. and DUBNER, S.J. (2005), *Freakonomics: A Rogue Economist Explores the Hidden Side of Everything*, William Morrow Ltd.

LONDON ECONOMICS, in association with STEFFEN HUCK and BRIAN WALLACE (University College London) (2010), 'The Impact of Price Frames on Consumer

Decision-Making', OFT Economic Discussion paper, May.

LONDON SCHOOL OF ECONOMICS (2004), 'The Economic Impact of Pharmaceutical Parallel Trade in European Union Member States: A Stakeholder Analysis', Special Research Paper, January.

MACKIE-MASON, J. and METZLER, J. (2009), 'Links Between Markets and Aftermarkets: Kodak (1997)', in J.E. Kwoka and L.J. White (eds), The Antitrust Revolution: Economics, Competition, and Policy, 5th edn, New York: Oxford University Press.

MAJORAS, D.P. (2001), 'GE–Honeywell: The U.S. Decision', Remarks of Deborah Platt Majoras, Deputy Assistant Attorney General, Antitrust Division, US Department of Justice, before the Antitrust Law Section, State Bar of Georgia, 29 November.

MARKARD, J., TRUFFER, B. and IMBODEN, D.M. (2004), 'The Impacts of Liberalisation on Innovation Processes in the Electricity Sector', Energy and Environment, 15:2, 201–14.

MARSHALL, A. (1890), Principles of Economics, London: Macmillan.

MARTIN, S. (1995), 'R&D Joint Ventures and Tacit Product Market Collusion', European Journal of Political Economy, 11, 733–41.

MCAFEE, B.Y. and BRYNJOLFSSON, E. (2000), 'Bundling Information Goods: Pricing, Profits, and Efficiency', Management Science.

MILGROM, P. and ROBERTS, J. (1982), 'Predation, Reputation and Entry Deterrence', Journal of Economic Theory, 27, 280–312.

MÖLLERS, T.M.J. and HEINEMANN, A. (2007), The Enforcement of Competition Law in Europe, Cambridge: Cambridge University Press.

MORRIS, D. (2003), 'Dominant Firm Behaviour under UK Competition Law', paper presented to the Fordham Corporate Law Institute, October.

MORWITZ, V., GREENLEAF, E., SHALEV, E. and JOHNSON, E.J. (2009), 'The Price Does Not Include Additional Taxes, Fees, and Surcharges: A Review of Research on Partitioned Pricing', SSRN Working paper series, February.

MOTTA, M. (2004), Competition Policy: Theory and Practice, Cambridge: Cambridge University Press.

—— and POLO, M. (2003), 'Leniency Programs and Cartel Prosecution', International Journal of Industrial Organisation, 21:3, 347–79.

NALEBUFF, B. (2003), 'Bundling, Tying, and Portfolio Effects. Part 1: Conceptual Issues', DTI Economics Paper No 1, February.

NASH, J. (1950), 'Equilibrium Points in N-Person Games', Proceedings of the National Academy of Sciences, 36:1, 48–9.

NELSON, D. (2006), 'The Political Economy of Antidumping: A Survey', European Journal of Political Economy, 22, 554–90.

NEVEN, D. (2007), 'Enhancing the Economic Assessment of EU State Aid Cases', presentation to the ESMT/EStALI State Aid Conference, Berlin, 8–9 October.

NIELS, G. (2004), 'The SSNIP Test: Some Common Misperceptions', Competition Law Journal, 3:4, 267–76.

—— and JENKINS, H. (2005), 'Reform of Article 82: Where the Link Between Dominance and Effects Breaks Down', European Competition Law Review, 26:11.

—— and TEN KATE, A. (1997), 'Trusting Antitrust to Dump Antidumping; Abolishing Antidumping in Free Trade Agreements without Replacing it with Competition Law', Journal of World Trade, 31, 29–43.

—— and —— (2004), 'Antitrust in the US and the EU: Converging or Diverging Paths?', Antitrust Bulletin, 49:1–2, 1–27.

—— and VAN DIJK, R. (2006), 'Market Definition in the Tourism Industry', in

A. Papatheodoru (ed.), *Corporate Rivalry and Market Power: Competition Issues in the Tourism Industry*, London: I.B. Tauris.

NIELSEN (1997), 'Loi Galland: Jusqu'où les Prix vont-ils Grimper?', Linéaires no. 1529, March, cited in C. Chambolle, 'Stratégies de Revente à Perte et Réglementation', Laboratoire d'Econométrie de l'Ecole Polytechnique, Paris.

OFFICE OF FAIR TRADING (2005), 'Positive Impact: An Initial Evaluation of the Effect of the Competition Enforcement Work Conducted by the OFT', December.

—— (2007), 'The Deterrent Effect of Competition Enforcement by the OFT', report prepared by Deloitte, November.

—— (2009), 'Road Testing of Consumer Remedies', July.

—— (2010), 'What Does Behavioural Economics Mean for Competition Policy?', OFT 1224, March.

ORGANISATION FOR ECONOMIC CO-OPERATION AND DEVELOPMENT (2002), 'Report on the Nature and Impact of Hard Core Cartels and Sanctions against Cartels under National Competition Laws', 9 April.

—— (2005), 'Enhancing Beneficial Competition in the Health Professions', Competition Committee policy roundtable, DAF/COMP(2005)45, 16 December.

—— (2006), 'Policy Roundtables: Remedies and Sanctions in Abuse of Dominance Cases', DAF/COMP(2006)19.

—— (2007), 'Dynamic Efficiences in Merger Analysis', DAF/COMP(2007)41.

O'ROURKE, K.H. and WILLIAMSON, J.G. (2006), 'Did Vasco da Gama Matter for European Markets? Testing Frederick Lane's Hypotheses Fifty Years Later', CEPR discussion paper no 5418, January.

OXERA (2003a), 'Assessing Profitability in Competition Policy Analysis', OFT Economic Discussion Paper 6, July.

—— (2003b), 'Consumer Survey Report', report prepared for the UK Office of Fair Trading, November.

—— (2004), 'Costs and Benefits of Market Regulators', report prepared for the Ministry of Economic Affairs (the Netherlands), October.

—— (2005a), 'What is the Impact of a Minimum Price Rule?', report prepared for the Ministry of Economic Affairs (the Netherlands), June.

—— (2005b), 'Buying Loyalty: South African Airways and the Ongoing Saga of Rebate Cases', *Agenda*, August.

—— (2007), 'Energy Sector Inquiry: A Third Way for Transmission Networks?', *Agenda*, January.

—— (2008a), 'Truth or Dare: Leniency and the Fight Against Cartels', *Agenda*, January.

—— (2008b), 'What is Network Rail's Likely Scope for Frontier Shift Enhancement Expenditure over CP4?', report prepared for the Office of Rail Regulation, 27 March.

—— (2008c), 'Dealing with Doping: A Question of the Benchmark', *Agenda*, July.

—— (2009), 'Vertical Functional Separation in the Electronic Communications Sector', report prepared for ICP-ANACOM in collaboration with Ellare, July.

—— (2010a), 'Should Aid be Granted to Firms in Difficulty? A Study on Counterfactual Scenarios to Restructuring State Aid', report prepared for the European Commission, February.

—— (2010b), 'Best of Both Worlds? Innovative Approaches to Modelling Merger Price Rises', *Agenda*, May.

—— ET AL. (2009), 'Quantifying Antitrust Damages: Towards Non-binding Guidance for Courts', report prepared for DG Competition, December.

PARETO, V. (1906), *Manual of Political Economy* (original in Italian).

PEASNELL, K.V. (1982), 'Estimating the Internal Rate of Return from Accounting Profit Rates', *The Investor Analyst*, 26–31.

PILSBURY, S. (2007), 'The Impala Decision: An Economic Critique', *European Competition Journal*, 3:1, 31–47.

POLINSKY, A.M. and SHAVELL, S. (2000), 'The Economic Theory of Public Enforcement of Law', *Journal of Economic Literature*, 38:1, 45–76.

PORTER, R.H. and ZONA, J.D. (1993), 'Detection of Bid Rigging in Procurement Auctions', *Journal of Political Economy*, 101:3, 518–38.

—— and —— (1999), 'Ohio School Milk Markets: An Analysis of Bidding', *RAND Journal of Economics*, 30, 263–8.

POSNER, R.A. (1976), *Antitrust Law: An Economic Perspective*, Chicago: University of Chicago Press.

—— (2001), *Antitrust Law*, 2nd edn, Chicago: University of Chicago Press.

PUGH, E. (1995), *Building IBM: Shaping an Industry and Its Technology*, MIT Press.

ROACH, K. and TREBILCOCK, M.J. (1997), 'Private Enforcement of Competition Laws', *Osgoode Hall Law Journal*, 34, 462–508.

ROCHET, J.C. (2003), 'The Theory of Interchange Fees: A Synthesis of Recent Contributions', *Review of Network Economics*, 2.

ROSCH, J. (2007), 'The Challenge of Non-Horizontal Merger Enforcement', paper for the Fordham Competition Law Institute's 34th Annual Conference on International Antitrust Law & Policy, New York City, 27 September.

SALOP, S. and SCHEFFMAN, D. (1987), 'Cost-Raising Strategies', *Journal of Industrial Economics*, 36:1, 19–34.

SANTANDER (2010), 'Britons Stay With Their Bank Longer Than Their Partners', press release, 16 August.

SCHERER, F.M. (2009), 'Retailer-Instigated Restraints on Suppliers' Sales: Toys "R" Us (2000)', in J.E. Kwoka and L.J. White (eds), *The Antitrust Revolution: Economics, Competition, and Policy*, 5th edn, Oxford University Press.

—— and ROSS, D. (1990), *Industrial Market Structure and Economic Performance*, 3rd edn, Boston: Houghton Mifflin Company.

SCHMALENSEE, R. (1982), 'Commodity Bundling by Single-Product Monopolies', *Journal of Law and Economics*, 25, 67–71.

SCHUMPETER, J. (1942), *Capitalism, Socialism and Democracy*.

SELTEN, R. (1978), 'The Chain Store Paradox', *Theory and Decision*, 9, 127–59.

SHAPLEY, L.S. (1953), 'A Value for N-Person Games', in H.W. Kuhn and A.W. Tucker (eds), *Contributions to the Theory of Games II*, Princeton: Princeton University Press.

SHENEFIELD, J.H. (2004), 'Coherence or Confusion: The Future of the Global Antitrust Conversation', *Antitrust Bulletin*, 44:1–2, 385–434.

SHEPHERD, W. (1988), 'Competition, Contestability and Transport Mergers', *International Journal of Transport Economics*, 15:2.

SLADE, M. (1998), 'Beer and the Tie: Did Divestiture of Brewer-Owned Public Houses Lead to Higher Beer Prices?', *Economic Journal*, 108, 565–602.

SMITH, A. (1776), *An Inquiry into the Nature and Causes of the Wealth of Nations*.

SPAGNOLO, G. (2004), 'Divide et Impera: Optimal Leniency Programmes', working paper 4840, Center for European Policy Research.

SPENGLER, J.J. (1950), 'Vertical Integration and Anti-Trust Policy', *Journal of Political Economy*, 58, 347–52.

STEPHAN, A. (2009), 'An Empirical Assessment of the European Leniency Notice', *Journal of Competition Law and Economics*, 5, 537–61.

STIGLER, G.J. (1968), *The Organization of Industry*, Chicago: University of Chicago Press.

SUGDEN, R. and WILLIAMS, A.H. (1978), *The Principles of Practical Cost–Benefit Analysis*, Oxford University Press.

SULLIVAN, L.E. (1995), 'Post-Chicago Economics: Economists, Lawyers, Judges, and Enforcement Officials in a Less Determinate Theoretical World', *Antitrust Law Journal*, 63, 669–81.

SWANSON, D. and BAUMOL, W. (2005), 'Selection of Compatibility Standards and Control of Market Power Related to Intellectual Property', *Antitrust Law Journal*, 73:1.

THALER, R. (1980), 'Toward A Positive Theory of Consumer Choice', *Journal of Economic Behavior and Organization*, 1, 39–60.

—— and SUNSTEIN, C.R. (2008), *Nudge: Improving Decisions About Health, Wealth and Happiness*, Yale University Press.

TIMMERMAN, A. (2006), 'Forecast Combinations', in G. Elliot, C.W.J. Granger and A. Timmerman (eds), *Handbook of Economic Forecasting*, vol. 1, Elsevier.

TREACY, P. and KOSTENKO, M. (2007), 'Safer Standard Setting', *Competition Law Insight*, 10–11.

VEBLEN, T.B. (1899), *The Theory of the Leisure Class: An Economic Study of Institutions*, London: Macmillan Publishers.

VICKERS, J. (2005a), 'Abuse of Market Power', *Economic Journal*, 115:504, 244–61.

—— (2005b), 'State Aid and Distortion of Competition', speech for the UK Presidency Event on State Aid, London, 14 July.

VINER, J. (1923), *Dumping: A Problem in International Trade*, Chicago: Chicago University Press (reprinted in 1991 by Augustus M. Kelley, Fairfield, NJ).

WALTERS, C. and REYNOLDS, G. (2008), 'The Use of Customer Surveys for Market Definition and the Competitive Assessment of Horizontal Mergers', *Journal of Competition Law and Economics*, 4:2, 411–31.

WATERSON, M. (2009), 'Beer: the ties that bind', in B. Lyons (ed.), *Cases in European Competition Policy: The Economic Analysis*, Cambridge: Cambridge University Press.

WERDEN, G. (1992), 'The History of Antitrust Market Delineation', *Marquette Law Review*, 76:23.

—— (1998), 'Demand Elasticities in Antitrust Analysis', *Antitrust Law Journal*, 66.

—— (2000), 'Expert Report in United States v. Interstate Bakeries Corp. and Continental Baking Co.', *International Journal of the Economics of Business*, 7, 139–48.

—— (2003), 'The Effect of Antitrust Policy on Consumer Welfare: What Crandall and Winston Overlook', Economic Analysis Group discussion paper, January.

—— (2006), 'Identifying Exclusionary Conduct under Section 2: The "No Economic Sense" Test', *Antitrust Law Journal*, 73, 413–33.

WHINSTON, M.D. (1990), 'Tying, Foreclosure and Exclusion', *American Economic Review*, 80, 837–59.

WILLIG, R. (1979), 'The Theory of Network Access Pricing', in H.B. Trebing (ed.), *Issues in Public Utility Regulation*, Michigan State University Public Utility Papers.

WILS, W. (2006), 'Optimal Antitrust Fines: Theory and Practice', *World Competition*, 29:2, June.

WOOLDRIDGE, J.M. (2005), *Introductory Econometrics: A Modern Approach*, 3rd revised edn, South-Western.

INDEX